An
EVOLVING
TRADITION

Maidun Collection / Alamy Stock Photo

An EVOLVING TRADITION

The Child Ballads in Modern Folk and Rock Music

Dave Thompson

Backbeat
Books

Essex, Connecticut

Backbeat Books

An imprint of Globe Pequot, the trade division of
The Rowman & Littlefield Publishing Group, Inc.
4501 Forbes Blvd., Ste. 200
Lanham, MD 20706
www.rowman.com

Distributed by NATIONAL BOOK NETWORK

British Library Cataloguing in Publication Information Available

Library of Congress Cataloging-in-Publication Data

Names: Thompson, Dave, 1960 January 3- author.
Title: An evolving tradition : the Child ballads in modern folk and rock music / Dave Thompson.
Description: Essex, Connecticut : Backbeat, 2023. | Includes bibliographical references and index.
Identifiers: LCCN 2022061477 (print) | LCCN 2022061478 (ebook) | ISBN 9781493068067 (cloth) | ISBN 9781493068241 (ebook)
Subjects: LCSH: Ballads, English—History and criticism. | Folk songs, English—History and criticism. | Child, Francis James, 1825-1896. English and Scottish popular ballads.
Classification: LCC ML3545 .T56 2023 (print) | LCC ML3545 (ebook) | DDC 782.42162/2—dc23/eng/20221223
LC record available at https://lccn.loc.gov/2022061477
LC ebook record available at https://lccn.loc.gov/2022061478

Dedication—to my beloved cousin Jane Thompson Dua, 1971–2022. As a child, she heard me playing "The Wee Wee Man" (Child 38) one day, and completely misunderstood what the song was about. Her interpretation still comes to mind when I hear that ballad.

CONTENTS

AUTHOR'S NOTES

Professor Francis J. Child, for whom the Child Ballads are named, compiled two collections of ballads during his lifetime. The first, published between 1857 and 1859 within the broader *British Poets* series, comprised eight volumes under the title *The English and Scottish Ballads*. The second, for which he is best remembered, and which is now commonly described as "The Child Ballads," was titled *The English and Scottish Popular Ballads*, and appeared between 1882 and 1898.

To avoid confusion, and to follow established convention, these two series are referred to in this book, respectively, as *ESB* and *ESPB*.

All 305 ballads in *ESPB* were numbered, 1, 2, 3, et cetera, and these numbers remain in common use when referencing a Child Ballad. This convention, too, is continued here, with the applicable Child number following ballad titles in parentheses (thus). It follows, therefore, that any song appearing without a number is *not* one of the Child Ballads, no matter how popular and/or widespread it might be.

For the purpose of clarity, this same numbering system is also followed in those instances where a ballad is referred to by an alternate title or has even evolved into a very different song from that which Child noted.

Be aware, however, that this book is concerned only with the Child Ballads as they have been sung in the English language. A number have since come to light sung in Irish and Scottish Gaelic and Welsh, while Child notes versions of the ballads hailing from Spain, across Scandinavia, central Europe, and even further afield.

Of "The Maid Freed from the Gallows" (95) alone, Child estimated in 1888 that there are "nearly fifty Finnish versions." Forty years later, the American performer Burl Ives met a Swede at the International House hostel in New York City who listened to Ives sing "Barbara Allen" (84) and responded, "That's a Swedish song."

Ives reflected on the incident in his autobiography, musing, "Where had this song come from and how far around the world had it wandered?" That, however, is a question for a very different book than this one.

Finally, ballad titles, lyrics and historical quotes are given as they were written or spoken at the time. Please be aware that these historical records may contain material that some might find offensive.

ALTERNATIVE TITLES

Although F. J. Child assigned a "preferred" title to every one of the 305 ballads that he included in the *ESPB*, he was aware that alternate titles existed for the majority of them; indeed, the "index of published airs" that appeared among his appendices includes some 800 such, and that was compiled in the 1890s. In the century-plus since Child completed his list, research has probably unearthed as many again of new titles and variations.

Some of these variations, then and now, are regional. In the far north of England, for example, "Scarborough Fair" was "Whittingham Fair." In certain parts of America, however, it became "An Acre of Land." Child's preferred title was "[The] Elphin Knight," but even in academic circles, it is often changed to "[The] Elfin Knight."

Changes were wrought for manifold reasons, from mispronunciation to mishearing, and even misspellings. Personal names are especially prone to change, in title and lyric alike. Thus, we find the same song recorded as "Lord Bateman" and "Lord Bakeman," or noted as "Johnny Armstrong" and "Johnnie Armstrong." Sometimes a word that one ballad treats as a compound (Blackjack) will reappear as two words (Black Jack).

Throughout this book, titles are given as they appear in the original source material, be it a ballad book, a record sleeve, or elsewhere. To avoid confusion, each of these variations is assigned the Child number associated with it. However, for ease of further reference, the following is a list of every variation mentioned in this book.

#1: "Riddles Wisely Expounded," "Lay the Bent to the Bonny Broom," "[The] Devil's Nine Questions," "Jennifer Gentle"

#2: "[The] Elphin/Elfin Knight" a.k.a. "[My Father Gave Me] An/Y'Acre of Land," "Scarborough/Whittingham Fair," "Sing Ivy," "True Lover of Mine," "The Cambric Shirt," "Love Letter and Answer," "O Say Do You Know the Way to Selin," "Strawberry Lane," "The Tri-Coloured House"

#3: "[The] Fause/False Knight/Knicht [up]on the Road"

#4: "Lady Isabel and the Elf-Knight," "May Colvin," "Pretty Polly," "[The] Outlandish Knight," "The False Hearted Knight," "[The] Willow Tree," "The Dapple Grey"

#5: "Gil Brenton"

#6: "Willie's Lady," "[The] Witch Mother"

#7: "Earl Brand," "Awake Awake," "[The] Bold Dragoon," "[The] Dragoon and the Lady," "[The] Seven Sleepers," "The Douglas Tragedy," "Sweet William"

#8: "Erlinton"

#9: "[The] Fair Flower of Northumberland"

#10: "[The] Twa/Two Sisters [of Binnorie]," "[The] Cruel Sister," "Minorie," "Binnorie," "[The] Wind and [the] Rain"

#11: "[The] Cruel Brother," "The Three Maids"

#12: "Lord Randal/Randall/Ronald," "Billy Boy," "Lord Donald," "John/Jimmy Randolph," "Henry My Son," "And Amhrán Nah Eascainne" (Gaelic), "Buried in Kilkenny"

#13: "Edward," "My Son David," "[The] Murdered Brother," "What's the Blood That's on Your Sword?," "The Blood of the Old Red Rooster," "The Blood on His Shirt Sleeve," "What Put the Blood on Your Right Shoulder, Son?," "The Old Yellow Mare," "The Ballad of Cain and Abel," "Baile Leo" (Gaelic)

#14: "Babylon," "[The] [Bonnie] Banks o Fordie/Airdrie/Virgie-O"

#15: "Leesome Brand"

#16: "Sheath and Knife"

#17: "Hind Horn," "[The] Bleacher Lassie of Kelvinhaugh," "[The] [Old] Beggar Man"

#18: "Sir Lionel," Bangum and the Boar," "Bold Sir Rylas," "Old Bangum," "Rockabello," "Wild Hog in the Woods"

#19: "King/Young/Sir Orfeo"

#20: "[The] Cruel Mither/Mother," "Fine Flowers in the Valley," "[Down by] [the] Greenwood Side/Sidey-O," "Wella Wallia," "Fine Flowers in the Valley," "The Lady from Lee"

#21: "[The] Maid and the Palmer," "Jesus Met the Woman at the Well," "[The] Well Below the Valley"

#22: "St. Stephen and [King] Herod," "Stephen"

#23: "Judas"

#55: "[The] Carnal and the Crane," "[King] Herod and the Cock"

#56: "[Dives and] Lazarus"

#57: "Brown Robyn's Confession," "William Glenn," "Sir William Gower," "[The] Guilty Sea Captain"

#58: "Sir Patrick Spens"

#59: "Sir Aldingar"

#60: "King Estmere"

#61: "Sir Cawline/Colvin"

#62: "Fair Annie," "[The] King's Daughter"

#63: "Child Waters," "Fair Ellen"

#64: "Fair Janet [and Young James]"

#65: "Lady Maisry," "[Bonny] Susie Clelland," "Mother, Go Make My Bed"

#66: "Lord Ingram and Chiel Wyet"

#67: "Glasgerion," "Glenkindle," "Jack O'Rion/Orion"

#68: "Young Hunting," "False True Love," "Henry Lee," "Love/Loving Henry," "[The] Proud Girl," "Lou Bonnie," "The False Young Man," "Earl Richard"

#69: "Clerk Sanders/Saunders"

#70: "Willie and Lady Maisry," "William and Lady Marjorie"

#71: "[The] Bent Sae Brown"

#72: "[The] Clerk's Twa Sons o Owensford"

#73: "Lord Thomas and Annet," "[Lord Thomas and] Fair Annie/Eleanor/Ellen/Ellendor," "[The] Brown Girl"

#74: "Fair/Lady/Little Margaret [and Sweet William]"

#75: "[The New Ballad of] Lord Lovel/Lovell," "Milk White Steed"

#76: "[The] Lass of Roch Royal," "Lord Gregory," "Roving on a Winter's Night" "[The] Storms Are on the Ocean," Who Will Shoe Your Pretty Little Feet," "Who's Going to Shoe Your Pretty Little Foot?"

#77: "Sweet William's Ghost"

#78: "[The] Unquiet Grave," "[Lost] Jimmy Whalen," "Cold Blows the Winter Wind"

#79: "[The] Wife of Usher's Well," "There Lived a Lady in Merry Scotland," "[The] Lady Gay"

#80: "Old Robin of Portingale"

#81: "[The Ballad of] Little/Lady Musgrave/Musgrove and Lady/Lord Barnard," "[Little/Lyttle] Matty/Mattie Grove/Groves/Musgrave," "Lord Banner"

#82: "[The] Bonny Birdy"

#83: "Child/Gil Maurice/Morice/Morris/Norris"

#84: "[Bonny/The Ballad of/The Cruelty of] Barbara/Barbry/Barb'ry/Barberry/Bawbee Allen/Ellen"

#85: "Lady Alice," "George/Johnny Collins"

#86: "Young Benjie"

#87: "Prince Robert," "Lord O'Bore," "Lord Abore and Mary Flynn"

#88: "Young Johnstone"

#89: "False Foodrage/Foudrage," "East Muir King," "King O'Lurve"

#90: "Jellion/Jellon Grame"

#91: "Fair Mary of Wallington," "Bonnie Earl of Livingston"

#92: "Bonny Bee Hom," "[The] Lowlands of Holland"

#93: "[Bo/Bol'] Lamkin," "Long Lankin"

#94: "Young Waters"

#95: "[The] Maid Freed from the Gallows," "Gallows Tree/Pole," "Derry Gaol," "[The] Hangman," "The Hangman's Tree," "Ropes I Man, Ropes I Man," "[The] Prickle/Pricklie/Prickilie/Prickly [Holly] Bush"

#96: "[The Gay] Goshawk"

#97: "Brown Robin"

#98: "Brown Adam," "Brown Edom"

#99: "Johnie/Johnnie Scot"

#100: "Willie/Willy o Winesbury/Winsbury," "[The]re Was a Lady Lived in the West," "Lord Thomas of Winesberry," "Johnny Barden"

#101: "Willie o Douglas Dale"

#102: "Willie and Earl Richard's Daughter," "Robin Hood's Birth," "The Birth of Robin Hood"

#103: "Rose the Red and White Lily"

#104: "Prince Heathen"

#105: "[The] Bailiff's Daughter of Islington"

#106: "[The] Famous Flower of Serving-Men," "Sweet William," "[The] Lament of the Border Widow"

#107: "Will Stewart and John"

#108: "Christopher White"

#109: "Tom Potts"

#110: "[The] Knight and the Shepherd's Daughter," "Knight William," "The Royal Forester"

#111: "Crow and Pie"

#112: "Blow Away the Winds/Morning Dew," "[The] Baffled Knight," "[The] Shepherd Lad," "Katie Morey"

#113: "[The] [Great] Silkie/Selchie [of Sule/Shule Skerry]"

#114: "Johnie Cock," "Fair John and the Seven Foresters," "Johnie O'Braidslea/O'Brady's Lea/O'Breadisley"

#115: "Robyn and Gandeleyn"

#116: "Adam Bell, Clim of the Clough and William of Cloudesly"

#117: "A [Little] Gest of Robyn Hode"

#118: "Robin Hood and Guy of Gisborne"

#119: "Robin Hood and the Monk"

#120: "Robin Hood's Death [and Burial]"
#121: "Robin Hood and the Potter"
#122: "Robin Hood and the Butcher"
#123: "Robin Hood and the Curtal Friar"
#124: "[The] Jolly Pinder of Wakefield"
#125: "Robin Hood and Little John"
#126: "Robin Hood and the Tanner"
#127: "Robin Hood and the Tinker"
#128: "Robin Hood Newly Revived"
#129: "Robin Hood and the Prince of Aragon"
#130: "Robin Hood and the Scotchman"
#131: "Robin Hood and the Ranger"
#132: "[The] Bold Pedlar and Robin Hood"
#133: "Robin Hood and the Beggar, I"
#134: "Robin Hood and the Beggar, II"
#135: "Robin Hood and the Shepherd"
#136: "Robin Hood's Delight"
#137: "Robin Hood and the Pedlars"
#138: "Robin Hood and Allen a Dale"
#139: "Robin Hood's Progress to Nottingham"
#140: "Robin Hood Rescuing Three Squires" "Robin Hood and the Three Squires"
#141: "Robin Hood Rescuing Will Stutly"
#142: "Little John a Begging"
#143: "Robin Hood and the Bishop"
#144: "Robin Hood and the Bishop of Hereford"
#145: "Robin Hood and Queen Katherine"
#146: "Robin Hood's Chase"
#147: "Robin Hood's Golden Prize"
#148: "[The] Noble Fisherman, or Robin Hood's Preferment"
#149: "Robin Hood's Birth, [Breeding, Valor and Marriage]," "Robin Hood's Xmas at Gamwell Hall"
#150: "Robin Hood and Maid Marian"
#151: "[The] King's Disguise, and Friendship with Robin Hood"
#152: "Robin Hood and the Golden Arrow"
#153: "Robin Hood and the Valiant Knight"
#154: "A True Tale of Robin Hood"
#155: "[Little] Sir Hugh/William," "[The] Jew's Daughter/Garden," "It Rained a Mist," "The Fatal Flower Garden"
#156: "Queen Eleanor's Confession," "Fair Rosemund"
#157: "Gude Wallace"
#158: "Hugh Spencer's Feats in France"
#159: "Durham Field"

#160: "[The] Knight of Liddesdale"

#161: "[The] Battle of Otterburn/Otterburne," "Lammas Tide"

#162: "[The] Hunting of the Cheviot," "Chevy Chase/Chace"

#163: "[The] Battle of Harlaw"

#164: "King Henry Fifth's Conquest [of France]," "[The] Fency King and the English King"

#165: "Sir John Butler"

#166: "[The] Rose of England"

#167: "[Sir] Andrew Barton/Baron/Bataan," "Henry Martyn"

#168: "Flodden Field"

#169: "[The Betrayal of] Johnie/Johnny Armstrong," "Johnny Armstrong's Last Goodbye"

#170: "[The] Death of Queen Jane," "Jane Was a Neighbor," "King Henry"

#171: "Thomas Cromwell"

#172: "Musselburgh Field"

#173: "Mary Hamilton," "[The] Four/Queen's Maries"

#174: "Earl Bothwell"

#175: "[The] Rising in the North"

#176: "Northumberland Betrayed by Douglas"

#177: "[The] Earl of Westmoreland"

#178: "Captain Car, or, Edom o Gordon"

#179: "Rookhope Ryde"

#180: "King James and Brown"

#181: "[The] Bonnie/Bonny Earl of/o Moray," "[The] Earl o' Murray"

#182: "[The] Laird [o] Logie," "Young Logie"

#183: "Willie Macintosh," "[The] Burning of Auchindoun/Auchindoon"

#184: "[The] Lads of Wamphray"

#185: "Dick o the Cow"

#186: "Kinmont Willie"

#187: "Jock o the Side"

#188: "Archie o Cawfield," "Bold Archer," "[The] Escape of Old John Webb," The Brothers"

#189: "Hobie Noble"

#190: "Jamie Telfer of/o the Fair Dodhead"

#191: "[The Lamentation of] Hughie Grame/Graeme/Graham"

#192: "[The] Lochmaben Harper," "[The] Blind Harper"

#193: "[The] Death of Parcy Reed"

#194: "[The] Laird of Warriston"

#195: "Lord Maxwell's Last Goodnight"

#196: "[The] Fire of Frendraught"

#197: "James Grant"

#198: "Bonny John Seton"

#199: "Bonnie/Bonny House o Airlie"
#200: "[The] Gypsy Davy/Laddie/Rover," "Black Jack Davey/Davy/ David," "Gypsies-O," "[The] [W]raggle Taggle Gypsies," "Seven Gypsies on Yon Hill," "Seven Yellow Gypsies," "The Black-Guarded Gypsies," "[The] Whistling Gypsy"
#201: "Bessy/Betsy Bell [and Mary Gray]," "Two Bonnie Lasses"
#202: "[The] Battle of Philiphaugh"
#203: "[The] Baron o/of Brackley"
#204: "Jamie Douglas," "[Oh] Waly Waly/Wallie Wallie," "[The] Water Is Wide," "[When] Cockleshells [Turn Silver Bells]," "Wade in the Water"
#205: "Loudon Hill, or, Dromclog"
#206: "[The Battle of] Bothwell Bridge"
#207: "Lord Delamere"
#208: "Lord Derwentwater," "Derwentwater's Farewell," "Lord Allen-water," "[The] King's Love Letter"
#209: "Geordie," "Georgie"
#210: "Bonnie James/George Campbell"
#211: "Bewick and Graham"
#212: "[The] Duke of Athole's Nurse," "Little Duke Arthur's Nurse"
#213: "Sir James the Rose"
#214: "[The] [Braes o] Yarrow," "[The] [Dowie] Dens o Yarrow," "Heathery Hills O'Yarrow"
#215: "Rare Willie Drowned in Yarrow," "[The] Water o Gamrie," "Wille Drowned in Ero," "Rare Willie," "Willie's Rare," "Annan/ Allan/Allen Water"
#216: "[The] Mother's Malison," "Clyde's Water," "Clyde Waters," "The Drowned Lover"
#217: "[The] Broom of Cowdenknows," "Bonnie May," "[The] Maid of the Cowdie and Knowes"
#218: "[The] False Lover Won Back," "Honey for the Bee"
#219: "[The] Gardener [Lad]," "[The] Gardener's Child"
#220: "[The] Bonny Lass of Anglesey"
#221: "Katherine Jaffray/Jaffrey," "[The] Green Wedding"
#222: "Bonny Baby Livingston"
#223: "Epie/Eppie/Eppy Morrie/Moray"
#224: "[The] Lady of Arngosk"
#225: "Rob Roy"
#226: "Lizie Lindsay," "Leezie/Lizzie Lindsay"
#227: "Bonny Lizie Baillie"
#228: "Glasgow Peggie/Peggy"
#229: "Earl Crawford"
#230: "[The] Slaughter of the Laird of Mellerstain"

#231: "[The] Earl of Errol"

#232: "Richie Story"

#233: "Andrew Lammie," "Mill O'Tifty's Annie"

#234: "Charlie Mac Pherson"

#235: "[The] Earl of Aboyne"

#236: "[The] Laird o/of Drum," "[The] Gates of Drum"

#237: "[The] Duke of Gordon's Daughter"

#238: "Glenlogie or Jean o Bethelnie"

#239: "Lord Saltoun and Auchanachie," "Johnny Doyle," "An[n]achie Gordon"

#240: "[The] [Bonny] Rantin Laddie"

#241: "[The] Baron o Leys"

#242: "[The] Coble o Cargill"

#243: "James Harris," "[The] D[a]emon Lover," "[The] House Carpenter," "Well Met My Own True Love"

#244: "James Hatley"

#245: "Young Allan"

#246: "Redesdale and Wise William"

#247: "Lady Elspat"

#248: "[The] Grey Cock," "Saw You My Father?," "Here's a Health unto All Lovers," "[The] Ghost Lover," "[The] Lover's Ghost," "[The] Night Visiting Song," "[The] Pretty Crowing Chicken," "[The] Bay of Biscay," "Fly Up My Cock"

#249: "Auld Matron"

#250: "[Young] Henry Martyn/Martin [Pirate Ballad]," "Andrew Bataan," "[The] Lofty Tall Ship"

#251: "Lang Johnny More," "Long John More," "Long John, Old John and Jackie North"

#252: "[The] Kitchie-Boy," "Lord Gordon's Kitchen Boy"

#253: "Thomas o Yonderdale"

#254: "Lord William, or, Lord Lundy"

#255: "Willie's Fatal Visit"

#256: "Alison and Willie," "My Luve She Lives"

#257: "Burd Isabel and Earl Patrick"

#258: "Broughty Wa's," "Burd Helen"

#259: "Lord Thomas Stuart"

#260: "Lord Thomas and Lady Margaret"

#261: "Lady Isabel"

#262: "Lord Livingston"

#263: "[The] New-Slain Knight"

#264: "[The] White Fisher"

#265: "[The] Knight's Ghost"

#266: "John Thomson and the Turk"

#267: "[The] Heir of Linne/Linne/Lynn"

#268: "[The] Twa Knights"

#269: "Lady Diamond/Dysie/Eliza"

#270: "[The] Earl of Mar's Daughter"

#271: "[The] Lord of Lorn and the False Steward"

#272: "[The] Suffolk Miracle," "[The] Holland Handkerchief"

#273: "King Edward the Fourth and a Tanner of Tamworth," "A Pleasant Ballad of King Henry II and the Miller of Mansfield," "King Jamie and the Tinker," "[The] King and The Tinker"

#274: "Our Goodman/Gudeman," "My Good Man," "Cabbage Head Blues," "[Three/Four/Five/Seven] Nights Drunk/Experience," "Seven Drunken Nights," "I Came in the Other Night," "I Came Home Drunk," "Wake Up Baby"

#275: "Get Up and Bar the Door," "[The] Barring o/of the Door," "John Blunt"

#276: "[The] Friar in/at the Well," "The Fryar Well Fitted"

#277: "[The Wife Wrapt/Wrapped [up] in] [a] Wether's Skin/Sheepskin," "Rissilty Rossity," "Risselty-Rosso/alty," "Nickety Nackety [Now Now Now]," "The Nick Nack Song," "The Women Are Worse Than Men," "[The] Wee Cooper O'Fife," "A Merry Jeste of a Shrewde and Curste Wyfe Lapped in Morelles Skin for her Good Behaviour"

#278: "[The] Farmer's Curst Wife," "[The] Devil/Divil and the Farmer/Feathery Wife," "[The] Devil out of Hell," "The Devil Song," "Lily Bulero," "[The] Old Lady and The Devil," "Little Devils," "O Daddy Be Gay"

#279: "[The] Jolly Beggar," "[The] Little Beggarman," "[The] Auld Beggar Man," "[The] Gaberlunzie Man," "Davy Faa"

#280: "[The] Beggar-Laddie," "[The] Beggar's Dawtie"

#281: "[The] Keach i/in/and the Creel," "[The] Wee Toun Clerk"

#282: "Jock the Leg and the Merry Merchant," "Yorkshire Bite"

#283: "[The] Crafty Farmer," "Oxford Merchant," "[The] Fair Damsel from London Town," "Well Sold the Cow," "The Oxford Merchant"

#284: "John Dory"

#285: "[The] George Aloe and the Sweepstake," "[The] Coast of High Barbary," "[High] Barbaree/Barbary"

#286: "[The] Sweet Trinity," "[The] Golden Vanity/Vanitee/Victory," "The Golden Fenidier," "Sinking in the Lonesome Sea," "The Merry/Merrie Golden Tree," "The Turkish Rebelee/Revery," "The Lowlands Low," "The Weeping Willow Tree," "A Ship Set Sail for North America"

#287: "Captain Ward [and the Rainbow/Streaker]"

#288: "[The] Young Earl of Essex's Victory over the Emperor of Germany"

#289: "[The] Mermaid," "[The] Raging Sea, How It Roars," "The Wave on the Sea," "The Merrimac at Sea"

#290: "[The] Wylie Wife of the Hie Toun Hie"

#291: "Child/Chylde Owlet"

#292: "[The] West-Country Damosel's Complaint"

#293: "John of/o Hazelgreen/Hazeldean"

#294: "Dugall Quin"

#295: "The Brown Girl," "[The] Rich Irish Lady" (relationship disputed).

#296: "Walter Lesly"

#297: "Earl Rothes"

#298: "Young Peggy," "Peggy and Jaime"

#299: "[The] Trooper and [the] Maid," "The Soldier and the Lady," "As I Roved Out," "[The] Brewer's Daughter"

#300: "Blancheflour and Jellyflorice"

#301: "[The] Queen of Scotland"

#302: "Young Bearwell"

#303: "[The] Holy Nunnery"

#304: "Young Ronald"

#305: "[The] Outlaw Murray"

INTRODUCTION

Let's get one thing straight from the start. This is *not* a book about folk music. Nor is it about folk musicians. It is, however, a book about the 305 songs that have frequently been described as the bedrock of what we know as traditional folk music, and how they have continued to be performed in the modern world with as much, if not more, enthusiasm than ever they were sung in centuries gone by.

For their age *is* numbered in centuries, with one or two pushing close to a millennium's worth, according to some researchers. Certainly all were commonplace in the Victorian era, and the Georgian Age before that. The Tudors knew many of them; the Plantagenets, too.

Some form the soundtrack to historical novels that tell tales from the age of the Norman Conquest. Others might have been sung at the battles of Agincourt and Crécy. They commemorate shipwrecks that history has long since forgotten, and personages of whom it may never have heard. Indeed, they *are* history, and yet they remain alive today via new recordings and fresh reissues from across the musical spectrum, from Joseph Haydn and Benjamin Britten to Led Zeppelin and Ritchie Blackmore; from Sonny Boy Williamson to a former First Lady of the United States.

They populate Spotify playlists and YouTube video channels; they soundtrack TV and movie epics. They are the Child Ballads, and they are what author Alan Garner night have been thinking of, in his novel *Treacle Walker*, when he conjured "a tune with wings, trampling things, tightened strings, boggarts and bogles and brags on their feet."

For they are that; and they are more besides.

Child's *English and Scottish Popular Ballads* was by no means the first book to bring together a selection of "traditional" songs. Child himself had already published the *English and Scottish Ballads* (*ESB*) in the late 1850s, the latest representative of a school of research that dated back to the 1600s.

These earlier collections, however, were just that. They collected ballads, often heedless of origin, history, and authenticity. The *ESPB* was the first to truly curate itself; to single out the ballads that represented the very cream of the crop.

The *ESPB*'s sheer longevity echoes that accolade, as Missouri-based folklorist Julie Henigan acknowledges.[1] "All of the academics and collectors I was aware of [regarded the Child Ballads as] the crown jewels."

Partly, she believes, this was because the ballads had clearly been handed down orally for centuries before the first pen consigned their words to paper; and partly because they were "of the people." Not the palaces, not the courts, not the mansion houses. These were the songs of the farmers and drovers and blacksmiths and sailors. And if that makes them sound a little like today's pop songs, then so be it.

But the Child Ballads are an extraordinary document for reasons beyond their undeniable quality, their venerable age and their extraordinary insights into the lives of our long-dead predecessors.

They are also thrilling, exciting, sordid, and sensational. For many listeners, their first exposure to the Child Ballads took the form of a murder mystery, a horror story, a tale of the supernatural. To delve into the Child Ballads is to slip so far from the most common perceptions of "folk music" that it is difficult to believe that these *are* folk songs.

The devil stalks the land, tempting some people, kidnapping others. Murderesses are burned, noblemen are slain, children are poisoned, lovers are drowned. Regiments are wiped out on the battlefield and entire ships' companies are lost at sea. Pregnant sisters are slain by the brothers who impregnated them.

Outlaws roam unchecked, pirates rampage unstoppable, fathers imprison their daughters, demons seduce damsels, queens are beheaded, and fair maidens die for love. Heroes are heroic, villains are villainous. Fairy queens transform unfaithful subjects into wild beasts, and newborn babies are thrown into the ocean to drown.

In one of the collection's most haunting tales, "The Great Selchie of Sule Skerry" (113), a young woman takes a seal for her lover, only to see both the seal and their presumably half-seal love child slain by a hunter.

In another, "Lamkin" (93), a mother and child are ruthlessly slaughtered by a psychopath and his sidekick.

In a third, "Little Musgrave" (81), an aristocrat returns home to discover his wife in bed with one of the villagers. He savagely murders them both.

It is as if every tabloid newspaper headline of the last century or so has been bound together into a single document, and then ferociously edited by a malevolent elf. Or, as musician and folklorist Dom Flemons put it,[2] "I remember hearing Grandpa Jones[3] do a version of 'The Brown Girl' and the first time you hear how he chops her head off and kicks it against the wall, you think, 'Man! This is so hardcore.'"

An early working title for this book was *We Will Stab Him with a Pin*, from a line in the aforementioned "Lamkin." Another was *A Grisly Ghost, Stamping*, from "King Henry" (32). That we eventually settled upon the present title should not be taken to mean the nature of the ballads has in any way been diluted.

They remain the saddest, sweetest, ghastliest and goriest stories ever told. Author, academic, and musician Polly Paulusma muses, "There's something we all recognize in them, something of our unconscious, something of our dreams in them. They feel like they have an echo back to our forefathers, or it's like sonar, a ping in the darkness, and you wait for the return. These songs give us some sense of cultural geo-positioning in that way."[4]

What they most certainly are not are folk songs. How can they be? Did Beethoven wake up in the morning and say, "I think I'll write some classical music today?" Did Marie Lloyd trot down to the theater to sing some "old time music"?

No. Beethoven wrote music, Marie Lloyd sang songs. The terms that we apply to their music today are simply disposable tags applied to entire bodies of work, regardless of its content, its age, and its intentions. So it is with what is now called "folk music."

The term came into popular use around the beginning of the twentieth century, abbreviated from the more all-encompassing term *folklore*—itself coined a mere half century previous by the author Ambrose Merton. In the August 22, 1846, edition of *The Athenaeum* magazine, Merton declared "What we in England designate as Popular Antiquities ... would be most aptly described by a good Saxon compound Folk-lore"—the teachings of the people.[5]

The term's accepted meaning today, and its heedless embrace of almost anyone with an acoustic guitar and a handful of songs, would have been meaningless to Merton. To his mind, the songs that were a part of his "folk-lore" remained firmly locked in the past, as much a part of our heritage as the ruins of Pompeii or the stones of Stonehenge ... and who could even dream of "modernizing" those?

Professor Child took this principle even further. He was interested in the ballads as poetry as opposed to performance pieces. They may have been a part of a culture's folklore, but they were not folk *songs*.

It is a contentious point, one of several that can be raised when discussing Child's work, and American singer Judy Collins speaks for many when she reflects, "Child ... did not consider the melody to be essential to the lyric and, quite frankly, I think that was one of the things that led [the folk scene] astray a little bit, because we look at this work without the music and consider it in some kind of odd way as literature. But a lyric is not a poem, and a poem is not a lyric, and I think it put us off on the wrong foot. A big piece of what tradition is about was missed."[6]

Not that Child's thoughtlessness sounded any kind of death knell for the songs. Many of the ballads were still current during the professor's lifetime, familiar and popular.

They might be sung in music hall and vaudeville performances, at medicine shows and family gatherings. They might be referenced in novels or reworked into new songs. Some were chanted in the schoolyard as children skipped rope or played other games. The ballad of "The Mermaid" (289), for example, was behind the Aberdeenshire game "Three Times 'Round Went Oor Gallant Ship."

They were present, too, in traditional witchcraft—that is, forms practiced in the decades prior to the development of Wicca in the early 1950s. The riddling that is familiar to us from ballads such as "The Devil's Nine Questions" (1), "The Elphin Knight" (2), and so forth was (and might still be) integral to several local traditions, and a northern English variant on "Allison Gross" (35) where the witch is the injured party was still being sung by a hereditary practitioner in the late-1970s, who learned it as a child in the 1930s.

In every such instance, Judy Collins continues, "The lyrics are important, the stories are important, but the original melodies are important too." They not only carry information, she says, but they broadcast our very DNA. "When a person is singing [a traditional song], there we are, sitting in the audience, it's dark, we're listening to this, and we're all going through our ancestral memories and musings, and [the singer] is, too."[7]

For the majority of people who witnessed the ballads in what we might call their "natural surroundings," the songs that have been singled out as the Child Ballads were a part of the musical furniture. Few cared—or even thought—about the qualities that Child appreciated. Songs were for singing, not for studying, and people sang them.

Not all of them. Child's remit was vast and, even at the time, many of the 305 songs he singled out across his balladry were already obscure. For every song for which he found a dozen or more different lyrics, there were others known only from a single old manuscript. Thus, while his books' title described its contents as *Popular*, many were already forgotten.

Singer and scholar Brian Peters explains,[8]

> When Child referred to "popular" ballads he was not using "popular" in its modern sense. If you want to get an idea of their relative popularity with

singers, look at Bertrand H. Bronson's *Traditional Tunes of the Child Ballads*.[9]
In those volumes you'll find some—such as "Barbara Allen" [84], "Lord
Thomas and Fair Ellender" [73], and "The Outlandish Knight" [4]—that are
each represented by 100–200 collected examples, whereas for many others
there are few or none at all. Having done some page-counting in my own
treasured set of Bronson, I find that ballads numbered #1–100 occupy over
950 pages, #101–200 take up 300-odd pages, and #201–305 about 650.

This can then be broken down further. Assembling his collection, Child
gathered songs together by theme. Romance and the supernatural dominated the first 100 or so; Robin Hood and general history consumed the
200s; and the remainder comprised what Peters describes as "'Anecdotal,'
some of which he didn't particularly like."

The popularity or otherwise of certain ballads was then skewed even
further around the midpoint of the last century. Peters continues,

> When the folk revival came along, a lot of singers were attracted to ballads
> with a vigorous singing tradition, since there were plentiful variants with
> tunes readily available that could be learned without much ado. [But they]
> focused also on some of the more Gothic ballads, particularly those dealing
> with witchcraft and the supernatural. Never mind their extreme rarity in oral
> tradition, and the fact that they usually required quite a bit of work; "King
> Henry" [32], "Kemp Owyne" [34], "Allison Gross" [35] and "Thomas the
> Rhymer" [37]. . . .

The same rules hold true today, too. Even within the most fervent circles,
there are many Child Ballads that almost nobody sings and nobody
remembers, unless they happen to rank among that doughty band of
online performers who set out to perform and record their own interpretation of every song in the *ESPB*.

Even Ewan MacColl, the Scots-born writer, performer, and radical
whose boundless fascination with the Child Ballads saw him release more
than twenty LPs dedicated to the subject, nevertheless recorded little
more than one-third of the full corpus.

The songs, however, survived. And, again, while the default setting for
anybody discussing the Child Ballads is to refer to them as "folk music,"
that is to completely disregard the sheer complexity of their lineage.

What were the first Child Ballads you ever heard?

For singer Judy Collins, it was Elton Hayes's rendering of "The Gypsy
Rover" (200) from the soundtrack of an early 1950s Alan Ladd movie, and
country star Jo Stafford's "Barbara Allen" (84).

To lovers of classical music, it might have been Gustav Holst's grandiose orchestration of "King Estmere" (60) or Ralph Vaughan Williams's
"The Baffled Knight" (112).

For the generation that came of radio-listening age in the mid-1960s, it was Simon and Garfunkel's chart-topping "Scarborough Fair" (2), or the Dubliners' "Seven Drunken Nights" (274). For rockers of the early 1970s, it might have been Led Zeppelin's rendition of "Gallows Pole" (95).

In more recent times, it could have been White Stripes' galloping "Black Jack Davey" (200), the Waterboys' manic take on Davey's close cousin "The Raggle Taggle Gypsies," or that veneficial rendition of "Barbara Allen" (84), conjured for Dolly Parton's *Heartsongs Live from Home* album, Parton and Irish singer Mairéad Ni Mhaonaigh trading verses in English and Gaelic.

Or thousands more besides.

Neither are we limited to music as we contemplate our initial exposure to the balladry. Roddy McDowall directed and Ava Gardner starred in a 1970 horror movie titled for, schemed around, and soundtracked by "Tam Lin" (39), and the melody of "Willie O'Winsbury" (100) haunts the cult celluloid of *The Wicker Man*.

Shirley Jackson published *The Daemon Lover* in 1949, with her title borrowed from Child 243. The paperback edition of Lindsay Barraclough's *Long Lankin* quotes a couple of lines from "Lamkin" on its front cover; Amanda MacLean's *The Flax Flower* is built upon the story of "Andrew Lammie" (233), in which a woman is beaten to death by her brother for loving a man that her family dislikes.

Angela Carter lifted elements from several Child Ballads in her novels and short stories and "The Maid and the Palmer" (21) haunts her "The Executioner's Beautiful Daughter." Virginia Woolf mentions "Mary Hamilton" (173) in *A Room with a View* (1929). There are references to the Child Ballads in James A. Michener's *The Drifters* (1971). Artist Charles Vess created the graphic novel *Book of Ballads* in 1997, drawing almost wholly upon the Child Ballads for his storylines.

These borrowings are not recent developments. Printed versions of the songs that became the Child Ballads (and many more besides), sold cheaply on the streets by peddlers and publishers, are likely almost as old as the printing press; and in 1839, no less a literary dream team than Charles Dickens, William Makepeace Thackeray, and artist George Cruikshank combined forces to publish their own interpretation of "The Loving Ballad of Lord Bateman" (53).

It matters not that we don't know who originally wrote the ballads, or when they were written. In many cases, we aren't even sure what their original melody was, and the musical term *contrafacta*—meaning, the substitution of one text for another without substantial change to the music—might well have been invented for the benefit of the Child Ballads, as folklorist Hester NicEilidh explains: "Ballad meter and structure are quite standardized, so there is nothing to prevent the lyrics from a supposed 'literary' ballad being sung to the known tune of another ballad."[10] She cites the popular air "Greensleeves" as a well-known example of this contrafacta, its melody having once been equally familiar as the tune of the popular nineteenth-century carol "What Child Is This?" NicEilidh goes on to say,

> Other Christmas and New Year's lyrics were associated with the tune as early as the seventeenth century. Similarly, the traditional tune to which Robert Burns originally set "Auld Lang Syne" is not the same one we are most familiar with today from New Year's celebrations. [Furthermore], printers . . . may not have bothered to specify a tune, as pretty much any ballad tune would work for anyone who wanted to sing rather than just read the ballad.

Thus "The Twa Corbies" (26) is most frequently sung to a melody first borrowed by Scots poet R. M. Blythman from the Breton tune "An Alarc'h" ("The Swan"); and singer James Raynard performs "The Loathsome Worm and the Mackerel of the Sea" (36) to the tune of "The Italian Rant"—which may or may not be appropriate for a ballad in which a witch turns her stepson into a hideous worm and his sister into a fish who drops by to comb his hair every week.

But it works, and this process of reinvention and reinterpretation continues to this day. For not only are original melodies malleable, so are the ballads' very plot lines.

Collector and performer John Jacob Niles once noted that the most common American version of "The Elphin Knight" (2), "My Father Gave Me an Acre of Land," had completely stripped away the supernatural elements that hallmarked the original, heedless of the fact that it's the supernatural that was the focus of the ballad in the first place.

Hearing the music of the fairies, a young girl dreamed of finding a supernatural lover. Summoned by her longing, the Elphin Knight appeared, only to reject her because she was too young. What followed was a battle of wits, the series of riddles that would, in later years, become the sole focus of the song.

In its original form, the ballad is playful, suspenseful, and even sexually suggestive. In its later incarnation, it is merely wheedling, the male protagonist issuing what amounts to a litany of demands, with only a vague promise if the young woman complies: "Tell her to make me a shirt," "tell her to plow my field," tell her this, tell her that, and maybe I'll fancy her when I see how well she does.

Look, also, at some of the other titles under which the Knight now does his business: "The Wind Has Blown My Plaid Awa'," "O Say Do You Know the Way to Selin," "The Fairy Knight," "Lord John," "The Cambric Shirt," "The De[v]il's Courtship," "Whittingham Fair," "The

Lover's Tasks," "The Parsley Vine," "The Shirt of Lace," "The Tri-coloured House," "Strawberry Lane," "Rosemary Lane," "Love, Letter and Answer." With just one or two exceptions, it's difficult even to recognize the old song.

What befell "The Elphin Knight" is neither an uncommon process nor is it an archaic one. Some eighty years after Niles made his observation in 1934, the duo of Jefferson Hamer and Anaïs Mitchell recorded another of the Child Ballads' great tales of magic and fairy—possibly even the greatest of them all. "Tam Lin" (39) is the story of a maiden's battle to win her lover back from the Queen of the Fairies. Or it was. Hamer and Mitchell, however, wanted to focus upon another aspect of the story, and dispensed with both the magic *and* the fairies. Hamer subsequently recalled, "Very early on, I gave up reading the online commentary. Some people were getting pretty hostile!"[11]

Yet change was inevitable, even when the ballads were young. There was no radio in those days, no records nor CDs, no songbooks nor lyric sheets. The majority of people were illiterate. Ballads were learned orally—somebody sang a song and, if you liked it, you'd ask them to teach you the words. Or you'd do your best to remember them as they were being sung.

This process continued even into the earliest years of the twentieth century. In 1975, collectors Jim Carroll and Pat Mackenzie interviewed Mikeen McCarthy, an aged Irish traveller—a "gypsy" in the vernacular of his generation—"who, as a youth, had sold . . . ballads around the fairs and markets of rural West Kerry with his mother. He told of how he would go into a local printing shop and recite some of his father's many songs over the counter to the printer, who wrote them down and printed them out to an agreed number."[12]

The procedure was not perfect; or, for our purposes, perhaps it was. Mishear a lyric and you've changed the song. Take out a reference to something that would mean nothing to your intended audience, and replace it with another, you've changed it some more. Alter the name of a primary character to fit, say, a local dignitary, make a few judicious edits to increase the tension or make the story flow more seamlessly, all of these things serve to alter the original composition, and when enough of them have taken place, that's when the scholars descend to proclaim the discovery of a new variation.

The shift might be geographical. To remain with "The Elphin Knight," the version known as "Scarborough Fair" most likely originated in the English county of Yorkshire, wherein the titular annual agricultural fair took place. Further north in Northumberland, however, the ballad was sung of the local "Whittingham Fair" (this version was recorded by Eliza Carthy and Nancy Kerr, in 1993). A ballad sung in Scotland would likely reference very different locales to its counterpart sung in England. But even in the smallest, closest communities, there can be signal differences.

Appalachian singer Jean Ritchie recalled visiting her Uncle Jason, just a short bus ride and a five-mile walk from her home in Viper County, and hearing him sing "Lord Bateman" (53), a song that she knew from her own family's repertoire. But there was something about it that was different, in the words, in the melody, in the very delivery. "It was always a wonder to me," she later wrote, "how families living close to one another could sing the same song and sing it so different."[13]

When the Ritchies sang the ballad that Child called "The Maid Freed from the Gallows" (95), but which they knew as "Hangman, Slack Your Rope," it was indeed a maiden who awaited rescue. However, when their near neighbors the Engles sang it, the felon was a male highwayman.

Sometimes, the difference could be merely a matter of removing an unfamiliar term. Jim Carroll recalls Ewan MacColl discussing "Sir Patrick Spens" (58) and pointing out a piece of weather lore in Child's earliest version (from the 1790s) that suggests the ballad was composed either by a farmer or a sailor, those being the professions that were most likely to notice if they "saw the new moon yestreen wi' the auld moon in its arms." But not every audience pursued those professions, and so some performers would dispense with that verse.

Always, however, the story remained, and one hopes it always will. American musician Timothy Renner, who has recorded more than a dozen Child Ballads under his Stone Breath alias (and also for his Strange Familiars podcast), nevertheless highlights some of the dangers that the ballads might face in the modern era:

> I think they are great stories and great melodies. Sometimes there were lessons being taught with the songs—or social justice—often in subtle ways and, in this, wisdom was being passed from generation to generation. Until relatively recently, the ballads were just memorized, learned from one singer to another, and when we lost that part of the tradition we may have lost some very powerful part of the equation, for better and worse. The ballads will continue to change and evolve, but in different ways than before. Now we have the written record, some traditional singers may feel like they can't add a verse or change things up. Or perhaps they will want to use only the earliest recorded version of the song, and there is value in that. But it takes out part of the equation of a sort of living/growing version of these songs. That said, these songs are very durable. They've lasted all this time—I'm sure they will survive any further changes that come their way.[14]

All of that is by way of explaining why there are so many different versions of so many of the ballads in circulation—not only in Child's original volumes, but also across a wealth of subsequent scholars' work. New discoveries continued to be made throughout the twentieth century and, hopefully, beyond as well.

This book discusses the nature of some of these finds, and the circumstances of their discovery. But it also looks at what was done with these discoveries *after* they had been found, and here we are fortunate in that we do have a very reliable record of this, in the form—appropriately enough—of audio recordings: wax cylinders, gramophone records, LPs, CDs, mp3s, video footage, and so forth.

The first audio documentaries of the still-living Child Ballads that we know of were those captured by folklorist and composer Percy Grainger in eastern England in 1906. As with all the other recordings Grainger made on these field trips, as such excursions were called, these particular renditions were recorded in or around the singer's home, on a portable recording machine, and were intended for Grainger's own use. Two years later, however, one of his earliest discoveries—an elderly man named Joseph Taylor—was recording again, but this time at a studio in London, for the His Master's Voice record label.

The aforementioned "Lord Bateman" was among the songs Taylor sang and, while the fragile shellac discs that resulted were destined to remain in obscurity, 1972 saw his performance find a whole new audience through its release on a compilation album titled *Unto Brigg Fair*. At which point, Ashley Hutchings's Albion Band started performing their own take on "Lord Bateman," and borrowed from Taylor for the occasion.

But changes were made, instrumentation was added, and the original Taylor performance, so quaint and old-fashioned to a hip seventies audience, was brought slam up to date by the Albions. And that, in a nutshell, is the story told here: the evolution of the Child Ballads from their earliest available recordings through to the most recent; and from the most pristinely traditional performances to the most far-reaching and far out.

Inevitably, and despite the affirmation that opened this introduction, we will meet a lot of what the modern world calls folk musicians. But we will also encounter rockers (both "classic" and "alternative") and jazzers, hillbillies, heartthrobs, bluesmen, vaudevillians, country stars, avant-garde improvisers, comedians, and classical composers.

We will not be discussing every version of every ballad. As of May 2022, the online Child Ballads Database[15] had noted over twenty-one thousand recordings, and it is by no means complete. How could it be when every year brings new recordings that add to the corpus? Discussions of collectors and performers, too, are limited by the sheer number of them.

This book's goal is to spotlight those people and performances that can be considered intrinsic to the ballads' overall story, whether as fleeting anecdote or life-changing revelation. Among the appendices, too, playlists will guide the curious toward key versions of the ballads, and the repertoires of those performers who have paid Professor Child's work the greatest attention. And, in following the convolutions and convulsions to which so many of these venerable old songs have been subjected, we will understand why the term *folk music* is both seriously overused and grossly misunderstood.

(Here, too, readers will find a download code for the London Experimental Ensemble's 2023 album *Child Ballads: The Final Six*, the first ever commercial recordings of the last six ballads in the *ESPB*.)

Because "folk music" certainly isn't the exclusive property of "folk musicians," and that has been the case for centuries. In case there is any doubt, however, ninety years ago no less an authority than the BBC took what any purists among their contemporary listeners must have considered a very bold step indeed, with a twenty-minute broadcast titled *A Recital of New Folk Song Settings*.

Aired on November 4, 1933, the program featured half a dozen traditional songs set to brand-new arrangements and sung by the acclaimed tenor David Brynley (1902–1981). A written preview in the BBC's *Radio Times* schedule guide then explained:

> The last fifty years has seen an enormous drive in the field of folk-music. Every nation has made its effort to preserve from oblivion before it is too late the priceless heritage of its native song and dance music. But it would now seem that the ground has nearly everywhere been dug over and little can remain still to discover.
>
> The interest, however, has scarcely begun, though the face of music has already changed considerably under the influence of the application of folk idioms to serious music. In another way, too, the fascinating study continues; the arranging and re-arranging of these lovely old tunes is a hobby with composers that never seems to pall.[16]

If only they knew.

Chapter One

THE VERY FIRST RECORD

On Friday, June 5, 1908, Canadian-born tenor Henry Burr (1882–1941) arrived at the fourth-floor suite that housed the Victor Talking Machine Company's new Victor Recording Studio in Camden, New Jersey, to record his next 78 rpm release.

The converted factory on Front and Cooper had been in operation for a little over six months; hitherto, Victor utilized premises across the river in Philadelphia, an imposing five-story brick building at 424 S. Tenth Street. That was where Burr recorded what were then his best-known performances, the traditional Scottish songs "Loch Lomond" and "Scots, Wha' Hae' wi' Wallace Bled."

This was not Burr's first trip to the new studio, however. He was in Camden in March to record "I Love and the World Is Mine." On this latest occasion, he had two songs in mind, "In the Shade of the Old Apple Tree," composed by the writing team of Van Alstyne and Harry Williams, and "Jock O'Hazeldean," another from his repertoire of Scottish numbers. And, in so doing, he stepped into history as the first artist ever to make a commercial recording of a Child Ballad.

"Jock O'Hazeldean" appears toward the end of Child's collection, numbered 293 out of the total of 305, a somewhat maudlin ballad in which a gentleman does his level best to dissuade a maiden from loving the titular Jock but is resisted at every turn.

Burr's version is not what academia would describe as "authentic," in that it is not wholly a traditional song. Rather, it was taken from an adaptation penned by Sir Walter Scott, which was based, in turn, upon what Scott's transcriber, a Mr. C. K. Sharpe, described as a manuscript "in a female hand, written probably about one hundred years ago" (i.e., the early 1700s).

Nevertheless, Child was impressed enough that he included this same manuscript in the *ESPB*.

We do not know if Burr was aware of the significance of his recording; we don't know, in fact, whether he even knew of Child's work. It's likely that he did not. Less than a decade had passed since the final volume of the *ESPB* was published, and it was largely the preserve of collectors and academics alone. Burr, on the other hand, was a popular singer with a vast repertoire of traditional songs. "Jock O'Hazeldean," in his estimation, was probably just one more in that canon.

A large man, with a high forehead and dark, piercing eyes, Burr was born Harry Haley McClaskey in 1882, in the Canadian border town of Saint Stephen, New Brunswick. A community built around the twin industries of timber and shipbuilding, the town's downtown and seafront were still recovering from the devastating fire of 1877, and sometime after Burr's birth, his candy-store-owning father relocated the family some sixty miles west to a house on Armstrong Street in Saint John.

Growing up, the boy proved a talented singer, regularly performing in church and at local exhibitions, where his already powerful, but always pleasant tenor caught the ear of Giuseppe Campanari, a baritone with the Metropolitan Opera. At Campanari's bidding, Burr relocated to New York City in 1902 and began recording for the Columbia label, before moving to Victor in 1905. There, he distinguished himself across a variety of musical fields (he claimed to have made over twelve thousand recordings), but especially so with his ventures into the world of his ancestral Scotland.

"Jock O'Hazeldean" was cut "live," the only means available at the time. There were no microphones in those days; rather, singer and any accompanying musicians would gather around a large sound horn, attached to a needle that converted the sonic vibrations into grooved patterns on a master disk. It was released just weeks later on Victor.

"Jock O'Hazeldean" was a popular song in those early years of the gramophone. Burr returned to it in 1911, for release under one of his multitude of pseudonyms, John Young, around the same time as New York baritone Reinald Werrenrath (1883–1953) released his own grandiosely orchestrated take on the same ballad, on the B side of that other Burr favorite, "Scots Wha Hae wi' Wallace Bled."

Werrenrath, like Burr before him, was built for the opera, with his debut in that field coming in 1907, before culminating with his appearances alongside Pagliacci at the Metropolitan Opera House in 1919. Nevertheless, he simultaneously commenced a stream of more accessible releases for the Victor label, of which "Jock O'Hazeldean" was just one.

Soprano Mary Garden (1874–1967) recorded the same ballad for Columbia around 1912, and Scots singer Archie Anderson (not to be confused with Burr's Alfred Anderson pseudonym) recorded yet another for The Winner label in 1914.

Clearly, then, "Jock O'Hazeldean" was a popular number, but not because it was a Child Ballad. Indeed, it is notable that, in every recorded instance, it was the artist's sole venture into the pages of the *ESPB*. Even Anderson, whose entire repertoire was based around the songs of his homeland, delved no deeper. Confirmation, then, that it was the Scottish element of the song, not its traditional standing, that caught their ears.

Henry Burr was the first performer to record a Child Ballad for commercial release. He was not, however, the first to be recorded *singing* one. For that, we have to thank Percy Grainger (1882–1961), as writer Bob Thomas demonstrated in the liner notes to the 1972 LP *Unto Brigg Fair*: "Were it not for [Grainger's] perception and enthusiasm . . . we would have no record of the performance style of English traditional singers at the time when more folk songs and ballads were being sung and collected than at any period before or since."

Australian by birth, Grainger was a prodigious pianist. At age thirteen, he relocated to Frankfurt to study music in 1895, financing the move wholly via the proceeds of an Australian tour. There he studied alongside fellow aspirant composers Balfour Gardiner and Cyril Scott before moving to London in 1900 to commence his career as a concert pianist and composer.

A tousle (some might even say wild)-haired youth whose photographs always seem to capture a glimmer of mischief in his deep-set eyes, Grainger arrived in the city at a propitious moment.

English folk music was undergoing a renaissance at the time. Inspired by the American Child's efforts on behalf of their homeland's musical history, a number of English collectors—such names as Marianne Mason, Sabine Baring-Gould, W. A Barrett, and Frank Kidson—were now publishing their own discoveries, documenting songs that they had personally collected from around the United Kingdom

Several of these people were also involved in the Folk-Song Society, founded in 1898 as a focus for the new enthusiasts. The *ESPB*'s own reputation was then given a further boost in 1904, with the appearance of an abridged, "student's edition" edited by Child's daughter, Helen Child Sargent, and his long-time associate George Lyman Kittredge. (This edition would remain the most readily accessible edition of the Child Ballads for the next half century.)

Elsewhere, old songs were being revived as music hall hits and sheet music publishers—who commanded, at that time, a far larger market than gramophone recordings—were taking note.

Percy Grainger in 1919. George Grantham Bain Collection / Wikimedia Commmons

So was Percy Grainger. He had recently fallen under the spell of the Norwegian composer Edvard Grieg, whose settings of his homeland's traditional music left the Australian entranced, and, in March 1905, he attended a lecture on folk song at the Royal Musical Association in London.

It was presented by Lucy Broadwood (1858–1929), the granddaughter of John Broadwood, founder of the piano manufactory that bore his name, but in her own right a major power in the world of traditional music. A founding member of the Folk-Song Society, she was now editor of the influential *Folk Song Journal*, as well as an acclaimed composer and performer.

Ms. Broadwood likely inherited her love of traditional music from her paternal uncle, also named John Broadwood. His 1847 book *Old English Songs* is regarded as the first English publication ever to marry both the words and the tunes to its subject matter, its contents being drawn from his personal collection of local Suffolk and Surrey songs.

A fresh edition of this was published in 1880 under the title *Sussex Songs*, appended by sixteen further numbers that Lucy had collected. Another family member, music critic J. A. Fuller Maitland (husband of one of Lucy's cousins), enlisted her as joint editor of 1893's *English County Songs*. Ten of the volume's 184 songs were versions of ballads that Child had collected.

At the time Broadwood met Grainger, at that 1905 lecture, she was working toward the publication of another book, *English Traditional Carols and Songs*, and making regular trips into the countryside in search of fresh material, often in the company of fellow enthusiast Frank Kidson. They were preparing now for a visit to the Lincolnshire town of Brigg, to attend the annual North Lincolnshire Musical Competition. Grainger was invited to accompany them as a pianist.

He was little more than an observer on this occasion, watching as his companions introduced themselves to the singers, explained their quest and then sat feverishly writing with pen on paper as the songs poured out. Food would be eaten, drinks quaffed, anything to put the singers— many of whom had never encountered such interest before—at ease.

Grainger was astonished at what he heard. A pianist and composer, he sensed in these simple old songs a musical strain that spoke louder to him than any he had hitherto played or studied.

He was intrigued, too, by the performers, most particularly one Joseph Taylor (1833–1910). According to Taylor's daughter Mary, interviewed by folklorist Peter Kennedy for the BBC on March 27, 1953, "[Grainger had] heard of my father singing and he came over to see him . . . and asked him to enter in the coming competition. He got the first prize." Among Taylor's fellow competitors, she continued, was "one old gentleman [who] started singing and they couldn't stop him . . . of course the audience was convulsed with laughter."

Grainger returned to Lincolnshire the following year to attend the Brigg Music Festival, and watch as Taylor won the competitive element of the event with performances of "Brigg Fair" and "Bold William Taylor." Grainger also played at the event, entertaining the audience with his own settings of half a dozen of the folk songs that were collected locally, "Brigg Fair" among them.

Now he resolved to commence his own collection of songs. Unlike the majority of other "ballad collectors" of the day, however, he eschewed pen and paper as a means of capturing what he heard. Instead, he brought with him a phonograph on which he could record the singers as they sang. One can only imagine the various singers' reactions to this strange new technology.

Grainger recorded onto wax cylinders, and later acknowledged that it was not necessarily the songs or the singers that interested him, but the actual performance.

As folklorist Steve Roud noted in his essay on Grainger, posted to the British Library website in 2018,[1] "He became fascinated with the minute details of performance and set out to devise a way of representing the nuances of pitch, rhythm, accent, and so on that a skilled singer brought to each rendition of a song.

"This approach was only made possible by the availability of *recorded sound*—the ability to play an otherwise ephemeral performance over and over again, and even to slow it down to really understand what the naked ear could only fleetingly register." Grainger himself wrote an essay entitled "Collecting with the Phonograph" for the 1908 volume of *Journal of the Folk-Song Society*.

Grainger was not the first researcher to employ such technology. In America in 1889, anthropologist Frank Hamilton Cushing (1857–1900) is believed to have captured the words that accompanied Apache, Zuni, and Navajo dances, while heading up the Hemenway Southwest Archaeological Expedition. The following year, the same organization's Jessie Walter Fewkes (1850–1930) used a mechanical recording machine to capture the songs and stories of the Passamaquoddy tribe of Maine.

In 1894, James Mooney (1861–1921) made a similar study of the Comanche and Arapahoe. The Russian ethnomusicologist Evgeniya Lineva (1853–1919) visited Ukraine in 1897 to record the polyphonic singing traditions of the region. By the early 1900s, the talking machine was a firm fixture in the worlds of ethnography and folklore.

Except in the United Kingdom. There, many collectors viewed the machine with suspicion. Responding to a draft of Grainger's article, another of the *Journal*'s regular contributors, Anne Geddes Gilchrist (1863–1954), complained,

> In my own experience of seeing records being taken by my brother of the performances of singers, both cultured and otherwise, we have found it not absolutely reliable as a recorder. . . . It is faulty both as regards "dynamics" and the timbre of the sounds recorded, and fails to reproduce sibilants—the initial "s" of a word particularly. As to pitch, I have also had some occasional doubts as to which instrument—the human or the artificial—was a little "out."

Fellow collector Cecil Sharp also disliked the phonograph's reproductive capabilities, although his complaint (in a letter to Grainger that same year) was that it was *too* accurate; that collecting required not "an exact, scientifically accurate memorandum . . . so much as a faithful artistic record of what is actually heard by the ordinary auditor."

He and Geddes Gilchrist both then proceeded to compare the perceived failings of the new technology to those of the camera, in that the "trained ear or eye of an artist is surely able to reproduce with more real truth—because of understanding and sympathy—the sounds or sights" before them than any kind of machine.

In the face of such animosity, voiced by some of the most influential figures on the folk scene of the day, Grainger was thus the first to deploy the gramophone for field work in the United Kingdom, and on May 7, 1906, he became the first person ever to capture a Child Ballad "in the wild," when he recorded a brief, unaccompanied performances of "Lord Bateman" (53), from a Mr. Thompson in Brigg. Days later, he would record Joseph Taylor for the first time.

Again, we do not know whether Grainger assigned any especial significance to this pair of "firsts." He was in the area for the express purpose of recording old songs, as performed by anyone he met who knew them, and it was immaterial to him, as it likely was to them, whether the song had been singled out for attention by Child or any other past collector.

Nevertheless, even if we focus solely upon the Child Ballads that Grainger gathered on this expedition, it was a profitable jaunt. On July 28, Joseph Taylor was recorded singing his own rendition of "Lord Bateman." Scant days later, on August 4, a most jaunty third was delivered by George Wray, and a mournful fourth by Joseph Leaning.

"Lord Bateman" is the tale of a young nobleman and adventurer who, on a visit to Turkey, is captured and imprisoned. He is rescued by Sophia, his captor's daughter, "the fairest creature my eyes did see," and the pair swear that neither will marry for seven years, during which time she will endeavor to join him.

The time passes, however, and she does not appear. Finally, the Lord weds another woman—only for his true love to arrive at his castle on his wedding day.

He turns to his new mother-in-law.

> *I own I made a bride of your daughter*
> *She's neither the better or worse for me*
> *She came to me with her horse and saddle*
> *She may go back in her coach and three*

The marriage is presumably annulled, and Lord Bateman marries Sophia.

> *I'll range no more in foreign countries*
> *Now since Sophia has crossed the sea*

Chapter Two

UNTO BRIGG FAIR

By the time Percy Grainger returned to London, his collection of newly recorded Child Ballads included a second performance by Joseph Leaning, "The Outlandish Knight" (4), alongside "Robin Hood and the Three Squires" (140), by Dean Robinson; and "The Golden Vanity" (286), hesitantly intoned by Theodore Button.

There was also George Gouldthorpe's passionate delivery of "Lord Lovel" (75), a genuine heartbreaker in which the titular nobleman returns home from a trip abroad to discover his sweetheart has died during his absence. Heartbroken, he follows her to the grave.

The pride of Grainger's collection, however, was Joseph Taylor, and that despite the old man's initial performances for the recording machine proving less than impressive. His first attempt at "Lord Bateman" eschews the lyrics in favor of confidently "la la la-ing" the melody; the second, for which Taylor does provide lyrics, is fractured and uncertain—evidence, perhaps, of Grainger's later observation that "his memory for the texts of songs was not uncommonly good."

Grainger was not downhearted. Further experience with the machine relaxed Taylor, and Grainger, comparing notes on the technology with Cecil Sharp two years later, was able to argue that the majority of his subjects were so excited that their performances were often improved. Sharp, of course, relayed the opposite findings.

Soon Grainger was able to report that this "courteous, genial, typical English countryman" was "a perfect artist in the purest possible style of folk-song singing. . . . Nothing could be more refreshing than his hale countrified looks and the happy lilt of his cheery voice."[1]

Joseph Taylor. History and Art Collection / Alamy Stock Photo

A handsome young man who grew into a kindly, if somewhat no-nonsense-looking mutton-chopped gentleman, Joseph Taylor was already into his seventies when Grainger "discovered" him—not that "discovery" is really the correct term.

Born on September 10, 1833, in the east Lincolnshire village of Binbrook, Taylor had been singing since his late teens. He learned his songs from whatever source could teach him. No matter that Binbrook was well off the beaten track for even the most itinerant musicians, Taylor wanted to hear music and hear it he did, walking as far as he needed to in order to hear what his granddaughter, E. Marion Hudson, described in her personal memoir of Taylor, as "a good concert."[2]

The most significant event, however, occurred in 1850, when Taylor was sixteen, maybe seventeen. Every year, on the eve of the annual Brigg Fair agricultural showcase,[3] a Traveler encampment would appear in the neighborhood, and Taylor had taken to hiding out in the field adjoining it, to listen to its residents singing at night.

The encampment was located in an area known as "the pit," across a field down an old cart track. On this occasion, Taylor passed the gate that led onto the track and made his way to the one that overlooked the pit itself, to be startled as he saw one of the men separate himself from the group and walk toward him.

Expecting to be sent on his way, Taylor nevertheless stood his ground, only to be surprised when it became clear that the man recognized him from previous visits. "Young man, you enjoy our singing."

Taylor agreed, and he was promptly invited to partake in the evening's entertainment, seated in the circle that formed around the campfire, listening and even joining in with the songs. In his own mind, the most significant of these was a song about the upcoming event itself, "Brigg Fair," about a young man heading there to meet his sweetheart. Taylor learned it that same evening. But there were others, too, that he picked up and which, Mrs. Hudson recalled, "in later years he sang . . . to his grandchildren."

Taylor could not, much as he may have wished, devote his life to song. A trained arboriculturist, he rose to become bailiff of a nearby estate, overseeing two villages and a number of small farms. He also had seven children, of whom at least one, John, followed in his musical footsteps. Indeed, Percy Grainger's first impressions of Taylor saw him remark that "his flowing, ringing tenor voice is well nigh as fresh as that of his son, who has repeatedly won the first prize for tenor solo at the North Lincolnshire musical competitions."[4]

Eighty-two when she was interviewed by the BBC's Peter Kennedy on March 27, 1953, Taylor's daughter Mary also had excellent powers of recall. "We were all singers and in those days, winter evenings, we would go into each other's houses and we'd have an old harmonium or something like that, and we'd sing . . . or we'd go to different houses and sing. I was so delighted when I got old enough to go to other houses to sing."[5]

The harmonium was not their sole instrument. Taylor himself would often accompany his songs with the fiddle; Mary continued, "He would sit back in his chair and he'd sing, he loved to sing, he sang because he loved to sing, and he liked us all to sing, and was very proud of us. The old folk songs that he used to sing, he'd put in the little turns and twiddles that you don't hear nowadays. I'd love to hear them now, I'd love to hear the choirs and the children sing the folk songs."

Meanwhile, Grainger was busy spreading word of his discovery even further afield, by introducing his own arrangements of Taylor's repertoire to the composer Frederick Delius.

Born in the Yorkshire town of Bradford in 1862 (it became a city in 1897), Delius was now based in Paris, from whence his renown swiftly spread to Germany. Indeed, Delius's native land had little interest in his work until he came to the attention of the great conductor (and future Knight of the Realm) Thomas Beecham in 1907.

It was in April of that same year that Grainger introduced Delius to Taylor's music—the pair had met for the first time only recently, brought together by their mutual friendship with Edvard Grieg. In the conversation, Grainger mentioned that he'd been working on creating new musical arrangements for a selection of folk songs.

"Delius's response is significant," wrote Robert Matthew-Walker in *The Delius Society Journal* in spring 2001. "'But our harmonics are identical.' He was not referring to the harmonics of the song; rather, he meant the similar harmonic language they used—for, as Delius also said to Grainger, 'we think alike.'"[6]

Now Delius was intending to use Grainger's arrangement of Taylor's "Brigg Fair" in a new orchestral work, premiered in Liverpool on January 18, 1908, and Birmingham on February 19, with the major London premier taking place in March, with the New Symphony Orchestra under the baton of Beecham. Taylor was among the guests of honor.

Mary Taylor recalled, "My father went up to London for the first performance in the Queen's Hall, and he was with Mr. Grainger, Mr. Grainger's mother, . . . Beecham and Delius himself, they all sat together and heard it for the first time. A friend of ours who was with my father, the schoolmaster here, was very much amused because he said when my father got the air, he was humming it."[7]

Returning to Lincolnshire, Percy Grainger undertook a second round of field recordings in 1908, on which occasion Taylor added "Barbara Ellen" (84) to the Australian's trove of Child Ballads—which the same trip expanded further with one Septimus Lowe's boisterous rendition of "Henry Martin" (250), a further restatement of "Lord Bateman" by Mary Packer, "Lord Lovel" (75) by either Amy Doughty or a Mrs. Teale; and "The Raggle Taggle Gypsies" (200) by a Mr. A. Lane.

Still it was Taylor who continued most to impress Grainger, prompting him to remark, "He most intelligently realizes just what sort of songs collectors are after, distinguishes surprisingly between genuine traditional tunes and other ditties."[8] It's an observation that makes one wonder whether Grainger was in fact the first of his ilk to encounter Taylor.

It matters not. Even if others had heard Taylor sing in the past, it is unlikely that the old man's repertoire would have changed so dramatically as to alter our perspective upon Grainger's collection, nor would it have altered Grainger's next scheme.

He was now working with the Gramophone Company record label's His Master's Voice subsidiary, compiling a series of discs that would be marketed under the title *Percy Grainger's Collection of English Folk-Songs Sung by Genuine Peasant Performers*.

Taylor was invited to contribute, and, in July 1908, he again made the 180-mile journey to the label's studio in London. There, from July 9 through 11, he recorded a dozen songs, of which nine would be included on the finished record album, a dominance best explained by Hudson's recollections of Grainger's enthusiasm for Taylor's "Lord Bateman": "He much preferred Grandpa's because he said 'his memory for tunes was infallible, and his singing more melodious.'"

Grainger's career as a collector lasted for two more years, and it is now best regarded as an adjunct to his primary aim of establishing himself as a composer. Lessons learned from his collecting days would become key to his own musical style, however. Edvard Grieg once described Grainger as the only pianist he ever met who could play the composer's "Norwegian Peasant Dances" "as they ought to be played. No-one in my country can!"

Neither did Grainger allow his work to waste in academic terms. In 1926, writing for *Success Magazine*, he remarked, "In the folk-song there is to be found the complete history of a people, recorded by the race itself, through the *heartoutbursts* of its healthiest output. It is a history compiled with deeper feeling and more understanding than can be found among the dates and data of the greatest."

(That invented term *heartoutbursts*, incidentally, would title a 1998 album of Grainger's collected folk songs by John Roberts and Tony Barrand, among them a "Lord Bateman" that was created from all the versions that Grainger collected. The duo also offered a most charming explanation for the ballad's continued appeal: "It's certainly a good tale, and it's nice to have an occasional long ballad that doesn't end in tragedy and death for all the protagonists.")[9]

Listening to Grainger's wax cylinders today is something of a chore. The medium was never designed for permanent storage and, while the more than three hundred cylinders that Grainger left behind were transferred to lacquer disc by the Library of Congress in 1940, the years had already taken their toll. Joseph Taylor's fifty-seven seconds of "Barbara Ellen," for example, are drowned by almost gelasmic surface noise, although the quality of his voice is undeniable.

Percy Grainger's Collection of English Folk-Songs Sung by Genuine Peasant Performers, on the other hand, remains as impressive today as it must have been at the time. What we now call the folk genre's first ever "compilation album" (the very term *album* was coined in the days when multiple 78s were packaged together), it is most readily accessed today via the LP *Unto Brigg Fair*, released in 1972 by Bill Leader's Trailer label.

All twelve of Taylor's HMV recordings are featured alongside nine other tracks (Thompson's "Lord Bateman" among them) drawn from Grainger's field recordings, "carefully remastered to eliminate as far as possible the technical short-comings of the period," as the liner notes put it and adding up to "the very finest performances of English traditional singing ever to be permanently collected."

The difference between Henry Burr's "Jock O'Hazeldean" and Joseph Taylor's "Lord Bateman," although they were recorded scant weeks apart, is unmistakable. Burr's was the sound of a man singing a song. Taylor's was the sound of a man *living* it.

The booklet accompanying the series explained Taylor's predominance.

> Mr. Joseph Taylor is in most respects the most exceptional folksinger I have yet heard. The ease and ring of the high notes, the freshness of his rhythmic attack, his clear intonation of modal intervals, and his finished execution of ornamental turns and twiddles (in which so many folk-singers abound) are typical of all that is best in the vocal art of the peasant traditional-singers of these islands.
>
> His mind was a seemingly unlimited store-house of melodies, which he swiftly recalled at the merest mention of their titles. His versions were generally distinguished by the beauty of their melodic curves and by the symmetry of their construction. He relied more upon purely vocal effects than almost any folk-singer I ever heard. His dialect and his treatment of narrative points were not so exceptional, but his effortless high notes, sturdy rhythms, clean unmistakable intervals and his twiddles and "bleating" ornaments (invariably executed with unfailing grace and neatness) were irresistible.[10]

Joseph Taylor passed away on May 4, 1910, following an accident that saw him thrown from the trap of his cart. Although he continued on about his business for the remainder of the day, even fetching the cows in from a field, he was clearly in pain and died before the doctor arrived.

Taylor's claims to fame are many, including his status as the first major English folk singer of the recorded age. From this book's perspective, however, he is also notable as the first English artist to release a Child Ballad on record. Indeed, while "Lord Bateman" alone made it onto disc, Grainger also recorded Taylor's versions of "Barbara Ellen" (84) and "Geordie" (209), alongside a host of other songs now integral to the folk canon.

Little can be read into the comparative paucity of Child Ballads in Taylor's repertoire. There are simply so many "folk" songs, some unique to particular locales, others more widely distributed, that it would be more bizarre had Taylor sung any more. Steven Roud's folk song index,[11] the standard reference for English traditional songs since the 1970s, contains some five thousand individual entries, and that is without considering the multitude of varieties that he documents. By comparison, the Child Ballads are a mere drop in the ocean.

But they are certainly the most significant one.

Chapter Three

2,000 YEARS BC (BEFORE CHILD)

Professor Child was not the first person to attempt to compile an at least partially authoritative guide to the best in British traditional balladry. How could he have been, in a field whose origins could be traced back centuries, if not millennia before he was born?

Take, for example, "The Elphin Knight" (2), whose story of love and riddles is common to folklore as far afield as China, Tibet, and *The Arabian Nights*,[1] and *The Life of Aesop* too, an anonymous Greek biography of the great storyteller written, it is believed, around the second century AD. Child's earliest printed rendering of the ballad dates from "about 1670," but it was clearly ancient already.

Or "Barring of the Door" (275), a musical setting for a tale commonly known as "The Silence Wager," in which a couple disagree over who should lock the door and resolve that the first one to speak should do so. So stubborn are they that, even when a party of strangers arrive and help themselves to their food and drink, neither husband nor wife says a word. Only when one (or more) of the strangers tries to kiss (or, again, more) his wife does the husband at last speak. His wife immediately sends him to bar the door. Some sources date this tale to the days of the pharaohs.[2] Child's earliest source was printed in 1769.

The great English singer and academic A.L. (Albert Lancaster) "Bert" Lloyd pointed out that the premise of "The Farmer's Curst Wife" (278), "The tale of the shrewish wife who terrifies even the demons,"[3] is included among the fables in the sixth-century Hindu *Panchatantra*. Lloyd ascribed similar age to "The Two Magicians" (44), the story of a young woman who avoids an unwelcome suitor's attentions by constantly changing into different animals and substances, until:

A
GARLAND
OF
NEW SONGS.

William and Margaret.
Death or Liberty.
Roy's Wife of Aldivalloch.
The Jubilee.

Newcastle upon Tyne:
Printed by J. Marshall, in the Old Flesh-Market.
Where may also be had, a large and interesting Collection
of Songs, Ballads, Tales, Histories, &c.

A later eighteenth- or early nineteenth-century garland featuring "William and Mary," a ballad (tentatively ascribed to David Malloch) that draws upon the same story as Child 74. Mike Butler/Bill Leader Archive

She became a silken plaid and stretched upon a bed
And he became a green covering and took her maidenhead

as Child's chosen version had it; or

She became a corpse, a corpse all in the ground
And he became the cold dark clay and smothered her all around

as Steeleye Span somewhat melodramatically preferred.

Lloyd observed, "In Hindu scripture, when the first man pursued the first woman, she thought to hide by changing into a cow, but he became a bull and so cattle were born. She turned into a mare and he into a stallion, she a jenny and he a jackass, ewe and ram, on and on till all the world was created, down to the ants."[4] Neither was that the extent of this story's spread. Lloyd noted, also, the ancient Greek myth of Peleus and Thetis, and how "she transformed herself into fire, water, lion, serpent and ink-squirting cuttlefish before yielding to his determined embrace."

In Lloyd's view, then, the greatest difference between "The Two Magicians" and its forebears was this: "In Latin countries, the metamorphosis fantasy became a pretty, rather insipid ballad, but in Britain it long remained tough and witty." Child, however, was unimpressed, describing it as the "base-born cousin of a pretty ballad known all over southern Europe, in especially graceful forms in France."[5]

Collector Ken Stubbs's book *The Life of a Man: English Folk Songs from the Home Counties* repeated claims that "Cruel Mother" (20) predates the Norman Conquest of 1066. Musician Ashley Hutchings declared "The Twa Corbies" (26) "goes back to the 13th century at least" in the liner notes for Steeleye Span's debut album; and Scottish singer Jean Redpath reported that "The prototype of the story included in Child as 'The Keach in the Creel' [281] appeared in French jest books of the 13th century."[6]

The origins of others are cloudier, but popular belief might well offer some clues. When collector Jim O'Connor met Traveller activist and singer Johnny Connors in Wexford, Ireland, in 1973, the singer introduced him to a song called "The Ballad of Cain and Abel," which he introduced (as O'Connor puts it) as an account of how "Travelers were first cast out of society and forced onto the road—a Traveler 'Origins myth.'" It was, in fact, "Edward" (13)

Are the ballads contemporary to the events they retell? Or memories thereof? The fact is, we do not know. The ballads of Robin Hood celebrate a hero who likely lived as far back as the 1190s, but the earliest of the ballads appear to date from some three centuries on. The anti-Semitic "Little Sir Hugh [or the Jew's Daughter]" (155) records a child murder/blood libel committed in 1255,[7] although the ballad would not be committed to print (that we know of) for a further five hundred years.

Also known as "Lady Dysie" (in which form it has been recorded by Martin Carthy), "Lady Diamond" (269) is aptly described by Bert Lloyd as "the brutal story of the king who kills his daughter's low-born lover and sends her his heart in a golden cup." It was, he wrote, "on the go in the Middle Ages. Boccaccio re-tells it in his tale of Ghismonda and Guiscardo [it was translated into English in 1566], and in later years it was several times made into a play in England and elsewhere."[8]

(Incidentally, Frankie Armstrong's self-composed melody for her rendition of the ballad, recorded on her 1975 album *Songs and Ballads*, surely holds the record for being written at a higher elevation than any other—at 35,000 feet over the Atlantic Ocean.)

And then there is "Judas" (23), the oldest Child Ballad for which we have written evidence, in a form that is still recognizable today. Taken down in Middle English sometime before 1300, it was preserved as a manuscript in the possession of Trinity College, Cambridge.[9]

> *Hit wes upon a Scere-thorsday that ure loverd aros;*
> *Ful milde were the wordes he spec to Judas.*
> *"Judas, thou most to Jurselem, oure mete for to bugge;*
> *Thritti platen of selver thou bere up othi rugge.*
> *Thou comest fer ithe brode stret, fer ithe brode strete;"*
> *Summe of thine tunesmen ther thou meiht imete.*

Other ballads can also lay claim to antique origins, in subject matter if not their actual composition. For example, "The Battle of Otterburn" (161) details a battle fought in Scotland in 1388 and captures what are professed to be the dying words of James, the second earl of Douglas—"My wound is deep, I fain would sleep."

Another Scottish skirmish, "The Battle of Harlew" (163), took place in 1411, fought between two claimants to the Earldom of Ross: Robert Stewart, the Duke of Albany (1340–1420) and Donald, Lord of the Isles (d. 1423). We have no hard evidence that either ballad is contemporary with the conflicts they commemorate (the earliest known printings date from circa 1550 and the early nineteenth century respectively). But neither do we have any that they aren't.

The text of "Riddles Wisely Expounded" (1) has been traced to a mid-fifteenth-century manuscript in the Bodleian Library, around the same age as "Robin Hood and the Monk" (119).[10] Likewise dated to this period, "St. Stephen and Herod" (22) and "Robin and Gendelyn" (115) are to be found among the so-called Sloan Manuscripts, collected by the physician Hans Sloane (1660–1753) and held now by the British Library.[11]

All told, Child's own list of sources notes several dozen ballads that existed in either manuscript or printed form prior to 1700, and that is without considering those whose titles are referenced, but whose lyrics are unpublished, in other manuscripts.

The Complaynt of Scotland was published in 1549 as a response to the increasingly brash efforts of English politicians to force union upon their northern neighbor, and it is effectively a compendium of all the things that the authors believed helped make Scotland Scottish—myth and legends, history and heroes. Ballads inevitably formed a part of this arsenal.

It is not an easy read in its original form, as the following excerpt from chapter six, the Monologue Recreative, makes plain:

> "Thom of lyn . . . the perssee & the mongumrye met . . . the hunttis of cheua . . . , the battel of the hayr lau . . . ihonne ermistrangis dance."

Translated, however, we find five Child Ballads staring out at us: "Tam Lin" (39), the aforementioned battles of Otterburn and Harlew, "The Hunting of the Cheviot" (162), and "Johnny Armstrong" (169).[12]

The *Complaynt* offers no words to the ballads, but we do discover the manner of accompaniment to which such entertainments were performed, and by whom: in this instance,

> "Ther vas viij scheiphyrdis and ilk ane of them hed ane syndry instrament to play to the laif. the fyrst hed ane drone bag pipe, the nyxt hed ane pipe maid of ane bleddir and of ane reid, the thrid playit on ane trump, the feyrd on ane corne pipe, the fyf [. . .] playit on ane pipe maid of ane gait horne, the sext playt on ane recordar the seuint plait on ane fiddil, and the last plait on ane quhissil. kyng amphion that playit sa sueit on his harpe quhen."

That is, seven shepherdesses, armed with drone bagpipe, a pipe made of bladder and reed, trumpet, cornet, goat's horn, recorder, fiddle, and whistle. There was also a male harpist.

The ballads continued to punctuate the literature of the day, and the private musings, too. On January 2, 1665, the diarist, Sir Samuel Pepys (1633–1703), documented an assignation with the actress Mary Knipp, or Knepp.

> Up by candle light again, and my business being done, to my Lord Brounkers, and their friend Sir J. Minnies and all his company, and Mr Boreman and Mrs Turner, but above all, Mrs Knipp, with whom I sang, and in perfect pleasure I was to hear her sing, and especially her little Scotch song of "Barbary Allen" [84].

(On another note, the correspondence that sprang up between the pair saw Mrs Knipp claim "Barbary Allen" as her romantic alias; Pepys, less poetically, would sign his letters "Dapper Dicky.")[13]

Neither was Pepys the only man in Restoration-era London to fall prey to that particular ballad's charms. Apparently, Nell Gwynne used to sing it to her lover, the reigning monarch Charles II.

Other mid-millennium memories open out. In his *An Apologie for Poetrie*,[14] English poet Sir Philip Sydney (1554–1586) describes the emotional impact of hearing "the old song of ['The Hunting of the Cheviot' (162)] performed by "some blind crowder with no rougher voice than rude style, which being so evil appareled in the dust and cobweb of that uncivil age, what would it work trimmed in the gorgeous eloquence of Pindar?"

A few years later, in 1600, Sir Thomas Overbury's *Miscellaneous Works in Prose and Verse* muses longingly of the "Faire and happy Milkmayde" who "dares go alone, and unfold the sheep i'th'night, and feares no manner of ill because . . . she is never alone, for she is still accompanied by the old songs."

She almost certainly sang unaccompanied, bar the bleating of her flock.

Although the modern ear is now well-accustomed to enjoying the ballads with musical accompaniment (and the *Complaynt of Scotland* would appear to say the same of medieval listeners), it is by no means accepted that this was the case in earlier eras, and it was certainly frowned upon by the collectors of the nineteenth and twentieth centuries.

John Hullah, professor of vocal music at King's College London and author of the once-popular 1866 *The Song Book: Words and Tunes from the Best Poets and Musicians*, explained, "The presentation of these songs without accompaniment has been dictated . . . by the desire to present them in their original forms. For, in almost every case, the tune is the only original part of the music of a national song; the addition even of a bass having been generally made by a later hand—not always guided by a sympathetic spirit."

Neither did this attitude change. Half a century later, collecting in the Appalachian Mountains, Cecil Sharp was happy to note that he encountered only one singer who performed to even a guitar accompaniment, and that was in the city of Charlottesville, Virginia.

When the 1950s brought a boom in "serious" folk recordings, Bert Lloyd and Ewan MacColl did much to popularize unaccompanied singing, and the latter's wife, Peggy Seeger, confirmed their stance in a lecture she gave during the 1960s; "The first thing to ask about accompaniment is 'Is it necessary? If it isn't, you should think twice about it.'"[15]

Collector Sandy Paton, discussing his investigations on Beech Mountain, North Carolina, in 1964, was equally unequivocal on this subject. "The folk of the Beech have obviously applied their own aesthetic, distinguishing between commercial music, which is all right for town, and the home-made music of earlier vintage, which is apparently more acceptable in the homes of the older residents. . . . This observation has led me to the conclusion that commercial music, from bluegrass to country and western belongs on the stages where it was nurtured, if not born, while more traditional music remains more appropriate in the quiet setting of the home."[16]

Modern-day folklorist Dom Flemons,[17] however, offers the most cogent reasoning for preferring the ballads in an a cappella setting, "because it does mould itself around the vocalists themselves. In [that] tradition, a lot of musical rules don't apply. When I started to hear those Peter Kennedy recordings, Bob and Ron Copper when they sing harmonies together, it's such a beautiful sound. Their harmony isn't a typical harmony that most people might sing, but it has a beautiful tone, and it helps with the storytelling, where they start to blend their voices. And that's the beauty. When you don't have accompaniment, you can do what you want. You can have breaks, you can have emphasis, you can break rhythm to emphasize the story telling, and this is what makes the Child Ballads so interesting in general.

Antiquarian John Aubrey's (1626–1697) *Remains of Gentilism and Judaism,*[18] published in the late 1680s, remembered the nurse who "had the history of [England] from the [Norman] Conquest down to the time of [Charles I] in ballads" (a span of some 600 years, 1066 to the mid seventeenth century); while any suspicion, based upon these rememberings, that the ballads were wholly the province of the lower orders was soundly dismissed when one of the most high-ranking personages of the age, the Bishop of London, Henry Compton (1632–1713), admitted that he thoroughly enjoyed listening to (and, one hopes, singing along with) "The Hunting of the Cheviot" (162), and that it was "no derogation to [my] episcopal character" to do so.

Well said, Your Excellency.

Chapter Four

BANNING THE BALLADS

It is through observations and recollections such as Aubrey's, Pepys's, and Compton's that we come to understand just how central a role the Child Ballads—and the traditional canon in general—occupied in people's daily life. They were sung as people worked in the fields or in the home; they were intrinsic to an evening's private entertainment; and they were performed on stage, both in instantly recognizable form and in the guise of modern "adaptations."

Julie Henigan writes of a ballad, published in 1710, explicitly titled "The Drinking Match, A New Ballad in Imitation of Chevy Chace" [162], written by 'a Person of Quality' and "The Tipling Philosophers," composed by author and satirist Ned Ward (1667–1731).[1] This was almost certainly intended to be sung unaccompanied, because Henigan then notes, "A version featuring a musical setting followed in 1720," which declared itself "set by Mr [George] Leveridge and sung at the theatre in Dublin."

Neither was "Chevy Chase" alone in such treatment.

Hindsight and scholastic interpretation both establish balladry firmly at the heart of period entertainment. Dom Flemons explains, "One of the things I find so interesting, thinking back on the theater of antiquity, is to see the way the ballads encapsulate the outward release of emotion and expression through the way they're written."[2] He cites "Barbara Allen" as an example, by recalling Pete Seeger's 1950s recording of the song, "the way he had Sweet William turn his head and 'just busting out a-crying.' The way he sings 'busting out,' gives you such a vivid impression of the pain of the scene. Even though the words are simple, the imagery and complexity of the scenes and emotions is very powerful."

It is that power that was translated on the long-ago stage and that remains so today. Flemons continues, "It's very interesting to see the ways in which each balladeer uses the words and how they decide to composite the words themselves. A lot of times it tells you something about the singer themself, which is also very interesting, particularly as a researcher."

Even as the ballads established a foothold in the theaters of the age, however, ballad singing "in public"—that is, away from those venues that were officially licensed to stage public entertainments—was not a risk-free pursuit, particularly among those characters whom the authorities might regard as itinerants—or, as Martin Carthy put it, "buskers."[3]

Queen Elizabeth I (r. 1558–1603) was the first English ruler to legislate against their ilk, although she certainly was not opposed to the ballads themselves; famously, a Romany performer named Alice Boyce sang "The Broom of Cowdenknows" (217) to her.

The early seventeenth century saw the rise of Mary Frith (1584–1659), a.k.a. the notorious underworld figure named Moll Cutpurse—so-named for her chosen method of relieving victims of their money. Her criminal activities notwithstanding, she was also a popular public performer, a talented lute player who, dressed as a man, performed comic and bawdy songs around London's taverns.

A biography of her in this guise, by one John May, was registered for publication in 1610—sadly, no copies of *A Booke called the Madde Pranckes of Merry Mall of the Bankside, with her Walks in Mans Apparel and to what Purpose* are known to have survived. Likewise, we have no record of Moll's repertoire, but several bawdy ballads from her era were included by Child,[4] and might well have been known to Ms. Cutpurse. Could May's book have been the first ever biography of a Child Balladeer?

If not, Moll might well attain that distinction regardless. In 1611, her antics were immortalized in the play *The Roaring Girl*, by Thomas Middleton and Thomas Dekker, and she is believed to have appeared in it, too, before it was closed down (and Moll was arrested) on account of its salacious quotient. Later, following her death from dropsy in 1659, her adventures appeared in a purported autobiography, *The Life and Death of Mrs. Mary Frith*, and several unofficial biographies, too.

Moll has a number of other, possibly dubious, claims to fame, among them being the first London brothel owner ever to cater to a female clientele by hiring male prostitutes. Her singing career, however, was curtailed both by old age and the law—the Puritan Commonwealth government of 1649–1659 banned balladry outright and declared street singing punishable with a flogging. Only when the monarchy was restored under Charles II, less than a year after Moll's death, did singing and

See here the Prefideffe o'th pilfring Trade
Mercuryes fecond; Venus's onely Mayd
Doublet and breeches in a Uniform dreffe
The Female Humurrift a Kickfhaw meffe
Heres no attraction that your fancy greets
But if her FEATURES pleafe not read her FEATS..

The legendary seventeenth-century balladeer Moll Cutpurse,
a.k.a. Mary Frith. Wikimedia Commons

dancing return to a legal standing; small wonder, then, that the London of Mrs. Knipp and Nell Gwynne fell so in love with "Barbara Allen."

It was a brief respite. King George III (r. 1760–1820) made several attempts to rid the city streets of balladeers, with punishments including fines, imprisonment, and the pillory awaiting any who were caught. Such prohibitions were not universally approved. Magistrate Patrick Colquhoun (1745–1820), striving at the time to establish London's first police force, argued that "even the common Ballad-singers in the streets might be rendered instruments useful under the control of a well regulated Police," in that they offered "a better turn to the minds of the lowest classes of the People. They too must be amused."[5]

Yet the ballads were seldom appreciated any more than the balladeers, particular after both old and new worlds were wracked by popular uprising and revolution toward the end of the eighteenth century and into the nineteenth too. Any art form that could be seen to give a "voice," or even succor, to the common people was to be repressed, if not for political reasons, then for moral ones.

Folksong, be it ancient or modern, certainly fell into this category. According to the legislators of the land, the "old songs" were coarse; common; largely obsessed with witchcraft, violence, death, and sex (all of which is true); and populated by incestuous siblings, murderous parents, vengeful spouses, and malevolent spirits. (All of which is also true.) The heroes were criminals, and the drama was glamorized, rich in macabre detail and bloody horror. The modicum of cautionary morality that might slip in to such a composition would probably have its throat slit in the night.

Despite such prohibitions, the ballads remained popular, and the advent of cheap printing presses furthered their spread, again in the form of both old and new compositions. "Broadside Ballads," as these offenders were known, were composed, and lustily sung, of recent crimes, scandals, disasters, executions, or political events. Some might mock the government, others could insult the monarchy and encourage sedition. Still others were simply sensationalist. In 1827, "The Murder of Maria Marten," supposedly immortalizing the last words of William Corder, before he was hanged for the savage slaying of his lover, was one of the best-selling broadsides of the age.

> *After the horrid deed was done*
> *She laid there in her gore*
> *Her bleeding, mangled body lay*
> *Beneath the Red Barn floor*

Another popular broadside told the bloody tale of the highwayman "Bold John Nevison," in terms that would have flattered the greatest warrior of the day.

> *Did you ever hear told of that hero,*
> *Bold Nevison it was his name,*
> *And he rode about like a brave hero,*
> *And by that he gained a great fame,*

It would be hyperbolic to suggest that the United Kingdom was in the midst of a moral panic over the pernicious influence of a few ballads. But reflect upon similar incidents in our own lifetimes—the comic book scare of the 1950s, video nasties in the eighties, social media in the 2010s—and we are speaking much the same kind of language. The street singers, and those who both printed and distributed the broadside—*ballad-mongers* was the favorite term—were regarded in much the same light as the perpetrators of those later outrages; although, in truth, their own motives seldom went beyond earning sufficient money to survive.

We know little of the actual men and women who pursued the trade, although a few names have lingered. Thomas Deloney was proclaimed king of the ballad-mongers in Shakespearean London; and his tradition was carried on by Martin Parker and Thomas D'Urfey. But there were countless others of whom we have no record, and Jim O'Connor, a mainstay of Ewan MacColl's Critics Group was not exaggerating when he wrote, in 1967, that it is these often anonymous souls that we have to thank for "the survival of many traditional ballads such as 'The Elfin Night' [Child 2] and 'Twa Sisters' [10] . . . due to repeated broadside publications."[6]

It was a precarious living. Some ballad-mongers were singers alone, hoping to be rewarded for the effort of singing itself, and perhaps selling handwritten copies of the ballads they sang. But others were effectively hired only to sell broadsides of both older songs and newly composed offerings, a proto-gig-economy form of unregulated servitude in which one's job was only as secure as one's latest sales figures. The printers at the top of this brutal chain doubtless did well out of the enterprise—why else would they have bothered? But their sales staff were substantially less well recompensed.

Neither was the law alone opposed to street ballad singers. English literature and art of the eighteenth and nineteenth centuries is frequently vociferous in its depictions of street ballad singers as among the lowest of the low, although historian Oskar Cox Jensen makes it clear that the balladeers were drawn from a multitude of societal backgrounds. The "typical" ballad-monger, he wrote, was "a boy of twelve, a girl of nineteen, a mother of three, a blind ancient; . . . an orphan, a spouse, a discharged veteran; lately of the Opera House, a jeweler's, a merchant bank; of the army, scullery or rookery; beggar, tailor, thief, writer, pensioner, weaver, prostitute, preacher."[7] The only common element was that they had fallen upon hard times, from which they were unlikely ever to recover.

Artist William Hogarth's 1741 engraving *The Enraged Musician* depicts what we are to assume is a typical ballad singer of the era, dowdy and yowling with a small child in tow. In her hand, she clutches a ballad pointedly entitled "The Lady Falls"; the enraged musician of the title is the gent outside whose home she, and a bevy of rowdy waifs, raucous street performers, and boisterous itinerant craftsmen ply their trades. Artist Sean Shesgreen in his *Images of the Outcast: The Urban Poor in the*

"The noisiest picture in English art"—Hogarth's *The Enraged Musician*. William Hogarth / Wikimedia Commons

Cries of London describes *The Enraged Musician* as "The noisiest picture in English art."[8]

Half a century later, in 1797, author Isabella Kelly's *Joscelena; or, the Rewards of Benevolence: A Novel* traces the vicissitudes with which the titular heroine is beset as she makes her naive way through the London of the day. In the midst of this, she falls in with a woman named Jessy, only to be warned away in dire terms. "Our manners will not suit your gentleness . . . our ways are low, our occupation very mean, and it requires a boldness and assurance which your modest nature could never assume. I am a ballad singer." Kelly is surely deploying a euphemism here. Jessy is, more likely, a prostitute. But, to eighteenth-century readers, was there really a difference? The insinuation that ballad singing is quite as low a profession is brought further home as Jessy outlines exactly what her profession entails, "sing[ing] in the street by night. Could you—could *you* do that?"

Irish novelist Maria Edgeworth (1767–1849) left even insinuation at the door in the pages of *The Ballad Singer; or, Memoirs of the Bristol Family: A Most Interesting Novel*. There, her orphan heroine Angeline finds herself faced with two possible careers, prostitution or ballad singing, and being not at all certain which would be worse.

Yet singer and song did have their literary supporters. Ballad singers feature, generally sympathetically, in the writings of Tobias Smollet, Mrs. Griffith, Laurence Sterne, Jane Austen, Eliza Haywood, Frances Burney, Thomas Hardy, and Elizabeth Gaskell. Emily Brontë has Cathy teaching Hareton Earnshaw to read by way of ballads in *Wuthering Heights*, while playwright Nicholas Rowe, in 1714's *The Tragedy of Jane Shore*, declared "those venerable ancient song-enditers soar'd many a pitch above our modern writers."

John Gay (1685–1732), striding with pen drenched in burlesque-tinted satire through his 1714 *The Shepherds Week in Six Pastorals*, devotes even more space to the subject as he tells of a most singular performance for an audience of "maids" and "swains." Gay offers only the briefest description of the material being performed, but that is all his audience required. They knew already precisely what he meant when he mentioned "[the] barbarous uncle, stain'd with infant blood! . . ." "What woful wars in Chevy-Chase befell . . ." "the squire, who fought on bloody stumps . . ." "Taffy Welch, Sawney Scot, Lilly-bullero Bateman, Robin Hood and the bower of Rosamond." At least four of what we now refer to as the Child Ballads are readily discernible in the full verse.[9]

The Irish-born novelist Oliver Goldsmith (1728–1774), too, proved himself a staunch champion of the old songs. In 1759, as editor of the London periodical *The Bee: Being Essays on the Most Interesting Subjects*, Goldsmith reminisced, "The music of the finest singer is dissonance to what I felt when our old dairy maid [her name was Peggy Golden] sung me to tears with the ballads 'Johnny Armstrong's Last Goodbye' [169] or 'The Cruelty of Barbara Allen' [84]."

Goldsmith replayed a similar happenstance in his novel *The Vicar of Wakefield* (1766), with the scene in which Farmer Flamborough and the Blind Popier serenade Parson Primrose with the same two "soothing ballad[s]." And in *She Stoops to Conquer* (1773), Goldsmith has the lovable Tony Lumpkin sing the opening lines of "The Knight and the Shepherd's Daughter" (110)—despite, as Julie Henigan notes, the ballad having never "been reported in the writer's native Ireland either in print or in the oral tradition."[10]

> *There was a young man riding by*
> *And fain would have his will*
> *Rang do didlo dee*

This apparent anomaly notwithstanding, research into the Irish spread of what was regarded as English and Scottish balladry was limited until the 20th century. Elsewhere, however, the halls of learning were treating the ballads with considerable respect, not necessarily as works of art or even literature, but as historical artifacts whose preservation was as pronounced an imperative as any old building or ancient belief.

No matter how grisly their subject matter might sometimes be, there was a romance to the old songs, a sense of innocence, purity even. But, more than that, there was something almost alchemical about the ballads' existence and survival, to the point where any individual human's involvement in their creation became less than secondary. The ballads simply *were*.

Chapter Five

A GARLAND OF BALLADRIES

It was Professor Child's single-minded adhesion to this romance, this alchemy, that so distinguishes *ESPB* from any of the collections that preceded or, indeed, succeeded it. The collectors of the past simply gathered the ballads. Child curated them and, in so doing, fashioned a work that can readily be ranked among the classics of English literature.

But he was not alone in having attempted this feat, as he was the first to acknowledge.

The aforementioned Samuel Pepys had collected, if not published, ballads in the form that was eventually released as *A Pepysian Garland — Black-Letter Broadside Ballads of the Years 1595–1639*.[1] Further "garlands," as they were known,[2] were published around the balladic adventures of Robin Hood later in the seventeenth century, while diverse other publications followed. Perhaps the most enthralling of all such works, however, was that conceived by Thomas Percy (1729–1811), bishop of Dromore in County Down, Ireland, in 1765.

Reliques of Ancient English Poetry, consisting of Old Heroic Ballads, Songs and Other Pieces was the culmination of an interest ignited—perhaps literally—one evening when Percy was visiting friends in the small market town of Shifnal, near Telford, in the west midlands county of Shropshire. A chambermaid was preparing the fire and lighting it with pages from what appeared to be an old manuscript that she had tucked beneath the dresser for this purpose. Curious as to what manner of book was considered so worthless that it could be used for kindling, Percy inspected the pages to discover it was a handwritten collection of old songs and verses—he estimated it to be at least a century old.

Bishop Percy's

Folio Manuscript.

Ballads and Romances.

EDITED BY

JOHN W. HALES, M.A.

FELLOW AND LATE ASSISTANT-TUTOR OF CHRIST'S COLLEGE, CAMBRIDGE

AND

FREDERICK J. FURNIVALL, M.A.

OF TRINITY HALL, CAMBRIDGE,

ASSISTED BY

PROF. CHILD, OF HARVARD UNIV., U.S.; W. CHAPPELL, ESQ., &c. &c.

Vol. I.

LONDON:

N. TRÜBNER & CO., 60 PATERNOSTER ROW.

1867.

The 1867 first edition of the complete Percy folio was partially financed by F. J. Child. Author's collection

Already of an antiquarian bent, Percy salvaged what remained of the manuscript from its intended fate and set about editing its contents towards what he believed might prove a successful book. He was fortunate in that much of the volume remained intact, although he despaired nevertheless at its overall condition.

It was, he wrote in the introduction to the book that modern convention refers to as *Percy's Reliques*, "a long narrow folio volume, containing 195 Sonnets, Ballads, Historical Songs and Metrical Romances, either in the whole or in the part for many of them are extremely mutilated and imperfect." The first and last pages of the volume were completely missing, and "of 54 pages near the beginning, half of every leaf hath been torn away and several others are injured towards the top or bottom line." He also found fault with the binding, "and even where the leaves have suffered no injury, the transcripts . . . are sometimes extremely incorrect and faulty, being in such instances probably made from defective copies or the imperfect recitation of illegitimate singers."

Now he was on a roll. "Miserable trash and nonsense [are] not infrequently introduced into pieces of considerable merit." He speculates that "the copyist grew so weary of his labour as to write on without the least attention to the sense or meaning." Rhymes were misplaced, misspellings were common. Percy was especially incensed, it appears, by the appearance of the phrase "want and will" for "wanton will," and "pan and wale" for "wan and pale."

Maybe the book was as slapdash as it sounds, although given that it appears to have been compiled for no reason other than its original owner's pleasure, it is more than a little presumptuous of Percy to have so vilified its execution. It is also possible that Percy protested too much; that he was simply defending himself against future allegations that he was little more than the fortunate rescuer of the original manuscript, and the even more fortunate beneficiary of an unknown predecessor's labors. No matter. What he wrought from his efforts was a thing of beauty, three volumes extensively annotated after Percy circulated both the original manuscript and his proposed text among his most learned friends, to seek out their opinions and guidance upon its content.

He haunted the archives of the Antiquarian Society in London, and his requests for more manuscript folios must have exhausted the staff of the British Library, the Ashmole Library[3] in Oxford, and the Pepysian Library in Cambridge. He composed a most erudite history of the English minstrel, and his introductory notes to the ballads both preempted and often surpassed Child's later offerings.

That *Percy's Reliques* was a signal influence upon the *ESPB* is undeniable, despite Professor Child admitting that he (like many others) doubted the authenticity of some of the included texts. Indeed, Child devoted many years to seeking access to the original folio, and when he was finally granted it, he discovered that his suspicions were correct. Percy had indeed made a number of corrections, amendments, and even additions to the original handwritten texts.

This in turn prompted Child to bring his influence to bear on bringing the original folio to the public, under the aegis of scholar Frederick J. Furnivall (1825–1910), the founder of the Early English Text Society and later, the Ballad Society. The first attempt to gain access to the folio was unsuccessful; its owner utterly rebuffed Furnivall's offer of £100 for permission to make a copy of it. Child then weighed in with a further £50 of his own, and the volume was secured, but its expenses had only begun. By the time the book was published, the total debt accrued through its production was in excess of £800. All concerned were satisfied, regardless. As Professor Child wrote to Furnivall in 1882, "Without the Percy MS, no one would pretend to make a collection of the English Ballads."

Yet Percy was not the sole guardian whose work was a significant influence upon what became the *ESPB*. As Child gathered together his research material, again and again he found his eye falling upon the work of Anna Gordon (1747–1811), the Aberdeen-born ballad collector from whom he selected no fewer than twenty-seven of what he described as his "A" texts—that is, the most important example of every ballad he included in his books.

His confidence was not misplaced. By Gordon's own account, every ballad she collected was learned from either her mother, an aunt, or one of her family's servants; not once did she have recourse to any printed form. Indeed, a friend of hers confided to Bishop Percy, "[She] does not recollect to have heard any of them either sung or said by anyone but herself since she was about ten years. She kept them as a little hoard of solitary entertainment."

Child was enthralled, and with good reason. "No Scottish ballads are superior in kind to those recited in the last century by Mrs. Brown [Gordon's married name], of Falkland," he declared, and when future generations came to visit the *ESPB* in search of material to perform and record, it was often Anna Gordon's discoveries to whom they turned.

The supernatural epics "Willie's Lady"(6), "King Henry" (32), "Kemp Owyne" (34), "Alison Gross" (35), and "Thomas the Rhymer" (37) were all, as folklorist and singer Brian Peters puts it,[4] "exhumed from her colorful repertoire, never mind their extreme rarity in oral tradition, and the fact that they usually required quite a bit of work."

It was Gordon's "The Cruel Sister" (10), which she learned from her mother, that Canny Fettle vocalist Steve Turner sang on his solo debut album, 1979's *Out Stack*; while "Gil Brenton" (5), "Burd Ellen and Young Tamlane" (28), "Young Beichan" (53), and "Sir Patrick Spens" (58) are among the other ballads whose preservation Gordon can lay some claim to having ensured. The first two, it is true, have scarcely been revisited since. The other pair are among the most frequently recorded of all Child Ballads.

Child also made abundant use of the collection of ballads and songs amassed by antiquarian Andrew Crawfurd (1786–1854) earlier in the nineteenth century, those that he gathered from one Mary Storie of Lochwinnoch. No less than thirteen of her fourteen offerings were included in the *ESPB*, including "False Knicht on the Road" (3), yet it is ironic that the one Child omitted has become one of the most popular Scottish ballads of all, "The Devil's Courtship."

Brian Peters, who recorded "The Devil's Courtship" on his 2010 album *Gritstone Serenade*, explains in his liner notes, "Child chose not to include [it] because the refrain alters from verse to verse, and he didn't approve of that kind of nonsense."[5]

One further key to Child's research was the vast archive of song revealed to him by two sisters living in the tiny highland hamlet of Fearn, in Perthshire. Amelia and younger sister Jane Harris were not collectors as such; rather, they wrote down songs that family tradition could trace back to the mid-1700s, and their mother Grace's childhood in the home of her grandfather, the Reverend Patrick Duncan, in nearby Tibbermore.

When Grace was orphaned at the age of seven, the Reverend took her in, placing her under the care of family nurse Jannie Scott, who had been in the family's employ since the birth of Grace's mother in 1745. It was Scott who taught Grace the ballads that she passed onto her own daughters, and there were more, too. Apparently Grace was known to mourn that she possessed "only a tithe [one-tenth] of old Jannie Scott's ballads."

The sisters' first attempt to publicize this trove came in 1828, when twelve-year-old Amelia sent handwritten copies of "Burd Helen" (258) and "My Luve She Lives" to antiquarian Peter Buchan, as he worked toward his landmark *Ancient Ballads and Songs of the North of Scotland*. He did not use the sisters' text, but he retained it in his manuscript collection, where it was discovered by Child some fifty years later.

In 1859, the Harris sisters tried again to interest the outside world, when a handwritten collection of their repertoire was sent to the author of the previous year's *Ballads of Scotland*, Professor William Aytoun at the University of Edinburgh. There appears to have been little follow-up. Indeed, when Child made contact with the women in 1873, the Aytoun manuscript was already long lost. Instead, Amelia sent him another of her handwritten collections, completed just the previous year. This time her efforts paid off. Over 50 percent of the Harris manuscript found its way into the *ESPB*, and close to half of the ballad airs were included in Child's appendix.

It would be 1955 before the Aytoun manuscript was rediscovered in an Edinburgh bookstore warehouse, where it could conceivably have lingered for close to a century; and it was almost half a century more before it was published in its own right, as the Scottish Text Society's *The Song Repertoire of Amelia and Jane Harris*, in 2002.

Two years later, singer and ethnomusicologist Katherine Campbell recorded a companion CD, *The Songs of . . . Scots Songs and Ballads from the Perthshire Tradition*, and the richness of the sisters' collection could at last be appreciated in its own right. Campbell performs no fewer than ten of the sisters' Child Ballads, including a fascinating four-stanza fragment of "East Muir King" (89); and a likewise incomplete "Brown Edom" (98) that Amelia had adapted for bagpipe.

> *East Muir king and West Muir king,*
> *And king o Luve, a 'thrie,*
> *It's they coost kevils them amang,*
> *Aboot a gay ladie.*

Published thirty years apart, and such oversights notwithstanding, the Buchan and Aytoun collections were invaluable to Child and other subsequent researchers. Yet they represent merely a fraction of the song and ballad collections that were published in the United Kingdom during the near century that separated Percy's *Reliques* from Professor Child's own first venture into the field.

Some of these books re-trod familiar ground, creating fresh gatherings from previous compilations; some ventured anew into the field. Many—like Percy—strayed occasionally from the balladic path; others (again like Percy) included original material in the guise of authentic ballads or bowdlerized existing material to create what were presented as fresh discoveries.

There was also a brief fashion for rendering the old ballads into surroundings that the most discerning upper-class listener could appreciate, exemplified by the 1791 publication of the first volume of William Napier's *A Selection of Original Scots Songs in Three Parts*, arranged for voice, violin obligato, and figured bass.

A keen violinist, Napier was also a renowned music seller, whose advertisements numbered King George III and Queen Charlotte among his clientele;[6] the works reproduced in his book, not cheap at one pound, six shillings, were duly credited to "Eminent Masters." Some eighty-eight ballads were included in this volume, their new melodies composed by such (today largely forgotten) names as Polly Barthélemon, Samuel Arnold, and William Shield. Numbered among them, we find several future Child Ballads, including "Gil Morice" (83), "Waly Waly" (204), "Allan Water" (215), and "The Broom of Cowdenknows" (217), in texts similar, but seldom identical, to those from which Professor Child drew.

Some 150 further ballads, among them "Barbara Allen" (84) would appear across two successive volumes. These editions, however, are

142   POPULAR SONGS.

BARBARA ALLAN

It fell about the Martinmas day,
   When the green leaves where falling,
Sir James the Graham in the west countr.
   Fell in love with Barbara Allan.

She was a fair and comely maid,
   And a maid nigh to his dwelling,
Which made him to admire the more,
   The beauty of Barbara Allan.

The illustrated heading for "Barbara Allan" in the 1835 garland *The Forget Me Not Songster*. Author's collection

treasured now not for their contents, per se, but because the arrangements were commissioned from the Austrian composer Joseph Haydn, resident in London since 1791. Even more astonishingly, Haydn is said to have provided the airs absolutely free of charge, to prevent Napier from being sent to debtors' prison. Again the subscribers' list published in the volumes impresses, and the success of the publications was such that folklorist George Thomson (1757–1851) very soon offered Haydn a commission of his own.

POPULAR SONGS. 41

CAPTAIN WARD.

Come all ye jolly sailors bold,
  That live by tuck of drum ;
I'll tell you of a rank robber,
  Now on the seas is come.

His name is called captain Ward,
  As you the truth shall hear ;
For ther's not been such a robber,
  This hundred and fifty years.

He wrote a letter to our king,
  On the fifth of January,
To see if he would take him in
  And all his company.

Another page from *The Forget Me Not Songster*, this time illustrating the adventures of Captain Ward. Author's collection

Renowned today as organizer of the forebear of the still vibrant Edinburgh Festival, in 1815, Thomson had long collected folk songs for his own entertainment. In 1793, however, he recruited poet Robert Burns to either write or revise around one hundred texts for publication as *A Select Collection of Original Scottish Airs for the Voice. To each of which are added Introductory & Concluding Symphonies & Accompanyments for the Violin &*

Piano Forte, by Pleyel. With Select & Characteristic Verses by the most admired Scottish Poets adapted to each Air, many of them entirely new. Also Suitable English Verses in addition to such of the Songs as are written in the Scottish dialect.

The undertaking was a success, and in 1799, with Haydn having now returned to Vienna, Thomson offered the composer the sum of 2 ducats for every fresh air he arranged. His goal was "to furnish a Collection of all the fine Airs, both of the plaintive and lively kind, unmixed with trifling and inferior ones; to obtain the most suitable and finished Accompaniments, with the addition of characteristic Symphonies, to introduce and conclude each Air; and to substitute congenial and interesting Songs [poetic verses], every way worthy of the Music." Thomson himself provided Haydn with some, if not all, the tunes that he would be using.

Haydn immediately responded with 30 airs and ultimately supplied Thomson with 208, among them a clutch more of the ballads that Professor Child would one day immortalize: "The Wee Wee Man" (38—Haydn also used the same tune for his setting of Robert Burns's "O Bonny was yon Rosy Brier"), "Fair Margaret and Sweet William" (74),[7] a new arrangement for "Gil Morris" (83), "Bessy Bell and Mary Gray" (201), alongside several veterans of the Napier collection.

Neither was Haydn alone in accepting Thomson's commission; Ludwig van Beethoven, too, did some work for him before the pair fell out over money and the composer's poor opinion of Thomson's musical aspirations. Nevertheless, he delivered 150 airs, of which 125 would be published. Thomson's *Scottish Airs* series ultimately ran to six volumes, with the final collection appearing in 1841; a similar project devoted to Welsh Airs ran to three volumes (1809–1817).

Barely had Haydn completed Thomson's commission than he accepted a third, this time from Edinburgh bookseller William Whyte. His *A Collection of Scottish Airs, Harmonized for the Voice & Piano Forte with introductory & concluding Symphonies; and Accompaniments for a Violin & Violoncello. By Joseph Haydn Mus. Doct.* was published in two volumes between 1804 and 1807, and, again beyond a wealth of non-Child material, included Haydn's airs for "The Braes of Yarrow" (214), and several further reprises.

Grand and grandiose though they certainly are, these works were not produced for public performance. Rather, they were intended for private entertainment, in much the same way as sheet music was marketed later in the pre/early gramophone age. There would be no concert hall premiers for what amounted to thirteen years' worth of Haydn's labors; and no great recordings of more than a handful of airs—those that were made were usually tacked on to the end of a disc devoted to one of the composer's so-called major compositions, although they were explored briefly by singer Jean Redpath on her 1984 album, the dryly titled *Haydn: Scottish Songs*.

It was not, in fact, until the twenty-first century that any attempt was made to bring the full scope of Haydn's folk songs to a wider audience, flawlessly performed by Lorna Anderson (soprano), Jamie MacDougall (tenor), and the Haydn Trio Eisenstadt. Both across individual collections and within the vast (160 disc) *Haydn Edition* box set, these efforts were distributed across an impressive 18 separate CDs. Furthermore, while the Napier, Thomson, and Whyte collections are certainly a lot more well-mannered than most interpretations of Child's ballads, one understands immediately the galvanizing effect that these familiar old songs, restaged amid such unfamiliar, even luxurious, surroundings must have had on contemporary listeners and performers. Yet, even as Haydn was perfecting this so-refined vision of traditional Scottish music, a young man named Walter Scott was doing his best to restore it to its most lowly roots.

Chapter Six

THE BALLAD OF SILAS WEGG AND THE TRIPE-SKEWER

Born in Edinburgh, Walter Scott (1771–1832) is routinely considered among the greatest novelists in British, but more specifically, Scottish letters. Singlehandedly, Scott pioneered the now endemic concept of the historical novel, but more importantly, he also dictated the cultural parameters that continue to map out the world's awareness of Scotland itself.

Certainly much of what we think of as Scotland's history flowed first from Scott's pen, and it was perhaps inevitable that his love for burrowing into the most obscure corners of that history would, at some point, introduce him to the nation's balladic heritage.

In the event, that fateful introduction came early in life. According to the memoir that Scott wrote between 1811 and 1826, and that was posthumously published in 1837 as *Memoir of the Early Life of Sir Walter Scott, Written by Himself*, he was just thirteen when he discovered Percy's *Reliques*.

As I had been from infancy devoted to legendary lore of this nature, and only reluctantly withdrew my attention, from the scarcity of materials and the rudeness of those which I possessed, it may be imagined, but cannot be described, with what delight I saw pieces of the same kind which had amused my childhood, and still continued in secret the Delilahs of my imagination, considered as the subject of sober research, grave commentary, and apt illustration, by an editor who showed his poetical genius was capable of emulating the best qualities of what his pious labor preserved.

I remember well the spot where I read these volumes for the first time. It was beneath a huge platanus-tree, in the ruins of what had been intended for an old-fashioned arbor in the garden. . . . The summer day sped onward so fast that, notwithstanding the sharp appetite of thirteen, I forgot the hour of dinner, was sought for with anxiety, and was still found entranced in my intellectual banquet.

To read and to remember was in this instance the same thing, and henceforth I overwhelmed my schoolfellows, and all who would hearken to me, with tragical recitations from the ballads of Bishop Percy. The first time, too, I could scrape a few shillings together, which were not common occurrences with me, I bought unto myself a copy of these beloved volumes; nor do I believe I ever read a book half so frequently, or with half the enthusiasm.[1]

The most obvious literary consequence of this infatuation was Scott's own version of Percy's *Reliques*. First published in 1802, Scott's *Minstrelsy of the Scottish Border: Consisting of Historical and Romantic Ballads, Collected in the Southern Counties of Scotland; with a Few of Modern Date, Founded Upon Local Tradition* would continue swelling until 1830, as the author added fresh additions and revisions.

Billed as a gathering of every authentically Scottish ballad of which Scott was aware, the *Minstrelsy* was compiled from years of both avid scholarship and hands-on exploration. He could be a harsh judge, too. Scott declared many of the ballads collected by Anna Gordon, and subsequently so beloved by Child, to be "inauthentic," although he committed several to print in his *Minstrelsy*.

He also hunted out ballads for himself. Alone, or in the company of close associates John Leyden and James Hogg, Scott devoted swathes of his leisure time to meeting and listening to singers and storytellers, and such was his power of recollection ("to read is to retain") that he did not even need to take notes of what he heard. He could return home and transcribe the evening verbatim.

Nor was this talent confined only to the *Minstrelsy*. The ballads inspired events in his novels, and even characters: the Antiquary, in the novel of the same name, who could "detect you an old black-letter ballad among the leaves of a law paper"; or, in the same tale, the "rascal" Edie Ochiltree, who knew "more old ballads and traditions than any man in this and the next four parishes."

Scott was a collector, but he was also an editor. His interest in the ballads was profound, and he cared deeply for authenticity, but only in as much as the ballad was genuinely ancient. Like Percy before him, he thought nothing of rewriting lines, or even entire verses, with which he was unhappy.

Child, investigating Scott's sources as he worked on his own book, learned very early on not to trust the published texts of the *Minstrelsy*. Neither was he surprised when one of his researchers, William Macmath, returned from perusing Scott's library to report that there were several ballads for which he discovered no original source—that Scott had, most likely, composed them himself.

Nevertheless, a casual comparison of Scott's *Minstrelsy* and Child's *Popular Ballads* reveals that more than half of the earlier book's ballads are included in the later one, among them some of the most beloved, and most discussed, ballads in the entire *ESPB*, and some of the most venerable, too: "The Douglas Tragedy" (7), "The Cruel Sister" (10), "The Twa Corbies" (26), "Kemp Owyne" (34), "Thomas the Rhymer" (37), "The Young Tamlane" (39), "Sir Patrick Spens" (58), "Clerk Saunders" (69), "The Wife of Usher's Well" (79), "The Battle of Otterbourne" (161), "Johnnie Armstrong" (169) and "The Daemon Lover" (243).

At least so far as we know, the great seventeenth-century diarist Samuel Pepys was the first to set down in writing Child 243, although he knew it under the grand title of: *A Warning for Married Women, being an Example of Mrs. Jane Reynolds (a West Country woman), burn [born] near Plymouth, who, having plighted her troth to a Seaman, was afterwards married to a Carpenter and at last carried away by a Spirit, the manner how shall presently be recited.* Small wonder that it was soon retitled "The Distressed Ship Carpenter," or even more succinctly, "The Daemon Lover."

It is under that latter title that the ballad became best known in England. In the United States, however, it became "The House Carpenter" and has been recorded by artists as far afield as Peggy Seeger (who described it as her "comfort song"), Richard Dyer-Bennett, Jean Ritchie, Joan Baez, the Doc Watson Family, and Bob Dylan.

Dom Flemons explains the ballad's popularity. He was already familiar with Clarence Ashley's 1930 recording, as captured on Harry Smith's *Anthology of American Folk Music*; it was upon hearing Joan Baez's version, and experiencing an entirely different vision of the ballad,

> that I realized there were variations. Joan has the ship spinning out of control and it sinks down, and she has the beautiful hills of heaven and the hills of hell motif. I thought that was so brilliant, and then comparing it to Clarence, it's so much more of a personal story, as opposed to a spiritual or metaphysical story. Then, when I read "The Daemon Lover" in its original form, it broadens out into such a mystical story that I think is brilliant as well, up there with Shakespeare or any of the great English poetry that's been handed down.[2]

"Twa Corbies," too, rates high among the *ESPB*'s most respected inclusions. Scottish singer and folklorist Grey Malkin reflects,

> I was initially drawn to "Twa Corbies" by its sheer sense of grimness and almost existential foreboding. A knight lies dead upon the ground, witnessed by two crows (corbies) who converse about making a meal of him. His life over, his hounds and hawks (and therefore symbolically his vestiges and material status whilst alive) have deserted him, allowing the birds free access

to his cadaver. The knight's lover too has fled with another man. In death he is nothing and has nothing. This remarkably bleak and stoic approach to mortality is lightened in the English variant "The Three Ravens," which allows the knight's hawks and hounds to remain loyal and protective even after his death and his pregnant lover (described as a "fallow doe") to tenderly lift and bury his body, denying the blackbirds their feast.[3]

Scott's version allows for no such solace. "Ye'll sit on his white housebane," one corbie tells the other,

> And I'll pike out his bonny blue een
> Wi ae lock o his gowden hair
> We'll theek our nest when it grows bare

Walter Scott's popularity as an author, and the attendant success of his *Minstrelsy*, did much to legitimize the well-researched historical novel in the eyes of the British literati, with the most skilled of these being Manchester-born William Harrison Ainsworth (1805–1882).

Best remembered today for his debut novel *Rookwood* (1834), the entirely fictional (but so supremely believable) source of the dashing mythology that still embraces the highwayman Dick Turpin, Ainsworth was, for a time, battling it out with Charles Dickens for the mantel of Britain's most successful young novelist. He was also a skilled balladeer, as *Rookwood* made clear, and many of his subsequent novels likewise featured what, on initial inspection, appeared to be authentic ballads, but which were in fact Ainsworth's own creations.

His chosen subjects of English history, witchcraft, and the supernatural loaned themselves readily to such treatments, and in 1855 Ainsworth published *Ballads Romantic, Fantastical and Humorous*, containing some eighty different pieces of his own invention. Nor was he at all averse to original sources. In 1858, Ainsworth turned his attention to a translation of the epic poem *The Combat of the Thirty*, subtitling it *From a Breton Lay of the Fourteenth Century* to confirm its pedigree.

William Makepeace Thackeray (1811–1863)—the author, later, of *Vanity Fair*, but hitherto a sly satirist whose pen dripped poison as much as it did prose—likewise made use of balladry, publishing a volume of his own imitations (*Ballads*, 1856); and also adapting an ancient verse for a modern publication.

But no obscure Breton lays for Thackeray, and his collaborators Charles Dickens and artist George Cruikshank. Published in 1839, just five years after *Rookwood* reinvented balladry for the modern reader, their selection, *The Loving Ballad of Lord Bateman*, seized upon a genuine piece of old English verse, and one of such renown and quality that Professor Child himself had no hesitation in adding it to his own collection, closing part

Lord Bateman as he appeared previous to his embarkation.

The Turk's only daughter approaches to mitigate the sufferings of Lord Bateman.

Two pages of Cruikshank art from *The Loving Ballad of Lord Bateman* (1839). Author's collection

two of the *ESPB* with the same ballad's supposed prototype, "Young Beichan" (53).

The mechanics of the partnership between these three titans of literature are foggy. Of course Cruikshank was the artist, delivering the eleven line drawings that illustrate the slim volume. But what of Dickens and Thackeray? How did they distribute the remaining labors? It is now generally accepted that Thackeray was responsible for the telling of the tale, and that Dickens penned only the introduction, before fouling the waters by assigning his words to Cruikshank, who promptly denies authorship in an autographed postscript to the introduction itself.

Whoever was responsible, there is a mocking tone to that intro that contemporary readers would instantly have appreciated: "In some collection of old English Ballads there is an ancient ditty which I am told bears some remote and distinct resemblance to the following Epic Poem." This, we are assured, is untrue. Rather, the author has it on very good authority that the sole author of the piece is "a young gentleman who can scarcely have numbered nineteen summers," who performed it regularly "on Saturday nights, outside a house of general refreshment." The only name by which he is known is "The Tripe-skewer."

His voice, we are told, was once "very melodious and plaintive"; if it subsequently lost those qualities, it was wholly the result of a diet of gruel, a consequence of six months spent on the treadmill following his arrest for vagrancy—and here we see that touch of social awareness for which Dickens is normally admired; *The Loving Ballad* was published in 1839, in the same year that the Act for Further Improving the Police in and Near the Metropolis was enacted.

This new vagrancy law levied a forty-shilling (two pounds) fine on offenders; of course it proved no more successful in cleaning the city streets than any previous prohibition, as William Wordsworth's *The Prelude*, in 1850, suggests:

> *. . . another street*
> *Presents a company of dancing dogs,*
> *Or dromedary, with an antic pair*
> *Of monkeys on his back; a minstrel band*
> *Of Savoyards; or, single and alone.*
> *An English ballad-singer.*

Later in the poem, we are stricken with the image of "files of ballads dangl[ing] from dead walls." But the penalties that the new law recommended were very real, and the Tripe-Skewer was surely an archetypal victim. Nevertheless, notwithstanding the man's incapacitation, the authors of *The Loving Ballad* had "taken down the words from his own mouth . . . and have been careful to preserve his pronunciation."

> *I in sevin long years, I'll make a vow*
> *For sevin long years, and keep it strong*
> *That if you'll ved no other woman*
> *O I will v-e-ed no other man.*

Interestingly, according to Professor Child, there appears to be some truth in this claim. Very much the same text is included among the sixteen different variants of "Young Beichan" in *ESPB*, where it is described as "the only English copy . . . derived from the singing of a London vagrant, [turning] the common English broadsheet . . . into the dialect of Cockagne" (Cockney).

Furthermore, "Lord Bateman" is one of three Child Ballads that antiquarian William Henderson, author of *Victorian Street Ballads: A Selection of Popular Ballads Sold in the Street in the Nineteenth Century* (1937), states were still being sung on the streets of nineteenth century London; he cites also "The Outlandish Knight" (4) and "Sir Patrick Spens" (58), with printed editions of all three known to date deep into the Victorian era.

There were likely more. Earlier in the nineteenth century, several ballads came into vogue as vehicles for stage comedians. Among these, Bert Lloyd noted a comedic rewrite of "Bonnie Annie" (24), now titled "The Watery Grave," which itself became so popular that, more than a century later, Shropshire farm worker Fred Jordan was recorded singing it for the

Topic album *Songs of a Shropshire Farm Worker*. The album also included a revision of "The Three Ravens" (26), which Jordan knew as "Three Old Crows."

Another old ballad "modernized" for Victorian theaters was "Lord Lovel" (75), which the Anglo-American comedian Sam Cowell (1820–1864) performed as "Joe Muggins," while folklorist Robert Bell[4] noted, "one Vauxhall Gardens' singer included the following verse in an otherwise more-or-less straight version of the song":

> *Then he flung his self down by the side of the corpse,*
> *With a shivering gulp and a guggle,*
> *Gave two hops, three kicks, heaved a sigh, blew his nose,*
> *Sung a song and then died in the struggle—uggle—uggle,*
> *Sung a song and then died in the struggle.*

"Lord Bateman" suffers somewhat more dignified treatment in *The Loving Ballad*, yet Dickens's involvement in the project is intriguing, if only because a balladeer's next appearance in one of his works, *Our Mutual Friend* (1864–1865), introduces us to one of the most dislikable characters in his entire canon. The publication date is significant in that 1864 saw the passage in Britain of the Street Music Act, which not only confirmed the forty-shillings fine on ballad singers but added three days imprisonment for those who couldn't pay. Surely Dickens, whose thirst for social justice and a fair deal for the poor hallmarked so many of his books, should have been among the very first literary figures to condemn such harshness?

Oddly, no. One-legged ballad singer and seller Silas Wegg is revealed to be as utterly loathsome a specimen of London life as could be imagined. Cruel, greedy, dishonest, and cunning, we encounter him for the first time at the outset of chapter 5, and assuredly Dickens offers us as accurate a description of a ballad seller's pitch as any we are likely to read.

Every morning at eight o'clock, [a man with a wooden leg] stumped to the corner, carrying a chair, a clothes-horse, a pair of trestles, a board, a basket, and an umbrella, all strapped together. Separating these, the board and trestles became a counter, the basket supplied the few small lots of fruit and sweets that he offered for sale upon it and became a foot-warmer, the unfolded clothes-horse displayed a choice collection of halfpenny ballads and became a screen, and the stool planted within it became his post for the rest of the day. All weathers saw the man at the post. When the weather was wet, he put up his umbrella over his stock in trade, not over himself; when the weather was dry, he furled that faded article, tied it round with a piece of yarn, and laid it cross-wise under the trestles: where it looked like an unwholesomely-forced lettuce that had lost in colour and crispness what it had gained in size.

Discovered selling his wares on the street corner close to Noddy and Henrietty Boffin's newly purchased house, Wegg is asked who composed his wares. He instantly, and dishonestly, takes credit for them and is hired to teach Mr. Boffin to read—a task he accepts despite himself being barely literate. He then proceeds to exploit his employer in every way he can, and few readers could have shed a tear when the loathsome Wegg was finally dragged out of the house and thrown out with the garbage. In much the same way as society seemed determined to do to his contemporaries.

Yet still the ballads lived on. In 1870, "Lord Bateman" was the subject of a full-blown theatrical presentation at the Globe Theatre in London. The ballad-sellers prospered too, unsuppressed by law, unashamed by literature.

Written in 1898 by A. Hall and George Le Brunn, "The Ballad Monger" was a popular number for music hall entertainer Arthur Reece (1870–1964) and reminded us that while topical ballads remained many listeners' choice, there was always a market for the oldies.

> *It is strange what some folks ask for,*
> *They don't like the songs that's new*
> *So I always keeps a stock of the old favourites, too*
> *Here's "The song that'll live for ever" sung since the year of dot*
> *Four and twenty in the parcel, bung the "stiver," take the lot.*

Chapter Seven

THE VOICE OF SOME PEOPLE

Francis James Child was fourteen when *The Loving Ballad of Lord Bateman* was published. The Boston born son of a relatively poor sail maker, he was then a student at one of the city's free schools, the English High School, where his friends knew him as "Stubby," on account of his diminutive stature. What the boy lacked in height, however, he readily compensated with intellect, and thirst for knowledge. Certainly Epes Sargent Dixwell, principal of the Boston Latin School, was impressed, arranging for Child to receive a scholarship to Harvard.

There, the boy proved as brilliant a scholar as his patron believed him to be, excelling at literature and the classics and, in 1848, Child published *Four Old Plays*, resurrecting, indeed, four plays dating from the early English Renaissance: the anonymously penned *Jack Jugler* and *Thersytes*, Heywood's *Pardoner and Frere*, and Gascoigne's *Jocasta*. The quartet was well-known to scholars, but Child's intention was to bring them to the attention of a wider American audience. He continued to prize such a goal when, in 1853, now installed as professor of rhetoric at Harvard, he oversaw the publication of *The British Poets*, a vast work that ultimately amounted to 130 uniform volumes concentrating on lesser- and even unknown works from throughout that nation's history.

It is very much a hack work. Child's brief saw him assume the role of collator as opposed to editor—there would be no critical commentary, no attempts at analysis. In fact, with the exceptions of the volumes concerning Elizabethan poet Edmund Spenser, Child farmed out the majority of the work to various friends and associates, ultimately involving himself only once the volumes themselves were complete and the actual publication process was underway.

Francis James Child. By Daderot—Own work, PD / Wikimedia Commons

However, he also made one decision that was to dictate the course of the remainder of his life. With his inclinations firmly on the side of those academics who believed traditional balladry was as valid a poetic form as the likes of Byron, Shelley, Chaucer, and Shakespeare, Child resolved to include such ballads in the series—eight volumes of them, in fact, drawn

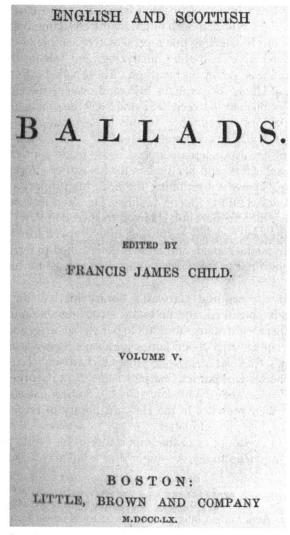

ENGLISH AND SCOTTISH

B A L L A D S.

EDITED BY

FRANCIS JAMES CHILD.

VOLUME V.

BOSTON:
LITTLE, BROWN AND COMPANY
M.DCCC.LX.

The title page to volume 5 of the original *English and Scottish Ballads* series, published in 1860. Author's collection

from the veritable mountain of some 150 earlier publications that he utilized as source material.

In a letter to the splendidly named English antiquary James Orchard Halliwell-Phillips (1830–1889), Child announced that he intended to include "every ballad of merit, except two or three too indecent to preserve."

English and Scottish Ballads (ESB) as this series-within-a-series was known, ultimately grew to embrace over 360 ballads with occasional duplication when Child was unable (or unwilling) to choose between two versions. But Child had been bitten by the collecting bug. No longer content with simply selecting one representative sample of every ballad, he was resolved upon gathering, analyzing, and tracing the origin of every variation he could lay his hands on. "These ballads afford me a very pleasant sort of labor," he wrote in 1855, and even as the eight volumes of *ESB* were published between 1857 and 1859, he was gathering fresh source material, and encouraging friends to seek out even more. What would become the *ESPB* was taking shape.

His circle of correspondents widened as he made contact with other scholars and collectors, and his disdain for his earlier efforts might well have increased likewise. Compiling the *ESB*, his primary concern was with the individual efforts' poetic qualities. He cared little for other collectors' editing; for whether Scott changed this word or Percy altered that one. Now, however, he grew suspicious of every well-turned phrase or anomalous rhyme he espied, and he was determined to ferret them out, to expose them if not to the wider public, then at least for his own satisfaction.

He had already scoured Harvard's library for balladic sources he had not already consulted, and he found a considerable number on the shelves. But there were many more still to peruse, so he set about convincing the librarian to order them: James Johnson's *Scots Musical Museum*, Allan Ramsey's *Tea Table Miscellany*, Moses Richardson's *Local Historian's Table Book*, Charles Kirkpatrick Sharpe's *Ballad Book*, George Thomson's *Select Melodies*, Alexander Whitelaw's *Book of Scottish Ballads*, and many more all owe their presence in the Harvard library to Professor Child's enthusiasm for their subject matter.

Child was in no doubt as to the importance of his work, and his reasoning still rings true today, as singer and academic Alasdair Roberts explains:

> I think that the best of the ballads have a sort of mythic, archetypal power. These ballads have human interaction reduced to its barest form, perhaps, and so that gives a sense of something that many people can enter into and associate with psychologically and emotionally very readily. The ones in which the characters are more like faceless ciphers or stock characters, as in Greek tragedy (or comedy–although the ballads are predominantly tragic!) perhaps. Pieces like "Lord Ronald" [12] "The Two Brothers" [49] or "The Cruel Mother" [20] have, for me, a sort of pagan, other-worldly eternal power to them.[1]

Canadian folklorist Ranald Thurgood makes a similar point: "To me, the main thing that shows me that Child was onto something is the commonalities in the structures and themes of these songs. I can almost always spot a Child Ballad when I hear one and have only run across two to five songs with those same characteristics that aren't in the collection. Stock phrases and repetition make these songs easy to learn and recreate. They [also] tend to be much better poetry than the broadsides and local ballads."[2]

It was with these goals in mind that Child and his agents sought material from across the United Kingdom and expanded their inquiries through Europe and beyond. They gained access to material that, held in private hands, had not seen daylight in decades. And every scrap of paper, every fragment of a ballad, was studied and, in turn, researched.

When Child started work on this latest project, he was still a young man of thirty or so. By the time the first volume of the *ESPB* was published by Houghton Mifflin in 1882, he was fifty-seven, and there were still at least seven further volumes to complete. In fact, when volume eight appeared a decade later, Child was telling friends there was yet one part more to come; when volume nine arrived in the fall of 1894, he was complaining that "the work on part ten is heavy," and admitting that he was already unhappy with the earlier volumes, not only regretting some of his past inclusions, but admitting he had reservations regarding ballads he had not even published yet.

His criteria for including a ballad in the *ESPB* was that it be histori-cally, aesthetically, and technically worthy. But the only existing text for "The Suffolk Miracle" (272) he had unearthed, for example, was "blurred, enfeebled, and disfigured." Should it be included? Ultimately, he decided it should. For, despite all its faults, it was also "representative in England of one of the most remarkable tales and one of the most impressive and beautiful ballads of the European continent."

Indeed, singer John Goodluck was sufficiently enamored with it to title his 1975 album for the ballad, while Packie Manus Byrne recalled an Irish version ("The Holland Handkerchief") that he learned from his cousins in Mín Uí Chatháin, Co Donegal, for his LP *Songs of a Donegal Man* that same year. In neither performer's hands was the ballad "blurred, enfeebled, and disfigured."

Other ballads that Child felt did not match his highest ambitions have likewise been recorded on several occasions, and revealed traits that, per-haps, he never even thought to seek. But still, he wrote, "Many things did not occur to me at first, and if I had the time and patience to do the whole work over again now, I should have the advantage of knowing exactly what to look for."

But he did not have the time. His health was failing and, while the bulk of this tenth volume was given over to indices, sources, glossaries and bibliographies, and a lengthy preface, in many ways it was the most onerous, and frustrating of them all.

There were, after all, no word processors or computers to hand in 1895. One could not simply make a list, block the text, and hit "sort ascending." There was no software that could scan a pdf and apply page numbers to key words and terms. Everything had to be done by hand, transcribed onto index cards which would, when the task was deemed complete, be copied onto paper . . . over and over until Child was finally satisfied.

He did not live to see the task completed. Professor Child died on September 11, 1896. His life's work was still unfinished. That final volume 10 was ultimately completed by Professor George Lyman Kitteridge, a former student of Child's, a Harvard colleague, and one of his closest collaborators throughout the creation of the *ESPB*.

Child's eldest daughter Helen Child Sargent, too, became involved. She shared her father's fascination with both the ballads and their study, and when publishers Houghton Mifflin agreed to push ahead with another of Professor Child's dreams—an abridged, single volume "student edition" of the balladry, it was Helen who went through her father's papers to select the single version of each ballad they would utilize.

Volume ten of the *ESPB* was finally published in 1898; the abridged version followed in 1904; and in 1912, the value of Child's work was broadcast to all when publisher J.M. Dent's Everyman's Library series produced *A Book of British Ballads*, volume 572 in one of the best-selling and longest-running series of low-priced literary classics ever marketed.

The Child Ballads are scattered throughout the volume; references to Child likewise. Indeed, Everyman editor R. Brimley Johnson's introduction is effusive in his praise for the *ESPB*, noting, "Every student of our old ballads owes an immeasurable debt of gratitude to the late professor F. J. Child, whose monumental collections have covered the entire field." He added, "I have naturally followed his guidance in the choice of texts and used his transcripts from manuscripts."

Together, the ready availability of the Everyman's title and the generous nature of the abridged Child brought ballad study and collecting to its highest peak yet, not only among the established great beasts of academia, for whom this was a golden age of folklore research, but among what they might have regarded as lesser beings—vicars' wives and maiden aunts, book-keeper's nephews and school music teachers, anyone, in fact, whose hobbies included collecting old ballads.

Throughout the decade or so that history now regards as the pastoral lull before the storm of World War One, membership and awareness not only of the official Folk-Song Society, but also a host of smaller, local organizations exploded. Traditional songs—not necessarily Child's chosen few, it is true, but a multitude regardless—soared in popularity. The British label His Master's Voice would never have countenanced the release of Percy Grainger's *Collection of English Folk-Songs Sung by Genuine Peasant Performers* had it not perceived a market for it, and if the modern mind recoils slightly at the description of the performers therein, perhaps that is further evidence of the newborn culture's attitude toward the music it was reclaiming.

The notion that the only people still singing "the old songs" had to be of the laboring class was not unique to Grainger; it was common throughout his era and, indeed, for over a century beforehand, back to the days of the German philosopher Johaan Gottfried von Herder (1744–1803). In 1773, he wrote, "The more distant a people is from artful cultivated thinking, language, and letters, the less will its song be written for paper." He mourned, "I am acquainted with folk songs, regional songs, peasant songs that certainly lack nothing when it comes to liveliness and rhythm, naiveté and strength of language. But who is collecting them?" [3] Thus he sounded a clarion call that many hastened to answer. But earlier remarks have remained a reliable canard, too. Indeed, their truth is only vouchsafed by such titles as Topic Records' long-running *The Voice of the People* series of historic field recordings and the bucolic sleeve art that adorns almost every such collection of note.

For the vast majority of British collectors at this time, it was only in the rural areas of England and Scotland that the best discoveries could be made. Industrial England sang industrial songs, dating back to the eighteenth century at best. It was on land and sea that the true salt of the earth was to be found, among the farmers, fishermen, and laborers, or within the family groups of caravan-borne Travelers who still crisscrossed the country, that the oldest songs thrived the best, and so the collectors set out to discover them.

Many of these new researchers were as dedicated to the task as Child had been, with enthusiasm for ballad collecting becoming even more pronounced once it became apparent that, just as Child had intimated on several occasions, *ESPB* was by no means complete. There were still myriad versions of the same ballads that had yet to be gathered, as Bert Lloyd made clear when he recorded "The Grey Cock" (248) in 1966. "Curiously enough Francis J. Child, in his enormous collection, never found a full set of it. [However], several good versions have turned up since Child's time."[4]

Percy Grainger's collections were the first to hint at the vast array of untapped material that still circulated, at least on a local level. His first mechanically recorded Child Ballads, that quartet of versions of "Lord Bateman" in 1906, followed almost word for word the version popularized by Thackeray, Dickens, and Cruikshank (albeit less than half the length). But Joseph Leaning's somewhat stumbling "The Outlandish Knight" (4) bears only some resemblance to any that Child documented

(4f and 4g are the closest), and George Gouldthorpe's "Lord Lovel" (75) strayed even further afield.

Further discoveries followed and, although it would be disingenuous to describe collecting now as a race to out-Child Child (collectors, after all, do not need any reason to collect beyond the sheer enjoyment of the pursuit), fresh urgency was perhaps added to the quest by the realization that, every time another old singer passed away unrecorded and not interviewed, every time another family mourned the grandparent who used to croon them to sleep with the old songs, another song died with them.

The sweet "Barbara Allen" that Mrs. Knipp sang to Samuel Pepys . . . we know that was written down. But what of Peggy Gold's serenades to the young Oliver Goldsmith? Did Child, or anyone else for that matter, succeed in transcribing her sweet song? Dickens and Thackeray preserved the words of one of the Tripe-skewers' ballads. But what of the remainder of that man's repertoire? All of this leads into an interesting debate, and one that has now exercised observers and academics alike for some two hundred years, still without a satisfactory resolution for either side.

Throughout the compiling of Walter Scott's *Minstrelsy*, one of Scott's closest collaborators was the poet James Hogg, and one of his most valuable sources for songs and stories was Hogg's mother, Margaret. Different sources offer different versions of the story but, effectively, when the woman realized that her songs were being written down and were likely to be published, she lamented that they "war made for singing an' no for reading; but ye hae broken the charm now, an' they'll never be sung mair."

THE MANY LIVES OF BARBARA ALLEN

What Shirley Collins described as "the dark lady of the ballads" has lived a multitude of lives. "She has been known to skip out of Jimmy's reach as he stretches a pale arm for her from his death bed," Collins wrote, "[or] laugh out loud as she sees Jimmy's ghost in the lane on her way home. But after her devilish behavior she always dies of remorse and finishes up in the churchyard with Jimmy."[5]

Dom Flemons continues, "In some versions [of the ballad], Sweet William's at fault because he slights Barbara Allen at a bar. Sometimes she's a barmaid and sometimes she's a high well-to-do woman. Sometimes she deserves it, sometimes she doesn't."[6] But, again, she always dies at the end.

In 1966, author and folklorist Ed Cray (1933-2019), writing for the Library of Congress, said of "Barbara Allen," "In the North American tradition, in spite of some seven hundred collected texts, there are but four basic versions of the ballad, each readily identifiable by its first stanza. . . . This lack of change is probably the result of the constant 'corrective' of print [and] a tribute to the popularity of the songster which reportedly had multiple press runs in the 1840s totaling one million copies."[7]

He already had a sizable corpus of recordings upon which to base his musings. One of the earliest commercial recordings of "Barbara Allen" dates from 1927, when operatic tenor turned hillbilly tragedian Vernon Dalhart, accompanied by guitarist and harmonica whizz Carson Robison, captivated American hearts with his reading of the song. The following year, Americans Frank Luther and his Pards and Scotland's Billy Dalton released their interpretations; in 1930, Bradley Kincaid followed suit; in 1934, The Vagabonds did likewise.

In 1936, Charles Seeger Jr., an active ethnomusicologist before the field was even named, captured a truly plaintive "Barbara Allen" when Tennessee singers Rebecca and Penelope Tarwater were invited to record at the Library of Congress; and, in 1938, John Jacob Niles produced one of the longest and, by his reckoning, most complete of all the circulating versions.

Josh White in 1943, Jo Stafford and Bob Atcher in 1948, country star Hawkshaw Hawkins (1953), Susan Reed (1957), the Everly Brothers (1958), Tennessee Ernie Ford and Marijohn Wilkin (both 1959), Joan Baez (1961), Bob Dylan (1962), all brought fresh stylings and sentiment to the song.

Singing actor Noel Harrison even rewired "Barbara Allen" for a distinctly groovy beat audience in 1965, but still his lyric was one that Child would have recognized instantly. And so it goes on: Art Garfunkel (1973), Almeda Riddle (1977), Dolly Parton (1994), Emmylou Harris (2000), Lucy Wainwright Roche (2007), Blackmore's Night (2010), Ellie Bryan (2012), Widow's Weeds in 2021 . . . even television's *The Waltons* (1973) got in on the game.

All adhered to type. Indeed, when Martin Carthy presented a very different take on the ballad in 1998, his explanation was almost apologetic: "I've known 'Barbary Ellen' all my life. The song I learned was very short and gave you nothing of her anger at being treated with such disdain and how that translates to the contempt with which she treats his rather late declarations of lurve."[8]

Carthy's version, set to a tune he took from Shropshire traveller Samson Price, amply compensated for that deficit, and shocked a lot of listeners in the process.

What had happened to the version they already knew?

Of course, Mrs Hogg was wrong. Her ballads continued to be sung, and they are still sung today. New versions appear, old ones are rediscovered, the charm remains far from unbroken.

It is true that the ubiquity of the Thackeray/Dickens "Lord Bateman," among Percy Grainger's first field recordings, suggests that once a ballad is committed to print, more people are likely to learn that version than any other. The advent of mechanical recording only emphasized this. It is true, too, that far more "cover versions" of a recorded Child Ballad are likely to appear than newly discovered, or even freshly confronted ones. But even "Barbara Allen"—alongside "Scarborough Fair," the most ubiquitous of the Child Ballads—has seen sufficient revision to prevent its absolute ossification.

Of course there are those audiences that do demand constancy; that would be happy to see "Barbara Allen" (and several other Child Ballads besides) as straitjacketed as any modern pop song, bound by copyright and guarded by suspicious lawyers. But although there was no prohibition, much to Margaret Hogg's dismay, to the ballads being written down, and nothing to prevent the charm from being broken, ultimately the fate she feared would never befall them.

They were far too tenacious for that.

Chapter Eight

SONGS AROUND EVERY CORNER

The canon continued to grow, both in terms of size and idiom. In 1907, the composer George Butterworth (1885–1916) heard "The Banks of Green Willow" (24) sung by a Mrs. Cranstone, in the village of Billingshurst in West Sussex. Home from that collecting expedition, he wrote his own piece of music, based upon the Child Ballad and bearing the same name. Was it still a Child Ballad in this new form? It doesn't matter. When the English singer Shirley Collins recorded Butterworth's vision in 2016, she did so because she had "always loved" it.[1] What better reason could there be?

Gustav Holst went even further. In 1903, the Latvian-born composer created a choral ballet around "King Estmere" (60), rescuing from absolute obscurity a ballad that Child knew only from Percy's *Reliques*. No other text of the ballad has ever surfaced, either in print or orally. Nevertheless, this gripping tale of knightly derring-do lent itself perfectly to Holst's approach, and perhaps it also offered fresh impetus to the collectors who were now wandering around the British countryside in search of song. Maybe, a few surely dreamed, they would discover their own "King Estmere."

They did not. But other rare finds surfaced regardless. In 1905, the Scottish author and collector Gavin Greig (1856–1914) and the minister James Bruce Duncan (1848–1917) unearthed an unknown variation on "Blow Away the Morning Dew" (112), now titled "The Shepherd Laddie," from a Mrs. Gillespie in Buchan, Aberdeenshire.

The wry tale of a persistent suitor who, invited to his intended conquest's home, is instead locked outside and tormented, it was just one of many new additions the pair were able to offer the Child collection and, a selection of their discoveries was published as *Last Leaves of Traditional Ballads and Ballad Airs Collected in Aberdeenshire by the Late Gavin Greig*.

Initially viewed as somewhat flawed (the pair included several examples of what contemporary critics regarded as "impure" or even indecent lyrics), *Last Leaves* would nevertheless go onto prove an outstanding wellspring for future artists, with the Scots band Malinky titling their 2000 debut album, *Last Leaves*, in tribute to the book. Later, in 2009, Katherine Campbell—fresh from restoring the Harris sisters' collection to daylight—edited a 150-strong collection of ballads from the Greig/Duncan collection, again including a number of Child variations.

Malinky cofounder Steve Byrne explains the book's personal significance. "My first interest [in traditional music] was really through my parents and groups like the Corries, who . . . included various ballads in their repertoire, such as 'Hugh the Graeme' [191], 'The Great Silkie of Sule Skerry' [113] and so on."

He says that he became more involved in the music in his teenaged years, however: "I discovered the Greig Duncan Folksong Collection in the local library, although I think at that time I didn't know what it really was, far less the fact that it contained a large number of Child Ballads." Nevertheless it led him to enroll at the School of Scottish Studies at Edinburgh University, and there, "I soon received a good grounding in ballad studies, which I carried through to my work with Malinky." Indeed, the first time he met future bandmate Fiona Hunter, it was at a Greig-Duncan ballads weekend organized by the Elphinstone Institute from the University of Aberdeen in 2000.

> [The aim of the gathering was] to get young singers singing the songs; it was led by the late Anne Neilson and Gordeanna McCulloch. Both are sadly no longer with us but were huge influences in the Glasgow singing scene and tutored people like Fiona who attended the then RSAMD (now Royal Conservatoire of Scotland) Scottish Music course.
>
> Two of Fiona's tutors were Andy Hunter and Alison McMorland; Andy had stayed for a time with Jeannie Robertson, so some of his versions of ballads, such as "Son David," that he taught to Fiona had come directly from Jeannie. We're very proud of that link and lineage. Alison McMorland is also a great champion of ballad singing and worked closely with Hamish Henderson, another huge influence on the band's thinking. We have taken forward some of Alison's ballad versions over the years in our group repertoire.[2]

Greig and Duncan were not alone in their endeavors. In 1906, Ann Geddes Gilchrist picked up a version of "The Golden Vanity" (286) while collecting in her native Lancashire. Grainger of course was at large that year, too.

Ralph Vaughan Williams, circa 1900. CCO 1.0 Wikimedia Commons

Perhaps the most astounding discovery, however, awaited George Gardiner (1852–1910) on a field trip to Hampshire, in southern England. There he unearthed no less than three versions of "George Collins," a hybrid of "Clerk Covill" (42) and "Lady Alice" (85) that had never before been encountered.

The question was, which came first—the hybrid or its component parts? As the editors of the 1959 edition of *The Penguin Book of English Folk Songs*, the composer Ralph Vaughan Williams (1872–1958) and singer Bert Lloyd, remarked, "Either ["Clerk Covill" and "Lady Alice"] are two separate songs which have been combined to form 'George Collins,' or (which seems more likely) they are two fragments of the completer ballad." They reiterated the fact that "'George Collins' has rarely been reported in England," a point which renders Gardiner's discovery all the more noteworthy. Two of the versions were found on the same day!

Vaughan Williams himself gathered a number of Child Ballads during the years he was most active on the folklore scene—an interest that persisted around his escalating renown as a composer. The versions of "The Outlandish Knight" (4) and "Broomfield Hill" (43) that he included in the aforementioned *The Penguin Book of English Folk Songs* were both drawn from his personal collection, while Martin Carthy reckoned it was "probably . . . Vaughan Williams' decision to follow Percy Grainger in using recording techniques to gather songs" that ensured the survival of the version of "The Banks of Green Willow" (24) that Carthy recorded on his 1972 *Shearwater* album, where he noted, "He recorded it from an old man in Hampshire and subsequently had great difficulty in transcribing it, so what he wrote is probably only the merest sketch of the tune."[3]

The same can be said for "Lord Allenwater," which Vaughan Williams transcribed in 1905 from Emily Agnes Stears of Horsham, Sussex, and which was recorded by the sisters Shirley and Dolly Collins on their 1978 album *For as Many as Will*; and in 2008 by the now-veteran Ian A. Anderson. Then working with the band Blue Bloke 3, Anderson is, in fact, Stears's great grandson, and he noted at the time, "History isn't able to register what Emily Stears might have made of her great grandson recording it with stubbly players of vintage Congolese guitar and electric saz [a kind of Turkish lute], though she did live to be 99."[4]

Equally recherché is what we might call an "extended version" of "There Lived a Lady in Merry Scotland," a reading of "The Wife of Usher's Well" (79) that Vaughan Williams collected from a Mrs. Loveridge of the Homme, a grand house in the Herefordshire village of Dilwyn, in 1908. In Child's versions, the titular woman is visited one last time, at Christmas, by the three sons she has outlived. In Mrs. Loveridge's rendition, not only do the children return from the dead, but we have what John Roberts and Tony Barrand described as "the extra supernatural element, more proper to the religious piece 'The Carnal and the Crane' [55], of the roasted cock crowing in the serving platter."[5]

> Then Christ did call for the roasted cock,
> Feathered with His holy hands,
> He crowed three times all in the dish,
> In the place where he did stand.
>
> He crowed three times all in the dish,
> Set at the table head,
> "And isn't it a pity," they all did say,
> "The quick should part from the dead."

Vaughan Williams also retrieved a "Robin Hood and the Three Squires" (140), sung to him by a Mrs. Goodyear in Axford, Hampshire, in 1909. Almost ninety years later, John Kirkpatrick looked to that rendition for a 1997 anthology by the Fellside label, *Ballads*. Another Hood ballad,

"Robin Hood and the Bishop of Hereford" (144), sung to Vaughan Williams by George Stone of Wareham, Dorset in 1906, was recorded by Tim Laycock in 1999.

Too many field recordings lay locked up in the archives, largely accessible for many decades only to academics. Yet it is airings such as these that truly reward the enterprising souls who collected the songs in the first place. They permit even the most obscure local variant of a traditional song to resonate once again.

Another key collection from this period was Ella Mary Leather's (1874–1928) *The Folklore of Herefordshire,* published in 1912 and destined, close to a century later, in 2009, to serve as a key resource for local musician Ian "Sproatly" Smith, as he worked toward his debut album. Smith explains, "I was researching songs that had an association with Hereford, and discovered the works of Ella Mary Leather. She was an avid and enthusiastic collector of folk songs from itinerant farm workers and from the local workhouse. She was encouraged to collect by Cecil Sharp, and Ralph Vaughan Williams had sent her an Edison phonograph to record on. They both made regular trips to Herefordshire to visit and record from the local gypsy encampments."[6]

Among Leather's discoveries was a version of "The Unquiet Grave" [78], sung by W. Hirons, a neighbor of Vaughan Williams's balladeering Mrs. Loveridge, in Dilwyn in 1909. But even more powerful was that which she and Vaughan Williams collected another from Traveler tenor, Alfred Price, in Monkland. A truly chilling ballad, "The Unquiet Grave" is the tale of a maiden whose grief for her dead lover is so strong that he finally returns from the grave, effectively to ask her to stop weeping, because he cannot rest while she does so. "One kiss from your clay cold lips," she replies, "one kiss, that's all I desire." But he warns her,

> *If you have one kiss from my clay cold lips*
> *Your days will not be long*
> *My lips are as cold as my clay*
> *My breath it is earthly strong.*

Leather's book *Collecting Folk-Melodies from Gypsies in Herefordshire* (1925) sets the scene for the Price version's discovery.

We all sat down on upturned buckets, kindly provided for us by the Gypsies, and while Dr. Vaughan Williams noted the tune his wife and I took down alternate lines of the words. It is difficult to convey to those who have never known it the joy of hearing folk-songs sung as we heard that pathetic ballad: the difference between hearing it there and in a drawing room or concert hall is just that between discovering a wild flower growing in its native habitat and admiring it when transplanted to a botanic garden.

Three years later, in the *Journal of the Folk-Song Society*'s 1928 edition, Vaughan Williams added his impression: "It was a cold, clear September night and we stood by the light of a blazing fire in the open ground of the gypsy encampment; the fire had been specially lighted to enable us to note down tunes and words in the growing darkness. Then out of the half light there came the sound of a beautiful tenor voice singing 'The Unquiet Grave.'"

Vaughan Williams's influence hangs, too, elsewhere in Sproatly Smith's career. "The other two Child Ballads that we've recorded thus far are 'Dives and Lazarus' [56] and 'The Carnal and the Crane' [55], from our album *Carols from Herefordshire*. In 1920 Vaughan Williams published *Twelve Traditional Carols from Herefordshire*, which included the two Child Ballads, [although] our version of 'Dives' is based on a song collected by Cecil Sharp, from Thomas Taylor from the Ross workhouse."[7]

Cecil James Sharp (1859–1924), despite the fierce competition of so many other collectors, is widely regarded as the preeminent British ballad collector of this age, primarily—if somewhat contradictorily—because of his later work in the United States.

A music teacher by profession, Sharp's interest in traditional song was initially aroused by what he felt to be a paucity of suitable songs for his pupils to sing. He commenced gathering his own selection from both popular and traditional sources, making his first excursions into this field in 1903 while visiting his friend Charles Marson (1859–1914) in the small town of Hambridge, in Somerset.

He proved a prodigious collector. Between 1904 and 1906, he and Marson published three volumes of *Folk Songs from Somerset*, while Sharp also made excursions to some fourteen other English counties. He was a student, too, of both Morris and Sword dancing; in 1911, Sharp founded the English Folk Dance Society (now the English Folk Dance and Song Society[8]), and another three-volume publication, issued between 1911 and 1913, was devoted to *The Sword Dances of Northern England*.

Sharp's contributions to the expansion of the Child Ballads are manifold. It was Sharp who unearthed, from a Mrs. Plumb in Armscote, Worcestershire, the version of "King Herod and the Cock" that John Kirkpatrick performs on the Fellside label's 1998 Christmas compilation *Wassail*. Another fascinating Sharp discovery was a unique variant of "The Mermaid," collected from an Anglican nun, Sister Emma, whom he met in Clewer, near Windsor. Sister Emma ran a home for abandoned boys, St Augustine's, and it has been speculated that she frequently called upon her vast repository of traditional songs to entertain her charges. In which case it makes sense that some of the grimmer ballads might be changed, so as to present her audience with a happy ending.

Mary Humphreys and Anahita sang Sister Emma's "The Mermaid" (289) on their 2003 album *Sharp Practice*, and remarked, "We love the way that the typical ending of the ballad (where the ship turns around three times and sinks to the bottom of the sea) is completely changed and everyone goes home happy ever after. Especially after the little homily by the 'good little boy' about the 'One who rules the waves.'"[9]

Valuable though these excursions and discoveries are, still these collectors were working in the shadow of Professor Child, and it is often considered ironic that the most important collection of English and Scottish traditional songs ever assembled should have been the work of an American professor. In fact, it was not so bizarre a turn of events. Although Child himself paid little attention to the survival of his chosen 305 in the New World, the sheer weight and nature of the Anglo-Scottish and Irish hordes who immigrated to the Americas guaranteed that, along with their accents and their family keepsakes, they would also bring their memories. And their songs.

Child was surely aware of this, as the occasional tantalizing snippet in *ESPB* reveals. The Child Ballad that Woody Guthrie would help popularize during the 1940s, "Gypsy Laddie" (200), Child notes, was discovered in Stockbridge, Massachusetts, and how coincidental is it that Stockbridge is the same town in which Woody's son Arlo set his breakthrough song "Alice's Restaurant"?

Child knew of "a little girl in New York derived, through her mother, from a grandmother born in Ireland," who contributed a version of "Little Sir Hugh" (155) to a book on the games and songs of American children.[10] Another "Gypsy Laddie" had been passed down from "the singing of Miss Phoebe Wood, of Huntington, New York, and perhaps learned from English soldiers stationed there during the Revolutionary War." And there were three contributions from an Emma Buckus of Polk County, North Carolina: "The Wife of Usher's Well" (79), "Lamkin" (93) and "The Maid Freed from the Gallows" (95).

Indeed, the American ethnomusicologist Alan Lomax, reflecting upon the popularity of "Usher's Well,"[11] explained that the ballad was considerably more common in America than the British Isles,[12] particularly "among mountain women, who feel deeply the cruelty of the mother who 'sent her babes way off yonder over the mountains to study their grammar.'" Lomax then goes on to explain that "grammaree" (from which the term "grammar" is derived) is "an ambiguous term, sometimes referring to general education and sometimes to the practice of magic, and in several versions of the song, the children return wearing (birch) bark caps, which is a sure sign of magic." This latter adornment is absent from Buckus's manuscript, but the British band Steeleye Span uncovered the reference, all the same.

It fell about the Martinmas,
The nights were long and dark,
Three sons came home to Usher's Well
Their hats were made of bark
That neither grew in forest green
Nor on any wooded rise,
But from the north side of the tree
That grows in Paradise.

Child added all three of these American variants as appendices to the primary entries for the relevant ballads. Yet had he possessed—we do not know whether it was the inclination or the time, but surely one or the other—how much more might he have gleaned from his own countrymen?

How many other ballads accompanied, for instance, "Little Sir Hugh" on the playgrounds of New York? What was the story behind the man on Clark's Island, in Plymouth Harbor, who taught his son, J. M. Watson, the words to "Archie O'Cawfield" (188)? What other songs did the "poor whites" of North Carolina sing, that Emma Buckus might have overheard?

Child did not inquire. Others, however, would.

The term "ethnomusicology" had yet to be coined (it is credited to the Dutchman Jaap Kunst [1891–1960], a renowned student of Indonesian music), but its exponents had already spread across the United States as the twentieth century dawned, and all the more so following the invention, and marketing, of the phonograph. As author Erika Brady[13] puts it, as early as the 1890s, "professionals and amateurs sought out and recorded the speech and music of cultures and communities the old ways of which were succumbing to the very world whose advent trumpeted from the phonograph's great horn."

The aforementioned Jesse Walter Fewkes was the first, taking a recording machine with him on a collecting trip to Calais, Maine, in 1890, to record the Passamaquoddy people. But others swiftly joined him, and they would continue to do so throughout the twentieth century and beyond. It is through their often tireless efforts that much of what we now know about the rural America of the past was ever preserved in the first place.

Occasionally, however, examining the mountains of discs, tapes, documents, and photographs that these researchers gathered, one becomes aware that one thing is absent, and that is the life stories of the sources themselves. Who actually *were* these people, one wonders, while perusing the lists of names, ages, and locations that were most collectors' sole acknowledgment that their sources were more than mere singing jukeboxes? What had they done, and what had they achieved, in the years before age, and perhaps straitened circumstances, lined them up as fair game for the magnificent mobs with their recording machines? They can't *all* have been manual workers, farm hands, Romani Rye, and rural grandmothers, can they?

Chapter Nine

THE MERMAID AND THE ASTRONOMER

In 1969, Ben Gray Lumpkin, a professor of English at the University of Colorado, Boulder, was nearing the conclusion of what had become a twenty-year search for folk song survivals in Colorado. Child Ballads accounted for but a tiny percentage of the two thousand songs he collected, and of those, the likes of "The House Carpenter" (243), "Barbara Allen" (84), "The Golden Vanity" (286), and "Old Bangum" (18) were by far the most widespread.

From the repertoire of seventy-five-year-old Edith Cummings Taylor, a widow living in Boulder, however, there emerged a couple of genuine rarities, "Robin Hood and Little John" (125) and "The Mermaid" (289), recorded by Lumpkin in September 1969 and February 1970, respectively.

Edith Cummings Taylor's voice was querulous and prone to losing its grip on the melody, hallmarks of course of her age. But her performances were powerful regardless. The band Finest Kind said of their 1999 "The Mermaid," "We like its sombreness, in particular the repetitive, knell-like introduction of each crew member who 'steps up' to lament his approaching doom."[1] They might have been thinking of Taylor's performance.

She also possessed a keen sense of humor, the same perhaps that glimmers from her 1915 university year book photograph, a very serious-looking young lady, but one whose expression belies the hint of amusement that flickers behind her dark eyes. Especially enjoyable is hearing the brief snatch of conversation between Taylor and Lumpkin as he questions her setting the non-Child "The Nightingale" in Chattanooga: "My father, Marion Taylor Cummings, was a southern man and Chattanooga was a big city he knew of and it rhymed. That's the way he sang it."

Born in 1894, Cummings grew up in Beatrice, in southeastern Nebraska, and gathered her repertoire from her father, and from regular visits from her Kentucky-born grandmother. "He knew songs that my grandmother didn't know," she said of her father, but it was grandma who taught her the "Robin Hood" ballad—a number that Lumpkin rightly points out is rarely heard in America.

"The Mermaid" had a wholly different origin, and Lumpkin is frustrated only because Edith, like so many other singers, did not wholly remember the complete song. He loaned her a copy of *ESPB* so that she might reconstruct her own version, and she was swift to point out the differences between the song as she learned it, and that which Child noted. "In some cases at the end of a line, in the Child Ballads, a word will be repeated, like 'a glass in her hand, in her hand'; the way I heard it, the word 'hand' is drawn out and the volume is increased, a crescendo.

"I think I learned ["The Mermaid"] from my Uncle Charles," she continued. "He was the son of my [maternal] great grandfather John Carroll. He was a sea captain and it seems very probable that it entered the family through him." He was also a keen abolitionist, and eventually gave up his seafaring career to work full time for his beliefs.

This story fascinated Lumpkin. But Edith, too, had led a remarkable life, as one of the early twentieth century's pioneering female astronomers. Studying at the University of Missouri through the mid-1910s, she graduated Phi Beta Kappa with a bachelors and a master's degree in astronomy—her master's thesis, "The Eclipsing Binary TV Cassiopeiae," was published in the *Laws Observatory Journal* in 1918. She was a recipient of the Laws Astronomy Medal, and further prestigious publications followed during her time as research assistant to Professor Robert Horace Baker, author of what were once considered the standard textbooks on the subject, *Astronomy* and *An Introduction to Astronomy*.

Professor Baker was especially impressed by Edith's abilities. "Miss Cummings," he wrote when he recommended her for graduate school, "was the most promising student I have had." He acknowledged the engrained chauvinism of the age with his confirmation that "unfortunately she is not a man"; nevertheless, "I believe she is hampered by her sex less than any aspirant I have known. In our extra focal work she has done a man's share. She has unlimited energy, health and strength to accompany it. She intends to make astronomy her life's work."

In 1923, Edith earned her PhD in astronomy from Berkeley, and her doctoral thesis, "The Photoelectric Photometer of the Lick Observatory and Some Results Obtained with It," described a machine, designed to measure the brightness of stars, that she built during her graduate years. Alongside the writings of the device's very inventors, P. Guthnik and R.

Prager, Cummings's thesis was for many years recommended among the highest authorities on the subject.[2]

Despite her earlier intentions, however, Cummings's days in astronomy were nearing their end. She was by now married—her husband, William Taylor, was a physics graduate who worked for the Bureau of Standards. They moved to Wisconsin, and the birth of their daughter in 1923 saw Cummings commence her drift away.

By the time Lumpkin caught up with her close to half a century later, that chapter of her life had long been closed. Nevertheless, when Edith mentioned her background during one of their interviews, Lumpkin sounds genuinely disappointed, almost disbelieving, to discover that she was so far removed from the popular (and persistent) stereotype of the "source singer" as anything but a farmer's wife or a fisherman's widow.

Inadvertently, but unmistakably, his response reminds listeners of a remark the American collector Elisabeth Bristol Greenleaf (1895–1980) once made, saying that too many of her contemporaries forgot they were talking with "singing people," and regarded them instead as "song repositories."

Folklorist Julie Henigan recalls,[3] "It was . . . during my time at University of North Carolina, Charlotte, that I gradually started to get away from the idea of orality as essential to traditionality, which probably had something to do with finding out more about how the terms 'folklore' and 'folksong' developed from scholarly ideas about the evolution of societies from primitive to civilized (a concept which predated Darwin—and which I doubt Darwin would have approved of)."

The irony—that the "educated" classes should expend so much time and energy investigating the culture of what they regarded as their less fortunate fellows, so that it might better be preserved for future generations of scholars (and let the primitives be damned)—would be amusing if it wasn't so patronizing. In the event, it is laughable because, in the eyes of many scholars, it is also patently muddleheaded. As Henigan continues, "There is nothing essentially oral or primitive about ballads or folksong in general. In a lot of cases, they came from or were based on court or upper-class culture."

Chapter Ten

THE ORIGINAL SOUTHERN JOURNEY

The death of Professor Child, and the publication of volume ten, did not spell the end of the *ESPB* project. Professor Kittredge continued to receive mail from people who were discovering "new" variants on the ballads in the books. In 1907, for example, Kittredge and a Knott County, Kentucky, schoolteacher, Katherine Pettit, coauthored an article for the quarterly *Journal of American Folklore* (volume 20, April–June 1907), documenting the songs she had heard being sung by one of her pupils, Josiah Cotton.[1]

Indeed, Kentucky and the Appalachian region was swiftly revealed to possess an Aladdin's Cave of unrecorded folk songs—including, as it transpired, a large portion of the Child Ballad canon. The mountain range itself reaches from Newfoundland, in the north, to central Alabama in the south, a concentration of some of the most glorious landscapes in eastern North America. At the time, however, it was also one of the most inhospitable, particularly at its southern extremes as it passed through Kentucky, the Virginias, Tennessee, and Alabama. Neither industry nor organized agriculture had fully reached into the region, and in the cities of the cosmopolitan North, it was regarded as backward and back*woods*, peopled by veritable savages, folks too stupid to accept any of the advantages that cities and civilization had on offer. There were no towns to speak of beyond small gatherings of dwellings; no paved roads except those built by the mining companies that were slowly attempting to gain a foothold; and the only halls of learning were the so-called Settlement Schools established by the missionary groups that ventured into the region.

Only gradually, through these missions, did news seep out that, far from embracing any of the stereotypes with which they were viewed, the people of Appalachia in fact presided over a vibrant culture that

Cecil Sharp, around the time of his 1916 Appalachian visit. Wikimedia Commons

was all their own, one that had remained largely intact since the first settlers moved in from Britain and Ireland, in which art was prized and songs were valued, and it was considered far better to live life free of the "advantages" of the modern world than it was to be enslaved by the corresponding disadvantages.

A number of folklorists were soon at work there. Local paintings, condescendingly tagged "folk art" by the gallery owners of New York and Boston, were being sold and collected. Local ghost stories, superstitions, and "folk wisdom" were finding their way into the hands of urban publishers; and the first whispers of a whole new species of folk song, too, were being heard.

Kittredge's correspondent Katherine Pettit was one such whisperer. Another was Olive Dame Campbell (1882–1954), whose husband, John C. Campbell, was the director of the Southern Highland Division of the

Russell Sage Foundation, a nonprofit organization concerned with "the improvement of social and living conditions in the United States."

Traveling the area with her husband, Campbell started collecting the ballads she heard being sung after being bitten by the bug, coincidentally enough, while visiting Josiah Cotton's alma mater, the Hindman Settlement School in Knott County.

There she overheard a little girl singing "Barbara Allen" (84), a song Olive knew from her own youth. It was, and remained, a popular song among children of the region—the singer Jean Ritchie, growing up in Viper County, Kentucky, in the 1920s, recalled how she and her sisters would sing "Barbara Allen" as they washed the dishes, to discover which they could finish first, the chore or the ballad.[2] Unhappily, the chore usually won, so they started singing the ballad increasingly slowly, "dragging out the tune until you could hardly recognize it . . . and in the saddest part of the song, too. I felt kind of bad because we were carrying on in such a disrespectful way, and both of them stretched out dying."[3]

The melody that Campbell was listening to at Hindman was completely different from any she had previously heard, and it was the tune, as opposed to the lyrics, that drove her to seek out further examples. And it was Campbell who first told Cecil Sharp about Appalachia, in 1915.

Renowned already for his tireless collecting efforts in the English countryside, Sharp was now working as choreographer for a New York City production of Shakespeare's *A Midsummer Night's Dream*. He was not sorry to leave England. War with Germany had broken out the previous August, and Sharp, too old for the armed services, was keen to take up new opportunities. How new they would actually become, he had no idea.

When Campbell first told Sharp of her collection, he was initially unimpressed. As he wrote in 1917,[4] "The effort that has been made to collect and preserve in permanent form the folk-songs of England during the last twenty or thirty years has resulted in the salvage of many thousands of beautiful songs. It was pardonable, therefore, if those who, like myself, had assisted in the task had come to believe that the major part of the work had been completed." Now he realized that "one important, albeit not very obvious, consideration had been overlooked; namely, the possibility that one or other of those English communities that lie scattered in various parts of the world might provide as good a field for the collector as England itself, and yield as bountiful a harvest."

Over the next three years, Sharp and his assistant, folk dance teacher and performer Maud Karpeles (1885–1976), traveled the Appalachians extensively, recording as many songs as they could. It is regrettable, however, that they did so only with pen, paper, and Karpeles's shorthand abilities. No less than back in 1908, when he complained of the recording machine's infidelities to Percy Grainger, Sharp continued to spurn the technology.

It was not only its perceived failings as an appropriate means of recording that he objected to. He was also opposed to the gramophone as a piece of furniture!

In her 1967 biography of Sharp, Karpeles wrote, "More than once it happened that Cecil . . . would be sitting quietly with an old couple, listening with enjoyment, when the peaceful atmosphere would be disturbed by the noisy entrance of the grandchildren, who would be shocked to find their grandparents singing their silly old songs to the gentleman, and would endeavor to reinstate the family reputation by turning on the gramophone with the latest music hall songs."[5] Sharp disliked, and even distrusted the recording machine. He was far happier taking everything down manually.

Basing themselves at the various Presbyterian Missionary Settlements that dotted North Carolina, Sharp and Karpeles would then venture forth, usually on foot, to meet whatever singers lived within walking distance. They would encounter some arduous treks, as Karpeles recalled.

> Walking over the rough mountain tracks where one had to pick every footstep was, as you can imagine, extremely exhausting, especially as we would often walk 15 or more miles a day. Cecil always maintained a steady trudge but my method of progression was to alternate a sprint with a full stop. On one occasion when I sat on a stone to rest, I found I had completely lost my will power and could not get up. With something like apathy, I saw Cecil's figure receding in the distance then he turned and walked back and somehow restored me to my right senses.[6]

Even the best roads were often little more than dirt tracks, the terrain was hilly, the weather hot. Sharp's asthma was as constant a companion as the buzzing, biting insect life, while a persistent (he called it "troublesome") cough often prevented him from sleeping, or even resting. Karpeles noted at the time, "Cecil . . . is never fully well. In Harrogate, Tennessee, he was so ill I dared not leave him alone at night, so I camped out on the floor of his bedroom. After some days, he recovered somewhat and he insisted on my scouting around for singers and bringing them to his bedside."

On their first visit to the region, the pair's perambulations took them to a host of communities scattered across Laurel County, North Carolina— White Rock, Allanstand, Allegheny and Carmen, Big Laurel and Hot Springs—all home to what Sharp described in his letters home[7] as "the direct descendants of the original settlers [from] England and, I suspect, the lowlands of Scotland." The pair also enjoyed longer sojourns in Rocky Park, Tennessee, and Charlottesville, Virginia. Sharp swiftly warmed to the locals. "The people are just English of the late eighteenth or early nineteenth century," he wrote early into that maiden expedition.

> They speak English, look English, and their manners are old-fashioned English. Heaps of words and expressions they use habitually in ordinary conversation are obsolete, and have been in England a long time. I find them very easy to get on with, and have no difficulty in making them sing and show their enthusiasm for their songs. I have taken down very nearly one hundred already, and many of these are quite unknown to me and aesthetically of the very highest value. Indeed, it is the greatest discovery I have made since the original one I made in England sixteen years ago.

The self-sufficiency of the region astounded him. "The people here are self contained," he wrote two weeks later. "They grow practically everything they eat, their corn, beans, vegetables, fruit and pork, which they call hog meat and it's the only meat they ever see. They make nearly all their own clothes, blankets etc, growing, carding, spinning and weaving their own wool. At the present moment they are busy preserving and canning the fruits and vegetables for the winter. The only crop they grow and sell is tobacco." Daily life itself appeared to be so far behind the times that he and Karpeles might have stepped back a century or more.

In his diary for August 24, 1916, he recalled, "Had breakfast at 7 and [then] sallied forth across the river with Maud. Crossed the river by punt with the aid of a wire manipulated by the ferryman. A perilous business."

But worse was to follow. Arriving in Hot Springs, the pair found the locals still cleaning up after what is now remembered as the Great Flood of 1916, with little or no assistance from the outside world. So much of the area was affected—if not by the flooding, then by the two hurricanes that swept inland in the course of just nine days. At least eighty people died, and Asheville, the nearest major city, was hit by a ten-foot tidal wave after a series of dam breaks. Hot Springs, however, was almost wiped off the map.

At the same time, it is very easy to romanticize their journey, as Dom Flemons points out: "If you go up to where he and Maud were staying in Hot Springs, the Biltmore Hotel is not a shack in the mountains. It's a very, very nice fancy hotel, very much in the gilded-age area. He's always portrayed as trudging through a J. R. R. Tolkien novel to find these singers, but it was a very fancy hotel, a real easy train ride, a beautiful resort town, very rustic but beautiful."[8] He would have been comfortable.

One of the pair's most treasured discoveries on this initial visit was the singer Jane Hitch Gentry. In 2016, Gentry's biographer Betty Smith told the BBC, "The first time he came, she sang twenty songs; I figured he thought he'd died and gone to heaven. He asked her on that first trip . . . I guess he thought this little mountain woman would be shy about singing . . . so he said, 'If you'd like you can sit in one room and sing, and I'll sit in the next room and write down the songs,' and she said 'well, if you can stand to look at me, I can stand to look at you.'"[9]

Sharp continues the story in his diary entry for August 24, 1916, celebrating in the process the discovery of a Child Ballad. "She sang till 11:30 some excellent songs." Included among these was "Awake Awake," a variant of "Earl Brand" (7), while Gentry also teased Sharp with a solitary verse from "The Golden Vanity" (286), and the promise of performing the entire song the following day.

Sharp wrote, "I told her not to die in the night or catch cold or do anything that would endanger me getting the song on the morrow." His caution, if a little lacking in taste, was not wholly misplaced. On a later occasion, Sharp and Karpeles made their way to the home of the singing Sloan family, only to discover that Mr. Sloan "had blown himself up with gunpowder and the family [was] too upset to sing. Our luck," Sharp concluded somewhat thoughtlessly, "has departed for the moment."

A week after meeting Gentry, Sharp and Karpeles were in Allanstand, where they encountered another precious find. Sharp wrote, "Mrs Mary Sands, the mother of nine children and expecting another fairly shortly, arrived soon after breakfast around 8.30 to sing. She proved to be a prize folk singer and started off with six first raters. . . . Maud danced to 'Jockey to the Fair,' I played the piano dreadfully out of tune."

The Sands family as a whole distrusted Sharp on sight. With World War One finally drawing the United States into the conflict, Sands's great grandniece Sheila K. Adams told the BBC,

> My granny . . . and her sister remembered him coming through . . . [but] they didn't sing for him because granny's older sister decided he was a German spy, because he wore a white suit and he talked funny. But Mary . . . said he was a perfect gentleman and the woman that was with him [Karpeles] was a very nice soft spoken woman, and they were probably took up, that's what the story was, that there was something going on besides just him and her recording the songs.[10]

The Sands clan was likely not alone in distrusting Sharp, either. Dom Flemons notes, "The First World War aroused so much animosity in the US, and these are the years leading up to it. I can only imagine there were certain biases, talk and commentary that was very common among people."[11] In many ways, he believes, we are fortunate that Sharp and Karpeles recorded as much material as they did.

Sheila K Adams's great aunt, Zephora Ross, also sang for the pair, as Adams recalled.

> She lived to be 112 years old. Her mind was as clear as could be, and she remembered the day they sat on the porch, what songs she sang for him. She

said, "I sang that old 'Seven Nights Drunk' [274], but I'll bet you a nickel to a dollar he only printed four of the verses," and she was exactly right. He did not print all seven verses because it goes south pretty soon after the fourth verse. . . . It's a bit vulgar. There's a line you just don't cross, and I think Sharp was a bit conscious of that line.[12]

There were many surprises. Collecting songs in England, Sharp revealed, he seldom encountered anybody aged under seventy who "possess[ed] the folk-song tradition." In Laurel County, he not only met young and old, but he also found himself "for the first time in my life in a community in which singing was as common and almost as universal as speaking." In England, singing was regarded primarily as entertainment. In Laurel County, it was intrinsic to life itself—one singer, lost for a particular lyric, lamented, "Oh, if only I were driving the cows home, I could sing it at once." On another occasion, Sharp heard "Young Hunting" (68) from the mouth of "a small boy" who had simply stopped by his lodgings because he "always likes to go where there is sweet music."

One criticism frequently leveled at Sharp was that he collected very little Afro-American music, and his writings seem largely to disparage it. His diary recalls one particular evening when, attempting to dictate a song to Karpeles, the "squalling" of nearby children and the sound of "negro music" proved so distracting that the pair finally fled to the drug store "and drowned our cares in soft drinks."

The key to this controversy, of course, is the belief that Sharp was interested only in collecting what he had set out to collect—namely, English folk songs. The music of other cultures, whatever they might be, was of absolutely no concern to him. Not so, says folklorist Brian Peters. "It's true that the ballads were what excited him most, but at the same time he collected a lot of American songs, including obviously recent compositions like Civil War songs, and some hymns, African American songs, and fiddle tunes, that a lot of researchers don't seem to have noticed, or don't want to notice."[13]

Besides, color proved no bar whatsoever when Child found what he was looking for. Visiting Nellysford, Virginia, in May 1918, for example, he was introduced to Aunt Maria, an "old colored woman," as he told his diary, who was formerly a slave belonging to Mrs. Coleman. She was freed following the Civil War, "and Mrs Coleman gave her the log cabin in which she now lives, which used to be the overseer's home."

Now eighty-five years old, Aunt Maria "sang very beautifully in a wonderfully musical way, with clear and perfect intonation." He collected from her a brief but lively "Barbara Allen" (84), recreated by Dom Flemons a century later for BBC Radio's *Folk Connections: Cecil Sharp's Appalachian Trail* documentary.

Folklorist Dom Flemons and musical friends. Photo by Nate Kinard / Courtesy 72 Music Management (72MM)

Flemons also disagrees with the accepted wisdom that Sharp actively disliked African Americans. What he didn't enjoy was their music.

> You have two things happening at one time. There's the vocal music tradition, and there's the composed music tradition. Cecil was in the United States in the first place because he was doing productions of *A Midsummer Night's Dream*, so there was very much a Shakespearean aesthetic quality that dominates his documentation. Also, he had led a symphony orchestra. I can imagine things like intonation and melody and certain types of musicality were part of the aesthetic that he was following. Whereas a lot of African American music, especially when you get to certain aspects of rural music, it's very hard to decipher how to transcribe it onto sheet music.

It was the age, Flemons continues, of the great

> coon song performers . . . people like Bert Williams, and there's an animosity there because, knowing Cecil Sharp didn't like music hall in England, to see there was an African American music hall style developing as well, I'm sure there was an aspect of him literally running to the hills. I see an aspect of Cecil's documentation as not wanting to have anything to do with that kind of ragtime influenced music anywhere within what he was collecting, which is why he had such a limited amount of African American people.[14]

Another element that must be considered is, as Flemons continues, going into the rural areas, he had to find the people that were willing to sing the songs in a way that he could transcribe into standard notation. Something I found in a string band context, the melody and the counterpoint and the rhythm and the polyphonic rhythm of the music are all things that have to be lived in the jam and lived in the music circle to really coalesce into a musical statement. When the parts are written out independently of each other, they may not make a lot of sense. If you're looking for a one-to-one ratio, you may not find it, especially if it's a very syncopated banjo song that might have two or three notes to it. A refined classical musician like Sharp might not know what to make of that. If Cecil Sharp heard James Brown, would he know what to do? I don't know. How would you transcribe that onto a piece of sheet music to show to someone else, while retaining all the dignity that James Brown shows? This is the crux of all these documentarians. They were trying to do it without any implication of ragtime, but African American people were so deep into ragtime that there was no going back.

Under these circumstances, Flemons says, "It's great that we even have one African American person being documented in this context, but when I read Cecil's commentary, what he's saying is, 'I hate this kind of music.' He's not saying it about the people, he's saying it about the ragtime musical style, the same way you might say 'I hate heavy metal.' He hated ragtime so bad, just like he hated English music hall so bad, and he did everything to make sure he never had to work with it."

However, even when Sharp and Karpeles did discover singers who met their criteria, one cannot help but wonder whether the families whom they visited actually understood why these two Britishers were making such a fuss about their songs?

Certainly the Ritchies of Viper, Kentucky, had little awareness of this new "folkology," although they were definitely familiar with the collectors. In fact, their daughter Jean later recalled that the room where her brothers slept doubled as that in which their parents would receive "strange folks from way over the ocean in England, wanting to hear mom and dad and the girls sing the old ballads."[15]

Jean's Uncle Jason was one of those who entertained Sharp and Karpeles. He was once, she wrote, "a celebrated play-party singer and has a fabulous repertory of songs still in his head. [He] was the sort of veritable walking one-man entertainment that for centuries before the radio astonished the country folk and endeared his type to all."[16]

He certainly thrilled Sharp and Karpeles when he delivered a whistled "Little Devils" (278)—Sharp had heard of such a thing in England, but this was the first time ever he encountered it for himself.[17] How ironic, then, that a notation error pitched the whistle a fourth too high, a mistake that would remain uncorrected until Jean herself recorded the ballad on her debut album in 1952.

In the liner notes to her 1961 collection of the songs her family had sung, Ritchie commented, "Back in the days when [her parents] Balis and Abigail Ritchie's big family was 'a-booming and a-growing,' none of them had ever heard of Francis J. Child, nor had anyone else in that part of the Kentucky Mountains, I believe. The word 'ballad' or 'ballit' meant, in our community, the written-down words for a song."

She recalled hearing one neighbor tell another, "Now I've got 'Barbry Ellen' up there in my trunk. Joe's Sally stopped in and she writ me out the ballit of it." The Ritchie family, on the other hand, had little need for "ballits." "These old songs and their music were in our heads, or hearts, or somewhere part of us." There was never a need to write them down.

The stories were key. Remembering hearing someone sing "Lord Thomas and Fair Ellender" (73), Ritchie recollected, too, the heads that would nod approvingly as Lord Thomas beheaded the wife who had just murdered his lover, and the murmurs that would interrupt the song. "Ain't that right, now? That's j'st what he ort to a-done to her."

Ritchie recalled how, as a child, she would sit out on the porch in the evening, looking up toward the row of apple trees that decorated a nearby slope, and were known as the Goat-on-the-Hill, because that is what they resembled. Her eyelids would droop and her mind would wander, "and the people in the ballads would pass before me out in the sparkly dusk." Sometimes, as she rocked on the swing, she would become one of those characters herself; "I was fair Ellender and the movement of the swing . . . became the slow graceful walking of the white horse. Hundreds of people lined the broad highway as I rode by, thinking I was some queen, as the song wound its way to the tragic ending. And so I died."[18]

The songs were as alive to the singers as their friends and family, as beloved as a shelf full of favorite novels, and as scandalous as the singer's own powers of interpretation might make them. To Sharp and Karpeles, on the other hand, the songs were curios, a lost world with ballads for brontosauruses, and they had little time to spare to ponder the ecology in which such creatures had survived. They cared only for the specimens they could take back to England to prod and peruse in the laboratory.

Chapter Eleven

APPALACHIAN AFTERSHOCKS

Sharp's *English Folk Songs from the Southern Appalachians* was published in 1917 (later editions appeared in 1932 and 1952—the young Shirley Collins purchased a copy of the latter, at a retail price equivalent to two weeks' wages). The book was credited to both Sharp and Olive D. Campbell, and included no less than 122 songs and ballads, alongside 323 tunes (39 of them from Campbell's collection). Furthermore, Sharp's introduction noted thirteen song texts that "I have [not] been able to discover in any standard English collection," and eleven new melodies that could "challenge the very finest of the folk tunes that have been found in England." Just one of the latter was recognizably an adaptation of a Child Ballad, "Katie Morey" (112). However, no less than 37 other *ESPB* veterans were uncovered, often very different from those that Child had gathered and, in a dozen instances, unrecorded even in the *Journal of the English Folk-Song Society* or any place else.

Three of the versions Sharp uncovered were, to the best of his knowledge, unknown even in American folklore circles—"Johnnie Scott" (99), "The Grey Cock" (248), and "The Suffolk Miracle" (272). But even among common ballads, there were so many variations to be enjoyed. Both Child and Sharp agree, for example, that the young lad waylaid by the "False Knight upon the Road" (3) is on his way to school. In the text that Sharp collected from Mrs. T. G. Coates of Flag Pond, Tennessee, however, the boy adds that he is going to "learn the word of God," a pious element that none of the Scottish texts include. Furthermore, while one of Child's versions concludes with the knight hissing, "I wish you were in yonder well" and the careless child rejoining, "And you were down in hell," Mrs.

Coates's text ends with the knight puzzling, "I think I hear a bell" and the boy triumphant, "Yes, and it's ringing you to hell."

Not every American ballad was so devout, of course. "Lady Musgrave and Lord Barnard" (81), the tale of a wealthy lady who seduces and beds a villager, only to be discovered by her husband who proceeds to kill them both, is as much a den of adultery and slaughter as any of its Child equivalents. But one version gives the story a modern twist when the cuckolded Lord Dannel [sic] kills his wife with a pistol, not a sword. In another, "he drew his sword, cut off her head, and kicked it against the wall."

There are bloodier conclusions to be found in Child—his "A" version, dated to 1658, sees the Lord

> . . . cut the paps from off her brest
> Great pitty it was to see
> That some drops of this ladie's heart's blood
> Ran trickling downe her knee

In two other texts, the Lady is pregnant, and her murderer is left mourning "my young son lies sprawling [another text says "weltring"; a third insists the fetus was "blobberin"] in her blood." Yet still there is something additionally disturbing about the image conjured by this Appalachian text, and the fact that it is repeated in certain versions of Child 73 does not lessen the horror.

"The Cruel Brother" (11) likewise remains cruel, and the sheer heft of material that Campbell, Sharp, and Karpeles gathered filled a crucial gap on the bookshelves, a role it continues to fulfill, as singers and performers alike turn to its pages in search of material.

In straightforward numerical terms, Sharp's earlier collecting around the United Kingdom has inspired far more re-recordings than his American journeys ever could. But, in terms of bringing to light some of the canon's most fascinating variations, and bearing in mind the conditions under which they were collected, *English Folk Songs from the Southern Appalachians* surely ranks among the most influential of all twentieth-century ballad collections.

For example, Sharp's discovery of "Love Henry," a variation on "Young Hunting" (68) that was sung by Mrs. Orilla Keeton of Mount Fair, Virginia, was recorded in 1962 by Frank Profitt, the old-time fretless banjo player whose arrangement of "Tom Dooley" has long been considered the model for anyone wishing to revisit it.[1] The ballad was also discussed by Bert Lloyd when he penned liner notes for Appalachian-born Hedy West's 1967 *Ballads* album. "Love Henry" was one of several Child Ballads included on the set. Noting how West's rendition deviates from the English, Lloyd explains,

Many of the changes come about naturally with the historical development of recognisable American characteristics of mood, outlook, personality. Stressing her proper pride in Americanised song . . . Hedy West expresses a fond romance of hers: that people can begin from similarity to expand their tolerance of differences to an appreciation of those differences. The ballad has been not uncommon in Scotland, very rare in England. In the U.S.A. its circulation has been limited almost entirely to the Southern states, but in more or less hillbillyized versions it has been carried widely by rural professional minstrels attached to medicine shows and such, notably through Virginia, Tennessee, Mississippi and the Ozarks.[2]

West also recorded a version of "The Cruel Mother" (20) that she took from Sharp's Appalachian journey; and in 1976, Frankie Armstrong reached back sixty years to record "The Wife of Usher's Well" (79), as Sharp took it down from Mrs. Zippo Rice of Big Laurel, North Carolina.

June Tabor used at least three of Sharp and Karpeles's Appalachian discoveries (including the tune contributed by James Chisholm of Nellysford, Virginia) to create her own haunting revision of "The Cruel Mother" for her 2003 album *An Echo of Hooves*. The same album's "Fair Margaret and Sweet William" (74) is the version that Sharp and Karpeles collected from Jeff Stockton of Flag Pond, Tennessee, in 1916.

Recording her 1997 album *American Stranger*, scholar, author, and singer Julie Henigan turned to Sharp for "John Randolph" (12), which she described as "the classic tale of food poisoning and living wills." Henigan adds, however, that this Virginia variant of "Lord Randall" was "actually learned from Maud Karpeles's *Eighty English Folk Songs from the Southern Appalachians*. In her notes she states that 'a couple of the stanzas' and, one assumes, the melody, came from Mrs. Ada Maddox of Buena Vista, Virginia. The rest of the text is taken from unidentified 'other versions.'"[3]

Belshazzar's Feast's 2009 seasonal album *Frost Bites* rounds up the most ubiquitous of the Christmas-themed ballads that Sharp and Karpeles collected, "The Cherry Tree Carol" (54), from William Wooton at Hindman, Knott County, Kentucky. And Steeleye Span fiddler Peter Knight's Gigspanner Big Band recorded the aforementioned Jane Hitch Gentry's "Awake Awake"[4] (7) in 2020.

Another Appalachian survivor is the version of "Little Margaret" (74) that the Carolina Chocolate Drops recorded for their 2006 debut album *Dona Got a Ramblin' Mind*. Dom Flemons, the band's leader, recalls, "Rhiannon [bandmate Giddens] had got to know Sheila K. Adams, and she used to sing 'Little Margaret.' Around North Carolina, 'Little Margaret' is a well-loved ballad, and the way Rhiannon was singing it was really moving people. She recorded it in one take, as well. She sang it the one time, everybody said that's a beautiful performance and that was that."[5]

Grander visions of the Appalachian journey have also appeared. Commissioned by the EFDSS and Shrewsbury Folk Festival in 2011, the Cecil Sharp Project comprised eight musicians closeted together for a week to work up a tribute to his work. Both live and on CD, however, the outing not only acknowledged Sharp and Karpeles's accomplishments but also utilized a number of original songs to further amplify them. Among these, "Mining for Song" compared the pair's digging to, indeed, the local industry of mining; "Black Mountain Lullaby" eulogized the landscape in which they worked; "Beautiful Maud" looked deep into Sharp and Karpeles's own relationship; and "Child's Song" took stock of the proceedings from the viewpoint of a young lady watching as her elders entertained the visitors. Singer Kathryn Roberts's voice captures all the excitement of the moment, and the spellbinding tragedy of which she sings. If a single performance could possibly capture the alchemy of those Appalachian evenings, Sharp and Karpeles seated silent while these ancient songs unfolded around them, "Child Song," and the "Barbara Allen" (84) that followed it, achieved that.

> Shadows hung on the fireplace on the night he came to see us,
> I stood in the door and I heard some more of the songs me ma won't teach us
> But I know more than she'll ever guess, I've grown with my ears open
> So I wait in the dark and I take his hand and I sing him 'Barbara Allen.'

Powerful, too, is the work of what *Living Tradition* magazine called "two of their respective countries' finest performers of traditional music," as 2013's *Sharp's Appalachian Harvest* CD combined American Jeff Davies and Briton Brian Peters across sixteen tracks drawn from Sharp and Karpeles's trek. Almost half of the album comprised Child Ballads.

The pair had been friends since the 1990s. It was Davies who first suggested the project, Peters recalled,

He mentioned an idea that [he] had been discuss[ing] years before [with other musicians], to put together a repertoire of Sharp's Appalachian material as a kind of transatlantic bridge project. It had come to nothing, but Jeff suggested we might revive it. The plan was that I would lead on songs that had more of an "English" kind of feel, and Jeff would do the more "American" songs, which meant inevitably that I would end up doing several ballads, though Jeff found some that he wanted to do himself. And, of course there are scores of wonderful versions of Child Ballads in Sharp's book.[6]

The ballads are not necessarily delivered precisely as Sharp and Karpeles would have heard them—an a cappella "The Banks of Green Willow" (24) is balanced by an accompanied "Barbara Allen" (84); a sparse "Edward" (13) by a jaunty "The Gypsy Davey" (200). But still there is an aura to the recording that could easily transport the attentive listener back to the Appalachia of a century ago, with Sharp and Karpeles feverishly taking notes as an even deeper past unfolded around them.

Perhaps the most ambitious of all tributes to Sharp's—or, more accurately, Olive Campbell's—work in Appalachia was delivered by the 2000 movie *Songcatcher*. The movie grew out of director Maggie Greenwald's research into the roots of country music, where she came across the stories of the first (predominantly female) teachers and missionaries to set up in the region, and how they were surprised to discover the "old songs" still a part of daily life. The movie's lead character, Dr. Lily Penleric, is at least partially based upon Campbell, although it takes several liberties with history. Campbell traveled to the region with her husband; in the movie, Penleric is alone, there to visit her sister, who runs a settlement school in the area.

Other incidents, however, are taken from life. Like Campbell, Penleric's initial exposure to the tradition comes from hearing a local girl (named in the movie as Deladis Slocumb) singing an unfamiliar version of "Barbara Allen." And later, as Penleric moves around the older inhabitants of the region, she encounters one with the delightfully resonant name of Mrs. Gentry—whose real-life counterpart's great grandniece, the aforementioned Sheila Kay Adams, was on board as *Songcatcher*'s traditional music adviser and vocal coach.

The movie unfolds as an exquisitely designed and intelligently soundtracked drama, into which are shoehorned several distrustful locals, a lesbian romance, a rapacious mining company, and a disastrous fire that destroys almost all of Penleric's collection. They are, however, mere distractions from the story itself. We learn to appreciate the sheer bulk, clumsiness, and operation of period recording machines, and are introduced at the end to one Professor Cyrus Whittle, an Englishman who is presumably based upon Cecil Sharp. (And also, ahistorically, traveling alone—there is no Maud Karpeles alongside him).

There are many moments of sharp dialog, including the sequence where Penleric first voices her belief that the ballads she is hearing "might be the purest versions in existence." Sheila Kay Adams, meanwhile, ensures a steady flow of those ballads, among them eight *ESPB* stalwarts, although "Barbara Allen" (perhaps inevitably) is the only one that is sung to its end, in the opening sequence by Penleric, and across the closing credits by Emmylou Harris. The remainder—"Lord Randall" (12) and "Matty Groves" (81) among them—are mere snippets.

It is an intelligent, and very well-researched movie, particularly if one views the various subplots as necessary links between Penleric's collecting adventures—and, perhaps, as a concession to twenty-first-century moviegoing tastes. It's hard, after all, to imagine an audience beset by such contemporary blockbusters as *Mission Impossible II*, *Gladiator*, and *The Perfect Storm* obtaining similar thrills from the discovery of a previously unknown tune to "The Trooper and the Maid" (299).

Sharp's work in the mountains did not go without a postscript. Many other collectors followed in his footsteps, among them Karpeles herself, and it was *their* work that was celebrated by the 2017 compilation *When Cecil Left the Mountains*, comprising audio recordings of songs that Sharp and Karpeles could only write down on their initial visit, but which were subsequently recorded by these later collectors.

Karpeles's contributions from her 1950 expedition, are the most affecting. We hear her return visit to Nellysford resident Dol Small, a full thirty-two years after their last meeting. Nevertheless, Small was able to furnish her with an almost identical rendering of "Little Sir Hugh" (155) to the one she had sung to Sharp.

There were others who emerged from the past as well. Florence Puckett, the daughter of the 1918 expedition's subject Florence Fitzgerald supplied four songs, among them "Jimmy Randall" (12) and "The Twa Brothers" (49); and Emma Hensley (now Mrs. Shelton), contributed eight, which included "The Gypsie Laddie" (200). She recalled for Karpeles her own first encounter with the English visitors, as a thirteen-year old in Madison County, North Carolina. She had been invited to attend a nearby mission school, but her family could not afford the clothes she needed. Sharp purchased them for her. Meeting Karpeles again all these years later, Emma was happy to reopen her arsenal of songs, accompanying herself on the harmonium.

Another glorious discovery, although it did not make the 2017 compilation, was a rare variant on "The Twa Brothers" (49), titled "Monday Morning Go to School," which was recorded by Dave Arthur on his 2010 album *No Use in Cryin'*.[7] There, Arthur notes that "One of [Karpeles's] verses that we've used as a chorus is almost identical to a verse collected by antiquarian William Motherwell from the recitation of Widow McCormick in Scotland in 1825."[8]

What is most remarkable, however, is the knowledge that many of the recordings on *When Cecil Left the Mountains* were made at a time when it felt as though the "old traditions" were finally dying.

Interviewed by the BBC in 2016, Sheila K. Adams spoke for many of her generation when she described how college life encouraged her to lose her Appalachian accent and mannerisms, in the awareness that the ever-encroaching outside world tended to mock the way her people spoke and stereotype the manner in which their forebears had lived.

Their traditions, too, were placed behind them; there was no room for the ballads in the modern world, and whereas Sharp and Karpeles had once marveled that, everywhere they went, even young people were singing the old folk songs as a part of their daily life, by the 1950s, it was the old-timers alone.

Revisiting the area, Karpeles also felt this.

> The fact is that life in the mountains has been completely revolutionized during the last twenty to twenty-five years and it is no longer the folksong collector's paradise that it once was. . . . Roads and electricity have brought "civilisation" to the mountains. . . . Whereas, formerly, there was little inducement for the people to grow more than they needed for their own requirements—and that was indeed little—markets have now been made accessible. Formerly there was leisure and time for the enjoyment of living; now everyone is so busy making money in order to acquire labour-saving devices and other amenities, that there is little leisure left and many of the social graces of life have had to be sacrificed. Judged from a material point of view the standard of life is certainly higher, but there seems to be a corresponding loss on the artistic and cultural plane.[9]

For Karpeles, touring the region in 1950, and to the performers themselves, an era was finally drawing to as significant a close, as Sharp himself determined at the conclusion of his third and final visit to the Appalachians in October 1918: "This was probably my last collecting expedition this year," he wrote, "and I suspect my last in the mountains and probably in America. I shall have taken down about 1,600 tunes and I believe they will represent pretty accurately the songs that are sung in the Appalachians. I'm sorry to have said goodbye to the mountain people but I suspect that I might have seen the last of them."[10]

Cecil Sharp died on June 24, 1924, but his influence has remained omnipresent, and discussions of his life and methods too. In May 2021, BBC Radio 3 even broadcast a new play, Neil Leyshon's *Folk,* inspired by Sharp's song-collecting in Somerset in the summer of 1903.

The story revolves around the relationship between Sharp, and two of the women he collected from, the sisters Louisa Hooper and Lucy White, residents of the village of Hambridge. Leyshon told the *Guardian,* "They were the daughters of a well-known singer who would have sung these songs to her children, songs that they knew by heart. I started to imagine what it might feel like if your body contained that many songs, enough to sing for days without repetition."[11] (Tragically, the two women's mother had died shortly before Sharp arrived in their lives.)

The sisters' repertoire was vast. Sharp transcribed well over 100 of their songs, including versions of "Lord Randall" (12), "Lady Maisry" (65), and "Barbara Allen" (84); nothing unusual or unexpected in terms of Child Ballads, but they delighted Sharp regardless. (He returned the favor by giving Louie a gift of a concertina that can today be seen in the museum in nearby Taunton.)

Leyshon's research into Sharp did not immediately endear the collector, although some of his outrage was certainly developed from second-hand sources, if not the misunderstandings or even outright prejudices of subsequent researchers—the accusation, for example, that Sharp *"refused to collect songs from Black American singers."*

One might also roll a weary eye at Leyshon's published claim that Sharp "promoted himself as the expert on folk song, building a career on other people's work." That is an accusation that can, and has been, leveled at every ballad collector at some point or other, but it is meaningless, spiteful, and perhaps even ignorant, all the same.

"[But he] had another side," Leyshon continued. "He had great respect for the country people who sang, and managed to collect about 5,000 songs that, were it not for his writing them down in his notebooks, would otherwise have been lost. That dissonance would be at the heart of the play."[12]

Indeed, as Leyshon told the Tradfolk website, as *Folk* moved to the Hampstead Theatre in London in early 2022, "The songs Sharp collected did lead to many types of new music, including the big folk revival in the '60s, which still feeds folk musicians today; it also led to new classical music from Holst, Vaughan Williams, and Butterworth,[13] which in turn inspired Benjamin Britten. We owe all of this to Sharp, but we also owe it all to a pair of little-known sisters who lived on the edge of the water, right in the heart of the Somerset Levels."

Chapter Twelve

CABBAGE HEAD BLUES

The early 1920s saw considerable advances in recording technology, not least of all sweeping away the old-fashioned method of gathering around a sound horn to record.

There was still no overdubbing to be done, or separate tracks for each instrument to be recorded onto, but neither were there such tight prohibitions on movement, and demand for intense concentration. Performers could suddenly perform at least a little, kicking away the often overly staid traits of the past, and letting fly.

The Child Ballads, too, were in full flow. Amid the host of Hazeldeans that descended upon the first two decades of the century, Margaret Woodrow Wilson (1886–1944) broke Jock's monopoly in 1915 with a heartfelt "Leezie Lindsay" (226)—and did so from a social height to which the ballads have never returned. Her father, Woodrow Wilson, was president of the United States, and it matters little whether his status influenced the Columbia label's decision to record Margaret (although it certainly inspired the addition of "Woodrow" to her stage name). A popular socialite and an avid Suffragette, Wilson really could sing.

"Leezie Lindsay" was recorded on February 27, 1914, in two takes—it was the second that made it onto a record, hauntingly orchestrated and confidently sung. Wilson, after all, was no novice when it came to recording; already that year she had recorded at least a couple of songs ("My Laddie" and "My Lovely Celia" were released in late winter). "Leezie Lindsay" followed in May, and Wilson would, in fact, record around ten sides for the label.

The death of her mother on August 6, 1914, and Margaret's subsequent elevation to White House social hostess (the role we now refer to as the

Margaret Woodrow Wilson, the first (and only) First Lady to record a Child Ballad. Wikimedia Commons

First Lady) curtailed her recording career somewhat. However, following her father's remarriage in December 1915, Margaret passed that role over to her stepmother and returned to her music. She toured the United States raising funds for the Red Cross, and cut several records more, including "The Star-Spangled Banner," with her share of the proceeds (25c per disc) being similarly donated. Following the United States' entrance into World War One, she also made several visits to France to perform for the troops. Very likely, "Leezie Lindsay" remained in her repertoire there.

Wartime expediency saw patriotic songs take precedence throughout the last years of the decade. By 1920, however, tastes had returned to normal, while the gramophone industry was experiencing what it termed a "hillbilly" craze—spreading in many instances from the same region that Cecil Sharp had so recently brought attention to. Moreover, it was ignited, to a great degree, by the interest aroused not only by Sharp but also the other collectors now at work around the United States.

It was very much the culmination of the process Sharp had so unhappily witnessed during his visits to the region: the coalescing of musical forms. Dom Flemons explains, "Traditionally, the Piedmont of North

Margaret Woodrow Wilson's "Leezie Lindsay" 78. Author's collection

Carolina is the hub of a lot of African American music. By the time Cecil Sharp was there, a lot of the urban places had already incorporated the guitar and the highly syncopated banjo into their music."[1] Now, it was time to let loose this new musical craze.

Impressive indeed is Bentley Ball's 1920 handling of two Child Ballads, "Gallows Tree" (95) and "Bangum and the Boar" (18), the former being the first known recording of the ballad that Led Zeppelin would later take to rock 'n' roll immortality; the latter, originally hailing from Appalachia, a romping sea of rolling r's and jovial piano, of which Cecil Sharp collected no less than four versions during his Appalachian journey. Not one could compare with Bentley Ball's. Though we know next to nothing about his upbringing, Ball himself was something of a pioneer in American traditional music. He is frequently cited as the first performer to record the cowboy songs "Jesse James" and "Dying Cowboy" in 1920, while other highlights of his repertoire included "Twankydillo," "The Little Log Cabin," "O Graveyard," and "Go Down Moses."

What fascinates, however, is that each of these releases, including "Gallows Tree" and "Bangum and the Boar," was released in Columbia Records' "educational" series, marketed primarily toward elementary schools. Ultimately short lived (1920–1921), the series was wholly dedicated to songs that, with application, could be applied to a schoolroom setting. They included the Princes Band performing the "Highland Fling," "The Forge in the Forest," and "Jolly Coppersmith"; the Columbia Band's "Star Spangled Banner" and "Dixie"; an orchestrated re-creation of bird song; Harry Humphrey reciting William Shakespeare and Abraham Lincoln; a wealth of hornpipes, polkas, and reels; children's songs, classics, Christmas carols. It is bizarre company in which to find a pair of Child Ballads, but it reminds us that the gramophone itself was not considered a wholly entertainment-led technology. Like radio and television, it was also regarded as a medium for information and elucidation, and the hope that young minds could be turned to the beauty of music was paramount,

The Child Ballads also maintained their appeal for the operatically inclined. In 1922, the Massachusetts-born baritone Royal Dadmun (1884–1964) recorded Eaton Faning and John Liptrott Hutto's buoyant arrangement of "Barbara Allen" (84), one of over two hundred sides he cut for the Victor label in a career that began in 1906. Dadmun also recorded his own "Jock O'Hazeldean," around the same time as Englishman Foster Richardson, an early star of British radio and, toward the end of the decade, vocalist for the Jack Payne Band, delivered the same ballad for the Zonophone label.

But increasingly, the ballads, and the audience for them, seemed to be slipping away from sonorously performed Scottish heartbreakers, and into more raucous territory. In 1926, Kentucky born Welby Toomey (1897–1989) recorded a jaunty, if somewhat clumsy "The Golden Willow Tree" for the Gennett label. And that same year, Lottie "Lena" Kimbrough, her brother Sylvester, and the Paul Banks Kansas Trio cut "Our Goodman" (274) as a weary, wired blues called "Cabbage Head Blues," for her manager Winston Holmes's Kansas City based Meritt Records in 1926.

Born in Craigshead County, Arkansas, and known as the Kansas City Butterball due to her weight, Lottie Kimbrough was one of the early queens of the blues. She possessed an enormous voice and, across a five-year recording career, between 1924–1929, she cut a string of dramatic sides for Paramount, Gennett, Champion, and Supertone, a near-clean sweep of the era's leading blues labels. Why she then ceased recording is a mystery; likewise, neither her birth nor death date have been confirmed, nor how she spent the rest of her life. "Cabbage Head Blues," however, is immortal, not merely representing the first suggestion that even the blues were not immune to the Child Ballads, but offering concrete confirmation that the spread of traditional British songs through the American heartland was not restricted to the white British immigrant communities alone.

Less than a decade later, after all, John Lomax would be recording both Lead Belly ("Gallis Pole"—95) and James "Ironhead" Baker ("Barbara Allen"—84), and Don Flemons observes that already, "there's a different aesthetic to hearing an Anglo-American singing [the same ballads], a different impression of the way the ballads were sung." That said, the ballad that became "Cabbage Head Blues," "Our Goodman," has little in common with what one would ordinarily expect from a traditional English folk song, even in its original form. One of the most ribald pieces in the entire *ESPB*, Child dates it back to at least Bishop Percy's time, from a copy unearthed among his papers titled "Old Wichet's Discoveries." He refers, too, to versions in Irish Gaelic and Flemish, and from as far afield as Sweden, Germany, Italy, France, and Catalonia.

It was also very popular in the United States. Less than a year after Kimbrough's recording, Kentucky's Earl Johnson and his Dixie Entertainers uncorked a glorious comic hoedown through the same song, now under the title "Three Nights Experience." One can only shudder at the thought of what Professor Child might have made of that.

Since that time, it has taken on a host of other titles, too: "Seven Drunken Nights" and "Coming Home Late" among them. Blind Boy Fuller used it as the basis for his 1936 recording "Cat Man Blues," and in the grip of another blues great, Sonny Boy Williamson, it became the super slinky "Wake Up Baby." And thirty-five years later, cabbage-headed once more, it was a barrelhouse boogie by Dr. John. Country, comedy, jazz, bar-room singalong, "Our Goodman" has probably worn more musical hats than any other Child Ballad. In every guise, however, it concerns itself with the same tale, of the man who arrives home late one night to discover what appears to be the irrefutable evidence of another man in the house.

> *The first night that I came home as drunk as I could be*
> *I found a horse stabled where my horse ought to be*
> *You come here little wifey and explain this thing to me*
> *How come a horse is stabled where my horse is meant to be.*

Oh, that's not a horse, his wife explains. It's a milk cow.

The second night he espies a strange coat on the rack. The third night, there's a head on the pillow. His wife, however, had an explanation for every one—this latest being the cabbage. Of course, she is lying every time, and we realize that long before the original ballad reaches its conclusion. What the most familiar versions do not capture is the sheer extent of the wife's infidelity. The copy owned by Bishop Percy is perhaps the most revealing.

> *I went into the chamber*
> *And there for to see*
> *And there I saw three men in bed lie*
> *By one by two by three.*

Oh, they're not men, she reassures him. "They're the three milking maids my mother sent to me." And her husband is left to ponder alone, with ejaculations of "heyday" and "Godzounds," the lingering image of "milking maids with beards on. The like was never known."

Around the same time as Kimbrough was titillating audiences with one of Child's most bawdy ballads, Holland "Si" Puckett (1899–1934) was having similar fun with another, the Peeping Tom of "The Keyhole in the Door" (27). Born in Patrick County, Virginia, and a bookkeeper by trade, Puckett was truly among the pioneers of what his label, Gennett Records, tagged "Old Time Singin' and Playin'." Recorded in May 1927, "Keyhole in the Door" was one of some twenty sides that Puckett cut for the label, a joyfully locomotive romp that Child plucked from William Motherwell's manuscript. Indeed, Child writes, "This ballad, if ever it were one, seems not to have been met with, or at least thought worth notice by anyone but Motherwell."

In that form, it tells of a king's servant who spies upon the princess through "a whummil bore"—hence the ballad's given title. In American hands, the circumstances were less grandiose, but Puckett's version nevertheless resonates with a devilry that absolutely contradicts the smooth, clean-cut, well-dressed, and short-haired young man who gazes out from Puckett's best-known photograph. Sadly, however, he would not live to become an old man—in July 1934, Puckett was stabbed to death during a dispute over a card game.

Puckett was not, of course, the only hillbilly artist who did not necessarily conform to visual stereotyping. Vernon Dalhart (1883–1948) was born in Jefferson, Texas, under the fabulously evocative name of Marion Try Slaughter; he took his stage name from the two towns between which he was employed as a cattle puncher during his teens. His family had, by that time, relocated to Dallas, following the murder of the young man's father by his brother-in-law in 1893. There, Dalhart learned guitar and mouth harp; he would study at the Dallas Conservatory of Music until 1910, when he uprooted his wife and two children and moved to New York City.

Like so many young singers of the age, Dalhart initially entertained dreams of an operatic career, and he did well, appearing in productions of *HMS Pinafore* and *Madame Butterfly*, at the same time as recording a string of light-classical and dance-music songs for Thomas Edison's eponymous label. He scored his first "hit" record in 1917 with "Till the Clouds Roll By" from the musical *Oh, Boy*. "Tuck Me to Sleep (In My Old 'Tucky Home)" arrived in 1921, followed by such charming ballads as "Dear Old Southland," "The Pal That I Loved (Still the Gal I Loved)." Biggest of them all, however, was "The Prisoner's Song," a 1925 ballad that US chart authority Joel Whitburn (1939–2022) described as "the biggest-selling non-holiday record of the pre-1955 era, with total sales of over seven million."[2]

But Dalhart hankered to escape the mannered singing with which he had become associated, and, under cover of various pseudonyms, he made several low-key experiments before stepping out later that same year with a "Wreck of the Old 97" that could have moseyed out from any of the great hillbilly recording sessions of the South. Dispensing with the strings that once accompanied him so sweetly, he teamed up with bandleader Carson Robison and recorded now with fiddle, harmonica, and guitar. And to anybody who accused him of faking it, he had this to say, in a 1918 interview. "When you are born and brought up in the South your only trouble is to talk any other way . . . the 'sure 'nough Southerner' talks almost like a Negro, even when he's white. I've broken myself of the habit, more or less, in ordinary conversation, but it still comes pretty easy." "In the Baggage Coach Ahead," "The Letter Edged In Black," "The Death of Floyd Collins," "The Wreck of the Shenandoah". . . the successes kept coming, and the Child Ballad "Barbara Allen," which he recorded on March 12, 1927, slipped effortlessly into this company. More than that, however, its success perhaps offered listeners in Britain a sense of how well *their* traditional songs adapted themselves to the New World.

It was little more than twelve years since Cecil Sharp had astonished Olive Dame Campbell with his insistence that he highly doubted America had *any* folk songs whatsoever. By the time he finished perusing the sheets of ballads that she had handed him, he was ready to admit, as she later put it, that this was "the first time he had come on any really original and valuable material." Now this "original and valuable material" was making itself heard wherever there was a gramophone player.

Buel Kazee (1900–1976) was a Kentucky-born banjo player who, in 1927, was invited to New York to record some trial sides for the Brunswick label—the first of many visits over the next few years. His "Lady Gay" (79) was recorded the following January, a belting banjo number that is as haunting as it is frenetic. Roy Harvey and the North Carolina Ramblers recorded "George Collins" (85) for Brunswick in February 1928, and, that same month, Ernest V. Stoneman and the Blue Ridge Corn Shuckers cut a variant on "The Mermaid" (289), called "The Raging Sea, How It Roars," for Victor. Another "Jock O'Hazeldean" (293) . . . the first in some years, it is true . . . would be recorded in 1931 for Columbia by Sandy MacFarlane, Glasgow born but a longtime resident of the Boston, Massachusetts, area; and the same year brought Lonesome Luke and his Farm Boys' deliriously exuberant fiddle-fired "Wild Hog in the Woods" (18).

Of all the Child Ballads and, indeed, their performers who flourished throughout this period, however, the best-remembered has to be bluesman Dick Justice (1903–1962), partly for his bright-eyed cover of Luke Jordan's "Cocaine," but mostly for the version of "Henry Lee" (68) that he recorded in Chicago on May 20, 1929. The performance itself is a relatively standard guitar strum, with Justice's down-home accent pitched just high enough to reawaken childhood memories of playing cowboy. In 1952, however, the American musicologist Harry Smith selected Justice's "Henry Lee" to open his monumental *Anthology of American Folk Music* in 1952, and it matters not that, in 1968, Smith declared, "[It's] not a good record. But it had to go first because it was the lowest numbered Child Ballad [on the album]."[3] Its very presence on that landmark collection assures its immortality.

Smith, in compiling the *Anthology*, does reveal a certain affection for the Child Ballads. No less than five appear across the first side of the two LPs that Smith devoted to ballads and folk music (subsequent volumes embraced blues and country), with surely the most peculiar being the disquietingly Hawaiian steel-led "The Fatal Flower Garden" (155) that the aptly named Nelstone's Hawaiians recorded in Atlanta, Georgia, on November 30, 1929.

Smith reintroduced his listeners to Clarence Ashley (1895–1967), a former member of the Carolina Tar Heels, whose peculiarly stark, nasal retelling of "The House Carpenter" (243), was recorded for Columbia in Atlanta on April 14, 1930. Coley Jones's "Drunkards Special," another variant on "Three Nights Experience" (274) follows, recorded in Dallas on December 6, 1929, for release the following year, but considerably more sober sounding than it might have been. It's certainly not the best version Smith could have chosen, and it is something of an outlier in Jones's own repertoire. As Dom Flemons points out, "If you listen to any of his other recordings he was a ragtime mandolinist, he ran a group called the Dallas String Band, and they're a real hot band."[4] But it is Bill and Belle Reid's "Old Lady and the Devil" (278) that steals the *Anthology* show, tearing out of the Columbia label's all-invited sessions in Johnson City, Tennessee, on October 17, 1928, with as much defiance as the titular female. It seems incredible on this evidence that the pair were granted just that single session.

Smith's *Anthology* is generally regarded as among the most important, and carefully curated collections of American traditional music ever compiled. Both as an introduction to the music, and a wellspring of future inspiration, its name and reputation glow across almost any discussion of the American folk boom of the late 1950s. Certainly the Child Ballads' own renown was greatly inflated by the significance that Smith accorded them, for it must be acknowledged that Smith's approval meant far more to a 1950s audience than the records ever did at the time they were originally recorded. Furthermore, the *Anthology's* contents only confirm what Sharp and Karpeles had already demonstrated: the depth to which the Child Ballads (and others, of course) were embedded in southern culture at the time. For the five that Smith highlighted were just a sampling of the plethora that was available to him, itself a consequence of a unique period in American musical history when a host of record labels set up temporary shop across the South, with the express aim of seeking out fresh talent.

Okeh Records was the first, heading for Asheville, North Carolina, in August 1925, and Winston-Salem, North Carolina, in September 1927. Victor pulled into Bristol, Tennessee, in July–August 1927 and again in October 1928, and emerged with the first-ever recordings by the hitherto unknown Jimmie Rodgers and the Carter Family. Brunswick was in Ashland, Kentucky, in February 1928, August 1929, and April 1930; and Columbia set up camp in Johnson City, Tennessee, in October 1928 and again one year later, both times under the auspices of producer Frank B. Walter.

Advertisements in the local press explained exactly what was required.

Can You Sing or Play Old-Time Music?
  Musicians of Unusual Ability—Small Dance Combinations—Singers—Novelty Players, Etc.
  Are Invited
  To call on Mr. Walker or Mr. Brown of the Columbia Phonograph Company at 334 East Main Street, Johnson City, on Saturday October 13th, 1928—9AM to 5PM.
  This is an actual try-out for the purpose of making Columbia Records.

Bill and Belle Reed were among the aspirants that descended in response to this advertisement.[5] They were a husband-and-wife duo about whom next to nothing is known beyond the fact that they had at least three children (a son and two daughters), who performed in their own act, the Reed Children, as well as accompanying their parents in a third, the Reed Family. Beyond that, even the suggestion that the clan was local to the Johnson City area is supposition.

As for their repertoire, we know it only from the two singles that were released from their audition session, one by Bill and Belle alone, the other credited to the children; and, it must be said, the parents' playful "The Old Lady and the Devil" is an anomaly both there, and across the overall day's worth of sessions, as authors Ted Olson and Tony Russell put it, when they describe "The Old Lady and the Devil" as "that not over-common thing in recorded old-time music, a British ballad known among Child scholars as 'The Farmer's Curst Wife.' The Reeds were the first to put it on record."[6] Yet the duo's comic presentation of what was already an extravagantly humorous song is so much "of its era" that it would be easy to have believed it a brand new composition. Only in those places such as Sharp and Karpeles had ventured a decade previous was it widely known that the ditty was almost as old as dirt. They had collected two versions of "The Farmer's Curst Wife," one from a Mrs. Sarah Buckner in Black Mountain, North Carolina, on September 19, 1916; the other, according to *English Folk Songs*, from Mr. N. B. Chisholm of Woodridge, Virginia, two days later, and we have another cause to marvel at the pair's dedication, crossing a 440-mile divide in such a brief amount of time. The ballad was well known much further afield than that, however.

Sadly, Columbia Records did not follow through on their original interest in the Reid clan, and the family and its music sank back into obscurity. For Dom Flemons, however, their recording of "The Old Lady and the Devil" ranks among the most significant touchstones of his career: "I think the very first time I became aware of the Child Ballads, and the only one I've really performed in public, was 'The Devil and the Farmer's Wife,' and I first heard it from Bill and Belle Reid on the *Anthology*. I heard that song and I thought it was so funny." His interest was further enflamed when he started at Northern Arizona University.

I [started] going to the record library, and the very first album they had in the catalog was the ten-record set *The Folk Songs of Britain*, and from the very first moment I heard Jeannie Robertson, I was completely transfixed by ballad singing. I guess I'd heard some before, like Jean Ritchie, Jean Redpath, Frankie Armstrong, I'd heard some stuff. . . . Doc Watson does a lot of stuff in the course of his catalog . . . so I had a sense of how the music fit into the broad spectrum of folk music. But then I found the Library of Congress's Child Ballad collections, at the same time as I was doing my BA in English, studying Chaucer and Shakespeare, John Donne, and it was a wonderful cross section of literature. I always kept an ear out for the Child Ballads, and I still think it's a beautiful body of work.[7]

Chapter Thirteen

SONG OF THE TANNER

Of all the acts swept up by the city-centric sessions of the late 1920s, the Carter Family are the most significant, at least in terms of their future renown. Originally featuring A. P. (Alvin Pleasant) Carter, his wife Sara, and her cousin Maybelle (who was married to A. P.'s brother Ezra), the Carter Family rapidly established themselves among the most commercially successful acts of the age, with a repertoire that bristled with traditional numbers and, across their career, a quartet of very well-wrought Child Ballads. The first of these, and probably the best loved of all the Family's Child appropriations, was "The Storms Are on the Ocean" (76), a somewhat loose, and occasionally disputed[1] variation on "The Lass of Roch Royale," itself a Scottish ballad that Professor Child had traced back to its 1776 publication in Herd's manuscript *Scottish Songs*.

It is a devastating ballad. Lord Gregory has gone away to sea when a pregnant woman arrives at his castle door, begging to see him. Though the visitor is clearly bearing her grandchild, Gregory's mother sends her away; in desperation, the woman attempts to follow her lover, only to perish in a shipwreck. But the tragedy is only half-done, for Gregory sees her death in a dream and goes out in search of her body. No sooner has he found it than he, too, dies, heartbroken. Child unearthed fifteen variations of the ballad. Steve Roud was ultimately to compile more than eighty, thirty of which sprang from Appalachian sources, and it was thence that the Carter Family derived their version—and that despite A. P. Carter, as would prove to be his career-long wont, promptly claiming the songwriting credit for the song.

"The Storms Are On The Ocean" was among the numbers that the Carter Family recorded at their maiden August 1, 1927, Victor sessions in

Bristol, under the eye of producer Ralph Peer. They had traveled twenty-five miles to the session, from Maces Spring, Virginia, tempted as much by the promise of $50 for every song they recorded, as by the prospect of making a record.

In the event, Peer had no doubts whatsoever as to the family's worth. Just three months later, Victor released the Carter Family's debut recording, "Wandering Boy" / "Poor Orphan Child"; a year later, it was followed by "Single Girl Married Girl" and "The Storms Are on the Ocean," and the record's success reminds us why A. P. was so fast to claim he'd written the Child Ballad himself. He received a half-cent royalty on every sale of the songs that he had registered.[2]

Indeed, A. P. now became something of a ballad collector himself, scouring southwestern Virginia with his friend, African American guitarist Lesley "Esley" Riddle, in search of new songs that he could "write." (He did also compose originals, and often they sounded as authentic as the traditional numbers.) The Carter Family's treatments of the Child Ballads all but bookend their period of greatest success. Following on from that original take on "Storms Are on the Oceans," "Sinking in the Lonesome Sea" (286) was recorded for the Vocalion label in May 1935, for release alongside a fresh recording of "Storms Are on the Ocean." Maintaining the seafaring flavor of the group's initial dip into the *ESPB*, this latest effort was a ballad that was originally learned in full from A. P.'s mother Molly—Child has examples with up to fourteen verses; Sharp and Karpeles captured one with ten; and the Carter Family's prototype was no shorter. On record, however, they had no alternative but to reduce it to just six stanzas, while a performance on Texas radio's XERA saw it carved down to three. Clearly, the feeling was, the ballad was already so well known that it did not need to be performed in full.

The third, and most dramatic, of the Carter Family's Child Ballads, "Black Jack David" (200), was recorded in October 1940 for the Okeh label. It was also, in recorded terms, the most familiar (although A. P. again claimed the writing credit). The story of a gentleman who returns home to find that his wife has run away with the titular Traveler, "Black Jack David" was first placed on disc by Professor and Mrs. I. G. Greer, for Paramount in 1929.

A decade later, it was cut for Decca by Kentucky-born steel guitarist and yodeler Cliff Carlisle, performing a version he learned from singer-songwriter T. Texas Tyler (David Myrick), with whom he'd worked on Texas radio. The Carter Family's version adhered very strongly to this particular prototype, as author Margaret Anne Bulger acknowledges, "It is uncertain whether the Carters were familiar with Carlisle's version; however, it is possible that their source for this ballad was the media rather than tradition."[3]

The Carter Family in 1927, around the time of their recording debut. Pictorial Press / Alamy Stock Photo

The following year, "The Wave on the Sea" (289) completed the Carter Family's trilogy of great seafaring ballads with the proven oldest of all their selections from Child (as "The Mermaid," its first printed reference has been dated to before 1632). It was recorded in New York City for the Bluebird label on October 14, 1941, and it was, perhaps fittingly, one of the final songs the original Carter Family would ever record. A. P. and Sara were already divorced; now she and her second husband, A. P.'s cousin Coy Bayes, were relocating to California. The band could not continue.

Its legacy, however, is colossal. Of all the performers that emerged from the turbulent waters of country music's genesis, and especially those that midwifed the music's shift away from the pure hillbilly sounds of the 1920s and into a more wholesome "down-home" landscape, the Carter Family are frequently ranked among the most influential in all of American music. The three hundred-plus recordings that they made[4] represent the very foundation stone of country and western music, and a key element in more besides.

For all the Carter Family's acclaim and success, however, one detects little variety across the Child Ballads in their repertoire, even when, as with the rerecorded "Storms Are on the Sea," A. P. took over the lead vocal from Sara. Certainly, they possess a great deal of charm, but the later recordings in particular are also moving dangerously close to the homogenization of a music that had once been characterized by its freneticism. No matter how successfully the Carter Family raised the profile of country and folk music, they also paved the way for its absorption into a musical mainstream that cared nothing for a song's history; only that it sounded sweet enough to become a "hit."

Of course there were plenty of exceptions to this generalization. Despite being blind since childhood, the consequence of a medical procedure gone wrong, Georgia-born Riley Puckett (1894–1946) was well established among the country's most accomplished guitarists, and a popular singer too. Regular appearances on local radio saw him earn the nickname of "the Bald Mountain Caruso," and in 1925, the Columbia label reckoned Puckett second only to Vernon Dalhart in terms of the company's best sellers. Another accolade describes Puckett as the first recording artist ever to yodel on a gramophone record, predating even Jimmie Rodgers, while his time with Gid Tanner and His Skillet Lickers—the preeminent hillbilly act of the late 1920s and early 1930s—brought him even greater acclaim. Puckett maintained a solo career throughout this period, although his "George Collins" (85) coincides with the Skillet Lickers' demise. It was recorded on March 29, 1934, in San Antonio, Texas, at the same session that marked the end of the band, but the lineage (like Puckett's guitar skills) is clear.

Sheet music for Clem the Melody Man's arrangement of "Barbara Allen." Author's collection

On the other side of the musical spectrum are the heavenly harmonies of the English Singers, who cut Ralph Vaughan Williams's unaccompanied arrangement of "An Acre of Land" (2) for the Roycroft label in the late 1920s. And Geoffrey Marston Haddock, the principal of Leeds College of Music, recorded "Edward" (13) for the little-known English label Musicraft in April 1923.

Thus did the Child Ballads continue their gentle percolation into the record-buying world. Chubby Parker's tongue-twisting take on "The Wife Wrapped Up in Wether's Skin" (277), now renamed "Nickety Nackety Now Now," was a novelty earworm in 1927; two years later, an even more ramshackle version was unleashed by Ridgel's Fountain Citians, as "The Nick Nack Song." Jess Young's Tennessee Band and Kyle Wooten both visited "Loving Henry" (68) less than a year apart, 1929–1930. Bradley Kincaid, a staple today of the Nashville Songwriter's Hall of Fame, recorded an infectious "Barbara Allen" (84) in Chicago on January 24, 1930, and the vocal trio the Vagabonds returned to the song in December 1933.

The original 78 rpm pressing of Maxine Sullivan's "Barbara Allen." Author's collection

The ballads were also reproduced in the form of sheet music. In 1935, for example, "Clem the Melody Man" was credited with a version of "Barbara Allen" that he laid out for ukulele and guitar, with a "special Hawaiian guitar chorus" arranged by Mick Manozof.

Homestead, Pennsylvania–born jazz and swing star Maxine Sullivan (1911–1987) followed her hit recording of "Loch Lomond" with her own surprisingly merry, and mellifluously orchestrated "Barbara Allen," and her delivery of the line "young man, I think you're dying" alone sets her rendering high above many, many others.

Perhaps the most significant release, however, came in 1937, when Columbia Records recorded Welshman Phil Tanner and brought British folk music its first homegrown superstar. Tanner was into his seventies

A 1938 CBS Radio shot of Maxine Sullivan. CBS Radio / Wikimedia Commons

In pre-WW2 Britain, Welshman Phil Tanner was the first folk-singing superstar. Sdoknfonfosijogij, CC BY-SA 4.0 / Wikimedia Commons

at the time; he was the youngest of seven children (six of whom were sons), born in 1862 to a family of weavers in Llangennith, near Swansea on Wales's Gower Peninsula. It was a small community, with no more than four hundred inhabitants, and weaving (alongside agriculture) was their primary occupation. Tanner worked in both professions throughout his lifetime.

He started singing early, and quickly showed a marked preference for English, as opposed to Welsh, songs, which he would pick up from whoever he heard singing them. Later in life, he recalled the names of some of those who had taught him his repertoire—William Taylor and Sam Phillips of Llangennith, Billy Gibbs of nearby Port Eynon, "Kitehole" John of Overton, "Morriston" Tom Lloyd, and a Cornish millwright named Osborne who was visiting Gower to dress stones. Tanner's grandfather David, a variety of uncles and brothers, and a cast of weavers, laborers, Travelers, and more also added to the songbook.

Nicknamed the Gower Nightingale by the locals, Tanner sang wherever he could, with the highlight of the year being the annual Mapsant, a celebration of St. Cennydd's Day, July 5. He was a familiar sight at Harvest Home, and he was also among the wassailers at Christmas. (Tanner's arrangement of the perennial "The Wassailing Song" was later recorded by Steeleye Span.) He also regularly entertained the customers at the public house, the Welcome to Town, of which his wife Ruth was landlady—Tanner was twenty-five when they met, Ruth a forty-one-year-old widow. When she passed the business to her daughter in 1898, the couple moved on; and when Ruth died in 1921, Tanner left Llangennith for a new start a mile away in Barraston.

He still sang—sometimes for the price of a beer at the local King's Head pub, but on more formal occasions too, and in 1932 he found himself performing at a holiday camp that a group of students had established to give local workers the chance of an affordable getaway. (It would be another six years before the United Kingdom passed the Holidays with Pay Act.) There he fell into conversation with one of the students, a folk singer named F. A. Bracey, who in turn brought him to the attention of Maud Karpeles at the English Folk Dance and Song Society.

It was Karpeles who arranged for Tanner to make his recorded debut. In November 1937, the Welshman (and his dog) was brought to London for the first time in his life, to record both for the English Folk Dance and Song Society and for BBC radio's long-running (1933–1960) Saturday-evening variety show *In Town Tonight*. It is said that, as his taxicab passed Buckingham Palace, Tanner demanded it stop so that he could sing the National Anthem outside the palace gates. The engagements fulfilled, Tanner returned home, but a month later, on December 21, the BBC was at the King Arthur Hotel in Reynoldston, a village some eleven miles from Llangennith, to record Tanner's "Christmas Revels," a battle of the bards in which, as the *Radio Times* put it, he "challeng[ed] all comers to a contest of folk songs and dances."

It was during this period that Tanner made his recordings for Columbia, a total of four songs: "The Banks of the Sweet Primroses," "Gower Reel," "Gower Wassail," and "Henry Martin" (250). He sings unaccompanied, and it cannot be imagined that his voice was but a patch upon that with which he had thrilled the people of Llangennith in his younger years. Still, his performances are exceptional, and it is astonishing to think that a full twelve years later, with Tanner now a longtime resident of Glan-y-Mor Nursing Home, housed in what was once the Victorian-era Gower Union Workhouse in Penmaen, he was still singing.

Encouraged by journalist John Ormond Thomas's profile of Tanner ("The Old Singer of Gower") in the March 1949 edition of *Picture Post* magazine, the BBC repeated one of his past recordings on the May 1 seventh-anniversary edition of the popular *Country Magazine*. The listener response was so encouraging that, a month later, the outside broadcast van returned to south Wales to record him once more—only to discover that his repertoire for the evening surpassed the number of blank discs they had thought to pack! Nevertheless, they captured thirteen songs, including fresh versions of three of the Columbia sides, and a soft, sad "Barbara Ellen" (84). *Phil Tanner (Songs and Ballads)* was broadcast on the Home Service on July 13, and it can only be added that the BBC's visit was most fortuitously timed. Little more than six months later, on February 19, 1950, Tanner passed away, aged 88. He was buried in St Cennydd's Churchyard.[5]

Chapter Fourteen

HUNTERS AND GATHERERS

Emboldened, or perhaps merely awakened by the success of Cecil Sharp and Maud Karpeles's expeditions, and the success of the songbook that followed, the postwar years saw a host of other collectors join the ballad-hunting fray. Karpeles herself led the way. As both the spiritual and actual successor to Sharp, her first trip was a fourteen-week excursion to Newfoundland in 1929–1930, a location that Sharp himself had been interested in visiting ever since a trip to Boston in 1917. There he met a woman from Harbour Grace, now working as a maid, who—while she admitted she was "no singer"—nevertheless provided him with "interesting information" on the region. In addition, he had visited Canada on several occasions in the past, on a lecture tour in 1915 and, the following year, when he and Karpeles were employed teaching folk song and dance at the University of Toronto and the Margaret Eaton School of Literature and Expression on Bloor Street, in that same city.

Karpeles's visit was not wholly impulsive. She had recently received an invitation to direct a folk music summer school at Massachusetts Agricultural College (the future University of Massachusetts) in Amherst. Classes were scheduled to begin in mid-August. Karpeles arrived in Montreal a full month earlier so that she might undertake some field work in Ontario and across the border in Vermont. From there she traveled south to Amherst, then, once the class ended, she left first for Halifax, Nova Scotia, before taking the steamer to Newfoundland. She arrived on September 9, apparently armed with no more local knowledge than a travel guide and a couple of letters of introduction. She had packed her camera, to create a visual documentary of her visit, and plentiful writing material. Sadly, she did not bring any recording equipment, preferring to work as she had with Sharp, with paper, pen, and typewriter.

Some preparatory work had been done by the men to whom she was being introduced, the lawyer Frederick Rennie Emerson, and John Lewis Paton (1863–1946), the president of Memorial College. A handful of potential singers and dancers had already been contacted, and she was also introduced to Gerald Coyle (1892–1956), a businessman and collector who had recently published the book *Old-Time Songs of New-foundland*, gathered from a variety of local sources, and distributed as a promotional freebie for the cod liver oil that underpinned his business. (The company he founded would publish further editions in 1940, 1955, 1966, and 1978.)

Beginning on September 12, when she boarded the Newfoundland Express to Trinity East, Karpeles visited some forty different settlements. Initially she was disappointed to discover that two American collectors, Elisabeth Bristol Greenleaf (1895–1980) and Grace Mansfield (1907–1981) had themselves been gathering Newfoundland folk songs earlier in the summer. Nevertheless, she returned home with a wealth of material, and plans to return again the following year to continue her investigations. Ultimately published in 1934 as *Folk Songs from Newfoundland*, Karpeles's eventual haul included an enviable crop of Child Ballads, among them local variations on "Riddles Wisely Expounded" (1), "The Outlandish Knight" (4), "Hind Horn" (17), "Proud Lady Margaret" (47), "Lord Bate-man" (53), "The Unquiet Grave" (78), "Little Musgrave" (81), "Lamkin" (93), "Lord Thomas of Winesberry" (100), and "The Lover's Ghost" (248).

Reflecting upon the trip later, Karpeles agreed that, while it was by no means as fruitful as the Appalachian journey, it compared "very favor-ably" with her experiences collecting in England. Certainly the years to come saw a number of artists delve into her notes for inspiration, among them George Deacon and Marion Rose, who adapted one of the melodies Karpeles discovered for their 1973 recording of "Sweet William's Ghost" (77) (their lyric came from Ramsey's *Tea-Table Miscellany*). More recently, Alasdair Roberts and Emily Portman sang Karpeles's "The Lover's Ghost" (248) on 2010's *Too Long in This Condition* album.

It would be 1950 before Karpeles undertook another major collecting trip, when she made the first of two return visits to the Appalachians. Most of her time now was spent in London, as honorary secretary at the English Folk Dance and Song Society, and editor of Sharp's vast archive. She organized the first International Folk Dance Festival and Conference in 1935, and was awarded an OBE for service to folk music in 1961. She also published two further books reflecting upon her work with Sharp, the biography *Cecil Sharp: His Life and Work* in 1967, and 1974's two-volume *Cecil Sharp's Collection of English Folk Songs*. Karpeles died in 1976.

Folklorist Jim Carroll met Karpeles several times toward the end of her life, and recalls, "I found her somewhat eccentric, but I have the highest respect for what she did with Sharp and for her own work, particularly in Newfoundland. Her collection has proved a major source for my [study of] Irish Child Ballads."[1] Indeed, Karpeles discovered Newfoundland to be a veritable trove of Irish versions of the Child Ballads.

Sadly, later in life "Auntie Maud" lost her hearing; it is said that one day, while clearing a cupboard in Cecil Sharp's house, she discovered a store of wax cylinders made by various early collectors. She had someone play them for her; the ones she couldn't hear she had destroyed. It was a shocking decision, but surely, the amount of music that she preserved for future generations more than outweighs that particular loss.

Even before Karpeles began planning her Newfoundland jaunt, other collectors were venturing forth. In 1921, American ethnologist Martha Beckwith (1871–1959) and anthropologist Helen Heffron Roberts (1888–1985) visited Jamaica to document the music of the Maroon community. Among the items with which they returned home were wholly unexpected versions of "Little Musgrove" (81) and "Sweet William" (7).

Beckwith recalled the discovery of "Little Musgrove," up in "the remote hill country about Maroon Town, called Accompong, in St. Elizabeth parish." William Forbes was "an unusually intelligent" man, "between seventy and eighty years of age" and, unlike some of the "entertainers" the pair had met, "he was no clown but a genuine enthusiast. He always sang with a shining delight and his feet going in time to the tune; I doubt if he could have remembered the words in any other way. He was, in short, a reliable source for the standards of old-fashioned art. Now when old Forbes first gave me the story of 'Little Musgrove,' he strung the verses upon a connecting thread of prose to carry along the action. Only when confronted with the phonograph did he sing the verses straight through without interruption."[2]

> *Raise up, raise up, my little Musgrove,*
> *An' put on you clo'es, Musgrove,*
> *For I won't 'low de worl' to got it to said*
> *I kill a naked man.*

> *An' turn to de woman an' said,*
> *Raise up, raise up, my gay lady,*
> *An' put on you clo'es, lady,*
> *For I won't let dis worl' to have it to said*
> *Dat I kill a naked woman.*

The late 1920s also saw the first field trips undertaken by Mississippi Methodist minister James Madison Carpenter (1899–1983), an adventurer whose collection ultimately spanned some thirty years into the mid-1950s, and contains some six hundred Child Ballads gathered from across the United States and the British Isles. All of his recordings reside today in the American Folklife Center at the Library of Congress.

University of California at Berkeley professor Robert Winslow Gordon (1888–1961) walked the San Francisco waterfront of the early 1920s, collecting songs from sailors. They were "Mostly shanties and other sea songs," wrote Ronald D. Cohen,[3] "but also some Child Ballads, blues, and bawdy songs." He also visited North Carolina, where his discoveries included Nancy Weaver Stikeleather's rendering of "Georgie"[4] (209). Gordon also edited the column "Old Songs Men Have Sung" for *Adventure* magazine, and several Child Ballads slipped into those pages, either submitted by readers (another version of "Geordie"), or taken from his own collection: "The Merrie Golden Tree" (286), as sung to Gordon by Ada Moss, a student at Cullowhee State Normal, appeared in the January 30, 1926, edition.

Anthropologist Herbert Halpert (1911–2000) recovered a number of Child Ballads in Virginia in 1939. Several of these, including such uncommon variants as "The Three Maids" (11—sung by Polly Johnson) and "The Turkish Rebelee" (286—collected from Horton Baker) were included on the 1978 *Ballads from British Tradition* album, released within the Blue Ridge Institute's Virginia Traditions series. Halpert himself later (1968) went on to close a circle of sorts as founder of the Memorial University of Newfoundland Folklore and Language Archive.

Others boldly struck out into less well-traveled regions; the aforementioned Ben Gray Lumpkin, who devoted twenty years, 1950–1970, to seeking out new songs in and around Colorado; and Max Hunter, a traveling salesman from Springfield, Missouri, who augmented his work schedule by recording singers and performers he met in the Ozarks, beginning in 1956. Hunter gathered some 150 Child Ballad recordings over a twenty-year span, including the delightful "Pretty Polly" (4) that folklorist Julie Henigan recorded on her 1997 *American Stranger* album.

Henigan recalled, "I went to hear Max Hunter talk about his collection and, discovering that much of it was available on cassette tapes, I was at them like a shot. Since I couldn't drive and do fieldwork, I had my own source singers on those cassette tapes. They got to be like old friends, and I learned a lot of songs (including both Child and broadside ballads) from them."[5] Originally sung by Donia Cooper of West Fork, Arkansas, in August 1959, Henigan describes "Pretty Polly" as "an Arkansas version of a ballad ('Lady Isabel and the Elf Knight') that Child said was more widespread than any of the songs in his collection. The appeal of the story for women, the primary carriers of the ballad tradition, is not far to seek: Bluebeard gets his just reward, thanks to the resourceful heroine, who fools her father in the bargain."[6]

None of these collectors focused on the Child Ballads alone, but they unearthed them regardless. One of Carpenter's discoveries during a visit to Scotland, the Aberdeenshire singer Bell Duncan, had no less than sixty-five Child Ballads in her repertoire. Two of them—"The White Fisher" (264) and "The Young Earl of Essex's Victory over the Emperor of Germany" (288)—have never been recorded elsewhere.

Another collector, Maurice Matterson, visited Beech Mountain, in Watauga County, North Carolina, in the early 1930s and returned home with, among other recordings, the repertoire of a local dulcimer maker named Nathan Hicks and his wife. "Barbry Ellen" (84), "George Collins" (85), "Bol' Lamkin" (93), and "The House Carpenter" (243) were among the Child Ballads sung by that couple.

Beech Mountain was to prove a remarkably fruitful collecting ground. Now renowned as the home to the internationally renowned Beech Mountain Resort, offering skiing, trail hiking, and some breathtaking views, it was previously a tiny, self-contained community of a few hundred people, best known as the highest town east of the Rocky Mountains, and seldom visited by outsiders.

Little had changed since Cecil Sharp became the first collector to visit the town. Beech Mountain was the kind of place, it was remarked, where there was little to do in the way of entertainment beyond singing; it is notable that, even today, Wikipedia's list of the town's "notable people" numbers just two, banjo player Frank Profitt (1913–1965) and storyteller Ray Hicks (1922–2003). There were, however, many more, including several other members of Hicks's own family.

In 1964, folklorist Sandy Paton (whose early Elektra label albums featured a handful of Child Ballads, including an irresistible variant on "Lord Randall" [12] called "Wee Croodlin' Doo") compiled a selection of his Beech Mountain discoveries into two LPs dedicated to *The Traditional Music of Beech Mountain, North Carolina*. Sensibly divided between "the older ballads and sacred songs" (volume one) and "later songs and hymns" (volume two), eight Child Ballads on the first LP include a retelling of "Sir Lionel" (18) by Buna Hicks, which, according to Paton, was only the second "serious version" ever to be recorded in America (the first, by another of Hicks's relatives, Samuel Haron, dated from 1939).

A somewhat jumbled but eminently enjoyable "Five Nights Drunk" (274) was performed by Hicks's daughter Hattie Presnell, while Paton also collected a rendition of "The House Carpenter" (243) that he believed predated the broadside versions popularized in the United States during the 1850s. Then there was a rare variant on "The Grey Cock" (248), known as "Pretty Crowing Chicken," sung to the tune of the Texan folksong "Willie Moore," and performed by the same Jane Gentry who so bedazzled Cecil Sharp half a century previous.

Chapter Fifteen

SEEKING FRESH DIRECTIONS

The Great Depression tore America's heartland to shreds, displacing millions and pushing more into unemployment. President Roosevelt's New Deal was launched to try and pull things back together, but it was not going to be an easy task. The South and the Midwest were particularly hard hit, with the crisis only exacerbated by the prolonged drought and soil depletion resulting in swathes of farmland turned into dust bowls. Thus was born the Resettlement Administration, to oversee the establishment of government-built homesteads, in which the displaced families could indeed be resettled.

Swiftly, however, the program ran into problems. Yes, it was a noble enterprise, but, as with so many such endeavors, good intentions were not sufficient. Workers were dispirited, despondent, and, in some places, rebellious; ripped from their own lands, they were now transplanted to unfamiliar climes and effectively instructed to begin their lives over. It was to try and quell their disquiet that the Special Skills Division came into being and, within that, a Music Unit, overseen by Charles Seeger Jr., founder of the University of California, Berkeley's pioneering musicology curriculum (the first in the United States) in 1913, and a cofounder of the American Musicologist Society.

Seeger's task was to oversee efforts to develop new recreational programs and entertainment around the settlements, encouraging the settlers to reconnect with their own cultural heritages and incorporate them into their new lives. He was also aware, however, that academics, social workers, and so-called "do-gooders" were the last people to whom the settlers would respond. He required people who not only would understand the settlements' needs, but would empathize with them, too. It is to his eternal credit that he made precisely the right choices.

In 1935, Seeger hired Margaret Brahan Valiant (1901–1982), a Mississippi-born singer whose career included several European productions and, according to the National Endowment for the Humanities (NEH) website, a stint as a Ziegfeld Girl. Most recently she had worked as a model and clothing designer, and had known Seeger since she met his fiancée, Ruth Crawford, on a transatlantic voyage in 1931. Valiant would initially be based at the Cherry Lake Farms homestead in Madison County, Florida (others were established in Tennessee, Virginia, and Pennsylvania); among her innovations was a series of fashion shows, at which the women sang their favorite songs while modeling home-made clothing. She also arranged boxing bouts, and accompanied them on guitar! Later, she moved onto homesteads across Tennessee, Alabama, North Carolina, and Montana, and migrant camps in California and Arizona, usually accompanied by the Music Unit's latest acquisition, a so-called "portable" (it weighed 130 pounds) Presto aluminum disc recorder, and a 75-pound case of blank recording discs.

Now resident in the Library of Congress, Valiant's recordings offer a startling glimpse into both the lives of the people she met, and their resilience. They include, too, some significant musical finds, including perhaps the earliest known recording by Chicano guitar legend Lalo Guerrero, the singing of children at a Native American school in Arizona, and the Okie ballad "Going Down the Road Feeling Bad" (subsequently recorded by Woody Guthrie). Amid such wealth, Child Ballads were scant, but a handful stand out nevertheless, including Blaine Stubblefield's renditions of "The Keyhole in the Door" (27) and "The Farmer's Curst Wife" (278), and the Skyline Farm Group's "Billy Boy" (12).

The ballads were, however, alive and flourishing around the settlements, as Seeger's next hire, California pianist and music teacher Sidney Robertson Cowell (1903–1995), would discover.

Sidney Hawkins, as she was born, already possessed a formidable musical background. As a child, she learned piano, violin, and dancing. She spoke French fluently and studied elocution. She was also astonishingly well traveled. She visited Europe regularly in the company of her piano tutor, while her father often took her on work-related trips across the West, then left her to her own devices while he went about his business. She devoted this time to exploring the towns and environs around her.

Having earned a BA in Romance languages at Stanford, Hawkins married her first husband, philosophy student Kenneth Robertson. She taught music at the Peninsula School for Creative Education in Menlo Park and studied what would now be called world music at the San Francisco

Conservatory of Music. After divorcing, she continued to work under her married name.

Sidney moved to New York in 1935, where she took a job directing the social music program at the Henry Street Settlement on the Lower East Side. The following year, a visit to Washington, D.C., introduced her to what was then called the Archive of American Folk Song (now the American Folk Life Center Archive). There, she so intrigued the staff with her curiosity and questions that they arranged a meeting with Seeger. He swiftly hired her and, following a quick apprenticeship under John Lomax (during which she was taught to operate a recording machine), Seeger sent her out to begin collecting, initially focusing upon the still fruitful Appalachian and Ozark regions.

Sidney Robertson Cowell, "government song woman." By Roger Higgins / Wikimedia Commons

The region must have been thoroughly sick and tired of collectors by this point. Ever since Sharp and Karpeles first unearthed the diversity of balladry to be found there, scholars, academics, and others had flooded in, all seeking out the "old songs." Indeed, what is regarded as the first doctoral thesis on the American survival of British ballads, by Professor Josiah Combs, was researched there, largely from the repertoire of his own family, the Combs of Knott County, Kentucky.[1]

Robertson won their hearts, regardless. Self-deprecatingly, she referred to herself as "a government song woman," and she was tireless. Over the next five years or so, she would travel over three hundred thousand miles across seventeen states, running three automobiles into the ground in the process. She traveled light, usually accompanied by nothing more than her Presto recording machine (purchased with the pay-out from a car insurance claim), a sleeping bag, and what she once overheard someone describe as "the lady about the songs' dog." All additional space was consumed by the twelve-inch acetate discs upon which she would record.

In 1938, Robertson established the Northern California Folk Music Project under the auspices of the Works Progress Administration (WPA, a pillar of Roosevelt's New Deal program) and cosponsored by the Library of Congress and the University of California, Berkeley. She would spend the next seventeen months heading up a team of twenty in one of the first ever concerted, large-scale investigations of the state's musical heritage. Robertson documented the project's aims in an interview with the *San Francisco Chronicle* in September 1938, a month before its official October 28 opening, and she courted controversy from the start.

Discussing the successive waves of immigrant workers who had settled in California, Robertson described them as "hard-working citizens," in stark contrast to such more commonly used and purposefully divisive terms as *immigrants, foreigners,* and *aliens.* Robertson not only loathed such terminology, but she also encouraged her staff to avoid it. She then shot down the popular orthodoxy that these people "contributed nothing . . . beyond the work of their hands."

"What traditions came with them?" she wanted to know. "Which have survived here, changed or unchanged. What were they thinking and feeling as they labored in mines and forests, herding cattle and sheep along our slopes? Plowing and harvesting in the valleys, and fishing along the coasts?

"Their songs will tell us, if we can find them."

Robertson was not, from all accounts, the "typical" collector. Early on in her time at the Resettlement Administration, she had witnessed the brusque, even demanding manner in which people were asked to perform for the recording machines. Robertson, on the other hand, made it clear that the singers were doing her a favor. As she put it in her writings, "I never asked the singers to sing for me or for the government, except as a preservation project. And I was never demanding of them. If they didn't want to sing, we skipped it for the present. And almost without exception, they revived the subject later themselves. I was careful, just as a matter of good manners, not to say 'I want.'"[2] Always, she made it clear that she loved their music and wished only to ensure that it was preserved for future generations to enjoy, and her hosts responded in kind. "This is what has made a wide variety of people willing and even anxiously determined that I should know and record the best they had."

What truly singles out Robertson's writings was the sheer enthusiasm that she brought to her quest. Previously, such expeditions had focused on little more than the most basic data—the singer, the song, where and when it was recorded, and so forth. Robertson, however, created what lecturer Catherine Hiebert Kerst described as "a vicarious experience for all of us of what it meant to do ethnographic field work at the time . . . more contextual detail, with numerous photographs, drawings and sketches, official field reports sent into the WPA, a variety of other field notes, and a wealth of Robertson's lively reminiscences about her own work and her often gossipy correspondence."[3]

As for how she found the singers in the first place, Robertson simply shrugged. They were everywhere. In her 1938 paper *Folk Music in California*, she described how, stepping out of the project's Shattuck Street office one day, she heard a man singing an old ballad while he changed a tire on his automobile. She promptly asked if he could sing it again while she wrote it down. Another time, accepting a package from a railroad delivery man, she recognized his signature as being a Basque name. She asked if he knew any old songs, and he did.

Robertson was even reunited with some acquaintances from her days collecting songs in Crandon, Wisconsin, for the Resettlement Administration in 1937. There she first met the incredibly musical Ford family; now the brothers Warde, Arthur, Bogue, and Pat, together with their uncle Rob Walker, were in Shasta County to work on the Shasta Dam, near Reading. "The Warde brothers sang a number of songs for me when I didn't have a recording machine," she wrote. "I noted some of them down, they've been sending me texts ever since."

The project's results are startling. Robertson returned home with some thirty-five hours of field recordings, sung in twelve different languages by 185 different musicians. Photographs and drawings of performers and their instruments were also gathered to flesh out the archive to even more enviable proportions. She met direct descendants of the '49 gold rushers; fiddlers who had once performed in medicine shows; a Finnish American who arranged for Robertson to record in the cafe he owned, Koljonen's

Cafe in Boomtown; and another, John Soininen, who sang her the dark tale of a man who murdered his brother, "Velisurmaaja"—a take on Child 13.

Robertson herself was surprised to discover a number of traditional English, Scottish, and Irish songs still circulating, with many of them brought to the region during the gold rush. Among these, there were some thirty Child Ballads, including George Vinton Graham singing a variation on "The Farmer's Curst Wife" (278), now titled "The Devil Out of Hell" (but known in Kentucky as "The Little Devils") and a "Lord Bakeman," rather than "Bateman" (53) he had learned from his mother. Warde Ford's repertoire was as rewarding as Robertson expected—he and Vinton Graham both sang her "Our Goodman" (274) and "The Lowlands Low" (286). There were the likes of Alex Barr, Virginia Meade, and Vinton Graham again, all offering up their own particular takes on "Barbara Allen" (84); and so many more.

The project came to an end in early summer 1940, when Robertson was shocked to learn that the WPA would not be renewing its funding. As it happened, however, Robertson's collecting would probably have ended around this same time regardless. The following year, she married the composer Henry Cowell—a close friend since her teenaged years. Although she continued to make occasional collecting excursions (she visited the Arran Islands in the 1950s), marriage to one of the era's most famous composers saw her become better known as his wife before, as Catherine Hiebert Kerst puts it, spending "a lot of time sort of being the composer's widow."[4]

No sooner had Robertson been forced to end her researches in northern California, however, than two City College of New York students, Charles Todd and Robert Sonkin, were embarking upon their own expedition into the state's central region. Inspired, at least in Todd's case, by John Steinbeck's portrayal of the San Joaquin Valley migrant camps in his pamphlet *Their Blood Is Strong*, the pair's destination was the worker settlements established by the so-called dust bowl diaspora. Making their way to the towns of Arvin, Bakersfield, El Rio, Firebaugh, Porterville, Shafter, Thornton, Visalia, Westley, and Yuba City, Todd and Sonkin originally saw themselves as simply documenting the life of the workers, and they commenced gathering everything they could—photographs, ephemera, even the crudely typewritten newsletters that various workers groups produced for their immediate communities. In fact, during 1942, Todd was writing an occasional column for one of these, *The Hub*, produced by the Tulare Farm Workers Community.

The idea of collecting songs, too, had never crossed their minds. It was Todd who first realized that, among the handful of possessions the communities had brought from home were the songs they once sang. He made contact with the Archive of American Folk Song at the Library of Congress, explained what he and Sonkin were doing, and was soon discussing his precise requirements with the Assistant in Charge of the Archive, Alan Lomax. A Presto recording machine and a supply of discs, needles, and batteries was soon making its way into the Southwest—very carefully. As America began planning so reluctantly for the possibility of the European war reaching its own shores, the aluminum that ordinarily was used in the manufacture of recording discs became increasingly scarce. Instead, the New Yorkers were sent the far heavier, and far more fragile acetate-on-glass discs, and while the majority arrived intact, they did not remain so. Among the discs that sadly shattered while being transported from one place to another was the pair's entire archive of Spanish-language performances.

Todd and Sorkin made two trips to the camps, the first in July–August 1940, the second exactly a year later. Neither was their quest a straightforward one, although it assures us a fascinating listen today. It was next to impossible to find a quiet location in which a song might be recorded; many of their recordings, then, are littered with background sounds ranging from sewing machines to passing locomotives, and all the other hubbub of a 1940s Californian migrant camp.

The pair also discovered that they were not alone in their researching; in his writings, Todd complained that some of the camps were "full of PhD scholars and do-gooders studying the real people." In fact, it later transpired that one particularly rich vein of songs that the pair collected, all dealing specifically with the lives of the migrants, had been written by what they disdainfully referred to as "a PhD from Vassa." Nevertheless, they persevered and returned home, finally, with some 436 recordings, songs and interviews alike, from which we can extract some fifteen Child Ballads—more than half of which comprise variations on "Barbara Allen" (84) and "Gypsy Davy" (200).

They are not, however, to be dismissed. "Barbara Allen" is represented by several lilting duets between two young ladies, Lois Judd and Rosetta Spainhard (one, sadly, is marred by the recording speed increasing, and reducing the voices to laughable chipmunks); while a woman named O. C. Davis not only delivers a joyously sauntering "Blackjack Davy," she introduces both herself and her song with the utmost confidence. Davis also performs "The Brown Girl" (295) with similar aplomb, having detailed how her version was written down by her cousin seventeen years before, when they were both thirteen, back in Oklahoma. Tragically the cousin died in a house fire, "so I kept the song to remember her because I loved her so much."

Helen Hartness Flanders (1890–1972) was another tireless investigator of the United States' less-traveled regions, and in 1930, she was approached by the Vermont Commission on Country Life's Committee

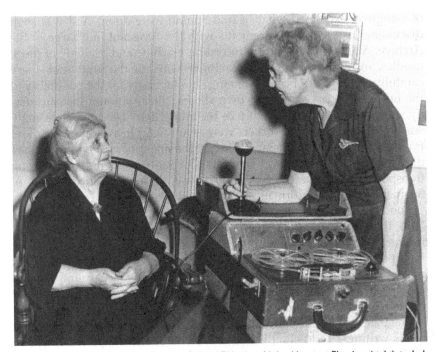

Mrs. John Fairbanks (left) delivered several Child Ballads to Helen Hartness Flanders (right), including "Barbara Allen," "The Bailiff's Daughter," and the rare "Little Harry Huston" variant of #155. Courtesy Middlebury College Special Collections, CC By 4.0

on Traditions and Ideals to begin searching out the traditional songs of the area. Flanders agreed, setting out her quest in an open letter published across the region's newspapers: "Do you know of any music—old songs or dances specially grown in Vermont?" She described her work, and that of the committee itself, as a survey, and promised that upon its conclusion the following May, "four writers hope to present a play and a pageant or two." There would also be a book. She added,

> I welcome material, or clues or suggestions from any friend of Vermont, and, in making use of it, I will, of course, credit the correspondent as my source of information. For instance, the song "Fair Charlotte" written in Benson, Rutland County, is recorded with some variants in states halfway across the continent. . . . Certainly there are others which grew into the story form of song. There must be Come-all-ye's and Shanties and French-Canadian dialect songs, Nursery Songs and altered Welsh, English and Scottish Ballads. Please try to remember where you have heard them and write me. Even fragments of this type will mean much to me.

This initial search was followed by others. In 1939, Flanders organized a competition offering two $50 prizes to whomsoever could offer up the greatest number of traditional songs, including "British—Scotch, Irish, and English—folk songs and ballads," and that July, she staged an all-day Festival of Folk Music.

By the fall, Flanders's archive comprised some 500 audio recordings and 140 manuscripts, a total that was then swollen when Alan Lomax, enchanted by Flanders's discoveries, spent nine days traveling Vermont for the Library of Congress, and depositing copies of all his discoveries in Flanders's own archive. Her own collecting work continued until the end of her life, and it naturally has attracted a number of musicians seeking fresh material. Singer Margaret MacArthur (1928–2006) was among the most devoted of these.

MacArthur discovered traditional music in the early 1930s when her forester father was employed on a timber marking crew in the Sierra Anchas in Arizona. A child of no more than five or six, she was fascinated by the songs that she heard the workmen singing, and began collecting and learning them for herself. The family continued moving around as work demanded, to the Ozarks, to California, to Louisiana. By the time she moved to Marlboro, Vermont, in 1948, the bug had surely bitten, and she was forever listening out for new old songs, ballads, broadsides, hymns, anything. MacArthur also came to know Flanders and, across the ten years that preceded the collector's death in May 1972, "she gave me invaluable assistance and encouragement." Thereafter, her estate "made available to me various of her manuscripts, letters and tapes."[5]

"Gypsy Davy" (200), which MacArthur recorded on her 1962 debut LP *Folksongs in Vermont*, was a ballad that she collected herself, from an Alice Snow Bailey in nearby Readsboro. But five of her other performances were drawn from the Flanders collection, and more would appear on *From the Mountains High* (1972). Here again, her Child choices were her own discoveries, "The Cambric Shirt" (2) and "The Old Yellow Mare," an unfamiliar title for a very familiar ballad, "Edward" (13). Accompanying herself on dulcimer, MacArthur performs the song exactly as she was taught it by one Florence Fowler, whose own memory had lost the first half of the opening stanza. We begin, then, with Edward already explaining how he came to be dripping with gore: "Tis the blood of the old yellow mare that plowed the furrow for me." It is the first of a wealth of implausible excuses he offers, before finally confessing that he has murdered his brother.

MacArthur also revisited both Flanders and Child for 1982's *Make the Wildwoods Ring*, an album recorded with, and co-credited to her daughter Megan and sons Gary and Dan. "Barbara Allen," she wrote, was taken from her own collecting, and the three days she spent recording the singing of Fred Atwood of West Dover, Vermont.[6] His father, a local mason named James, had sung the same song for another local collector, Edith

Jonathan Moses (L), Lena Bourne Fish (C), and Asa Davis (R) provided Flanders with almost thirty different Child Ballads. Courtesy Middlebury College Special Collections, CC By 4.0

Barnes Sturgis,[7] around 1919; apparently, he was hired to work on the Sturgis family chimney, and she overheard him singing while he worked. He taught his songs to his son, but evidently did not always pass on their origins. Of "Barbara Allen," MacArthur wrote, "Fred told me that this tragedy happened over west of Bennington, near the border of York state."[8] (Fred was not alone in such a belief. In 1954, a singer from Canterbury, in the English county of Kent, Charlie Scamp, informed the BBC that "Barbara Allen" took place just twenty miles away, in the port town of Dover, where a sailor on leave was courting a "rich, handsome girl.")

"The Weeping Willow Tree" (286) was a prime Flanders discovery. It was one of thirty-six versions published in Flanders's *Ancient Ballads Traditionally Sung in New England* (Child gives three, and none under this title), collected from Lena Bourne Fish, of East Jaffrey, New Hampshire, and MacArthur described it as "our favourite, in which the cabin boy emerges triumphant. In our minds eye, we see him as the lone survivor."[9]

Flanders, Sturgis, and MacArthur were not the only investigators scouring the high Northeast for song. In Maine, in the 1920s, local singers such as Annie V. Marston and Susie Carr Young were intriguing members of the Concord Summer School of Music with both the depth and breadth of their knowledge of the old songs—intriguing because, as three of those students, Phillips Barry, Fannie Hardy Eckstorm, and Mary Winslow Smith, admitted in 1929, "So few old ballads have been reported from New England . . . that it has been taken for granted that they do not exist here." And that despite the fact that New England "has long been the beacon-light of all students of balladry."[10] In just eleven days that September, one of their number, George Herzog, collected no less than 199 "desirable old airs" from visits to Bangor, Calais, and Mount Desert alone. That many of these, and other finds besides, in some way duplicated great swathes of the Appalachian songbook was an even greater surprise, and discovery. At last, agreed Barry and company, "a New England superstructure [had been] built upon Professor Child's well-laid foundations."

These discoveries also punctured, at least in part, the insistence that the ballads were the songs of the common folk. In Maine, it was now declared, "the singers are all literate and often well educated." That said, they had no awareness whatsoever of their beloved ballads' heritage. Comparing the songs of Maine with their equivalents in *ESPB*, the team reported, several of the singers were "disturb[ed] to find the ballad they have always known as 'Lord Bateman' [53] listed under 'Young Beichan'; [and] why should we call 'Lady Isabel and the Elf Knight' [4] when there is no Lady Isabel in it, and no Elf Knight?" And thus we discover another example of the loss of a ballad's supernatural elements sometime after it crossed the Atlantic.

The material that Barry, Eckstorm, and Smith gathered from these excursions was published by Yale University in 1929 as *British Ballads from Maine: The Development of Popular Airs with Texts and Airs* across a door-stopping 535 pages. In scope, it features no less than 94 of Child's original 305, often in multiple texts, and its contents span not only the course of the recent collections, but earlier gatherings too, both predating and apparently eluding Professor Child's studies. These include a broadside of "The Elphin Knight" (2), retitled "Love Letter and Answer," that was published in Boston in the mid-1830s, and from 1842, a gripping recitation of Captain Ward's pursuit by, and escape from, the king's ship the *Rainbow* (287).

The texts themselves intrigue. We find a "Lord Banner" (81) in which the wronged husband first slaughters the adulterers and then puts an end to his own suffering, too; an Irish "Barbara Allen" (84) that boils down the entire story to just five rhyming couplets; and a "Cruel Mother" (20) sung by a woman who mentioned that the same version was also known to her husband, only he considered this epic of illegitimate birth, unsuccessful abortion, ultimate infanticide, and finally, awful denouement, "too smutty to repeat." She apparently had no such qualms. There is also a fine "Young Hunting" (68), which would be recorded in 1998 by Nancy Kerr and James Fagaan for their *Starry Gazy Pie* album.

Neither had Maine surrendered all its secrets. Thirty years on, in the mid-1950s, Sandy Ives (1925–2009) was collecting folktales and songs for his own enjoyment, while also researching the life and music of poet and songwriter Larry Gorman. He was not necessarily overly impressed by his discoveries. "Anyone who collects songs in Maine and the Maritimes is struck by the homogeneity of the material," he wrote somewhat dismissively. "A song that is known in Maine will also be known [elsewhere] and, what is more, often to the same tune."[11] How interesting (yet also typical of collectors of all pursuits) that a discovery once regarded with such delight should now be regarded with equal disdain.

His sources, too, were somewhat dogmatic. Ives noted that the tunes he was hearing were, in general, the only tunes that could be sung to the songs, suggesting that attempts to apply any other melody were by definition doomed to failure. He also discovered, in common with so many of his 1950s-era contemporaries, "old singers are sometimes made uncomfortable by hearing the songs sung to any accompaniment." Echoing Cecil Sharp's observation of forty years previous, Ives heard just one song sung with any form of accompaniment.

It could, then, be assumed that Ives had a thoroughly miserable time collecting the ballads he gathered, although there were certainly moments of triumph. He was overjoyed to unearth what he described as "one of the rarest [Child Ballads] to be found in America," a "Hind Horn" (17) that his source knew as "The Old Beggar Man." Unfortunately, every silver lining has a cloud. Beyond a handful of tantalizing scraps, he was never able to collect what he deemed a "good version of the ballad." Indeed, when he came to record the song for his 1959 *Folk Songs of Maine* LP, he placed his own discovery to one side and turned instead to *British Ballads from Maine* and the version collected from Thomas E. Nelson of New Brunswick in 1928, who had learned it in turn from his Irish mother.

Chapter Sixteen

BRITTEN, IVES, AND NILES

John Jacob Niles was a teenager when he started collecting the songs that he heard sung around his home in Louisville, Kentucky. Born in 1892, he knew nothing of collecting as an academic pursuit, and neither, it seems, did his family or acquaintances: if anybody ever remarked upon the lad with his ever-present notebook and pen, it was (as he recalled) to call him "quaint and cute." He was also determined. His goal was to develop a repertoire of songs that he could sing in public, and preferably ones that were not common to other performers. To this end, he also noted down any other scraps of interest that he chanced upon. Local folklore, riddles and jokes, nursery rhymes, church sermons, anything that caught his fancy was fodder for his notebook, including—one hot day in July 1907—a ballad of twenty-five quatrains that he heard while working in a surveying party for the Burroughs Corporation of eastern Kentucky. It was called "Lord Bateman" (53).

Money was tight. Niles's first notebook cost him what he felt was an extortionate 10 cents, and it was so shoddily made that he considered it was scarcely worth half that. His second, then, he purchased used, despite it already having been filled in with a previous owner's poetry. He erased it all and started again. By 1935, the year in which he first began considering the book for which he is best remembered, *The Ballad Book of John Jacob Niles*, he had fourteen such notebooks, all crammed with material.

Niles also had an enviable musical education. Following the Great War, in which he served (and was wounded) in the US Army Air Service, Niles moved to Lyon, France, to study music. From there he relocated to Paris, where he attended the Schola Cantorum; back in the United States in 1920, he enrolled at the Cincinnati Conservatory of Music. Studying

A waxed platinum print of John Jacob Niles by Doris Ulmann, circa 1931, now to be found in the National Portrait Gallery. By Doris Ulmann—National Portrait Gallery / Wikimedia Commons

now under the composer Ralph Lyford, Niles fell into the same kind of musical double life as the likes of Henry Burr and Reinald Werrenrath had once enjoyed, turning his talents to both opera and traditional music. The latter, however, was always destined to win out, especially after Niles began appearing on local radio, drawing his repertoire from his own now sizable assemblage of material.

He continued collecting. Niles moved to New York City in 1925 and, two years later, landed the post of assistant to photographer Doris Ulmann as she set out on the first of four trips to the southern Appalachians, gathering material for what became author Allen Eaton's *Handicrafts of the Southern Highlands*. Talking with the people they encountered, Niles naturally asked if they knew any songs, and he was ready to transcribe them if the answer was yes.

He was also performing regularly, a dazzling figure in white tie and tails that quite contradicted his adopted stage persona of Johnnie Niles—Bone Creek Boy. Music hall audiences adored him, medicine show crowds too. He would sing for anybody, anywhere, from college campuses to churches, from lowly cabin porches to the best-appointed auditoriums. He also often performed at the assemblies staged by Chautauqua, an adult education and entertainment movement that spread from humble beginnings on the banks of Lake Erie in 1873 to become a major force across the rural landscape of the 1920s and 1930s.

By now, Niles was publishing sporadically a series of small octavo pamphlets featuring folklore and verses drawn from his collection. He also landed a recording contract with RCA Victor and, by 1941, he had released two volumes of *Early American Ballads*, bound collections of three and four shellac discs, respectively. All, again, were drawn from his notebooks, and included performances that ranged from "Frog Went a Courting" and "Who Killed Cock Robin" to "The Gypsy Laddee" (200), "The Wife of Usher's Well" (79), "The Death of Queen Jane" (170), "Little Mattie Groves" (81), and onto the now ubiquitous "The Ballad of Barberry Ellen" (84)—albeit sung in a tone that surely chilled the blood of any who knew the song solely from its more popular renditions.

Niles's interpretations were not necessarily popular within the folklore community. On several occasions, he found himself accused of bogus scholarship and deceptive methodology, while his performance style was frequently dismissed as eccentric, at best. He was criticized, too, for not sticking to one musical form. Niles's repertoire merrily ranged from traditional ballads to self-composed numbers, and embraced the full scope of his own collecting interests—the music of the African American community, nursery rhymes, even songs he picked up from soldiers during the war.

It must also be admitted that the Niles voice was a singularly peculiar beast, and certainly an acquired taste. Pitched high, but with glorious range and effortless expression, he described it as the "electrifying effect of the male C# alto." Decades later, attempting to convey the same sound to a younger, modern, readership, writer Gabe Melline suggested they imagine the Violent Femmes' "Country Death Song" being performed by a neutered Nick Cave, then compared the result to the sounds of a feral turkey being slowly boiled.[1]

But the ballads were the ideal vehicle for such a tone, and the more emotional or sensational the lyric, the better Niles was equipped to convey it. "Little Mattie Groves" was a song he learned in July 1934, toward the end of his time with Ulmann (she passed away that August), from a cook working for a preacher's wife in Asheville, North Carolina. Plainly, the song's blatant treatment of adultery and murder shocked the old woman, even as she merrily sang it to herself. When Niles asked her to teach him the words, she insisted on whispering the entire eighteen verses. Niles's version, though far from being delivered in a whisper, nevertheless captures some of that secrecy; he sings as though he is relating the most scandalous slice of gossip (which, of course, he was, albeit several hundred years late). When Mattie Groves initially rejects the overtures of Lord Arling's wife, you can hear the panic in his voice; when she attempts to reassure him, you can hear her conviction. And when Lady Arling follows her lover to the grave, Niles can barely conceal his delight.

He took his wife by the lily-white hand and he led her to the hall
And he cut off her head with his bitter sword and he stove it against the wall

"The Ballad of Barberry Ellen," too, retains a taste of its discovery. Niles learned it originally from his father, but every place he went, it seemed, he would hear another version: "If I had wanted to clutter my already overstuffed notebooks, I might have gained this doubtful benefit by putting down every 'Barbara Allen' I encountered."[2] Instead, he created a hybrid, a little from one source, a little from another. There was one, he recalled, that was collected from twelve-year-old Florrie Medars of Caldwell County. She knew the song, she assured him, but she refused to sing it for him. It was, she declared, too sad. Instead, she wrote it into his notebook herself.

By 1933, Jacob Niles's rendition of "Barbara Allen" had reached ten quatrains, which he believed was quite enough. That was until one day that fall, as he was walking along Puncheon Camp Creek and met Carter Sizemore, a scruffy young man with all his worldly belongings carried in a small poke, and a guitar tied to his back. He was on his way to Lexington, he said, to join the army. They fell into conversation, and then into music, Niles on his dulcimer, Sizemore on guitar. And at some point in their reverie, Sizemore struck up a "Barbara Allen" half as long again as Niles's own. Of course Niles marveled at the six extra verses—they tied the entire tragedy together, and Sizemore offered to "loan" them to him. This is the version that Jacob Niles performs on his debut, its length necessitating it being split across two sides of a disc, and he is right. The tragedy is complete.

It was with the release of these early albums that Niles learned another of the pitfalls of possessing such a unique repertoire: the "imitators and an ever increasing group of young ballad enthusiasts went about the disturbing business of pirating my collection by way of my published works and my recordings."[3]

His efforts to complete his proposed ballads book ended there, and it would be 1961 before he was finally sufficiently at ease to publish his *Ballad Book*. Indeed, his career as a public performer, too, came to a halt while he turned his attention to his own songwriting. It would be 1952 before Niles resumed recording ballads, when he self-released the album *American Folk Love Songs to Dulcimer Accompaniment*, recorded in his own living room.

One Child Ballad found its way into the set, a truly haunting "Oh Waly Waly" (204), the older Niles voice now an ethereal being that floats above his stark instrumentation. By now, however, the folk scene was shifting again, and Niles suddenly found himself ranked among its most venerable elder statesmen. It was a role to which he swiftly became accustomed.

The publication of *The Ballad Book* was echoed by the release of a new album, titled for the book and comprising twenty-four favorite Child Ballads, in the most distinct variants that Niles had collected. Many are unusual, some are still rare, a few were even unique. Known to Child as "King Henry V's Conquest of France" (164),"The Fency King and the English King" had never been recorded in the past, and it would wait over forty years before being heard again, until the now seventy-one-year-old Margaret MacArthur included it on her final album, 1999's *Ballads Thrice Twisted*.

Five years later, it was revisited by Richard Thompson, as he surveyed *1,000 Years of Popular Music* for a 2003 release. He comments:

I've never heard a recorded version of the song. I found it in a book[4]—possibly *The Ballad Tree*—which shows seven or eight verses [actually eleven], and mentions that it was collected in Cades Cove, in the Appalachians, in the 1930s. The book notates the tune, presumably as sung to the collector, as I don't think any written tunes exist for it, and it seems to have long disappeared from Britain as part of the sung tradition, although some manuscript versions do exist.[5]

At the same time as John Jacob Niles was gathering the traditional songs of his Kentucky home, the young Woody Guthrie was doing much the same, first in Oklahoma, and then in Pampa, Texas, accumulating (and composing) a repertoire that is as much the gold standard of American "folk" music as the Child Ballads are of the British Isles. What he did not collect, or at least seldom record, were any of the Child Ballads that might have leaked into the region. His focus was on songs that spoke directly to or of the American people, and it is for that he is most widely renowned. Two of the ballads did, however, settle into his repertoire; "The Golden Vanity" (286) was included in his July 1941 sessions for General Records; and he recorded it again, as a duet with Cisco Houston, for Asch Records in April 1944. Around the same time, Guthrie also laid down his version of "Gypsy Davy" (200), a song that he learned from his mother, and of which his son Arlo reflected, "I . . . loved my father's ability to take an old song and rewrite it to update the original. 'Seven Little Gypsies' was the song he used for . . . 'Gypsy Davy' and it's not all that different from the original song. However, in the original ballad, the un-named hero gets hung along with his friends for daring to seduce the lady in the lord's home. In my father's version, the lord becomes the 'boss' and the hero ends up with the girl. Times change."[6]

Indeed they do. But in some ways, they remain the same. "The chief attractions of English folk songs," the English composer Benjamin Britten (1913–1976) told the American magazine *Modern Music* in 1941, "are the sweetness of the melodies, the close connection between words and music, and the quiet uneventful charm of the atmosphere. Folk songs are concise and finished little works of art." Britten was explaining why he had taken to deploying folk songs as the intro and outro to concerts he was giving in the US at the time. He and his lifetime partner, pianist Peter Pears, had left their British homeland on the eve of World War Two, morally repulsed by the prospect of the upcoming conflict, basing themselves first in Canada and later New York. Perhaps, then, there was another element to his newfound appreciation for traditional song—he was homesick.

Despite the British embassy advising the couple to remain in America as "artistic ambassadors," Britten and Pears returned to England in 1942. Officially registered now as conscientious objectors, they offered recitals to such organizations as War Relief and the Council for the Encouragement of Music and the Arts. These endeavors, too, brought folk songs into sharp relief, with Britten composing whole new settings for the familiar lyrics, much as Joseph Haydn had 150 years before.

In 1943, he published the first volume of seven folk arrangements, with three further volumes of English and Scottish songs (and two devoted to Ireland and France) following. In between publications, Britten frequently premiered new material as soon as it was completed, with the bulk of his arrangements being composed between 1942 and 1947. He continued to dabble throughout the remainder of his life; the final volume in the series was published shortly before Britten's death in 1976.

It is uncertain where Britten turned for his sources, although tenor vocalist Mark Milhofer declares the aforementioned John Hullah's *The Song Book: Words and Tunes from the Best Poets and Musicians* was certainly among them.[7] For where else, he might have asked, was the discerning ear likely to find so many pieces that, as Hullah declared, "fully answer to the popular idea of a song—a thing, the first condition or qualification of which is that it can be sung." It is surprising, then, to discover just two future Child Ballads within the work. "Barbara Allen" (84) is taken from Percy's *Reliques*, "Oh Waly Waly" (204), is a version that Child ignored and that Hullah took from one of Scottish collector Robert Chambers's publications.

Britten, however, was familiar with several more, with "Oh Waly Waly" joined by "The False Knight upon the Road" (3),"King Herod and the Cock" (55), "Little Sir William" (155), "The Bonny Earl O'Moray" (181), and "Leezie Lindsay" (226) all numbered among his folk arrangements, with "False Knight" clearly drawn from the version Cecil Sharp collected from Mrs. T. G. Coates of Flag Pond, Tennessee, in September 1916. Elsewhere, "The Ballad of Little Musgrave and Lady Barnard" (81) is numbered among his chorale works (1943), and "The Golden Vanity" (286) appeared as a lengthy "Vaudeville for Boys and Piano after The Old English Ballad" (1966).

Multiple recordings of the shorter pieces have been made over the years, most notably the Naxos label's *English Folk Song Series*, with Philip Langridge taking an understated, but nevertheless powerful tenor role. His delivery of "Leezie Lindsay" (226), the tale of a Scots lass being courted by a rich Highland lord, is especially spry. The earliest (and probably the greatest) of these recordings, however, are Britten and Pears's own renditions, the first of which appeared across three shellac discs in 1948. Here, "Little Sir William" (155) and "The Bonny Earl o'Moray" (181) represent England and Scotland in a collection that spreads across the entire British Isles. These shorter arrangements are, as one would expect, impeccably performed and mannered, although the question of how happy any marriage of traditional song and "classical" music can be remains as potent here as it was in Haydn's time.

The longer pieces, however, are considerably more successful in telling their stories as the "original" performers intended. "The Golden Vanity" is especially grandiose, the marriage of playful piano to stamping feet summons up the image of the decks of an old sailing ship as she makes her way toward disaster. Listening to it, it is possible even to forget that the ship is indeed crewed exclusively by schoolboys. Ten minutes of "The Ballad of Little Musgrave," meanwhile, prove as engrossing in the guise of a dark and moody chorale, as any folk or rock performance. The flight of Lord Barnard's servant to alert his master to the Lady's infidelity is a frantic helter-skelter; the murderous finale is as mournful as it is gore strewn.

Like John Jacob Niles, Britten was a major influence upon the US music scene of this period. However, if any single figure can be said to encapsulate the development of popular American traditional music as the postwar era got underway, it was Burl Ives (1909–1995).

Born in Hunt City, Illinois, Ives was the son of a gardener and one of six children, siblings whom the young Burl would often entertain with his singing. He learned his first tunes at the elbow of his clay pipe–smoking grandmother Kate White, and allowed his enthusiasm further rein from there. "Sometimes she would sing for hours," Ives remembered. "She would sing 'Barbara Allen' [84], 'Pearl Brian,' 'The Riddle Song' [46] and many other ballads in an easy, flowing style." But she only sang when her husband was out working in the fields, "because he forbade her to sing them. He said they were sinful songs, songs about killing and about unfaithful love. . . . Man should use his voice only to sing in praise to God." To her grandson, contrarily, they represented "excitement and color . . . pictures, romance, passion, bravery, gallantry, sorrow, joy."[8]

Although it's unlikely Ives thought of himself as a collector, he became one, encouraging older neighbors and their friends to sing him songs, and learning those he fell in love with. "The Devil's Nine Questions" (1) was one such; Ives was partial to a version he heard somewhere, originally collected in Virginia in 1922, titled "Ninety-Nine and Ninety." Close to seventy years later, singer Jeff Welsey recorded this same version on the cassette album *Brisk and Bonny Lad*, and it is clear why Ives found it so appealing.

One day, out in the garden with his mother, Ives was singing as he so often did, when a passing uncle, Ira Vance, overheard him. Vance stopped to listen for a time, and then invited the youngster to sing at an old soldiers reunion that was taking place in town. Ives agreed and, on the night, blew the audience away with the "Barbara Allen" (84) he had learned from grandma. He had been promised 50 cents for his performance; in fact, Uncle Ira was so thrilled by the performance that he doubled the boy's payment. Ives spent his earnings on hot dogs, lemonade, and a bunch of rides on a nearby merry-go-round.

As a youth, Ives's ambition was to become a teacher and, in 1927, he was accepted into Eastern State Teacher's College. Less than two years later he dropped out. Seated in a lecture on the great Anglo-Saxon poem *Beowulf*, he suddenly realized he had absolutely no interest in either the subject or, indeed, college. He rose and walked out of the room, breaking the window on the door as he slammed it, and never returned, at least as a pupil. In April 1990, however, the now eighty-year-old Ives had a school building named after him.

His mind now set on a career as a singer, Ives was granted an audition by Gennett Records in Richmond, Indiana, in July 1929. He sang "Behind the Clouds," but clearly did not do it very well—he was rejected, and the trial recording made that day was apparently destroyed a short time after. Unperturbed, Ives took to the road, living on whatever he could earn from part-time jobs and his musical abilities (he accompanied himself on banjo), following the hobo lifestyle of riding the trains, singing for his supper, and occasionally enduring a night in a jail cell after being picked up for vagrancy. Nevertheless, by 1931, he had secured an occasional residency at WBOW Radio in Terre Haute, Indiana, a fifteen-minute slot titled *The Wayfaring Stranger* and starring "The Blond Tenor with His Guitar." He was one of just three singers to hold down such a position, alongside "The Melody Lad" Claude Fitzsimmons, and "The Matinee Songster" Harry Frey.

Settling now, Ives returned to full-time education at Indiana State Teachers College before, in 1933, moving to New York City. There, however, his attempts to introduce his old songs and ballads into metropolitan life were met with constant rejection and scorn. Even Ives's girlfriend complained "nobody wants to hear those old moss-grown tunes," while an NYU professor Ives was hoping might take him under his wing was even more disdainful. "We don't want any of that stuff around here." Prior to coming to New York, this professor was music supervisor at a Midwestern school, and he complained, "all those hillbillies wanted to do was pick guitars and sing through their nose." It had taken the professor seven years, he told Ives, before he was finally able to get "some nice choirs together to sing Brahms and the classics." Ives responded, "Sir, you have missed the whole point of music," and stomped back to his room, where he consoled himself by singing the songs he loved to himself: "Barbara Allen," "The Riddle Song" (46), "Lord Thomas and Fair Eleanor" (73), and so forth.[9]

Ives would, in the end, locate a teacher who wanted to hear him sing *his* songs, and not attempt to make his way through the classics and popular favorites of the day. "I sang 'Lord Thomas and Fair Eleanor.' I watched her face. What a joy to sing these songs for her. I sang and sang and sang. Her next student arrived and became part of my audience [and] she said when I finished 'The minstrels of old must have sung that way.' No man ever received greater praise."[10]

Slowly his career took off. Ives made his Broadway debut in 1938, in Rodgers and Hart's *The Boys from Syracuse*, and the following year he moved to Hollywood. A year after that, he was hosting his own radio show on CBS, again titled *The Wayfaring Stranger*. The earliest surviving recording of Ives performing a Child Ballad, several of which were in his repertoire at the time, is presumably from his own show, a 1940 radio broadcast of "Lord Randall" (12). It's a very straightforward rendering, but the Ives voice is unmistakable, and he injects such excitement into both his playing and the lyric that few listeners could fail to have been touched.

Over the next two years, until he was drafted into the US Army, Ives made a number of guest appearances on other radio shows, including an August 1940 spot on *Columbia Presents Forecast*, a popular show previewing new radio dramas and comedies, with musical interludes. Woody Guthrie was among the guests that day, and soon Ives would be alongside Guthrie, Pete Seeger, and others in the earliest incarnations of the radical folk group, the Almanac Singers.

Ives also cut his first album for Okeh, four discs featuring twelve songs familiar from his radio show. Included was "The Riddle Song"—Ives introduces it as "a song from down Kentucky way, sometimes called 'I Gave My Love a Cherry,'" but it is familiar too as that so-treacly corruption of Child 46 that Child himself noted but did not comment upon. (In which regard, we will follow his inclination. Not for nothing was a performance of the same ballad, in the 1978 movie *National Lampoon's Animal House*, curtailed by a toga-clad John Belushi breaking the hapless singer's guitar against the wall.)

Ives's second album, recorded for Moses Asch, was also titled *The Wayfaring Stranger* and featured the nineteenth-century broadside "The Foggy Foggy Dew"—a number that once landed him in jail in Utah during his traveling days, for the crime of performing "bawdy songs." He also tackled "Henry Martin (Pirate Ballad)" (250), a marathon composition in *ESPB*, where Child includes four versions of between 64 and 82 verses. Ives's version, adapted from one he unearthed in Cecil Sharp's writings, is, needless to say, considerably shorter.

In truth, Ives's recordings of the Child Ballads—and traditional song in general—hold little interest to serious folklorists. There are certainly some terrific performances in his repertoire, including a suitably raucous "What Shall We Do with a Drunken Sailor," and there is no doubting his love of the music. But, in keeping with his reputation as an all-round entertainer, ubiquitous on TV and film alike, he approaches them very much from a "light entertainment" direction. Ives's earliest discs really are little more than showcases for his voice—certainly the "Cockleshells" (204) that graced 1945's *A Collection of Ballads and Folk Songs* passes by almost unnoticed (although that might also have something to do with its brevity; it clocks in at just ninety-one seconds). Grandmother Katy's

"The Devil's Nine Questions" on 1948's *Ballads and Folk Songs, Volume II* is similarly bland; Ives even reduces the usually so uproarious "The Divil and the Farmer" (278), from 1949's *The Return of the Wayfaring Stranger* to little more than a pleasant meander.

At the same time, however, for artists of a certain generation, the presence of Burl Ives in their parents' record collection was as likely to act as a gateway to traditional music as anything else. Canadian singer Maura Volante, Australian Raymond Crooke, and German-Canadian Rika Ruebsaat all credit their childhood exposure to Ives's music with kickstarting their interest in folk, with Crooke recalling, "One of the first songs I ever learned to sing was 'Barbara Allen'," from one of his parents' Burl Ives albums. "I used to act it out with my brothers and sisters and later in my early teens I made a film of it, again with my brothers and sisters, with my father's Super 8 camera. It was only later that I knew it was a Child Ballad."[11]

In more recent times, Ives's "The Turkish Revery" (286) on 1959's *Ballads with Guitar* album, inspired the band The Outside Track to record the same song a full fifty years later, with vocalist Norah Rendell learning it from guitarist/singer Dáithí Sproule, who in turn found the song (and album)—where else?—in his mother's record collection. Indeed, any criticism of Ives's style or approach is by definition harsh. He worked within the dictates of the music industry of the age, and his own status as a star of that industry. Besides, like so many traditional performers, Ives's true forte was live performance.

Returning to "The Divil and the Farmer," that same song opens the *Coronation Concert* live album, recorded at London's Royal Festival Hall on May 28, 1953, in very different temperament to its studio counterpart. Ives's introduction is brief. "A number of people have asked me to repeat this one song that I did in my last concert here; it's an old Irish song, the story of the devil who comes up to the earth and takes a farmer's wife down below. And she causes so much trouble that the old boy has to bring her back." A jaunty guitar, an Irish accent, and an appreciative audience laughing in all the right places gives us a taste of why Ives so readily came to dominate the popular American folk scene of the age. "Henry Martin" (250) and "Waly Waly" (204) also appear during the show, and both likewise erase all memory of Ives's overly mannered studio versions.

Altogether, Ives recorded around a dozen Child Ballads throughout his long recording career. And though some people might scorn his versions, his success went a long way toward opening other ears to the potential of traditional song.

Chapter Seventeen

A NOVA SCOTIAN SONGBOOK

In 1898, folklorist Phillips Barry—coauthor thirty years later of the afore-mentioned *British Ballads from Maine*—published what is believed to be the first traditional song ever "collected" in Canada, "The Gypsie Lad-die" (200) that he heard being sung in Nova Scotia. His discovery marks the start of what has, over the ensuing 125 years, proved simultaneously to be a surprisingly fruitful, and a disappointingly underappreciated, investigation into the musical history of the nation. An investigation that also offers up one of the earliest examples of a Child Ballad having taken hold in the Black tradition (performed by William Riley), and birthed the first indigenous singer to have performed Anglo-American folk songs to a major audience, the Piapot-Cree Buffy Sainte-Marie.

That the theme should be so overlooked is, says folklorist Ranald Thur-good, a consequence of Canada's own cultural history.

[Although] we are a multiethnic and multilingual country, we have a long history of being influenced by both British and American (cultural, financial) colonialism, and often look outward for "culture" and "entertainment."

I think Canadians, as a group, have less interest in our collective folk heritage than people in almost any other country. Many Canadians tell of traveling and, when others are singing their folk songs, having nothing to contribute.

We are also coming to grips with the fact that Canada itself is a colonial power, ruling over most of the northern part of the North American conti-nent, and ruling the peoples already living there. We have surprisingly few people who listen to Canadian folk songs in the "traditional" sense. It would be very hard to find songs that most Canadians would accept as part of our folk heritage.[1]

Regardless, there were early students. Entranced by his native soil's isolation and entranced by its then-sparse beauty, W. Roy MacKenzie, author of 1928's *Ballads and Sea Songs from Nova Scotia*, commenced collecting around 1910. Names such as F. W. Waugh, W. J. Wintemberg, and the Quebec-based Marius Barbeau contributed further to the slowly growing canon. So did a local cod liver oil magnate named Gerald Doyle, the publisher of *Old-Time Songs and Poetry of Newfoundland*.

British Ballads from Maine, despite its title, nevertheless included some thirty Child Ballads that were excavated from across the northern border, largely in New Brunswick, but it was Maud Karpeles's maiden expedition to Newfoundland that truly kickstarted Canadian collecting. She returned home with twenty-four Child variants (Mackenzie gathered nineteen), and there were few surprises among them. Across the entire scope of Canadian collecting, "Barbara Allen" (84) is as omnipotent north of the border as it is south; "Lady Isabel and the Elf-Knight" (4), "Lord Randal" (12), "The Cruel Mother" (20), "Little Musgrave and Lady Barnard" (81), "The Gypsy Laddie" (200), and "The Farmer's Curst Wife" (278) are close behind. It is within the variations upon each that we discover that, no less than in the Appalachians, the ballads had no objections whatsoever to adapting to their new home. Indeed, throughout the first half (and more) of the twentieth century, the Montreal based farming weekly *Family Herald* regularly published Child Ballad texts in its "Old Favourites" column, usually in response to reader's requests.

In 1950, University of Pennsylvania professor MacEdward Leach (1897–1967) followed in Karpeles's footsteps to Newfoundland (and also Cape Breton), returning with some 585 songs, and a total of forty-one hours of field recordings—the first ever made in that region. Many of them were locally specific, pieces such as "The Towering Heights of Newfoundland" and "Newfoundland Hornpipe"; there were songs of the sea, of wrecks and tragedies, and, as Karpeles discovered, a wealth of Irish survivors. (The Cape Breton leg of the journey afforded around eighty Gaelic performances.) W. Roy Mackenzie speculated on why that should be, finally determining that "there came a time when the Scottish Protestants put aside their old ballads as fit only for the ungodly, preferr[ing] hymns to worldly songs. Fortunately, the Catholics had no such prejudices."[2]

Leach also retrieved a handful of Child Ballads, with several especially notable for their deployment of melodies that had rarely, if ever, been encountered elsewhere: Gerald Aylward's 5/4 time rendition of "Barbara Allen" (84), the singer sounding far older than his thirty-three years, and a similarly distinctive "The Golden Vanity" (286), intoned by James Maher—who also offered up a firsthand tale of hearing fairy voices while at sea, off Seal Cove. From the fabulously named Raymond Noseworthy, a resident of Pouch Cove, there came a fine "Lord Bateman" (53); and from Din Dobbin of St Vincent's, a "Matty Grove" (81) that he precedes by warning, "I'm sort of hoarse today."

"That doesn't make any difference," responds Leach, and so Dobbin launches into one of the most detailed accounts of precisely what happened, that fateful day when Lady Daniel took young Matty Groves to her marital bed—including the seldom-sung moments that could have saved both of their lives:

> *Young Groves he had not been asleep*
> *These words to her did say*
> *I think I hear Lord Donald's horn*
> *I think I hear it say*
> *Anyone that's in bed with another man's wife*
> *Its time they be jogging away oh*
> *Its time they be jogging away*

Lord Donald's wife, however, informs him that he is mistaken.

> *Come huddle me come cuddle me*
> *Just keep me from the cold*
> *For that is my father's shepherd she said*
> *And he driving his sheeps to fold*
> *And he driving his sheeps to fold*

The inevitable then unfolds.

> *He huddled and he cuddled her the two fell fast asleep*
> *And when they awoke to their great surprise*
> *Lord Donald stood at their feet*
> *Oh Lord Donald stood at their feet*

First Matty is killed, and then Lady Donald, but here we are privy to another uncommon development, as her husband is punished for his misdeeds.

> *The bells of Scotland ring tonight*
> *They always ring for sorrow*
> *Lord Donald killed young Groves and his wife*
> *And he'll be hung tomorrow*

Nor would Karpeles and Leach exhaust the area's capacity for delight. Newfoundlander Anita Best's 1997 album *Cross-Handed* was comprised wholly of songs that she had collected from the region. On it she offered up ballads in both Irish Gaelic and French, as well as English, opening the set with a "Lord Bateman" (53) that she learned in 1973 from Kate Wilson, the near-eighty-year-old daughter of a Fox Harbour fisherman and,

Ketch Harbor Store; Donald Gallagher with guitar, Helen Creighton recording. Courtesy Nova Scotia Archives

according to Best, "one of the few [local] women" who took an active part in the town's "Paddy's day concerts."[3]

Helen Creighton (1899–1989) was another assiduous explorer who gathered some four thousand songs during her lifetime, including thirty-three titled Child Ballads in around two hundred different performances, for the most part collected around her native Nova Scotia, but also in New Brunswick and Prince Edward Island. These included a "Cruel Mother" (20) set to "one of the best tunes ever taken down [for it]," from a Mrs. John Smith; "The Famous Flower of Serving Men" (106) from Mrs. Duncan, resident in the white-cottaged fishing village of South East Passage ("a rare and definite discovery"); and an unexpected "Bold Pedlar and Robin Hood" (132) from Catherine Gallagher, whose husband operated the lighthouse at Chebucto Head.

There was also a remarkable rendering of what Creighton described as "that most popular of all ancient ballads here, 'Bonny Barbara Allen'" (84), sung by Ada Tanner from the island of Black Rocks. The emotional impact of the rendering was, however, somewhat offset when, "no sooner [had] the rose and briar entwined above the [lovers'] graves than [Ada] looked at me and . . . remarked, 'You got fat legs, ain't it?'"[4]

But the Child Ballads were responsible, too, for moments of staggering poignancy. Creighton never tired of recalling the day in 1940 when she stood on Halifax Harbor with Catherine Gallagher, watching as a sea fog rolled in. Suddenly, they became aware of a navy convoy departing for a perilous voyage across the U-Boat-infested North Atlantic. As the vessels' masts became visible above the banks of fog, Mrs. Gallagher suddenly struck up a soft "The Bonny House of Airlie" (199), the tale of a long-ago raid, a ghostly accompaniment to what was already an eerie sight.

From her home in Dartmouth (now part of the Halifax Regional Municipality, but proudly separate during Helen's lifetime), Creighton initially embarked upon a career in broadcasting, as children's storyteller Aunt Helen. In 1928, however, her long-standing interest in folklore was given fresh impetus by the publication of MacKenzie's *Sea Songs and Ballads from Nova Scotia*. Acting upon the suggestion of Dr. Henry Munro, the superintendent of education for the province of Nova Scotia, Creighton set out to add to MacKenzie's work, often in the company of Doreen Senior of the English Folk and Dance Society, aboard a touring car they named Cecil, after the redoubtable Mr Sharp.[5]

One especially enjoyable anecdote that has grown up around Creighton is that she occasionally accompanied her singers on a melodeon that she pushed around in a wheelbarrow—at least until it encountered one bump too many and wheezed its last. Sadly, her friend, biographer and archivist Clary Croft reports, "This almost never happened, and the famous image of Helen with a wheelbarrow carrying the melodeon occurred only a couple of times."[6]

From 1938, Creighton and Senior also oversaw a weekly half-hour show on CBC radio, which featured regular appearances from several of her Nova Scotian discoveries, alongside a professional male quartet. Each singer received $10 per broadcast, and Creighton set out the show's parameters very early on, kicking off the maiden episode with "The Bold Pedlar and Robin Hood" (132), performed by the most loquacious of her sources, Ben Henneberry, the coxswain of the sole lifeboat stationed on the sparse and desolate Devil's Island, at the mouth of Halifax Harbor. Just seventeen houses dotted the rock, and three of those were empty. The first version of the ballad ever to be published in North America, "The Bold Pedlar and Robin Hood" was one of nine Child Ballads in Henneberry's repertoire. It was also, as Creighton noted in her autobiography, "a long one and difficult to sing," but was chosen for the radio show because "it gave an immediate impression of antiquity combined with a beautiful modal tune."[7] Interestingly, the same ballad was also known to Catherine Gallagher.

Nova Scotia remained Creighton's focus. While she did later visit neighboring New Brunswick and Prince Edward Island, she was aware that another collector, fellow broadcaster and folk song enthusiast Louise Manny (1890–1970), was also operating in that area, and broadcasting many of her discoveries on her weekly CKMR radio show.

Creighton also worked with Alan Lomax, at whose suggestion she began regularly employing a recording machine. According to Clary Croft, "she used a wax cylinder machine in 1933 with limited success, but I cataloged a couple in her collection at the archives." Lomax would feature four of her finds, including Daughter Smith's "Cruel Mother," (20) on the Canada volume of the Columbia World Library of Folk and Primitive Music. She also retained fond memories of meeting John Jacob Niles during her days at the Institute of Folklore, at Indiana University. He was a guest lecturer, illustrating his talks "with the beauty of his music," and then interrupting himself to call across to her, "Ma'am, have you anything like *that* in Nova Scotia?"

Creighton herself published a number of books, commencing with 1932's *Songs and Ballads from Nova Scotia*, a splendidly decorated volume that became a staple for libraries and college course work, and that still stands out on any bookshelf of ballad collections. It was followed by volumes devoted to Lunenburg County, Gaelic, French Acadian, and Maritime folk songs, and even a book of the regional ghost stories that she also collected on her travels, *Bluenose Ghosts*. It is recommended reading for anyone who enjoys a chill with their balladeering.

Eleven Child Ballads were included in *Song and Ballads*, plus four more that were clearly derived from them, and Ben Henneberry's repertoire dominated. It was he who provided Creighton with her second Robin Hood ballad, albeit a mere fraction of "Robin Hood's Progress to Nottingham" (139), and a "Cruel Mother" (20) that is not simply longer than almost any other known version, it also—like the "Little Matty Groves" (81) that so enamored MacEdward Leach—feels a lot more complete. For in this version, once the mother has slain her children, the little rascals not only return to haunt her, but she is also saddled with that most Shakespearean of curses, a blood-soaked murder weapon that cannot be cleaned, and cannot be discarded, either.

> *She stuck her penknife in the green*
> *All alone and a-loney*
> *The more she rubbed the blood was seen*
> *Down by the Greenwood siding.*

> *Then she threw it far away*
> *All alone and a-loney*
> *The farther she threw it the nearer it came*
> *Down by the Greenwood siding.*

Another gem was "The Golden Vanity" (286), sung by another South-East Passager, Richard Hartlan, and differing from most known verses in the nature of the enemy vessel. Usually, it was the Turk, the Spaniard, or the Frenchman who were the foe. In this recitation, it was the "Roosian," prompting Creighton to wonder whether this particular version was being sung while Britain (and, therefore, the rest of her empire) was fighting the Crimean War of 1853–1856.

The sheer vastness and endless fascination of Creighton's collection is not, sadly, reflected in the number of artists drawing from its depths. In 1975, Creighton herself reflected that, "in concert and on professional records, our songs have been most widely sung by Alan Mills and Ed McCurdy."[8] The latter, in fact, would often mention her by name during performances and broadcasts, introducing songs as being from "Helen Creighton's fine collection." Mills, who recorded a stream of Canadian-themed albums for Folkways during the early 1950s, devoted one wholly to the *Folk Songs of Newfoundland*.[9]

In more recent times, attempts to popularize the Creighton collection have seen the Helen Creighton Folklore Society release several CDs of her work. *Songs of the Sea*, with four Child Ballads among the first half dozen tracks, is an especially enjoyable collection, expanding as it does Creighton's own 1962 Folkways album, *Maritime Folk Songs*. There we find a "Lord Bateman" (53) performed in September 1950 by David Slauenwhite of Terence Bay, and an intriguing note from Creighton herself, explaining, "You will notice that the singer speaks the last word. This is customary among the older generation and means that the song is over."[10] (This is also apparent from the MacEdward Leach collection.) Creighton's biographer Clary Croft also recorded a number of her discoveries, several Child Ballads among them, on his 1986 album *False Knight on the Road*.

Another fascinating facet of the Creighton collection is its focus on Black Nova Scotians, a field to which she was alerted in 1943, when she heard the songs sung by the wards of The Nova Scotia Home for Coloured Children. In the town of Cherry Brook, she was introduced to the singer William Riley, who initially sang her the southern antislavery song "No More Auction Block for Me." However, she also recorded him performing several other songs, both solo and with his daughter Rose Mann, among them the Child Ballad "The Cherry Tree Carol" (54). It is a brief (seventy-one seconds) performance but was finally released in 1997 on a two-CD collection produced by the CBC and the Black Cultural Centre of Nova Scotia, *Lord You Brought Me a Mighty Long Way: An African Nova Scotian Musical Journey*. Fully one-half of the set was drawn from Creighton's collection.[11]

Folklorist Ranald Thurgood explains, "Creighton wrote a memoir, *A Life in Folklore*. It's a good read. She was a working woman, a journalist who began collecting as part of her work. She originally collected just about everything, but was influenced by the folklorists and scholars of her day to focus on the British canon (Child Ballads, British broadsides). She was then criticized by later folklorists and scholars for this conservative focus." She was, he continues, also "disappointed by how the popular Canadian show *Singalong Jubilee*, broadcast from Halifax, focused on American folk-song revival music and largely disregarded her collection, though Catherine MacKinnon's singing of 'Farewell to Nova Scotia,' collected by Creighton, on the show, popularized that song."[12] Nevertheless, it must have been infuriating for her that neither Buffy Sainte-Marie nor Ian and Sylvia, Canada's biggest exports during the early 1960s folk revival, looked toward their homeland's repository of traditional songs when delving into those waters.

Problematic, too, is the fact that Creighton's field recordings were, for many years, accessible only to academia—the task of digitizing the collection for public access was just coming to an end in mid-2022. Ranald Thurgood points out, "Field recordings are another common source of folk songs. Baez, Dylan, [Jerry] Garcia, and many others were learning songs and tunes from Folkways recordings, including *The Anthology of American Folk Music*. I think commercially available field recordings may be important in getting songs out to singers who can't read music. Record companies made albums of Helen Creighton's field recordings, but only real folk-song nerds find these."

Creighton passed away in December 1989. Her friend Clary Croft was among her final visitors, and recalls standing beside her to offer her one final gift. Holding her hand, "I sang 'The Cherry Tree Carol,' the beautiful song that she had first collected from William Riley many years before. She didn't even know I was there. There again, perhaps she did. It didn't matter. I knew."[13]

Chapter Eighteen

A CANADIAN CACHÉ

Despite the paucity of acknowledgment throughout her lifetime, Helen Creighton's work has since inspired a number of other artists to revisit her discoveries. Nova Scotia singer Blue Lobelia (Rachel Bruch)'s 2021 release *Folk Songs and Broadside Ballads from the Helen Creighton Collection* includes several of her Child Ballads, among them, a foreboding vision of "The Cruel Mother" (20), a menacingly fiddle-led "Geordie" (209), and the ubiquitous "I Will Give My Love an Apple" (46). Canadian singer Maura Volante is another to delve into the Creighton archive.

> I grew up in Scarborough, a suburb of Toronto. My parents had albums by the Clancy Brothers, Burl Ives, Harry Belafonte, Paul Robeson and a few others who did folk songs, so I kind of grew up with folk music, though nothing Canadian at that time. In my teens I was a fan of some Canadian singers and some of them (Ian and Sylvia, Buffy Sainte-Marie and Bonnie Dobson) included some traditional songs. I was mostly aware of the Americans: Joan Baez, Judy Collins, Pete Seeger, and the great plethora of singer-songwriters that were inspired by folk songs but only sang their own songs.[1]

It was a chance encounter with the non-Child "A Maid I Am in Love," sung to Creighton by a Mrs. Stan Marshall, that truly turned Volante's head. "I was riveted by the sound. The recording quality was poor, and the voice was not in its prime, but the simplicity of the style conveyed the meaning of the words better than any complex arrangement could. The lesson for me was to let the song take precedence over the singer." Ben Henneberry's "Well Sold the Cow," a variant on "The Crafty Farmer" (283), was included on Volante's 2022 album *Safe and Sound: Traditional Canadian Folk Songs*, with the singer explaining, "I chose the Child Ballads already in my repertoire that no one else had recorded to modern engineering standards. Some of the songs are on Folkways albums that are available to purchase. But these old recordings are mostly field recordings."[2]

More of Volante's material was drawn from the archive of one of Creighton's proteges (and Volante's tutor in Ballads and Folk Songs at York University), the Canadian broadcaster Edith Fulton Fowke (1913–1996). The author of 1954's *Folk Songs of Canada* (and a companion LP of the same name, by Joyce Sullivan and Charles Jordan), Fowke oversaw a number of folk-related radio specials for CBC. Beginning in 1956, she also made a remarkably fruitful study of Ontario Province and, despite remarking that few of the ballads that came to Canada with settlers from the British Isles have survived ("the greatest treasure trove is found in small villages of Newfoundland and Nova Scotia, where farmers and fisher folk have preserved [them]"),[3] she gathered some sixteen Child Ballads in Ontario, including a version of Child 4, titled "The Dapple Gray," and a "Little Musgrave" (81) in which the titular character is now "Lord *Banner*'s Wife." Her first expedition saw her collect some four hundred songs; altogether, it is estimated that she made around two thousand field recordings throughout her most active years in the field.

Another of Fowke's discoveries was the singer LaRena Clark, whose 1965 album *A Canadian Garland: Folksongs from the Province of Ontario* includes her versions of four Child Ballads. More still reside in the Fowke Collection, a resource that, like Creighton's, has lain strangely, and sadly, untapped in recent years, despite containing some uniquely Canadian variations. Maura Volante explains,

> Most English-speaking Canadians have no idea about traditional folk songs and their place in Canadian history and culture. Most recorded sources of Child Ballads are British and American, so that is where anyone learning songs tends to look. Only the dedicated folk nerds think to find the field collections of Fowke and Creighton, and even among those who might be interested in looking at books, access is very limited. Most of the books are out of print. Even the *Penguin Book of Canadian Folk Songs*, Fowke's most accessible and internationally available book, has been out of print and unavailable for decades.[4]

Geography, and the sheer size of the country, too, plays a part. Ranald Thurgood adds, "Most collecting has been done in eastern Canada (Newfoundland to South Ontario), so we may have a lopsided view of how widespread singing traditions were in Canada. Other regions may have been rich in folk song, but we'll never know."[5] (The handful of Child Ballads retrieved from Acadian Canada are generally assumed to be translations from English to French, as opposed to survivors of the French balladic tradition. Child certainly notes no French versions of them.)

It was Edith Fowke who became the first to place a song drawn from the Creighton Collection on vinyl, when a reading of "The Farmer's Curst Wife" (278), uniquely set in Nova Scotia, was included on the *Songs of Canada* album. It was accompanied by "The False Young Man" (68), which Fowke's liner notes describe as "a complaint about the faithlessness of men . . . from a small Irish community on the Gatineau River north of Ontario." Fowke also oversaw an album of songs from the traditional singer, O. J. Abbott, *Irish and British Songs from the Ottawa Valley*, its contents drawn from the eighty-plus songs she recorded from him over a five-day span during the summer of 1957. The pair met through Abbott's daughter Ida, who wrote to Fowke at the CBC; "She told me that her father knew a great many old songs, so I wrote back asking for the names of some of them. When I saw the list, I realized that he had a real treasure trove of traditional songs and decided to record them as soon as I could."[6] There were few Child Ballads in Abbott's repertoire, but the album (which was released in 1961 by Folkways) did include one, "The Gypsy Daisy"—a version of Child 200, Fowke wrote in the liner notes, that "is fairly rare, although it has been found in Nova Scotia. Mr. Abbott learned it from Mr. O'Malley."

These releases aside, Fowke would wait until 1975 before her own collecting was celebrated on record with the release of *Far Canadian Fields*, a companion to her *Penguin Book of Canadian Folk Songs*. From that set, Calumet resident Eva Bigrow's rendering of "Willie Drowned in Ero" immediately became the basis for Scottish-Canadian singer Margaret Christl and Ian Robb's recording that same year. Their album, *The Barley Grain for Me*, was also dedicated to Fowke, who in fact introduced the duo to the album's producer, Sandy Paton. Louis and Sally Killen also recorded this variant of the ballad that Child knew as "Rare Willie Drowned in Yarrow" in 1976, and Jon Bartlett and Rika Ruebsaat followed suit in 1979.

The popularity of this version raises an intriguing point. Child published eight copies of the ballad: three in which Willie drowns in the River Yarrow, close by Sir Walter Scott's home town of Abbotsford; five in which the action takes place farther north in Gamery, on the Moray Firth. The Ero of which Bigrow sings, on the other hand, appears to be wholly fictional, yet the title has found at least a modicum of favor among singers whereas the Gamery variant remains wholly unrecorded.

Ranald Thurgood suggests, "It seems most likely to me that 'Ero' is simply a misinterpretation of 'Yarrow,' especially as your average Canadian has never heard of the Yarrow River. As well, I don't know if the spelling of Ero came from Eva Bigrow, the song's source, or from Edith Fowke, the collector, or whether Ero should be pronounced as 'arrow' or as a rhyme to 'hero.' I've heard Canadians sing it both ways (all versions returning to Bigrow)."[7]

Fowke's academic leanings were certainly influential upon those who studied under her. Maura Volante recalls,

> Her Ballads and Folk Songs course . . . was my first education in the distinctions between traditional folk songs and modern folk songs of our time, as well as an introduction to Child and the various other forms of folk songs. (Broadsides, sea songs, lyric laments, work songs, etc.) She was sixty-eight when I met her, prim and proper, soft-spoken and analytical. She taught in the English department, and her focus was always the words. Mostly we did text study of the songs. She was certainly biased towards the Child Ballads and showed us some of the characteristics of the different kinds of ballads as well as the other types of folk songs.[8]

Ranald Thurgood first met Fowke at the Mariposa Folk Festival during the mid-1970s, and also studied beneath her.

> Her lecturing was sometimes very dry—Edith was not given to theatrics— and her course seemed tedious for those looking for nothing more than a little variety in their English programs. However, for those of us with a real interest in folksong, Edith's class was an Aladdin's cave with its own tour guide. [She] conveyed to her students the love of ballads and folksongs in their traditional forms and an appreciation of the singers. By her use of tapes [from her own collection] and accompanying comments, she was able to communicate the aesthetic qualities of traditional singing.[9]

He rounded out his portrait by recalling a side of her that, sadly, many people may not have been aware of: "In spite of her appearance as a dear old lady, Edith . . . was a feisty woman who enjoyed a smoke, a drink, and an off-color song."[10] In fact, at the time of her death, Fowke was putting the finishing touches to a new book, *Bawdy Songs from Ontario and Newfoundland*, written with American folklorist Kenneth S. Goldstein, until his passing just a few months earlier.

Thurgood, too, acknowledges the importance of Fowke's work. "I've learned songs from *Far Canadian Fields*, which [also] includes 'Seven Gypsies on Yon Hill" (200). I also learned 'I Came Home Drunk' (274), from Edith's tapes in the York University library, but only seriously disturbed folk-song nerds go that far."[11]

Maura Volante's album is perhaps the work of one such. *Safe and Sound* included no less than three of LaRena Clark's offerings to Fowke: "The Dapple Grey" (4), "Gypsy Davy" (200), and "The Golden Vanity" (286). Volante also revisits a Sandy Ives discovery, "The Beggar Man" (17), which he heard from Edmund Doucette of Prince Edward Isle; and "Bonnie Banks of Virgie-O"[12] (14), as sung to collector and classical composer Kenneth Peacock (1922–2000) by a Mr. and Mrs. Monks. (Another prime Peacock discovery, "Sweet William's Ghost" [77], was one of five Child

Moira Cameron, 2017. Photo by Michael Nabert

Ballads recorded by Bill Shute and D.C.-based singer, collector, and academic Lisa Null on their 1977 album *The Feathered Maiden and Other Ballads*.)[13]

Fowke was also an influence on Toronto-born singer Moira Cameron, through the older woman's friendship with Cameron's father, Scots-born but Ontario-raised folk singer Stewart Cameron (1947–1989). "Edith was a big fan of my father's, and always made sure to see him perform if they happened to be at the same musical event," Cameron recalls.

I don't know when they first met, but I believe one of the first times they connected was at some sort of workshop or educational setting in which Edith talked about ballads she had collected, and had my father "demonstrate" them. The last encounter they had was the one that sticks in my mind the most. It was a Mariposa festival in 1987 or '88, when it was held at Molson Park in Barry. My family was living in Sudbury at the time, and we had formed a Mummer's Troupe called Mums the Word. We were hired to perform at the festival, and since we were there, they had my father perform as a solo singer in a couple of festival workshops. Edith was in the audience, coming specifically to hear my father. He was sharing the stage with a few other performers including Paul Morris, who invited me up on stage to sing a loud and raucous music hall song about a Salvation Army band. Unbeknownst to me (someone told me this after I got up off the stage), each time the rollicking chorus came along in my song, Edith stuck her fingers in her ears quite unashamedly.[14]

Moira learned many of her first songs from her father—"he was a stay-at-home dad. He practiced his ballads daily, and I learned them by osmosis even before I could talk, and certainly long before I understood the words."

In fact, she made her stage debut at the age of just three, performing "Bonny Susy Cleland" (65) ("an ancient Scottish ballad," she explains on her website) on stage at the Fiddler's Green Folk Club in Toronto.

> My father became a member of the Toronto folk group, Friends of Fiddler's Green. He also sang duet with Margaret Christl, and performed with her and the Friends and as a solo performer regularly. Every Friday until I was five years old, we went to the Fiddler's Green folk club in Toronto where I heard my father perform, as well as other great balladeers like Louis Killen, Frankie Armstrong, John Roberts and Tony Barrand, Peggy Seeger, Eric Bogle—the list goes on and on. It was at one of those Fiddler's Green nights, during a break between guest sets when everyone had gotten up to get refreshments, I crawled up on stage, grabbed the nearest mic, and began singing (with a lisp), my father's rendition of "Bonny Susy Cleland." To this day, I wish I knew which version that was.

Cameron's official debut at the club followed when she was eight, by which time "I had actually developed a consciousness about ballads." She performed three songs, two duets with her father and a "Pretty Polly" (4) that she learned from a Peggy Seeger album (probably the second of Seeger and Ewan MacColl's *The Long Harvest* collections).

Margaret Christl was another influence. Cameron recalls her excitement upon hearing her second album, 1978's *Jockey to the Fair*: "She had recorded a Canadian version of Child #14, 'Banks of Airdrie-O.' I learned it instantly, and when I saw her at that summer's Mariposa, I pulled her to the side and insisted she listen to me singing the ballad back to her."

By the 1980s, Cameron was regularly performing semi-professionally around Sudbury and Toronto, before moving to Yellowknife, in 1990. Her debut album *One Evening as I Rambled* followed in 1991. Partially funded with a Northwest Territories Arts Council Grant, it introduced her largely a cappella approach to the *ESPB*, with a wonderfully echo-soaked "Outlandish Knight" (4) and that Christl-inspired "Banks of Airdrie-O," alongside a spoken-word folk tale and much more. "My father practiced many songs over and over again in preparation for performances, and then didn't really sing them again–like 'Bonny Susy Cleland.' But there were several he came back to again and again, too many to list, but quite a few of his ballads I recorded on my albums. 'Jock O Hazeldean' [293—from Cameron's 1997 sophomore album *Lillies among the Bushes*], for instance, was one he initially sang solo, and then we sang as a duet."[15]

Lillies among the Bushes and 2007's *Sands of the Shore* both lean heavily toward the Child Ballads, between them featuring sixteen of the professor's choices, both the well-known—"The Elfin Knight" (2), "Barbara Allen" (84), "Lamkin" (93), "Willie O'Winsbury" (100), "The Demon Lover" (243), "Jock O'Hazeldean" (293) all feature—and the completely unexpected. From *Sands of the Shore*, her "The Whummil Bore" (27) brings new life to a song that only Steeleye Span (just one year previously) had hitherto recorded, but which also was present in her father's repertoire. "I remember him singing it at several concerts, teasing the audience because they couldn't sing along to the tongue twister chorus."

> *With my glimpy glimpy glimpy eedle*
> *Lillum too tee a ta too a tee a ta a tally*

Another Steeleye staple, "The Wee Wee Man" (38—from their 1973 *Parcel of Rogues* LP) makes a rare reappearance; she learned it, of course, from her dad who, in turn, took it from Ewan MacColl.

Cameron reintroduces, too, "Young Benjie" (86), a song whose best-remembered past appearance came from Peter and Chris Coe in 1976. Cameron does not recall her precise source.

> I was sharing a car ride from Sudbury to Toronto with Paul Morris, and he was playing something in the tape deck which had a woman singing that ballad. I fell in love with it, looked it up and learned it from Bronson's *Traditional Tunes*. I think one of the first things that tunes me into a ballad is the melody and how well it works as a vehicle for transmitting the emotional content of the story. "Bonny Susy Cleland," for example, . . . I mentioned I have no recollection of which version it was that my father sang. He never sang it again after those early years. I have long searched for a version which I feel inspired enough to sing. But each version I have found has a melody which seems to me to be at odds with the storyline. I like Lisa Null's version[16] the best, but even hers sounds a bit too jolly for my taste.[17]

Princeton-based Jon Bartlett and Rika Ruebsaat are also renowned for their allegiance to the Child Ballads, as musicians and as academics. English-born Bartlett credits the Aldermaston Ban the Bomb marches of the early 1960s with his introduction to what he has called "Scottish parodies of American folk tunes"; that led him into the country's then fervent folk club culture, before he immigrated to Vancouver, British Columbia, in 1968. There he joined the Vancouver Folk Song Society, which is where he and Ruebsaat met. German born, but living in Canada since 1952, she had hitherto worked solo, and in a duo alongside Jack Nissenson.

First singing together in 1976, the pair's primary focus as both performers and academics was Canadian folk songs. They were a familiar sight presenting folk workshops at schools and colleges through the late 1970s, and in 1979 they produced *Songs and Stories of Canada*, a sixteen-part radio series for the CBC's schools programming. An album, *The Green Fields of Canada*, was drawn from the series, but also celebrated, at last, the publication of what the couple described as "the last of the major collections of traditional folk songs," Phil Thomas's *Songs of the Pacific Northwest*. (Thomas's collection of logging, gold rush, and railroad songs was also the subject of the duo's *The Young Man from Canada* album.) That same year also saw the release of *Come to Me in Canada*, featuring their take on "Willie Drowned in Ero," alongside a dark "The Unquiet Grave" (78), their source the Greenleaf and Mansfield expedition that reached Newfoundland just ahead of Maud Karpeles in 1929. That is the extent of their recorded visits to the *ESPB*.

However, Bartlett and Ruebsaat's 2006 paper on Child 39, "Lamkin: The Terror of Countless Nurseries," was published in editors Roger deV. Renwick and Sigrid Rieuwerte's acclaimed *Ballad Mediations: Folksongs Recovered, Represented, and Reimagined—Ballads and Songs*. They have staged ballad workshops; and are also responsible for creating a series of cassette tapes of ballad performances, each featuring multiple versions of every one of the Child Ballads, to offer students a sense of how dramatically the songs have changed over the years—and how they continue to do so.

Chapter Nineteen

THE LOMAX CONNECTION

In terms of recorded evidence, Alan Lomax is the most successful and certainly the best-known song collector in the history of that endeavor. His archive contains more than seventeen thousand sound recordings, gathered over some fifty years spent in the field, with a global reach that laid the foundations not only for countless subsequent researchers, but a myriad of musicians too. His contributions to the Child Ballads canon, on the other hand, are comparatively scant, with fewer than seventy recordings, many of them performed by Ewan MacColl, to whom Lomax was introduced by folklorist Peter Kennedy on his first trip to the United Kingdom in 1952.

By the time he visited London, Lomax was already considered a powerhouse in American folk circles. Indeed, most of his family shared a similar status. Born in 1915, he was the third of four children born to author and folklorist John A. Lomax, a renowned collector of Texas cowboy songs. Three of his offspring were destined to follow in his footsteps, as daughter Bess and his eldest son John Jr., both accompanied Alan into the field.

Alan Lomax was seventeen when he undertook his first collecting expeditions, joining his father on several trips sponsored by the Library of Congress. Two books coauthored by the pair documented their findings, *American Ballads and Folk Songs* (1934) and *Negro Folk Songs as Sung by Lead Belly* (1936). In between those two publications, Alan joined anthropologist and film-maker Zora Neale Hurston and folklorist/activist Mary Elizabeth Barnicle on a summer 1935 tour of the American South and the Bahamas, where he recorded an "Our Goodman" (274) as sung by Simeon Rolle in Mangrove Cay. Another expedition took Lomax and his wife, Elizabeth (they married in 1937) to Haiti.

Alan Lomax onstage at the Mountain Music Festival, Asheville, North Carolina, circa 1940. Wikimedia Commons

That same year saw Lomax become assistant in charge of the Archive of Folk Song of the Library of Congress and, two years later, he was responsible for commissioning one of the most singular versions of a Child Ballad recorded thus far, when he arranged for Charles Seeger Jr. and his wife, Ruth Crawford, to compose new musical works based upon American traditional ballads. Seeger chose "John Henry." Crawford, on

Ruth Crawford Seeger's adaptation of Child 277 ranks among the mid-twentieth century's most audacious ballad recordings. Wikimedia Commons

the other hand, embarked upon a medley of three songs, the non-Child "Equinoxial and Phoebe" and "The Last of Callahan," plus the tongue-twisting earworm that is "Rissolty Rossolty" (277).

Writer Jeanne Trembeth captures the consequences.

I love how Ruth begins the piece with a 20th century flair, the first few notes slightly similar to the beginning of the fourth movement of her 1931 "String Quartet." Woven throughout this piece are American folk songs interspersed with decidedly dissonant harmonies. She bonds the piece together with ostinatos and repeated short motives along with the return of the folk melodies. [Then] the texture deepens, polyphony becomes very evident and chaotic along with a lot of dissonance. The horns become quite intense in dynamics as if announcing an upcoming musical event which does indeed occur with the triumphant tonal entrance of the trumpets with a folk song melody.[1]

It is certainly not a conventional reading, and Lomax adored it.

Lomax continued traveling. He toured the Great Lakes region in 1938, while 1941 saw him visit Mississippi for the first time, where he met Muddy Waters. He was actually searching for Robert Johnson at the time, and was shocked to learn that the great man was dead. He recorded Woody Guthrie and worked, too, with Big Bill Broonzy and Jelly Roll Morton. He hosted two series of CBS's *American Folk Song* and *Wellsprings of Music,* targeted at some two hundred thousand schools across the country and again introducing the likes of Guthrie, Pete Seeger, and Josh White to a wider audience. After leaving the Library of Congress in 1942, he continued both broadcasting and producing.

In 1950, Lomax resumed his traveling with a trip to Ireland in the company of folksingers Robin Roberts and Jean Ritchie, the extraordinarily talented Kentuckian whom he first met at the Henry Street Settlement School in New York, where she worked at that time. He was now embarking upon a truly Behemothic project, compiling for Columbia Records a vast (Lomax originally estimated between forty-five and sixty LPs)[2] *World Library of Folk and Primitive Music,* drawn both from existing sources around the world and from Lomax's own adventuring. The label—for whom the LP, or long-playing record, was still a brand new plaything, introduced just a year or so earlier, and whose possibilities felt endless— gladly financed Lomax's wanderings, and the Irish visit was undertaken with that country's LP firmly in mind.

From Ireland, he made his way to London—of course the *World Library* would include a volume dedicated to English and Scottish folk song. He also arranged to record a three-part radio series for the BBC, *Adventures in Folk Song.* Two others would swiftly be commissioned, *Patterns in American Folk Song* and *The Art of the Negro,* all featuring material from his own earlier expeditions.

Ewan MacColl—or Jimmy Miller, as he was then known—met the visitor for the first time at the BBC studios. Characteristically, MacColl was at the microphone, recording a "Barbara Allen" (84) when Lomax first clapped eyes upon him. Already a known actor, playwright, and singer, as well as a committed left-wing firebrand, MacColl had a reputation as something of an authority on the Child Ballads. Indeed, it was said that he was originally discovered by BBC producer D. G. Bridson, busking "rare old Scots Border ballads and songs in Gaelic" in a Manchester cinema queue during the 1930s. He was swiftly hired for an upcoming radio production.

MacColl's first ever recording date, at the English Folk Dance and Song Society's studio, saw him cut three Child Ballads in one session, "Lord Randall" (12), "Sir Patrick Spens" (58), and "Eppie Moray" (223), plus the Australian convict lament "Van Dieman's Land." All four would see release by the HMV across two 78s released in 1951; around the same time, MacColl also recorded "The Keach in the Creel" (281) for a Topic label 78.[3]

It was not, MacColl was amused to discover, a ballad that Professor Child himself especially admired.

[He] concludes his notes on the ballad with a peculiarly prim comment: "No one looks for decorum in pieces of this description but a passage in this ballad, which need not be particularized, is brutal and shameless almost beyond description." These are harsh words for a scholar whose stock-in-trade was stories dealing with mayhem in all its forms and it is difficult to imagine what prompted them. It is, of course, possible that Child was shocked by the use of the word "keach" on which considerable play is made in the song. Used as a noun the word denotes bustle or fluster, when used as a verb, however, it can mean "lift" or "hoist" or alternatively it can mean to void excrement.[4]

MacColl's early performances were harsh, unaccompanied and heavily accented, and they could be disquieting, too—unsurprisingly, in the case of "Eppie Moray," as it was a song he associated with childhood days spent with his father, William Miller, at the deathbed of a family friend named Jock Sinclair. Lying in his bed, Jock would ask for a song, and MacColl, reflecting upon these moments later, admitted, "I ha[d] heard my father sing this song many times, but this [was] the first time I ha[d] listened to the words, really listened, and I [was] stirred."[5] More than twenty years had passed since Sinclair passed away, but MacColl's rendition snares the listener's imagination just the same.

According to MacColl, all four of the songs he had chosen to record for HMV were too long to fit onto one side of a disc. The only solution left to him was to sing them at twice his normal tempo. Lomax assured him that he'd be able to take his time at their first session.

Born just sixteen days apart, MacColl on January 15, 1915; Lomax on January 31, the two men swiftly bonded. Politically they were certainly cut from the same cloth—Lomax was defiantly left wing, and under regular surveillance by the FBI as a consequence; MacColl was a committed and outspoken socialist, a trait he inherited from his parents. Indeed, according to MacColl, his father—an iron molder by trade—was forced to move to England after being blacklisted by virtually every iron foundry in Scotland.

But, MacColl continued, he was only an iron molder by profession. By inclination he was a folk singer,

and he'd been a folk singer all his life. He knew hundreds [of songs] and, the last two years of his life, I began to take them down. I'd learned many of them already from him, but the long ballads I'd never taken the trouble to learn in any great detail so when it was obvious that his health was failing I began to take them down. I took "Sir Patrick Spens" [58], "Hughie Graeme" [191] . . . and about sixteen others in detail, and quite a number of lyric songs and fragments too.[6]

It was William, too, who awakened MacColl's interest in the history, and roots of the old songs. For example, curious to learn more about what was generally considered one of the great Scottish ballads, the seafaring epic "Sir Patrick Spens" (58), "I asked him about [it], and he said Spens was not a Scots name. He'd never come across it in Scotland. But it was his opinion that [the name] was *Spence*, it was young Patrick *Spence*, but the hard C was hard to sing so they softened it into 'Spens' because you could hold the note longer that way. The name usually appears in the third line where the note has to be held."[7]

Like his father, MacColl swiftly became a fount of similar lore and detail, although William Miller was only one of the primary sources for MacColl's early repertoire. Other relatives, too, were also a repository of song. Indeed, in the liner notes to the Campbell Family's 1965 *The Singing Campbells* album, the group credit MacColl's aunt, Margaret Logan, for the tune they selected for their "The Cruel Mither" (20).

(Jim Carroll reflects he was initially skeptical when he heard MacColl credit different ballads to the family. That changed, he says, when "I spent an afternoon with Salford historians Ruth and Eddie Frow. They were contemporaries and neighbors of Ewan's parents and told me 'William knew hundreds of bits and pieces of old Scots songs and always sang them when he'd a few pints down him.' I suspect that Ewan learned these bits and filled them in from the ballad collections long before the revival was a twinkle in anybody's eye."[8])

MacColl was inevitably invited to contribute to the *World Library*'s English and Scottish volumes, while Lomax continued to record him on subsequent visits to Britain in 1953 and 1958. The recordings they made together are seldom ranked among MacColl's most essential. They are, however, among his most immediate, and they include a number of Child Ballads (or variations thereon) that had rarely, if ever, been recorded before. Their first session together, on February 12, 1951, comprised a staggering sixty-six songs (and fragments thereof), among them ten Child Ballads. These included a new version of the seldom sung "Kemp Owyne" (34), "The Laidley Worm" (34); and "The Jew's Daughter" variant of "Little Sir Hugh" (155), while MacColl's treatment of "Nickety Nackety" (277) spun far beyond even the song's riotous American incarnations in the 1920s, to be delivered at breakneck speed in a thick Scottish brogue.

MacColl did not consume all of Lomax's time. The American worked and recorded, too, with Bert Lloyd (it was Lomax who introduced

MacColl to Lloyd); while he also journeyed north to Scotland, accompanied by the Scottish poet, academic, and collector Hamish Henderson, and the brothers Calum and Sorley MacLean. There, he recorded everything from Gaelic work songs and pipe tunes to the inevitable Robert Burns,[9] and a handful of Child Ballads surface across his endeavors.

Henderson (1919–2002) undertook most of the required introductions. Head of the School of Scottish Studies at Edinburgh University, he fell into ballad collecting while serving abroad during World War Two, collecting (and eventually publishing) a number of popular military songs as *Ballads of World War Two*.

He turned his attention to his native Scots balladry following the war, and his influence on its subsequent study was immense. As a collector, he was a major source for the BBC's archive, while his discoveries of singers include such pleasures as Martha Reid, Willie Mitchell, Rab Morris, and Charlotte Higgins, and they have been celebrated, too, with a number of CD compilations.

ALLAN CUNNINGHAM—FANTASIST OR FABULOUS?

Child trusted few of his sources. Even the most venerated of past ballad collectors were, in his eyes, under suspicion for embroidering their discoveries. Bishop Percy, Sir Walter Scott—reputations tumbled before the professor's dark doubts.

Few men, however, were so sorely mistrusted as the Scottish poet Allan Cunningham (1784–1842), and with good cause. Cunningham had already pulled the wool over the eyes of Robert Hartley Cromek, compiler of the 1809 collection *Remains of Nithsdale and Galloway Song*, submitting his own verse as "genuine" ancient ballads; thus, the moment Child caught even a glimpse of Cunningham's name, the alarm bells went off in his mind.

The ballad "Gil Brenton" (5) especially aroused Child's ire; at one point, he remarks that "forty or fifty" of Cunningham's verses "could be excised in one mass" from that single ballad alone.

It is crucial to remember, however, that Cunningham was very good at what he did. Like a master forger who passes undetected by all but the most suspicious minds, Cunningham's work might still lie, free from reproach, within scholarly sources.

His influence, too, lingers.

It was Hamish Henderson's recordings of Martha Reid that inspired Oakland, CA, balladeer and blogger[10] Sarah "Djiril" Brody to record a unique, aching "Gil Brenton" (5)—one of the multitude of Child Ballads for which no traditional tune has ever been noted—in 2013.

"I stole the melody and chorus from Martha Reid's singing of 'The Elfin Knight' (2) on [Henderson's] *Songs and Ballads from Perthshire Field Recordings of the 1950s* [album]," she admits. But her lyric borrows happily from Allan Cunningham.

> Child often mentions . . . Cunningham, who was in the habit of trying to pass his own poems and verses off as traditional. In this case, Child believed that he had added a chunk of his own writing into the middle of "Gil Brenton." He included the ballad in his collection as version "C," with the suspected Cunningham verses removed, but included them in a footnote at the end. I sang the first few verses of version "C," and then finished them with a few of the suspected Cunningham verses, letting the story trail off from there.[11]

In other words, Djiril performs the ballad much as Cunningham thought it should be, and—for all we really know—as close to its reality as it might ever be. Child's opinion is more or less moot.

Jessie Murray of Buckley, who told Lomax that she learned the old songs "from my mother when I was a wee girl," offers up "Lord Thomas and Fair Ellen" (73), but the Lomax archive also includes her first-person "Barbara Allen" (84) recorded during the 1951 Edinburgh Fringe Festival, where Lomax and Henderson staged the first People's Ceilidh, on August 31, 1951. Another great Scots singer, John Strachan, also appeared at the Ceilidh, adding a stoutly sung "Johnny O'Braidislea" (114) to the handful of other Child Ballads that Lomax recorded at the Aberdeenshire farmer's Crichlie home in July. Lomax's other great highland source was William Mathieson (1910–1995), a Turiff farmworker to whom he was introduced by the great, in terms of reputation at least, 1930s collector James Madison Carpenter.

Behind the wheel of his Austin 7 motor car, Carpenter was seeking songs throughout northeastern Scotland when he heard about the cattleman on the Dunlugus Estate, near Turiff, who was always singing songs. Mathieson invited him to his home, and there Carpenter both recorded his songs . . . just a stanza or two for the most part, to get a sense of the tune . . . and took down the words on a portable typewriter. He came away from Mathieson's home with more than 100 songs, including almost three dozen Child Ballads. Neither did Carpenter exhaust Mathieson's repertoire. According to the singer's own reckoning, he'd been writing "old songs" down in a ledger since the age of seven or so (he was born in 1879) and now knew around 650.

Mathieson himself was a diligent collector, walking for miles if he heard of somebody singing a song he didn't know, and then doing whatever was necessary to learn it from them. The most common means of exchange was a song for a song, but others he purchased from the itinerant ballad sellers who went door to door selling their wares; or, in his younger years, his father might pick one up at the market for him. For all his love of song and singing, however, Mathieson had no particular urge to sing in public. He was twenty-two before he was finally prevailed upon to do so, at a wedding at a hotel in Rhynie. Then he went back to his notebooks and ledgers, his day job, his marriage, and life. Which is not to say he never sang for his friends or joined them as they sang. On one occasion, while being interviewed by Hamish Henderson, Mathieson remembered sitting with four other people, all of them singing 'The Dowie Dens of Yarrow" (214), all to a different melody. Neither was this unusual. He had, he later remarked, frequently encountered singers who sang the same song, with the same words, but all to their own tune. Lomax's own collection of Mathieson's songs was tiny in comparison with Carpenter's, but his take-away included five Child Ballads that he did not already possess, including the still seldom-sung "The Bonny Rantin Laddie" (240), the tale of a woman who bears the bastard child of the titular "rantin laddie," only to discover he is the Earl of Aboyne.[12]

Lomax's researches continued, and his collection of Child Ballads swelled accordingly. In Ireland, Lomax met with Elizabeth Cronin, seventy-two years old but still widely proclaimed as "the Queen of Irish Song." His trawl through the BBC's archive, meanwhile, saw him select several Child Ballads for the World Library series, including: Maud Karpeles's recording of Phil Tanner's "Barbara Allen" (84), Walter Lucas's "The Prickle Holly Bush" (95), and a raucous "The False Hearted Knight" (4) from Jumbo Brightwell, recorded in 1947 at the Eel's Foot by the Anglo-Irish composer Ernest. J. Moeran (1894–1950).

More, too, would follow. Again, Lomax was not looking specifically for Child Ballads, but they found him regardless, on subsequent trips to the United Kingdom in 1953–54 and 1957–58, when Jeannie Robertson and one of MacColl's most gifted proteges, Isla Cameron (1927–1980), were numbered among his sources. They abounded across the American South in 1959 as well, with the young Shirley Collins as his accomplice; and in San Juan, Puerto Rico, in 1960, when his old friend, Texan folksinger Hally Wood, surprised him with "Fair Ellender" (73). Professor Child even awaited him as far away as St. Eustatius in what were then the Netherland Antilles, where Lomax and assistant Joan Halifax were vacationing in 1967. The majority of what he recorded there were either whaling songs or Christmas carols. But tucked away among the tapes was the sound of an unknown woman singing "Barbara Allen," accompanying herself on guitar while a roomful of onlookers sing along, and revealing a fresh take on the opening lines:

> *In yonder town in yonder place*
> *Two sweethearts they were drinking . . .*

Like Burl Ives before him, Lomax discovered that, no matter how far you traveled, "Barbara Allen" had arrived there first.

Recordings from Lomax's archive had been appearing on record almost from the moment he completed his first field trip. For this book's purposes, however, among the most significant of all these discs were his contributions to the Library of Congress two-volume LP series *Child Ballads Traditional in the United States from the Archive of Song.* Commissioned from Bertrand H. Bronson and released in 1959, shortly after the publication of volume one of his *Traditional Tunes*, this visionary series called upon a number of collections, not just Lomax's, in search of material. Sidney Robertson Cowell, Robert F. Draves and Helene Statman-Thomas, Maud Karpeles, and Laurence Powell were also numbered among the contributors, alongside Lomax's father John, who supplied a quavering rendering of the seldom-heard "The King's Love Letter" (208), concerning the arrest for treason of Lord Derwentwater, as performed in Newberry, Florida, by a Mrs. G. A. Griffin in 1940.

Indeed, the two discs are unique in that they offer us, if not the earliest recordings of several ballads ever to be made, certainly the earliest to become readily available. Warde H. Ford's "Andrew Bataan" (167), "The Oxford Merchant" (283), and an epic ten-minute "The Bishop of Canterbury" (45) were captured in 1938 by Robertson Cowell in Central Valley, California, and the latter certainly inspired Dom Flemons. The two-album set was another of his discoveries at the University library, and "The Bishop of Canterbury" was, for a time, a song he loved to sing—at least until "I gave up because it's so esoteric. I loved that ballad because—for one, I studied Chaucer and so I was interested in hearing a ballad about Canterbury, and—for two, it's so rude to King John! It's such an intriguing ballad and it has a beautiful melody. I used to sing it a bunch, but most audiences were like 'huh?' I'd like to revisit that one."[13]

The albums' magic remains as strong today, and the foresight of the collectors whose work it celebrates remains a vivid beacon. We hear the fruits of Robert F. Draves and Helene Statman-Thomas's visit to Wisconsin on the very eve of the outbreak of World War Two, in the form of two selections, "Well Met My Own True Love" (243), warmly delivered by

Pearl Jacobs Borusky in Antigo, and "A Ship Set Sail for North America" (286), a rare variant known to Ollie Jacobson of Pearson. We marvel as Emma Dusenbury of Mena, Arkansas, singlehandedly out-performs the Carter Family with her haunted retelling of "The Mermaid" (289). But most of all, we wonder at the sheer dedication that Lomax showed to his calling. It was he who was responsible for the lion's share of the recordings and, while later years would see a host of compilations, both vinyl and CD (and latterly, downloads) made available, all drawing from Lomax's archive, still there must be a special place on the shelf reserved for *Child Ballads Traditional in the United States from the Archive of Song*.

As much as any other manifestation of Professor Child's masterpiece, and more than the vast majority, it remains one of the most influential record sets of the twentieth century.

Chapter Twenty

BROADCASTING THE BALLADS

Alan Lomax was to prove influential in the early careers of any number of future British folk music legends, from MacColl, Lloyd, and Jean Ritchie, to Isla Cameron and Shirley Collins. Another figure with whom he was to work closely during his first visit to the United Kingdom was Peter Kennedy (1922–2006), a sometimes controversial character who is nevertheless regarded among the doyen of British collectors and broadcasters. Ewan MacColl described Kennedy as "an indefatigable collector of English folk songs,"[1] but the tall, willowy figure with his impeccable accent and upper-class mannerisms was also responsible not only for preserving the voices and songs of countless traditional singers and musicians but also for broadcasting many of them on BBC radio, publishing several highly regarded books on the subject, and overseeing a number of LP (and, later, cassette and CD) releases, too.

Like Lomax, Kennedy had folk music in his blood. London born, he was the son of Douglas Kennedy (1893–1988), Cecil Sharp's successor as president of the English Folk Dance and Song Society, and Helen Karpeles, the sister of Maud. His grandfather, David Kennedy, was a renowned Scottish folk singer, and his great aunt Marjory Kennedy-Fraser was an early ballad collector who published her discoveries in the multivolume *The Songs of the Hebrides*. It was surely inevitable that Kennedy would follow in the family footsteps.

In 1935, at age thirteen, Kennedy was part of the team filming the first International Folk Dance Festival in London. In 1948, he joined the English Folk Dance and Song Society staff full-time. He also worked for the BBC's Folk Music and Dialect Recording Scheme, but his most significant step in popularizing both traditional music and its performers would be as one of the hosts of a new BBC Radio Light Programme series, *As I Roved Out.*

Kennedy's arrival at the BBC was most propitiously timed, coinciding as it did with a great upsurge of enthusiasm for traditional music that now swept through the Corporation. Because of founder William Reith's insistence that the BBC was to both entertain and educate, traditional music had long had a presence in the scheduling. Neither was it restricted to the homegrown variety. Canadian folklorist Helen Creighton recalled, "the usual way to hear folk song programs was by short wave radio from England, since we had few [Canadian shows]." It was via the BBC, in 1938, that she first heard songs from her own collection on the radio, tuning in one night to learn that one particular show's fare would include music "from Nova Scotia, where Helen Creighton has discovered."

"I didn't wait for the rest," she wrote, "but ran downstairs to tell [the family] the exciting news."[2] Her debut was, in fact, one of at least three programs featuring, or even dedicated to Canadian and French-Canadian folk music aired by the BBC that year, while that October saw the "Beeb" also give airtime to the CBC's *Fifth World Concert*, subtitled *A Musical Picture of Canada*, which featured sea shanties, an old time orchestra, and a yodeling cowboy.

The corporation's focus upon British folk song was most pronounced, however. Within a year or so of commencing operations in 1922, programs such as *Folk Songs and Ballads*, *Mainly Folk Music*, and *Scotch Night* were being aired. Irish singer Winifred Fisher was the star of a two-part broadcast in 1924; and that same year, on January 3, "I Will Give My Love an Apple" (46) was performed by baritone Ernest Eady on *A Night with Folk Songs*. This was probably the first Child Ballad ever to be heard over the British airwaves.

Traditional songs were (and would remain) an integral part of children's broadcasting, courtesy of baritone Esmond Bristol, while the death of Cecil Sharp on June 22, 1924, was marked the following year by both a special presentation of his discoveries by singer Helen Henschel, and a commemorative program described in the *Radio Times* as being comprised "entirely of songs and themes collected by Cecil Sharp from the peasant folk of the English counties."

On July 1, 1927, Maud Karpeles offered BBC listeners a lecture on "English Folk Songs, collected in the Appalachian Mountains of America." And when Helen Henschel performed "Jock O'Hazeldean" (293) on *Romantic Music and Folk Songs* on March 14 that same year, the *Radio Times* went so far as to print the lyrics in that week's issue. In 1932, the corporation even marked the twenty-first birthday of the English Folk Dance Society with a special broadcast. When occasional BBC contributor Bert Lloyd approached his bosses with his own idea for a folk-themed broadcast, then, he was not entirely shooting into the dark. His concept, however, was to have far-reaching effects.

A young man in his late twenties, whose background included stints spent working the land in Australia and aboard a whaling ship in the south Atlantic, Lloyd had recently befriended author and folklorist Leslie Morton. When the latter relocated to the neighborhood of Eastbridge, in Suffolk, part of the region known as East Anglia, Lloyd and his first wife, Norma, were among the friends he would regularly invite to visit.

Perched in rolling wetlands two miles from the North Sea, Eastbridge was a picture-postcard-perfect English village. A ruined twelfth-century chapel stands on the site of what once was the grand Leiston Abbey, there was a working windmill and a parish church, St. Peters, with a well-preserved rounded tower and a thatched roof. The village pub, the Eel's Foot Inn, could trace its origins back to 1533, and it abounded with tales of smugglers and their crimes. For students of military history, there was even the crash site of a German zeppelin, brought down in flames in 1917.

It was his visits to the Eel's Foot that Lloyd most anticipated. By his own admission, he was a latecomer to English traditional music, stumbling upon it only shortly before he first published his thoughts and theories on the subject in an article for the socialist *Daily Worker* newspaper, "The People's Own Poetry" on February 10, 1937. There he stated that, while "the English ballad . . . goes on developing," it no longer did so in England. Rather, its homelands now were "the primitive communities of English origin and culture . . . in the Appalachian Mountains of the United States, or in Newfoundland."[3] One evening spent at the Eel's Foot disavowed him of that misconception. Every Saturday night, he discovered, local farm workers and fishermen would gather for an evening of singing, dancing, and merriment. Morton himself, having grown up in the area, knew many of the songs by heart; indeed, he once sorely embarrassed Lloyd's wife, Norma, with his recitation of an especially bawdy "Five Nights Drunk" (274).

By the time Lloyd returned to London a few days later, his head still spinning from his first ever encounter with the living folk tradition, he had conceived the idea of a radio program based exclusively around a Saturday night at the Eel's Foot, and recorded wholly in situ. The BBC was as enthused as he was. The art of outside broadcast was now in full swing, with the BBC commanding a fleet of mobile Direct Disc Cutting Studios just itching to be dispatched around the country. And so, on May 13, 1939, Lloyd, Morton, and their partners, accompanied by producer Maurice Brown and a BBC engineer, parked outside the old inn to record *Saturday Night at the Eel's Foot*. Broadcast on July 29, at the somewhat contrary hour of 3:30 in the afternoon, *Saturday Night at the Eel's Foot* included no Child Ballads. It paved the way, however, for the BBC to amass one of the largest and most unique collections of traditional music in the world.

The outbreak of World War Two just six weeks after the broadcast curtailed whatever immediate plans either Lloyd or his employers may have had. But producer Douglas Cleverdon would, in February 1942, travel to Hambridge, a small village near Langport in Somerset, to record Cecil Sharp's informant Louisa Hooper and some of her neighbors; and the following year, he visited the Isle of Purbeck in Dorset.

The program *Country Magazine*, already mentioned in connection with Phil Tanner, started life in May 1942 and ran until 1954. It proved to be one of the most influential music-based shows of the era. The fifteen-year-old Shirley Collins wrote to *Country Magazine* informing them that she wanted to be a folk singer when she grew up, and expected to hear nothing more. Instead, she received a personal visit from Bob Cooper, whose folk singing family were staples of the BBC's traditional output. His interest in her ambition only amplified the teenager's fascination.

In 1945, Ernest J. Moeran returned to East Anglia to record for the Beeb; and in 1947, he staged a second revelry at the Eel's Foot in Eastbridge, where his captures included that grandly enunciated unaccompanied "The False Hearted Knight" (4) that would be selected for the Library of Congress's Child Ballads LPs. That same year, Brian George, the BBC's head of Central Programme Operations, undertook the first experimental field recordings in Ireland, returning there in 1949 and, by the early 1950s, the corporation's management was firmly committed to recording (and often broadcasting) as many traditional folk singers as its researchers could possibly find. These included a number of startling finds, paramount among them "King Orfeo" (19), a ballad that had not only evaded capture in the past, but also was not even known to have a tune. Professor Child described it simply as a "whisper from the Middle Ages," when it was apparently conceived as a medieval retelling of the story of Orpheus and Eurydice, with Elfland standing in for Hades. Recorded in 1947 by Patrick Shuldham-Shaw from one John Stickle, in Lerwick, in the Shetland Isles, the performance subsequently appeared within the Caedmon label's 1961 anthology *The Folk Songs of Britain*, where the liner notes offered a stirring description of its discovery:

> That a tune in the midst of the 20th century be recovered . . . was as little to be expected as that we should hear a horn from elfinland blowing. . . . Child printed one version only of the ballad, but when Patrick Shaw went to the Shetland to look for songs he was shown [a] text that had appeared in the *Shetland Times*, written down from the recitation of Bruce Sutherland of Turf House, North Yell, in 1865. Still no tune has ever been recorded for the ballad. Then one day Mr. Shaw was visiting John Stickle in the island of Unst

and the two began talking about nonsense songs. "Have you ever," said Mr. Stickle, "heard anything as nonsensical as this?" Mr. Stickle then proceeded to sing him the song here reproduced, and he failed to understand how his London friend could be so excited over a bit of nonsense that he had never been able to get out of his mind.[4]

Stickle's rendition subsequently inspired versions of "King Orfeo" recorded by, among others, Archie Fisher (1970), Steeleye Span (1976), and Frankie Armstrong (1996), and it was not alone. As much as any collector of previous decades or even centuries, the BBC opened the traditional music of the entire United Kingdom up for inspection, with every corner of the land being visited and recorded. Roger Glover of the hard rock band Deep Purple reflects upon the impact of this policy:

> Growing up in the 50s in England, we had the BBC, and they played every kind of music there was. And, though we complained about it, in retrospect that was a great education. Without the BBC, we'd not have heard gospel music and classical music, folk, blues and jazz. They'd dip into everything, and it wasn't done with any style or anything. But in retrospect it wasn't so bad, because you look at kids growing up now, they get force-fed a particular sub-genre of music, and that's it. They don't have the wide overview. They're very channeled.[5]

Several hundred Child Ballad performances repose in the BBC archive, including versions sung in Welsh and both Irish and Scots Gaelic, and almost all of them were recorded in the field. As a snapshot of the Child Ballads (and, indeed, traditional song's) survival into the second half of the twentieth century, the collection has few peers, and it is a source of regret for researchers and listeners alike that so little of this venerable stash has seen the light of day on record. Caedmon's aforementioned *The Folk Songs of Britain* series released in 1961 (1968–1969 in the United Kingdom, when it was picked up by Topic Records), is the fullest readily available survey of the BBC's holdings. This was a mighty ten-volume set that included two volumes dedicated exclusively to the Child Ballads, alongside such themed collections as *Songs of Seduction, Songs of Ceremony,* and *Sailormen and Servingmaids.* Even here, however, we hear just forty performances, and not all were BBC recordings. (Revised editions with bonus tracks appeared on CD in 2000.)

Drawing upon the efforts of no less than eight collectors, including Karpeles, Kennedy, Lomax, Irishman Séamus Ennis, and in Sussex Bob Copper, the greatest revelation among these albums was Lucy Stewart of Fetterangus in Aberdeenshire. Born in 1901, she was first recorded by American folklorist Kenneth S. Goldstein, who spent close to a year living with her family in 1959–1960. During this time, he recorded everything he could—ballads, stories, riddles, children's games, the lot. He later revealed it was not an easy task.

> Lucy's tradition was a wholly private family matter. In the very village in which she lived, no one outside of her family even knew that she sang. She was extremely reticent to sing in the presence of persons not related to her, and it took more than two months to pry loose from her the first song. Once we had established full rapport—and I was almost literally adopted into the Stewart clan—her song flowed in a seemingly endless stream.[6]

Regardless, Stewart's unique style and performance inspired many. The great Norfolk singer Peter Bellamy based his "Two Pretty Boys" (49) on her rendering; Martin Carthy, Alison McMorland, and Emily Smith have all borrowed her "Cruel Mother"; Tom Gilfellon took Stewart's "The Two Sisters"; and more.

Thomas Moran (1876–1960), of County Leitrim, Ireland, is another performer who especially sparkled. Across several BBC sessions between 1952 and 1954, he served up some forty-five songs, of which close to a dozen were Child Ballads. Remarkably, they were taped in just one visit in December 1954 by Séamus Ennis.

Sam Larner (1878–1965), a fisherman from the village of Winterton in Norfolk was first recorded in 1956 by a producer for BBC Birmingham, Phillip Donnellan, although his local renown as a singer greatly predated that. Whenever the fleet returned home, or put into any other port, Sam once explained in an interview, "We used to get in the old pub, have a pint or two around, give 'em the four-handed reel. A drink, a song and a four-handed reel. Round we'd go and up we'd go and we used to have a rare old, good old time."[7]

Judy Dyble, a founding member of Fairport Convention in 1967, had family from Winterton. Her grandfather, Walter Dyble, was the last coxswain of the Winterton Life Boat, the *Edward Birkbeck,* and she remembers hearing how the local pubs, The Fisherman's Return and The Three Mariners, "were apparently full of singers, most of whose names have now been forgotten: the brothers Bob and Dick Green, Jack George, Sam's own father George Larner, and many more."[8]

Larner's fame swiftly traveled. Ewan MacColl wrote the song "The Shoals of Herring" about him, and later recorded the material that appeared on Larner's LP *Singing the Fishing.* He appeared in an installment of MacColl's *Radio Ballads* radio series,[9] and in the Donnellan-produced television film *The Singer and the Song.* He was also an occasional guest on the British folk club circuit of the late 1950s and early 1960s, prompting Martin Carthy later to exclaim, "[his singing] confronted everything I had thought made a musical sense, and changed it."[10] On another occasion, Carthy described Larner as one of the "two people in the late 1950s whose

NOW IS
THE TIME
FOR FISHING
songs and speech by
SAM LARNER
of Winterton, England

Collected & edited by
Ewan MacColl & Peggy Seeger

A 1961 Folkways/Topic records LP of singing fisherman Sam Larner. Author's collection

unforgettable wildly different performances—one at the Troubadour Folk Club in Earl's Court and the other at Ewan MacColl's Ballads and Blues Club in the upstairs room of a pub in the Edgware Road—decided for me the musical direction which my life was going to take."[11] (The other was Séamus Ennis, whose renown as a collector was eclipsed only by his talent on the Uillean pipes.)

Larner laid claim to a repertoire of some sixty songs, and a number of Child Ballads were included therein—not, necessarily, the great seafaring epics (although "The Drowned Lover" (216), "The Lofty Tall Ship" (250), and "The Golden Fenidier" (286) were present and correct), but also several landlocked airs—"Barbara Allen" (84) and "Blow Away the Morning Dew" (112), recorded in March 1958, and "The Outlandish Knight" (4), which he sang for the BBC in September 1959.

Also hailing from Norfolk, and destined for similar renown, was Harry
Cox (1885–1971). A farmworker, he was "discovered" by Ernest J. Moeran
in 1921—a year before the BBC was even founded. In 1934, he cut several
sides for Decca Records. Peter Kennedy recorded him for the Beeb on several occasions between 1953–1956, and it remains a thrill to hear Cox's so
distinctive tones wrap themselves around "The Black-Guarded Gypsies"
(200) and "Georgie" (209). Cox is present within the Caedmon anthology, as indeed is Ennis, with "Captain Wedderburn's Courtship (46), but
it should here be remarked that the series was never aimed at a general
audience. Although there is certainly a charm to hearing some truly
unique characters sing the songs of his or her youth, these collections
were very much targeted at more scholarly inclined minds, or toward
musicians seeking "fresh" versions of familiar songs. Indeed, their very
existence was an act of encouragement for aspiring folk singers, proof that
these songs were still being sung as a part of daily life across the United
Kingdom and Ireland.

The teenaged June Tabor was one of the series' most devoted disciples.
Her first job upon leaving college found her working as a librarian in
Tottenham, north London. There she discovered a full set of *Folk Songs
of Britain*; borrowing the discs, she took them home to record, and pho-
tocopied the accompanying booklets. The repertoire with which Tabor
first made an impact on the British folk scene of the mid-1960s was built
upon those records' foundation, and listened to today, they still offer an
intoxicating glimpse into all that the BBC was to accomplish during the
late 1940s and 1950s.

Not that the corporation was forever receptive to fresh ideas. Bert Lloyd
had several folk-related program proposals rejected, including a four-part
series that was to be titled "The Foundations of Folk-Music" and a single
documentary dedicated to "British Ballad Survivals in the USA," calling
upon the work of the vast array of collectors who were now active in the
new world. But when Peter Kennedy suggested a new weekly folk show,
to be broadcast every Sunday morning at 10:30, it received the green light
almost immediately.

Titled for what Kennedy considered to be a "mild derivative" of
"Trooper and Maid" (299), *As I Roved Out* was born just as the long-
running *Country Magazine* was winding down. Yet it was never viewed
as a replacement. It was an entirely new start. Debuted on September 27,
1953, the show laid out its intentions in that week's *Radio Times* listing magazine: "You are invited to listen to some of the folk songs and music still
sung and played in the British Isles." Journalist and author Colin Harper,
profiling Kennedy's cohost Séamus Ennis in 2015, described the show as

in effect the national shop window for the work Séamus, Peter Kennedy
and others were doing as folk song collectors for the BBC. The collectors

would talk about their song-hunting adventures across the British Isles and introduce recordings they had made. Occasionally, as with Donegal fiddler Frank Cassidy and Galway Gaelic singer Colm Ó Caodháin, Séamus would enjoy an opportunity to profile his favourite discoveries. At least two episodes across the six series were broadcast from rural pubs, and Séamus often enjoyed an opportunity to perform something himself.[12]

Speaking with Harper, Ennis recalled, "I tried always to paint a word picture of the district, the person singing and the house he lived in—just little unimportant details about my visit there, like 'At that moment the dog came in,' for instance."

That maiden broadcast featured appearances from Isla Cameron and Irish singer Sarah Makem (1900–1983), before Kennedy introduced "some of the people [I] met in Mrs. Makem's kitchen," while Ennis discussed the Buckinghamshire singer Amos Becket. Liam Clancy, who met Sarah Makem for the first time while accompanying collector Diane Hamilton around Ireland, described her for *R2/Rock'n'Reel* in 2008: "[She] had worked in the linen mills with hundreds of other girls. There was no radio at the time, so while they worked all day they would sing. She had a memory like a vice grip. So she remembered ancient songs . . . old versions of 'Barbara Allen,' 'The Month of January,' some of the great Child Ballads. She was a remarkable woman." Already locally renowned, Makem was now to become a key figure in what Kennedy, Lomax, MacColl, and Lloyd saw as an ongoing "folk revival," despite her very existence questioning whether there was even a need for a revival. Scots singer Alasdair Roberts reflects, "To call it a 'revival' to me implies a lack of continuity, whereas I think that there has been a continuous strand of interest and celebration of this kind of song and music."[13]

Makem was living proof of that; so was the decision that she should sing the new show's theme song. Makem made her first appearance on record soon after, via Jean Ritchie's 1954 *Field Trip* album and, although just one LP was credited wholly to Makem, 1967's *Ulster Ballad Singer*, her recordings remain a key inclusion on compilation albums (including the Topic label's multivolume *Voice of the People* series) to this day. Her "Barbara Allen" (84) can be heard on a host of discs; "You and I in One Bed," her unique interpretation of "Captain Wedderburn's Courtship" (46) and "As I Roved Out" are not far behind. Makem's BBC exposure inevitably contributed to her renown.

In the weeks that followed its debut broadcast, *As I Roved Out* spread its wings ever further afield. On October 4, Maud Karpeles revisited the Somerset locales where she and Cecil Sharp had collected songs half a century previous. On October 18, the show spotlighted another Irish singer, Elizabeth Cronin. On November 15, listeners were introduced to Colm Keane, a Connemara, Ireland, performer whose repertoire stretched to two hundred songs in both English and Gaelic. Ewan MacColl, who made his first appearance on *As I Roved Out* on November 1, returned to the show three weeks later, and continued as an occasional guest into early 1954. On December 20, Karpeles and Kennedy went in search of Christmas carols in Hertfordshire and Gloucestershire; and the following week, the show went to Rottingdean, Sussex, to join the Copper family's Christmas celebration.

Close to seventy years on, *As I Roved Out* is little more than a fading memory, with only a handful of isolated editions known to circulate among collectors and old-time radio enthusiasts today. Those that have survived, however, contain some marvelous moments, including Frances Kitching's Welsh-language performance of "Lord Randall" (12) from the January 3, 1954, edition (MacColl also appeared on that show); "Binnorie" (10) sung by Dorothy Fourbister of Flotta in a May 10, 1956, broadcast dedicated wholly to the music Kennedy recorded on his trip to the Orkney Islands; and "Lord Gregory" (76) by Elizabeth Cronin (aired on December 31, 1954). And those are just the Child Ballads that were broadcast in those particular shows. Kennedy's personal archive, which also incorporates his contributions to the BBC's storehouse, contains some 167 Child Ballads and their variants.

Much of Kennedy's holding would see commercial release, albeit in sometimes cruelly limited quantities, by his own Folktrax label, inaugurated in 1957. At the time of its closure in 2007, its catalog numbered close to five hundred CDs. Sadly, however, it is largely the activities of the label that have so darkened Kennedy's name in certain circles. Tales abound of Kennedy being loaned tapes of singers for his personal listening, only for them to then find their way into the Folktrax catalog; of moneys being promised to performers, but never delivered; of arrangements being copyrighted not in the name of the arranger, but in Kennedy's own.

Such stories, of course, are sadly all too commonplace in the music industry, and they have been since its inception; many old-time blues singers suffered exactly the same injustices when their music first began to be heard on a wider scale. Nevertheless, although Kennedy's alleged business practices have certainly sullied his reputation among many in the folk world, his legacy—which reveals nothing but love for the music to which he devoted his entire life—remains unimpeachable.

Chapter Twenty-One

THE GIRL FROM VIPER COUNTY

"Memory," wrote Jean Ritchie, "is a wonderful thing. My reason tells me that I must have had many unhappy times as a child, as psychoanalysts today tell us all children must. But what I remember is a long chain of hazy-golden years of almost total happiness."[1]

Jean Ritchie was born on December 8, 1922, in Viper, an unincorporated community in Perry County, Kentucky. Perched within the Cumberland Mountains, it was named for the sheer number of those snakes that were common to the region, although Ritchie admitted she was more worried about another of the region's purported inhabitants, "the scaly grampus, [because] if a grampus grabbed hold of your toe, he wouldn't let go until sundown."[2]

Her family was steeped in song. One of the first books the infant Jean ever read, and learned by heart, was *Lover's Melodies*, a songbook compiled and self-published by her father, Balis Wilmer Ritchie, in 1910, based upon the most popular songs at the nearby Hindman Settlement School—a favorite hunting ground, a few years later, of Cecil Sharp. (Most of the Ritchie children, of whom Jean was one of fourteen, attended Hindman.) Just twenty pages long, printed on the press he ordered through the mail—which was delivered on a mule-drawn wagon—and bound with the family sewing machine, *Lover's Melodies* combined the songs he knew from his own youth, with more recent compositions he heard around town.

Inevitably the book's contents slipped into young Jean's repertoire, while other songs were gifts from her Uncle Jason, a true aficionado of the ballads; it was he who taught her "The Lyttle Musgrave" (81), "The Cherry Tree Carol" (54), and, excitingly for any passing collectors, "The

Jean Ritchie. Mirrorpix / Alamy Stock Photo

Unquiet Grave" (78)—"something of an Appalachian rarity," wrote collector Mike Yates. "Once relatively well-known in Britain, it has seldom surfaced in America."[3] Another of what Ritchie described as Uncle Jason's "old ones" was "False Sir John" (4), and she points out that, while the song was descended from one of the great otherworldly epics, "Lady Isabel and the Elf Knight," in the Ritchies' hands, "the Elf-Knight is no longer a supernatural being but plain old False Sir John, and Lady Isabel has become simple May Colvin."[4]

Music was the family's life, the soundtrack to both work and play. In an interview with the BBC, Ritchie explained, "[My family] sang along with whatever they were doing. My mother had a sweeping song she liked to sing when she was sweeping because it had a good brushing rhythm. When she was churning, it was something else more quick and bouncy to go with the dasher coming down on the butter. For rocking babies there were lullabies, sometimes an old ballad where everybody gets killed in the end, but it had a nice soothing tune and the baby didn't understand the words."[5] (Singer Nancy Kerr tells a similar story, of how her mother Sandra used to sing her to sleep with "The Great Silkie of Sule Skerry" [113], the tragic tale of a woman who bears a child by a shapeshifting seal, in the knowledge that both her lover and baby will be shot dead by a hunter. The difference was, young Nancy *could* understand the words, and it terrified her.)

Ritchie also recalled the first gramophone, or "talking machine," the family ever owned, purchased long before she was born, around 1905, but still in regular use.

> My dad sent away to a mail order company. And then he had to take the mule and wagon to go about sixty miles to the nearest freight office and pick it up. Along the way home he'd stop at people's places and stay the night, and to pay for his lodging, he'd play them some music on the talking machine. It was one of those record players with a big horn in front, and you'd crank it up. They'd all run around, look behind, to see what was making the sounds. They all thought there must be a little man in there making music.[6]

Ritchie, who also played dulcimer, frequently performed at local fairs and other events. At Cumberland Junior College she studied social work. And in 1946 she graduated Phi Beta Kappa with a BA from the University of Kentucky at Lexington. Echoing Henry Lumpkin's dismissal of Edith Cummings Taylor's background as one of America's most talented astronomy students, Maud Karpeles later insisted Ritchie could not be described as a folk singer "because she has been to college."

It was around this time that Ritchie was recorded for the first time, singing with sisters Pauline, Edna, and Kitty, for collectors Mary Elizabeth Barnicle (1891–1978) and Artus Moser (1921–1988). She took her songs, too, to New York, where she was hired as a social worker at the Henry Street Settlement. There, she taught children the music that she had grown up with and, as word of her talents spread, she began catching the attention of the New York folk scene. She made her first New York live appearance at the Little Greenwich Mews Theater in 1948 and, just weeks later, was alongside Woody Guthrie, Pete Seeger, and Betty Saunders at the Spring Fever Hootenanny.

In that same BBC interview, Ritchie exclaimed,

> The Village was a very exciting place. A few of us used to go down into the subways and sing, because the acoustics were so good; we'd sing rounds and madrigals and things, down there. Nobody had seen a dulcimer before; I used to carry it on the subway wrapped in a scarf and once people found out it wasn't a gun, they wanted to see what it was, so I'd take it out and they'd say play it for us . . . I'd pluck it—bing—and they'd all go "wow!"

The following April, Alan Lomax invited Ritchie to record at his tiny West Third Street apartment, upstairs from a pizza parlor. Seated in front of the tape machine, Ritchie's pure tones rang out across a room strewn with tapes and books and records, the tools of Lomax's collecting trade. In the course of those sessions, Ritchie made her way through a dozen Child Ballads (and more).

Ritchie also came to the attention of the Canadian-American folksinger and humorist Oscar Brand (1920–2016), who recruited her as a regular on his popular WNYC radio show *Folksong Festival*. They went on to record three albums together and, later in the decade, co-headlined the show (alongside David Sear) released in 1959 as *A Folk Concert in Town Hall, New York*. Brand's take on "Lord Randall" (12—the accompanying booklet misnumbers it as 21) is one he first heard in Mineheart, Georgia, in 1942, and rates among his finest ever recordings.

Ritchie's career, by that time, was in full flow. In 1951, she signed with Elektra Records, newly launched by New York doctor's son Jac Holzman as a focus for his love of folk music. Ritchie was, in fact, among Holzman's very first recruits.

Although the singer later revealed that her debut album was recorded at the wrong speed ("I sound like I'm about 12 years old"),[7] *Jean Ritchie Singing the Traditional Songs of her Kentucky Family Home* remains a landmark album, both musically and commercially. It can also be classified as the first true folk LP ever released, in that Ritchie was recording the music as she knew and loved it and not, as could be said of the likes of Oscar Brand, Ed McCurdy, Burl Ives, and the Weavers, with at least a degree of either popular entertainment or agitation in mind. "Take me as you find me," she seemed to be saying and many people did.

Years later, writer Mick Houghton reflected upon the album's impact. "To everyone who knew anything about authentic folk music, Jean Ritchie was the undisputed queen of New York City."[8] Ritchie, on the other hand, attributed her record's success at least in part to Holzman's insistence that she come and sit in the Elektra store with her greyhound Lady Gay—named, of course, for the Child Ballad (79)—to greet customers and, perhaps, convince them to purchase her record.

She did not rest upon her laurels. Having applied for a Fulbright Scholarship to allow her to travel to the United Kingdom to trace the origins of her family's songs, Ritchie learned that she had been successful around the same time as her LP was released. Accompanied by her husband, photographer George Pickow, she departed almost immediately.

Crossing paths occasionally with Alan Lomax, who was also in Britain at this time, Ritchie amassed several hundred hours of material, and did so with considerable cunning. She discovered that when she asked people to sing her their old songs, they normally rewarded her with music hall numbers, "or something about shamrocks," as she put it. But, when she asked if they knew "Barbara Allen" (84), they immediately knew what she wanted. "They would bring out beautiful old things that matched mine and were variants of the songs that I knew in Kentucky. It was like coming home."[9] (Collecting in Nova Scotia, Helen Creighton employed a similar trick, asking potential sources if they knew "the one about the milk white steed," in the knowledge that "many songs have this phrase, and they are usually Child Ballads."[10])

It was close to four years before Ritchie boiled her tapes down to a single LP's worth of songs, 1956's *Field Trip*, with the finished item encompassing both rural discoveries and professional performers (Sarah Makem, Ewan MacColl, and Isla Cameron all feature), bell ringers, and pipe bands. She chose the eighteen songs on the album carefully, and while it was perhaps inevitable that "Barbara Allen" would find her way in, courtesy of a Mr. Rew, she also captured Douglas Kennedy, father of Peter, performing "The Death of Queen Jane" (170), the harrowing tale of a monarch's death during childbirth.

Ritchie's recording career continued apace. Her second and final Elektra album, *Kentucky Mountain Songs*, was released in 1954; thereafter, her material appeared on a variety of labels, among them the cream of the now-emergent folk revival's most perceptive outlets: the Clancy Brothers' Tradition, jazz labels Prestige and Riverside's folk subsidiaries, but most of all, Moses Asch's Folkways—active since 1948, but capable of drawing upon more than a decade's worth of earlier Asch productions, featuring Woody Guthrie, Burl Ives, Lead Belly, and more. Indeed, Folkways was swiftly to become the dominant force on the American folk scene, not only for its "current" releases (Pete Seeger alone recorded some sixty albums for the label), but also its attention to the past, with albums that delved into the roots of American traditional music in all of its many guises.

It was Folkways who released Ritchie's *Field Trips*; Folkways, too, who commissioned her to record two volumes of *British Traditional Ballads in the Southern Mountains*, comprising twenty-one Child Ballads from across her repertoire. Her liner notes speak of the special place the ballads occupied in the family's daily life:

> Of course we hummed them about the housework, and when walking along the roads and out in the fields, but that wasn't really singing them. It had to be a quiet time for that, as when the family gathered on the front porch, evenings, and after awhile the house clatter ended and the talk dwindled and died. Then was the time for "Lord Bateman" [53] or "The Gypsie Laddie" [200] to move into our thoughts.

The two albums reflect those "quiet times" as accurately as any gramophone record being played in a modern home possibly could.

With Child Ballads having already populated her earlier LPs, an under-taking such as this might have exhausted Ritchie's repertoire. But no. She and Oscar Brand had a fine time duetting "The Devil's Nine Questions" (1) for an eponymous LP in 1967; "Johnny Collins" (85) made its way onto 1971's *Clear Waters Remembered*.

In later years, Ritchie's focus shifted as her own songwriting came into its own, largely fueled by her feelings as the landscapes she grew up in were torn asunder by logging and strip mining. Nevertheless, she included her family's own version of "The Riddle Song" (46), again fea-turing Brand, on 1977's *None But One*.

With additional guest appearances from Susan Reed, Mary Travers, and Janis Ian, and released by Sire—a label better known at that time for its patronage of the New York City punk scene—*None But One* earned Ritchie the Folk Artist of the Year category in *Rolling Stone* magazine's Critics Music Awards. There, writer Paul Nelson described it as "a gen-tler, distaff *Basement Tapes* . . . eschew[ing] both portent and pretense, only to find greatness anyway, more through inherence than ambition. What we hear is not the questing for, but the realization and celebration of an identity—and that identity is as timeless and universal as it is beautiful."

In 1995, Ritchie celebrated fifty years of recording with the album *Mountain Born*; the title, too, of a documentary on her life screened the following year by Kentucky Educational Television. Judy Collins, Emmy-lou Harris, and other artists have acknowledged Ritchie's importance over the years; others have reached fresh heights from the music that she brought forth. Shirley Collins took her version of "Lady Margaret and Sweet William" (74) from that which Ritchie collected from Justus Begley of Hazard, Kentucky. Nowell Sing We Clear learned "The Cherry Tree Carol" (54) "from the Ritchie family of Kentucky." Pentangle credited Ritchie with their 1969 take on "The House Carpenter" (243). The Owl Service picked her "Geordie" (209) from the Alan Lomax archive. Across six decades, Ritchie's influence on the music she loved remains strong even today.

Ritchie passed away, aged ninety-two, on June 1, 2015. Her health had been failing in recent years; a stroke in 2009 was followed by her hus-band's death in 2010, shortly after they celebrated their fiftieth wedding anniversary. After two-thirds of a lifetime spent in New York and there-abouts, her last years were spent back home in Kentucky.

Chapter Twenty-Two

THE BIRTH OF THE BOOM

By the late 1940s, it was clear that a folk boom of some description was underway in America. In part, it was nurtured by political dissent. This was the age of the atom bomb (and its even more sinister cousin, the hydrogen bomb), of virulent anti-Communism and the creation of the House Un-American Activities Committee. A flood of sympathetic artists poured their emotions out in what the media referred to as folk songs.

But tradition lived on regardless. Richard Dyer-Bennett (1932–1991) was a self-styled "twentieth-century minstrel" who, though born in Leicester, England, made his career in the United States. Recorded in September 1941, his first album, *Lute Singer (Ballads and Folk Songs)* includes versions of "The House Carpenter" (243) and "The Golden Vanity" (286), alongside a "Drunken Sailor" that in turn surely helped influence Burl Ives's treatment of the shanty. A steady stream of releases through the late 1940s and 1950s included excellently executed versions of "Lord Randall" (12), "The Wife Wrapped in Sheepskin" (277), "The Willow Tree" (4), "Binnorie" (10), and more, and even the album of children's songs that he recorded toward the end of his career found ways of squeezing Child into the proceedings: "The Devil and the Farmer's Wife" (278) and "The Soldier and the Lady" (299) both appear on 1964's *Stories and Songs for Children and Their Parents*.

The duo of John and Lucy Allison included a dramatic American take on "Archie O'Cawfield" (188), and "The Escape of Old John Webb" on their 1943 album *Early American Ballads*, replacing the original Scottish border raider with a Massachusetts forger. Four years later, the so-called "thinking men's hillbillies" Homer and Jethro recorded a very merry "Three Nights Experience" (274).

Child Ballads even made it into the movies. Ritchie Blackmore, famed as guitarist with the hard rock band Deep Purple, recalls, "One of my favorite films is *Tom Brown's Schooldays*, the 1940 version [starring Cedrick Hardwicke and Freddie Bartholomew], and 'Barbara Allen' is being played in the background throughout the film."[1] On that occasion, the music was fully orchestrated by veteran soundtrack composer Anthony Collins. Other Child-infused movies, however, recruited genuine folk singers. African-American Josh White (1914–1969) performs a gentle acoustic "I Gave My Love A Cherry" (46) in Randolph Scott's 1949 movie *The Walking Hills*, while British folk singer Elton Hayes (1915–2001) enjoyed a film career on both sides of the Atlantic.

In the United Kingdom during the 1940s, Hayes was a familiar sight on the social and folk club scenes, long before he was moved into radio with a regular spot on the BBC's *In Town Tonight*. He toured the United States and, in 1948, made his movie debut in the British wartime comedy *A Date with a Dream*. His unnamed character appears in the credits simply as "the Singer." Four years later, he played Alan O'Dale in Disney's *The Story of Robin Hood and His Merrie Men*, and again the role had a musical element, as he performed "Whistle, My Love." Now, in 1954, he was cast as "the Minstrel" in Alan Ladd's Arthurian epic *The Black Knight*, and the writers turned to Professor Child for Hayes's contribution to the soundtrack. It was only a brief performance, but it certainly made a powerful impression upon one aspiring young musician as she listened to the radio one afternoon in spring, 1954.

Judith Marjorie Collins was born in Seattle in 1939, but was now living with her family in Oneida, East Denver. With an Irish grandfather who was forever singing, and a father who hosted local radio and played guitar and sang, it was a musical family, although hopes that Judith might follow in their footsteps were built around her apparent love for classical piano. Collins studied under the great Dutch pianist and conductor Antonia Brico and, on this particular day, she was supposed to be practicing Bach's Second Piano Concerto for an upcoming symphony date with the orchestra Brico led. She was, she recalled, "14 and a half, maybe 15. I happened to turn on the radio, and I heard Elton Hayes singing 'The Gypsy Rover' [200] on a score for the Alan Ladd movie *The Black Knight*."[2]

Abandoning Bach, Collins hastened to the local Wells Music store to purchase a copy of the soundtrack album, noting from the label that Irish songwriter Leo McGuire (1903–1985) was credited with having composed the song—which he titled "The Whistling Gypsy"—himself. The man behind the counter swiftly disavowed her of that impression, however. He explained how this was just one of many versions of the song, some of them dating back centuries before McGuire was even born, and Collins was intrigued.

She and her friends Marsha and Carol had recently been performing a musical skit based around the story of *Little Red Riding Hood* at various venues around town. Now they were actively searching for another story to adapt, and Collins thought she had found it in "The Whistling Gypsy." Unfortunately, she sat on her copy of the soundtrack album almost the moment she got it home, breaking the fragile shellac into pieces. The popularity of the soundtrack recording, however, ensured there would be plenty of future opportunities to learn the song from the radio, and soon Collins' and her friends' interpretation of *The Whistling Gypsy* was being performed across Denver and "our heads were filled with dreams of . . . taking [it] to Las Vegas."[3]

She was, as she has said on many occasions, hooked on traditional music; or she would be, very soon. A short time after, "I was listening to the same radio station and they played 'Barbara Allen,' sung by Jo Stafford. And those two songs, "Barbara Allen' and 'The Gypsy Rover,' ignited my folk music career."[4]

"Barbara Allen" was one of six songs Stafford recorded for her 1948 album *Jo Stafford Sings American Folk Songs* (Burl Ives's signature "Wayfaring Stranger" was another). Her version drips strings and emotion, a driven rendering and one more in the long stream of hits she was then enjoying.[5] Collins was certainly smitten. "I immediately went out and bought the record, and it's a funny story because, of course, Jo and I were politically at very opposite ends of the pole. But I was able, many years after, to write the foreword to her box set!"[6]

With this story, Judy Collins, as she swiftly became better known, introduces us to an entirely new breed of folk musician. In the distant past, and more recently too, songs (and not only songs, but traditions as well) were passed between performers through social interaction—one thinks of Joseph Taylor learning his first songs from the Travelers on their way to Brigg Fair, or Burl Ives hearing them sung by his grandmother. The gramophone record, although it was now over half a century old, was still a newcomer in those terms. But it was making ever deeper inroads into the popular consciousness, through radio, television, and movies, and suddenly there was a world of learning to be garnered without even leaving the house. It does not sound at all unusual today for a traditional singer to admit to learning their repertoire from old records in their collection. Collins's generation was the first for whom that was possible.

Besides, Jo Stafford was certainly a superlative teacher. Collins recalls how she already knew Stafford's voice from her past hits. "She had a voice as smooth as honey, rich in tone, and clear in diction. She had sung with the Pied Pipers as well as Frank Sinatra."[7] The English singer Shirley Collins likewise recalls Stafford, "who sang folky pop songs such as 'Shrimp Boats,'"[8] as a radio favorite while she was growing up.

Jo Stafford in 1948, shortly before recording her version of "Barbara Allen." Wikimedia Commons

In terms of her musical choices, Stafford was as far from traditional music as it was possible to get. But her voice was perfect for so bereft a ballad as "Barbara Allen," and the man at the Wells Music doubtless explained that song's roots, too, to Judy Collins when she rushed in to buy a copy of *American Folk Songs.* "I was hooked, and the minute I got hooked, I began searching and hunting and buying books and buying records, joining the Denver Folklore Society and going up into the mountains, listening to all these folkies playing their instruments and learning at great pain how to play the guitar.

"It was an education and a study of American and of course English, Scottish and Irish history. Now I have a great collection of books and resources, shelves and shelves of books . . . and everything that I read and get involved with in terms of the history of folk music is very important to my choices of songs I sing."[9]

Collins was still some years away from taking her place among the ranks of America's most-beloved traditional singers. Now that she was paying attention, however, it was clear that there were many places in which she should be looking for further information and inspiration. Beginning with a crash course in the work of Pete Seeger, son of the near-legendary Charles Seeger Jr.

Born in New York on May 3, 1919, Pete Seeger—like Alan Lomax—was very much following in his father's footsteps when he turned toward folk music. His parents divorced when he was seven; ten years later, his father married composer Ruth Crawford, and it was this marriage that confirmed the folk singing Seeger dynasty, with all four of its progeny, Mike, Peggy, Barbara, and Penny becoming performers. All, too, were deeply steeped in traditional music—family lore reports that, when Peggy was two and hospitalized with a burned foot, her parents found her room by following the sound of someone singing "Barbara Allen" (84).

It was alongside his father and step-mother, too, that Seeger discovered the instrument that would carry him through his musical career. The family was attending the 1936 Mountain Dance and Folk Festival, staged near Asheville, North Carolina, when he heard the five-stringed banjo being played by Bascom Lamar Lunsford (1882–1973). Instantly enamored with its sound, the teen would spend the next four years learning to master the instrument (and published the now-classic *How to Play the Five-String Banjo* in 1948), while also taking his first steps as a public performer.

From there, Seeger's career—both as a musician and as a political activist (and often both simultaneously)—took off. He formed the Almanac Singers in 1941; that group metamorphosed into the Weavers in 1950; and the canon of songs those two groups amassed represents perhaps the most influential catalog in modern American music, while simultaneously delving deep into the traditional songbook for some genuinely under-sung ballads.

The Almanac Singers recorded three Child Ballads (although more were apparently included in their live repertoire): "The Coast of High Barbary" (285), "The Golden Vanity" (286), and a thoroughly revamped "Lord Randal" (12), retitled "Billy Boy." With its lyric furiously realigned against the military complex, and including the decidedly untraditional line, "it wouldn't be much thrill / To die for DuPont in Brazil," the sing-along chorus of "Billy Boy," "he's a young boy and cannot leave his mother," completes a magnificent reinvention.

The Weavers, too, were more committed to comment than the majority of Child Ballads would allow. "You Old Fool" is a breezy recital of "Our

Goodman" (274), performed with wry humor by Lee Hays and Ronnie Gilbert, from their 1959 album *At Home*. But it was left to Pete Seeger alone, recording as a solo artist throughout the careers of both groups, to fully embrace the Child Ballads' continued resonance on the American scene.

The albums *American Ballads* and its successors *America's Favorite Ballads* volumes two and three, are particularly laden with such survivors. He revisited "The Golden Vanity" (286) and "My Good Man" (274), toyed with "Gypsy Davy" (200), broke hearts with "Barbara Allen" (84), raised laughs with "The Farmer's Curst Wife" (278), and more. Indeed, Seeger's eye for the humor in the ballads is confirmed by the breathless "Risselty-Rosselty" (277) that graced 1956's *With Voices Together We Sing*; while his 1962 *The Bitter and the Sweet* live album captures his showmanship at its very best, as he leads the audience through the tales of "Barbara Allen" (84) and "The False Knight upon the Road" (3).

Seeger's repertoire also acts as an accurate gauge of just how inextricably certain Child Ballads were bound up with the American folk experience. He was, after all, an entertainer far more than he was an explorer, and so chose the songs that an audience was most likely to recognize: "Lord Randall" (and its variant "Henry My Son") (12), "The Riddle Song" (46), "The House Carpenter" (243), and "Fair Margaret and Sweet William" (74), which he described as "one of the first [ballads] I ever learned . . . from the country lawyer and old-time banjo picker of Asheville, North Carolina, Bascom Lunsford." He pointed out, too, that the ballad's final verses, "describing the conversation between Lady Margaret's ghost and her false lover, are as close as we get to superstition in this LP."[10]

Bascom Lamar Lunsford described his own discovery of the ballad. "This fine text and melody is a centuries-old tale, with supernatural overtones that make it peculiarly effective. One time when visiting the Roaring Forks section of Madison County, N.C., I heard little nine-year-old Alice Payne sing this song, just as given here. She had learned it from her mother and grandmother and had never seen a written copy."[11] (Another effective banjo-fired version of the same ballad, from a different source, appeared on Obray Ramsey's 1957 LP *Banjo Songs from the Blue Ridge and Great Smokies*.)

Only occasionally would Seeger dig deeper into the *ESPB*. Teamed with Frank Hamilton to record a couple of songs for *Nonesuch and Other Folk Tunes*, he turned in a rare "Lady Gay" (79); and "The Half Hitch" (31) was among his choices for 1961's *Story Songs*. Most fascinating of all, however, was Seeger's inclusion of "Elder Bordee," an Adirondack variant on "Sir Andrew Barton" (167), on an album investigating the work of Marjory Lansing Porter (1891–1973).

Smithsonian Folkways' *Music from the Champlain Valley* brought into focus a collection that began, as Porter herself wrote, completely by chance. She was visiting a resort on Lake George when she happened to meet "Grandma" Lily Delorme, an old woman who was giving a spinning demonstration to the vacationers.

> Her story of pioneer life in an Adirondack valley was set to a musical hum as she paced, now close to the big wheel, now away from it. Grandma's saga continued in lively conversation as she rode home. She spoke of her grandfather, Gideon Baker, and of his muzzle-loader and bullet mold from the War of 1812. Did she, by any chance, happen to know a ballad composed by the wife of General Macomb during the battle of Plattsburgh, The Banks of Champlain? Why, yes, it went this way, "'Twas autumn and round me the leaves were descending"—Her thin, reedy voice told the whole story in a score of verses.[12]

That meeting was "the seed for a constructive activity—the collection of folksongs, ballads and lore illustrative of life in the Adirondacks and its adjacent Champlain Valley." Another hitherto hidden source was revealed.

Considering the vast impact Seeger had on the emergent folk revival, his relationship with traditional songs in general, and the Child Ballads in particular, was tenuous. His importance, then, is as a vehicle by which other performers might hear and learn the rudiments of the folk tradition; his goals were less concerned with developing a text or an arrangement than they were in nurturing an appreciation of the music, and the principles (political and cultural) that he believed were integral to it. It is in his own songwriting that we see Seeger at his finest; the ballads are simply the space-fillers around which he arranged his own material.

In this, of course, he is scarcely that different from many of the other performers that arose during the first decade of the folk revival—Dick Wilder, Hermes Nye, Susan Reed, and more all made albums that can be said to have cared more for preserving traditional arrangements than offering them any kind of future.

Yet all have their role to play in the growth of the folk revival. Reed (1926–2010), in particular, enthralled. Shirley Collins credits Reed's performance in the 1948 movie *Glamour Girl* (released in Britain as *Night Club Girl*) for sparking her love of folk music in the first place. It is the story of a Tennessee folk singer, played by Reed, discovered by a talent agent in her Appalachian home, and brought to New York to become a superstar.

Reed's career, while never following that particular trajectory, nevertheless saw her record some eight different Child Ballads over the course of half a dozen albums,[13] the majority on her Elektra label debut, 1954's *Susan Reed Sings Old Airs (From Ireland, Scotland and England)*. A pure, warm voice and her deft touch on the harp was an especially winning combination in a scene that often felt extraordinarily male dominated.

A CD reissue of Susan Reed's eponymous 1957 LP. Author's collection

Her "Barbara Allen" (from 1957's *Susan Reed*) is particularly powerful, building to a positive crescendo of grief as it approaches its end, with the death bell knelling its condemnation of Barbara's hard-heartedness. It is not too great a leap to suggest that it was Reed's success within folk circles that opened the door, over the next few years, for the emergence, in rapid succession, of Carolyne Hester, Joan Baez, and Judy Collins.[14]

Equally of note, and echoing Reed's penchant for less familiar instrumentation, were Bob "Fiddler" Beers and Evelyne, whose 1960 album *Walkie in the Parlor* saw Evelyne's crystalline voice accompanied by the psaltery, a plucked instrument in the zither family. "Lord Randall" (12) is one of several songs learned from Bob's grandfather, George Sullivan, that were featured on the album; others include the perpetual ear worm "Sulphur Molasses," the lyrically askance "Hindside Before," and the frankly odd title track. Grandad George was a homesteader in North Freedom, Wisconsin, around the time of the Civil War. Hailing from an Irish settlement in Pennsylvania, he was said to be a locally renowned storyteller, and the best-known fiddler for a radius of fifty miles. Bob Beers first played the instrument alongside his grandfather at age seven, the first steps toward developing an act that saw him perform in the guise of an old time fiddler.

Beers met Evelyne Andresen, a founding member of the famed Virginia City Players, in 1943; according to the *Montana Kaimin* newspaper, she was once described by Hungarian-American composer Sigmund Romberg as "having the most beautiful voice he had ever heard. Strangely enough, Evelyne Beers has never had a voice lesson, nor can she read music."[15] Initially, Evelyne acted as her husband's business manager. By the mid-1950s, however, they were touring together, and in 1960 their folk-themed television show *On Strings of Song* was voted "the best TV music program in the western states" by *TV Radio Mirror Magazine*. Recorded with daughter Martha at their home in Montana, the Beers's "Lord Randall" is indicative of the family's love and respect for Grandpa Sullivan's repertoire. "This is the Sullivan version," the album's liner notes remark, but the fifth and the final verses were added by Bob Beers "from other sources" so as to complete the narrative.

Chapter Twenty-Three

THE CURIOUS TALE OF ROBIN HOOD

It is often suggested that, if Child miscalculated any element whatsoever of *ESPB*, it was his inclusion of so many ballads pertaining to Robin Hood. One entire volume within the original series, totaling almost forty ballads (117–54) was devoted to him (the equally renowned King Arthur receives just three, 29–31), with Child's introduction explaining,

> There is not one of the royal heroes of England that enjoys a more enviable reputation than the bold outlaw of Barnsdale and Sherwood. His chance for a substantial immortality is at least as good as that of stout Lion Heart, wild Prince Hal, or merry Charles. His fame began with the yeomanry full five hundred years ago, was constantly increasing for two or three centuries, has extended to all classes of society, and, with some changes of aspect, is as great as ever. Bishops. sheriffs, and game-keepers, the only enemies he ever had, have relinquished their ancient grudges, and Englishmen would be almost as loath to surrender his exploits as any part of the national glory. His free life in the woods, his unerring eye and strong arm, his open hand and love of fair-play, his never-forgotten courtesy, his respect for women and devotion to [the Virgin] Mary, form a picture eminently healthful and agreeable to the imagination, and commend him to the hearty favor of all genial minds.

We should not be surprised by Child's generosity toward the Hood. Compiling the earlier *ESB*, he devoted one complete volume of that work, too, to Robin; no less than fifty-three titled pieces. On both occasions, incidentally, Robin's ballads were placed in volume five.

For all his fascination with the ballads, Child is not altogether convinced by Robin's place in history. "Securely established as Robin Hood is in popular esteem," he continues, still he reminds us that "'a tale of Robin Hood' is an old proverb for the idlest of stories." Nevertheless, the ballads needed to be preserved, and the green-clad hero would ultimately consume over one-tenth of the complete collection, relaying or replaying the myriad adventures and exploits for which Robin was renowned. Yet they remain largely untouched even today.

Singer and folklorist Alasdair Roberts ventures to explain perhaps an element of the Hood ballads' comparative obscurity, and that of other historical pieces:

> I think it's telling that a lot of the ballads which haven't remained so popular into the present day are the ones which are more specific—perhaps about certain battles, feuds, locations, individuals or historical situations—rather than the ones which have that sort of anonymous, timeless universality. It reminds me in a way of political campaign songs—during the Scottish Independence Referendum [2014], for example, many songs were written and sung for the period of a few weeks leading up to the day of the big vote, but I doubt whether anybody will ever sing most of them ever again. They're too specific to that time. It's similar with a seldom-sung ballad such as "The Battle of Otterburn" [161] or whatever—people nowadays might sing it as a curiosity, out of historical interest, but it's difficult for most listeners to relate to it emotionally or psychologically (unless your ancestors fought at Otterburn, of course, in which case I apologise).[1]

At the same time, however, has Robin Hood ever relinquished his hold on the popular imagination? In print, on the radio, television, and the cinema, we have never had a shortage of presentations both repeating and embroidering the original adventures, including several that made genuine efforts to portray their period with a degree of authenticity—the BBC's 1956 *Robin Hood* series even recruited Alan Lomax as an adviser on the music that was deployed throughout the series.

For all their comparative obscurity, however, a closer look at the ballads illustrates precisely what Professor Child was trying to achieve in his curation of *ESPB*. He was aware that their inclusion was not necessarily wholly justified. In one letter, he described his decision to begin part five with Robin as "bold"; in other correspondence he conceded that his intention of restricting the collection's tales of derring-do to historical figures and events was seriously undermined by the belief that Robin Hood himself may never have existed. Some of his inclusions even flaunted his insistence that the included ballads genuinely *were* ballads; of "The Tale of Robin Hood" (154), for example, Child mused that although "it might contain much traditional material not elsewhere found," he nevertheless regretted not simply reducing it to an appendix. "I wish . . . I had not given it a number." His personal fancies were for the earliest ballads, an opinion analogous today to the music fan whose tastes are steeped in classic rock, and who regards more modern sounds as little more than crass commercialism. "The earliest of these ballads," Child wrote, "are among the best of all ballads, and perhaps none in English please so many and please so long. . . . On the other hand . . . a considerable part of the Robin Hood poetry looks like char-work done for the petty press, and should be judged as such."

Neither was he alone in his distaste for what he considered to be these latter-day concoctions. A century earlier, antiquarian Joseph Ritson—author of the highly acclaimed *Robin Hood: A Collection of All the Ancient Poems, Songs, and Ballads, Now Extant . . .*—seized upon one particular ballad, "The King's Disguise, and Friendship with Robin Hood" (151), as having been "written by some miserable retainer to the press, merely to eke out [a] book; being, in fact, a most contemptible performance." Bertrand Harris Bronson poured his scorn out on "Robin Hood and the Prince of Aragon" (129) and its "forty-six rather deplorable stanzas,"[2] with his fury further compounded by the revelation that this admittedly slight offering not only survived in England, it was one of the ballads that made the crossing to North America as well, in the repertoire of the earliest settlers (it would eventually be retitled ". . . the Prince of *Oregon*").

One can understand such points of view, of course. There is a beauty to the earlier ballads that is quite lacking from many of their later counterparts, a sense that the first writers wrote for the love of the song and the joy of their audience, while those that came after them were motivated more by the lure of filthy lucre. Here is Child discussing "Robin Hood and the Tinker" (127), a verse that almost certainly dates from the eighteenth century: "The fewest words will best befit this contemptible imitation of imitations." Or "Robin Hood and Maid Marian" (150): a "foolish ditty." He rages on. "Robin Hood and Queen Katherine" (145) is "a piece of regular hack-work"; and while the professor admitted that "Robin Hood's Chase" (146) is "a well-conceived ballad," he still cannot resist a most elitist poke at it. "[It] needs to be older." "Robin Hood and the Pedlars" (137), on the other hand, might well be a genuinely ancient piece. But he would nevertheless "be glad to be rid of it."

Cecil Sharp was the first post-Child collector to encounter the ballads of Robin Hood in the wild, when eighty-two-year-old Blind Henry Larcombe sang him "Robin Hood and the Tanner" (126) in September 1903.[3] Three years later, during his first ever collecting trip, Percy Grainger captured a performance of "Robin Hood and the Three Squires" (140), from Dean Robinson. Others were found as far afield as Hampshire, England, by Vaughan Williams and Nova Scotia, Canada, by Helen Creighton. James Madison Carpenter's collection boasts two Robin Hood ballads; Ben Gray Lumpkin gathered "Robin Hood and Little John" (125) from

Edith Cummings Taylor; and in October 1943, the BBC recorded Peter Sandry, a singer and storyteller from Helston, Cornwall, performing a version of "Robin Hood and Little John" that local tradition had repurposed for the Mayday festivities and retitled "The Helston Furry Song":

> *Robin Hood and Little John they both are gone to fair-o*
> *And we will to the merry Greenwood*
> *To see what they do there-o*
> *With hal an tow, jolly rumble-o*

Doubtless there were other people singing these songs, who weren't captured by a passing collector. Nevertheless, given the sheer number of Robin Hood ballads noted by Child, these are very slim pickings indeed, and it has been suggested that this paucity of performance might be the result of Robin's sheer ubiquity elsewhere in the modern world. It is, after all, ironic that the most oft-recorded of all the Robin Hood ballads, "The Birth of Robin Hood" (102) is not, by Child, considered to even be a part of the cycle. Rather, it is the tale of two lovers who, having fled their homes rather than confess to pregnancy, hide out in the woods and give birth to a son who, in some versions, is named Robin Hood. Child titled this same ballad "Willie and Earl Richard's Daughter."

Researcher Bob Askew, speaking at the English Folk Dance and Song Society in 2015, argued that movie and television adaptations have lifted Robin Hood clear out of the folk milieu, and established him instead as a product of modern mainstream mythology—the kiss-of-death, of course, in a medium that prides itself on unspoiled tradition. It is true, as Askew pointed out, that two Robin Hood plays were more popular than Shakespeare in the late sixteenth century. He continued, however,

> In the romantic era, Walter Scott made [Robin] an Anglo-Saxon fighting Norman oppressors. In the 19th century he became a children's book hero who did not kill anybody, and who robbed the rich to give to the poor. He became a film hero once cinema was invented, and later a TV hero. . . . He has been depicted with involvement with space travelers [the Canadian animated series Rocket Robin Hood and the Doctor Who episode "Robot of Sherwood"]. The ballad stories have been used as a basis in every major adaption. So I think that Robin Hood's continuing popularity is the real reason why the ballads are not sung much nowadays. He seems to be current, rather than from the mysterious past.

Yet it is the very stubbornness of the ballad stories that maintains the "modern" Robin's links to his ancient forebear. "The Bold Pedlar and Robin Hood" (132) was still being sung in England as late as 1846, as James H. Dixon revealed in his *Ballads, and Songs of the Peasantry of England*, published that same year. "An aged female in Bermondsey, Surrey, from

THE CURIOUS TALE OF ROBIN HOOD

whose oral recitation the editor took down the present version, informed him that she had often heard her grandmother sing it . . . ; he [Dixon] has of late met with several common stall copies"—that is, printed copies of the ballad being sold on the streets. These were probably the work of James "Jemmy" Catnach, the prolific broadsheet publisher who issued a broadside of the song sometime between 1813 and 1838.

Furthermore, collector Mike Yates discovered the same ballad in the repertoire of George Trainer, of Haywards Heath, as late as 1964, around the same time as another researcher, Frank Purslow, discovered one elsewhere in Sussex. Yates concluded, "So, at one time, it seems that 'Robin Hood and the Pedlar' was relatively well-known, at least in one part of Sussex." (It was Trainer's rendition that the singers Emily and Hazel Askew performed on their 2005 album *Six By Two*.)

According to Grey Malkin, whose The Hare and the Moon project ranks among the Child Ballads' most imaginative modern interpreters,

> One of the aspects about the Robin Hood ballads that I am personally intrigued by is how little has changed in their telling over the centuries, as if the authors or storytellers hit the nail on the head from the word go and tapped into something in the storytelling form that was almost perfectly constructed and timeless. [However], by the folk revival heyday of the late 1960s and early 1970s, Robin Hood was associated with green-tighted Errol Flynn style heroics and was simply not viewed as being very cool, happening or "authentic." In hindsight, this glaring omission could be viewed as a genuine shame, for such an illustrious and potentially counter-cultural figure to be so excluded. However, arguably Robin has instead found an alternative and potentially more timeless home in interpretations on both television and in cinema.[4]

If the Robin Hood ballads were seldom performed "in the field," then they were even scarcer onstage. Which means singer Wallace House was certainly taking a step into the arcane when, in 1953, he released the album *Robin Hood Ballads*, sensibly comprising nothing but tales of the man in tights. Born in Guernsey, in the Channel Islands, in 1900, House moved to Toronto at the age of nine. There he became involved in theater work and, by 1920, had relocated to New York City, where he made several appearances on Broadway. Rising to become a professor at New York University, House also found his way onto radio, a folk performer with an especial affection for tales of the American West. However, he also ventured further afield. His first album, in 1952, was called *English Folk Songs*, although it was utterly devoid of Child Ballads.

He made amends with *Robin Hood Ballads*. Of the ten tracks on the album, only one ("Robin Hood's Morris," first collected in 1860 by Sabine Baring-Gould) was omitted from *ESPB*. He chose well, too. "There are

Grey Malkin of the Hare and the Moon disappears into the Greenwood. Courtesy Grey Malkin

probably over fifty authentic Robin Hood ballads which have been handed down and preserved," the smartly mustachioed House wrote. "I have selected [those] which tell of his life and the well-known figures associated with him." To add further charm to his performances, or what he called "an authentic 13th Century atmosphere," he accompanied himself on a flat-backed twelve-stringed Spanish guitar, thus to suggest "the quality of the instruments of the period, the lute and the cithern."[5]

Opening with the story of how the Earl of Huntingdon became Robin Hood in the first place ("A True Tale of Robin Hood"—154), he goes on to recount Robin's initial encounters with Friar Tuck ("Robin Hood and the Curtal Friar"—123), the animal catcher ("The Jolly Pinder of Wakefield"—124), Little John ("Robin Hood and Little John"—125), and Arthur a'Bland ("Robin Hood and the Tanner"—126); his rescue of the three poachers ("Robin Hood and the Three Squires"—140); and his fights with the forester ("Robin Hood and the Ranger"—131), and the disguised Maid Marian ("Robin Hood and Maid Marian"—150). It is from this same sampling that what we can now describe as the most frequently (yet still sparingly) recorded Hood ballads have been drawn, although a handful more have since come to life, including versions of "Robin Hood and the Fifteen Foresters" (139) by Ed McCurdy (1973) and English folk singer John Goodluck (1974).

House was very much a voice in the wilderness, although he did open the door a little for other admirers of Robin to creep through. Charles Finnemore included "Robin Hood Rescuing the Three Squires" (140) on 1953's *Burly Banks of Barbry O* collection of eight traditional British-American ballads; and Bert Lloyd recorded "Robin Hood and the Tanner" in 1956.

The most significant nod to Robin, however, came the following year, when Hermes Nye (1908–1981) recorded two of his Child Ballads, "Robin Hood's Golden Prize" (147) and "The Death of Robin Hood" (120).

What Jean Ritchie meant to the traditions of Kentucky, Nye represented for East Texas—despite having been born in Chicago. A lawyer by trade, and a liberal activist by inclination, Nye was also a folk singer, a folklorist, a novelist, and a humorist—a point firmly made with the title of his 1965 songbook, *How to Be a Folksinger: How to Sing and Present Folksongs; or, The Folksinger's Guide; or, Eggs I Have Laid.* His focus was primarily upon Texan or, more generally, Civil War and military music. However, Nye's first LP, the *Anglo-American Ballads* collection, for Folkways in 1952, delivered ten ballads of that description; and he returned to the theme five years later with the grandly titled *Ballads Reliques: Early English Ballads from the Percy and Child Collections.* Almost unnecessarily, he remarked, "I have a sneaking fondness for the English things from Percy and Child, especially when I can find Texas versions."[6]

He did not always succeed, but the twenty songs on the album, all Child Ballads, nevertheless offer a unique snapshot of Nye's interests, his gently melodic voice resonant against a simple acoustic guitar accompaniment. He acknowledged the greatest difficulty facing the modern balladeer; namely, "Child, as a professor of literature cared nothing for the tunes, and these have had to be dredged out here and there. The best books I have seen on the tunes are *Ballads of Britain,* by John Goss, Editor,

The Bodley Head Press, 1937, and, for the Robin Hood tunes, a superbly produced *Song of Robin Hood*, Anne Malcolmson, Editor, Houghton Mifflin, 1947"[7]—hence, in the latter instance, his choice of songs.

Ballads Reliques is a magnificent album. Nye's eye throughout is trained upon either historical ballads or tragedies: "Queen Eleanor's Confession" (156), "The Queen's Maries" (173), and the story of Scottish legend Rob Roy's marriage (225) rank among the former; "Binnorie, or The Cruel Sister" (10), "The Three Ravens" (26), and "The Lament of the Border Widow" (106) among the latter. And the humor that dignifies his performances is evident in his text too. Of "Binnorie," he writes, "Sir Walter Scott collected [this song], and probably had enough integrity not to add to it, although we can never be sure about those old boys."[8]

There is room, too, for the supernatural, as "The Outlandish Knight" (4) and "Sweet William's Ghost" (77) are joined by a full blooded "Thomas the Rhymer" (37). "Thomas of Ercildoune was his true name," explained Nye.

> He was known as a poet, but first of all as a seer and prophet. He was carried off to Fairyland by the Queen of the Fairies, where he got all his lore. He was then allowed to come back to earth, to spread the good word among his Scottish countrymen; he was to go back to Fairyland, however, whenever the Queen called him. One day as he was birling at the wine (the red, red wine, the wine butt and the beer), a hart and a hind wandered down the village street. Thomas left his birling, followed them into the forest and has not been seen to this day. Those who doubt the story may go to Ercildoune and see, not the Eildon Tree, now long since cut down, but the Eildon Tree Stone which stood close by, and Bogle Burn (Goblin Brook) where the Queen appeared.[9]

"Thomas the Rhymer" is now placed within the upper echelons of the *ESPB*, compliments of the manifold recordings it has spawned—and Ewan MacColl notwithstanding, Nye was responsible for the first of these. It is his appreciation of the ballads of Robin Hood, however, for which he might best be celebrated.

"Robin Hood's Golden Prize" (147) reminds us of the occasion when Robin disguised himself as a friar and begged for charity from two passing monks, who turned out not to be very charitable whatsoever. "The Death of Robin Hood" (120), which was also recorded by Wallace House, meanwhile, tells the tale that leads up to the fateful moment when Robin, mortally wounded, shot an arrow out the window. Wherever it landed, he declared with his final breath, was where he should be buried. In both instances, we get the impression that Nye selected his ballads for their length as much as their content: "Most of the Robin Hood songs," he writes, "run to sixty or even a hundred verses." And why? Because, in those days, "there was nothing to do but to listen to the lute, and the minstrel singing the sun down the sky in the court-yard of an afternoon."[10]

Perhaps the greatest contribution to the modern survival of the Robin Hood ballads, however, was offered by anthropologist and folklorist Hester NicEilidh. In 2005, she launched the Robin Hood Project with the intention of making fresh recordings of all the Robin Hood ballads included in the *ESPB*. Her interest, she explains, grew out of her love of the 1980s British TV series *Robin of Sherwood*, with Michael Praed a glowering hooded man, and a haunting theme by Clannad.

> I was intrigued with the show's pagan interpretation of the legend. This led me to explore parallels between the Robin Hood ballads and older pagan mythological narratives. Generally, if a tune is not specified for a ballad in the extant printed/written sources, and the ballad is not part of the surviving performed folk repertoire, it is usually assumed that the ballad was "literary" and originally intended to be read, not sung. This is certainly Child's assumption for the oldest extant Robin Hood ballads, such as "The Gest" and "The Monk" (119). (*ESPB* cites dates, respectively, of "probably" 1489 and 1450.) In response, I began to search for recorded versions of the Robin Hood ballads, but they were few and far between.[11]

Among those she located were recordings by Wallace House, Bert Lloyd, Ed McCurdy, and Herman Nye in the 1950s, Barry Dransfield and Steeleye Span in the 1970s, Estampie and, most recently, Bob Frank's album-length country-style rendering of the marathon *A Little Gest of Robin Hood* (117). A handful of others. But if she wanted to hear all of the ballads being performed, she realized, she would have to perform them herself. "For many of the ballads, particularly those said to have 'no known associated tune,' I could find no recorded versions. That led me to the idea of trying to record some of my own versions around 2005–6, even though I was a very novice singer, and to try to encourage other singers and musicians to look at the Robin Hood ballads as potential performance material."[12]

She remedied the first pitfall by marrying "orphaned" lyrics to tunes from other ballads: "Robin Hood and The Monk, pt. 1" (119) she set to the traditional British folk tune "In Summertime," "Robin Hood's Xmas at Gamwell Hall" (149) was allied with "Robin Hood and the Ranger" (131); "Robin Hood and the Pedlars" (137) to "The Three Ravens" (26), and so forth. Ultimately, the Robin Hood Project never did fulfill its aim of recording all of the Robin Hood ballads, although that is not to say it was a failure. NicEilidh continues,

> My attempts to record the ballads were always intended primarily as a demonstration that the supposed literary "text" could in fact be easily paired with traditional tunes from other sources. I do not have any musical training, other than some brief singing classes for adult beginners at the Royal Conservatory of music in Toronto. I don't read music or play an instrument. So, I was hoping to inspire some real musicians to attempt to revitalize some

of the "orphaned" Robin Hood ballads and re-integrate them into the performed folk music repertoire. Alas, my "Robin Hood Ballad Project" did not exactly go viral.[13]

Yet, within a year or so of the project launching, YouTube balladeer Raymond Crooke had recorded all thirty-eight of the Robin Hood ballads as part of his drive to record every one of the 305 Child Ballads. There have also been recordings by Brass Farthing, the Owl Service, Spiers and Boden, Bob Lewis, Kate Locksley, and the Unquiet Grave, among many others, with the latter's Randall Krieger confessing that his band's decision to record "The Ballad of Robin Hood's Death" (120) was predicated wholly upon it being "one of the few ballads that still makes me cry. This tale of his death, which includes archaic practices like bloodletting, is not one I have heard the likes of before."[14]

Robin Hood's ballads cannot be ranked among the most popular, or even the most immediately obvious, inclusions in a book that is said to represent the very best in English and Scottish balladry. But they're still out there, hiding in the shadows, creeping between the trees, and leaping out when you least expect them to. And long may they continue to do so.

Chapter Twenty-Four

DOWN BY THE RIVERSIDE

If any single event can be said to have brought the Child Ballads back into focus not simply as an academic tool, but also a public resource, it was the republication in 1956, of the full *ESPB*. Out of print for most of the century, its restoration had long been among the greatest goals of the Folklore Press, one of the key specialist publishers of the American 1950s. Hitherto, as noted by folklorist Kenneth S. Goldstein (1927–1995), copies had otherwise been available only "at exorbitant prices."[1]

Goldstein, in fact, led the project to republish the work and, no sooner was it complete, than he set about a similarly grandiose quest, a series of LPs that would allow readers to actually listen to at least one version of each ballad as they perused the book. It was a mammoth task, one that consumed almost two years spent seeking suitable performers and a record label that would finance it. Finally Goldstein made contact with Bill Grauer, whose self-named production company oversaw the next eighteen months of recording and production work. It was Grauer who arranged with the American Riverside label to handle the actual release.

The men voicing the collection would be Ewan MacColl and Bert Lloyd. MacColl had cut several records more since that awkward HMV session, often in the kitchen of his apartment in Croydon, south London, with his five-year-old-son Hamish in attendance as "recording engineer." Now, however, the same team was tasked with recording a nine-LP set of *Popular Ballads of England and Scotland*, with eight discs devoted to Child, and the ninth to *Great British Ballads Not Included in the Child Collection*.

Destined to become a staple in both university and public library collections for decades to come, the series comprises some seventy different Child Ballads, all recorded in that small Croydon kitchen. Years later,

FOLK MUSIC OF THE WORLD SERIES — WASHINGTON 715

THE ENGLISH AND SCOTTISH POPULAR BALLADS (THE CHILD BALLADS)
SUNG BY EWAN MacCOLL AND A. L. LLOYD
edited and produced by Kenneth S. Goldstein

Volume 1   Lord Randall (12) • The Devil And The Ploughman (278) *The Farmer's Curst Wife* • The Laird O' Drum (236) • Herod And The Cock (55) *The Carnal And The Crane* • Thomas Rhymer (37) • Our Goodman (274) • The Unquiet Grave (78) • Minorie (10) *The Twa Sisters* • Hind Horn (17)

Volume One of the Riverside series of LPs, the most influential recordings in the entire history of the Child Ballads. Author's collection

MacColl remarked that he could still hear his young son's "small, commanding voice shouting 'three-two-one-go!,' can still picture the lovely curly head poised intently as he turns the cumbersome dials on the elephantine old Ferrograph."[2]

That this was the most ambitious, and the vastest approach ever to the Child Ballads goes without saying. Leaving aside field recordings, MacColl and Lloyd recorded more individual ballads during those few weeks of sessions than the entire Anglo-American music industry had captured in fifty years; and while they did not fulfill Goldstein's dream of covering *every* Child Ballad, their cross-section was unimpeachable.

It has been said that *Popular Ballads of England and Scotland* was already outdated at the time of release, as collectors continued collecting. In the very same year that Lloyd recorded "George Collins" (85) for the Riverside series, Sussex folklorist Bob Copper was listening to eighty-year-old Enos White, of Axford in Hampshire, singing his own, hitherto unrecorded version of the same ballad.[3] (Twenty years on, Lloyd's reading inspired a moving echo from Louis and Sally Killen.) Yet it remains a landmark release, even today. We hear MacColl sing "The Cruel Mother" (20), a ballad he had known since he first heard his Aunt Mag perform it at the family's Hogmanay parties when he was still a child, and one that Shirley Collins in turn learned from him. We hear Lloyd intone "The Demon Lover" (243), a performance that twenty-first-century singer Emily Portman admits "gives me goose bumps. I've since heard many beguiling variants but I always return to this one for its poetic turns of phrase and eerie tune."[4] MacColl also offers what remains a very scarce airing of "Jock the Leg and the Merry Merchant" (282), a Robin Hood-esque adventure in which the titular merchant befriends one of Scotland's most notorious thieves, only to be betrayed and attacked. Fighting back, he kills five of Jock's men, but rejects the offer to join the gang himself.

The albums alternated performances by the two performers—Lloyd's so immaculately imposing and occasionally stentorian tones, MacColls's gravelly Scots-accented exuberance—but the approach was immediately attuned more to the academic ear than the listener who simply wanted to sing along. Compare Lloyd's almost hectoring take on "Robin Hood and the Tanner" (126), with the careless bonhomie of Wallace House's, and it immediately becomes apparent what the latter intended when he noted in his liner notes, "In my singing I have attempted to preserve the lusty flavour of the English rustic ballad singer rather than to use the 'arty' approach of the formal musician. Although these ballads make interesting reading, they were in general created to be sung."[5] And sing them he does. Lloyd, and MacColl to a lesser extent, emote them, as if to lay out the template for how the ballads *ought* to be handled, now and forever more.

MacColl in particular never turned his back on the Child Ballads. Time and again over the subsequent decades he returned to those pages, shedding new light not only on the ballads that had already ascended to the common vocabulary of what was universally regarded as the "folk revival," but also to those that had yet to make it so far. Omissions from the Riverside series were regularly repaired, although listening to the "Child Owlet" (291) that MacColl recorded in 1976, it seems incredible that this was the first time he had ever recorded it. (A second version would be included in the *Blood and Roses* series five years later.) It is, after all, one of the great murder ballads, as MacColl reveals:

A death in the family is a common ballad feature and the instruments of death are fairly common as well: the knife, the axe, the stake, the pistol, the noose, all take their toll. Sisters, brothers, fathers, mothers, aunts, uncles, nephews and nieces kill each other by stabbing, shooting, decapitating, drowning, smothering, strangling and poisoning. There is something off-beat about having one's nephew torn to pieces by wild horses but, as Professor Child has observed, "the last two stanzas are unusually successful." In fact, dialect notwithstanding, the last three are among the most graphic in the entire *ESPB*.[6]

Steeleye Span's Maddy Prior—no stranger to some of Child's most grisly discoveries—learned the ballad from MacColl's performance and, recording it in 1997, she shuddered, "If there is a lesson to be learned from this ballad it is that hell really hath no fury like a woman scorned. Also that being honest and upright does not necessarily result in affirmation and happy endings. Sometimes the cost of principles is very dear."[7]

> *They put a foal to ilka foot*
> *And ane to ilka hand*
> *And sent them down to Darling muir*
> *As fast as they could gang*
>
> *There was not a cow in Darling muir*
> *Nor ae piece o rind*
> *But drappit o Childe Owlet's blude*
> *And pieces o his skin*
>
> *There was not a cow in Darling muir*
> *Nor ae piece o a rash*
> *But drappit o Childe Owlet's blude*
> *And pieces o his flesh*

For all its suggested failings, the Riverside collection—indeed, the Riverside label's output as a whole—proved immensely influential. Singer Peter Bellamy recalled,

The search for authentic blues recordings—not too easy in Norfolk around 1959—brought me my first contact with British Isles traditional music. An American anthology LP [1957's *Riverside Folk Song Sampler*] was borrowed from a school mate because it contained a track by Reverend Gary Davis, but there with it was Something Completely Different: someone called Ewan MacColl was singing "Lord Randall," learned from his mother, Betsy Miller. A new world opened up; the high drama of the performance of this dark mediaeval tale grabbed me, literally by the throat, and never let me go. A pilgrimage to the Singers' Club in 1962 or '63 brought me face to face with the man himself, and I can't deny that the impression he made has been a major influence on my approach to performance unto the present.[8]

The young Moira Cameron devoured the series ("I remember listening to it from volume one to the end"[9]); and Julie Henigan recalls discovering the full breadth of the Child Ballads via, "those MacColl/Lloyd Riverside albums, which a lot of English departments used to have around, especially back when they thought that ballads belonged in the medieval lit.

section instead of (as they eventually figured out) the eighteenth-century lit. section. Dad brought them home when I was about twelve." She was, she admits,

> already hooked on what I call "old stuff," by which I mean old players and performances—like Clarence Ashley's "Coo-Coo Bird" (which I first heard when I was ten, along with Ewan's "Geordie" [209] and Jean Ritchie's "Nottamun Town," on the Elektra *Folk Box*)[10] or Hobart Smith's "Pateroller," which was on an album called *Instrumental Music of the Southern Appalachians*. But Dad was something of a folklore buff himself, so he bought me the cheap Dover edition of the [*ESPB*] when I was thirteen or fourteen, along with whatever else he could find.[11]

The Riverside albums allowed her to put melody and phrasing to the words she was now reading, and she continues, "I learned 'Hind Horn' [17] from one of those Riverside records and was paid the ultimate compliment by a Scottish singer (who, perhaps, should remain nameless) when, after I played and sang it for him at a party, said, 'I cou'd roll ye on the fleer for that'!"

At the same time as they were recording the Riverside series, MacColl and Lloyd were also overseeing the newly opened Ballad and Blues Club,[12] upstairs at the Princess Louise pub in High Holborn. There, among the most regular visitors was a newcomer to MacColl's circle, Pete Seeger's sister Peggy. She was first introduced to him by Alan Lomax during rehearsals for Lomax's upcoming TV series *The Ramblers*. There, Seeger had astonished her future husband with a dynamic performance of "The House Carpenter" (243), her high heels banging on the wooden floor, her five-string banjo—as MacColl put it—"far removed from the metallic plinkety-plunk of the average tenor banjo."[13]

The club itself was named for a three-part radio show written by MacColl and produced by Denis Mitchell for the BBC in 1953, and described by the *Radio Times* as "a series of programmes in which folk singers and jazz musicians find a common platform in modern and traditional folk music from both sides of the Atlantic." Among the others involved were the perhaps inevitable Lomax, Lloyd, and Isla Cameron and, for the non-folk element of the entertainment, band leader Humphrey Lyttelton. The folk club's members met every Sunday evening, with entertainment by MacColl, Lloyd, and resident guitarist Fitzroy Coleman always guaranteed. Later, once Peggy Seeger relocated to London,[14] she too became a part of the inner circle, sharing in MacColl's delight and astonishment as word of the venture began to spread, and similar folk clubs began opening up across the United Kingdom.

The club's influence was not entirely an unintended happenstance. Gatherings at the Princess Louise always began with someone handing out song sheets of the material they could expect to hear that evening. Within a couple of weeks, MacColl reckoned, you'd hear the same songs being sung at venues as far away as Sheffield and Newcastle.

That said, the club's repertoire was extremely varied. MacColl remembered the "surprising number" of singers who would choose to perform Russian, French, Greek, and Israeli folk songs. Peggy could add Spanish and Italian to that brew; while MacColl also had a stock of American numbers. This would gradually change, as it became apparent that the club members were exerting an awful lot of time and energy singing songs in a language they didn't understand, about a culture they could barely imagine. Seeger, in particular, "found it difficult to keep a straight face when she heard cockneys and Liverpudlians singing Leadbelly and Guthrie pieces,"[15] and was never too proud to admit that any passing Catalonian might have felt the same way as her pristine Massachusetts tones contorted themselves around a slice of Spanish heritage. It was MacColl's decision to put a stop to such foolishness that laid out the landscape upon which the British folk revival would take shape.

Chapter Twenty-Five

MACCOLL'S LONG HARVEST

The Ballads and Blues Club was adamant. If you wanted to perform there, you could only perform songs whose heritage you shared. Americans could sing all the Woody Guthrie they liked, Spaniards could sing their civil war marching songs, Canadians could sing their whaling ballads. And the British were saddled with British folk song.

It was not a popular decision to begin with, attendance plummeting as the regulars realized they could no longer listen to German tourists singing Mexican folksongs. Other clubs, too, looked askance at the policy, and took to describing MacColl and Lloyd in particular as running a dictatorship—"folk fascists" was a popular insult.

Yet the policy was rooted in a very sound reasoning, far beyond the desire to no longer hear misshapen tongues strangling foreign culture. In terms of the popular musical vocabulary, it was a cold hard fact—the English, in particular, had no idea that there were English folk songs they could sing. Yes, they knew "Early One Morning" and "Greensleeves" and the like. The more adventurous might know "Barbara Allen" (84) and "I Gave My Love A Cherry" (46), although it was more likely they'd learned them from an American recording. MacColl and Lloyd wanted to send them in search of "the real stuff," the songs that their forebears had sung. And that meant doing some research—which was useful for both Lloyd and MacColl, both of whom had recently published books that would satisfy the hungriest acolyte.

In 1944, Lloyd published the first edition of his book *The Singing Englishman*, destined to become one of the most influential (if, in the eyes of subsequent scholars, not necessarily accurate) studies of traditional song yet produced. Heavily influenced by his left-wing leanings (Lloyd described the book as a "socio-political" history), *The Singing Englishman* viewed traditional song as the art of the proletariat. His friend Leslie Morton described it as "a model for the application of Marxist ways of thinking to cultural questions"; Lloyd himself told *Folk Review* in September 1974, "Marxist applications are particularly valuable in arriving at . . . why song styles have changed with . . . social changes."

This view would flavor many of Lloyd's writings. His 1951 songbook *The Singing Englishmen* (note the plural) was published by the Workers Music Association, and its twenty-three folk (and other) songs—within which number we find "Dives and Lazarus" (56)—were those, Lloyd claimed, that best "mirror the life, work, and aspirations of the British working population."

His chosen Child Ballad certainly deserves that appellation. When the Young Tradition recorded it for their eponymous debut LP, the liners described it as "a simple but eloquent version of the story of rich old Dives who slighted the beggar Lazarus and got his desserts for doing so. The song must have appealed to the countryfolk, who would have appreciated the idea of Lazarus, downtrodden on Earth, finding a place in Heaven, where he sits on an angel's knee."[1]

As they had in Lloyd's political publications, so the Child Ballads fell effortlessly into the Ballads and Blues club repertoire, aided first by MacColl and Lloyd's own vast repertoire of material, and then by their involvement in the Riverside anthology.

Like Lloyd, MacColl and Seeger's politics were also forever on display, a thread that ran through many of the albums they recorded and the songs they wrote, with folk ballads frequently subverted to the cause of making a wider point. One of the finest of the resultant hybrids was Peggy Seeger's "The Landlord's Nine Questions," firmly based upon "Riddles Wisely Expounded" (1) and dedicated to the St. Pancras Rent Strikes of 1960. There, a rent increase imposed by the local council saw renters not only withhold payment, but also erect such formidable barricades against the inevitable eviction squads that finally, an army of police was called upon, not only to effect entry to the disputed buildings, but also keep myriad TV crews and sympathizers in order.

First recorded by Seeger in 1960, before being rerecorded by singer Sandra Kerr on the MacColl/Seeger-led Critics Group's 1966 LP *Sweet Thames Flow Softly*, the song (which is also known as "Hey Ho! Cook and Rowe" after the strike's leaders, Don Cook and Arthur Rowe) gleefully took its lead from the Child Ballad, all the way down to the sequence of riddles that offer such piquancy to the original.

> *What is higher than a tree?*
> *And what is lower than a flea?*

My rent is higher than a tree,
And the landlord's lower than a flea.

What goes on and never stops?
And what is gentler than a cop?
The tenants' fight will never stop
And the devil is gentler than a cop.

Neither was MacColl averse to eyeing popular trends. Few observers could overlook him turning his attention to "Matty Grove" (81) only after Joan Baez began including a marathon rendition in her live set. Regardless of whether he was reclaiming the song for its homeland, or aiming to show people how it "ought" to be recorded, its inclusion on 1961's *Two Way Trip* likely caught casual browsers' attention as much as it snagged the imagination of more specialist observers. (Baez's own version would not appear on vinyl until the following year's *In Concert* LP.) It is also possible, however, that it was a complete coincidence—notably, MacColl never did record that other great staple of the American folk boom, "The Great Silkie of Sule Skerry" (113), while he avoided "The House Carpenter" (243) until 1966 saw him and Seeger conceive a project even more ambitious than the Riverside series, the ten-volume *The Long Harvest*.

The series was inspired, MacColl explained in the liner notes, by the sheer proliferation of versions of the ballads over recent years. One example was "Lamkin" (93), a piece that he claimed had only been "introduced to revival audiences in the spring of 1965 and within four months, five distinct versions were in club circulation, two of them collected from field singers by revival singers."

Each of the ten albums, released over the course of three years, would include between four and five different Child Ballads (a handful of non-Child inclusions also crept in), taken from a variety of different texts. For example, on volume 1, five distinct renditions of "The Cruel Mother" (20) include English and American versions of the original ballad, followed by two retitled and sometimes redrawn variations: the American "Down by the Greenwood Sidey-O" and the English "The Lady from Lee."[2] "Lord Randal" (12) on the same volume, runs to three American, two Scots, and one English version; six takes on "The Elfin Knight" (2) on volume 2 include "O Say Do You Know the Way to Selin," "The Cambric Shirt," "My Father Had an Acre of Land," and, perhaps acknowledging Simon and Garfunkel's latest hit single, "Scarborough Fair." "Barbara Allen," on the other hand, is offered up in just three forms, Scots, English, and American, out of deference, perhaps, to the work of Peggy's father, Charles Seeger, author of the paper "Versions and Variants of the Tunes of 'Barbara Allen.'" As sung in traditional singing styles in the United States and recorded by field collectors who have deposited their discs and tapes in the Archive of American Folk Song in the Library of Congress, Washington, D.C." No fewer than thirty different versions are to be found there.

The key to inclusion in *The Long Harvest*, MacColl and Seeger insisted, was "whether a ballad has entered into tradition both [in Britain] and in North America, and been subjected to the same folk processes that operated on most of the ballads included in the Child canon."[3] Sensibly, they chose ballads with which they were already familiar, and, in seeking out representative variations, they drew again from memory, supplemented by field recordings and reading (all of their sources were noted in the accompanying booklets). Occasionally, two different versions might be brought together in one.

The Long Harvest is a remarkable collection, if not wholly as a listening experience (it is especially heavy going if one chooses to listen to all ten LPs in one sitting), then as a reference work. As with the Riverside series, the target audience was more academic than popular, and the series was especially well-received in those circles. Indeed, one can regret only that the harvest was not quite as long as MacColl and Seeger originally planned. Two further volumes were recorded, one of Child Ballads, the other of further traditional pieces, but both remained unissued until MacColl's estate placed digital versions online in 2019.

But the couple were not finished with the *ESPB*. In 1979, they embarked upon yet another major Child Ballads project, five volumes of *Blood and Roses*. Released on their own Blackthorne label and financed from the proceeds of MacColl's own songwriting (principally the much-covered "The First Time Ever I Saw Your Face"), fifty Child Ballads were this time undertaken, and remarkably with minimal duplication from *The Long Harvest*—in terms of ballads selected, let alone variations. With gentle musical accompaniment often supplied by Seeger's banjo or mandolin, and occasional flourishes of concertina and psaltery, the duo outlined this latest work by detailing "our own feelings for the ballads" that they represent "something that we have nurtured throughout most of our joint working life as singers. Time and again we have returned to this or that ballad and discovered something new in it. Occasionally we have been led to conduct major explorations into territory that we thought we already knew. The end result has been a complete reworking of the ballad."[4]

Much of this was the result of fieldwork, others' if not their own. Tackling "Sheath and Knife" (16), MacColl laments that, "of the four texts given by Child, only one . . . can be said to be more than a fragment."[5] It was 1960 before folklorist Helen Mennie Shire published a full twenty-six-stanza version, taken from the newly discovered Dalhousie Manuscript.[6] MacColl's recording, while amounting to just sixteen stanzas, was based "almost entirely" on that particular text. "Young Hunting" (68) was drawn from Cecil Sharp's discovery of Jane Gentry of Hot Springs; "Child Waters" (63) came from Rebecca Gordon of Cat's Head, on Saluda Mountain, also in North Carolina.

"The Laird o'Drum" (236), the story of a rich lord who falls in love with a working girl, despite his friends and family's opposition, is one of the few ballads for which MacColl does not offer a source. It would, however, also prove influential. Recording the ballad in 1997, the Glaswegian singer Gordeanna McCulloch recalled,

> When I went down to sing in London for the first time Ewan MacColl and Peggy Seeger gave me a bed for the week I was there. But more importantly, I had free access to Ewan's books, records and tapes! I spent every free minute listening and copying words, and this song was one that attracted me instantly, although I wanted to tackle it more vigorously than MacColl seemed to. It wasn't until very many years later when I heard Peggy accompany him on guitar on what was possibly their last visit to Glasgow, that I heard the underlying rhythm of horses hooves, which is the feeling we have tried to re-create here.[7]

Two other selections from *Blood and Roses* would make it onto McCulloch's 1997 album *In Freenship's Name*, "The Laird o'Warriston" (194) and

Ewan MacColl and Peggy Seeger at the Singer's Club. Courtesy Jim Carroll

"Chylde Owlet" (291). "I've always loved the big ballads," she wrote, "perhaps because I love a good story well told, and I shiver to imagine a 16 year old child bride saying 'Strike aff this dolwie heid o' mine.'"

Blood and Roses was Seeger and MacColl's final major contribution to the Child Ballads, and it completes a catalog that stands with neither peer nor reproach—to which, for sure, can be added such one-off projects as *Classic Scots Ballads* (1959), and two further volumes of Child Ballads recorded for Folkways in 1961. Further ballads appear in isolation across the couple's vast discography. Indeed, the sheer weight of influence that MacColl exerts over the modern popularity of the Child Ballads and the manner in which they are performed can never be measured. Across so many decades since the release of the Riverside albums, his efforts remain the gold standard of what we might call traditional Child Ballad recordings, not only for musicians but for many others as well—even runaways!

The young Jessica Simpson learned her first Child Ballads from MacColl, and her 1996 recording of "The Gardener's Child" (219), recorded with then-husband Martin for their *Red Rain* album, was indeed born out of her experiences as "a sixteen-year-old runaway. I came to a University town with a folk music school, and made friends with musicians who had books and cassettes to share, who knew songs I didn't know." She had always sung with her mother, a Texan of Irish/English heritage; now, "I was voracious, and people turned me on to lots of singers and bands. I learned about Child Ballads from their books, and that's how I heard Ewan MacColl sing 'The Gardener's Child.' I wanted to sing it but had to figure out what the words meant. It was strange, unusual, mysterious with a tune to match. I did my best to put it into English without messing it up. I didn't know that it had [already] been done, of course; I was just a kid, and so learned the song that way."[8]

Chapter Twenty-Six

JUDY AND JOAN

Judith Collins had not been idle since "The Gypsy Rover" (200) and "Barbara Allen" (84) diverted her musical focus away from classical piano. Her library of books and records alike was swelling, her knowledge of folk songs and tradition was deepening. Her steel-faced Guild guitar accompanied her everywhere, and the Denver Folklore Center proved an irresistible strain upon her finances as she bought every new disc and volume she could find.

There, too, she met with other acolytes, all of them as obsessed with collecting and learning songs as she now was. There were no barriers—her father often used to sing around the house, and Collins had written his repertoire off as show tunes and popular hits. Now, however, she realized that salted among these were the traditional tunes that he also loved. She learned them.

She befriended an army veteran named Lingo who sang the songs of Pete Seeger and Woody Guthrie, and often performed them on his own Denver radio show. Collins asked him to teach them to her. When she and her partner Peter landed a job as caretakers at Fern Lake Lodge in the Rocky Mountain National Park, she would stage impromptu folk song concerts for the guests. By 1959, when she was twenty, Collins was performing regularly at Michael's Pub in Denver, regaling the audience with the likes of "The Gypsy Rover" and noting the songs—that was one of them—that received the most attention.

She was taking a chance appearing there, at least at first. No folk singer had ever trod those boards before; no local venue had ever booked an entertainer with such a repertoire, and the beer-and-pizza-loving crowd was naturally suspicious. Even the club's namesake, owner Mike Bisesi,

Still recording, performing, and singing the Child Ballads, Judy Collins today. Photo by Shervin Lainez / Courtesy Cleopatra Records

introduced her onstage with a wink—"a folksinger who will now entertain everyone with her . . . folk songs!" And when she completed her audition (which was also her first gig there), he took her to one side to inform her that he hated folk music. But he hired her regardless.

Word spread; other bookings followed. The Gilded Garter in Central City, the Exodus in Denver, just a stone's throw from her old piano tutor's studio. Those days, however, seemed long ago. The Exodus was big time, the only dedicated folk club in the state's largest city, and a draw not only for local performers but national acts too—Josh White, Bob Gibson, and the Tarriers among them. Collins knew their music already; now she was meeting them, hearing their compliments and basking in their praise.

Another Child Ballad slipped into her repertoire, the mournful majesty of "The Great Selchie of Shule Skerry" (113). Even Bob Gibson was reduced to tears by Collins's rendition; audiences did not stand a chance. When he returned to his Chicago base, Gibson was still talking about Collins and her ballad, and his excitement promptly landed her a six-week residence at the Gate of Horn, a club that was co-owned by his manager, Albert Grossman.

Collins was recovering from a skiing accident at the time, a double spinal fracture that left her in a cast for months. Grossman's partner Alan Ribback was hardly impressed as he saw her make her way painfully onto the stage that first night. But as she came off again at the end, he told her she could sing in a cast as often as she wanted, so long as she sang "The Great Selchie of Shule Skerry."

Five years later, when Collins was interviewed by Chicago DJ Studs Terkel, he admitted that he had been fascinated by the song ever since he first heard her perform it at that same venue.

"The Great Selchie" remains a magical touchstone for Collins. "There was a kind of sorcery in its strange lyric," she wrote. "A song that originated in the Hebrides, many of whose natives would not eat the meat of seals because they believed them to be bewitched sea-men, this song has a link to the history of magic in traditional ballads."[1]

Collins made her New York debut at Gerde's Folk City, on Greenwich Village's West Fourth Street, in February 1961. The city itself was an eye-opener, particularly after she visited Izzy Young's legendary Folklore Center. There were records she had never heard of, books she had only dreamed of finding. Imported British compilations. It was paradise, and Folk City was no less impressive.

Just eight months had elapsed since the club replaced the building's previous occupant, a similarly themed venue called the Fifth Peg, but its success was immediate. The night Collins made her first appearance, she faced what she quickly discovered to be a blood-freezing audience of folk superstars: Cisco Houston, Ramblin' Jack Elliott, Eric Weissberg, even Woody Guthrie's thirteen-year-old son Arlo was there. The figure that transfixed her, though, was Joan Baez—herself freshly arrived upon the American folk scene, but already being proclaimed its queen.

Two years Collins's junior, born on Staten Island, New York, in 1941, Baez developed her love for singing in the school choir, and via the hits of the day. Folk music she did not discover until she heard Jamaican American calypso singer Harry Belafonte, as he rose to prominence in the early 1950s, first in the folk world, and then on a much wider stage. In 1956, his *Belafonte* album became the first LP ever to sell a million copies. Baez was entranced instantly upon hearing Belafonte's soft, mellifluous tones, and a friend, sensing her excitement, introduced her to the music of Pete Seeger and Odetta. Then, upon Baez's arrival at Boston University in 1959, a new friend named Debbie truly inducted her into the music.

Debbie tutored her guitar playing and taught her her first folk songs— "Fair and Tender Maidens," a song that Professor Child had included in *ESB* but omitted from *ESPB*; "All My Trials"; and—most significantly for this book's purposes—"Geordie" (209), in which a young wife pleads for the life of her husband, condemned to hang for poaching. Baez's repertoire was not wholly confined to traditional song; she took other routes, too. But her delivery, so crystalline and pure, could not avoid the folk connotation, and she quickly realized that she was in the ideal location to follow where that led.

Judy Collins appearing on *Hootenanny* in 1963. By ABC Television / Wikimedia Commons

Club Mt. Auburn 47—a coffee house named for its street address off Central Square in Cambridge, Massachusetts—opened on January 6, 1958, with a diet of jazz, occasional movies, and poetry readings. Gradually, however, a different crowd began drifting through the doors, one that was picking up folk music from another newly opened venture on the same street, the Turntable record store, and needed some place to go and talk about it. Baez was, if not the first folk singer to perform at Club Mt. Auburn 47, the first one that anybody recalls. She would not be the last, although it initially felt touch and go.

The audience for the first set of her opening night numbered eight people—her parents, her sister Mimi, three friends, the club owner, and her partner. Not quite the proverbial one man and a dog, but close enough. A handful more appeared for the second set, but Baez was scarcely looking forward to her next appearance at the club—only to discover, on the night, that that handful of witnesses had not remained quiet about their discovery. The place was packed.

Rapidly, Cambridge developed a scene of its own, and it was cutthroat as hell. Not quite an echo of Ewan MacColl's Ballads and Blues club in its demand for "authenticity," it was nevertheless possessed of high values, with the self-appointed arbiters of taste drawing their red line between what they regarded as "true" folk music, and the commercial pap that could be heard on the radio of the day. The sort of music a young Tom Rush was listening to, for example.

Rush was one of the wide-eyed folkies who arrived in Cambridge with his ears full of the folky hits of the day: Josh White; San Francisco's Kingston Trio (whose first album topped the *Billboard* chart four years before Bob Dylan was heard of); Connecticut's squeaky-clean Highwaymen; the Elektra label's Limeliters, led by Glenn Yarborough; and so forth. "I had to be totally reeducated," Rush recalled. "It was like being sent to a camp by the Communist Party, to cleanse your aberrant belief. I was told that Josh White was commercial and that was bad."[2]

Initially the emphasis around the clubs was on the songs of the African American experience, learned for the most part from old records or other local performers. For some, it was the popular artists whose catalogs were mined—the Weavers, Oscar Brand, Theo Bikel, and Cynthia Gooding (who joined forces to perform both "Katherine Jaffray" (221) and "As I Roved Out" (299) on their 1956 album *A Young Man and a Maid Sing Love Songs of Many Lands*). For others, it was the more obscure output of Folkways and Riverside. Others still hunted through boxes of dusty old 78s.

Whatever his sources, and wherever he chanced upon it, what Rush's educators demanded, the singer continues, "was ethnic, and the ethnic guys were of course the old actual sharecroppers, coalminers, chain gang etcetera. Incredible music. So I was reeducated, and I did my best to be ethnic, although it was difficult for all of us because we were a bunch of Harvard students singing about how tough it was in the coal mines and on the chain gang." He threw himself into that mission regardless, but other music was also beginning to make itself heard. "As for the ballads, I studied them in an English course on the oral tradition at Harvard and, more importantly, heard them performed by some old masters and some of my contemporaries in the coffee houses around Cambridge and Boston."[3]

Several English and Scottish ballads made their way into his repertoire.

> Part of what drew me to the ballads, I think, was the idea that no one person wrote them, that there was no "correct" version, that every village and every generation had their own variants. It gave me a sense of freedom when dealing with other writers' songs, one which sometimes got me in trouble. The one I can remember recording was "Barb'ry Allen" [84].[4] I used an open tuning and a slide (a kitchen knife), thinking that blending the blues guitar style with the old Scots lyrics might be interesting.[5]

Indeed it was; in fact, when English singer Steve Tilston recorded the same ballad for his 2005 album *Of Many Hands*, it was Rush's version that intrigued him. "I loved [what he did] and wanted to do something that was kind of similar, which had echoes of being an earlier British song but also with certain American sensibilities to it."[6]

Cambridge and New York City were not the sole magnets for young would-be folk singers. In 1961, twenty-four-year-old Jean Redpath (1937–2014) arrived in San Francisco from her native Edinburgh, Scotland, where she had taken medieval courses at the city university, while also working with folklorist Hamish Henderson at the School of Scottish Studies. Redpath already had a vast repertoire of traditional songs that she learned, in the main, from her mother, and a voice that was ideal for singing them. It was not until she relocated to California, however, that she started performing professionally. Then, moving to New York, she cut a single album for Prestige International before signing with Elektra in 1962.

Redpath is probably best remembered for undertaking the mammoth task of recording every song associated with Robert Burns, a series that was originally envisioned stretching to twenty-two volumes, before the death of her collaborator Serge Hovey in 1989 saw it curtailed after just seven. She also held several academic positions, lecturing in folklore both in the United States and Scotland, and later was appointed artist in residence at Wesleyan University in Middletown, Connecticut.

Her knowledge of traditional music was far-reaching and vast, and her repertoire of Child Ballads was considerable. Over the course of her long career, Redpath recorded some three dozen, beginning with "The Cruel

Mother" (20) and "The Barring o' the Door" (275) on her debut *Skipping Barefoot through the Heather*. Her first Elektra album, *Jean Redpath's Scottish Ballad Book*, followed, and it is almost wholly consumed by Child, with her liner notes reinforcing her performance's familiarity with the songs.

"The Wee Cooper O'Fife" (277), for example, was "one of the earliest songs I can recall learning from my mother"; for "Gypsie Laddie" (200), her text was taken from Gavin Greig's *Folk-Song of the North-East*, but her melody was learned from Jeannie Robertson. Her "Clerk Saunders" (69) was introduced to her by Hamish Henderson, despite the ballad having apparently died out in the British Isles; "Barbary Allen" was collected from Mrs. Jean Turriff of Fetterangus, Aberdeenshire, by folklorist Arthur Argo. "This exquisite melody," Redpath noted, "is thought to be the only uniquely Scottish one so far found."[7] Her canon has proven a fruitful hunting ground for other performers, too. It was Redpath's 1977 recording of "Clerk Colven" (42) to which Alasdair Roberts turned in 2018, and he is not alone in his admiration.

For everybody rising up the folk stakes, however, Joan Baez was the act they had to follow. The dark-eyed, Sphinxian lady with her long dresses and sandaled feet was an immediate sensation and, as her fame spread, other venues pricked up their ears. Soon, Baez was recording her first ever album—or at least, half-an-album, nine songs on a disc shared with fellow Cambridge folkies Bill Wood and Ted Alevizos.

"Waly Waly" (204) is there, the sole Child Ballad on *Folk Singers 'Round Harvard Square*, but it was Alevizos—more commonly known for his repertoire of traditional Greek songs—who performed it, soft, graceful, and, if the term can even be breathed in the presence of the young Baez, angelic. Baez's offerings did not even include her live staple "Geordie."

Nevertheless, Baez was the star of the show; in years to come, copies of the *Harvard Square* album would be shipped emblazoned with a sticker proclaiming, "This is the historic album featuring the original first recordings of America's most exciting folk singer" (the latter in block capitals) and, in even larger lettering, "the best of Joan Baez."

Things moved fast. Albert Grossman added her to his managerial roster and booked her into the Gate of Horn. Other venues fell at her feet. But it was Baez's performance at the 1959 Newport Folk Festival, as a guest of Bob Gibson, that cemented her ascent.

Chapter Twenty-Seven

CHILD GOES TO NEWPORT

Even at its height, the Newport Festival was never all about folk music. Blues, gospel, and "old time music" also had their moments in the sun. Nevertheless, it was the biggest event on the folk calendar, the August weekend when the entire scene, it seemed, made its way to Rhode Island.

Things were a little different in 1959. Twenty-nine years old at the time, entrepreneur and jazzman George Wein had been staging jazz festivals in Newport since 1954, and initially intended folk to simply be given an afternoon to itself. But he also ran a club in Boston, Storyville, and had seen how the college crowd, in particular, responded when he booked Odetta for a week of shows. He'd heard the Kingston Trio topping the American charts with "Tom Dooley." And he had come to know Albert Grossman. Soon, what Wein originally intended to be a single afternoon of featured folk performers had morphed into two full days and nights, featuring the Weavers, the New Lost City Ramblers, Pete Seeger, Jean Ritchie, the Kingston Trio, Bob Gibson, the Stanley Brothers, Jimmy Driftwood, and Leon Bibb, the cream of contemporary folk, and blues and gospel too. Topping the bill was Odetta.

Alabama-born Odetta Holmes (1930–2008) studied music at Los Angeles City College and dreamed, in her youth, of becoming an opera singer. She doubted, however, that she would succeed. There was scant African American representation in the opera world of the day—and fewer still were female. Although she was only nine years old at the time, Odetta remembered when the great contralto Marian Anderson (1897–1993) was refused permission to perform to an integrated audience at Constitution Hall in D.C., because of her color. It took the intervention of First Lady Eleanor Roosevelt to force a change—the performance took place, instead,

Odetta Sings Folk Songs included her dramatic "The Golden Vanity." Author's collection

on the steps of the Lincoln Memorial. But not every aspiring singer could rely on presidential approval to smooth their way. Instead, Odetta moved into theater, and it was while touring with a production of *Finian's Rainbow* in 1949 that she encountered a group of radical balladeers in San Francisco. Their music appealed, as did their politics, and Odetta's future course was set. Within a year she was performing regularly around the city (and further afield) and in 1954, she and her accompanist Larry Mohr cut their eponymous debut album onstage at the Tin Angel.

Further albums followed, but it was the live arena in which Odetta truly came to life, that the power of her performance, and the conviction of her beliefs pushed her to the greatest prominence. Following her death, *Rolling Stone*'s Daniel Kreps described her as "The Voice of the Civil Rights Movement." *Time* magazine reported that Rosa Parks and Martin Luther King Jr. both ranked among her fans.

Odetta was a major force throughout the burgeoning folk revival; indeed, Judy Collins insists that the movement would have been "far less" than it became were it not for Odetta, and recalled the first time she saw her perform, at the Gate of Horn in Chicago. "She sang big, completely embracing songs," Collins declared, and paramount among them there was a "terrifying song called 'Gallows Tree' (95)."[1] It was one of just two songs from the *ESPB* that Odetta regularly performed (the other, from her 1963 album *Odetta Sings Folk Songs*, was "The Golden Vanity"—286), but Collins is correct. Odetta's "Gallows Tree" *is* terrifying, more so than any other to be found, and she readily added it to her own live repertoire.

Odetta, then, was the undisputed headliner of the 1959 Newport Festival. It was Bob Gibson and Joan Baez who grasped the headlines, however, sharing the stage for a brief set of "The Virgin Mary Had One Son" and "Jordan River" that, as Baez put it in her autobiography, combined with her "long tresses, no makeup and Bible sandals" to portray her as "purity itself." The following day's press described Baez as both "the Madonna" and "the Virgin Mary." True, the *Providence Journal* also spelled her name wrong ("Byers"), but the case was made. Baez soared to fame; a record deal was hers for the taking (she signed with Vanguard), and now her career began to take off, both commercially and as a gateway to a host of fresh careers.

Judy Collins's star was likewise ascending and, over the next five years, both performers—adored perhaps as much for their image and attitude as for their voice and repertoire—ensured that their audiences were soon on the most intimate terms with balladry in general, and Child in particular. "I started by recording traditional songs, or mostly traditional songs," Collins recalled, and pointed out that it was—perhaps inevitably, at this stage—her performance of "The Great Silkie of Sule Skerry" that captured the attention of Elektra Records. Jac Holzman, like so many other of the people who shaped her career, "was very smitten with that."[2] The funny thing, she says, is that she has no recollection whatsoever of where she heard and learned the ballad in the first place. Only that the melody that she employed was composed for the ballad by Columbia University's Dr. James Waters early in the 1950s.[3]

A Maid of Constant Sorrow, Collins's debut album, was released in 1961, bursting with her own unique interpretations of the traditional repertoire, and across the half-decade that ensued, Collins recorded or performed at least nine Child Ballads. In her repertoire, "The Great Silkie" is joined by "The Cherry Tree Carol" (54), "Lord Gregory" (76), "Barbara Allen" (84), "The Prickilie Bush" (95), "The Gypsy Rover" (200), "The Dens of Yarrow" (214), "O Daddy Be Gay" (278), and "The Cruel Mother" (20)—a song that English folklorist Sproatly Smith unhesitatingly acclaims for its "beautifully dark and gruesome lyrics" and singer-songwriter Gillian Welch refers to as "a good example for me of the richness of poetry that's in some of these songs and the touching upon spiritual and the invisible."[4]

Baez's repertoire, across much the same span, included thirteen: "The Greenwood Side" variant of "Cruel Mother," her own interpretations of "The Cherry Tree Carol," "Barbara Allen," and even Collins's signature "Silkie," plus "I Gave My Love a Cherry" (46), "The Unquiet Grave" (78), "Lady Gay" (79), "Matty Groves" (81), "The Death of Queen Jane" (170), "Mary Hamilton" (173), "Geordie" (209), "The House Carpenter" (243), and Burl Ives's old favorite "Henry Martin" (250). Yet, despite the similarities in their material, there are profound differences in their treatment of it. With Baez, the immediate impression is the voice, an instrument of such startling purity that it held listeners literally spellbound.

With Collins, it is the experience, the unfolding of the story in a tone that feels almost firsthand, as though the singer herself was present at the events of which she sang. A sign, she affirms, of just how powerfully traditional song impacted upon her. "[It] made an incredible inroad into my life, so it's been not only a career in terms of being my work; it's quite a deep study."[5]

She cites "Anathea," the song that opens her sensibly titled third album, *Judy Collins #3*, and which some sources feel is somehow related to the Child Ballad "The Maid Freed from the Gallows" (95) as an example of this.

> I don't know who sang it, or where I heard it, but it's a very oddball song. I don't think it's a traditional song, I think it was written. It's a very eclectic choice to move from "Barbara Allen" to "Anathea," but murder ballads had a lot to do with this choice that I made. I think that some of these songs that have to do with women . . . the ones who have their hair pinned to the ground, and "Anathea," about murder, the judge who rapes her also hangs her brother . . . have to do with women's issues, and the way women are treated and thought of. It's a very, in a way, disturbing background. Historically, women are not treated very well, but the whole study and search for the songs has always had a sociological and political edge to it, so it's no wonder that I started singing things that were more overtly political, like Woody, the anti-war songs . . . and they have a history too, things from centuries ago that are talking about the same things we're talking about today.[6]

The ballads' impact upon the performers' fan base, too, was immediate.

Melanie Safka's early 1970 anthems "Candles in the Rain" and "Look What They've Done to My Song, Ma" (released, as have most of her records, under the singular name of Melanie) posited her among the most likely superstars of the new decade. When she recalls her earliest days as a musician, however, she talks of learning her first songs from the likes of Baez and Collins, and—following their emergence over the next few years—Bob Dylan and Phil Ochs. But the Child Ballads were a vital component in her repertoire even before that.

Melanie Safka. William Morris Agency, Neighborhood Music / Wikimedia Commons

I remember "Matty Groves," "Barbara Allen," "Geordie," and "I Gave My Love a Cherry" from when I was a little girl. In fact, "Barbara Allen" was in an esoteric play called *Dark of the Moon* that I was in. I had just graduated from the American Academy of Dramatic Arts, and I was very hesitant in going to auditions, but I came across the casting call for a girl to play Barbara Allen. I took it as an omen, as I think I was the only person in my acting school who could play the guitar and sing; and not only that, but I knew all twenty-eight verses. I came in from New Jersey for the audition, and when I got to the address, the Brill Building on Broadway, I didn't have a room number. I didn't know where to go, so I wandered into the wrong office . . . which led to my meeting Peter Schekeryk, my future husband and record producer.[7]

Melanie's recording career—one that would swiftly establish her as one of the most inventive songwriters of her age—would not begin in earnest until 1967, and already she had no need to reach back into her past repertoire for material. Nor is it easy to detect the influence of the ballads on her music, any more than one could single out the gospel, jazz, and cabaret tones that also color her palette. But, like those, it is there, and when Melanie's second daughter was born, "I named her after the ballad, Jeordie . . . spelled with a *J* because it looks more feminine to me."

Chapter Twenty-Eight

THE CLANCYS LEAD THE WAY

It is ironic—or maybe it isn't—that paramount among the forefathers of the American folk boom, and constantly active throughout it, were the Clancy Brothers and Tommy Makem, an Irish act who had not even intended a musical career when their founders first arrived in the country. Not only was the band responsible for ensuring that Ireland's traditional music became a key component of the American experience, but they also operated one of the key record labels of the movement's infancy, Tradition Records. Ed McCurdy, Paul Clayton, Jean Ritchie, Odetta, Séamus Ennis, Isla Cameron, Oscar Brand, Carolyn Hester, and Ewan MacColl all released music on Tradition, alongside the Clancys themselves, both collectively and individually.

The roots of the Clancy Brothers lay in the meeting, back in Ireland, of Liam Clancy and Tommy Makem—the son of singer Sarah Makem. Clancy was accompanying ballad collector (and Guggenheim heiress) Diane Hamilton on her tour of Ireland, with the Makem home as one of their destinations. While Sarah sang and Diane recorded, Liam and Tommy struck up first a conversation, and then a friendship, which was only strengthened when the youths discovered that they were both on the verge of immigrating to the United States to take up careers, they hoped, in acting. Clancy arrived first, accompanying Hamilton now on her visit to the southern Appalachians, where she was collecting ballads with Paul Clayton. Then, once the collecting season was over, he settled in New York to focus on Off-Broadway plays.

Makem, meanwhile, had also reached America and was working in summer stock. Any musical "career" the pair had during this period was simply a sideline, performing the songs of their homeland (most of them

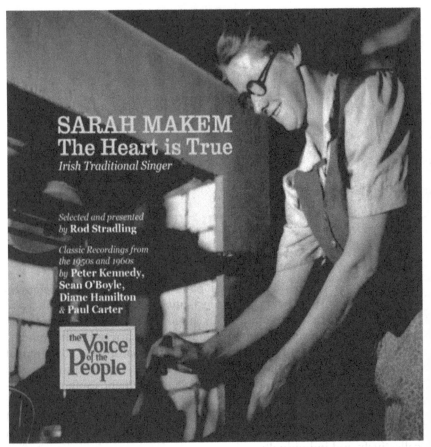

SARAH MAKEM
The Heart is True
Irish Traditional Singer

Selected and presented
by **Rod Stradling**

*Classic Recordings from
the 1950s and 1960s*
by **Peter Kennedy,
Sean O'Boyle,
Diane Hamilton
& Paul Carter**

the **Voice**
of the
People

Volume 24 of Topic Records' *The Voice of the People* CD series was dedicated to Sarah Makem.
Author's collection

learned from Tommy's mother) in bars and taverns between acting gigs. There, they were astonished to discover that, even with the folk boom under way, "there was a limited American repertoire, and we had a whole new batch of songs that nobody had ever heard. We were taking the old songs that had been slow and solo back in Ireland, and we picked up on the American rhythms and the attack of the Kingston Trio and the Weavers, and we'd put a bit of punch and drive into the songs. We added the banjo. Pete Seeger was on our first record."[1]

With Clancy's brothers Tom and Pat now also on board, the Clancy Brothers and Tommy Makem swiftly established themselves, the sheer energy and effervescence of their performance completely rewiring the popular notion of how "folk music" should be played—and where it could be recorded. Overseen by Diane Hamilton (who also financed the venture), the first release on their Tradition label, *The Lark in the Mountain*, bears the distinction of being the first record of traditional Irish music to be recorded in Ireland. Credited to Liam Clancy and Makem alone, it also featured a variety of friends and family, including Tommy's mother, and singer Thomas Baynes, who closes the disc with a dark a cappella "Barbara Allen" (84).

Academia has long debated how the Child Ballads (and other English traditional songs) were disseminated in Ireland. Julie Henigan writes, "Irish-language variants of ballads like 'The Cherry Tree Carol' [54] and 'Lord Randall' [12] are derived from early—and, probably oral—imports; although who composed the [Gaelic] translations is unknown, and the ballads themselves are few in number."[2]

That said, Jim Carroll asserts, "Ireland is poorly represented in Child. Bronson makes up for that to a degree in his *Tunes*, but that still falls far short of what there actually was. Travellers, of course, don't feature. I was staggered when [Irish folk song collector] Tom Munnelly gave me a list of 49 Child Ballads taken from Irish sources in the second half of the twentieth century."[3] Working with his partner Pat MacKenzie, Carroll's own collecting, which began among the traveller community in west London in 1973, before crossing the sea to County Clare, Ireland, saw him add "over twenty" further Child Ballads to that number. Even more surprising, "Many on the list had disappeared from the oral traditions elsewhere."

Many of the ballads circulating in Ireland, says Henigan, likely arrived as printed broadsides from England—she cites "Chevy Chase" (162) and "Lord Bateman" as prime examples, and perhaps Goldsmith's Peggy Golden learned her rhapsodies in this manner. She remarks, too, upon a peculiar two-way trade between Britain and Ireland, describing how

> an Irish version of "The Lass of Roch Royal" (76) appears in a Glasgow chapbook of 1799, having apparently circulated orally throughout Ireland and returned via a ballad sheet (now lost) to Britain in its Hibernicized form. It [is] possible that only a few copies of a song may have been necessary to perpetuate it in oral tradition: oral versions of "The Holland Handkerchief" [272] have been collected throughout Ireland, while only one extant printed copy of the ballad is known.[4]

That, however, might speak as loudly for the poor survival rate of Irish printed ballads from before the late eighteenth century as for the paucity of available editions. For certainly they circulated, and in such numbers that several period poets took issue with what Dáibhí Ó Bruadair (1625–1698) condemned as "the chanters of the frigid sheets."

However they arrived in Ireland, the ballads took hold. Visiting Galway for the BBC in 1954, Sean Ennis recorded Irish Gaelic versions of

"Lord Randall" (12) from Colm Keane in June, and Colm MacDonagh two months later—they knew the song, however, as "S ceard a fuair tu ar do bhreicfeasts" ("What Did You Have for Breakfast?"), while Julie Henigan writes of two fascinating, if somewhat stomach-curdling, lyrical twists that have also made their way into the Gaelic versions of the ballad. "In the British variants, Lord Randall eats 'a dish of sma' fishes,' 'eels boiled in brue,' and so on; more colourfully, one Irish variant describes the meal as 'escainn a raibh lúb uirthi/Nimh fuinte brúite uirthi' ('a coiled eel / with kneaded and mashed poison on it') and another as 'sicíní nimhe ar phláitíní óir' ('poisoned chicken on golden platters')."[5]

Elsewhere in the BBC archive of Irish recordings, there lurk English language versions of "The Elfin Knight" (2), "Edward" (13), "The Cruel Mother" (20), "Captain Wedderburn's Courtship" (46), "The Cherry Tree Carol" (54), "The Farmer's Curst Wife" (278), and more. There is also a distinctly Irish revision of "The Maid Freed from the Gallows" (95), retitled "Derry Gaol,"[6] in reference to one of the most notorious and feared prisons in Ireland. Sarah Makem's repertoire contained "Barbara Allen" (84) and company; Elizabeth Cronin's included "Lord Gregory" (76), in a version that, almost half a century later, floored singer Alasdair Roberts. "I first heard 'Lord Gregory' sung by the great Shirley Collins, before hearing the version of the singer from whom she learnt it, Elizabeth Cronin. Both of their recordings, in their different ways, I have at certain times found almost emotionally devastating, and I feel that my own recording of it contains only a fraction of that power. I recorded it in 2000 or so, and still sing it and it still grows with me. In fact, I [recently] had the pleasure of hearing the song sung by Elizabeth Cronin's granddaughter, Eibhlis, in Skibbereen."[7] (Mick Pearce and Kitty Vernon also used Cronin's variant for their 1998 album *Dark the Day*.)

Among the BBC's other Irish discoveries are Londonderry singer Eddie Butcher's vision of "Tam Lin" (39), "The Bride Stolen by the Fairies," which was collected by Hugh Shields in 1968; and, indeed, the dozen other Child Ballads, performed by ten different singers that join it on that same year's *Folk Ballads from Donegal and Derry* LP. But few, if any, of the source singers could match the sheer unrestrained exuberance of the Clancy Brothers and Tommy Makem's treatment of the ballads. "The Whistling Gypsy" (200) on their 1961 live LP absolutely deserves the album's subtitles "a spontaneous performance recording . . . and a 200 voice singing audience"; "The Mermaid" (289) is equally hearty; and "Wella Wallia" (20), recorded live in Dublin in 1964, is introduced as a popular children's song, and has certainly been heavily adapted for the purpose, even if the lesson remains the same as the original "Cruel Mother" intended.[8]

The moral of this story is,
Weela weela walya
Don't stick knives in babby's heads
Down by the River Saile

Tommy Makem quit the group for a solo career in 1969 (the split also necessitated a shortening of the band's name; he was replaced by another Clancy brother, Bobby). Still, further Child Ballads would leak into both acts' repertoires thereafter. "Jennifer Gentle" (1), "When Joseph Was a Man" (54), and "The Prickly Holly Bush" (95) were among them, while the 1992 TV special *Songs of the Sea* hosts a truly moving take on "The Great Silkie," with Makem's tin whistle accompanying Judy Collins's vocal and guitar.

The Clancy's influence upon the future course of Irish folk (and, in due course, folk-rock) cannot be quantified, although it would be several years more before it truly flowered. In the meantime, in the United States and elsewhere, the sudden rebirth of so many old songs among popular young singers took a lot of people by surprise.

Sheila K. Adams, great grand-niece of Cecil Sharp's discovery Mrs. Gentry, told the BBC how, after years of local youngsters trying to escape their Appalachian heritage, hearing "the old songs" on the radio gave them the confidence to reclaim it again:

When my family started hearing these old songs being sung on the radio, I remember granny plainly saying "Well, they're not singing that song right," and she started singing the same song, only she sang the entire thing, and I was just blown away. Then there was the folk revival, and then in the '70s, they started encouraging what granny called "real people" to come out of the woodwork so that they could send them off to the Smithsonian Folklife Festival in 1976 with all of these old traditions and everything. We celebrated our 200th birthday [the US Bicentennial] and they had the [festival] on the mall in Washington, D.C., and all the old ballad singers got to go and sing on the stage.[9]

It was not only the performers who were being swept along by the momentum of the folk boom. The fortunes of both Elektra Records and Vanguard, too, were exploding. Indeed, despite the competition of Tradition, Folkways, and others, those two labels were *the* ustorious lights of the US folk scene of the 1960s, their far-reaching vision of what "folk" actually entailed ensuring that it constantly plowed a broad swath through the contemporary music scene.

The Vanguard label was launched in June 1950, by the brothers Maynard and Seymour Solomon, built upon a $10,000 advance from their father, Benjamin. The brothers' forte was jazz and classical music, and two labels were established to cater for their tastes—Vanguard itself, and The Bach Guild, an ambitious project intended to release recordings of all of its namesake's chorale work. Original Vanguard releases, in keeping with industry standards, were issued on ten-inch LPs, and between 1953 and 1955, Vanguard released some twenty different jazz albums in this format, including well-received and respected titles by Vic Dickenson, Sir Charles Thompson, Joe Newman, Buck Clayton, Don Elliott, and Ruby Braff—many of them produced by the legendary John Hammond.

However, a glimmer of the label's future came in the form of *Brother John Sellers Sings Blues and Folk Songs*, a collection released in 1954. Then, in 1956, Vanguard released its first album by Pete Seeger and the Weavers—a courageous move at a time when the group's political stance saw them all but boycotted by the rest of the industry. (Paul Robeson, another performer blacklisted for alleged "un-American" sympathies, joined the Weavers at the label.) Releases by Martha Schlamme and Cisco Houston followed and, by the end of the 1950s, Vanguard was essentially the biggest folk game in town, without ever being solely concerned with folk.

One of the label's most intriguing early signings, for example, was Alfred Deller (1912–1979), an English-born countertenor specializing in Baroque and Renaissance music and working as a peerless interpreter of John Dowland and Henry Purcell before forming his own Deller Consort in 1948. His musical focus, perhaps, led listeners to anticipate a repertoire comprised largely of religious music, Bach and Handel. In 1955, however, he and lute player Desmond Dupré released *The Three Ravens (Songs of Folk and Minstrelsy out of Elizabethan England)*, with the title track and four further cuts besides ("I Will Give My Love an Apple" (46), "Barbara Allen" (84), "The Death of Queen Jane" (170—retitled "King Henry," but not to be confused with Child's ballad of that title), and "Waly Waly"—204) all drawn from Child and rendered in the most pristine manner.

Four years later, *The Cruel Mother and Other English Ballads and Folksongs* followed suit, with "When Cockleshells Turn Silver Bells" (204), "Geordie" (209), and "The Lover's Ghost" (248) joining the titular "Cruel Mother" (20); and, on either side of these releases, some nine other Child Ballads made their way into Deller's courtly repertoire. It was all a very far cry from what the average record buyer would regard as a sound labelmate for Joan Baez and company, but the connection was unimpeachable regardless.

Other Vanguard artists were similarly prone to take the ballads in fresh and unexpected directions. Bob Jones unleashed a startling "Black Jack Davy" (200) for the *New Folks 2* label sampler; Lisa Kindred included a slinky shuffle through "The Water Is Wide" (204) on her debut LP *I Like It This Way!* Enthralling, too, was Georgia-born singer-songwriter Patrick Sky, a dynamically contrary performer whose gentle, reflective songs were, singer Dave Van Ronk memorably mused, "peopled by bits of verse, horrible puns, unprintable lyrics, japes, jibes and a beer river flowing gently over your grandmother's paisley shawl."[10] Who better, then, to record a new version of "The Farmer's Curst Wife" (278) for his second Vanguard album, *A Harvest of Gentle Clang*?

Vanguard's biggest stars beyond Baez were the Canadian duo Ian (Tyson) and Sylvia (Fricker). It was Albert Grossman who recommended the couple to the label and, in 1962, their *Ian and Sylvia* debut album saw them emerge not only as their homeland's first folk superstars, but also the first to introduce a local audience to the kind of songs that Helen Creighton and Edith Fowke had dedicated so many years to uncovering. Ian and Sylvia did not, it is true, delve into those collections for their material. But still, the complex harmonies of their "The Greenwood Side" (20) and "Jesus Met the Woman at the Well" (21) from their *Four Strong Winds* sophomore album; and "Captain Wedderburn's Courtship" (46), "The Ghost Lover" (248), and "The Little Beggarman" (279) from the succeeding *Northern Journey*, unquestionably opened the door for a new generation of Canadians to begin investigating their heritage.

It was Ian and Sylvia's appearance at the 1963 Newport Festival—where their set included a captivating "The Greenwood Side"—that launched them to stardom. No less than Baez in 1959, the duo (accompanied by guitarist Eric Hord) were the incontestable highlight of the event. They returned to the festival two years later, and for evidence that little of what they recorded in the studio matched the magical intensity of their live performances, 1996's *Ian and Sylvia Live at Newport* retrospective CD captures them at the very peak of their powers.

Chapter Twenty-Nine

ENTER . . . AND EXIT . . . BOB DYLAN

Beyond Vanguard's doors, Albert Grossman remained an indomitable figurehead, and a schemer par excellence, too. With Joan Baez already on his books, he had ensnared the hearts of the teenage folk boom. Now he planned putting together a sweetly harmonic folk trio, and courting the tastes of their parents, too. Dave Van Ronk and Carolyn Hester were among the Greenwich Village habitués he initially considered recruiting, and both were grand choices. They, ultimately rejected his overtures. But Pete Yarrow, Mary Travers, and Noel Stookey proved more interested, and in 1961, the threesome made their debut at the latest Greenwich Village folk club, Bitter End, as Peter, Paul (Stookey's middle name) and Mary.

Born in Baltimore, Maryland, in 1937, Stookey arrived in New York City upon graduation from Michigan State University, with a head stuffed full of jazz, pop, and R&B. He recalled,

> I listened to a lot of doo wop, Black music, when I was in high school; I had a rock group called the Birds of Paradise, so when I came to Greenwich Village what folk music meant to me was . . . it was like a curtain parting on the capacity of music to inform. I thought music was entertainment only, and suddenly I became aware that, in a perfect world, you could do both. So all of the songs that I've either written or chosen to perform since that point, with very few exceptions, have a point behind them that's beyond just the music and the physical enjoyment.[1]

A crash course in folk music followed—after a fashion.

> A lot of dope and working in the village. There were some excursions, but I wouldn't call it a crash course, I would call it gradual immersion. Because, at

the same time, I'm going to Randalls Island to hear the jazz festival, because my fave musicians at the time were Charlie Byrd, who played jazz on classical guitar; the Brubeck Quartet, who had a sense of propriety when it came to improv because they could work in counterpoint, they could work with all the same devices that Bach and Haydn had used, that was genius music to me. Probably the most pivotal album for me was [Brubeck's] *Dave Digs Disney* [released in 1957]. . . . It was taking common themes from Disney movies and translating them into this give-and-take that Brubeck and [saxophonist Paul] Desmond had, that was particularly lovely.

That, he says, was the spirit that Peter, Paul and Mary, too, epitomized. "I was once asked when I knew that Peter, Paul and Mary were magic, and I realized that it was the way we approached singing."

The first song the trio ever sang together was "Mary Had a Little Lamb," selected because they couldn't agree on the lyrics of any folk tunes. "But even there, there was a sensitivity to each other's voice. We almost immediately understood this was a give-and-take process, so we sang sensitively with each other and that translated to our personal interaction on stage as well. I think that, to a large extent, is what the audience ultimately came to see and hear, three people who were willing to concede to each other a portion of their ownership of the moment."

Across a career that delivered no less than twenty-one Top 100 hits, including major hits "Puff the Magic Dragon," Dylan's "Blowing in the Wind" (both 1964) and the number one "Leaving on a Jet Plane" (1969—their last ever hit), Peter, Paul and Mary recorded several Child Ballads, including "Jimmy Whalen" (78) and "Hangman" (95) in 1965. After reforming, they later tackled "The Cherry Tree Carol" (54) and "Golden Vanity" (286). Stookey's own favorite performance, however, was the brittle reading of "The Three Ravens" (26) that appears, alongside "Jesus Met the Woman at the Well" (21) on the trio's 1964 *In Concert* album.

I loved performing "The Three Ravens" with Dick Kniss, who was our bass player for certainly nine out of the first ten years we were together, and all of our remaining years from the eighties until Mary passed away in 2009. He never played the same part twice. It depended on the mood, and you know the song . . . "there were three ravens . . . black as they might be. . . ." Dick would go between the arco, which is a bowed bass, and the plucked bass, and he would pick his entrances. Now this is a jazz bassist from Woody Herman; he's part of the reason why I'm the jazz junkie I am, because I realized he was making this thing come alive every night. His attitude was the same as Frank Sinatra when he sang, if he didn't get it down in two takes, forget about it, because he realized that to beat it to death is to take all the life out of it, so some of his phrasing is just remarkable. I always tried to do that in my singing, with the trio and personally, I always find myself delivering the message as though it were the first time. So "Three Ravens" was not only special to me because of its moodiness. It's Shakespeare, it's tragedy, and yet it's the setting for the normal consequences of life against the span of life. The fact that the deer should be dead and the ravens should eat the flesh of the deer, this is life in its rawest form. So, approaching that story each time as though it were new just became a valuable lesson that I learned from Dick, and tried to apply to all the music that I do.

Carolyn Hester was already a known force on the emergent scene when she turned down Grossman's invitation to join his gestating trio. Barely twenty-one when her debut album, *Scarlet Ribbons*, was produced by Buddy Holly's regular producer Norman Petty in 1958, already her voice and presence were captivating—particularly, from this book's point of view, with her supreme restatement of "The Riddle Song" (46). Three years later, now a regular on the Greenwich Village scene, Hester came under the aegis of the Clancy Bothers, whose Tradition label issued her eponymous second album. And perhaps it was her "The Water Is Wide" (204) that introduced the song to Noel Stookey, sixty years before he recorded his own version of the song for his solo album *Fazz*.

Stookey admits, "When I first thought of 'The Water Is Wide,' I said, 'Oh, I'm not going to include that; it's such an old folk tune.'" This was an echoing of English singer Louis Killen's confession that "I don't know where, or how, I learned this song, probably by osmosis; or perhaps it was forced into my head at school."[2] But Stookey continued, "I do love the additional verse that I wrote and I can hear in the tenor of my voice that I was missing my wife when I sang it."

Hester's original recording of the ballad is positively shimmering, but perhaps even it is shaded by the rendition that appears on her 1965 *At the Town Hall* live album. "Here's one of the best-loved American ballads," she announces, before going on to demonstrate exactly why that should be the case.

In 1961, A&R man John Hammond signed Hester to Columbia Records—the unknown Bob Dylan made his official recorded debut that same year on her third album, also titled *Carolyn Hester*. His own debut album followed quickly after, however, and with it came the greatest shift ever in the concept of what "folk music" is—the move from reinterpreting the old songs to the creation of new ones. At the same time, however, it cemented the traditions even deeper into the soul of popular music.

In the eyes of the general American public, Dylan was initially sighted as the nasally-toned protege of the contrarily pristine-sounding Joan Baez, before arising to become her equal. His appearance at the 1963 Newport Festival was, for many people, the point at which they realized his fame was inevitable. But it was also the moment when he started to turn away from the traditional music that had both inspired and sustained him throughout his development.

The King and Queen of Folk—Joan Baez and Bob Dylan, 1963. Rowland Scherman / Wikimedia Commons

Dylan never attempted to camouflage his influences across his earliest albums—how the opening lines of "A Hard Rain's A-Gonna Fall" were based around those of "Lord Randall" (12); how "Lay Down Your Weary Tune" took its melodic lead from "Waly Waly" (204), and "Boots of Spanish Leather" from "Scarborough Fair" (2). And many more non-*ESPB* examples, too.

Many listeners appreciated these borrowings. Of course they were Dylan's acknowledgment, if such was needed, of his formative listening, but they were also evidence that the folk tradition itself was still alive— that one song could yet become another, and another still, until just a handful of words and a few snatches of melody remained to prove the relationship. It was Child's ceaseless search for such lineage that gave the *ESPB* much of its value, ensuring that it could never be mistaken for just another ballads book, when it was so obviously evidence of an evolving tradition. The activities of so many subsequent ballad collectors had only furthered that transformation, and Dylan was a part of the process.

To this list of Dylan's borrowings, after all, can be added those Child Ballads that he has performed in their traditional form. Among the earliest known recordings of the unknown Robert Zimmerman, "The Two Sisters" (10) arises from a tape he made at friend Karen Wallace's apartment in St. Paul, Minnesota, in May 1960; "Jesus Met the Woman at the

Well" (21) and "Gypsy Davy" (200) from what collectors know as the Gleason Home Tape, recorded in East Orange, New Jersey, the following year. Dylan performed "Barbara Allen" (84) at the Gaslight in New York in 1962, and he has occasionally revisited it during his ongoing Never Ending Tours, alongside "The Golden Vanity" (286).

Early studio sessions included a variant on "The House Carpenter" (243) that he likely learned from Dave van Ronk,[3] and in 1993, the album *World Gone Wrong* saw Dylan rolling back the decades to revisit "Love Henry" (68). Of course, Dylan is rightly most highly regarded as a songwriter in his own right. But a mix tape of his Child Ballads makes as solid a listen as many of his regular, early albums.

Following Dylan's lead in allowing traditional songs to infiltrate her own writing was Buffy Sainte-Marie, a Cree singer-songwriter born on February 20, 1941, on the Piapot Reserve in Saskatchewan, Canada, and signed to Vanguard in 1964. Her debut album *It's My Way* largely comprises her own material. However, Minneapolis-born artist and mouth bow virtuoso Ellie Bryan is not alone in tracing Sainte-Marie's "The Incest Song" back to the *ESPB*, and the Scots ballad "Sheath and Knife" (16)—which Walter Scott first remembered hearing being sung by his nurserymaid!

It was *It's My Way* that introduced Bryan to the Child Ballads. Describing her younger self as "an angsty teenager," it wasn't until her first year of college that Bryan began listening to folk music, largely inspired by the cousin who borrowed *It's My Way* from the local library, "and essentially played on repeat in both of our stereos, computers, and cars for a year."[4] Two songs from that album were part of Bryan's repertoire when she first began performing in the mid-2000s: "Sir Patrick Spens" (58) and "Waly Waly" (204). "The Incest Song" was on her mind, too, but it did not crystalize until she heard "Sheath and Knife."

[It] was . . . sheer luck and coincidence. I found a playlist that someone had compiled, clicked on a few links, and eventually landed on "Sheath and Knife." The version that was uploaded to the playlist was by Broadside Electric, who had a modern folk-rock approach. [But] the song's dark and tragic nature instantly appealed to me, and, with another quick search, I found the lyrics. There were many parallels between "The Incest Song" and "Sheath and Knife," such as the opening line of the incest song, "Word is up to the king's dear daughter, and word is spreading all over the land," and "Sheath and Knife": "It is talked the world all over, The king's daughter goes with child to her brother. Go down to the broom no more." The story of "The Incest Song" goes on to describe a young man who after discovering his pregnant lover is his sister, kills her. But in this version she begs for her life . . . to which he replies: "Too late too late for change my sister, My father has chosen another fair bride." Essentially the two songs share the same story,

Ellie Bryan's 2012 *Am I Born to Die* CD, featuring her spellbinding reading of Child 16. Author's collection

but one where the girl is willing to die, and one where she is not. Within moments of drawing the parallels, I knew instantly that these songs were about the same people, which put into place so much more weight and magic into the idea of these old, old songs having been about real human beings who once lived, and their stories had made an impact on at least one person who saw fit to write about them. And now, hundreds of years later, through word of mouth and song over the generations, here I am having heard of this tragic story of two lovers, for the second time.

Like Dylan, Sainte-Marie was an infrequent visitor (if a less recalcitrant magpie) when it came to the pages of the *ESPB*. But again, her example could only strengthen the canon's hold on the folk musician's imagination—no matter what convolutions it was now about to be pushed through.

If the folk revival had spent the past decade bubbling beneath the surface, only to break through in the admittedly anodyne form of the Kingston Trio, the emergence in such swift succession of Baez, Collins, Dylan, and more brought fresh energy and respect to the music. It also raised dollar signs in the eyes of industry heads the nation over.

There were folk music TV shows (ABC's *Hootenanny* was frequently taped on college campuses), folk music radio shows, even a folk music movie, *Hootenanny Hoot* (1963), starring Johnny Cash, George Hamilton IV, the Gateway Trio, and Elektra's latest sensation, the six-foot-one Judy Henske, who sings "Wade in the Water" (204) from the confines of a Beverly Hills swimming pool, glamorously sporting a Louise Brooks wig.

Inspired by Newport, local folk festivals became the rage. Most faded after just a year or two. But others would at least outlive the folk boom, among them the St. Olaf Folk Festival in Minnesota.

Recordings from this particular event are sparse; among those that do circulate, however, is the local trio of John Koerner, Dave Ray, and Tony Glover powering through an extraordinarily locomotive, jugband-shaped "Black Jack Davey" (200).

The same ballad, sung by Tossi Aaron, appears on an LP celebrating the first edition of the still-active Philadelphia Folk Festival, as it briefly followed Newport's lead by releasing its own souvenir live albums; in fact, "Gypsy Davy" was one of three Child Ballads included on Aaron's debut album, *Tossi Sings Folksongs and Ballads*. Today, Aaron is best remembered for her 1960 recording "I Know You Rider," thanks to its subsequent life in the Grateful Dead's repertoire, but the two albums she recorded for Prestige International demonstrate just what a crapshoot "folk stardom" was. So many talented performers were birthed, so many memorable performances were given. But in an industry that was as merciless as it was rapacious, there was only so much room at the top table and, once Dylan broke through and rearranged the furniture, there was even less.

Dylan has never forgotten his roots, any more than Collins, Baez, and Stookey have forgotten theirs. Much of their audience, however, certainly did forget, an accusation that can be backed up with a survey of Professor Child's appearances at the Newport Folk Festival. John Jacob Niles appeared at the 1959 event, sixty-seven years old but still capable of causing a stir. In fact, his set, which included "The Hangman" (95) and "Matty Groves" (81) was among the best-received of the day.

The former is especially impressive, Niles's barely audible guitar offering mere interludes between verses that are declaimed in a bewildering tangle of tones and pitches as he excavates every ounce of fear and imploring in the maid's remarks, and an almost sadistic glee in the responses of her watching family. "I come to see you swinging-swinging high from that hangman's tree." One witness, posting on the festival's Facebook site in 2015, recalled, "Aside from Josh White, Pete Seeger and The Kingston Trio, I was still learning about the different folk groups and musicians in the early days of the festival. I was unfamiliar with John Jacob Niles, but upon hearing his high-pitched Kentucky soprano singing traditional English songs at Newport, I realized the depth and breadth of the music in the folk world, into which I was dipping my toes for the first time."

Ed McCurdy, best known at the time as composer of "Last Night I Had the Strangest Dream," but also renowned for the three-volume *When Dalliance Was in Bloom* collection of erotic Elizabethan balladry, silenced the crowd with a sonorous "When Cockle Shells Turn Silver Bells" (204). And, among the younger generation of players, Frank Hamilton, still in his mid-20s, offered up a frenetic "Lady Gay" (79), his banjo a blur beneath the words.

The following year, 1960, saw a solo Tommy Makem regale the masses with a gentle "Whistling Gypsy" (200), while the veteran Oscar Brand made his festival bow by retelling the tale of "The Great Selchie of Shule Skerry" (113). Will Holt delivered a sinister "Edward" (13); and Mike Seeger (whose sister Peggy was also on the bill alongside husband Ewan MacColl) introduced a quirky "Fair Ellender" (73). Few performers introduced their songs *as* Child Ballads, but with a new edition of *ESPB* now in production,[5] and earlier volumes being passed eagerly around college campuses and coffee houses, it is likely that anybody who cared was already aware. The live albums that Vanguard recorded across those two festivals capture both the rapture and the respect with which audiences received these performances.

What they don't capture, however, is the near riot that ensued on the Saturday night of the 1960 event as thousands of ticketless fans attempted to storm the festival grounds, to be repelled by both the police and the Rhode Island National Guard. Flying bottles and beer cans were met with fire hoses and tear gas, and no less than 182 people were arrested. A further 27 were picked up when the unrest continued the following day on the beach. The city responded furiously. The bulk of the remainder of the 1960 festival was canceled (only an afternoon blues workshop was permitted to go ahead), local taverns were closed, and the festival, it seemed, was finished. Applications for a license to stage the 1961 event were rejected,[6] and, while a Newport Festival took place in 1962, it was restricted to jazz alone.

By then, of course, the demand for a folk event was even greater. This was the very apex of the Folk Revival, with an entirely new generation of performers arising. Perhaps sensing that if Newport continued to play hard to get, any number of other cities would happily welcome an army of excited folk fans and their bulging wallets, the city lifted its ban in 1963. This latest event, however, was more carefully curated than many of the twenty-seven thousand attendees might have wished. For them, a full three days of folk would have been nirvana. Instead, afternoon workshops ensured that blues, country, and bluegrass, and old time music, too, were well represented, and when Vanguard released their 1963 Festival recordings, each of those specifications received an LP in its own right.

The sea change ushered in by the music's new popularity is instantly clear. Although traditional songs were scarcely at a premium throughout the 1963 festival itself, just one Child Ballad made it onto vinyl, and that by a performer who was not even booked to play! West Virginian Jenes Cottrell was a furniture maker who sang for fun; he had one banjo tuning, and a handful of songs, and only attended the festival at the insistence of a student friend, Ken Davidson. He found his way onto the stage, however, and his "The Devil and the Farmer's Wife" (278) still raises a smile today.

The following year's festival saw no less than seven discs preserve the weekend's action. But Child, again, was scarcely present and even he would scarcely have recognized his contribution to the proceedings, as Koerner, Ray, and Glover reprised their monstrous "Black Jack Davey" (200). The festival's delineation between "folk" music and "old time music" remains one of those dividing lines whose repercussions were felt for years after.

Writing the liners to Tom Rush's first album for Elektra Records, journalist Paul Nelson coined the term "city folksingers," to encompass the growing coterie of performers who, while continuing to utilize the instrumentation and form of traditional song, were now happiest when writing their own material. And, whereas Dylan's transition from one to the other is easy to trace through his aforementioned borrowings of traditional melody, those who emerged in his wake presented themselves as fully formed. Their influences were clear, but they were adamant that they wanted to sing of their own lives and times, not those that had passed centuries before. Neither were they straitjacketed by the "folk" genre into which, by virtue of acoustic guitars and the like, they were most commonly placed. Rush's second Elektra album, *Take a Little Walk with Me*, featured organist Al Kooper—fresh from Dylan's *Highway 61 Revisited* noise fest—and dedicated its first side to a clutch of rock'n'roll covers.

Increasingly, the impression was—even the folkies found folk music old-fashioned.

Chapter Thirty

SHIRLEY SHINING

While the American folk scene focused on creating the superstars of the future, its British counterpart continued to investigate the dustiest corners of Cecil Sharp House, the repository of that man's collections, or pursue old-timers across the countryside, demanding to hear their songs. It was not, however, a practice that everybody condoned. In a momentous book titled *The Horn Book: Studies in Erotic Folklore and Bibliography*, American author and folklorist G. Legman lamented what he calls the "fakelorists" who "go out now to every corner of the English-speaking world . . . heavy laden with high-priced hi-fi recordings traps, and will look at you with heartbreak engraven on their face if some thoughtless 'native' sings a note before the machine is turned on." And why? "They are all out for the money. Most of them have no other job than the hoked up 'folklore' they are peddling." They could not, he condemns, conceive of ever undertaking any labor more intensive than that required to "exploit and debase the unpaid art-production of country people, factory hands, itinerant singers (if there are any left, God help them) and the historic folk-arts to be found in 'public domain.'" Neither will they "sing, record, or print one bloody word or note without a brassbound contract for a cut of the box office take."[1]

It's a damning condemnation, and doubtless period readers had a high old time trying to guess precisely whom Legman was targeting with his wrath. But Ewan MacColl described *The Horn Book* as "magnificent" in his liner notes for *The Wanton Muse*, a 1968 collection of erotic folk songs; and besides, whether or not Legman was wholly accurate at the time, innumerable examples have since come to light of collectors doing all that he accused them of, and worse.

Shirley Collins in the Sussex countryside, 2016. Andrew Hasson / Alamy Stock Photo

To tar every collector with this same brush would, of course, be wrong. Many did undertake their collecting for fun, anxious only to share their discoveries with as much of the world that could be said to care. Others saw it almost as a form of civic duty to ensure the survival of old songs for the sake of history itself, consciously or otherwise obeying the request in 1925, from the League of Nations' International Congress of Popular Arts, that every government in the world make efforts to record its peoples' traditional songs and melodies.

And for some, it was for the love of song itself.

For Shirley Collins, all three factors came into play. Collins was already well known in academic circles for her associations with Alan Lomax; as the 1950s came to a close, she was also leading the British folk revival with a stream of peerless releases. Born in the southeastern coastal town of Hastings, Collins moved to London in the early 1950s and immediately impacted upon the local club scene, a regular at the Troubadour in Earls Court and the 44 Club on Gerrard Street, in Soho.

Author Mike Butler describes how "two versions of 'The Maid Freed From The Gallows' [95] could be heard at the 44 Club. . . . Redd Sullivan sang it as the Leadbelly-derived 'Gallows Pole'; for Shirley, it was 'The Prickle Bush' and sung with proper sacramental feeling."[2]

John Hasted, a physicist who was also editor of *Sing* magazine and a performer in his own right ("the nearest Britain ever had to Pete Seeger," according to Bill Leader),[3] was one of those who could lay claim to having "discovered" Collins, as organizer of the left-wing London Youth Choir. Collins was a member of the choir, accompanying it on visits to Warsaw and Moscow in the mid-fifties. He also witnessed her folk club performances and was especially enamored by her interpretation of "Prickle Bush": "The symbolism would assume such importance that the audience never unravelled the mystery of who killed who, or why," he wrote in his *Alternative Memoirs* autobiography.

Twenty years old, Collins had just returned from the London Youth Choir's trip to Moscow when she met Alan Lomax at a party thrown by Ewan MacColl, marking the American's latest visit to London in 1955. She was already familiar with Lomax's work from his radio broadcasts; the big American (he reminded Collins of a bison, she later said) swiftly discovered that the youngster was a repository of song. She had all but committed Cecil Sharp's books to memory and supplemented that with hours spent at the English Folk Dance and Song Society. She played the five-string banjo, eschewing the common dictate, no matter how fervently her authenticity-driven peers demanded, that the ballads be performed a cappella.

Lomax was instantly smitten—he later described her as a "young girl singing alone in the house or garden, dreaming of love," and the pair swiftly became lovers. Lomax was still working on the Columbia Records world music project, and Collins was drawn into that as a researcher, while also assisting him on his in-progress book, *The Folk Songs of North America*. She would also become involved in his own musical project.

The mid-1950s saw the British airwaves invaded by the latest American invention, rock'n'roll. Simultaneously, however, a peculiar form of folk was taking control, in the form of skiffle—a literally DIY concoction within which almost any instrument could be replicated with a common household object, be it a washboard for percussion, or a broomstick with a string attached for bass. It was American music that dominated this upstart genre, the songs of Lead Belly, Woody Guthrie, and so forth, with any semblance of British traditional music most likely to be performed à la the Stateside folkies. "The Golden Vanity" (286) was part of skiffle superstar Lonnie Donegan's show (it also appeared on the B side of his monster hit "My Old Man's a Dustman"). The Chris Barber Skiffle Group recorded "Gypsy Davey" (200), while Nancy Whiskey, the so-glamorous vocalist alongside Chas McDevitt on the latter's 1957 Top 5 hit "Freight Train," recorded an alluring "The Trooper and the Maid" (299) for that same year's *Nancy Sings* solo album. When Lomax, MacColl, and Collins formed their own skiffle band, the Rounders (under which name they appeared on Granada TV) and later, Alan Lomax and the Ramblers, it is no surprise that they, like their skiffle contemporaries, looked westward for inspiration.

The Ramblers' solitary EP (extended play) comprised two American work songs, "Railroad Man" and "Oh Lula," alongside two MacColl originals ("Dirty Old Town" and "Hard Case"). And while Child 204 appeared in their repertoire and was also included in *The Skiffle Album* songbook that Lomax and MacColl masterminded in 1957, it was in its American "The Water Is Wide" incarnation, as opposed to the Scottish "James Douglas."

It is true that individual members of the band were among the mammoth cast for Lomax's 1957 BBC spectacular *Sing Christmas and the Turn of the Year*, a gathering that brought singers and performers from across the British Isles, and was surely highlighted by Shirley Collins and her haunting "The Cherry Tree Carol" (54). Otherwise, however, the American variants ruled, suggesting that many skiffle artists did not even realize they were delving *not* into the foreign traditions that they loved, but the ones from which they were born. MacColl's fellows at the Ballads and Blues Club must have looked most askance at the contradiction.

Despite this, the impact of the skiffle fad on the incipient British folk scene could not be impugned, and the country at large was offered a glimpse of the sheer variety of forms that fell beneath the folk music banner by a concert staged at the Royal Festival Hall in London on July 5, 1954. On a bill nominally dominated by the Ken Colyer Skiffle Group, attendees were treated, too, to Scottish country dance; solo sets by Isla Cameron; Bert Lloyd (who also performed a song with Colyer's outfit); Ewan MacColl, who silenced the venue with a drama-soaked "Dowie Dens of Yarrow" (214); and a variety of sea shanties, calypso, and more.

Furthermore, Shirley Collins was not the first future British folk performer to serve an apprenticeship in a skiffle combo. Guitarist Martin Carthy was first sighted in such combos as Redd Sullivan's Thameside Four and the Three City Four; broadcaster Wally Whyton, a staunch supporter of both folk and country music, was first heard in the Vipers (where he played alongside future members of Cliff Richard's Shadows); and the young Frankie Armstrong sang with the Sort Valley Skiffle Group.

She recalls, "I went to the local trad jazz club with some girlfriends to see Mick Mulligan and George Melly, when Mac Jones, who was the leader of the Stort Valley Skiffle Group, asked me to dance. We were jiving away and I told him I'd enjoyed his band when I'd seen them. He said he was looking for a girl singer, did I know one, and without hesitating, I said 'Yes, me.'"[4] A star was born that night.

Lomax's skiffle band, like the fad itself, did not live long. The upcoming release of the first volumes in the Columbia world music series naturally occupied much of his time, but he was also dealing with the fall-out unleashed by the British government's continued suspicions that he was somehow an undesirable alien, a notion that the FBI had been encouraging all decade long.

Lomax had ascended to a certain degree of local stardom by now, a consequence of his radio and TV appearances. The satirical magazine *Punch* even lampooned him with a 1957 cartoon depicting a lonesome farmer seated on the steps of his shack, singing "I got those 'Alan-Lomax-Ain't-Been-Round-To-Record-Me-Yet' blues." Nevertheless, he left the United Kingdom in 1958, his parting gift to Collins being the two day recording session (set up with Peter Kennedy) at which she recorded all thirty-seven of the songs that comprised her first two LPs, 1959's *Sweet England* and *False True Lovers*.

Collins had already released two EPs, *The Foggy Dew* and *English Songs*, for the tiny Collector Records; across all four records, she performs eight Child Ballads, among them a rare airing for a "Ritchie Story" (232) that she learned from Ewan MacColl, who in turn picked it up from his father; and "The Unquiet Grave" (78). The studiousness of youth is certainly apparent in her performances, however, and it required one more encounter with Lomax to bring her to full voice.

Collins and Lomax remained in contact following his departure, completing their collaboration on the Caedmon label's *The Folk Songs of Britain* series by mail, before he sent her a boat ticket to join him in New York. Together they made their way first to Chicago, where Lomax was due to appear on Studs Terkel's radio show. Then it was on to California, where Lomax was directing the Berkeley Folk Music Festival, and where Collins joined him onstage for a Talking Folk Music panel. They returned to the East Coast for the Newport Folk Festival before then heading south to record in the field for another Columbia records project, *The History of Jazz*.

Collins remained in America until January 1960; the "Southern Journey," as it came to be known, having taken the couple through eight states in three months, where they captured—for the first time in stereo— the likes of Texas Gladden, Wade Ward, Almeida Riddle, and "Mississippi" Fred McDowall.

It was an eye-opening journey for the young Collins, musically and culturally, too. But her memoir of the trip, *America Over the Water*, preserved some singular observations, too, such as Texas Gladden's response to Lomax asking her if she ever visualized the characters in "The Devil's Nine Questions" (1), which she'd just sung. "Oh yes. The girl is dressed in a crinoline, very blonde, delicate and soft. The Devil is very swarthy, but not a bad looking guy. He's tall and lanky, has a Roman nose, but he's very good-looking and has a definite persuasive way about him." She might have been describing one of her visitors.

Despite their jazz brief, Lomax and Collins recorded everything, from spirituals to prison songs, from work songs to blues, and a handful of Child Ballads as well. The most valued source for the latter was Almeda

Riddle (1898–1986), whom Lomax now met for the first time at her home in Greers Ferry, Arkansas. Encouraged in her love of music by her father, a renowned fiddler and shape note singer, Riddle was introduced to Lomax by local folklorist John Quincy Wolf, who had encountered her a short while before. (It is Wolf's recording of her "The Merrimac at Sea" (289) from which Vic Shepherd and John Bowden with Linda Lee Welch sourced the version on their 2015 CD *Still Waters*.)

Collins, in *America Over the Water*, described Riddle as "a singer of such composure and quiet intensity that you were compelled to listen." The twenty-three songs she and Lomax recorded on that trip laid the foundation for Riddle's 1964 Vanguard Records release *Songs and Ballads of the Ozarks*, released alongside her much-admired appearance at the Newport Folk Festival.

Just three of Riddle's Child Ballads made it onto Lomax's recorder: "The Hangman's Tree" (95), "The House Carpenter" (243), and "The Merry Golden Tree" (286). The Vanguard album would reprise "The House Carpenter" and add "Lady Gay" (79) and "Black Jack Davey" (200). Later in her career, Riddle would record some half dozen more, including distinctly local versions of "Edward" (13), known to her as both "The Blood of the Old Red Rooster" and "The Blood on his Shirt Sleeve," and "The Merrimac at Sea" (289).

Riddle remained on Shirley Collins's mind long after she returned to England. That "rare and admirable quality of serving the songs, rather than the songs serving her" was something that escaped many singers, regardless of their age and experience. But the next time Collins appeared on record, across a succession of folk compilation albums prepared by Peter Kennedy,[5] and her own *Heroes in Love* EP, it was clear the lesson had sunk home.

Collins was now married to Austin John Marshall, himself a figure who bestrides the story of British folk in the 1960s (and beyond) like a colossus.[6] They met when Marshall was commissioned to design sleeves for the Kennedy compilations; now Marshall was preparing for Collins's next LP by introducing her to mercurial jazz guitarist Davy Graham (1940–2008). The resultant hybrid, *Folk Roots, New Routes,* is today widely regarded as one of the very foundations of all that was to follow in terms of folk's musical destiny, yet Collins later admitted that Marshall wanted the duo to take things even further than they did, until finally she put her foot down.

"John loved jazz," Shirley said, "and I hated it—too fidgety for my taste—and I thought it was inappropriate for English folk music, so I resisted having any further jazz influence on *Folk Roots*. What Davy Graham did was different, and it worked with my songs." Again, however, she reiterated, "That collaboration was John's idea."[7]

In the end, Marshall stood back from producing the album, in favor of Ray Horricks (1933–2005), fresh from sessions with the Scottish folk band the Galliards and balladeer Kenneth McKellar, while the engineer was a young man barely starting out in his career, Gus Dudgeon (1942–2002). Speaking in 1986, the latter recalled the sessions as "nerve wracking. Davy was very unpredictable, John [Marshall] could be domineering, and Shirley could be stubborn."[8] The album as a whole he regarded as "a success, but it was not an easy one"—and this from a man whose later jobs included producing David Bowie, Elton John, and the Bonzo Dog Doo Dah Band.

Collins was largely responsible for choosing the material on the album, two songs apiece from the Scottish and Irish traditions, three from the English and seven from America, including two that she learned on the southern journey, Texas Gladden's "The Bad Girl" and Vera Hall's "The Boll Weevil." Just one Child Ballad, however, was included, "The Cherry Tree Carol" (54), and when journalist Karl Dallas (1931–2016) described *Folk Roots, New Routes* as being "there at that instant that Electric Rock . . . Folk Rock, call it what you will . . . was born" (by virtue of attitude, if not electricity), "The Cherry Tree Carol" could probably exempt itself from that company.

Besides, no matter what the critics said, the collaboration with Graham was, in artistic terms, an absolute dead end. He and Collins both moved on.

Chapter Thirty-One

TALKING THE TUNES

By the end of the 1950s, Professor Child was discovering ways of invei-
gling himself into all manner of different company. *Unexpurgated Songs
of Erotica* was produced by the US-based Fax label and, while erotic folk
songs were scarcely a new or shocking development (Legman's *The Horn
Book* treated of nothing else), they were normally released by "respect-
able" labels, who knew the context into which they should be placed—
releases such as Argo's *The Wanton Muse*, Topic's *The Bird in the Bush*, and
Transatlantic's *Songs of Love, Lust and Loose Living*. They certainly weren't
accustomed to becoming labelmates to such innuendo-strewn delights
as *Stories for Sex-Minded Males*, *Nights of Love in Lesbos*, *Hollywood's Most
Intimate Smoker Stories*, to name but a few of Fax's line in adult-themed
gramophone recordings.

But "The Friar at the Well" (276) slipped seamlessly, even glibly, into
such company regardless.

> *There was a friar as I been told*
> *Fancied a girl sixteen years old;*
> *Come begging to her in the middle of the night,*
> *Would he sleep with her till the broad daylight.*
> *Till me ay fall lal diddle air o dee*

This particular version was performed by singer Frank Purslow and John
Pearce, the latter a renowned authority on the dulcimer. Indeed, his first
book, *The Dulcimer Book*, was subsequently reprinted as *How to Make and
Play the Dulcimer*, while he also presented a UK TV series on the subject,
and later had his own branded instrument, manufactured by the British
company Rosetti.

267

Neither was this the performance's sole appearance under such circumstances. It also appears on the charmingly titled *Rap-A-Tap-Tap—English Folk Songs Miss Pringle Never Taught Us*. If *Unexpurgated Songs of Erotica* is the Child Ballads reveling at the lowest end of the artistic spectrum, however, the work of actress Kathleen Danson Reid takes it to altogether opposing heights.

In 1959, following two earlier albums of spoken-word poetry, the Lancashire-born Danson Read released *Spoken Literature of Early English Ballads* and effectively torpedoed even the most tightly woven interpretation of how the old songs should be performed. The theory that the ballads, in their original form, were not ballads at all, that they were originally written to be read (and perhaps acted out) as stories, is of course impossible to prove one way or another. It is, however, an attractive theory, one that chimes with the ballads' popularity in the southern American play parties of the nineteenth century, and accrues further credibility through the belief that the Robin Hood ballads developed out of plays. Danson Read was perfectly placed to take this notion further. She studied dramatic art and elocution, subjects which she later taught in her hometown, Burnley. She frequently appeared at festivals and Eisteddfods, and was recipient of the elocution gold medal at the Wallasey Music Festival.

The texts employed on *Spoken Literature of Early English Ballads* were principally drawn from Child's own primary versions. Only "Chevy Chase" (162) significantly differed, as Danson Reed's liner notes explained: "The version I am about to read [and she does indeed "read" the ballads] was popular during the reign of King James I of England (1604–25) and though lacking some of the dignity of the earlier ballad, contains fewer difficulties of wording that make it easier to understand and appreciate." The poem, she conceded, "has been slightly abridged"; nevertheless, it numbered 57 stanzas and, at close to ten minutes duration, is by far the longest recitation on the album.

In all fairness, *Spoken Literature of Early English Ballads* is not a popular listen today, despite—or perhaps because of—Danson Reed's award-winning elocution. One could imagine her clipped "BBC English" tones emanating from a particularly sober schoolmarm, of the breed delightfully parodied by the English comedian Joyce Grenfell. Distance oneself, however, from such perceptions and the notion that these pieces were indeed once performed as spoken-word passages does not seem so unlikely. The stories themselves still fascinate, and they simply do not *need* music to touch an audience. For they possess a musicality in their internal rhyme and rhythm that is only a step or two away from the unaccompanied singing that the ballad collectors toured the world in search of.

Besides, the success of Danson Read's project can be gauged from the release, that same year, of C. R. M. Brookes's beguilingly grumbled *Poetry*

John Laurie, as *Dad's Army*'s Private Frazer, his best-remembered television role. AA Film Archive / Alamy Stock Photo

of Robert Burns and Scottish Border Ballads, with its inevitable cargo of Child Ballads, and the similarly themed *Jupiter Book of Ballads*. Released by playwright and author V. C. Clinton-Baddeley's (1900–1970) Jupiter label, a specialist in spoken-word and poetry, this latter contained seventeen ballads, including eight from Child, either being sung or, more thrillingly, spoken by a trio drawn from the upper echelons of British acting.

Clinton-Baddeley himself delivered "Saint Stephen and King Herod" (22—a retelling of the martyrdom of Saint Stephen) with a panoply of voices; then joined with a dramatically ghostlike Pauline Letts (1917–2001)—Cleopatra in the 1951 British movie version of *Anthony and Cleopatra*—for an "Unquiet Grave" (78) that is as forlorn as it ought to be.

From Dumfries-born actor John Laurie (1897–1980), "Alison Gross" (35) is coyly devilish; his "Wife of Usher's Well" (79) likewise. Anyone who enjoyed Laurie's role as the doom-foreseeing Private Frazer on British TV's *Dad's Army* will instantly recognize the intonation he deploys. Neither was this Laurie's sole dalliance with the Child Ballads. The following year, Clinton-Baddeley invited him back to voice "Jock O'Hazeldean" (293) for Jupiter's *A Junior Anthology of English Verse Part Two*. And, again, Laurie turns in a performance that is, quite possibly, even more authentic than the authenticators themselves.

That the Child Ballads should be viewed as literature of some sort is not in dispute. They would, however, soon be forming the basis of literature in their own right.

Angela Carter, folk singer and novelist. INTERFOTO / Personalities / Alamy Stock Photo

In 1964, the University of Bristol's *Nonesuch Magazine* published an article, "For the Love of Singing," by twenty-four-year-old Angela Carter, a doctoral student working on a dissertation on the etymology of the English folksong text "The Streams of Lovely Nancy." It's a fascinating piece of writing, very much "of its time," but also fiercely confrontational. "Much of what is loosely termed revival singing is curiously irrelevant to the real why and wherefore of authentic folk song," she argues at one point. "[I]t is well-nigh impossible to write convincingly in the style of a folk song . . . if you haven't got the specific sort of talent," she declares later, before condemning "most of the 'composed' folk song one hears so much about these days" as "species of historical rant that are more bastard descendants of Brecht and Weill (whose hypothetical parents, screaming in horror, would disown them) than anything to do with folk song."

Throughout the piece, she references the great old men of English traditional song—the farmworker Harry Cox; "the wild and passionate Scots tinker singer" Davy Stewart; the Irishman Joe Heaney; and the fisherman Sam Larner, so recently brought to wider attention by the release of his Folkways album *Now Is the Time for Fishing*. As Carter put it, "One will learn more about folk song from listening to them than could ever be gleaned from books."

Carter herself had been a key figure on the Bristol folk scene for five years at this point. Born in May 1940 in the south coast town of Eastbourne, in 1959 she married Paul Carter (died 2012), a singer and sound recordist for Topic Records, to this day the single most important folk label in the United Kingdom.

It was Paul Carter who accompanied collectors Ken Stubbs and Bill Leader on trips to record the Willett family, father Tom and his sons Chris and Ben, for the 1962 Topic album *The Roving Journeymen*—Tom opens the album with a rousing "Lord Bateman" (53), notable for the singer's decision to omit the opening verses and leap straight into the action. With Sean O'Boyle, he recorded Sarah Makem in 1967 and Phoebe Smith in 1969, to name just a few.[1] It was Carter, too, who selected the material included on the two EP volumes of Willie Clancy and Michael Gorman's *Irish Pipe and Fiddle Tunes*, and it was Angela who wrote the uncredited portion of the liner notes that accompanied them: "The Bedfords Arms is almost a legend. The draught beer must not have been great, but the music was wonderful." She would write other Topic liners, too, anonymously as was often the case in those days, and she frequently accompanied her husband on his recording trips, including one around the so-called singing pubs of Sussex.

Back home in Bristol, meanwhile, the pair ran, and performed at, the Folksong and Ballad Club, in a room above the Lansdown public house.

(It later relocated to the Bear on Hotwells Road.) They also visited other clubs—it was at one of these, in Cheltenham on January 15, 1967, that a recording of Angela herself was made, singing the non-Child "The Flower of Sweet Strabane," and playing polka music on her English Concertina. It was from this immersion that the seeds were sewn for Carter's future as a best-selling author of some of the darkest, yet most haunting novels and short stories of the late twentieth century.

In 2021, musician, author, and researcher Polly Paulusma released *Invisible Music*, a collection (as the subtitle makes clear) of *Folk Songs That Influenced Angela Carter*. With each of its nine tracks preluded by a reading from one of Carter's novels or stories, the set includes Paulusma's mercurial interpretations of four Child Ballads: "Lady Isabel and the Elf-Knight" (4), "The Maid and the Palmer" (21), "Lucy Wan" (51), and "Barbary Allen" (84). The themes that run through those songs—incest, revenge, and frustrated love—all have deep echoes within Carter's earliest fiction.[2]

Paulusma discovered Carter's writings at university in the 1990s, in the years following the author's 1992 death.

> I was always struck with the musicality of her writing, but I couldn't put my finger on how she was managing to do it. In 2012 I set up a small record label and I found myself at the English Folk Expo in Bury, listening to loads of traditional folk songs and signing Maz O'Connor[3] to my label . . . and getting a pretty rapid education in English folk. I had Carter['s books] with me on that trip, because I'd been booked by chance to teach a Cambridge student doing a Carter dissertation, and I think it was the bringing together of my two lives, the singer/songwriter/label founder and the teacher, that led to my realization that Carter knew the folk songs I was hearing very well. I was really overwhelmed with a sense that she knew how to sing them. At first it was a singer's instinct. But then I went down a rabbit hole of discoveries and realized that she had been much more involved in the Bristol folk scene than the critical community realized at that point.[4]

Carter was not the first, and certainly not the last author to draw inspiration from folk songs in general, and the Child Ballads in particular. But she did not simply "draw inspiration." Her novels are suffused with the very substance of the songs, and purposefully so.

Paulusma explains, "Carter left a paper trail. And it's a wiggly trail, not obvious but definitely present. I do think, however, that her folding in of the music into her writing can be seen as a form of positive onward evolution of the form, and she did state in a letter in 1966 that this was her intention. So . . . there is actually quite a lot of textual evidence out there."

Carter was astoundingly prolific; seven novels in the six years that followed her debut *Shadowlands* (1966) were accompanied by a welter of short stories, poetry collections, a couple of children's books, and a mass of nonfiction journalism, too. She reviewed Dylan's 1966 UK tour for *London Magazine*, interviewed a retired busker for *New Society*, and discussed the musical preferences of a Bristol pub for the same publication, alongside a wealth of reviews, commentary, and observations. And it is Carter's earliest work that best reflects her relationship with traditional music. *Invisible Music* pairs an excerpt from Carter's second novel, *The Magic Toyshop* (1967), with Paulusma's performance of the incest-ridden "Lucy Wan," while a reading from *Several Perceptions* (1968) preludes "The Maid and the Palmer." A reference to the short story "The Lady of the House of Love" introduces "Barbary Allen."

"[Carter] went very very quiet about folk singing after she and Paul Carter broke up [in 1967]," Paulusma reflects. "Some might speculate that she perhaps associated folk song with her first marriage and that when the marriage ended, she put her folk singing past behind her. Others might wonder if she maybe grew ambivalent about the scene itself, in particular the ways in which collecting, writing down and recording songs had a negative impact on their more 'natural' progress through communities. It's hard to say."

Recording her album, Paulusma focused upon versions of the ballads that Carter herself might have listened to. "My 'Lucy Wan' is my homage to the amazing version I found sung by Martin Carthy on *Byker Hill*, from 1967." But she also threw herself into the folk tradition itself, admitting,

> "Lady Isabel," I just made up. Really the whole recordings project fell out of my research, because I was listening to these wonderful recordings and just itching to sing them for myself, to have that body understanding of the songs as well as a brain understanding of them, to breathe them and have them inside-out, not just outside-in. And for some of them, I loved the versions I heard, and some not so much. It just became about cherry-picking really, taking what I fancied, discarding what I didn't, and making up the bits in between. I wasn't very scholarly about it. I just followed my musical sensibility wherever it led. It was great for me to have that freedom.

The first public airing for the project came in March 2017, during the *Strange Worlds: The Vision of Angela Carter* exhibition at the Royal West of England Academy in Bristol. Performing "Lucy Wan" and the non-Child "Jackie Monroe," Paulusma appeared alongside various of the musicians and singers who actually performed alongside Carter at the Folksong and Ballads Club, among them Dave Byrne and Marianne McAleer (singing "The Maid on the Shore"—43).

Paulusma's album followed four years later, to considerably more acclaim than the artist anticipated. "I didn't expect anyone to pay much attention to this project. It felt very much like I had disappeared down my own little pit for a few years and very much made this album self-ishly, made it for myself just to understand the songs a bit better, have a real experience of occupation with them. To be able to share that, and for people to enjoy the connections I've been able to make, is a true honor and privilege."

Like his wife, Paul Carter drifted away from involvement with the traditional scene following their parting, and he remained modest about his accomplishments at Topic. "I think you overestimate the importance of my recording these various singers," he wrote in a 2012 message that has since been posted online.[5] None of them were my 'discoveries' if you like. All I did . . . was to press switches."

Bill Leader, with whom he undertook several field trips, laughs away the latter. "No, he had a far better understanding of things. That would be a better description of me than of Paul. I knew him as a great enthusiast."[6] Leader also credits Paul Carter as the voice that convinced Colin Pomroy, owner of the specialist Jazz Collector independent label, to launch the even more specialist Collector label for folk releases in 1959. He adds, "Aside from what he was doing for Topic, Paul had an almost parallel career with Collector Records, doing a lot of recording."

Séamus Ennis, Robin Hall and Jimmie MacGregor, Sandy Paton, Steve Bembow, Shirley Collins, and Joe Heaney were numbered among the label's releases over the next five years, and Carter was involved in many of them. He also handled Dominic Behan's *Down by the Liffeyside*, with his marvelous reading of "The Farmer's Curst Wife" (278), retitled "The Women Are Worse Than Men" and described in Behan's liners as "enshrin[ing] a libel against womankind the origins of which are lost in the mists of antiquity, but which comes with perennial freshness from the lips of male singers. A classical lady who went to Hell and came back again was Alcestis; but her errand was to fetch home her husband. She is no relation of the virago of this song."

Jeannie Robertson's recording of one of Angela's favorite songs, "The Handsome Cabin Boy," was Carter's handiwork; so, very likely, was her *Twa Brothers* EP, with its bewitching rendition of a song Robertson learned from her mother, "Davy Faa" (279). He oversaw, too, Bert Lloyd's vinyl companion to the 1960 edition of *The Penguin Book of English Folk Songs*, and an EP *England and her Folk Songs*, that included no less than three Child Ballads among its four tracks.[7] Also numbered among his accomplishments were Robin Hall's distinctive versions of "The Dowie Dens of Yarrow" (214) and Leezie Lindsay" (226); a number of Shirley Collins performances; and, over at Topic, the first EP by an astonishing young singer named Anne Briggs, *The Hazards of Love*.

Chapter Thirty-Two

THE CRITICS GROUP

Barely out of her teens when she recorded *Hazards of Love*, Nottinghamshire-born Anne Briggs moved into folk circles through her friendship with Bert Jansch. They met when Briggs and a friend hitch-hiked to his hometown Edinburgh, and it was through Jansch's encouragement that Briggs became a fixture on the folk club circuit of the day, before making her recorded debut aboard a live album celebrating the 1963 Edinburgh Festival.

Briggs was an uncompromising performer. Reviews from the period pile on such epithets as "tempestuous," "feral," "untamed". . . "tense and volatile to the point of being the bad girl of folk," wrote *Sounds* journalist Jerry Gilbert in 1971. She was unpredictable, too, for she abandoned music in 1973 and, a quarter of a century later, journalist Colin Harper wrote in *Mojo*, "If British folk needs one single Robert Johnson figure, Anne Briggs could be it." She was, he continued, "sexy, wild, mysterious, otherworldly and vulnerable all at the same time."

Briggs recorded just two Child Ballads, but the unaccompanied treatments of "Willie O'Winsbury" (100) and "Young Tambling" (39) that appear on her eponymous debut album are certainly among the finest of them all. Even Bert Lloyd—whose "Young Tambling" Briggs recorded—sounds modest as he remarks, in *Anne Briggs*'s liner notes, how the ballad was "cobbled . . . together, in part from Child, in part from recent collection; the tune is derived from one used for this ballad by gypsies."

Briggs's repertoire was broad, then, and though she would not cut that first album until 1971, it was in the years prior that she made her greatest impact, plying the folk club circuit, recording sporadically, and, through the turmoil of her personal life, weaving the legend that still clings to her today. She did not enjoy performing, then or later. Turning her back on performance following her second album, *The Time Is Now*, Briggs remained out of sight until 1991 brought a brief resurgence.

Little survives from that period. Memories of a handful of shows with Carthy and Swarbrick and a few solo appearances are precious, although she later said she "didn't enjoy [them] at all."[1] But, most transcendent is Briggs's February 1992 appearance on the BBC's *Folk On 2*, during which she performed a (perhaps inevitable) "Willie O'Winsbury" (100), and a gripping "Maid on the Shore" (43), delivered with all the character and grit that ever stunned audiences in the past.

Sadly, the return was short lived. Even at the peak of activity, "I used to love busking and impromptu stuff far more," she insisted in 2007. "I didn't like being on the stage, I didn't like being looked at, so I'd shut my eyes half the time, trying to shut it out." But writer Alexis Petridis nevertheless confirmed, "Her voice was unaffected, at turns vulnerable and lusty, capable of breathing new life into a 200-year-old ballad, and it seems to have inspired virtually every significant folk artist since."[2]

Bert Lloyd was certainly a fervent admirer. Briggs's first ever studio recording, in 1963, was for an album of industrial songs that Lloyd, as artistic director at Topic Records (a post he had held since 1958) was compiling for Topic, *The Iron Muse*. The following year, he contributed the liner notes to her *Hazards of Love* EP, and in 1966, he recruited her to another thematic collection, the aforementioned round-up of erotic folk songs titled *The Bird in the Bush*. Lloyd's own interpretation of "The Two Magicians" (44), recorded with fiddler Dave Swarbrick, opened the set; and we are given a glimpse into Professor Child's reluctance to include any overtly sexual material in the *ESPB* by the fact that only one other Child Ballad, "The Maid on the Shore" (43), appears on the record, courtesy of another of Lloyd's proteges, Frankie Armstrong.

Much had changed since Armstrong's days with the Stort Valley Skiffle Group, although her band mates had not. "We changed our name," she explains,[3] "but I can't remember to what, and were largely singing songs from the Weavers, Jack Elliott, and Woody Guthrie, so I was singing every part in every song that Ronnie Gilbert ever sang. Then in 1962 we transmogrified into the Ceildh Singers and shifted to entirely British and Irish material."

The Ceildh Singers' greatest influence now was the Ian Campbell Folk Group. Formed in 1958, but generally confined to the club circuit immediately around their Birmingham base, that band's debut EP, *Ceilidh at the Crown*, had just been released by Topic, to be followed swiftly by another, *Songs of Protest*. Armstrong continues, "They had a big influence on me, all of them—certainly [vocalist] Lorna Campbell. They did the ballads and the folk songs, and all the wonderful protest songs as well. I would definitely say they had the biggest impact on me at that time."

Frankie Armstrong's 1972 debut LP *Lovely on the Water*. Author's collection

As for the Campbell Group's wider import, Armstrong points out that they were among the first British folk bands to release an LP, 1963's *This Is the Ian Campbell Folk Group!* As such, it offered up the first opportunity for British record buyers to hear the Child Ballads performed by a home-grown ensemble. Lorna's unearthly reading of "The Unquiet Grave" (78) would have proven a highlight of their debut, whether Child had selected it for his book or not. "I think other people tend to get more attention than they did," reflects Armstrong. Even with the young Dave Swarbrick in the band's ranks, "[the Campbell Group] didn't make a splash like some people, and they didn't have much in the way of marketing, they didn't go in for that. They just ran their club in Birmingham and did gigs in the same way the rest of us did. None of us had agents or marketing managers in those days."

One evening in spring 1963, just a few months after Armstrong relocated to London from her hometown Hoddesdon, she and her flatmate decided to visit a folk club in nearby Catford. "And there was Louis Killen. I was sitting in the front row, and I thought 'Ooh this man is totally gorgeous, apart from being a tremendous singer and instrumentalist,' so I went up and said hello."

From there developed a relationship that Armstrong ranks among the most important in her entire career, a rapid ascent that saw her initially joining Killen onstage for occasional duets, before being booked as a performer in her own right. "We'd play and afterwards, someone would come up and ask if I'd come back on my own. I'd say, 'Yes, that would be lovely,' and then they'd ask 'What's your fee,' and I hadn't a clue. In the end, I just halved Louis's fee and thought that was a reasonable amount."

It was Killen who encouraged Armstrong to listen to Ewan MacColl and Bert Lloyd's Riverside albums and to pick up the collections of source singers that were now beginning to appear. But his most important lesson was teaching her how best to sing the material she was learning. "I had what was probably a good voice, but it was somewhat rounded. I remember Louis saying, 'You can take it up and harden it, or take it down and harden it, but it needs to be less round and edgier.' And that started me off on a whole different aspect. I started running my own voice workshop in 1963, from listening to the people Louis told me to listen to, and listening to Bert Lloyd's folk music of Bulgaria,[4] going 'Oooh, how do they produce that sound?'"

Lloyd was a part of Armstrong's circle now, as were Ewan MacColl and Peggy Seeger. She became a regular visitor to the Singers Club and soon a resident performer; she also joined MacColl's Critics Group, a regular gathering of likeminded souls for an evening of discussion, argument, and song that ultimately ran for close to a decade, with some forty-plus members coming and going throughout that span. "It was a musical feast," Armstrong continues. "There was the core of us who probably stayed there for seven or eight years, and then there were various people who came and went, either because of geographical relocation or because they had a row with Ewan. It was an interesting experience, but most of us stayed there longer than we should have."

Meetings took place on Tuesday evenings at MacColl and Seeger's home in Beckenham, on the outskirts of south London. There, "We listened to traditional singers and talked about their style and the songs, their context and their history and influences, so there was lots of interesting stuff. Ewan obviously led it, but we all got our word in, and we also did this sequence where one of us would put together a half-hour performance, as if we were doing it at a folk club, to be critiqued by the others."

Among Armstrong's presentations was her rendering of "The Cruel Mother" (20), to which she had been introduced by Lloyd, who in turn took it from Cecilia Costello's repertoire. "I think it was the first Child Ballad I ever performed; either that or 'The Grey Cock' [248], which was also Mrs. Costello's." It was Lloyd, too, who first recorded Armstrong, inviting her to perform three contributions (two non-Child) to *The Bird in the Bush,* and the following year, he suggested she record a solo album for Topic Records. She declined. "I thought long and hard about it and said 'I'd love to, but not yet, I'll let you know when I feel I've got the range of repertoire and on top of my material sufficiently to do a whole album.'"

In the meantime, she contributed a plaintive "Geordie" (209) to Critics Group's 1968 release *The Female Frolic,* and was also heavily involved in a gallant attempt to introduce traditional song to high school–age students, when the Argo label embarked upon a fourteen volume series of albums titled *Poetry and Song.* A follow-up of sorts to the same label's 1965 series *Rhyme and Rhythm: Poems and Songs for Children,*[5] this latest collection was largely schemed under the auspices of MacColl and the Critics Group, with the intention, as the liner notes put it, "to present poetry and song as an exciting adjunct to everyday language." The artwork for each album was selected from the winning entrants to the *Sunday Mirror* newspaper's Children's Art Competition.

Released across a two-year span, spring 1967 to summer 1969, the series is scarcely remembered as avidly as other, earlier, attempts to reach the same age group. However, singer Raymond Crooke recalls volumes being in use during his schooldays in Australia, and Critics Group alumnus Jim Carroll recalls, "Around the time of their issue, Ewan and Peg held meetings with a number of schoolteachers, at least one of [whom] joined The Critics Group, Alwyn Cooper." An illustration on the online Discogs collectors site, meanwhile, depicts a copy of volume two in the series, adorned with a sticker denoting it as the property of the English department of the Liverpool Institute of Higher Education.

Regardless of the series' ultimate penetration, it was a very well-conceived effort, and Frankie Armstrong was one of a host of performers called upon to contribute to the "song" aspect of the series. Alongside MacColl and Seeger, there were offerings, too, from Lloyd, Pete Seeger, Sandra Kerr, and a panoply of Critics Group regulars. For the "poetry," a wealth of familiar names from radio and television were enlisted, among them Patrick Wymark reading Hillaire Belloc, and future *Fawlty Towers* actress Prunella Scales reciting Thomas Hardy. MacColl himself delivered a spoken word "Alison Gross" (35) that is not quite as nightmare-inducing as John Laurie's effort of a decade previous but could nevertheless make a few hairs stand on end.

Armstrong and Child Ballads alike appear on several of the albums in the series. We hear her paired with Sandra Kerr for "Scarborough Fair" (2); and alone, performing "The Outlandish Knight" (4). Kerr delivers a desperate "Prickle Holly Bush" (95), and pairs with John Faulkner for a rousing "The Sweet Trinity" (286). MacColl adds even more, among them an epic "True Thomas" (37), a performance that Armstrong ranks among his very best: "It's one of my favorite ballads, and I do think it needs an authentic Scottish accent to pull off, and Ewan had a good enough one. That's him at his best. It wasn't too mannered, it wasn't over dramatized, and the ballad itself, the language is so phenomenal, and the imagery is so powerful."

Armstrong continued gigging throughout this period, but it was 1972 before she started work on her debut album, a year after the vision problems that had dogged her since childhood rendered her legally blind. *Lovely on the Water* rates among the most pristinely lovely traditional albums of its era. Armstrong sings unaccompanied throughout, and her choice of material is irreproachable, with no less than five Child Ballads nested among its fourteen tracks. Her signature "The Cruel Mother," of course, is there, alongside "The Two Sisters" (10); a return visit to "The Maid on the Shore"; "The Unquiet Grave" (78) and, perhaps the finest of all, "The Brown Girl" (295), a version she learned from fellow Critics Group member Floyd Kennedy, who also composed its distinctive tune.

Kennedy's interpretation in turn came from the collection of author Sabine Baring-Gould (1834–1924), an oft-overlooked accumulation from the counties of Devon and Cornwall that was published across four volumes between 1889 and 1891 as *Songs and Ballads of the West*. "Well, he collected it," Armstrong affirms, "but it's suspected that he did a rewrite. Baring wrote such dramatic novels, so the story of the brown girl, whether you think of her as a peasant, a Romany, a witch, or whatever, it could be quite novelesque." And quite bloodthirsty, as Dom Flemons has noted.

Angeline Morrison, whose 2022 recording of the same song, she acknowledges, was wholly inspired by Armstrong's, was likewise transfixed. "There are two versions of this text in the Child Ballads, the slightly longer one known as 295(b) includes tantalizing sections where The Brown Girl takes off her golden rings and strikes the faithless lover with a white wand. It makes you wonder if maybe she also had some witchy tendencies or knowledge."[6]

Other Child Ballads in Armstrong's arsenal, unsurprisingly, came from Lloyd. "'The Unquiet Grave'—I'm certain Bert must have given me that one, and the actual origin is cloudy, because he never said specifically 'this comes from the singing of . . .', or such and such a collection, so it might be one of his rewrites. Or, as I prefer to say, improvements. 'Maid on the Shore' is from Bert definitely, a rewrite from a Newfoundland version I think."

"The Two Sisters" (10), however, was one of Armstrong's own discoveries, taken "mainly," as Lloyd's liner notes put it, "from a set noted by Frank Kidson from an Irish singer in Liverpool." Armstrong looks back on *Lovely on the Water* with affection. "I don't often listen to my own albums, but I do think it's actually a very good one. It really paid off to not do it back in 1967."

Armstrong's career continued apace, a series of albums across which a wealth of further Child Ballads emerged and culminating in 1997's *Till the Grass Grew O'er the Corn*, a dozen *ESPB* staples recorded with guest appearances from John Kirkpatrick and Maddy Prior. Impressively, only two of the album's inclusions had ever appeared in her repertoire in the past. "Lady Diamond" (269) featured on her 1975 album *The Garden of Love*, and it ranks alongside "Tam Lin" (39) and "The Farmer's Curst Wife" (278) among what she describes as "the three great ballads of my life." "Hares on the Mountain," meanwhile, first appeared on a 1980 collaboration with Sandra Kerr, Alison McMorland, and Kathy Henderson, *My Song Is My Own — Songs from Women Over the Centuries*, although Armstrong acknowledges the latter was a controversial choice for an album dedicated wholly to the *ESPB*. Unmentioned by Child, "Hares on the Mountain" has since been viewed by many scholars as a distant cousin to "The Two Magicians" (44). However, as Armstrong put it in her liner notes, "The conceit is surely obvious enough to have been independently invented and all traces of magic (and story) have disappeared, leaving us with a genial day-dream of lyric."

Otherwise, the entire album comprised material she might have long thought about recording but never had, and Armstrong fondly recalls the hours she spent in the bowels of Cecil Sharp House researching its contents—an epic "Child Waters" (63), an ethereal "The Lover's Ghost" (248), and so forth. "I managed to get a research and development grant from the Arts Council to have people come to Cecil Sharp House with me, because I had to have somebody both to read the text onto cassettes, and then musicians to dot out the tunes for me. I made a whole project of it." *Till the Grass Grew O'er the Corn* emerged as one of the crucial collections of Child Ballads, richly detailed and dynamically arranged, and when the twenty-first century dawned, and brought with it a whole new underground "wyrd folk" boom, *Till the Grass Grew O'er the Corn* was there and waiting, a fresh crash course for a new generation of balladeers.

Armstrong speaks for many, then, when she explains how she selects the ballads that she records.

It's a song that says "sing me." A song that speaks to me. I can look back and think there were some songs that I like, but the big songs, the ones that are still with me, they really say something to me about the world in which we live, archetypes, emotions, and situations—how and why those situations are still with us in different ways and different cultures. I don't like thinking of art having to be relevant, but all art *is* relevant, because it comes out of the human condition and its creativity. Those are the things I'm looking for in a song.

Like so many others, she finds them in the Child Ballads.

Chapter Thirty-Three

NIGHTCLUBBING

In March 1966, the *New York Times*'s Robert Shelton reported, "There are about 500 active folk clubs in England and Scotland, many with memberships running into the hundreds. The clubs meet weekly, often in a room adjoining a pub, and the meetings have an atmosphere of sociability and mutual learning that few American folk cabarets or coffeehouses enjoy."

It was within these confines, which were often upstairs or back rooms at tiny pubs, run by enthusiastic part-timers and musicians, that the folk-rock movement of the 1970s was born. A training ground, then, but also a trading post for songs. More than from books or field recordings, or even records, ballads were heard and learned firsthand from fellow performers.

Leo Kelly of Ireland's Tír na nÓg, for example, recalls learning "The Unquiet Grave" (78) from Christy Moore. "I didn't know it was a Child Ballad at the time, but I remember asking him to sing it when I saw him play at a small folk club in London. . . . It was my favorite of the songs he sang." Tim Hart, later of Steeleye Span, spoke of adding "Our Goodman" (274) and "The Farmer's Curst Wife" (278) to his repertoire after hearing them performed "at a club in the midlands, somewhere. They were always good songs for waking up sleepy audiences." Frankie Armstrong agrees, describing "The Farmer's Curst Wife" as one of the ballads that has remained by her side her entire career long, "Deliciously supernatural but silly, the dear old devil getting his comeuppance."

She recalls, too, hearing Bert Lloyd perform his dramatic recital of "Tam Lin" (39) one night at the Singer's Club, "and I thought 'This isn't just *about* magic, this *is* magic. There was a transformational quality to his performance, that kind of story being put across as it should be, with no ego, just for the sheer power and beauty of the story and the melody and the nature of the words, and how they are framed."

Similar encounters in clubs up and down the country inspired countless others, too, to learn, and then develop their own multi-stanza impressions of what Lloyd's biographer Dave Arthur refers to as "the benchmark Ur-rendition" of the ballad.

Other accolades descend across the country. For anybody looking to master "Geordie" (209), perhaps the single most popular of all the Child Ballads on the British scene of the 1960s, Sandy Denny's timeworn take had few peers.[1] Willie O'Winsbury" (100) was best learned from Anne Briggs's impassioned performances, likewise a key element in her live show long before she recorded it for her eponymous debut album. And the only place to hear all of these performers and performances was in the clubs.

Folk clubs had been a presence on the UK scene since the early 1950s, although beyond MacColl's Ballads and Blues Club, few made more than a local impact at that time. They sprang from a variety of inspirations; some clubs were launched by enthusiasts alone, others by musicians looking for a place to perform on a regular basis.

Ballad collectors, too, became involved. In Horsham, Sussex, Tony Wales launched the Horsham Songswappers club around the release of his first album for the American Folkways label,[2] a collection of nineteen songs that he had collected locally—among them, four unusual Child Ballads. Performed entirely by Wales himself, the album led off with a most uncommon variant on Child 2, "Sing Ivy"; it also featured "The Bailiff's Daughter of Islington" (105); a hybrid "Henry Martin" (250) that married two verses collected by Sharp with three new ones Wales heard from a Mr. C. Potter; and "Our Goodman" (274). And this set was simply a sampling of the 170+ different performances that Wales had collected, many of which received their first public airings at the club.

The manner in which many of the folk clubs operated was for the headliner to be preceded by an open mic system; that is, anyone who showed up with an instrument or a repertoire and wanted to perform. It was strictly first-come, first-served basis; the aspiring performer would add their name to a list and wait for the compere to shout it out.

Al Stewart, whose first ever job in London was manager of the legendary Les Cousins, in London's Soho district, recalls,

> I went down there shortly after it opened for the first time, made friends with the owner, Phil, and he asked if I'd run the all-nighters for him. What that meant was, there was a major name act who was booked, whoever that would be, and then whoever had been playing the London folk clubs drifted in after their gigs at 1 or 2 in the morning, and I'd put them on the stage. They'd do two or three songs, and my job was to put people on stage and

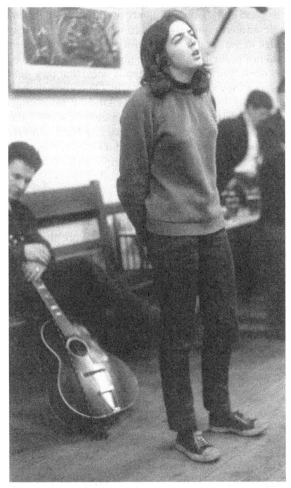

Anne Briggs—"the bad girl of folk"—performing at Cecil Sharp House. THOMAS, Eddis/EFDSS/Heritage Images / Alamy Stock Photo

take them off, and have a running list of all the people who wanted to play. There were usually twenty or thirty people with guitars down there, amateurs who wanted to do three songs, but around about 4 a.m. I'd run out of people, so I used to put myself on.[3]

Richard Byers of Suffolk Punch, a four part harmony band modeled upon the Watersons and the Young Tradition, continues,

Floor singers could be a mixed bunch. There was a good deal of unaccompanied singing—solo or in groups. Most singers had some chorus songs in their repertoires, so good clubs featured plenty of full-throated ensemble singing that the whole audience joined in with, often in harmony. Some singers might specialize in sea songs and shanties, which offered loads of opportunities for audience participation. And clubs would have their own favorite songs (bawdy ones, lyrical ones, sentimental ones) that they got really good at singing because they were sung regularly. On a good night, these could take the roof off. But there would be other kinds of floor singers too—the politically committed (like singing Irish republican songs); the sleek and suave (as in imitators of Peter, Paul and Mary or Nina and Frederick); the wildly creative (people who wanted to read their own poems or sing songs they had written); and sometimes the downright awful. Folk clubs provided (and sometimes still provide) an outlet for it all.[4]

Many of the later folk/folk-rock movement's biggest names. Briggs, Denny, Stewart, Armstrong, Martin Carthy, Bert Jansch, Roy Harper, and more learned their trade in this fashion. They were the unknown names and faces in the crowd until their own strengths and talents pushed them up into renown to become headliners in their own right.

Judy Dyble fell into this milieu by default.

"I never had eyes for that particular prize, and I didn't have the repertoire, either." She played the folk clubs, she said, because there were precious few other places where she could play her beloved autoharp to an audience that at least had a vague idea what it was. "My 'repertoire' essentially consisted of three numbers, all among the usual songs you

WHEN A CHILD IS NOT A CHILD

Away from the folk clubs, Marianne Faithful—the teenaged protégé of Rolling Stones manager Andrew Loog Oldham—recorded an entire album of traditional and folk music, 1965's *North Country Maid*. Included were a fragile "Scarborough Fair" (2), and one song that could well be mistaken for a Child Ballad ("When Cockleshells Turn Silver Bells," a variant of "James Douglas"–204), by virtue of both sharing a similar first verse.

Faithful, however, confirmed, "'Cockleshells' is not a folk song. It was written by a guy called Mick Taylor who was a friend of Donovan. He wrote that song and I liked it and wanted to record it, so I did. But it's not folk."

That said, she reflects, "My father played the guitar and sang, he had a beautiful voice, and he also played the violin. I grew up in that kind of atmosphere, folk dancing and all that. . . . We used to go camping in a large group of people and we'd sit round the campfire and my father would play the guitar and we'd all sing."[5]

Pausing between folk club gigs, Judy Dyble and her autoharp, 1966. Photo by Len Lavington / Courtesy Judy Dyble Estate

heard in folk clubs back then: 'Kum Bay Yah,' 'Come All Ye Fair and Tender Ladies' [which she also recorded, as a demo, with her first band, Judy and the Folkmen] and 'The Water Is Wide' [204], which I probably first heard courtesy either of the Kingston Trio or Joan Baez."[6] If an evening went particularly well, she had one further song. "I remain convinced that I was the only person *ever* to transpose Bert Jansch's 'Strollin' Down the Highway' for autoharp. Why would anyone else want to?"

Her other lingering memory of the era, and it's a story that every folk/traditional musician of the age can tell, was, "It was always a bit of a trek to get to these places, and I didn't especially like going on my own. Remember, I had to lug my harp around with me in its heavy duty black plastic bag and rushing up and down escalators or getting on and off buses was not the easiest of things. And I frequently dropped it with the resulting clang of strings, which startled quite a few people."[7]

Frankie Armstrong also recalls the bitter cold of many of the rooms where folk clubs were held, and the fact that the ladies bathroom often doubled as their "dressing room." And June Tabor remembers attending clubs around her Leamington Spa home. As she told biographer David Burke, "I liked the social importance of a folk club. It was a way of associating with other people with something in common, without it being too confrontational. You could make friends in a general way. For someone like me who was an only child of older parents, who had friends at school but not at home, it was a very good way of establishing some kind of social network."[8]

Singer Steve Tilston agrees. "My earliest influences were Elvis, the Beatles, the Stones, the old blues singers, and that's how I got into folk music, through the blues, and out of convenience. The folk clubs were a place to go and sing a few songs. And that's how I think I got into the folk bracket." His local folk club was based at the Victoria Hotel in Leicester, and his first ever visit was to prove massively influential. "The first time I went down there, I saw Hedy West. I thought she was fantastic, and I went again the next week hoping to see her again, not realizing she was touring, I was only fifteen; I thought she was going to be on every week."[9]

She wasn't, but the Appalachian-born West was a common sight on the English folk circuit in the mid-1960s. Raised in a family that, like so many of her contemporaries, was forever singing traditional songs for its own enjoyment, West was stunned when she arrived in New York for university in 1959 to discover the "folk revival" she'd heard tell of back home was, in fact, the very same music she grew up with. Certainly her background, not to mention her repertoire, impressed her new peers—Pete Seeger was an early supporter, and in 1961, West signed with Vanguard Records. Three years later, she moved to London and was promptly snapped up for Topic Records by Bert Lloyd.

Child Ballads permeated West's releases as much as they did her repertoire, with her liner notes making it clear that the versions she sang were more or less unique to either her family or friends. For her 1965 recording of "The Wife of Usher's Well" (79), for example, she combined a variant learned from her grandmother with another "that Nan Perdue of Fairfax, Virginia, learned from her mother-in-law Eva Samples."[10] Of "Little Matty Groves" (81), she remarked,[11] "Both Grandma and Gus [her Uncle Augustus]'s wife Jane sing a fragment that breaks off before Lord Arnold discovers his wife and Matty Groves in bed together. Neither Grandma nor Jane ever knew more of the ballad."

West's influence on the British scene, largely communicated through her live appearances, was immediate. It was West who originated the 9/4-metered tune with which Fairport Convention conclude their "Matty Groves." Martin Simpson learned "Beaulampkin" from West's 1967 album, having purchased a copy from her when she played the Scunthorpe folk club. He recorded it initially in 1976, then returned to it in 2019 for the Topic label's eightieth anniversary album, where he described West as "one of my biggest influences for 50 years."[12]

Another West fan was John Wright. In 1997, he recorded a "Matty Groves" that was based almost equally upon versions by West and Jeannie Robertson; while Canadian singer Moira Cameron credits West wholly with breathing fresh energy, in her opinion, into "Barbara Allen":

I have heard dozens of different versions, and I had never liked the song, mostly because of the message in the story. I felt annoyed by how it portrayed the woman, and then, after she realizes how "cruel" her rejection of her lover had been, she feels so guilty she dies repentant. Bah! It just offends my more feminist sensibilities. Then I heard Hedy West's version. I was utterly transformed. Somehow, the melody of her version made me connect for the first time to the emotion in that story. I empathized with the characters in a way I had never been able to before. Hedy's very simple banjo-strummed accompaniment just accentuated the story and the realness of the feelings. I managed to duplicate the effect of the strumming of the banjo with a very simple and repetitive plucking pattern on my dulcimer. The sound was different, but the effect was the same. So I changed my perspective of the ballad and learned it. Mind you, I always paired it in my performances with Frankie Armstrong's "The Brown Girl" [295], which seems to be the feminist version of "Barbara Allen." And thus my inner balance is maintained.[13]

With or without further appearances by Hedy West to tutor him in the art of folk performance, Steve Tilston's education continued. Within weeks of his first visit to the Victoria Hotel, Martin Carthy, Davy Graham, and Bert Jansch all passed through its doors. "I saw all the greats, standing three or four foot away from them, a real baptism. It really was one of the best ways of experiencing music, and becoming a musician yourself."

Indeed, although he swiftly became known for his own original song-writing, Tilston's early repertoire included several Child Ballads, among other folk staples.

> There were always a few songs that I would throw in occasionally, the first I ever did was "The Foggy Dew" when I was about fifteen. Then I did "The Water Is Wide" [204] and, early on, I did the "The Dowie Dens of Yarrow" [214], which was very different from the one that I recorded, so I'd always looked in that direction. I played it very differently, and I slightly changed the melody for the record, just to put my own stamp on it. But I used to sing a very straightforward version that's kind of commonplace.[14]

Steve Ashley—who, with the Albion Band and producer Austin John Marshall, would go on to record one of the all-time great versions of "Lord Bateman" (53)—recalls his own first steps onto the west London circuit, where venues like the Troubadour in Earls Court also encouraged the audience to take the stage and do a song or two. He performed unaccompanied and, like the majority of his peers, he lifted his material from the songs he heard elsewhere. "Any ballads I sang in my youth were learned from albums by Ewan MacColl, Bert Lloyd, Shirley Collins or Louis Killen," learning the songs either from recordings, "or the singing of others."[15] The sad epic of poisoning, "Lord Randall" (12); the murderous tale of "The Cruel Mother" (20); the seductive devilry of "The Demon Lover" (243), "and one or two other ballads," all became highlights of his early repertoire.

It was when Ashley left London to attend Maidstone Art College in Kent that he first made his mark. Alongside fellow student Peter Bellamy (1944–1991), the pair made regular appearances at the Medway Folk Club in nearby Rochester, while they also enjoyed a residency at the Wig and Gown pub on Maidstone's Week Street. Indeed, Ashley later became the club's MC and part of an organizing committee under whose aegis the Wig and Gown hosted a plethora of now legendary faces and names that passed through. "We booked Ewan MacColl and Peggy Seeger, Anne Briggs, Bert Jansch, Roy Harper, Al Stewart, Bert Lloyd, Shirley and Dolly Collins, Alexis Korner's band, Wizz Jones, John Foreman, The Young Tradition—and Linda Thompson too, but she was Linda Peters then, in a duo with Paul McNeil. There were so many great singers . . . I can't remember them all now."

The hyperactive Incredible String Band was a particular favorite. "The imprint of traditional music was clear, but the Incredible String Band took things further. Their song structures were more innovative, and the trail they were blazing was brilliant, and a very eclectic and international one." Even the Incredibles, however, could not resist the siren call of the Child Ballads, recording and performing inimitable versions of "Black

Jack Davy" (200) and "Geordie" (209), and taking both to entirely new musical extremes.

Of all the performer at the Wig and Crown, however, it was Bellamy who made the greatest impression.

> Peter was one of my oldest friends in the folk scene. I met him on a round-about, hitch-hiking in Cornwall in the summer of 1964. By coincidence he was at Maidstone Art College doing a painting course, and I was due to be starting there in a month's time. So we met up there in September. Pete taught me how to play the penny whistle, and also let me have a few songs he'd learnt. We were close chums and spent a lot of time together. He was a remarkable character, playing his anglo-concertina and tin whistle every-where. His singing was amazing in its power.

Bellamy dropped out of college in 1965, at Anne Briggs's prompting. She had heard him sing, knew his ideas, and was adamant. He needed to perform on the largest stage he could find. Ashley recalled, "Pete was doing a painting course and not enjoying it much. In the end he decided to jack it in to try his luck as a singer in London."

In 1968, Norfolk-based Bellamy included two full-throated Child Ballads, "Geordie" (209) and "The Lofty Tall Ship" (250), on an a cappella album dedicated to the songs and folklore of his home county's best-known balladeers, Harry Cox and Sam Larner: *Mainly Norfolk—Songs and Ballads*. These in turn became the first in a canon that saw Bellamy's distinctive tones and talent tackle close to twenty Child Ballads. It was a repertoire that certainly impressed singer Sylvia Barnes, as she cast about for a version of "Fair Annie" for her 2007 CD *The Colour of Amber*: "I first heard this ballad from the late Peter Bellamy."[16]

Martin Simpson, who recorded "Fair Annie" earlier in the decade, was similarly influenced. "'Fair Annie' was given to me on a cassette of a show that Peter [Bellamy] did at McCabe's Guitar Shop in Santa Monica. My friend Josh Michael thought that I might like the song and, indeed, he was right. I looked for other versions, but found nothing so succinct, or with such a sting in the tail. I wonder to what extent Peter altered the lyrics?"[17]

Steve Ashley continues, "A short while after he left Maidstone, Peter started singing in a duo with Royston Wood, and the pair of them stayed over with me one night after a gig they'd done in Rochester. They sounded very good together."[18] The Bellamy-Wood duo became a trio with the arrival of Heather Wood (no relation) and, naming themselves the Young Tradition, they recorded four albums together before splitting in 1969. All feature Child Ballads and are noteworthy in that, numbered among them were several from the less well-frequented corners of the *ESPB*—but which the Young Tradition's example would see become far more popular: "The Bold Dragoon" (7), "The Rolling of the Stones"

(49), "Dives and Lazarus" (56); and "Knight William and the Shepherd's Daughter" (110).

Of these, "The Rolling of the Stones" is especially fascinating. Child knew it as "The Twa Brothers," while also noting such variations as "The Cruel Brother," "The Wood o'Warslin," a Massachusetts' children's chant called "John and William," and "The Perthshire Tredgey" (Tragedy). "The Rolling of the Stones," however, is—as Grey Malkin explains,

> an almost singularly American variation, mostly found in the Appalachians and the southern mountains. There is admittedly still a certain lineage from the "The Twa Brothers" (in the theme of accidental death), but "The Rolling of the Stones" then takes its own very unique and almost inexplicable path indeed. One aspect I find especially interesting is the power that Susie wields as a female protagonist in puritanical, God-fearing and patriarchal early America. She effectively, with the use of her mysterious "tablet" and her "charms," resurrects her lover so that "he could no longer rest." Is this witchcraft, perhaps necromancy? Or something more symbolic and pertaining to Christian beliefs such as the rolling of the stone from the tomb of Jesus and his rising from the dead? I do find it most curious that a commonly recited ballad and stalwart of regional folk tradition would place something so potentially sacrilegious and ambiguous (or at least to me!) in such plain sight. A woman raises her lover, Lazarus like, from the dead using some form of spell craft; surely this is heretical, unspeakable even? Or, if this is a Christian aphorism, why coat it in such (for the time) signs of ambiguity and possible incendiary allegory? This was an era where superstition was rife and everyday people were quite ready to cry "witch" and point the finger, usually at innocent women.[19]

The Young Tradition also partnered Shirley Collins across her old favorite "The Cherry Tree Carol" (54), while a live album recorded at Ohio's Oberlin College in November 1968, added "The Two Magicians" (44) to the Young Tradition's canon. The trio's performances remain still among the most exhilarating of all unaccompanied Child Ballad performances.

Immediately upon the band's breakup, Bellamy launched a solo career—one that is as dramatic as it is volatile. Several proposed album projects were abandoned through a lack of record company interest, although he nevertheless maintained a stream of releases throughout the remainder of his life, and audiences never lost their taste for his near-Shakespearean performance style.

Moira Cameron recalls, "One of my most revered memories is seeing Pete Bellamy perform as a last-minute substitution for a sick Louis Killen at a club in London in the summer of 1991. It was, as it turned out, one of the last performances Pete made before he committed suicide."[20] The final word on Bellamy, however, and indeed the folk clubs, belongs to Steve

Ashley and the fond remembrance of those days that he included on his 2001 album *Everyday Lives*, "Down among the Hop Poles."

> *We sang the doom of Andrew Rose*
> *The Bonny Broom of Cowdenknows*
> *Filled the room*
> *when Jones's Ale Was New*
> *There we met John Barleycorn*
> *sailed a passage round the horn. . . .*[21]

Chapter Thirty-Four

THE BALLAD OF PAUL AND MARTIN

It was into this fertile universe that a young American singer-songwriter named Paul Simon stepped in the early spring of 1964. Back in New York, he and singing partner Art Garfunkel had enjoyed a modicum of success with Simon's contributions to the City Folksinger genre—they had at least signed a record deal, with Columbia, and released their debut album, *Wednesday Morning 3 AM*. In terms of all that the duo would go on to achieve, however, they were still unknowns, and even more so in the United Kingdom than at home. What was to become their maiden hit, "Sound of Silence," had yet to commence its mercurial ascent up the US chart, and Simon's British excursion saw him visiting the smallest folk clubs around the country, just one of the myriad roving troubadours strumming for his supper in the furthest outposts of the British music industry.

Simon's London visit was, essentially, born of hopelessness. The New York folk scene to which he and Garfunkel had attached themselves was . . . not dying, but certainly ailing. Earlier in the year, the Beatles had arrived in the United States in a cloudburst of wild hysteria and even wilder haircuts, and what had once been a thriving scene of earnest young singers filling coffee bars with music, and equally devoted listeners nodding thoughtfully to their revelations, was already shifting on its axis.

Last month's folkie was this month's beat musician, and for those performers who had not taken the next step up the live circuit, it was a case of adapt or die.

Simon, however, did not want to adapt. Not yet.

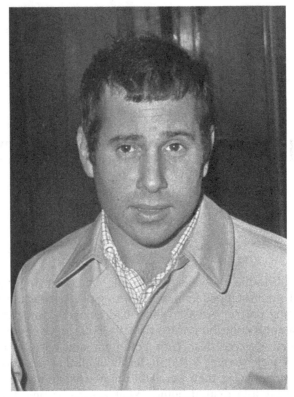

Paul Simon in 1966. Joost Evers, CC BY-SA 3.0 NL / Wikimedia
Commons

Traveling first to Paris, Simon fell in with a young Englishman named
Dave McCausland, who ran a folk club at the Railway Hotel in Brent-
wood, a small town in Essex, about an hour outside central London. He
was offered both a place to stay, and a gig at the club. Arriving in London
on the boat train on April 20, 1964, Simon was onstage just twenty-four
hours later.

Over the next few months, Simon endured several changes of address,
circulating though the more-affordable hinterlands of the metropolis,
while also enrolling at King's College, close by Waterloo Bridge. And,
inevitably, he infiltrated the folk scene, gigging not only around London,
but also around the country.

The influence of the performers he heard on this trip was profound.
A recording exists of a live show Simon played at his old alma mater,
Queen's College in New York, following his return to the United States
later in the year. For obvious reasons, the bulk of his repertoire was

self-composed. Opening the show, however, were two songs that he had adopted on his travels—"Scarborough Fair" (2) and "The House Carpenter" (243).

A third Child Ballad, "Barbara Allen" (84), was also on his mind during sessions for Simon and Garfunkel's second album, *The Sound of Silence*. Ultimately it would be left on the shelf, not to see release for forty years— by which time, the duo's straight-faced, strait-laced rendering had been absolutely superseded by Garfunkel alone, a strings-and-things-driven re-envisioning that became one of the highlights of his 1973 debut solo album.

Garfunkel abridges the ballad somewhat—he disposes of it in just nine stanzas. But the gist of the song remains the same, and, in that single, sad, performance, the singer achieved a career high that even he has admitted would be difficult to better.

"When I listen to ['Barbara Allen'], I think 'Oh man, were you blushingly crimson,'" Garfunkel confessed to *Mojo* magazine in 2015. "Songs are different colors and that one is red, red. I'm doing so much breath control and the heart is way out on my sleeve."[1] It was Simon and Garfunkel's "Scarborough Fair," paired with Simon's "Canticle," however, that was to cause the greatest stir, both commercially and professionally.

Within a year or two of the ballad's appearance on the duo's third LP in 1966, some fifty further versions had appeared across the pop and light entertainment firmament, from names as far apart as Charlie Byrd, Jeff Afdem and the Springfield Flute, Percy Sledge, and a bevy of orchestras— and only a handful that bore comparison with what they clearly regarded as the "original" version.

Among these, the pairing of Bobbie Gentry and Glen Campbell is certainly the most inspired selection on their joint 1968 LP, a showcase for harmonies that the remainder of the set paid scant attention to, while an alternate version recorded without the album's string accompaniment surpassed even that.[2]

"Scarborough Fair" is a deceptive song; misleading in as much as the melody and the most recurrent lyric ("a true love of mine") paint it with a romantic sheen that its true origins utterly belie. Even the title is open to interpretation, "Scarborough Fair" being just one of several titles by which the ballad is known. The earliest appears to have been "The Elphin Knight," to which a somewhat longer title was abridged when it appeared in a volume of *Ancient Scottish Poems* in 1673: "The Wind Hath Blown My Plaid Away, or, a Discourse betwixt a Young [Wo]man and the Elphin Knight."

Passing time, and the ministrations of other singers and performers saw the ballad undergo considerable alteration; the "wind has blown" chorus was lost, and with it a great deal of exposition. Soon, all that remained were the riddles: "tell her to sew me a holland sark, and sew it all without needle-wark" . . . "tell her to wash it at yon spring-well, where ne'er wind blew nor yet rain fell," with each command beautified by the pledge "and syne we'll be true lovers again." (Contrast this with Ewan MacColl's 1964 recording of the same ballad's "Proud Lady Margaret" variation, in which it is the riddles that are expunged, "the story being confined to the wooing.")

Recording the ballad's "The Elfin Knight" variant, Ewan MacColl outlined the original story:

> A universal theme of both folk tale and ballad is that of impossible tasks. In this ballad, the form it takes is that of the courtship, with one flirtatious lover setting a series of tasks and his companion meeting the challenge by setting an equally difficult series. In early forms of the ballad, an elfin knight posed the tasks, to be answered by a maiden who remains free by devising tasks of no less difficulty which must be answered first. Modern folk have made both characters mortal enough. Child had nineteen versions of this ballad, which he traced in his affinities through many languages of Europe and Asia. It is well known in England and America.[3]

Shirley Collins, who recorded it as "Scarborough Fair" in 1960, pointed out that the ballad's "test-by-riddle is a heritage from remote antiquity. The survival of this ancient piece of folklore is assured by the fact that all the couplets in this song contain gentle, but evocative erotic symbols."[4]

The version that is most common today trims even more away. In 1810, the unimpeachably titled *Gammer Gurton's Garland* offered up a version that replaced the earlier refrain of "sober and grave grows merry in time" with the now-familiar "parsley, sage, rosemary, and thyme"; and, by the time Lucy Broadwood and J. A. Fuller Maitland published their *English Country Songs* in 1893, even the Scots setting was displaced.

> *"Is any of you going to Scarborough Fair?*
> *"Remember me to a lad as lives there."*

Versions of the ballad, in different forms, were already commonplace on the British folk scene of the early 1960s, and on record, too. Aside from MacColl and Collins, Bert Lloyd and the Copper Family had all recorded versions by the time Paul Simon reached London, while he learned the song from Martin Carthy—for a time, his neighbor in a bedsit in Belsize Park, north London.

Carthy was a familiar face around the club scene, performing his own vivid arrangements of favorite ballads in a voice that was as distinctive as his guitar style. And, although he would not record the song for another year or more ("Scarborough Fair" appears on his self-titled debut album in 1965), his unique arrangement of a song that he in turn learned from Ewan MacColl and Peggy Seeger, was already one of the high points of his repertoire. In the liner notes to that album, Carthy wrote, "Folklorists and students of plant mythology are well aware that certain herbs were held to have magical significance—that they were used by sorcerers in their spells and conversely as counter-spells by those that wished to outwit them. The herbs mentioned in the refrain of 'Scarborough Fair' (parsley, sage, rosemary and thyme) are all known to have been closely associated with death and also as charms against the evil eye." In other words, the maiden might be tormented by the Elfin Knight, but clearly she had defenses of her own. In fact, Carthy continued, "Sir Walter Scott in his notes to *Minstrelsy of the Scottish Border* recalled hearing a ballad of 'a fiend . . . paying his addresses to a maid but being disconcerted by the holy herbs she wore in her bosom.'"

The version of the song with which Simon opened his Queens College concert and also appears on (and, via its refrain, titles) Simon and Garfunkel's *Parsley Sage Rosemary and Thyme* LP, is clearly modeled upon Carthy's own. Sadly, however, Simon did not think to credit the donor.

Simon was not the only American to pass through London, there to be impressed by Carthy's arrangement of "Scarborough Fair." Bob Dylan shared a stage with him at central London's King and Queen folk club on New Year's Eve, 1962, and would subsequently appear to have borrowed several arrangements from Carthy. Nevertheless, Paul Simon's omission rankled. If nothing else, a simple "arranged by Martin Carthy" would have been polite. Neither did Simon make amends when the song was released as a single in March 1968, destined for a berth in the *Billboard* Top 5 and, in the process, becoming the biggest "chart hit" in the entire history of the *ESPB*—although, in truth, it did not have much competition.

The previous year, Ireland's the Dubliners released a riotous "Seven Drunken Nights" (274), which they learned in turn from the singing of Joe Heaney. Indeed, it was *so* riotous that it was banned from the radio in their homeland—despite Heaney himself having successfully performed the song several times on Irish radio, albeit taking the precaution of singing it in Gaelic.[5]

The Dubliners even lobbied the then Taoiseach Jack Lynch to ask his help in having the prohibition lifted. Their efforts were to no avail. As Dubliners front man Ronnie Drew once remarked, "In 1967, Ireland or parts of it, were living in the '30s when you couldn't mention such things as S.E.X. . . . You could spell it but you certainly couldn't say it."[6] Not that he and the band were especially crestfallen by the prohibition. The resultant publicity sent "Seven Drunken Nights" soaring, topping the charts in Ireland and reaching number 7 in Britain.

The Dubliners' success remains unique in the United Kingdom—the only band ever to have scored a Top 10 hit with a Child Ballad.[7] Even Steeleye Span, at the height of their commercial success in 1974, could not scratch the charts with their 45 rpm edit of "Thomas the Rhymer" (37); and, unbelievable though it seems, nobody has ever landed either a British or American hit with "Barbara Allen" (84).

Simon and Garfunkel's "Scarborough Fair," however, triumphed spectacularly, both on single and album. *Parsley Sage Rosemary and Thyme* went triple platinum, and the song was inescapable. Still Carthy himself did not get a mention, and for decades, he barely even acknowledged Simon's existence in conversation or interview. It would be thirty-five years before the dispute was finally salved, when Simon invited Carthy onstage to perform the song with him at London's Hammersmith Apollo in 2000.

Chapter Thirty-Five

ANOTHER CHILD OF SKIFFLE

It was the skiffle boom of the mid- to late 1950s that drew the young Martin Carthy into music, when he borrowed an old guitar from his father and began teaching himself his first elementary chords. Like so many of his generation, his fascination lay in skiffle's American roots, and his earliest bands, Redd Sullivan's Thameside Four and the Three City Four, bore this out. It was only slowly that he came to comprehend just what a vast world he was tapping into, as he listened to a rival skiffle band led by one of Carthy's own schoolmates, Joe Lloyd. Their repertoire was rife with songs that Carthy had never heard before, and he asked Joe where his group learned them.

"From my dad," Lloyd responded. "He's a singer." In fact, he was Bert Lloyd.

That was a name Carthy already knew. Even as the Three City Four landed a deal with Decca Records, and cut their debut album, Carthy's band work was interspersed by a growing presence on the folk scene. He earned a residency at the Troubadour in Earl's Court, and in 1963, he joined Alex Campbell, Bob Davenport, Louis Killen, and others on *Hootenanny in London*, a Decca Records entry into the folk boom overseen by onetime Vipers Skiffle Group front man Wally Whyton.

Carthy's material on the *Hootenanny* album offered little suggestion as to his musical future. His contributions lean toward the novelty end of what was then passing as folk: "End of Me Old Cigar" and "Your Baby 'as Gorn Dahn the Plug 'ole," and the album is best remembered today for the prominent, and still spellbinding photograph of Anne Briggs that appears on the cover, without her actually being involved in the record. Such frivolities were crucial, however. Even as the at-home listener chuckled along to the sad tale of the disappearing baby ("so skinny and thin he should have been washed in a jug"), Carthy was building both a repertoire and a reputation as one of the most individual of all young English guitarists, and his self-titled 1965 debut solo album gave vent to both.

Ewan MacColl's influence is clear throughout *Martin Carthy*, alongside that of Bert Lloyd, and the Child Ballads are a constant presence, too. The then seldom-recorded "Broomfield Hill" (43) and "The Two Magicians" (44) join "Scarborough Fair" on the record, and it was perhaps history's misfortune that Paul Simon's ears should have fallen upon Child 2 when he first heard Carthy perform. Imagine Simon and Garfunkel recording "Two Magicians"!

Carthy was accompanied on this album—and so many more thereafter—by fiddle player Dave Swarbrick, the mercurial dynamo behind the Ian Campbell Folk Group. Prior to that, he was yet another refugee from the skiffle circuit, as a member of Beryl Marriott's Ceilidh Band, a preternaturally talented player who met Ian and sister Lorna Campbell when both they and "Swarb" were hired to appear in Ewan MacColl's latest Radio Ballad, 1961's *The Big Hewer*. Swarbrick met Carthy for the first time at the Troubadour in Earl's Court, and after guesting on

Martin Carthy and Dave Swarbrick at the BBC Radio 2 Folk Awards, 2007. Bryan Ledgard, CC BY 2.0 / Wikimedia Commons

the guitarist's first album, the pair were soon a regular and increasingly popular sight on the club circuit. Indeed, one of the finest British folk recordings of the 1960s has to be *Both Ears and the Tail*, a live recording of the pair onstage at the Folkus Folk Club in Nottingham on June 16, 1966. (It was released in 2000.) Again, Child is represented with "Broomfield Hill" and "Two Magicians," but throughout, the live interplay between Carthy and Swarbrick is nothing short of breathtaking.

Carthy's second album, sensibly titled *Martin Carthy's Second Album*, was now out, again an excellent set, although perhaps history reflects upon it more as a portent of Swarbrick's future than Carthy's. A version of the album's closing track, the epic "A Sailor's Life," would be Swarbrick's first ever recording with Fairport Convention, whom he would join in 1969. The duo's live performance also included the show-stopping "The Hen's March/The Four Poster Bed," a fiddle medley that Fairport would subsequently make their own.

The album is also singular in terms of the Child Ballads, as Carthy first delivers a moving "Lowlands of Holland" (92), before delving deep into his copy of Bronson's *The Traditional Tunes of the Child Ballads* to secure "Fair Maid on the Shore," listed there as a variant on "Broomfield Hill" from his previous album. And so it is, thematically, as Carthy and Swarbrick made clear by performing both songs during the Folkus Club set. From the stage, "Fair Maid on the Shore" is introduced by Carthy as "a story about a sea captain. He's sailing along and he's passing an island where he sees this young girl walking up and down. He sends his sailors after her, and they go and get her and unfortunately, for him, things don't work out as he had hoped."

"Broomfield Hill," on the other hand, is best described by Eileen Pratt, from a 1976 BBC recording of her and husband Graham performing at the Phoebus Awakes folk club in Catford, east London:

> It's about a girl who makes a bet with her boyfriend that they can meet in a secluded wood and she can still retain her maidenhead. But he doesn't think she can do this because he's all big and lusty and hairy, and desperate as they say, and she's just a frail ninny of a girl. Fortunately . . . she suddenly has the help of an old witch who tells her about broom blossom, the magic perfume of which makes lusty lovers drop off [to sleep]. The girl tries this, and scatters the blossom around her lover, and he carries on sleeping, and when he wakes up he's still madly randy and very angry, so he takes it out on his poor old horse. And that's the end of the song.[1]

It is not, however, the end of the versions of it that circulate, with one of the most impressive arriving courtesy of Malinky. Steve Byrne explains, "We got [the tune] from a recording of the poet Norman MacCaig singing it, discovered through my work as a cataloguer on the Kist o Riches/Tobar an Dualchais project."[2] The ballad is, Byrne continues, a popular live number, a factor he credits to "the somewhat obscure chorus, 'Leatherum thee thou and aw, madam I'm wi you, and the seal o me be abrachee, fair maiden I'm wi you.'"[3]

Carthy's liner notes for his second album, too, make clear the sources from which he was drawing, a Cecil Sharp manuscript here, the Cyril Tawney collection there, the journal of the Folk Song Society and, of course, "the vast repertoire" of Bert Lloyd.

Again, however, it is Carthy's approach that raised him above so many of his contemporaries, to the point that, even as he worked to establish his own reputation, he was already being spoken of as a member of the same company that he drew upon. By the time of his and Swarbrick's next release, 1967's *Byker Hill*, *Melody Maker* journalist Karl Dallas—the doyen of British folk writers—was describing Carthy and Swarbrick as "one of the most creative partnerships in British folk music."[4]

Two weeks later, in the same paper, Dallas declared that *Byker Hill* "really marks a peak in the development of their partnership which is underlined by [Swarbrick's] name getting equal prominence to Martin's on the sleeve,"[5] before singling out the album's lone Child Ballad, "Lucy Wan" (51—Carthy learned it from Bert Lloyd) as the peak of Swarbrick's contributions. "Swarbrick . . . anticipat[es] the next move of the jagged tune (fitting so well the tale of incest and murder) . . . allowing Carthy complete freedom to tell the story in his own way."

"I knew the stories backwards," Swarb reflected.[6] "So when Martin suggested we try it, I already knew where the emphasis needed to be, or where something dramatic was about to happen, or even when to just shut up. The funny thing is, I don't remember having to rehearse too often. A lot of the ballads sing and play themselves, and we were just busking along."

Carthy's own explanation for the success of his Child Ballads is equally modest. "You do have to sometimes kick the buggers into life, find them a tune, give the lyrics a kick here and there. And they can take it; they're fabulously resilient. I really do believe there's nothing you can do to these songs that will hurt them—except for not singing them."[7]

Another key exhumation in the duo's repertoire was "Long Lankin" (93), the song that Ewan MacColl believed had only recently entered the folk boom's consciousness. Carthy and Swarbrick recorded it for their fourth LP together, *But Two Came By*, and the album's liner notes lay out a considerably longer genesis.[8]

His primary source was the "extensive essay" that Anne Geddes Gilchrist contributed to the first ever issue of the *Folk Music Journal* magazine, noting how the song has developed in two distinct forms: "The first which she titles 'Lamkin, the Wronged Mason,' is the Scottish version and the second, found from Northumberland to the south coast of England, she called 'Longkin, the Border Ruffian,' but, she says, the second might have arisen from the first when the verse was lost as the motives appear to be the same, i.e., revenge."[9]

Carthy's version was taken from that included on volume 4 of the Lomax/Collins/Kennedy curated *The Folk Songs of Great Britain* in 1961 (it appears there as "Cruel Lincoln"), although Carthy expanded the text somewhat "largely from the singing of a nun, Sister Emma of Clewer, Bucks." Even today, there are few mental images so surreal as the thought of a nun entertaining her charges with the tale of Lamkin. First, he slaughters the baby . . .

> *We will pinch him, we will prick him*
> *We will stab him with a pin*
> *And the false nurse held the basin*
> *For the blood to flow in*

. . . and then the lady herself.

> *There was blood all in the kitchen*
> *There was blood all in the hall*
> *There was blood all in the parlor*
> *Where my lady she did fall*

Carthy mused,

> It has been suggested that Lamkin was . . . a leper seeking to cure himself by bathing in the blood of an innocent, which was often believed to be successful, but attractive (if that is the word) though this idea may seem, I myself incline to the view that it is a simple "bogey man" song, for, after all, if children have bogeymen, why not adults? They just call them by different names (nowadays, "neurotic fancies" et al.). Indeed, according again to Anne Gilchrist, until a few years ago a mother near Whittle Dean, Northumberland, had but to go outside, shake a bunch of keys, and cry "There's Long Lankin!" to recall her straying children at nightfall.[10]

Also included on *Two Came By* was one of the Child Ballads best associated with Carthy, "Jack Orion" (67), and, once again, he credits Bert Lloyd for his own enthusiasm. "[Bert] has done exceptional work in many fields, especially, to my mind, in knocking into singable shape songs that were lost in tradition, but have attractive and not to say very powerful story lines: *Jack Orion* is such a one."[11] Lloyd's interpretation of "Jack Orion" is, in fact, a fine example of contrafacta. It was based upon the ballad "Glasgerion," but, as Lloyd noted, that ballad "dropped out of tradition long ago."

Its story, however, "was an engaging one and it seemed to me too good a song to be shut away in books, so I took it out and dusted it off a bit and set a tune to it and, I hope, started it on a new lease of life."[12] The melody Lloyd selected for his reading was, in fact, borrowed from the Scots novelty "Donald, Where's Your Troosers," although the subject matter is far from comical. That said, Martin Carthy later recalled how, when he first approached Lloyd for the lyric, the older man responded with a wry obscenity inserted within the nineteenth verse:

> She says, "Surely you didn't leave behind
> A bracelet or a velvet sock,
> Or are you returned back again . . ."

The final line, Carthy left to his listener's imagination. Suffice to say, in Lloyd's own original version, the "velvet sock" was a velvet *glove*, to rhyme with "To taste more of me love."[13]

His LPs aside, one other archive of Carthy recordings from this period exists, in the form of the wealth of sessions he performed for the BBC, both solo and alongside Swarbrick, during the 1960s. The BBC had maintained its interest in traditional music since the days of *As I Roved Out*, with the mid-1960s particularly well-served. Shows such as *Bright as a Button*, hosted by Jimmie MacGregor and Robin Hall between 1964 and 1966; the same pair's *Folk Spin* (1966) and the long-running *Folkweave* tour of the nation's folk clubs all poured out of the radio,[14] while television viewers were very well served by American singer Julie Felix's TV series *Some Folks Like to Sing* (1966–67) and *Once More with Felix* (1969).[15]

Paramount among these programs was *The Song Carriers*, a multi-part series overseen by Ewan MacColl in 1965, drawing upon both his own performances and the BBC archive to present a thematic overview of traditional song.

The Child Ballads play only a minor role in the overall project, and most performances last just thirty seconds or so, with McColl's commentary the show's focal point. Nevertheless, the music selected for the series spans the decades between Cecil Sharp's first pioneering recordings to pop singer Anthony Newley's "Strawberry Fair" (2), more than half a century later. Sadly, *The Song Carriers* and a few isolated scraps from elsewhere notwithstanding, we have little recorded evidence of the BBC's traditional output throughout the 1960s. The chief exception to this, however, might also be the most significant—a series of transcription discs, marketed to foreign radio stations interested in broadcasting another MacGregor/Hall presentation, *Folk Song Cellar*.

Close to forty surviving discs provide us with a vivacious snapshot of the state of British folk in the mid-1960s. Recorded before a live audience in the basement of Cecil Sharp House, with a cast that included a host of lesser-known artists alongside the likes of Carthy, Sandy Denny, and Shirley Collins, *Folk Song Cellar* is the closest the modern listener can come to a genuine 1960s folk club atmosphere, singalongs, laughter, and partisan audiences included.

It delivers, too, a portrait of the Child Ballads' own absorption into the milieu. Carthy's five surviving appearances on the show saw him perform just two, "Scarborough Fair" (2) and "The Bonny Earl of Moray" (181).[16] Many more, however, are delivered by such guests as the Ian Campbell Folk Group, Felicity Johnson, Rosemary and Hugh Gentleman, Val and Roy Bailey, Nigel Denver, Jack Armstrong and Patricia Jennings, Colin Ross and Forster Charlton, and more. Few of these are household names today. But the folk clubs rang to their voices all the same.

Another regular guest on the BBC (and another highlight of *Folk Song Cellar*) was the group then known as the Strawberry Hill Boys. Between their radio debut on the long-running *Saturday Club* on March 18, 1963, and 1967 (when they shortened their name to the Strawbs), what started life as a duo of Dave Cousins and Tony Hooper appeared at least twenty-five times across the corporation's circuit of folk and light entertainment radio shows.

The Strawberry Hill Boys, as Cousins acknowledges today, were more concerned with bluegrass than English folk. "One time, Tony and I cycled to Cecil Sharp House (a twenty-five-mile round trip) to go to the library. We were disappointed, as they had none of the records we were interested in in the shop, although I do remember buying a ten-inch Jack Elliott album on the Dobell label, a limited edition of ninety-nine copies."[17]

At least part of the Strawberry Hill Boys' appeal was the sheer exhilaration of their performance. "I was the fastest banjo picker in England," Cousin affirms, and beyond the band's own activities, he recorded sessions with Leonard Cohen, as well as the Clancy Brothers and Tommy Makem. The Strawberry Hill Boys also accompanied Steve Bembow on his 1965 *Songs of Ireland* album, home to a dynamic "Little Beggarman" (279).

Unfortunately, there is little further evidence of the original Strawberry Hill Boys' music available today. It would be 1967 before they were offered a recording contract,[18] and the vast majority of the BBC tapes were wiped long ago. Nevertheless, Cousin confirms, "We did a helluva lot of shows, and every time we did one, I wrote and thanked the producer. Then I wrote to the producers of every other show going and said, 'We've just done *Saturday Club*, we've just done this and that, will you consider us for your program,' and inevitably we did virtually every program."

One performance that has survived is their reading of "Two Sisters of Binnorie" (10), recorded for *Folk Song Cellar* in 1966, and heard by Cousins for the first time in over fifty years, in 2021. "I didn't remember how many songs from England, Scotland, and Ireland we sang at that time," he marveled. "Minnorie," as he knew it, is joined by a wealth of non-Child material, with Cousins laughingly admitting, "I had no idea that 'Minnorie' was a Child Ballad!"

Chapter Thirty-Six

PLUCKING THE PENTANGLE

By the end of the 1960s, in terms of the musical mainstream, both the folk boom and Professor Child were all but forgotten in the United States. Two of his most successful recent acolytes, it is true, appeared at the great festivals of 1967–1969—Simon and Garfunkel at Monterey, Joan Baez at Woodstock—but neither performed any song from the *EFSB*. The market for traditional releases contracted accordingly.

The music was by no means dead in America. The specialist labels, led by Folkways, continued issuing interesting material, but no longer matched the quantities of even a few years previous, as blues, international music, and even electronics shoved the folkies to one side. Labels like Vanguard and Elektra continued active and still bore the imprimatur of their "folkie" reputation. But outside of their longest-serving signings, few of their releases matched that designation. Even the likes of Joan Baez and Judy Collins had moved away by now.

On the other side of the Atlantic, however, matters were only growing more potent. Topic's long-awaited UK release of the Caedmon Child Ballads collections, and MacColl and Seeger's *Long Harvest* project were both underway, while a new record label, Folk Heritage, had sprung up specifically to cater to artists whose careers were unlikely to extend beyond the clubs. Indeed, the albums as a rule were available only from the clubs, sold by the bands who recorded them and rarely pressed in quantities beyond a couple hundred.

In 2022, the Cherry Red label released a three-CD anthology of Folk Heritage releases, *Before the Day Is Done: The Story of Folk Heritage Records 1968–1975*, spanning the label's entire seven-year lifespan. Several Child Ballads are included, including Preston folk club favorites the Wayfarers,

Pentangle in Amsterdam, 1969. Jac. De Nijs / Anefo, CC0 / Wikimedia Commons

with a defiantly mandolin-powered "Matty Groves" (81); a lilting "Lord Lovell," by The Minor Birds, hosts of the Warrington club; and the Horden Raikes duo's driving "Two Magicians" (44). Even with close to seventy tracks (and no shortage of enjoyable music), however, *Before the Day Is Done* is scarcely representative of either Folk Heritage's full output or its contributions to the Child canon.

The very first release on the label, the MacDonald Folk Group's *Take One*, in 1968, featured a spirited "Geordie" (209); the second, Rosemary Hardman's *Queen of Hearts*, includes "The Golden Vanity" (286) and an epic ten-minute "Lady Barnard and Little Musgrave" (81), recorded live at the Bate's Hotel folk club in Macclesfield, shortly after Christmas 1968. The Blue Water Folk highlighted their eponymous debut with "The Trooper and the Maid" (299), and then delivered "The Mermaid" on 1972's *All the Good Times*. All told, the fifty or so albums Folk Heritage released represent as great an insight into life in the folk clubs of Britain through the late 1960s and early 1970s, and the *ESPB*'s importance to the repertoire, as *London Folk Song Cellar* represents for the mid-1960s.

Neither was such grassroots activity confined only to the folk clubs and record stores. The so-called summer of love, 1967, saw a new ballad collection arrive on the shelves, and what an appropriate title it bore. *The Seeds of Love* was collected, and compiled by Stephen Sedley, a spinoff, he explains, from an LP which I put together for Transatlantic Records, a company set up by my college friend Nat Joseph. His ambition was to be a stage impresario, and his first (brilliant) enterprise was to hire the Mermaid Theatre for a one-off concert of folksong and poetry. We got Tony Britton, who had never sung on stage, and the folksinger/actress Isla Cameron to perform, and Isla got her old lover Robert Graves to come over from Mallorca to anchor the show and to read some of his own work. I did the research and arrangements, and (with Ralph Trainer) the guitar accompaniments.

On the back of the concert, Joseph then conceived what Sedley describes as

a classic LP, [released] under the idiotic title *Songs of Love, Lust and Loose Living*, which pretty well killed it. By then I had begun to amass a sizable file of unpublished material. Some was in obscurely catalogued broadside collections in the British Museum (now the British Library). Some was in the MS collections of Gardiner, Hammond *et al.*, held on microfiche at Cecil Sharp House. Some was in long out of print books. It was Nat who suggested using the material for a book, and who got Essex Music ([until] then only sheet music publishers) to take it on. I think it took me from 1962 to about 1966, working on and off, to collate, compile, select and edit the contents.[1]

Meanwhile, Sedley had also launched the career in law that would ultimately see him work as a judge of the Court of Appeal of England and Wales, one of the highest legal bodies in the land (ranked second only to the Supreme Court). He was knighted in 1992 and became a privy counsellor in 1999. At the time of the album's release, however, he was still at the very outset of that journey, as he recalls. "I was called to the bar in 1964 and I was able to start practicing straight away. One of my first acquisitions, when I began earning, was a Uher reel-to-reel tape-recorder, probably the best investment I ever made." For now he could supplement his library excavations with balladic finds of his own.

Sedley's earliest excursions were to the Lake District in 1965–1966 where, among several discoveries, he met and recorded a retired quarryman named Frank Birkett. The non-Child "Dido Bendigo" that Sedley taped him singing was recorded by the Watersons for their 1966 eponymous LP.

Sedley's next excursion took him to the opposite end of the country, to the southeastern county of Kent.

In about 1967, a kindly and decent Sevenoaks solicitor, Peter Kingshill, who had come here in his teens as a refugee from Nazi Germany, started briefing me on legal aid to take on what seemed hopeless defenses for local gypsies. By pure good luck, I started by winning a group of thirty-two appeals in one go on the ground that the police had not proved that my clients [fell] within the ambit of the 1959 Highways Act. After that, a welcome was assured in every caravan in Kent.

Often, that welcome included music. Sedley acknowledges, " I don't think I had the good fortune to encounter any Child Ballads as a collector." Nevertheless, *The Seeds of Love*, almost one-quarter of which comprised Child's children, did as much to germinate the British folk-rock scene as any other printed contribution.

Not that every major event on the scene at this time was "good news," as November 1967 saw the disbanding of the Watersons, one of the most critically admired of all the acts on the club scene. Neither was it simply a matter of four musicians going their separate ways. The Watersons were family, and a hitherto tightly knit one. But Elaine, known as "Lal" (1943–1998), the youngest of the three Waterson siblings, was relocating to Leeds to be with her husband; brother Mike (1941–2011) was looking toward a new life as a local businessman; eldest sister Norma (1939–2022) would soon be immigrating to the Caribbean island of Montserrat, where she worked in local radio; and the final member of the group, cousin John Harrison, wanted to move into photography.

In the event, it was not a permanent sundering. The group would both reform in the 1970s and continue to work in a variety of other partnerships—Lal and Mike reunited in 1972 to record *Bright Phoebus*, an altogether unique and captivating album that sundry twenty-first-century writers tend so unimaginatively to describe as the *Sgt. Pepper* of folk (it is worth so much more). Mike alone would deliver his own epic interpretation of "Tam Lin" (39) on his 1977 solo album. Norma's marriage to Martin Carthy in 1972 was responsible for a string of magnificent records and performances, and their daughter Eliza would grow to become one of the brightest lights of the 1990s folk scene.

As for the original group, their occasional excursions into the *ESPB* remain visionary; "Herod and the Cock" (55) was certainly a highlight of their 1965 debut, the *Frost and Fire* year-round calendar of traditional folk songs; "The Broom of Cowdenknows" (217) was their instantly recognizable contribution to a Topic label sampler the following year. It is difficult to escape the irony, however, that it was the very scene that supported the Watersons that, ultimately, forced their breakup.

When the group started out, they scarcely needed to leave their hometown of Hull, on England's eastern coast, where they had opened a folk club of their own. As their renown grew, however, and particularly once Bert Lloyd signed them to Topic Records, they found themselves joining the touring treadmill. "The real reason [for the breakup] is health," Norma Waterson explained at the time. "The pace has been cruel, and we have all been suffering from bronchitis." Health, however, was only a part of the equation. Norma continued, "We are also fed up with all the pettiness on the folk scene. . . . It seems to us that a lot of people have forgotten what the whole revival is about. Someone started criticizing our 'image' the other day. Bloody nonsense! It's the songs that matter, not anyone's image."[2]

She was correct. But the "pop scene," even on those fringes where the Watersons and their contemporaries existed, is ferociously image conscious. Increasingly, it seemed, the day of the unaccompanied, or at least acoustically based, folk singer was, if not nearing its end, at least being seriously overshadowed. Audiences wanted movement! Action! Drama! And, wherever possible, electricity.

Pentangle formed in 1967 around the nucleus of singer Jacqui McShee, who both ran and performed at a folk club above the Red Lion pub in Sutton, just outside London, and two of the acts she most regularly booked to play there: guitarists John Renbourn (1944–2015) and Bert Jansch (1943–2011). Both men had long solo careers behind them around the folk clubs, and a clutch of albums, too—in 1973, journalist Jerry Gilbert proclaimed, "Individually and collectively, Bert Jansch and John Renbourn shaped the course of contemporary folk music during the mid-'60s and did precisely the same with the beginnings of contemporary rock. The underground following they enjoyed in the States through their Vanguard recordings was probably larger than anyone would care to believe, and this probably alludes to the huge following that Pentangle were ultimately to enjoy."[3]

Neither, however, was especially feted for their adhesion to traditional songs. Jansch's third album, 1966's *Jack Orion*, was his first to seriously investigate the field, with the title ballad (67) joined by "The Gardener" (219), and "Henry Martin" (250). But, even here the emphasis was on the mysterious, moody Jansch persona, and his correspondingly coruscating guitar style. Renbourn, on the other hand, was better regarded for his jazz stylings, and the *Bert and John* album that the pair made in 1966 again did much to distance their work from any other characterization.

Nobody denied that the basic inspiration behind Pentangle lay in Shirley Collins and Davy Graham's *Folk Roots, New Routes*, and that maiden collision of folk and jazz. That experiment, however, was just that, a one-off project from which both players quickly escaped. Pentangle was intended to follow through on the album's premise, and to do so on the largest scale possible. Far from the folk clubs and tiny theaters in which the members had previously cavorted, Pentangle's debut concert took place at the Royal Festival Hall on July 6, 1968. The gig sold out effortlessly.

The musicians were aware that their hybrid was controversial. Renbourn reflected, "There were all sorts of ideological discussions going on in the folk movement . . . all kinds of directions–whether the music should be kept exactly as it was; whether it should be taken further; whether you should take elements of the music and remold it. . . . But in practice you didn't talk about that sort of stuff. I think people would have laughed in your face if you did."[4]

Completed by the rhythm section of Danny Thompson and Terry Cox, Pentangle certainly had a powerful punch, but they were capable of moments of delightful tenderness, too. Indeed, it was Pentangle's eclecticism that excited audiences. No less than the Incredible String Band, Pentangle offered a no-holds-barred glimpse into the futures not only of folk, blues, and jazz, but also the "psychedelic" sound that was sweeping the United Kingdom at this same time.

It was the heyday, after all, of Syd Barrett's Pink Floyd, the twenty-four-hour technicolor dream and so many other unparalleled flights of musical fancy. Simply by virtue of their musical and lyrical expanse, Pentangle—like the Incredibles—were welcomed warmly into this latest devil's brew.

Naturally, the folk purists gnashed their teeth in outrage, bemoaning the paucity of traditional music in these so-called folk groups' repertoire, and then berating the occasions when a familiar ballad did fall into their clutches. It was an old argument already—Ewan MacColl positively eviscerated Anthony Newley's "Strawberry Lane" (2) when he had played it in an episode of *The Song Carriers*, two years previous. His words on that occasion, however, remained potent:

> Is it animal, mineral or vegetable? There are those who consider it to be folk music. It certainly began life as a folk song. Both the words and the tune were conceived in the folk idiom and it has been sung by generations of folk singers. And yet, there are many people who would deny that it is still a folk song when performed in that particular manner. What then, has happened to it? Its utterance has been translated, its idiom changed to that of pop-music. It is as if we were to take over a pop song and recast it in a classical mould, and then have it performed by a string orchestra whose natural metier was, say, the Beethoven quartets. Do you think it would still be pop music? Conversely, if we took one of those same quartets and performed it on three electric guitars and bongo drums, would it still be Beethoven? It would not. The imposition of styles and idioms foreign to a particular form results in that form being transformed. It becomes something different. Not necessarily something worse or better, just different.[5]

In fact, few of Pentangle's re-envisionings of the Child Ballads (or any other traditional numbers) are overly demanding of censure. Their reworking of Jean Ritchie's "The House Carpenter" (243—from 1969's *Basket of Light*) is faithless only in the unexpected insertion of Renbourn's sitar alongside Jansch's banjo on the latter. Likewise, the title track (10) from the following year's *Cruel Sister* album is positively angelic. True, the same LP's reworking of Jansch's earlier assault upon "Jack Orion" (67) can be regarded as cluttered and concerned, again, more with virtuosity than the ballad's natural vitality, but compared to the kaleidoscopic bolognese of the Incredibles' early albums, Pentangle's Child Ballads are almost painstakingly reverential.

Besides, far more alarming, not to mention louder, events were taking place elsewhere on the London underground scene.

Chapter Thirty-Seven

ANY FAIRPORT IN A STORM

Looking back a decade from the end of the 1970s, Ewan MacColl and Peggy Seeger left nobody in any doubt as to what they thought of "folk-rock." Discussing the "challenge" that a great ballad offers an aspiring performer, the couple observe that "occasionally" that challenge has led them to a "less than encouraging" outcome. Perhaps recalling his own very first excursion into recording Child Ballads, MacColl lamented the recent fate of "Sir Patrick Spens" (58), re-wrought "with spangles and a rock accompaniment." Elsewhere, he complained, folk-rockers had "dragged 'Barbara Allen' (84) protesting, into the Middle Ages to the (albeit skilled) thrumming of shawms and crumhorns. But the ballads don't lend themselves to this kind of treatment. They don't make good 'production numbers.' The poetry gets in the way." The end result, he determined, was akin to placing "a silk garter on the Venus de Milo. It seems overdressed."[1]

Fairport Convention, although they never laid a hand on Barbara Allen, were likely the dressmakers he had in mind, although Dave Swarbrick shrugged the criticism aside. "It's not folk-rock. It might be traditional songs played in part on rock instruments, but that doesn't change the essence of the song itself, anymore than the shift from lute to dulcimer, if there was one, changed it. 'Tam Lin' [39] is still 'Tam Lin' whether Bert [Lloyd] is singing it, Martin [Carthy]'s singing it or Sandy [Denny] is singing it. Janet still gets her man at the end."[2]

In fact, when Fairport Convention first emerged onto the London scene in 1967, it was into the heart of that aforementioned psychedelic era and, like Pentangle and the Incredible String Band, they were an awkward fit, albeit for quite different reasons.

The original Fairport Convention in the garden of the Fairport house in Muswell Hill, 1967. Pictorial Press / Alamy Stock Photo

Guitarist Richard Thompson (no relation to Pentangle's Danny—or to this book's author) was another of his instrument's most gifted practitioners, but in the age of wild men like Jimi Hendrix, Pete Townshend, and Jeff Beck, he was scarcely visible. Judy Dyble was a beautiful but not especially overconfident vocalist. Simon Nicol was a solid but never showy rhythm guitarist. Ashley Hutchings and Martin Lamble (1949–1969) comprised a strong but scarcely Brobdingnagian rhythm section. Fairport did not take drugs, they did not tote around their own light show, they didn't perform lengthy improvisations at excruciating volume. Rather, they followed the guidance of their Boston-born producer, Joe Boyd, and trailed a gentle North American vibe, covering Joni Mitchell, Judy Collins, and Bob Dylan, and writing their own material to similar parameters.

Thompson recalls his own influences. "I've always listened to all kinds of music. Growing up in a big city [he was born in Notting Hill, London, on April 3, 1949] where most things were available, and being a bit of an art student in my early days, I'd listen to Stockhausen, John Cage, weird stuff. Ravel, Debussy, I really like twentieth-century classical music, all the jazz, all the country music which nobody thought had any redeeming factors at the time. I kind of got schooled in everything."[3]

A vital component in this education, although Thompson did not realize it at the time, was the influence of his Scottish father. "My father was obsessed with Robert Burns. Robert ruled in our house. So did Sir Walter Scott. So I grew up with all that stuff, reading Scottish ballads. 'Sir Patrick Spens' [58] was something I was familiar with since I was six. And, even though I culturally rejected that entire thing for a long time as not being useful, eventually I found it so. All that stuff, Jimmy Shand, Scottish dance music, at some point I just regurgitated it."

That point commenced riding into view with the birth of Fairport in 1967, a band that was destined to, first, rewrite the rules of the English folk club circuit, and then those of English folk music itself. Not that such lofty attainments were ever on the band's mind at the outset. "We got into folk . . . not by accident, but not by design either," Thompson reflects.

We all had the same, very cosmopolitan musical backgrounds, and the same kind of taste for everything. So, if someone heard that there was a gig going at a folk club, we'd learn a few folk songs and go along saying we were a folk band. We'd be a blues band to get a gig at the local blues club, and we put together an acoustic group that included Judy to play at the folk club—I think it was myself, Judy, Tyger [Hutchings], and Simon. In the repertoire were things like "The Coming of the Roads" and "Pack Up Your Sorrows." We schooled ourselves in various traditions, and the first album [1967's *Fairport Convention*] shows that. It's all over the place; it's a bit chaotic. But it was also very rootsy, we were a rootsy band, and I think that was one of the things you could do in 1967, which you maybe couldn't get away with today. In fact, one of the greatest role models for Fairport was the Lovin' Spoonful, because they had that same thing going. They were a pop band, but they were stealing tunes from Memphis jug band, Henry Thomas, and country music. *Hums of the Loving Spoonful*! I played that album to death.

"Folk," however, has never been a term with which Thompson has been comfortable, as even he admits,

I always thought it was a sad day when the folk page disappeared from the *Melody Maker*! I always saw [Fairport's] role as being kind of revivalist, resurrectors of a tradition . . . bringing a tradition that was defamed and unpopular back into the cultural mainstream. To some extent we succeeded because Fairport were and still are very well loved. But to some extent we failed, because the music never really became popular—and the version that did become popular, which was Steeleye Span, immediately got pigeonholed as a novelty by the Brits. Their own culture was a novelty! So we were cursed before we started.

The group's awareness of that curse began early and, in many ways, fueled the band's own ambitions.

We'd always hung out in folk clubs and part of the diet, the general broad diet, was that we were completely out on a limb. There was a very deliberate, intellectual plane that we thrust ourselves out on, because we were a sub-urban grammar school clique, and because our music was so much further away from what anyone else was doing. It was snobbery, completely, but for us, what we were doing was the absolute cutting edge, a lot more than being Jethro Tull, the Rolling Stones, any of the more intellectual manifestations of the sixties and seventies. We were going absolutely against the current and working in an area where there were enormous barriers of prejudice against us. The fact we got any coverage whatsoever was amazing.

Fairport did not approach the folk milieu wholly unprepared. Dyble was recruited to the lineup when they were booked to play their first folk club, being the only person they knew who looked and sounded the part. She, however, was not necessarily impressed. "When I first started going along [to the band's rehearsals], they were doing a lot of Richard and Mimi Fariña, early Dylan, and really hackneyed folk songs. They even played my own *pièce de least-résistance*, 'The Water Is Wide'" (204). That first folk club gig took place on September 3, 1966, and Judy Collins's influence was apparent in the inclusion of "The Coming of the Roads," a Billy Edd Wheeler song that the band learned from her 1965 *Fifth Album*—"it showed off the sweetness, and delicacy of [Dyble's] voice to best effect," Thompson reflected.

Traditional song, however, altogether fell out of the band's repertoire as the group, influenced now by Joe Boyd, steered even closer to the American singer-songwriter idea, only to ricochet back following Dyble's departure, with her replacement by Sandy Denny (1947–1978).

Two years Dyble's elder, Alexandra Maclaine Denny trained briefly for a career in nursing before enrolling at Kingston College of Art, where John Renbourn was among her fellow students. Her home life had not been especially musical—she learned some Scottish folk songs from her grandfather, but her parents discouraged any musical ambitions she may

Sandy Denny was already a folk club veteran when she joined Fairport in 1968. KEYSTONE Pictures USA / Alamy Stock Photo

have shown. Student life, however, brought them to the fore, and she played her first live performance, at the Barge in Kingston, in late 1965. Like so many others, her repertoire at this time was largely rooted in American influences, but both her own compositions and British traditional song quickly made inroads into her repertoire. Tim Hart, later of Steeleye Span but a fellow denizen of the folk circuit at that time, was one of several witnesses who recall her performing "a fantastic" "Geordie" (209), "especially if an audience had been responsive."[4]

Denny had sung in a band before, performing live and recording with both Johnny Silvo's combo and the Strawberry Hill Boys. It was the latter link that proved strongest. Denny was briefly a full member of the band, her arrival coinciding with the group finally unearthing a record company that was interested in signing them.

Dave Cousins recalls, "I went to Denmark to do a little tour on my own, first time I'd ever done it, and I bumped into a guy named Tom Browne. He interviewed me for a folk show he was doing on Danish radio, and we got on famously. Tom . . . took the demo tape to Sonic Records in Copenhagen, played it to them, and they said they wanted to sign us. So we went over to Denmark and made our first album in 1967." Laughing, Cousins revealed that the deciding factor for Browne might have been Denny's involvement in the band. "I told him we had a new girl singer, Sandy Denny. He said, 'Good God, I used to go to the cinema and hold hands with her when we were fifteen.'"[5]

Nothing came of the album at the time, while demos for an LP of Denny's own fell on fallow ground, despite news that Judy Collins was recording one of Denny's songs, "Who Knows Where the Time Goes," as the title track of her next album. By spring 1968, it felt as though the solo Denny had risen as high as she was likely to. Her union with Fairport, then, was as logical as it was inspired. Denny met a band that, while not directionless, was in search of identity; they met a singer who, while scarcely anonymous, needed a change in direction.

The musicians' willingness to follow Denny's lead into more overtly folk-influenced quarters was broached on their first album together, *What We Did on Our Holidays*; and solidified on the succeeding *Unhalfbricking*, with its electrifying, and electrified, revision of the traditional "A Sailor's Life," with the guesting Dave Swarbrick a willing participant.

By summer 1969, as they worked toward their third LP together, a full concept came into sight. Before that, however, the band also encountered tragedy. A road accident as the band returned to London from a gig in Birmingham, in which both drummer Lamble and a friend, Jeanie the Tailor, were killed, forced the group into hibernation.

Sequestered on a rented estate, Farley Chamberlain near Winchester, Hampshire, Fairport welcomed Swarbrick in as a new full-time member, while at the same time auditioning for a new drummer; they settled upon Dave Mattacks. Influenced, if not necessarily counseled by Denny and Swarbrick, the band began searching for that elusive new direction, and discovered it in the notion of what Denny called "heavy traditional folk music."

Bert Lloyd was by their side throughout the process; he was already a fervent admirer of Fairport Convention, and would remain one. Giving a lecture to the University of Mississippi in 1980, he recalled the "gnome-like and somewhat gnomic" Swarbrick once telling him that he was "attracted to amplified music because he liked the sound, and because it offered great possibilities of exploring the dramatic content of the songs." Lloyd waxed lyrical, too, about Denny, "a sweet, plump lady to whom I was devoted." The band became regular callers to his office. Thompson later recalled "hours on the phone with Bert Lloyd saying things like, 'We have to find a better 32nd verse for 'Tam Lin'" (39).[6]

The not-altogether crystalline nature of period telephone lines, meanwhile, was responsible for a nomenclatural variation in "Matty Groves" (81); whoever was taking down the lyric from Lloyd misheard Lord Arnold's name as "Lord Darnell," although of course the error did not hamper the magic of the ballad. In 1980, Christy Moore of Planxty, discussing his band's newly released version of the same song, remarked, "I was first drawn to this song by its length. The first verse appealed to me because I too went to Mass to look at girls."

Those features remained paramount in Fairport's version, too.

Two further Child Ballads made it into the *Liege and Lief* album sessions at Sound Technique Studios in London late that summer. Based around a melody that Swarbrick got from Ewan MacColl, Thompson's beloved "Sir Patrick Spens" (58) was joined, at least in spirit, by "Willy O'Winsbury" (100), included on the album via Thompson's borrowing of the melody for his lyric "Farewell Farewell."[7]

Ashley Hutchings recalled the sessions for his biographers Brian Hinton and Geoff Wall. "We'd drift down one by one and have breakfast casually, and then drift into the room where all our equipment was lined up permanently. I remember a sense of excitement coming down the stairs for breakfast thinking 'What are we going to do today? Oh, we're going to look at jigs and reels today, or we're going to tackle that ballad 'Tam Lin' that we had a look at yesterday." He continued, "I'd got the [*ESPB*] here, we'd look up maybe compiled verses. I remember . . . one time with Dave Swarbrick, getting on the phone to Ian Campbell and saying 'we need a tune for one of the ballads.'"[8]

Everybody offered suggestions for material, with Thompson especially vocal about the need to include some original numbers, and Swarbrick quick to pick out favorites among the material he had previously recorded with Martin Carthy. Included in that category was "Tam Lin" (39), which future Fairport drummer Bruce Rowland (1941–2015) described as "a tune called 'The Kid on the Mountain'—a slip jig which Swarb learned from Martin Carthy and then masterfully adapted from 9/8 to 7/4."[9]

And it was "Tam Lin" that most clearly illustrated what this newfangled "folk-rock" business should be—not simply a rocking up of traditional song, with electric instruments instead of acoustic (the Irish band Sweeney's

Men had already made that transition, after all), but of expanding its horizons via that electricity; by permitting the instrumentation to flow as freely as the story, and along similar lines. Indeed, the greatest criticism of "Tam Lin," as voiced by Brian Hinton and Geoff Wall, is that "after Sandy has finished her triumphant tale, the music seems to peter away,"[10] and perhaps Fairport were aware of that. Rerecording the song in session for the BBC's John Peel soon after, the band jams thrillingly on for a further seventy-five seconds, an assault against which the LP version sadly pales and—if the fade-out is anything to go by—they could have played on even longer.

For Bruce Rowland, it was Denny's performance that gave "Tam Lin" its greatest impact. "Her essence was profoundly English, and she was a very old soul. I bet she dreamed in seventeenth-century English. She made the text—particularly of 'Tam Lin'–sound like an improvised story told at the fireside. Her sublime phrasing and unique vocal technique always unobtrusive, she was riveting."[11]

In Rowland's estimation, only Martin Carthy ever equaled Denny's ability to interpret the Child Ballads. Released earlier in the same year as Fairport's version, Carthy and Swarbrick's *Prince Heathen* LP (titled for Child 104) also included "Little Musgrave and Lady Barnard"—Fairport's "Matty Groves"—and it is no less compelling than theirs, even without the sound of a rock band going hell-for-leather behind the lyrics. And his choice of melody ("I pinched [it] from a version of 'The Holy Ewell,'" Carthy confessed in the liner notes) may even have been superior.

"Martin and Sandy brought the songs alive," continued Rowland. "For years, I was blissfully ignorant of the *ESPB*, in spite of being familiar with a good few of the ballads, and I was intrigued by the power of the lyrics interpreted and heard rather than read." At the same time, however, he poured scorn on the band's—and their supporters'—attempts to label this new approach "folk-rock."

> When I heard the early Fairport material with Dave Mattacks, I was well impressed. I also read interminable articles—largely the most abject bullshit—about "folk-rock" being variously an "unwelcome" or an "overdue" evolution of the tradition. Evolution my arse. A watershed moment perhaps, but folk music, in the right hands—even those in Arran sweaters, with fingers in ears and nanny goat vibratos—had always rocked. The only difference was, with amplifiers—and about time too—even the acoustic bands could be heard at the back of the hall. I was spitefully amused by the anguish of the purists who could not cope with "folk-rock" due to their proprietary attachment to the history and poetry of the tradition (viz. Pete Seeger's peevish attempt to sabotage the newly electric Dylan at Newport).[12]

Nevertheless, Hutchings's biographers are not mistaken when they describe Fairport's "Tam Lin" as "perhaps the most culturally important song Island [Records] released outside of Bob Marley." It not only created the ultimate template for a multitude of successors but also brought traditional music howling back into the focus of the British media, print and broadcast, and alerted the industry as a whole—record labels, producers, managers, an entire panoply of necessary evils—that traditional music could, and would, do the one thing it had so seldom succeeded at in the past—sell to the masses.

And so it could. Fairport, after all, were no strangers to the UK charts at this point. Their French language rendering of Dylan's "If You Gotta Go, Go Now," "Si Tu Dois Partir," had just missed the Top 20 a few months previous; *Unhalfbricking* reached number 12 on the album listings. If anything, *Liege and Lief* disappointed, as it peaked at number 17. But subsequent albums *Full House* (1970) and *Angel's Delight* (1971) were destined for numbers 12 and 8 respectively, and continued critical acclaim for *Liege and Lief* certainly played its role in that success.

"Tam Lin" is frequently singled out as the culmination of Fairport Convention's accomplishments. It was the album's other epic, "Matty Groves," however, that was to scale the greatest heights, at least in terms of Fairport's own convoluted future history. In swift succession, Denny and Hutchings both quit following *Liege and Lief*. Thompson departed in the wake of *Full House*, Nicol left in 1971, Mattacks in 1975. By the time Fairport Convention broke up in 1979, only Dave Swarbrick could claim uninterrupted membership since the days of *Liege and Lief*, with Hutchings's replacement, bassist Dave Pegg, a close second.

"Matty Groves, " on the other hand, stayed put, a regular in the live set no matter who was playing the tune. For each of the lineups that performed as Fairport over that decade, and for all those that have existed in the years since the group's full-time reformation in 1985, it is *the* ultimate Fairport song, capable of lasting ten, fifteen, even twenty minutes when the fancy takes them.

Rowland (who replaced Mattacks in 1975) described the song's omnipresence in the band's repertoire thus: "It's about Dead Matty Groves, whose monument is to have his story told late at night to a congregation of thousands of word perfect punters, by a motley cast of elderly, over-refreshed folk-rock greats who can, these days, barely manage the 'Orange Blossom Special' coda at the ludicrous tempo which over the years, thanks to Swarbrick's competitive streak, has become *de rigueur*. One day it will catch up with them and there will be some sort of group coronary." But he acknowledged, also, "It's a monster song which rocks even when the lyrics are recited as poetry and the tune is American. I would love to record an a cappella version."[13]

Fairport Convention never eschewed their folk-rock identity, nor did they abandon Professor Child. Dropped from the running order for *Liege and Lief,* "Sir Patrick Spens" (58) was the first of the Child Ballads to be recorded following the departure of Hutchings and Denny, a whole new arrangement, which also, sadly, dropped the fifth verse that Denny so atmospherically sang on the original recording:

> *Last night I saw the new, new moon*
> *With the old moon in her arms*
> *And that is the sign since we were born*
> *That means there'll be a deadly storm*

This new version, however, rapidly became a concert favorite, as well as a dominant feature of both 1970's *Full House* and the live-in-Los Angeles album that memorializes the accompanying tour. *Angel Delight* includes a typhonic "Sir William Gower" (57), and while the *ESPB* was then left to gather dust for a time, 1978 brought a towering rendition of "Jack O'Rion" (67) on what was intended as the band's final album, *Tippler's Tales.*

Bruce Rowland recalled recording the latter. "Swarb had the whole arrangement worked out before we got to the studio (a Fairport first!). The tune was traditional via Bert Lloyd–I can't remember if it was originally to 'Jack O'Rion,' or something else. The instrumental links evolved by a trial and error process at rehearsals (another Fairport first!), and I had not heard the song before, so had no preconceptions." This, he admitted, was fortunate.

> Otherwise, I should have had the echoes of Martin [Carthy]'s and Bert Jansch's compelling versions in my head. Having listened to both versions all this time later, I know I could not have escaped their influence. Swarb was born to lead; Simon [the now-returned Nicol], Peggy [Dave Pegg] and I were comfortable with this and could follow and complement. On a good night, Swarb would be on fire, and we would toss him about like a feather in the wind. I do have a very pleasant recollection of putting "Jack O'Rion" together.[14]

"As to the difference from other versions, this is difficult to pin down." When Rowlands joined the band, among the most mystifying of comments he heard from among his new bandmates was the accusation that he played "too American." The irony was that it was Jerry Donahue, Fairport's Manhattan-born guitarist, who made the accusation.

Rowland acknowledged, however, that "with this version of 'Jack O'Rion,' it does have a sort of bluegrass feel here and there, and I was always aware that my 'rock' input into English folk-rock might just have been on the wrong side of mid-Atlantic. But, heigh ho!"

Chapter Thirty-Eight

LEADER OF THE PACK

Liege and Lief was not the sole seismic event to shake the folk world in 1969. That year also saw the publication of *The Oxford Book of Ballads*, a weighty volume compiled by James Kinsley that served effectively as an abbreviated (150-ballad) edition of the *ESPB*.

Indeed, it will swiftly become apparent that many of the Child Ballads that were pressed into service over the next few years were those that had appeared within these pages. Shirley Collins acknowledged outright that no less than four of its inclusions made it into the sessions for 1970's *Love, Death and the Lady* album, the first album she recorded after sister Dolly gave her a copy of the Oxford collection for her thirty-fifth birthday.

The final year of the decade also saw the British film company Commonwealth United Entertainment begin work on a movie adaptation of "Tam Lin" (39). Produced by Stanley Mann and Alan Ladd Jr., the latter newly relocated to London from Los Angeles, *Tam Lin* also featured a screenplay by American William Spier, best known for his work on the 1940s radio series *The Adventures of Sam Spade*, and it marked the directorial debut of actor Roddy McDowall. The cast, meanwhile, included Ava Gardner, Ian McShane, Cyril Cusack, and what the language of the day would have regarded as a smorgasbord of "dolly birds"—among them Joanna Lumley, Sinéad Cusack, Jenny Hanley, and Madeline Smith.

It's not a great movie, and it was not a success. Despite being shot on location around Peebles, Scotland, through the summer of 1969, with fabulous weather and pleasing scenery certain to catch the eye, a less than enthralling script and McDowall's inexperience in his new role both litigated against the movie's hip horror intentions; its release in Britain, shortly before Christmas 1970, was limited to just a handful of showings, and the United States didn't even see the film until 1972. There, it was retitled *The Devil's Widow*, but it sank without trace regardless.

For some viewers, the movie's greatest fault was that, in attempting to modernize the story of the original ballad, the plot effectively lost all relationship to it—IMDb's dismissive description of it as "an older woman uses witchcraft to keep her young jet set friends" is, sadly, a very accurate takeaway.

But it was not entirely a lost cause. With the film's backers seeking at least some semblance of "authenticity," Pentangle—fresh from the *Cruel Sister* LP sessions—were recruited to provide the movie's theme, together with some incidental music. They duly turned in an absolutely spine-chilling rendition of "Tam Lin."

Overall, it is seven minutes in length. Jacqueline McShee's vocal is crystal clear over her bandmates' brooding accompaniment and rendered all the more effective by the use to which it was put. Never permitted to stretch out as a single piece of music, Pentangle's "Tam Lin" is instead sliced across the film to act as a form of narrative between different scenes, with the accompaniment necessarily adapting accordingly. The effectiveness of this can then be gauged by comparison with the version of "Tam Lin" recorded by Sproatly Smith for their second album, 2010's *Pixieled*, wherein dialogue from the movie is interspersed with "a few of the twenty-one verses that Sandy Denny sang on Fairport's different version."[1] Indeed, Smith proudly remembers one review describing the result as bringing "a straight-faced, soap-opera slant to the song, with unwelcome news through spoken passages interweaving with beautifully sung verses."

"Tam Lin," like *Cruel Sister*, was produced by Bill Leader, head now of his own Leader and Trailer record labels, but a longtime presence at Topic and Transatlantic and, before that, one of Britain's most diligent ballad collectors. Across Topic's *Voice of the People* series, and elsewhere too, Leader's name is attached to some of the most significant field recordings of the age, and the same can be said for his output as the head of two record companies. Leader explains the division:

> We thought that the whole thing of producing material for sale could only be commercial if it was done via post. Record shops weren't interested in carrying it, so we had to appeal directly to the enthusiasts, working by mail through newsletters and written information. So it was important to be as clear as possible as to what we were doing, and what I pictured was. If we were trying to advertise a record called *Folk Songs of England* and just sent out a letter about this, nobody would have a clear idea of whether it was performances by some folk club singer or some country singer. So we decided to have two labels, Leader for traditional roots material and Trailer for entertainment material.[2]

Both labels were responsible for some of the key folk and traditional records of the age. Leader, who admits that his working knowledge of the Child Ballads is basically confined to "I knew they existed," would also oversee the release, and often the recording, of some of the most exciting and imaginative renditions of the canon.

It was the Leader label, for example, that released the historic *Folk Ballads from Donegal and Derry* collection of thirteen Child Ballads recorded in the field in Ireland. Leader, too, reissued the Percy Grainger recordings that made up *Unto Brigg Fair*, drawn from the now-sixty-plus-year-old cylinders that brought Joseph Taylor and his mighty "Lord Bateman" (53) back to life.

Leader explains the album's genesis. "We got approached by a fellow named Bob Thomson, who was doing his PhD on Percy Grainger. It was intended as evidence of publication of his work, and we liked the idea, so he brought us the material, he did all the research and we cobbled it together into a record." Recordings by Séamus Ennis and the Copper Family, and compilations of bluegrass and Scots balladry also populated the catalog; alongside Topic, Leader was indeed leading the way in making available the very soul of British and American traditional song.

Trailer, on the other hand, was to pick up some of the key acts on the so-called folk-rock circuit, whether the musicians themselves rocked or not. The High Level Ranters from Northumberland and the brothers Robin and Barry Dransfield were among the label's earliest releases; later, the Scottish-Irish quartet The Boys of the Lough delivered a dramatic "Andrew Lammie" (233) on their eponymous 1973 album. And Tony Rose's 1970 *Young Hunting* album can be said to have reintroduced Robin Hood to the new folk audience—his LP opens with "Robin Hood and the Bishop of Hereford" (144).

In terms of future legend, and homage to the Child Ballads, however, Trailer's key signings were the solo performer Nic Jones, and the duo of Dave and Toni Arthur, the founders of east London's Phoebus Awakes folk club. Leader does not recollect how he and the Arthurs first met; only that their first album together was the couple's debut, *Morning Stands on Tiptoe*, released by Transatlantic in 1967. He oversaw, too, their sophomore set, *The Lark in the Morning*, for Topic.

It was the duo's first for Trailer, however, that became their masterpiece. Whereas their earlier albums were best described, in the words of *Fortean Times* writer Bob Fischer, as "beautiful essays in unaccompanied traditional song with a distinct leaning towards the pastoral,"[3] *Hearken to the Witches Rune* was an exploration not only of traditional music, but magical lore as well, created by a couple who were versed in both fields.

Avid collectors of the supernatural, the Arthurs prepared for the recordings by traveling across the United Kingdom, "tracking people

Dave and Toni Arthur's epochal LP *Hearken to the Witches Rune*, produced by Bill Leader.
Author's collection

down and interviewing them," as Dave Arthur told Fischer. "Travellers and canal barge people, fairground people and—particularly farmers. Talking to them and recording them." Fragments of these researches were published in the hand-typed four-page insert that would accompany *Hearken to the Witches Rune*, titled *Magic in Ballads*.

The album was recorded, as were most of Leader's productions, in his two-room flat in Camden Town, with the studio itself sometimes referred to as his bedroom, sometimes his living room. In fact it was both. Or neither, as Leader explains:[4] "I lived, worked, recorded, stored records and slept in the same two rooms, so the division between what you could call a bedroom and what you might call a living room was fairly ambiguous, and it changed from time to time as we decided to move the record stock from one room to another, or stick the stamps on envelopes in a different room. In fact, the only room that remained the same was the bathroom."

Such everyday surroundings are in no way apparent listening to the record, its eight tracks shifting between spell craft and fairy legend, and drawing upon some of the most opulently visual ballads in the entire *ESPB*—a jaunty "Alison Gross" (35); an elegiac "The Cruel Mother" (20), a fiddle-and-whistle fired "Broomfield Hill" (43), and a positively blood-freezing "Cold Blows the Winter Wind" (78), its lyric taken from Alfred Williams's 1923 publication *Folk-Songs of the Upper Thames*.[5]

The highlight, however, was the brittle, naked "Tam Lin" (39), a duet not only between Dave and Toni but also protagonists Margaret and Tam, and even the fairy queen, set to a melody collected by Hamish Henderson and first performed by Bert Lloyd. Up there alongside Anne Briggs and Frankie Armstrong, this was "Tam Lin" as the story was meant to be told.

Nic Jones was less dramatic but, in many ways, equally powerful. "I can't recall how we got started with Nic," admits Leader. "I don't know who made the first move there, but so many people look back on him now with respect. He was very good at searching out new material; he was very good at that, although I don't think I realized just how good he was, at the time."

Across five solo albums cut across the early and late 1970s, opening with the Leader-produced *Ballads and Songs* in 1970, Jones's sonorous voice, versatile guitar, and keening fiddle brought fresh energies to some twenty Child Ballads. He also guested effervescent on the Arthurs' *Hearken to the Witches Rune*, and, perhaps most impressively of all, ranked among June Tabor's favorite sidemen, at a time when she was best regarded as an unaccompanied performer. Small wonder, then, that his supporters (of whom there are many) regard him among the most unique solo artists to approach the Child Ballads in the last fifty years.

Chapter Thirty-Nine

KEEPING UP WITH THE JONESES

Born in Orpington, London, on January 7, 1947, and taking his guitar playing lead from such early sixties heroes as the Shadows and Duane Eddy, Nic Jones's early absorption of traditional music followed his recruitment to a schoolboy folk band, The Halliard.

There he picked up the fiddle; there, too, he started training himself to rearrange the songs he wanted to play, both to better suit his own abilities and to raise them above the more conventional airings that other performers were offering. Jones recalled his early efforts:

My approach to learning songs was quite undisciplined and somewhat lazy. I used to trawl through a variety of books such as the Child Ballads, [Dean William Christie's 1876 work] *Traditional Ballad Airs*, Bronson, and the *English Folk Dance and Song Society Folk Song Journal*, and listen to old recordings of traditional singers. Rather than conscientiously learn the songs by writing them down and working out the arrangement, I tended to absorb them over a period of time. Add the facts that I couldn't read music very well and had a terrible memory even then, the end result was words and tunes were not always remembered correctly, nor, in some cases, were the sources.[1]

Indeed, he took a very early fancy to the *ESPB*; the earliest circulating recording of Jones, from a folk club gig circa 1968, is a raw "Demon Lover" (243), while his love of "The Outlandish Knight" (4) was such that he recorded it for both his 1970 debut album, *Ballads and Songs*, and his second, 1971's *Nic Jones*. He excused himself in the liner notes for the latter: "I find that certain songs appeal to me on the strength of certain phrases or words that are enjoyable to sing due to their inherent lyrical quality. This is one of them."

Nic Jones at the Essex Folk Festival, August 1981. Tony 1212, CC BY-SA 4.0 / Wikimedia Commons

His notes also reveal the instinctive awareness of what was "good" or "not-so-good" that he poured into his selections. On that debut album, the melody employed for "The Outlandish Knight" was straight out of Cecil Sharp's *English Folk Songs*. But "Sir Patrick Spens" (58) was unearthed from Christie, and was later proclaimed by Bellowhead's Jon Boden as "One of the finest ballad melodies going,"[2] and by Martin Carthy to be "the best tune to carry" a song he had known since he was "seven or eight, [when] my mother first showed me 'Sir Patrick Spens.'"[3]

The melody accompanying "Little Musgrave" (81), on the other hand, was largely Jones's own composition, albeit with what he described as a few nods to an American variant. It would also prove to be among his most influential pieces, with the Irish band Planxty acknowledging a considerable debt when they recorded the same ballad for 1980s *The Woman I Loved So Well*. Having found the ballad's words on some loose printed pages that fell out of a book at an auction house, Christy Moore was despairing of ever finding a suitable tune until bandmate Andy Irvine drew his attention to Jones's arrangement. That became the basis for Planxty's otherwise wholly individual rendition.

The melody of "The Banks of the Green Willow" (24), on Jones's second album, was also, if not wholly self-composed, at least pieced together from "a mixture of various phrases that were already in my head. I have known this song for some years but have never sung it as none of the many tunes had particularly appealed." And then, a revelation. "Whilst looking at it again in *The Folk Song Journals* I began singing it to the present tune."[4]

Another Child Ballad, "The Bonnie Banks of Fordie" (14) was numbered among Jones's offerings for the *First Folk Review Record*, a sampler album produced by the magazine of the same name; wryly, he sought out the most Americanized version of the ballad he could, a seething nest of outlaws, rattlers and all, and then set it to another melody he discovered in *Traditional Ballad Airs*, "The Laird of Drum" (236).

Further Jones solo albums *The Noah's Ark Trap* (1977), *From the Devil to a Stranger* (1978), and *Penguin Eggs* (1980) followed; all but the latter included a Child Ballad apiece, "Anachie Gordon" (239) and "The Blind Harper" (192), respectively. He also became a somewhat regular fixture on John Peel's radio show, a total of eight performances across a five-year span including four Child Ballads. He made a ninth visit in 1978 as a member of Bandoggs, the short-lived group he formed with Tony Rose and Peter and Chris Coe for a self-titled album in 1978, and their versions of three Child Ballads, "The Dragoon and the Lady" (7), "Hind Horn" (17), and "Laird Logie" (182) effortlessly illustrate a vision, and a collaboration, that deserved to have been taken further.

Sadly, Jones's career was about to shatter.

Returning home from a club gig on February 26, 1982, Jones's car was involved in a horrific collision with a truck. The accident broke almost every bone in his body and left him in a coma from which he would not emerge for several months. While he would eventually recover and even return to occasional live work, he has not recorded a note since. "Everything on my right side was bust," he told *The Guardian*'s Colin Irwin (1951–2022) in 2012, on the eve of one such "comeback."[5] "Eyes, ears, arm. Elbow smashed to bits. Wrist. Everything had to be replaced. I've got a metal arse, a false eye, false teeth, everything is false. I'm an illusion. The only thing that wasn't bust was my guitar."

Yet, across these silent years, Jones rose to be acclaimed among the greatest traditional musicians England has ever produced, among fans, critics, and peers alike. "As an interpreter of ballads Nic is *sans pareil*," June Tabor once remarked. "'Little Musgrave,' 'Annan Water' [215], 'Annachie Gordon,' [239], they all still leave me speechless."[6]

Martin Simpson agrees. Intending to record "Little Musgrave" for his 2007 CD *Prodigal Son*, he wrote, "I spent several years reading, listening and considering [different versions], when one day I remembered Nic

Jones' recorded version on his first album. I didn't go back and listen, I just started to play."[7]

John Roberts, too, looks back on Jones with awe. "I learned Nic Jones' version of 'Sir Patrick Spens' quite a few years ago, when I was asked to sing some ballad examples in an English class at Union College. It lay dormant for a while, but I gradually started wondering if I could work out a concertina arrangement for it."[8]

Since that time, Jones has captured the attentions of performers as far afield as Anaïs Mitchell, Kate Rusby (who learned his arrangement of "The Blind Harper" (192) for her *Underneath the Stars* album in 2003), and Canadian Paddy Tully; Jones's influence can certainly be heard in her "Blind Harper" and "Annachie Gordon," from 2015's *The Roaring Jewel*.

And all this affection was aroused, it must be added, despite the majority of Jones's recorded catalog lying in obscurity or out of print. Bill Leader recalls being approached by a radio journalist for an interview about Jones's career: "He was a great enthusiast, and was aware that I had something to do with Nic, but in conversation it became obvious that the only album record he knew by Nic was [1980's] *Penguin Eggs*, because that was the only one that was available! The ones that I'm most pleased and proud of, that I did with Nic, he'd never even heard of."[9]

Nevertheless, the tributes continued. In 1999 alone, the magazines *Mojo* and *Folk Roots* offered up fulsome profiles, Martin Carthy included both a written tribute to Jones and a musical one on his latest album, and Jones himself had a song featured on Rhino's acclaimed three-volume *Troubadours of British Folk* collection. Most remarkably of all, however, that same year also saw the release of John Wesley Harding's *Trad Arr. Jones* album, a full-blown tribute to the missing genius.

Harding himself was among the host of younger musicians transfixed by Jones, even as he acknowledged, "Nic Jones is not really a familiar name, but I think in fact most people know at least a couple of songs by him, or associated with him, people into folk-rock, or maybe into Dylan, or Christy Moore, or Mary Black. All these people have sung songs which are heavily associated with Nic, even if they don't necessarily spell it out."[10] Dylan's take on the traditional "Canadee-i-o," from 1992's *Good as I Been to You* album, for example, has been described as a genuine nod toward Jones's *Penguin Eggs* arrangement, and he was scarcely alone in doing that. Harding continued, "When someone covers one of his songs, they don't think, 'Ah, that's a Nic Jones song.' A lot of these folk songs go back a long way, a lot of the great tunes as well. But he rearranged a lot of them for his own records, and those rearrangements are the ones people know now. That's why I wanted the name of the record to be *Trad. Arr. Jones*, so there's no doubt that this album is somebody else's songs."

Harding's own introduction to Jones's music came surprisingly late in the day. Born in Hastings, England, in 1965, Harding relocated to the United States in 1991 and was living in San Francisco when the crucial discovery came about. "I met someone who said, 'Oh, you're into folk music, you should hear this album *Penguin Eggs*, it's so good.' So, finally I picked it up and . . . it's very difficult to find the other records, but I persisted, and in fact, I had to go and visit Nic himself to get copies of his first two. But I just fell in love with the albums, I became totally obsessed with them, and slowly the idea of doing this record came to me."

Musically and stylistically, *Trad. Arr. Jones* was a considerable departure from past Harding opuses. For starters, for a long time he didn't even like English traditional music. "I was always very standoffish about the English stuff, it really didn't appeal to me. I started with Dylan, I learned to play acoustic guitar, then I discovered John Prine and Steve Goodman. It was only later, after I started collecting the literature, being in love with the literature of the English ballads, that I started wanting to hear musical versions of the songs. These songs are full of great stories, so for me to plunder this fantastic treasure trove, this museum of terrific stories, it was paradise."

Five of Jones's eleven songs on *Trad. Arr.* investigated its subject's explorations of the *ESPB*, including all three of those that rendered June Tabor "speechless," plus "Edward" (13) and "William Glenn" (57). Harding admitted,

> It was a very low panic situation for me. Folk songs are very durable, and whether I record "Little Musgrave" or whether I don't, it's going to make very little difference to the song itself. I could do a great version, or a bad one, it doesn't matter. This song is going to live forever regardless. It's already been around since at least 1611. So that knowledge made the making of this album a huge, huge pleasure, because when I do my songs, I'm really the only person who's ever going to do the "definitive" version of them. But with these songs, there's none of that. You do your version, someone else does theirs, someone else does theirs. And nothing any one of you do is going to make those songs any better, or any worse.

At the same time, however, he acknowledged that Jones generally did everything "better."

> Nic's from that school where it was kind of bad to write your own songs, where it was better to say, "It's traditional," and claim not to have written it. Now, this may seem really strange today, when some idiot will write three seconds of crap on a commercial, and make a million out of it, but this is a whole different culture, and these people were very into folk music. So, I think Nic wrote stuff which he then claimed was traditional, because that

was the style he wrote it in, but also because that was the world he lived in. It's all very well for him to say, "Well, 'Canadee-i-o' was my tune," which he did say to me, but I think the bottom line is, not only could he have claimed to have written some of those folk songs, as Bob Dylan has, as Led Zeppelin have, but Nic actually *did* write them. And another thought behind *Trad. Arr. Jones* was to actually give him back some of the credit which he didn't take, maybe even didn't want, in the first place.

Harding first met Jones in 1998, shortly after Nic's own Mollie Music label released the album *In Search of Nic Jones*, a collection of concert recordings gathered together by fans and friends in the weeks following his car accident, for Jones's wife, Julia, to play at his bedside, in hopes of bringing her stricken husband back to consciousness. The record was available only from the Joneses themselves, so when Harding sent away for a copy, he included a little note with his check: "I was going to England on holiday, staying in Yorkshire, and I wrote to Nic and his wife, 'My name's John Wesley Harding, there's no way you'll ever have heard of me, but I'm a huge fan, and I'm coming up to Yorkshire next week.' And Julia wrote back and said, 'Please stop by for a cup of coffee, and as it happens, we have heard of you, through some friends of ours.'"

The album was inspired by that meeting. "I moved up to Seattle to live on an island, and all I do is sit around waiting for ferries, or sitting in my house, with all this time to listen to music. So I was playing Nic's albums, getting more and more into them, listening to them, wanting to think about what the songs meant, listening to them closer and closer, and finally, it all just fit together."

Choosing the songs was relatively easy. Across his five studio albums, Jones recorded a total of forty-eight songs; there's another dozen, including a take on that most surreal and sinister of children's songs, "Teddy Bear's Picnic," on *In Search of Nic Jones*. "I picked my favorites," Harding affirmed. "But I also picked the songs which I thought I could add something to."

Harding initially intended to self-release the album.

But then the record company [Zero Hour] heard about it through my manager, and they said, "We'd like to put it out—we're hardly a folk label, but it sounds like an interesting project." And somebody who works there was actually a Nic Jones fan, so it just fell into place, because the moment they said that, suddenly I was looking at a budget to go into the studio, to bring in a producer [Kurt Bloch of Seattle bands the Fastbacks and the Young Fresh Fellows], to have a nice cover, and to know it's going to get out there.

Still he was surprised, touring before the album was released, to find his audience responding enthusiastically to the Jones material—which, of course, would have been brand new to many of them. Even more astonishing, however, was his own response to the music.

> People send me these CDs which they've burned of my shows, and I was looking at one of them, at the track listing, and suddenly I saw "Annachie Gordon," and the time next to it is 10 minutes 41. [on *Trad. Arr. Jones*, the tune clocks in at 6:43.] And I just thought, "Fucking hell, how did that go on so long?" Because all I did was sing the song, I didn't have a long speech in the middle of it, I just sung it, and people seemed to be as caught up in it as I was. . . . I mean, I got an encore immediately after it. So the thing is, most of my fans don't listen to Nic Jones; they've never heard of him. But that's what I like about music, it's a long stream, a big river of tradition, and it's good to dabble your toe in there and see if the people who like you like the other things you like. And with Nic Jones, it seems like they do.

Chapter Forty

PITY POOR STEELEYE SPAN

Possessing one of the most distinctive and extraordinary voices on the British folk scene of the 1960s, and one that no amount of electricity could ever overshadow, Madeleine Edith Prior originally found her musical interests on the American side of things—Joan Baez, Woody Guthrie, and company. Born in the northwestern seaside town of Blackpool in 1947, the daughter of television scriptwriter Allan Prior, her tastes shifted in her teens when her family moved to St. Albans, an ancient town some twenty-five miles northwest of London, and a hub of musical creativity.

The beat group the Zombies hailed from there; it was home, too, to the Scottish-born singer Donovan as he burst onto the UK scene under the unwanted tag of the British Dylan. Prior, who was more interested in the original Dylan, quickly found herself at musical odds with almost everybody she met there, a conflict that was finally resolved the day that two friends of hers, singers Sandy and Jeanie Darlington, suggested she quit trying to sing with an American accent and focus on her own. As added encouragement, they handed her a pile of English folk tapes to listen to.

Prior was not immediately impressed, but gradually, she succumbed. She caught the bug, too, for delving into old ballad collections, especially after she met, and started singing in a duo with Tim Hart, the son of a local vicar. Early arrivals to the duo's live repertoire were a couple of choice offerings from Thomas D'Urfey's eighteenth-century songbook, "Long George" and "Pills to Purge Melancholia."

A visit to Cecil Sharp House was an inevitable next step. "Basically we went there one day and didn't come out until we'd heard every scrap of music in the place," Hart—possibly exaggeratedly—remarked. "It took a long time."

He added, "We were going to the clubs every night and, after the initial excitement of hearing somebody perform an old ballad you'd never heard before, you realized that the following night, everybody would be doing it. So we decided to look for songs that other people weren't doing, and make certain that we did them in a way that people would remember. So it wouldn't matter who else started doing it, ours would be the 'original.'"[1]

It wasn't always easy, but across two volumes of *Folk Songs of Old England*, the albums Prior and Hart cut for recording engineer Tony Pike's Tepee Records label during 1968–1969, the duo did indeed tap some striking wellsprings. These include the seldom-heard "A Wager's a Wager" variation of "Broomfield Hill" (43); "Captain Wedderburn's Courtship" (46), "Earl Richard" (68), "Queen Eleanor's Confession" (156), "The Gardener" (219), and "Bay of Biscay" (248). Ewan MacColl and Hermes Nye notwithstanding, there were no readily circulating recordings of any of these ballads to be found, although it must be said that the duo's sources were very much hiding in plain sight.[2]

"Captain Wedderburn's Courtship," for example, was described in their liner notes as "an Anglicised collation of a number of Scottish versions, the brunt of which comes from the collection of F.J. Child." "Earl Richard" and "Queen Eleanor's Confession" were drawn directly from *Motherwell's Minstrelsy Ancient and Modern*. So, they were out there. It's just that nobody else had looked at them.

Bert Lloyd also became a close associate, frequently suggesting songs for the duo to try. "The Gardener" was one of his gifts; a variation on "Proud Maisrie" (219) was another, a text he had collated from various printed sources and feels all the more comprehensive because of it. (Prior would revisit "The Gardener" on Steeleye Span's 2016 album *Dodgy Bastards*.)

The duo was considering their third album when they were confronted with a very intriguing proposition. Ashley Hutchings's departure from Fairport Convention, shortly after the release of *Liege and Lief*, was a most unexpected side product of that band's exploration of traditional music. For Thompson, Swarbrick, Nicol, and Mattacks, it had been an experiment—their interests, while not abandoning the music altogether, lay more in continuing to record original material. Hutchings, however, wanted to delve deeper.

For a time, there was talk of him joining Sweeney's Men. When that fell through, he and Terry Woods, the Irish band's mandolin player, together with Woods's wife, Gay, broke away on their own. Now Hutchings ran into Hart and Prior at the 1969 Keele Folk Club. The pair was invited to dinner at Hutchings's home a short while later, and what became Steeleye Span was launched that same evening.

A visit from Martin Carthy gave the new group a name. He was leafing through one of Tim Hart's ballad books where he came across the Norfolk ballad "Horkstow Grange," and quoted a lyric from the chorus: "pity them that suffer, pity poor old Steeleye Span," and mentioned it as a great band name. Hart agreed.

Late in 1969, the band borrowed a friend's house in Wiltshire to begin rehearsals. Hutchings, meanwhile, had been introduced to Sandy Roberton, a record producer in the throes of establishing his own company, September Productions. Roberton had recently been working for Blue Horizon, a UK label that specialized in British blues music and found massive success with the band Fleetwood Mac. Now Roberton wondered whether a similar operation could be formed around the folk movement. "There was a huge folk scene," he says, "with clubs solely booking those kinds of acts. There was a kinship in the folk world that I don't see any more."[3]

September Productions would not become involved in the actual manufacture of the records. Rather, Roberton favored the direction taken by Fairport's early producer, the American Joe Boyd, signing artists to his own production company (Witchseason, in Boyd's case), recording them, and then leasing the records to a major label.

Thus, across the next four years, September Productions was responsible for a plethora of albums, including no less than three from Hutchings and Steeleye Span, and that long-delayed third album by Hart and Prior alone, *Summer Solstice.* Other September Productions triumphs included Shirley and Dolly Collins's *No Roses*, and a well-packed shelf's worth of albums that are constantly being rediscovered and reappraised: sets by Robin Scott, Al Jones, Spirogyra, Marc Ellington, Shelagh McDonald, Andy Roberts, Decameron, and more.

From this book's perspective, *Summer Solstice* is the key to much of the label's popularity among students of the Child Ballads. Hart and Prior's existing repertoire was swollen by recordings of "False Knight on the Road" (3) and a variant on their last album's "Bay of Biscay" (248), "Fly Up My Cock." But the couple's fascination with the lesser frequented corners of the *ESPB* was shared across the September Productions stable.

It is true that jazzman Harold McNair's adaptation of "Scarborough Fair" (2) was little more than a change in mood for Paul Simon's arrangement, even with Pentangle's rhythm section backing him. But singer Marc Ellington cut a stirring "Yarrow" (214) for the company's *Clogs* showcase compilation, and still Roberton's greatest discovery was yet to come.

Edinburgh-born Shelagh McDonald was an accomplished songwriter in her own right, but a brilliant arranger too, cutting two shimmering albums for September Productions in the early 1970s, before vanishing into self-imposed legend for the next forty years. (She returned in 2013 with *Parnassus Revisited*.)

The sole non-original on 1971's sophomore *Stargazer*, McDonald's arrangement of "The Dowie Dens of Yarrow" (214), is oceanic in its immensity, the crashing waves of percussion tossing the listener from side to side, with only McDonald's assured voice to cling onto. Later that same year, Elton John would take a similar approach to an early take of his "Madman across the Water," and it would be presumptuous to suggest he was influenced by McDonald's masterpiece. But played side by side, it's easy to see why one might want to.

Steeleye Span themselves spent much of their early career in a state of chaos. Gay and Terry Woods departed following the first album, 1969's *Hark! The Village Wait*, with the band still to play its very first live show. It is ironic, then, that the only recorded evidence of the Woods's next project, uniting with the progressive rock band Dr. Strangely Strange under the name Strangewoods, should be a live recording from a February 1971 show at Les Cousins. It includes a muffled, but nevertheless enthralling "Lowlands of Holland" (92) slower than that which highlighted Steeleye Span's debut album *Hark! The Village Wait*, but just as emotive.

Steeleye, meanwhile, were stunning all observers when it was announced that Martin Carthy—at something of a loose end since Dave Swarbrick split for Fairport—would be joining the band. With violinist Peter Knight expanding the sonic spectrum even further, this incarnation of the band cut two further albums, *Ten Man Mop or Mr. Reservoir Butler Rides Again* and *Please to See the King*, in 1971. It was with this lineup that the group went out on the road for the first time, touring the United Kingdom and recording a BBC Radio session for John Peel's *In Concert*, at which their full energies were on open display. "Who knew Martin Carthy could play so loudly?" asked one shocked witness.

Writer Jerry Gilbert captured the enormity of Carthy's recruitment. "Martin Carthy was the man who set alight the blue touch paper—at least so far as the folkies were concerned. Many failed to see why the champion of the revival, who enjoyed a near idolatry following, had lent his name to the propagation of electric folk music, nor could they understand why that doyen of the folk movement, A. L. Lloyd was condoning and even supporting the new direction." [4]

The band undertook other exercises, too. Hutchings, Hart, and Carthy were recruited to accompany singer Ray Fisher (1940–2011) across her debut album, *The Bonny Birdy*, titled for the ballad of the same name (82), and also featuring renditions of "The Silkie of Sule Skerry" (113) and "Mill O'Tifty's Annie" (233). Knight also joined Carthy backing Roy Bailey on his eponymous debut album for Trailer (Bailey had replaced

Carthy in the Three City Four), and one can only regret that the two guests' contributions did not stretch to joining Bailey on the album's "Clerk Saunders" (69).

Steeleye Span's own contributions to the Child canon, spread across the three albums they recorded under Hutchings's leadership, were equally noteworthy, best illuminated by "The Twa Corbies" (26), a delightfully unruly "Four Nights Drunk" (274), and a return to Hart and Prior's favorite "False Knight on the Road"(3) that Jerry Gilbert described as the album's highlight, because of "the unusual metre and accentuation, and the way the voice is used as another instrument."[5]

Steeleye's lifespan, however, appeared to have reached its end. Reflecting upon these years in 1973, Tim Hart claimed Steeleye Span never felt like a "real" band. "It all became so diversified and there just wasn't any direction . . . apart from just coming together and playing together. There was no career feeling about it—you just did it because you enjoyed it and because it was a fun thing to do. We never had that feeling of actually going anywhere. We played the gigs because we were committed to them, but really it was just a coming together of solo musicians."[6]

Neither was Hart alone in feeling this way. Carthy quit following the third album and then Hutchings, too, departed. And while Steeleye Span would recover, for the moment it was Hutchings whose activities most caught the eye, as he formed the first in what became a seemingly endless sequence of Albion Bands, initially as accompaniment on Shirley Collins's next album, *No Roses*.

Jointly credited to Collins and the Albions, *No Roses* also marks a critical highpoint in Roberton's early producing career, although hindsight now layers the entire September Productions roster with renewed luster. "It's nice to see that those albums are still getting talked about," Roberton muses. "They had a certain style and quality. Today, a lot of processed pop forgets to add the subtleties and sensitivities."[7]

It was from the musicians involved in *No Roses* that the first incarnation of the Albion Band was drawn, although the initial lineup of Hutchings, Collins, Royston Wood, and Richard Thompson was shorn very early on, after Thompson drifted away. Around the same time, however, Wood introduced Steve Ashley to the proceedings.

Ashley was working on his projected debut album at the time, under the aegis of producer Austin John Marshall, and the latter—whose marriage to Shirley Collins had ended a couple of years earlier—was initially uncertain whether it was the right move. Steve, however, had no doubts. "Royston told me that the new band he was forming with Ashley Hutchings would probably like to do a couple of my songs. Then, a little while later, Ashley called me himself and invited me to join the band for a rehearsal."[8]

The line-up continued evolving; Collins stepped back and, by the time Hutchings was ready to unveil the Albions, the group comprised Hutchings, Wood, Steve Ashley, American violinist Sue Draheim, and Fairport's own Simon Nicol and Dave Mattacks. By early 1972, the Albion Country Band was locked into place.

With Hutchings's avowed intent of taking his own electric folk visions further than either of his past bands had managed, the group threw themselves into the scenario with gusto. Steve Ashley recalled a considerable amount of their Island Records advance being spent on the most esoteric instruments the musicians could find—Draheim picked up a bass viol, Nicol chose a hurdy-gurdy, Ashley himself became the proud owner of a crumhorn.

Rehearsals brought any number of ideas into the group's remit, including the Chingford Morris Men (Hutchings was working on his *Morris On* project at the time), and amid reports in the UK press that an album was imminent, the group made its live debut at Sussex University on June 9, 1972. Two weeks later, on June 23, they were headlining the Kings Cross Cinema, blasting away the 2 a.m. cobwebs with Richard Thompson's "The New St George." July saw the band record a BBC session, with further British gigs and a short Dutch tour preceding a headline berth at the Courtyard Arts Trust Festival near Gloucester in August.

Their set was dynamic, a combination of the members' own compositions and ideas, together with select favorites from elsewhere. Typically, Draheim opened the set with a violin instrumental that led into "The New St George." Later in the set, the Shaker shape note hymn "Babylon" was "as American as apple pie," as Draheim put it, while the Morris set caught every audience unawares. But the big number, for band and audience alike, was "Lord Bateman" (53).

The Albions' treatment was pieced together from the cylinder recording of Joseph Taylor which Bill Leader had just released on the album *Unto Brigg Fair*. "That's where the tune came from," Steve Ashley recalled. "The other verses came from Bronson, as far as I remember. We sat down together and went through the verses. I imagine it must have been a similar process to the one Fairport used for 'Matty Groves' and 'Tam Lin.' It was a rare occasion in the Albions where the whole band came together to structure the song in a way that would give the drama maximum impact. The links and tags between the verses were vital in maintaining interest, while Dave's drum fills punctuated the narrative."

It was a process that might have made traditionalists blanch, but the Albions' treatment of "Lord Bateman" nevertheless demonstrates the sheer energy that fired the folk revival—the refusal to accept any single interpretation of a given ballad as "definitive," even if such a thing were possible. Yet it also revealed the sheer versatility of the ballads in general, and "Lord Bateman" in particular—a point reinforced later in the decade, when a Turkish theatrical company visited the United Kingdom to perform a stage play based around their own culture's retelling of Lord Bateman's adventures.

Professor Child published no less than fifteen different texts of "Lord Bateman" in the *ESPB*, under his preferred title of "Young Beichan." Ewan MacColl, the New Lost City Ramblers, and Steve Ashley's friend Peter Bellamy were among those who had already recorded versions by the time it arrived in the Albion Country Band's set. Sandy Denny, John Kirkpatrick, Planxty, and Sinead O'Connor all covered it thereafter.

Not one was as magnificent as the Albions' version.

Steve Ashley continued,

> It was a real highlight of the gigs we did. It was quite a responsibility too, with seventeen verses to remember. But it was a joy to sing in front of that rhythm section. It was like driving a train. The main focus for me was Dave Mattacks. I felt like he was responding to the vocal all the way through, whilst I was relying on the rhythms he was driving. Simon, Sue and Ashley [Hutchings] were always inventive on it but it was Dave's drumming that I was singing to. Of all the gigs we did, there was one in Gainsborough, Lincolnshire where I felt we really cracked it.

Shirley Collins was watching from the sidelines as Hutchings prepared to hit the road with the band that she had cofounded. "I recall feeling uneasy about [the Albions] at the time, but that might be because I was disappointed at not being in the lineup, when I had really been the originator with Ashley of the Albion Country Band."[9] For her, too, "Lord Bateman" was the highlight. "I can still hear it in my head, the intensity, passion, and integrity of Steve's singing of it."

Sadly, it looked as though "in my head" would be the only place "Lord Bateman" could be heard, as Hutchings concluded the latest round of live shows by breaking up the band. He would soon have a new lineup underway; the rest of the group moved on to other projects, and Steve Ashley returned to his long-gestating solo album. The problem was, as Austin John Marshall recalled "I was shopping [Steve's] tape around and it kept on getting passed up. And then Steve had the idea of recording the Albion's big feature 'Lord Bateman'."[10] The burning question was, would the old Albion Band agree to re-form for the occasion?

They would. "It had taken so much work and was undoubtedly a highlight of our gigs," Steve Ashley reflected. "It seemed like a nice opportunity for us to get together one more time and do something positive. I was really pleasantly surprised that everybody was up for it."[11]

Marshall immediately contacted Cliff Adams, the head of Sound Techniques Studio in Chelsea, to book a session, and he recalled the ensuing action for American journalist and DJ Edward Haber. "Steve got fired from the Albions, along with Royston Wood. . . . Everyone who works for Ashley Hutchings fears the brown envelope, he always fires people with this note in a brown envelope. But we reassembled them and . . . it was a very tense session, Ashley [Hutchings] and I weren't really speaking, and Shirley and I weren't really speaking." Regardless, he was very enthusiastic about "Lord Bateman."

The interesting thing about the Bateman ballad is, going right back to when John Renbourn [worked with Shirley], we were thinking about early music. We let him have a tape of something called *the Triple Ballade* by Guillaume de Machaut. Now, about this time, John's girlfriend was a lady called Sue Draheim, who was the fiddle player in the Albion Band, and when they were putting the Bateman ballad together, Sue put in *the Triple Ballade*, so that piece did a full circle. It's a wonderful interlude in this marvelous ballad that I think Steve has done the only good contemporary version of. I think it's a fantastic track.[12]

Steve Ashley's debut album *Stroll On*, featuring an epic "Lord Bateman." Author's collection

Finally released in 1974 aboard Steve Ashley's *Stroll On* debut album, the resultant six-and-one-half minutes of "Lord Bateman" rank among the most tumultuous *any* Child Ballad has ever experienced. Rising gently from its first forty-five a cappella seconds; the drums come rolling in, then the guitar and bass, everything building slowly, verse following and layering on verse.

Then, just when you think it's all over, with a moment of silence at two minutes and fifty, the pace changes and now the Albions are in full flood behind Ashley, every instrument in exquisite clarity and the story driving toward its conclusion, seventeen verses on from the outset. Simply listening to it leaves you breathless.

Chapter Forty-One

DON'T PITY POOR STEELEYE SPAN

Bereft of both their founder and their best-known member, Steeleye Span rebuilt. Guitarist Bob Johnson had previously played in a duo with Peter Knight; bassist Rick Kemp had been a formative member of the band that became David Bowie's Spiders from Mars. Producer and manager Sandy Roberton, too, was sidelined in favor of American Jo Lustig, who had previously managed Pentangle. And immediately the changes paid dividends.

With a new label, the major Chrysalis putting its weight behind them, the band's next album, 1972's *Below the Salt* brought Steeleye Span their second UK Top 50 album chart entry and, as the new year dawned, the group suddenly found themselves viewing the future from a wholly unexpected perspective. No longer the sole property of the folk scene, they were suddenly being courted by the mainstream music press—and not for the folk columns alone.

On January 6, 1973, the band appeared on the cover of the best-selling *New Musical Express* beneath the headline "Steeleye Spantastic." Their next album, *Parcel of Rogues* broke them into the Top 30 in mid-1973; while Christmas delivered the unforgettable image of Steeleye Span on British television's weekly *Top of the Pops*, intoning a Latin-language song that was first heard in 1582. The a cappella "Gaudete" brought the band a thoroughly deserved UK hit single, but to an audience accustomed to being drip-fed the glam rock of Slade, The Sweet, and T Rex, Steeleye Span weren't simply weird. They could have been spacemen.

Steeleye Span did not, after all, merely further establish the traditional folk song in the rock milieu. They also suggested that a group didn't nec-essarily need rock instrumentation to do so. Indeed, just two years after

Steeleye Span visit the Royal Albert Hall in London, 1973. KEYSTONE Pictures USA / Alamy Stock Photo

Fairport Convention, Steeleye Span wholly rewrote the rules of electric English folk. Innovation is rarely a lifelong attribute (and, in Steeleye's case, it can be measured in a mere handful of albums), but the quartet of releases bookended by 1972's *Below the Salt* and 1975's *Commoner's Crown* can be regarded not only as flawless examples in themselves, but also ones that rearranged perceptions of the *ESPB* for a generation of schoolchildren.

Music lessons and English classes still utilized traditional ballads under certain conditions, both in print and on any still-playable copies of the Riverside albums, or the marginally less-scratched *Songs and Poetry* series. For young teenagers, however, the horror implicit in, for example, "King Henry" (32) or "Long Lankin" (93), was often diminished by the archaic nature of the texts themselves. And then Steeleye Span came along and neither song would ever read the same again.

"King Henry" was first, a gargantuan romp through what Martin Carthy described as "a heavily anglicised Scottish way of telling the Beauty and the Beast story, the only difference being that the sexes are reversed."[1] On another occasion, Carthy added, "This ballad originated in the Gawain strand of the Arthurian legend. The King Henry in the ballad probably never existed, since the point of the tale is that chivalry has its own rewards."[2]

> *Tak aff your claiths, now, King Henry*
> *And lye down by my side*
> *"Oh God forbid," says King Henry*
> *"That ever the like betwide*
> *"That ever the fiend that won in Hell*
> *"Should streak down by my side."*

> *When night was gane and day was come*
> *And the sun shoine through the ha*
> *The fairest lady that ever was seen*
> *Lay between him an the wa.*

For the listener, however, Steeleye's "King Henry" is anything but chivalrous. The poor King is effectively raped by the monster, even if the story does have a happy ending.

"Below The Salt was a very mild album," Bob Johnson told *Sounds.* "We were careful not to rush in."[3] "King Henry," however, surely undid all the good mild work that the remainder of the album had put in, as the guitarist admitted later, "I remember doing the rock solo in 'King Henry' and thinking how lucky I was to get away with it."

"Even though it wasn't the last track on the record, it felt as though the whole *Below the Salt* album was building up to 'King Henry,'" Tim Hart explained. "You have 'Gaudete,' an unaccompanied Latin Christmas carol, there's the jigs that every folk-rock band was now including, there's good old 'John Barleycorn,' 'The Royal Forester' (110), the 'Spotted Cow,' and 'The Saucy Sailor,' and it's all very traditional, not too electric, not too rocky. And suddenly you're dropped into the middle of this Hammer horror scenario, complete with sound effects from Peter [Knight] and Bob."[4]

Even the accompanying liner notes were pregnant with menace: "The shrill cry of an owl echoed to a woodland hut telling 'The Daughter of King Under-Waves' of the approaching knight. She moved her misshapen form (cursed on her by a wicked step-mother) through the doorway. At every step the ground was shaken, at every turn there blew a storm, the very sky darkened as she passed. But would tonight be the [k]night."

The performance was guided, Hart continued, by a remark Peggy Seeger was fond of making, that unless accompaniment added to the telling of the story, there was no need to add it to the song. "I could see both sides of that argument. If you listen to our 'King Henry,' we open a cappella and yes, we could have continued like that for the full seven minutes and it would have worked fine. We'd have told the story. But that's not what we wanted to do. We wanted to make a movie."

It was a process that Steeleye Span would certainly follow across the next three albums, and Hart admits that the Child Ballads offered the most receptive vessel for their efforts. "It's in the very nature of the ballads." Again, however, Steeleye were offering fresh twists, most notably with the announcement that their next album, 1974's *Now We Are Six*, was to be produced by Jethro Tull's Ian Anderson and feature a cameo appearance from Rick Kemp's old bandmate David Bowie.

"Thomas the Rhymer" (37) and "The Two Magicians" (44) both reeled out of the *ESPB* during the sessions, with Hart recalling,

> Bert Lloyd definitely suggested "Two Magicians," because that's something we'd always loved by him, and because it was a challenge working out a "Steeleye" version of a ballad that probably is best served up as an unaccompanied narrative. "Thomas," on the other hand, lent itself perfectly to us, and the only downside was, when the label was looking for a follow-up single after "Gaudete," that's the one they chose. But it was too long [six and a half minutes on the LP], so they edited it down, which of course you can't do with something like that because the story is so important, and people still complained that it was too complicated, only now they didn't have a clue what was going on.[5]

THE TALE OF TRUE THOMAS

While the legend of the Rhymer, Thomas of Erceldoune, his encounter with the fairy queen, and the seven years he spent in Fairyland can be dated back to the thirteenth century and is as familiar in narrative form as it is in song, very few versions have come to light over the years.

Child, having traced the story and Thomas's gift of prophecy to a date prior to 1320, nevertheless notes only three manuscript versions—the first collected by Alexander Fraser Tyler from a Mrs. Brown in April 1800, a second that he believes to have been "corrupted here and there but only by tradition"; and the third published by Walter Scott.

In recorded terms, it was for a long time similarly underrepresented. Beyond Ewan MacColl, who tackled it several times, and Hermes Nye, only the poet C. R. M. Brookes had hitherto ventured into Thomas territory prior to Steeleye Span's rocking rendition of the Fraser Tyler version.

It would be another decade, however, before "Thomas the Rhymer" was captured "in the wild," when collectors Jim Carroll and Pat Mackenzie met with the renowned traveller singer Duncan Williamson (1928–2007) and his American-born wife, researcher Linda Deigh, at the cottage where they were staying in Fife, Scotland, in 1985. According to Carroll, "Linda had visited him to record songs, and stayed. She did magnificent work in collecting and

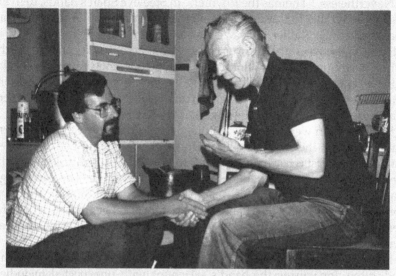

Jim Carroll and Duncan Williamson, at the Traveller's Fife cottage in 1985. It was during this visit that Carroll collected the first ever field recording of "Thomas the Rhymer." Courtesy Jim Carroll

publishing his ballads and stories." (Over the years, the pair were responsible for a number of published collections of Duncan's stories.)

Carroll and Mackenzie were in fact visiting in their own pursuit of the latter. They were gathering material for a cassette collection of British and Irish storytelling, to be released through the Vaughan Williams library, and Carroll recalls, "We'd gone expecting stories. . . . Duncan had the largest repertoire of 'big stories' I knew of [and], unlike any of the [other] storytellers we met, Duncan tended to play to the crowd, which made him the darlin' of the storytelling 'luvvies set.' But when he realized we liked songs, he just sang for us. We spent three glorious days recording Duncan. He was a (sometimes difficult) but very interesting character, a typical example of a singer who collected from his fellow travellers."

The pair collected three Child Ballads on that excursion, including rare versions of "The Brothers" (188) and "Bonny George Campbell" (210), learned from "an old Traveler woman away up in Aberdeenshire, shortly after the war"—Williamson, born in 1928, would have been in his teens at the time.

It was "Thomas the Rhymer," however, that mesmerizes. It runs eight minutes, with Williamson accompanied throughout his epic rendering by Linda; those are her ethereal, almost thoughtless, harmonies that occasionally float lightly behind his voice. And he ends it by declaring, "I heard it from an old man many years ago, and I think I'm the only person in Scotland at the present moment who knows the true story of Thomas the Rhymer."

Nevertheless, "Thomas the Rhymer," in Steeleye Span's hands, delivers a stinging rebuke to those who argue that instrumentation detracts from the storytelling. Rather, Steeleye's arrangement absolutely enhances it, alternating between the "power chords" that accompany, and drive, the actual narration, sung by Prior and Hart together; and the gentler, pastoral breezes that accompany Prior alone, as she speaks the lines of the fairy queen. Let loose in the pop singles marketplace, "Thomas the Rhymer" was a predictable flop. On the album, it was a triumph.

Steeleye Span were certainly not the first performers to spot the potential for edge-of-the seat storytelling in the likes of "Long Lankin" (93—a number they first recorded in 1971 for the BBC), 'Alison Gross' (35), "The Demon Lover" (243), "Thomas the Rhymer" (37), and "The Two Magicians" (44). Up there with "Tam Lin" (39), they rank among the most compelling of all the Child Ballads, at least for listeners of a supernatural bent. But they are also among the most malleable, and that is where Steeleye made their mark.

Bob Johnson was responsible for most of Steeleye Span's arrangements and, often, for pairing the band's selections with unexpected melodies. Hag-ridden and ear-splitting though it was, Steeleye's "Alison Gross" was nevertheless set to a tune that Bert Lloyd knew as the Christmas carol "Down in the Forest." In so doing, Johnson established the template for what would become folk-rock in the 1970s. The guitarist outlined his methodology to Jerry Gilbert:

> I always take a powerful line around which I write the chorus, for example "700 elves from out the wood and foul and grim they were." Apart from that, there was no bowdlerization—I used a powerful minor melody because it's a grim story and needs powerful rock chords. It just seems the most natural medium for that kind of ballad—not tinkling guitars. It's just pure fluke that someone like myself happened to have in his influence a combination of traditional melody and an upbringing of rock and roll and modern music——if you didn't have one or the other you couldn't do it.[6]

"Alison Gross," for example, had been recorded but rarely over the years, although its airings were certainly striking. Having been forebodingly growled by John Laurie on *The Jupiter Book of Ballads* in 1959, and again by Ewan MacColl in 1967, it was also in the repertoire of Lizzie Higgins, whose version was subsequently adopted by Malinky.

It was recast as a vocal jig by Dave and Toni Arthur in 1970 and given a comedic twist by Jon Rennard the following year. Nobody, however, had ever thought to apply it to crunching chords, feedback, and screaming solos; nobody had ever conceived a sound effect so apt for the line in which the song's narrator is turned into an ugly worm. And nobody, for sure, had ever dreamed of ending the song not with a coda, but the kind of tortured electric bellow that the Who, at the height of their pop art auto-destructive days, would have bowed down before.

The last (from this era, at least) of Steeleye Span's most enduring contributions to the Child Balladry is "Long Lankin" (37), from their 1975 album *Commoner's Crown*. Coproduced by the band and Robin Black, and featuring a guest turn from actor Peter Sellers (voice and ukulele on the closing "New York Girls"), *Commoner's Crown* found room for four Child Ballads, as sensational and murderous as ever, and all delivering the goods. "Lankin" is joined by the vicious infanticide of "Little Sir Hugh" (155), the foreboding "Demon Lover" (243), and the plaintive "Elf Call" (40), the latter noteworthy as the first ever commercial recording of the ballad Child knew as "The Queen of Elfan's Nourice," in which a human mother is lured away from her own newborn, to suckle instead a fairy baby. But "Long Lankin," as was always his nature, slaughters them all.

Grey Malkin recalls his first exposure to the ballad . . . courtesy of Steeleye Span: "'Long Lankin' has held a particular fascination for me ever since I first heard Steeleye Span's haunted and eerie version at the tender age of around eight or nine whilst listening to my father's cassette collection. There was something about the combination of Maddy Prior's delivery, that unsettling high register she sings the piece in, along with the text itself that I found (and still find) utterly bewitching." For the Hare and the Moon's own version, recorded for 2010's *The Grey Malkin* album,

> It felt imperative that the element of the otherworldly was invoked and captured. I wanted to illustrate something of the quiet, horrific inevitability of the unfolding scenario, as well as the moments of uncontrolled, extreme violence. My intention was also to capture the nightmarish, dreamlike quality of a figure, perhaps not human, entering the relative safety of a home and committing acts most unnatural. If I have captured even a glimpse of the uneasy, haunted quality that I found so attractive in Steeleye Span's "Long Lankin" that I first heard all these years ago as a child, then I am a happy man.[7]

"There was always a degree of mischief making, at least on my part," Hart conceded.

> The Child Ballads have always been raised up so high, to the point where you can call them the sacred cows of traditional music. No other printed collection has ever been treated with the same care as Child—how many albums can you think of built around the songs in Pepys's *Garland* or Percy's *Reliquary*? Of course that respect is thoroughly deserved. It is what Child intended it to be, a collection of the best ballads he could find. But that doesn't mean it has to be handled with kid gloves, every ballad shown due reverence, and because I was aware that a lot of people in the traditional field would listen to what we did with the Child Ballads, I wanted to make sure they'd get a shock when they did.[8]

Chapter Forty-Two

SILLY WIZARDS AND
THE SPRIGUNS OF TOLGUS

Steeleye Span were not the only band delivering such surprises to the traditional community. In 1970, recording their third album, Led Zeppelin turned their attentions toward "Gallows Pole" (95), a ballad popularized by Lead Belly in the 1930s, but very much reintroduced to British folk fans by Redd Sullivan, a regular on the club circuit of the early-mid 1960s. It was not wholly an unexpected step for Led Zeppelin to take. Vocalist Robert Plant had frequently spoken of his love of traditional music, and guitarist Jimmy Page's past as one of Britain's most in-demand session men saw him record with the likes of Donovan, Al Stewart, Marianne Faithful, Roy Harper, and Vashti, among many more. Page had also been listening to a lot of Bert Jansch and Davy Graham recently; Plant looked back to a teenaged fascination with American guitarist John Fahey; while "Gallows Pole" itself was based upon a version Page found on the Folkways album *Gallows Pole and Other Folk Songs*, by American singer and luthier Fred Gerlach (1925–2009).

Gerlach's own version, according to his liner notes for the album, was "based on one of Lead Belly's songs, which itself has a long history dating back hundreds of years in England. The rhythms and finger-picking styles have taken me four years to evolve. It is my favorite number, but it is so strenuous that I must perform regularly for a week before I'll attempt it."[1]

"He was one of the first white people on Folkways records to get involved in Lead Belly," Page explained. "We have completely rearranged it and changed the verse. Robert wrote a set of new lyrics. That's John Paul Jones on mandolin and bass, and I'm playing the banjo, six-string acoustic, 12-string and electric guitar. The bloke swinging on the

Led Zeppelin's Robert Plant and Jimmy Page during an acoustic interlude in 1973. Heinrich Klaffs, CC BY-SA 2.0 / Wikimedia Commons

gallows pole is saying wait for his relatives to arrive. The drumming builds nicely."[2]

Plant, too, has enthused about the performance, telling *The Guardian*, in 2014, that it proved integral to the development of his own singing style. "The outro of Gallows Pole is great, with all the manic singing I'd over-cooked horrendously prior to that. It started having some meaning. I was learning how to syncopate. I was flourishing."[3]

Led Zeppelin III met a mixed reception. Arriving just a year after the blues bludgeoning megalith that was *Led Zeppelin II*, its acoustic base and wide-open airs outraged the group's core constituency. But traditional folkies, too, were unhappy, dismayed by both the treatment of "Gallows Pole" and by Zeppelin's reputation as one of the giants of heavy metal.

Tim Hart, on the other hand, "thoroughly enjoyed it. It proved how versatile the ballads were, beyond the folk world, and it rattled some cages as well." It was also, he reckoned, "the opening shot" for the rancor-ous public debate that prefaced the following year's Keele Folk Festival, at which chairman Ian Campbell oversaw a heated argument discussing the merits of amplified folk music. "It was our own Newport '65,"[4] Hart concluded succinctly, referring back to the response to Dylan's decision to "go electric" at that event. The seeds had already been sewn—the English Folk Dance and Song Society itself was divided over the growing spread of electric instrumentation, with members resigning, or at least resigning themselves to denouncing the heretics who were suddenly massing at the gates.

Accusations that the electric musicians were simply "doing it for money" flew, at the same time as the complainants completely ignored the fact that very few people—at that time—had ever made any money from the English folk scene. If you were looking to "get rich quick," pumping several thousand volts into "Early One Morning" really wasn't the way to go. The debate itself was never settled, for how could it be? As an enraged, and provocatively leather jacket–clad Martin Carthy snapped, "Why can't we just accept that some people like electric folk music, and some people don't?"

He was in good company, too. As Bob Johnson told *Rolling Stone* in 1974, "A. L. Lloyd, who's one of the greatest experts on folk music any-where in the world, was saying that he liked Steeleye Span and thought we were perfectly valid because, in whatever age folk music has been performed, it has always been played on the instruments available at the time. This, in effect, is exactly what we're doing. We just try to make it live again."[5]

Neither were Steeleye alone in this ambition. New names were mak-ing themselves heard, it seemed, every time you stepped out. In cult (if not critical) terms, a handful of names from this period has since been elevated to various degrees of immortality. But there was room, too, for Spirogyra, Al Jones, Synanthesia, Andy Roberts, Gryphon, the JSD Band, Hedgehog Pie,[6] and many more. And that was aside from the already established folk club favorites who now stepped out of the shadows to stake a claim on the public ear—Anne Briggs released her first album in 1971, Frankie Armstrong followed suit in 1972.

In Paris, the reclusive Tia Blake (1952–2015), born in Columbus, Geor-gia, but now living in France, was recording the album *Folk Songs and Ballads* with local musicians for the French SFPP label. "Hangman" (95) is the record's sole Child Ballad, but Blake's warm presence enfolds an entire LP's worth of well-chosen traditional numbers. Ireland, too, was making its mark with the emergence of Tír na nÓg, Planxty, and Horslips, among others.

Planxty were the most "traditional" of the three, in that they were the least concerned with self-composed material. Three albums between 1972 and their breakup in 1974 saw them regularly dip into the folk canon, with a stirring "Raggle Taggle Gypsy" (200) among the highlights of their self-titled second album.

Their third album, meanwhile, was titled for a variant of "The Well Below the Valley" (21) that had never been found "in the wild" in either Britain or Ireland, until collector Tom Munnelly heard John Reilly of

Boyle, Co. Roscommon sing it. It now stands as more or less the definitive rendition of the ballad.

Neither did Planxty ever lose sight of their roots; indeed, band member Donal Lunny would soon be producing the debut album by countrymen Mick Hanly and Michaél Ó Domhnaill, 1974's *Celtic Folkweave*—home to a soothing "Heathery Hills O'Yarrow" (214). When Hanly returned to the ballad for 1980's *As I Went over Blackwater*, he extended it with further verses and composed a new tune, too, with Lunny and bandmate Andy Irvine again in attendance.

Julie Henigan remains a Hanly fan:

> One of the greatest figures in the Irish folk revival! I love his first two solo albums, as well as his contributions to *Celtic Folkweave*. He decided to become a singer/songwriter, however, so I didn't follow him as much after that. However, I got to open for him at a little club in Dublin sometime in the '90s. He was so sweet, and told great jokes. He also gave me permission to feature his famous composition "Jessica's Polka" in my first guitar book.[7] I don't know for sure whether he influenced my guitar style (I was already playing mostly in DADGAD), but he probably did—certainly, there are a lot of similarities in our guitar playing.[8]

Tír na nÓg, too, had their traditional roots. Although the duo was conceived as a songwriting vehicle for Leo O'Kelly and Sonny Condell, both had frequented the Dublin folk club scene, such as it was, during the 1960s. O'Kelly recalls:

> It was not at all as vibrant as the British scene. The clubs were confined to a handful in Dublin, and were as much social as musical. One of the first, and best, was The Auld Triangle in Mount Street. A couple of us would pool petrol resources and take the trip up from Carlow in the early/mid-60s. A lot of people who are still playing now would play there completely acoustically. You could on a night see The Wolfe Tones, Paul Brady, Tony McMahon, members of The Dubliners. . . . A few other clubs started, The Coffee Kitchen and The Universal, which Sonny and I frequented in '69, but the Child Ballads would have probably mainly been heard in the more "serious" clubs, like The Auld Triangle, though I never heard anyone referring to them.

Indeed, he readily admits "I know little about them myself," but looking back, "I find I sang a few: 'Geordie' [209], 'Willy O Winsbury [100]. . . . I even sang 'Lord Randall' (12) with The Tropical Showband in my mid-teens! I'd heard the Jean Ritchie version, and we did it as an old time waltz."[9]

"Willie O'Winsbury" remained in Tír na nÓg's live repertoire even after their relocation to London; and, years later, following their 2015 reunion, the duo cut a new version during the sessions for that year's *The Dark Dance* album. "It sounded lovely, but I doubt if we'll use it," O'Kelly admitted. "Ours is the same version most people sing nowadays; it is really Andy Irvine's, of Sweeney's Men [and Planxty], version, and apparently came about as a result of him mistakenly matching lyrics and music from the Child Ballads."

For folk-rock aficionados, these really were golden years. Throughout the previous decade, acts such as these would have seen most, if not all, of their efforts confined to the handful of independent record labels that then catered for the folk audience—Topic, Transatlantic, and Trailer. Now, however, the major labels were paying close attention.

One didn't even need to be a folk band *per se*. Newcastle's Lindisfarne certainly met some of the criteria when they achieved their first UK hit with "Meet Me on the Corner," an original composition that nevertheless sounded as though it could be steeped in history. But Dublin's Thin Lizzy were an undisguised hard rock outfit when they pumped up the traditional "Whiskey in the Jar" for their first smash.

Away from the pop charts, too, a host of acts on the progressive rock scene dipped into folk stylings, if not necessarily songs, as they cut albums for nominally rock-oriented labels such as Vertigo, Charisma, Dawn and Harvest: Magna Carta, Comus, Dando Shaft, Renaissance, Bridget St. John, Keith Christmas, Dr. Strangely Strange, Daddy Longlegs, ex-Fairport founder Judy Dyble's Trader Horne.

Elsewhere, Tír na nÓg preceded Steeleye Span to Chrysalis, Dick Gaughan and Horslips proved unlikely labelmates for Elton John at DJM, Gay and Terry Woods joined Planxty at Polydor, and the JSD Band linked with EMI's Regal Zonophone imprint. Some were destined to enjoy lengthy careers; others flared briefly but brilliantly. And most of them included Child Ballads in their repertoire.

Trees, who formed in early 1969 and signed with CBS before the summer was out, were a quintet cast somewhat in the Fairport mold, but eminently distinguished by the silken tones of Celia Humphries (1950–2021). They cut just two albums, 1970's *On the Shore* and 1971's *The Garden of Jane Delawney*,[10] and throughout both, Trees rage and range across a variety of stylistic canvases. The key, however, was in the manner in which they blended them into an overall band sound.

Their "Glasgerion" (67) has been described (by *Electric Eden* author Rob Young, who refers to it by its more familiar rock-era title of "Jack Orion") as "a romping Grateful Dead-style freakout." Their "The Great Silkie" (113), on the other hand, is akin to entering an empty room and wondering where the sound of singing is coming from—at least until the band breaks into earshot. "Lady Margaret" (74) and "Geordie" (209) also made it onto Trees' albums; "Prince Heathen" (104) was included in their live show, and a BBC session. All radiate such light that it is a tragedy that Trees were felled so soon.

Not every aspirant found a record deal. Vulcan's Hammer developed a dedicated following around their native county of Kent around 1973, a quartet whose live repertoire included a quirkily choral "The Two Magicians" (44) that, sadly, did not make it onto their one and only LP, 1975's self-released *True Hearts and Sound Bottoms*. Hopes that they might take the next step up the ladder, however, were dashed.

Things moved slowly, too, for the marvelously-monikered Spriguns of Tolgus. Formed in 1972, very much in the shadow of Steeleye Span, the band's first recordings date from 1974 and a privately produced cassette, *Rowdy Dowdy Day*. A heroic and indeed adventurous outing, it saw the band turn their hand to two Child Ballads, both of which were courageous in their own way: "Matty Groves" (81)—for who could hope to eclipse Fairport Convention? And "The Laily Worm and the Mackerel" (36) because nobody had ever tried to electrify those particular waters before.

Steeleye's own Tim Hart was especially impressed, taking the band under his wing and encouraging their next album, *Jack with a Feather* (complete with the band's interpretation of "Two Magicians," recorded by Steeleye just the previous year) released by their own Alida Star label. That in turn finally alerted major label Decca, which had largely lain silent throughout the folk-rock boom, and *Revel, Weird and Wild* followed in 1976.

Now the band (who had shortened their name to Spriguns) could really let rip. They revisited the Laily Worm, tackled "The Outlandish Knight" (4) and "Lord Lovel" (75), but most impressive of all was "Sir Colvin" (61), a gripping recitation rendered all the more thrilling for distilling to a mere six minutes a ballad known only from the original Percy manuscript that runs to 200 verses (including what Child describes as "a large omission after the 125th verse").

Of course much of the original drama is absent from Spriguns' rendering; we join the song as the King sends his daughter to take bread to the ailing Sir Colvin, and he pledges his love to her. But her challenge that he go into battle with the Eldridge Knight is here, with the clash itself following in a musical passage that is heavily redolent of Steeleye's "King Henry."

The abbreviation of the ballad is not without its casualties. In the original, the Knight is a giant with five heads, every one of which must be removed. Here, sadly, it takes only the loss of one *hand* to prompt the Knight to concede defeat, and off rides Sir Colvin to marry the King's daughter.[11] But the performance is relentless regardless, and the album as a whole certainly deserved a greater response than it actually received.

Across this same period, when the movement was at its commercial peak, British folk-rockers and their more traditional kin were responsible for upward of two hundred different Child Ballads finding their way onto vinyl and into the marketplace. Often, they picked the same source version. In 1972, both Dave Burland and Tom Gilfellon delved into the pages of Gavin Greig's *Last Leaves of Traditional Ballads and Ballad Airs* when they approached "The Cruel Mother" (20), although for very different reasons. According to Gilfellon, that book provided the basic source for his version; Burland, on the other hand, lifted his tune from Greig (from the ballad "Bonnie Annie"—24) but does not say where he found the lyrics.

The Clutha's 1973 recording of "Blue Flowers and the Yellow" (25) likewise came from Greig; their "The Gaberlunzie Man" (279) in 1974, from Ramsay's *Tea-Table Miscellany*. Another variant on "The Cruel Mother" was unearthed by Linda and Paul Adams for their 1975 album *Far Over the Fell*. "The Sun Shines Fair on Carlisle Wall" was learned, by Linda, from her English teacher, Ann Dickens (also a singer of some repute around their native Cumbria), the title replacing the familiar "Greenwood sidey-o" chorus. The entertainingly named Silly Wizard also recorded the version, as "Carlisle Wall," on their self-titled 1976 album and, in so doing, inspired Alasdair Roberts's version (as "The Cruel Mother") in 2005—"The melody and refrain of this version of the ancient infanticide ballad are adapted from the singing of Andy Stewart," Alasdair notes.[12]

Dick Gaughan learned the fratricidal "The Bonnie Banks of Fordie" (14) from a child's skipping song his mother used to sing, and twenty years later, in 1992, the band The Old Blind Dogs learned his version for their own album *New Tricks*.

Derek and Dorothy Elliott took their 1972 interpretation of "Lady Maisry" (65) from Cecil Sharp, while Martin Carthy recorded more than a dozen Child Ballads during this period, spread across the albums *Landfall* (1971), *Shearwater* (1972), *Sweet Wivelsfield* (1974), and *Crown of Horn* (1976). Among these was numbered the seldom-recorded "Betsy Bell and Mary Gray" (201), sung in duet with Maddy Prior; and "King Knapperty" (33) in which the titular character goes a-wooing, only to discover his prospective bride has "tauchy teeth and kaily lips . . . wide lugs . . ." and an eye like "a rotten plumbe."

There again, her suitor was not exactly an oil painting, and when the couple kissed, "the slaver that hang between their mouths wad hae tethered a two year auld bull." One alternate title for the ballad, says Child, was "Queen of All Sluts."

Carthy was also rightfully proud of his own tempestuous take on "King Henry" (32), "a song that I very much wanted to do for a very long time," only to be frustrated by his failure to find a satisfactory tune. He finally settled upon the traditional American tune "Bonaparte's Retreat," and, as he put it in his liner notes, "with respectful nods towards Mike Seeger, Doc Watson and many others, I swiped it."[13]

Others have been "swiping" from him ever since, with the same respectful nods. Timothy Renner, of Stone Breath recalls recording his own vision of "The Famous Flower of Serving Men" (106), a song Carthy first recorded on *Shearwater*.

> To my ears, when Carthy does a ballad, he often attacks the guitar in such a way that it feels really similar to clawhammer banjo. So what I did was not try to learn a "banjo version" of what Carthy was doing on guitar—but instead feel out something that would still support the vocal melody. I do all of this by memory. I'm not playing Carthy's version and trying to do what he did. I couldn't if I tried. So, I guess I'm injecting a bit of the "folk process" back into the proceedings. That's not entirely intentional or unintentional, really, but more the way I approach music.[14]

Bruce Rowland reflected,

> Martin, despite most of a lifetime spent practicing and evolving a technique to frighten the life out most of the rest of us, has found time for seemingly endless research. In the many lists and archives of the Ballads, very few have tunes and I am grateful for his time and boundless good nature in providing me with info. Martin solo or in company is, as everybody knows, something to behold. His renderings of the ballads are beyond perfection. To my ear, the heavyweights are "The Maid and the Palmer" [21] to an English Country Dance tune called "From Night to Morn"—to be found in the *Sussex Tune Book* by Vic Gammon and others; "Prince Heathen" [104], to the tune for "The Broomfield Wager" to be found—he thinks—in *Last Leaves of Aberdeen Ballads* by Gavin Greig; and "The Famous Flower of Serving Men" [106].[15]

That latter title, which Carthy set to a melody borrowed from Hedy West's recording of the song (and which in turn was lifted from the American folk song "The Maid of Colchester") remains one of Carthy's most impressive Child Ballads. Rowland described it as "probably the best either Martin or F. J. Child has ever sounded."

Another great Carthy Child Ballad is "Long John, Old John and Jackie North" (251), from 1979's *Because It's There*. Carthy referred to it as a reworking of "Long Johnny Mor," the story of a fourteen-foot-tall giant and his love for the king's daughter, and correspondingly "full of swash and buckle." The same album also included "The Death of Young Andrew" (48), "a reworking of a severely holed set of words."[16]

Later still, Carthy would piece together the first ever "complete" text of "Rockabello," a "Sir Lionel" (18) variant for which Child gave just one verse, from a manuscript titled *Antiquities of Worcestershire*.

Sir Rackabello had three sons
Wind well your horn, brave hunter
Sir Ryalash was one of these
And he was a jovial hunter

Recorded with wife Norma Waterson in 1996, it was created "with the help of every version I could lay my hands on, a shoe horn, a great tune from a Hertfordshire woman called Kathleen Williams (actually for the song 'The Crabfish') and a great band." And thus, "the story of the slaughter of the giant's pet pig is given full rein."[17]

Chapter Forty-Three

THE ELECTRIC MUSE

Steeleye Span dominated the folk-rock scene of the 1970s, their reign culminating in 1975 when the Mike Batt produced *All Around My Hat*, spun off the British Top 5 hit of the same name. Nor is it likely to be coincidental that this same year also saw the release of the key folk-rock document of the age, the book and accompanying four LP box set *The Electric Muse: The Story of Folk into Rock*. The work of journalists Karl Dallas and Robin Denselow (for the British side of the story), and Dave Laing and Robert Shelton (handling the US), and published in the United Kingdom only, *The Electric Muse* was very much written for an audience whose knowledge of the subject was predicated around artists who had either enjoyed radio play or had impacted upon the UK chart in recent years, a feat that a growing number of so-called folkies had mustered.

Steeleye Span and Fairport aside, such Les Cousins regulars as Al Stewart, Roy Harper, and Sandy Denny were all selling in appreciable quantities, while Ralph McTell had reached number 2 on the British chart with his "Streets of London" earlier in the year. In telling the stories of where artists such as these had come from, *The Electric Muse* also shone daylight upon a host of "lesser" names, a task that the accompanying album echoed with exquisitely selected highlights. But oddly, just a smattering of Child Ballads—Fairport's "Tam Lin" (39) and Martin Carthy's "Scarborough Fair" (2) among them.

However, *The Electric Muse* also informed readers (and listeners) that, for all their popularity, Steeleye by no means had the field to themselves. Fairport Convention were still at work, with Sandy Denny having returned after a six-year absence, in time for 1975's *Rising for the Moon*.

(She departed again, soon after.) Martin Carthy was at his prolific best, and fellow Steeleye escapees Gay and Terry Woods too.

There was even a folk-rock concept album, *The King of Elfland's Daughter*, by Steeleye's Peter Knight and Bob Johnson. It was only later that it was revealed the pair had been on the brink of departing the band, and Chrysalis okayed the project in the hope of convincing them to stay. The ploy failed, as did the album.

But was folk-rock truly as preeminent as its acolytes liked to believe? Probably not. Ewan MacColl was still a major force to be reckoned with, while October 1977 saw Jean Redpath host the first of two BBC TV series, *Ballad Folk*. Across five episodes in 1977 and four the following fall, Redpath's guests included the Gaughers, Lizzie Higgins (who performed "Willie's Fatal Visit"—255), Jimmy Hutchison ("The Beggarman"—279), and Archie Fisher—who also appears on *The Electric Muse*, performing "The Twa Corbies" (26) with wife Ray. His broadcast rendering of "Fine Flowers in the Valley" (20) was no less inviting, as he breathed new life into a fragment discovered by Robert Burns.

The most dramatic performance, however, awaited listeners to BBC Radio 3. At 6.30 p.m. on Friday, July 1, 1977, the station broadcast the sixth and final part of *Arthur's Folk*, a series hosted by Dave Arthur, and billed as his own "personal account of folk music of all kinds." The episode was titled "Tamlin," and the *Radio Times* breathlessly described it as "the magical story of a head-strong girl who lost her honour in the woods and battled with supernatural forces to win back her lover—retold in a new folk-rock-radiophonic setting."

Although Arthur had both guested upon and hosted folk radio in the years since he and wife Toni ceased recording, he was scarcely one of the music scene's most visible denizens. In fact, it was Toni who was better known at that time, as a regular presenter of the children's television staple *Play School* since December 1971. Now she hosted the international edition of BBC Radio's *Folkweave*.

To listeners, however, *Arthur's Folk* fascinated not only because it reached back to what many people, as the seventies neared their close, regarded as a simpler, happier era than the strife-ridden, strike-happy, punk-lashed landscape of modern Britain, but because he shared, with Toni, authorship of one of those old LPs that everybody seemed to have on their want lists but few were ever likely to find, *Hearken to the Witches Rune*. There, "Tam Lin" (39) had already received a devastating workout, a furious, drama-laden recital that was only amplified by a live performance in which the elements appeared to play their own part in the action. Appearing at Rochester Cathedral in Kent, Toni had just reached the line "out then cried the Elfin Queen" when a massive roll of thunder was followed instantaneously by a dazzling flash of lightning. "I nearly wet myself, the whole audience went aah, and the next line is 'an angry queen was she.' God, it was really, really frightening."[1]

Eight years later, the final part of *Arthur's Folk* was to give the Arthurs the opportunity to relive that same moment when they linked with Paddy Kingsland of the BBC's Radiophonic Workshop to recreate "Tam Lin," not as mere folk-rock, for that had been done so many times now, but as *electronic* folk-rock. The Radiophonic Workshop's forte, after all, was creating outlandish and even alien music for such BBC shows as *Doctor Who*, and Kingsland approached this latest project with gusto.

The version started conventionally, wholly unaccompanied. Slowly, carefully, a basic folk-rock sound emerged—drums, guitar, keyboards, and Toni's recorder. Then, percolating into that, before building to a massive crescendo, the swirls and shrieks of Kingsland's other-worldly electronics. It was shattering.

Arthur's Folk was the opening segment of the *Lifelines* magazine program, and if copies of the broadcasts exist today, then they have been well hidden. Back issues of the *Radio Times*, however, offer a taste of the six broadcasts. Part one, "From Ragas to Riches," told "the story of how the unlikely marriage between Indian Ragas and Irish folk song gave birth to a new and exciting brand of British music." Part two, "Tiger and the Hand-Jive," was billed as "an unfinished story featuring Mr. D'Arcy Ferris, Jinky Wells, an Aberdeen weaver who sings Gaelic mouth-music to Navajo Indians, and Albion, whose future is in the past." June 10 brought part three, "Virtuosi or Vagabonds," and its "stories of folk musicians who delighted audiences in Connemara [farms], drummed them up at street corners and horse fairs and brought traffic to a standstill in Dundee." Part four, "Revival of the Fittest," was "an everyday story of country folk with Tom Forrest, Webb's Wonders, singing Coppers, Silly Sisters, Dransfields, Watersons and Rakes"; part five, "A Once and Future Nation!" investigated "the developing story of Celtic music, from Gaelic psalm singing to Breton rock 'n' roll with bagpipes." All leading up to the cataclysmic climax of "Tamlin." And all, too, at a time when history insists that British popular music in general was so bound up in punk rock that it had absolutely no time for anything else.

Tell that to Professor Child.

It is true that in terms of media exposure, popular awareness, and, yes, overall record sales, the first half of the 1970s marked a high-water mark for traditional music that was at least as profound as that which it had experienced in the United States ten years previous. But whereas that earlier flowering was ultimately stymied by the artists themselves moving away from traditional song and into original composition, the 1970s generation was less readily swayed. The splits that ended Steeleye Span and Fairport Convention in 1978 and 1979 were shattering of course (both bands would re-form), but their examples could not help but live on—presided over, perhaps, by the now omnipresent Martin Carthy and Ashley Hutchings, but free to choose their own directions. Indeed, by the time Ewan MacColl and Peggy Seeger delivered their own declamation of "folk-rock" in the liner notes to *Blood and Roses*, also in 1979, such protestations sounded so old-fashioned that they themselves might have been lines from an ancient ballad.

In strict chronological terms, it was a period that opened with Bob Dylan's onstage reunion with Joan Baez, as she joined his fall 1975 Rolling Thunder tour of America, and the nightly interlude during which the two duetted rekindled bittersweet memories of times gone by. "Blowing in the Wind," "Never Let Me Go," and Merle Travis's "Dark as a Dungeon" all drew roars from the audie,nce, but surely the moment that came closest to time travel was when they paired up for an elegantly countrified "The Water Is Wide" (204), a song that, if the truth be known, they probably grew tired of even hearing, let alone singing, as they circulated the folk clubs of early sixties New York. It was inescapable then; it remains endemic today. But for the five or so minutes that they devoted to the ballad on those alchemical nights that fall, you could see the years slip back from both Dylan and Baez.

As for punk rock, perhaps the most significant indication of its true impact can be drawn from the program notes for BBC Radio disc jockey John Peel's nightly show, so often described as the upstart new genre's most fervent and devoted champion. January 1977 saw him playing music by the Chieftains, the Bothy Band, and the Boys of the Lough, alongside rhapsodic devotions to new albums by Emmylou Harris and Pink Floyd.

In February, John Martyn, Leo Kottke, Roy Harper, and Ralph McTell were among the acts he championed, alongside a specially recorded studio session from June Tabor, her third in just two years. And so it went on, with Nic Jones, Martin Carthy, Michael Chapman, the Albion Dance Band, Five Hand Reel, Dick Gaughan, and Fairport Convention all as likely to be heard as any punk talent. And at year's end, when Peel dedicated a show to his twelve favorite sessions of the year, there was Tabor again, with twelve minutes of unaccompanied folk song.

June Tabor first came to mainstream attention in 1976, as one half (the other was Maddy Prior) of the Silly Sisters. She was, however, scarcely a newcomer to the folk world. Born in Warwick on December 3, 1947, Tabor credited Anne Briggs's 1965 EP *The Hazards of* Love—a gift from her sister, who had also just given June a record player—with launching her musical career. Writing the liners to the Briggs compilation *A Collection*, Tabor recalled, "I went and locked myself in the bathroom for a fortnight and drove my mother mad. I learned the songs on that EP note for note,

June Tabor, onstage in Boston, 20212. candyschwartz from Boston, USAderivative work: Alison ♥, CC BY 2.0 / Wikimedia Commons

twiddle for twiddle. That's how I started singing. If I hadn't heard her, I'd have probably done something entirely different."

She told author David Burke, "Then I got The *Stewarts of Blair* topic album. This was a completely different style of unaccompanied singing, the travellers' way, the swoops and long held notes, quite a nasal way of singing. I was really captivated by that as well, so I taught myself how to do that too, just by copying the recording. Then the two styles got very gradually mixed into the way I sang."[2]

The result was exquisite. Introducing Tabor on BBC Radio's Folkweave in the late 1970s, singer (and host) Toni Arthur remarked, "To my mind, what makes her special is the depth and huskiness of her voice, whilst at the same time she manages to get amazing clarity on the higher notes."

Martin Carthy was another influence, sartorially, at least. Tabor told *The Guardian* in 2011, it was the sight of the leather jacket–clad Martin Carthy appearing on Sunday evening television that prompted June and her friend Frances to visit the recently opened Heart of England folk club in nearby Leamington Spa, a smoky room above the Fox and Vivian public house. There, Tabor was horrified when her friend marched up to the organizers and announced that her friend was a singer. Aged sixteen, Tabor's first ever public performance comprised "Michael, Row the Boat Ashore" and "Kumbaya."

A couple of Dylan numbers followed them into her set as she spread her wings, songs she learned from records by Briggs and Shirley Collins too. By the time Tabor arrived at Oxford University, where she became treasurer of the Heritage Club, she was absorbing traditional music from every direction. She moved onto the local club circuit, and, over the next decade, was occasionally captured on record. When one of her regular haunts, the Stagfolk folk club, announced it was compiling an album of its most popular regulars, Tabor was among the contributors. Released in March 1972, *Stagfolk Live Folk* included her versions of the folk songs "Searching for Lambs" and "The Bleacher Lassie of Kelvinhaugh," alongside tracks by fellow local luminaries Ron Simmonds, Clan Mountain Dew, Colin Grant, Rod Bayton, Dick Taggart, and Bonded Boots, who offered up the album's sole Child Ballad, "The Banks of Green Willow" (24).

Two years later, a somber reading of "The Fair Maid of Wallington" (91) was among three Tabor tracks included (alongside Nic Jones) on Folksound Recording's 1974 *First Folk Review Record*, and proved somewhat prescient in its very first line—"When we were silly sisters. . . ." It was Maddy Prior, whom she'd met a year or so earlier, who introduced her to the song, the story of a woman who, having seen five sisters die in childbirth, demands that her baby be cut out of her stomach. Tabor pulled together her lyric from among the seven different versions published by Professor Child.

Tabor told *Street Life* magazine, "Maddy and I had been singing together for a bit in a purely fun sort of way. We'd been at a festival together singing harmonies on choruses and things—and it sounded nice—so we decided to actually try to do something. Then we did floor spots at folk clubs—not paid—just turning up, and that gradually built up over about two years or so."[3]

The following year, 1975, saw Tabor invited to record a session for John Peel. Prior's bandmate Tim Hart promptly volunteered his services to accompany her for the occasion. "And then Maddy was going to do a solo album and she decided that she wanted to do some of the stuff that we'd been doing. That's how the [Silly Sisters] project got off."[4]

Tabor had already been offered the opportunity to record an album, by Topic around 1973. She turned it down because she couldn't decide what she wanted to include on it, and only returned to the idea once the Silly Sisters project was complete.

Three Child Ballads appear on their eponymous debut—the unaccompanied "Burning of Auchindoon" (183—Hedgehog Pie performed and recorded a very different live version at the Brum Festival that same year); a gentle "The Lass of Roch Royale" (76), which Prior first heard from Paddy Tunney; and Tabor's solo "Geordie" (209), based upon the version Child found in Johnson's *Musical Museum* of 1792, and with Martin Carthy accompanying her on guitar. And they alone spoke volumes for the respect with which Tabor viewed the *ESPB*.

Work on Tabor's much delayed solo debut album commenced soon after, and again Prior's influence was felt in the song selection. Commenting on her "The Broom of Cowdenknows" (217), Tabor described it as "a compilation of several texts, anglicised with the aid and inspiration of Maddy Prior." She regretted, too, the need to abandon (for undisclosed reasons) one particular verse, accredited by Child, via William Motherwell, to "the recitation of Mrs. Thomson of Kilbarchan, a native of Dumbarton where she learned it":[5]

> *Whan twenty weeks war past and gane*
> *Twenty weeks and three*
> *The lassie began to spit and spue*
> *And thought lang for blinkin' ee*

Sadly, upon returning to the ballad for her 1996 *Singing the Storm* album, Tabor did not restore the errant verse.

"Waly Waly" (204), "Young Waters" (94), and "Bonny May" (217) completed Child's contributions to *Airs and Graces*, with the latter pair intriguingly featuring instrumentation—a doom-laden harmonium from Cajun Moon keyboardist Jon Gillaspie and Nic Jones on fiddle and guitar. (Gillaspie also accompanied her on her return to the John Peel show, where she showcased "Young Hunting" (68) and the rarely performed "Young Alan" (245).

Tabor acknowledged it was an awkward transition.

When I worked with Maddy's back-up band, I found that very odd. . . . I'd convinced myself that I couldn't sing accompanied anymore. I had tried it with various people but I've been unaccompanied for so long that I've got into this business of sorta free time, as opposed to being within a strict rhythm. I never sing anything the same way twice–I just change from verse to verse, singing it first one way and then another. All of which is not exactly conducive to singing accompanied.[6]

Child was alongside Tabor once more at the BBC in February 1977, when she opened her third, wholly unaccompanied, John Peel session with a rousing "Lord Bateman" (53). However, Jones and Gillaspie both returned to her side for *Ashes and Diamonds*, Tabor's long-playing contribution to the soundtrack of 1977, most notably for an "Earl of Aboyne" (235) that opens upon a playful Jones guitar pattern, effortlessly setting a mood that is rudely and abruptly disrupted by Gillaspie's synthesizer bursting in as the song nears its climax. It's a startling juxtaposition, suggested perhaps by Dave Arthur's reworking of "Tamlin" for the BBC earlier in the year. Certainly, it is the first overt appearance of a synth on a commercially released Child Ballad, at a time when the instrument was still considered a novelty even within progressive rock and disco circles.

Punctuating Tabor and Jones's performance with little apparent regard for the song itself, without doubt, the Earl's tale would have been told equally effectively without it. At the same time, however, it can only be considered a successful intervention, and one that was to presage a host of subsequent synthi-folk hybrids.

Tabor would not rank among these conspirators, but she has remained a captivating interpreter of the Child canon across a stream of subsequent solo albums as well as a further Silly Sisters adventure with Maddy Prior, in 1988. Two years later, a union with the Oyster Band saw them include "Annachie Gordon" (239) in a John Peel session. It was Tabor's sixth appearance on the show.

Her ear for fascinating variations, too, has remained keen. In 1983, Tabor's *Abyssinians* LP saw her turn to a "Bonny Hind" (50), which she learned from singer Peta Webb in the early 1970s. Tabor, in turn, passed it on to Tony Rose (who recorded it on his 1976 album *On Banks of Green Willow*) and Martin Carthy, who included it on 1998's *Signs of Life*.

Another tremendous performance was Tabor's return to "Young Hunting" in its "Love Henry" variation, a cut that she and violinist Mark Emerson demoed but did not immediately release in 1990. It had, she admitted, been savagely revised once it left its Scottish homeland and resettled in North America. "I've often found it amusing and distressing," she remarked in the liners to her *Always* anthology,

the way the great ballads metamorphosed when they crossed the water. Something as disturbing as "Young Hunting" with its supernatural references, with the corpse bleeding when the murderer approaches and the real weight of horror that is in that tale of murder and the attempted concealment by the former true love, turns into a kind of Disneyfied version that becomes "Love Henry." And yet it still has so much strength. Now I appreciate much more the power of the Appalachian versions, whereas I might once have said, "Yes, but it's not as good as the original." This one sneaked through because it's got so many good lines in it. Particularly, *"Then up and spoke a pretty little bird / Exceeding on a willow tree"* You've got to sing a song with that in it! The bird flies away into the sunset to star in the sequel, while everybody else dies unhappily ever after.[7]

The following year, touring with Emerson and fellow fiddler Giles Lewin, "The Wind and the Rain" (10) found its way into the live show. A recording made in Germany that April also made it onto the anthology, with Tabor noting, "There were lots of versions of this song about." The version she heard from American banjo player Jody Stecher, on 1977's *Going up on the Mountain* LP, however, "had a kind of immediacy on it. "I like the refrain—probably it's the English in me; talking about the weather—but it was particularly the verse about making a little fiddle out of her breastbone and how the sound would melt a heart of stone. I thought that was a really nice way of putting it. It told the story very strongly. It's a good one to do with voice and fiddles. Mark put a tune called 'The Falls of Richmond' in the middle."[8]

An Echo of Hooves in 2003 saw Tabor devote an entire album to the Child Ballads, revisiting old favorite "Lord Maxwell's Goodnight" (195), but also serving up shimmering versions of "Sir Patrick Spens" (58), "The Duke of Athole's Nurse" (212), and more. She uncages, too, the most stygian of all takes on "The Cruel Mother" (20), adapting her text from Cecil Sharp and Maud Karpeles's Appalachian collection, most notably the version sung to them by James Chisholm of Nellysford, Virginia, in 1918. The finest of all, however, was the coarsely fiddle-led "Hughie Graeme" (191), set to a tune "mostly adapted" from the Appalachian piece "The Falls of Richmond." Incredibly, Tabor promptly surpassed the album version when she appeared on BBC TV's *Later . . . with Jools Holland* that same year, and drew it to even wilder extremes.

Tabor's influence has never waned. Across the decades, and particularly in more recent years, her versions of the Child Ballads have inspired a plethora of fresh interpretations, often with her direct involvement. Planning a recording of "Clerk Saunders" (69) in 2005, Martin Simpson called her up "to remind me of the verses she had sung to conclude her text."[9]

The following year, Chris and Siobhan Nelson credited Tabor's teachings for their "Young Waters" (94) on the album *Day Has Dawned*; Damien Barber and Mike Wilson adapted Tabor's "Bonny May" (217) for 2011's *The Old Songs*; and Kate Burke and Ruth Hazleton's 2015 recording of

"Waly Waly" (204) was "learned from the singing of June Tabor." And when Jack Rutter unearthed "Fair Janet and Young James" (64) for his 2019 album *Gold of Scar and Shale*, he took the melody from Tabor's recording of "The Old Garden Gate"—*not* a Child Ballad, but a popular Irish traditional song known also as "As I Roved Out."

Chapter Forty-Four

OLD ROOTS, NEWER ROUTES

Looking back from 2012, *The Guardian* journalist Colin Irwin reflected, "The decades following [Nic] Jones's accident were largely barren for British folk music."[1]

Nine years later, journalist Robin Denselow opined, "Folk and folk rock fell from fashion after the glory years of the seventies."[2] Jeanette Leech, author of 2010's *Seasons They Change: The Story of Acid and Psychedelic Rock*, mourned that, by the end of the 1970s, "most mainstream rock journalists had lost or shunned their collective folk vocabulary."[3]

Even John Jones, whose Oyster Band was one of the brightest sparks of the decade, remarked, in a *New Musical Express* interview in 1988, "The folk world's become part of the heritage industry. Everyone went into their various specializations in the '70s, getting their Morris steps right and creating this village way of doing it, you know, 'We're gonna dance Ducklington' etc. . . . and turning out on special days . . . dress[ed] up as bloody cobblers."[4]

The temptation, then, to regard more or less the entire span of the 1980s as a traditional musical wasteland, then, isn't simply tempting, it is all but prescribed. But how easy can it be to so readily dismiss a decade that began with Paul Simon performing "Scarborough Fair" (2) on *The Muppet Show*, and the release of Jean Redpath's *Lowlands*, with her so haunting approach to "Riddles Wisely Expounded" (1)? And that closed with Stone Roses' borrowing of "Scarborough Fair"[5] for the melody of their "Elizabeth My Dear"; and Current 93's near-nightmarish invocation of "Oh Thou Coal Black Smith" (44)?

A decade that saw the birth, in late 1981, of broadcaster Fiona Ritchie's still vibrant tribute to Celtic music, *The Thistle and Shamrock*, on

The Oyster Band onstage in Wickham, August 2006. SGBailey, CC BY-SA 3.0 / Wikimedia Commons

WFAE-FM, Charlotte. That witnessed the emergence of Home Service, Pyewackett, the Pogues, and Brass Monkey; the returns of Pentangle and the Watersons, represented both by the original generation, and a second, as Lal's daughter Maria Knight and Norma and Martin Cathy's Eliza took their own first steps toward their birthright?

That saw the release, as a privately produced cassette, of Peter Bellamy's leviathan *The Maritime England Suite*, broadcast (as *We Have Fed Our Sea*) over two parts in December 1982 / January 1983, and dignified by epic retellings of "Sir Patrick Spens" (58) and "Sir Andrew Barton" (167)?

Or one that was so beautified by the Ballet Rambert's 1986 production *Sergeant Early's Dream*, "a folk ballet," as one of the accompanying musicians, Steve Tilston puts it,[6] its stunning Christopher Bruce choreography accompanied by nine traditional songs, including "Barbara Allen" (84) and "Geordie" (209)?

Perhaps this book is biased, as it looks only toward how the Child Ballads fared very nicely throughout what so many people dismiss as a doomed decade. Beyond that, however, the only thing this period truly lacked was indeed the collective responsibility toward traditional music itself that John Jones alluded to. Because, what the media called—and the public referred to as—folk music instead underwent the same factional splintering as sundered so many other musical genres of the period.

In commercial terms, the most significant of these was that which the likes of poet Attila the Stockbroker and the Anglo-Irish bar band The

Pogues (featuring Terry Woods of the earliest Steeleye Span) led out of the punk movement, all octane and energy and impossible to ignore. There were others, however, including some whose names are not even memories any longer. For example, the blonde youth who played to a crowd of maybe eight or nine at a west London folk club around 1978 and whose set included an acoustic Sex Pistols–shaped approximation of Child 239, snappily retitled "Annachie Gordon in the UK"; and Germany's Subway to Sally, a self-styled folk-metal band that emerged in the early 1990s and, for a short while at least, led traditionalists to a very merry jig.

Folklorist Hester NicEilidh, whose online Robin Hood Project did so much to relaunch the *ESPB*'s entire canon of Robin Hood ballads, happily acknowledges, "I'm a child of the punk revolution, so my introduction to folk music was through punk-folk artists of the early '80s, such as the Pogues, Billy Bragg, and the Mekons." But it was only a steppingstone, because "that initial exposure led me to explore the music of the '60s British folk revival, and eventually led me even to obscure field recordings of oral tradition singers of Canadian logging songs and Scottish bothy ballads."[7]

American singer-songwriter Gillian Welch, too, "was a modern girl, I'd grown up listening to punk rock," and had performed as bassist in a goth band and drummer in a psychedelic surf combo. But, interviewed by the BBC in 2016, she was adamant that, when you "connect" with traditional music, "you realise they're human stories . . . rife with wisdom and knowledge and they were offering lessons about life. [Besides,] the unflinching subject matter of these songs, the sometimes dark, sometimes tragic, sometimes brutal and murderous content really appealed to me because I recognized that also was a truth." She then performed a "Cruel Mother" (20) that was part of an entire repertoire of songs that never made it onto record or even stage. "This is something [musical partner David Rawlings and I] just play in our living room, never performed this, never even played it on stage; these are songs for around the house, this is stuff that kind of informs everything else we do."[8]

Punk-infused folk even reached Australia. Based in Yass, New South Wales, songwriter Daniel Kelly heard his first Child Ballad from Scottish-born singer Alistair Hulett, of what has been described as Australia's answer to the Pogues, Roaring Jacks. That band broke up in the early 1990s and Hulett launched a solo career that included three albums with Dave Swarbrick and the version of "The Fair Flower of Northumberland" (9), which Kelly heard on ABC radio one day.

"That was my first exposure to the Francis Child collection that I remember," says Kelly. "A few years later a local Gaelic singer from the group Triantan lent me some of Alistair's albums, which include many settings of the Child Ballads."[9] Kelly's 2022 album of Child Ballads, *Love, Murder, Magic and Song*, includes many that he first heard from Hulett.

Among acts such as these, traditional music played only an incidental part in the overall performance; it was the *sense* of traditional music, whether conveyed by historic lyric, archaic language, or simply the deployment of seemingly appropriate instrumentation, that was the gateway to further investigation. Even the Home Service, whose 1986 album *Alright Jack* was feted by *Melody Maker* as "a landmark-cum-watershed in the annals of the electric muse," favored their own material over the traditional, although when they did merge the two, such as in the medley of the self-composed "Sorrow" and the Trad. Arr. "Babylon" on that same record, the effect was dynamic.

Under such conditions, the Child Ballads found themselves, for the first time since at least the mid-1950s, sinking back into the hands of either popular entertainers, longtime veterans, or thoughtful aspirants. Where were the new Spriguns of Tolgus? The next Hedgehog Pie? Ewan MacColl and Peggy Seeger's *Blood and Roses* collection of the *ESPB* was a child of the 1980s, but so was light entertainment superstar Cliff Richard's "The Water Is Wide" (204). So was the American heavy metal act Queensrÿche's sphacelated mutilation of a song they'd first demoed as the unknown Myth in 1982, "Scarborough Fair" (2). An excruciating excursion, Led Zeppelin's "Gallows Pole" it certainly isn't.

The reformed Steeleye Span recorded a live album at the Siego Club, in Rimini, Italy, in August 1982, but could only recycle those ballads that they had recorded up to a decade earlier. A subsequent handful of barely satisfying studio recordings offer better documentation of the band's ever-changing lineup than any fresh assaults upon expectations. And it would be some years more before Steeleye Span returned to the musical peaks they had hit so frequently in the mid-1970s. Nevertheless, the group's continued existence today renders them still the most successful folk-rock band of all—and one that is still capable of asking fascinating questions about ballads we feel we already know backwards.

Discussing Steeleye's 2006 recording of "The Whummil Bore" (27), Maddy Prior remarked, "I have been fascinated by this ballad for many years, and have thought of it as a fragment, but on further reflection it is the most unique snap-shot of a moment." The tale of a servant who spies upon the princess as she dresses, "it tells a massive story in so few words. It also leaves the mystery of many questions. A whummil is a gimlet or piece of drilling equipment and the bore is the hole made by it. Which adds a rather bewitching dimension. Who bored the hole?"[10]

Who indeed?

Yet Steeleye were very much outliers. Fairport Convention, reconvening as a working band after half a decade spent merely regrouping for their annual Cropredy Festival, had little time for any ballads beyond "Tam Lin" (39) and "Matty Groves" (81), and even that was little more than a shade of the sometimes twenty-minute workouts to which they once subjected folk's most famous double murder.

Pentangle, re-forming in 1983 around a nucleus of founder members Jacqui McShee, Bert Jansch, Terry Cox, and Danny Thompson (John Renbourn was initially involved but departed to work toward a music degree), would record a very distinctive, and truly characteristic "Yarrow" (214) on 1984's *Open the Door* comeback album, but the key was that it was very characteristic.

The Irish band Planxty, too, were back in circulation, reforming in 1979 after six years away, and the following year's *The Woman I Loved So Well* certainly lived up to expectations with its epic recital of "Little Musgrave" (81) and a dramatic "Johnny of Brady's Lea" (114). But how old were those expectations? "Lord Baker" (53) was also on their agenda as the band worked on through the 1980s, but live performances reached back to the Child Ballads that highlighted the original group's catalog— "The Jolly Beggar" (279), a song that tradition claims was written by King James V of Scotland; and "The Raggle Taggle Gypsy" (200).

Of course, Martin Carthy was still out there, departing the reformed Watersons, with whom he'd performed since 1977, and uniting with accordion virtuoso John Kirkpatrick in a new band, Brass Monkey. An eponymous 1984 debut album delivered a stupendous "The Maid and the Palmer" (21), and in the eyes of the faithful, Carthy could again do no wrong. But again, where were the *new* thoughts and *fresh* directions? Or, perhaps more accurately, where were the critics with the experience and understanding to recognize progress when it was standing in front of them?

The Oyster Band's roots were laid down at the University of Kent in Canterbury in 1976, a loose collective of friends and musicians that only slowly consolidated into a full-time lineup—and then did so under two names, the Oyster Ceilidh Band and Fiddler's Dram, both with much the same musicians. Signing with Dingle Records, it was Fiddler's Dram who debuted first, with the album *To See the Play* in 1978; the Oysters followed up with 1980's *Jack's Alive*, only for the spotlight to fall back on Fiddler's Dram after a cut from their two-year-old debut album, the lighthearted music hall–esque "Day Trip to Bangor" became a shock UK top-three hit.

It was a strict one-off, in terms of both success and execution. Both its parent album and the Oyster's records comprised genuine traditional fare, with *To See the Play* boasting enthusiastic (if perhaps over-fiddly) versions of "False Knight on the Road" (3), "Keyhole in the Door" (27), and "The Two Brothers" (49). But it was "Day Trip to Bangor" that audiences wanted to hear when they went to see Fiddlers Dram in concert, and those expectations spelled the end of the group.

An eponymous second album was necessarily constructed around the bonhomie of the hit, including a suitably jolly "Farmer's Curst Wife"

(278), set to the melody of seventeenth-century composer Henry Purcell's "Lillibulero"—wryly, the same tune was then employed as the theme to the BBC World Service hourly news broadcast. It was the group's final gasp. The Oyster Band, however, continued on, maintaining the light-hearted edge of their alter-ego, but retaining their original eye for well-curated traditional favorites. Or, as the *New Musical Express* put it in 1987, "Once upon a time, admitting to a fondness for English folk was akin to confessing a savage case of crabs. Then came The Oyster Band, the accept-able face of Anglo-folk; a band that walked the line between trad dads and rebel rhythm kings; that dragged Uncle Tom Cobbley and all bodily, screaming, into the '80s."[11]

"Annan Water" (215) was a highlight of the Oyster Band's superbly titled 1982 album *English Rock 'n' Roll: The Early Years 1800–1850*; "Bonnie Susie Cleland" (65) and what they called the "Banstead Downs" variant of "Geordie" (209) highlighted 1985's *Liberty Hall*, following original vocalist Cathy Lesurf's departure for the Albion Band. By 1988, the *New Musical Express* was referring to the group as the leaders of something called "the New Wave of British Folk"—ultimately a very short-lived movement that probably meant more to the critical establishment than the musicians themselves. However, the Oyster Band's 1990 collaboration with June Tabor marked the high point of their career, the album *Freedom and Rain* allowing both artists the space to be themselves, while simultaneously merging into a cohesive whole.

Tabor later claimed that the rendering of "Annachie Gordon" (239) that they premiered on their joint John Peel session in 1990 was deemed such a failure that they never returned to the ballad again. Such judgments were harsh, but perhaps its exclusion made space for one of the other Child Bal-lads that was included in the union's repertoire, "Susie Clelland" (65) or a "Dives and Lazarus" (56) that opened like a spy theme and turned into a surf rocker. It was absolutely unexpected, and joyfully brilliant.

Chapter Forty-Five

MURDEROUS BALLADS

When David Tibet concluded his first full Current 93 album, 1984's *Dogs Blood Rising*, with two minutes of whispered a cappella distortion that merged a scarifying invocation of Paul Simon's "Sound of Silence" with a comparatively angelic "Scarborough Fair" (2), it was most widely regarded as a dislocating finale to an album that was otherwise rooted in Gregorian chant, combined with Tibet's own interpretative meditations.

Nobody, Tibet included, foresaw it becoming the first step toward an eventual career shift that not only saw Tibet position himself among the most extreme of all Child Ballad interpreters, but also ignited a new musical genre through which folk traditions as a whole were reborn for the upcoming new century. The fact that Tibet apparently had no real awareness of what the Child Ballads were, and certainly little interest in "folk music" itself, only heightened the dichotomy.

Originally full-body straitjacketed in the experimental/industrial music that uglified the fringes of early 1980s rock culture, the Current 93 project has woven itself, since then, through a variety of stylistic changes, dictated wholly by Tibet's personal brand of mysticism and esoterica. It was a process that, by 1989, had led him to *Swastikas for Noddy*, an album cast deep in the shadow of one of Tibet's most recent discoveries, Shirley Collins, if also—albeit inadvertently—shot through with more than the passing specter of Spirogyra.[1]

Collins had not recorded any fresh music since 1978's *For as Many as Will*. Her marriage to Hutchings had collapsed, and, with all self-confidence ripped away, she simply stopped. The music she had recorded beforehand, however, was still available, and Tibet was smitten. "As soon as I heard Shirley she was immediately goddess," he told author David

Martyn Bates and Mick Harris's *Drift* album includes nightmare-inducing visions of "Lucy Wan" and "Long Lankin."

Keenan.[2] "She just sounded like somebody's heart singing without coming through their mouth."

Acting, too, on the impetus of a handful of other recent discoveries, including the Incredible String Band (*The Hangman's Beautiful Daughter* was a particular favorite) and Trees, Tibet set about creating an album that was wholly individual, but shot through nevertheless with a mood that was half sinister nursery (Noddy is a popular British children's book character created by author Enid Blyton), half the sense of rural menace that dominated such early-seventies cinema fare as *Straw Dogs* and *The Wicker Man*.

Leafing through an old book of English folklore, Tibet came upon a set of lyrics that slipped effortlessly into the overall mood of the gestating album, a lengthy ballad of seduction and shapeshifting called "Oh Coal Black Smith." It was Child's "The Two Magicians" (44), but Tibet did not know that; was unaware, too, that so many artists before him had recorded it. He just knew it was right for *Swastikas for Noddy*.

Performed over a gentle acoustic guitar bed and a faint backing chorale, Current 93's "Oh Coal Black Smith" is a fascinating, not to mention disquieting, performance, although it should not be surprising that the ballad was so willingly put to such apocalyptic use. In 1982, Kate Bush took the shape-shifting flavor of the ballad for her own, similarly cataclysmic "Get Out of My House" (from the album *The Dreaming*), and acknowledged Bert Lloyd's influence in the process.

Neither was Tibet wholly unaware of what he had created, although he was being defiantly ironic when he dubbed it "apocalyptic folk," not once suspecting that the term would, as author Jeanette Leech noted, "[become] a genre title itself." Thus, she wrote, "Current 93's music marked the first sustained radical folk music project since punk."[3] Nevertheless, Tibet is quick to disown any suggestion that he was now making, or was even interested in, anything that could be termed folk music. "*Swastikas for Noddy* wasn't a folk album at all, and if it pushed [anyone] toward a 'folk' trail, then they would completely have missed said trail. I had/have no interest at all in 'folk' music, apart from the early 'true' recordings, and a few ÆONS such as Shirley, Peter Bellamy, and Anne Briggs."[4]

The Current 93 albums that followed *Swastikas for Noddy* nevertheless continued in what the faithful saw as a similar direction. Tibet returned to the traditional canon to create a tempestuous ten-and-a-half minute "Tamlin" (39); he also made contact with Shirley Collins and, in November 1992, finally drawing her out of seclusion to contribute vocals to his *Thunder Perfect Mind* album. That same year, Tibet's Durto label released a compilation of Collins's earlier work, *A Fountain of Snow* (a live anthology, *Harking Back*, would follow in 1998), and in 1996, she appeared on Current 93's *The Starres Are Marching Sadly Home*.

Neither had he finished with the Child Ballads. Tibet appropriated the melody of "The Rolling of the Stones" (49) for the track "AntiChrist and Barcodes" on 1998's *Soft Black Stars* album. Even more dramatically, he and Shirley's sister Dolly were actively scheming an entire album of Child Ballads together at the time of her death and had even drawn up a tentative track listing.

Current 93's deployment of traditional and folk themes did not go unmarked; nor, for that matter, did it spring from naught. The year before "Oh Coal Black Smith," the *New Musical Express*'s Len Brown declared that "wild things are afoot in the folk world. In the wake of The Pogues' inebriated, reeling conquest of this planet, The Oyster Band and their ilk have gone mad. Things may never be the same again at the church youth club."[5]

Acts such as Millions of Dead Cops, the Horseflies, and Polkacide were invoked to back up his claim, and neither were these outfits alone, as Grey Malkin adds such names as "The Iditarod, Drekka, and the Jewelled Antler collective. Kitchen Cynics had been quietly working away prior to then too."[6] And looking back from a distance of a quarter of a century, in 2015, Portland musician and Child Ballads devotee Timothy Renner reflected on the late 1980s,

There seemed to be something in the air as Current 93 and friends started going folky in the UK and Swans [1989's *The Burning World* album] went acoustic [in the States]. Those were important albums to kind of confirm that my desire to explore acoustic/folk music—to see that others were experimenting with these sounds and songs as well. I was on the path already, loving early music and finding Nick Drake and, especially, Leonard Cohen before I ever heard Current 93. But having still one foot in more extreme and experimental music as well. Hearing bands that were attempting to marry these things which seemed so disparate before—it was like a signpost saying "what you seek is this way" or something similar.[7]

He was not alone. In 1991, American musician Bobin Eirth—known as B'eirth—launched In Gowan Ring at a tiny eatery, Café Haven, in Provo, Utah; two years later, he was recording his debut album on an eight-track cassette in his attic room in Salt Lake City, "inspired by various folk music from around the world, Middle Eastern to British Isles, and . . . a naive yearning to capture something of these feelings in my music."[8]

It was, by his own admission, a tentative beginning. Reviews of the ensuing *Love Charms* compared B'eirth's music to the Incredible String Band and the German art group Amon Düül II, acts he had never heard before. He investigated them, at the same time throwing himself into Celtic mythology, and relocating to record the next album, *The Twin Trees*, in Asheville, North Carolina.

Like Current 93, In Gowan Ring's music can be termed folk—apocalyptic or otherwise—in spirit far more than execution. Found sounds, improvisation, and personal mythologies and discoveries are the guiding principles, with the musical aspect touched upon more in subject matter than delivery. Still, a 2001 album recorded under the name Witch Hunt—in actuality, B'eirth alongside the Blood Axis duo formed by authors Michael Moynihan and Annabel Lee—included two versions of "The Rolling of the Stones" (49), one by the conjoined bands, one by In Gowan Ring alone; the following year the same team tackled "Two Magicians" (44) for their album *The Rites of Samhain*.

Another enthusiast was Martyn Bates, whose band Eyeless in Gaza rose out of the post-punk UK scene of the early 1980s. In 1994, seven albums into a parallel solo career, Bates linked with Mick Harris, from the equally unexpected ranks of the hardcore bands Napalm Death and Scorn, to record *Murder Ballads (Drift)*, a meditation on four folk ballads, among them "Lucy Wan" (51) and "Long Lankin" (93).

"You might say that my approach is akin to that of a kind of poacher, filching what I need from the surviving body of British folk song," Bates muses.

I hated school . . . in so many ways I feel that music was my education, my key to a wider world—seeing as how I shut myself off from the formal side of access to knowledge. The radio, and music . . . backs of album jackets, books . . . and in that way I began building up my own education, my own picture. Also, I had a kindly uncle who used to take me along to folk clubs to see people like Martin Carthy. That was quite an experience to be exposed to stuff like that so young—singing which included the Child Ballads, and their myriad meanings/predilections/musings.[9]

The union with Harris came about after Bates heard *Dreamt about Dreaming*, the drummer's first album under the name Luli. "Mick had pretty much just began an amazing departure, or side-step, from his stuff with Napalm Death and Scorn"—wholly ambient, but menacing too, his electronic soundscapes evoked all manner of emotions in Bates but, most pronounced of all was a sense of "Eureka! I'd occasionally sang 'Long Lankin' and 'Lucy Wan' totally a cappella—sometimes just to friends, and occasionally on stage when the setting seemed 'correct.' [But] for years, I'd been scratching my head trying to figure how on earth to present these thousand-verse, static/linear [ballads] to the audience that I already had."

Luli answered that question. "The music *spoke to me*—it felt dark, sinister, yet benign somehow . . . mythic and open—all that kind of stuff: it was the perfect vehicle with which these songs could interact beautifully. A music that was already much fashioned along the child song/murder ballads axis, in that everything slowly unfolded, everything dropped away to create an enlightening/illuminating revelation. To me, it seemed as if all this empty space seemed laden with mythology, with archetypes, with storytelling."

Murder Ballads (Drift) would be followed by two further volumes, *(Passages)* and *(Incest Songs)*, and while Bates consciously avoided making any changes to the texts that he selected ("it would seem like a kind of sacrilege; to consciously fuck with them [is] asking for trouble"), he admits to taking "screeds of liberties" with the melodies that he draped over Harris's backdrops. "The Bonny Hind" (50), for example, borrowed the melody of "The Christ Child Lullaby," as Bates explained:

"The Lullaby" is a quite beautiful song in itself, but I have to confess that I was chiefly interested in the way the magical/mythological aspects of "The Christ Child" song rubbed up against those of the murder ballad. The intent was purely playful, kind of alchemical. Singing those words, and that tune to this juxtaposing kind of estranged, moonstruck soundscape, it does something to you, turns your head around for that twelve-minute duration. And then, it leaves you with its effect—as both a singer and/or as a listener. You have to really listen and get right inside, though . . . focus/meditate/tune in.

A very different rendition of "Long Lankin" accompanied Bates alone onto Dutch radio in 1996, based this time upon a borrowing from the Incredible String Band.

I've always loved [their] music. It's hard to minimize their long-term, far reaching, sweeping influence, in terms of the polyglot stew they dished up for us all—musically, lyrically, and in terms of acting as a scattershot introduction to a whole smorgasbord of splintered world music. There is an amazing, (and often dismissed) fantastic suite of soundtrack tunes that they laced together as side two of the *Be Glad for the Song Has No Ending* album [1970], one of [which] sounds to me like a cracked marriage between some ancient Eastern European and Asiatic strains of music. I love all of *Be Glad*, but that particular tune—a tune that I *know* I've also heard somewhere on one of the Alan Lomax/David Lewiston collections—it's particularly haunting. So, I set it to "Long Lankin," and . . . *voila*, here's something really happening.

Neither were these projects, magnificent as they are, the end of Bates's relationship with the Child Ballads. Eyeless in Gaza recorded several for 2000's *Song of the Beautiful Wanton* album; and across one half of 2005's *Leitmotif*, Bates alone took a simple banjo-powered "The Twa Sisters" (10), then broke it up between "some moonstruck sketches, [which] allowed space to step right inside the things that the words and music are making happen in terms of painting that particular picture . . . a bit like a flickering signal from a wonkily tuned radio station, drifting in and out and off to unasked-for places."

The following year Harris and the sound artist John Everall (d. 2014) introduced Bates to experimental composer Max Ester. The pair quickly started work on an album that Ester initially wanted to title *Sit a Spell*, speaking to "the storytelling side" of what they intended to create; it was ultimately released, in 2007, as *Songs of Transformation*, a fitting title for a set that included versions of "George Collins" (85), "The Two Magicians" (44), "The Cherry Tree Carol" (54), and "The Cruel Sister" (10).

Again, the approach taken is absolutely unlike any other treatment to which the Child Ballads had hitherto been subjected; Bates continues, "It's music of the wind, the elements, played by the elements, on invented instruments. Therefore, it just made sense to sing magical/transformative songs when putting together this project. We met, I sang the songs to him, and then later we improvised the songs, recording them live in the studio as we did so."

The Child Ballads remain an integral part of Bates's repertoire. His Twelve Thousand Days project, launched with Alan Trench in 2000, included a wiry "The Cruel Brother" (11) on their 2021 album *The Birds Sing as Bells*.

But were one to seek out Bates's most influential Child Ballad recording, it would be his "Seven Yellow Gypsies" (200)—not for the performance itself, but because it found inclusion, alongside Witch Hunt's "Two Magicians," on *Hand/Eye*, a compilation album released in 2002 by the American h/e label.

The collection's intention was simple—to introduce what had by now become a dizzying community of acts working beneath a bewildering host of banners, all apparently spun off from David Tibet's Apocalyptic folk genre—Neo-folk, psychedelic folk, acid folk, wyrd folk, and more. Grey Malkin explains "The *Hand/Eye* compilation was an eye opener for a lot of people I know,"[10] not only for the sudden corralling of some twenty-six acts working within the traditions, but also for the stark glare it shed on the Child Ballads as the apex of all that the new genre(s) espoused.

Witch-Hunt and Bates were joined by contributions from Amps for Christ ("False Knight on the Road"—3), which opened the two-CD set, and Alasdair Roberts ("Willie-O"—248), a stylistic gamut that embraced everything, it seems, from near silence to deafening noise. Also present were the aforementioned Stone Breath, the vision of Oregon-based musician Timothy Renner. His repertoire, too, positively boils with repurposed Child Ballads, although on this occasion, he was represented by an original composition.

Chapter Forty-Six

OF OWLS AND HARES

Like so many other artists operating around the turn of the millennium, Timothy Renner's musical background developed out of

the most extreme music. I grew up listening to hardcore punk, then moved on to grindcore and, eventually, harsh experimental music. However, when I was in college, I started seeing an early music ensemble somewhat regularly—I think this was the beginning of me starting to really appreciate the textures of acoustic music. However, I always try to find deeper sources, the influences of bands I may like . . . and their influences, and so on. So, I got really into the folk revival stuff and then anything I could get my hands on as far as field recordings. At this same time, I'm learning how to play music and learning how to write songs. I began to realize I am quite drawn to ballads—these old storytelling songs—and most of what I know about songwriting, about phrasing, and how songs are put together—that comes from playing and singing those old ballads. A lot of my lyrics contain ballad-type phrasing. The language of song, for me, was largely informed by the ballads. As to what I like about them—well, someone once said that bad songs don't get to become traditional. They are great stories with great melodies—and they often explore these topics that appeal so much to me—spells and murder and witches and lost love. Wonderful![1]

A key influence on Renner's musical development was Tom Rapp (1947–2018), whose own band Pearls Before Swine has since been anointed among the founding fathers of this new strain of folk, while barely touching traditional song. Renner and Stone Breath bandmate Prydwyn worked as Rapp's backing band throughout the late 1990s and early 2000s; in fact, it was Rapp who gave Renner his first copy of the complete Child Ballads.

Renner hurled himself into those pages, acknowledging,

I'm fairly obsessive about ballads. I often try to find the most complete version of the story. Our version of "The Famous Flower of Serving Men" [106, from 2014's *Children of Hum*], for instance, was over thirty verses—but it's such a great story filled with amazing images! I didn't want to cut out one verse. In doing that, I think I'm trying to be a service to the story, but this also means combining verses or chopping them up in other ways so maybe a verse from version B which was sung with a different melody gets tweaked a bit and shifted to fit in the melody of version A. These changes though—it's all part of the folk process which, in my view, isn't terribly concerned with freezing things in time. What gets passed down is the story—and maybe the melody stays with it—but the songs mutate and change and probably take new meaning as they go from generation to generation.

Stone Breath's "The Famous Flower of Serving Men" started life through his love of Martin Carthy's version.

In fact, I'm not sure I've ever heard another version, now that I think about it.[2] Usually with trad songs, I learn the vocal melody, then figure out the instrumental melody—in this case cello banjo . . . and then I set about figuring out the lyrics. "Famous Flower" is such a great story—with so many great lines and symbols from Eleanor cutting her hair upon her child's tombstone to the king sitting upon that same stone as the dove cries tears of blood and tells the tale of her son's murder—and there's probably twenty to thirty more fantastic lines/images throughout the ballad. Some of the imagery in that song just gives me chills—it's incredible. It would make a beautiful film, I think. So, I had the Child Ballad books Tom gave me and I had Martin Carthy's version and I had the internet. I don't know exactly what I took from which source in the end—I think I have several verses that Carthy didn't use—but I'm sure the lyrics we used are 80 percent or better from Carthy. [But] I know I added a couple lines and jammed a couple verses together. That's one of the most exciting parts for me in doing ballads—just researching the lyrics in different versions, choosing my favorite lines/verses, and making them fit into the melody if they don't already.[3]

Renner's love of the *ESPB* bled over into his work with others, too. Teaming with Tara from the dark wave band Lycia under the name Black Happy Day in 2006, he introduced "Edward" (13) to sessions for their album *In the Garden of Ghostflowers*. And there was a genuine meeting of the minds when he linked with the Hare and the Moon's Grey Malkin for "The Cherry Tree Carol" (54—released beneath the alias of Antler and Ivy).

Grey Malkin and Tim Renner met through mutual friend (and Antler and Ivy bandmate) Neddal Ayad, and via Malkin "buying everything Stone Breath have ever put out from Tim." Like Renner, Malkin traces his own love of music to a source far removed from folk, although in his case it was

> a cassette copy of Jeff Wayne's musical version of *War of the Worlds* on a small, old-fashioned tape player. To a five-year-old, it was absolutely real and truly terrifying. To this day, I can't hear the bizarre prog/disco/musical/David Essex fusion that it actually is; I can only hear the sound of impending Martian apocalypse. I think this might explain my relationship with music, and why the Hare and the Moon sound the way they do. Fear, doom and [Moody Blues vocalist] Justin Hayward suddenly infected everything.[4]

According to Malkin, his earliest musical excursions, playing guitar in a bedroom duo with his friend Simon Shaw (later bassist for the Trembling Bells), are best described as "a kind of Nick Cave grizzled delta blues 'my woman has left me' type thing, which was ill-fitting as we were fifteen-year-old schoolboys; it also evidenced quite a poor sense of geography, given we were in Inverness." However, Malkin also underwent a lengthy immersion in folk and folk-rock before debuting the Hare and the Moon in 2009. Indeed, despite his unknown status, the album (also titled *The Hare and the Moon*) immediately affirmed Malkin's status among the twenty-first century's most visionary interpreters of the *ESPB*, and traditional song in general.

We encounter "The Three Ravens" (26) and "The Rolling of the Stones" (49), a dynamic "Barbara Allen" (84) and most bewitching of all, "The Unquiet Grave" (78)—the first Child Ballad that the Hare and the Moon attempted to set to music, inspired by Malkin's love for versions by Pamela Wyn Shannon[5] and Shirley Collins.

> When it came to making the first The Hare and the Moon album I wasn't particularly keen on or interested in using my own lyrics or words and had already become somewhat obsessed with Child Ballads from listening to Steeleye Span, The Young Tradition, and Pentangle. It felt like an ideal way to incorporate another passion within the music I was putting together if I could do these ballads some kind of justice. It felt important to be sympathetic and respectful to the ballads themselves, but not be overly precious about their setting or how they ought to be performed; they are stories after all, and are meant to be told in whatever manner feels appropriate. So, when recording "The Unquiet Grave," it felt imperative that something of the tangible sense of doom and dread in the ballad was evoked musically. Here, the dead are not only disturbed from their sleep, but they are also communicating and warning of a potentially terrible fate for the young protagonist. Moreover, they are irritated and angry. This, then, is a text that was not going to be convincingly framed with a twee acoustic backing; accordingly, I attempted to convey the level of terror and fatal consequence with an equally dramatic musical setting, the sense that something against nature was occurring.[6]

"Edward" (13) was Child's contribution to the second Hare and the Moon album, the semi-eponymous *The Grey Malkin*. Like Child, Malkin sees "Edward" very much as "a conclusion of sorts" to "The Twa Brothers" (49), and acknowledges, "For me, this is one of the most poetic ballads; Edward's protestations and excuses to his mother when she questions where the blood that adorns him has come from are exceptionally beautifully written (although I read that Child himself became frustrated with some of the later verses as Edward's explanations become more far-fetched)."

For his "The Rolling of the Stones," Malkin initially acknowledges the influence of Current 93's use of its melody in 1998. More to the point, however, was the Owl Service's faithful rendering of the ballad, as that band set out on its own voyage of discovery with their 2006 debut *A Garland of Song*. It was their version that opened Malkin's mind to the "eeriness and oddity that so distinguishes it from the other Child Ballads. It stands out as being deeply allegorical or symbolist, as opposed to a more straightforward oral form of storytelling."

The Owl Service, at heart, was yet another one-man operation, and another that might not have been anticipated if one judged by founder Steven Collins's early musical tastes—eighties electronica and heavy metal. It was in the early nineties that he discovered traditional music: initially "all the usual stuff—people like Anne Briggs, Shirley and Dolly Collins, Young Tradition, Pentangle, Steeleye, Fairports/Sandy." Others followed as the internet expanded and ever more obscure music from the era began finding its way onto blogs and download sites.

"All of this stuff was massively influential for me when I began recording as The Owl Service. But essentially what I was trying to do at the start was to somehow capture in sound the feel of some films and TV shows that had a major effect on me as a child—things which, for reasons I can't explain, have always evoked the same feeling in me as my favorite folk music."[7]

At the time, this confluence of music, film, television, and art was very much a fringe interest; a decade-plus later, it is generally regarded as a multimedia phenomenon in its own right, under the overall banner of Folk Horror.

Therein can be found everything from *Doctor Who*'s television encounter with "The Daemons" (1972), in which a prehistoric burial mound, witchcraft, devil worship, and a troupe of malevolent Morris dancers descend upon a hitherto idyllic English hamlet, to the previous year's *Blood on Satan's Claw* movie, where a similarly bucolic community is consumed by ancient magic. From another British television series, *Children of the Stones*, came a tale in which a prehistoric stone circle awakens to exert its powers over a modern village, and then there was the BBC's annual adaptations of M. R. James's ghost stories. All (and more) have been pressed into service as founding fathers of the movement, but essentially, Folk Horror is the point where modern realism encounters folk beliefs and, for the most part, comes off second best.

The movies *The Wicker Man* and the Roddy McDowall–directed *Tam Lin* likewise slip into this company, while further confirmation of Professor Child's influence upon the genre lies in the acclaimed 2022 Folk Horror documentary *Woodlands Dark and Days Bewitched*, and the so-effective—even startling—presence within of an electrifying "Lamkin" (93), as performed by Jim Williams and Lisa Abbott, and, elsewhere in the soundtrack, material by modern-day Child lovers The Hare and the Moon and Ellie Bryan.

Collins's Owl Service bandmate Diana Collier offers a very succinct summary: "English folk song set against a backdrop of sound that is influenced by many strands of music from the sixties onwards, including English folk revival, psychedelic, and electronic soundscapes."[8]

Collins accepts no credit for the emergence of Folk Horror as anything more than a feeling that a lot of people seemed to share. Neither does he claim any kind of expertise on the Child Ballads. "I'm no authority on folk music of any kind, and I don't approach it in that scholarly fashion which so many do. I don't know a great deal about Frances Child or the songs he collected, and my general folksong knowledge is limited. I guess, like many, I initially saw the name Child cropping up on the sleeves of many folk records I picked up, without having the slightest idea what it meant. But they always seemed to be the best songs!"[9]

The Owl Service debuted with a self-released EP, *Wake the Vaulted Echo* in 2006, and a fine rendition of "The Two Magicians" (44). Versions of "The Gardener's Child" (219) and, remarkably, "Robin Hood and the Bold Pedlar" (132) followed during the sessions for the first Owl Service album, alongside the aforementioned "The Rolling of the Stones."

The Owl Service has not consumed all of Collins's time, however; he works, too, alongside bandmate Diana Collier on her solo projects, and the pair also teamed up as Greanvine. Both of these projects have brought fresh dimensions to even the most oft-recorded Child Ballads; Collier's first album, 2013's *All Mortals Are at Rest*, includes powerful versions of "The Cherry Tree Carol" (54) and "The Two Brothers" (49); its successor, 2020's *Ode to Riddley Walker*, includes "The Bonny Hind"(50), while Greanvine's *Witch Song* EP includes an icy "The Prickle Holly Bush" (95).

Collier is very aware of the tradition that these projects represent. "One of our loveliest gigs with The Owl Service was supporting Martin Carthy at Canterbury in a Georgian building. It was very meaningful to be singing songs we got from his repertoire and from Anne Briggs who he knew, and then to sit and share wine and food with him. A proper gent."

The Owl Service's immersion into the roots of British folk music grew deeper when the band commenced collaborating with Alison O'Donnell, in some circles already a legend from her role in the late 1960s Irish band Mellow Candle and, later, during a spell in South Africa, Flibbertigibbet.

"The music was in my blood from the beginning and I just didn't know it," O'Donnell reflects.[10] She recalls "singing a few traditional songs here and there from the age of fifteen onwards," but she looks askance at Mellow Candle's posthumous labeling as a folk band, and dates her involvement in the genre to Flibbertigibbet—by which time she was twenty-five and utterly unprepared to discover how the band's mix of traditional tunes and songs felt so natural to her. "I took to it like a duck to water, but I didn't quite understand why."

Only by delving into her family history did she begin to see the linkage. "My grandfather and his two brothers were born into a military background in India and learned traditional tunes from their father. He was a boy musician when he emigrated from Ireland in 1867. I didn't know they had been involved in traditional music until well after the Flibbertigibbet era." Nevertheless it was, as they say, in her blood. "Finding a great trad song and making a good arrangement of it is just as satisfying as writing from scratch, and I have researched a number of traditional songs and created my own version of them."

She became a regular at the Góilín Traditional Singer's Club in Dublin, and her knowledge of the Child Ballads as an entity in its own right sprang from that. "I [always] asked more questions about the provenance of songs, as it is a really important thing to give credit to the origins of a song. If I am going to give the best rendition that I can, it is essential to know what there is to know about the song. When I am writing lyrics for my own songs, I often spend a considerable period of time researching a subject before I write a word."

O'Donnell's first session with Collins and the Owl Service was a case in point. "I looked around for a song with a strong and passionate story and settled on 'Flodden Field' (168)." The song, detailing the battle of that name fought between the English and Scots in September 1513, was new to O'Donnell—she had never heard any previous versions, while Collins's sole exposure was a version recorded, he thought, by Vulcan's Hammer in 1975. O'Donnell continues, "Together we created an arrangement for our 2008 EP *The Fabric of Folk*. I just had the basic melody so that I could make it my own. I try never to do a cover or a traditional song unless I can really put my own spin on it." The strength of the ensuing version is illustrated by its inclusion in the Greentrax label's 2013 *The Flooers o' the Forest*, a compilation marking the 500th anniversary of the battle itself. O'Donnell also voices the Owl Service's "The Lover's Ghost" (248).

(Another key partnership for O'Donnell was with Ireland's United Bible Studies, although she was absent from their most gripping visit to the *ESPB*, a positively terrifying "The Pricklie Bush" (95), included on the mid-winter themed *Soregh- Murne and Fast* album.)

The Owl Service itself, meanwhile, would make a number of subsequent visits to the *ESPB* before the band ceased operations in 2016, before returning in 2022 at the behest of a local art gallery, intending—as Collins puts it—"to produce a new sound work for a project of theirs which is showcasing fifteen South-end-based artists who work with music, poetry/spoken word, and found sounds."[11]

The Owl Service's offering was a collection of songs drawn from David Occomore and Philip Spratley's 1970s publication *Bushes and Briars; An Anthology of Essex Folk Songs*. "Few are of Essex origin," Collins notes, and none are Child Ballads. But included among them was a local variant on "Worcester City" that Percy Grainger collected from Joseph Taylor back in the 1900s; and "Newport Street," a number recorded by Nic Jones on 1978's *From the Devil to a Stranger*. Even apart from the *ESPB*, the lineage remains palpable.

Chapter Forty-Seven

AND OTHER STORIES

The so-called "old guard" was by no means silent as this new wave of talent pushed into the field.

It is true that many veterans had withdrawn somewhat, at least from what they regarded as the more onerous obligations of their profession, a stance that prompted younger researchers to ponder the irony of artists whose entire careers were based upon their elders being willing to share their knowledge and repertoire now refusing to make similar concessions themselves.

Many, however, at least continued to record and perform live, and often with stellar results. With Steeleye Span's 1996 album *Time* inviting Gay Woods back into the ranks, that band embarked upon a trilogy of albums that could hold their own even against the classics of the seventies. Even Maddy Prior's temporary departure for a solo career in 1997 could not weaken the succeeding *Horstow Grange* (1998) and *Bedlam Born* (2000) albums, and the two Child Ballads included therein rank among Steeleye's most perfectly realized—"The Prickly Bush" (95) and "Lord Randall" (12).

Martin Carthy, too, remained a force to be reckoned with, particularly across the two albums that reunited him with Dave Swarbrick for the first time (barring guest appearances) since *Prince Heathen*. *Life and Limb* in 1990 and *Skin and Bone* two years later were both deserving of their rapturous reception. A young Angeline Morrison was among those who listened with utter amazement.

In 2022, celebrating as her album *The Brown Girl and Other Songs* was unanimously feted across the UK media, Morrison reflected that her first exposure to her own title track was

Among the plaudits awarded to Angeline Morrison's 2022 album *The Brown Girl and Other Stories* was the Cambridge Folk Festival's Christian Raphael prize. Courtesy Angeline Morrison

by the inimitable Martin Carthy and Dave Swarbrick, on their *Skin and Bone album* [1992]. It absolutely thrilled me. I couldn't stop listening to it. I loved the lively tune they set it to, "Sweet Kitty." I especially loved Carthy's lilting refrain, which I couldn't get out of my mind. I just loved Kitty. [She] wasn't going to let rejection crush her—though the handbrake-turn of the former lover's loyalties always make me feel this song is more of a revenge fantasy than a murder ballad. This also helps me feel OK about loving a heroine who might have killed someone.[1]

Also listening keenly to the past, while planning diligently for the future was Australian singer Nick Cave, who—with his band, The Bad Seeds—had been cutting a violent swath through the alternative rock underground since the early 1980s. In 1996, Cave released *Murder Ballads*, an album that comprised ten tracks that more than justified such a portentous title. "Where the Wild Roses Grow," a surprise UK hit that saw Cave duetting with pop diva Kylie Minogue, was cut clearly from cloth that Child would have recognized, but it was Cave's "Henry Lee" (68), a duet with PJ Harvey,[2] that confirmed the *ESPB*'s influence.

Brian Peters reflects, "I think the sheer darkness of the Child Ballads appeals to a certain kind of person as well—the folk revival has always

had a taste for the Gothic, and every so often rock musicians like Nick
Cave discover all that darkness in Child and think 'I want some of that.'
And, of course, Gothic songs can take screaming electric arrangements
very well."

"Henry Lee" was Cave's second visit to the *ESPB*, following "Jesus Met
the Woman at the Well" (21) on 1986's *Kicking against the Pricks*. This time
around, the singer explained,

> [I wanted] to make a record where I could stand outside and tell a lot of
> stories. The idea that it would be a collection of murder ballads is one that's
> been around since the beginning of [his solo career]. We had two [self-
> composed] songs floating around, "O'Malley's Bar" and "Song of Joy,"
> which were long and unwieldy, and didn't sit comfortably on any of the
> records we'd made, so the idea came along that we'd write some more
> murder ballads and stick them on a record, more for our fans, who would
> appreciate it, than for the masses [who] I thought . . . would hate it.[3]

In fact, it became his most successful album yet.

Brian Peters himself was now carving out a distinct niche in the annals
of Child Balladeers. Indeed, since his 1985 debut album *Persistence of
Memory*, he has recorded close to three dozen of Child's children, including one full album, 2008's *Songs of Trial and Triumph*, and the aforementioned tribute to Cecil Sharp's Appalachian journey with Jeff Davies.[4]

It was Peters's "Kemp Owen" (34) that Frankie Armstrong recorded
for her album *The Garden of Love* in 2000, pointing out that this particular
variant would have been impossible to realize had Peters not wholly
reconstructed the ballad. Featuring the only tune ever found for what
Armstrong called "this weirdest of weird ballads," sung by a Mrs. Brown
of Falkland, Aberdeenshire, it appeared to have been "taken down . . . by
her nephew who wasn't very good at that kind of thing."[5]

Peters's introduction to the Child Ballads is very much the story of
many children of the British late sixties/early seventies:

> The first one I heard was probably Fairport's "Sir Patrick Spens" [58] and,
> although I'd never heard of F. J. Child at the age of fifteen, I was aware that
> this was a different kind of a song from your average folk-rock, with a story
> seemingly harking back to the medieval world. When I was seventeen, one
> of my friends had some Steeleye Span records which I was very impressed
> by. I bought *Below the Salt* and *Parcel of Rogues*, and particularly enjoyed the
> ballads . . . "Alison Gross" [35] and "King Henry" [32]. That was the big one;
> I even persuaded the rock band I was in to include it alongside the Status
> Quo and Free numbers we covered. A bit later on, I had a girlfriend who was
> a big fan of Martin Carthy, and I think it was the sleeve notes of his records
> that taught me that "Child Ballads" were a special part of the folk repertoire.
> "Willie's Lady" [6] was a favorite from Carthy's repertoire.

Another of Peters's top picks, again from the Steeleye Span catalog, was "Lamkin" (93), recorded for his debut album "because it was gruesome, and I was trying very deliberately to get away from the cozy, easy-listening kind of folk music that a lot of people seemed to be doing in the 1980s." Also included was "Demon Lover" (243), again a Steeleye classic, although, on this occasion, the inspiration came from "one of the residents at my local folk club. . . . I thought it a massively dramatic tale and tune—I still do, though I came to dislike my original instrumental arrangement and have sung it without accompaniment for years."

The *Trial and Triumph* collection grew out of Peters's conviction that a full live set devoted to the Child Ballads "might go down well at folk festivals, and I also felt that there were a lot of misapprehensions about him in the folk world—many people still think he was a field collector, for instance—so it would have an educational value." Peters already had "a number of meaty ballads" in his repertoire but set about gathering more, having also decided to create a themed CD for sale at shows.

> The challenge then was to learn a bunch of new material, and make an album within those narrow Child-only limitations that would have sufficient variety not to be boring. So, I decided that I would have some real heavy-duty material but also some lighter songs. I used every kind of arrangement, from unaccompanied vocal, through guitar and vocal (my default setting for the longer ballads), a few with squeezebox, and a couple of American old-time settings—I'm a hobby old-time musician as well. Oh, and of course there was the big electric setting of "The Three Ravens" (26) which was my homage to early Steeleye, really, and was a lot of fun to build in the studio.
>
> As with all of my material, I picked out either the less well-known ballads, or found alternative versions of familiar ones. It would be a complete waste of time (in my eyes) to cover anything that Carthy or Steeleye had done before me. "Sir Aldingar" [59] and "False Foudrage" [89] were both ballads that very few people had ever sung, and I did a lot of restoration work on both, so I knew they would be pretty much unique to me—I'd recorded "False Foudrage" before [on 1991's *The Seeds of Time*], but I really wanted it as part of that CD.

To further mix things up, Peters purposefully indulged in a little contrafacta, while also adding fresh verses in order to smooth the stories:

> There's a story behind the assembly of pretty much every one of those ballad versions, apart from a couple (like "The Golden Vanity" [286]) that were already unusual versions that I chose not to alter. Then there was my "Drunken Nights" [274] rewrite, which I did to lighten things up a bit—the tune for that comes from different versions collected by Sharp. A friend of mine who'd been studying the collector George Gardiner gave me "Lucy"

[51], though I had to find extra verses. "Green Broom" [43] was from a field recording made in an English pub in the 1960s.

Which, in the annals of British traditional music, is where a lot of the best ideas are found.

The son of folk singer Alan Roberts (d. 2001), Alasdair Roberts was first heard on record in 2001. His debut album, *The Crook of My Arm*, is initially deceptive; few instruments intrude beyond Roberts's own acoustic guitar, but such a description belies the manner in which Roberts's voice not only draws the listeners in, but also leaves them feeling culpable for whatever dark deeds were committed across the course of the album. Two Child Ballads were included on the disc, "Lord Gregory" (76), which he learned initially from Shirley Collins, and "The Wife of Usher's Well" (79), and he thanks his father (who sadly died in the same year *Crook of My Arm* was released) for introducing him to the canon.

> I have a recording of Alan made at a folk festival in Germany in 1977 sing-ing "The Fair Flower of Northumberland" (9), and it's one which is now a regular part of my own live repertoire. Another song that he sang—it's not in Child's collection but I think it shares something of the atmosphere of many of those songs—was "The False Bride." It's probably that song, with its strange imagery of strawberries growing in the salt sea, which Alan played for me when I was nineteen or twenty years old, that led me to seek out other such songs. Certainly I listened a bit to [other] musicians and dug through my auld man's record collection, and over time I acquired a library of books relating to these songs. . . . It all led me to dig deeper into specifically Scottish variants of these songs from pre-"revival" singers . . . the noncommercial singers who were recorded "in the field" by people such as Hamish Henderson.

Since that time, Roberts has included one or more Child Ballads on almost every one of his albums, among them some deliciously obscure variants—"The Tri-Coloured House" (2) on his 2012 collaboration with Mairi Morrison, *Urstan*; "What Put the Blood on Your Right Shoulder, Son?" (13) on 2010's *Too Long in This Condition*; "Johnny o' the Brine" (114) on 2018's *What's News*, with Amble Skuse and David McGuinness; and others. The majority of the ballads he selected, he explains,

> are learnt pretty much fully formed. But sometimes I piece them together–for example "The Daemon Lover" [243] on *Too Long in This Condition*, or "The Laird o' Drum" [236] on *Urstan*. Both of these were derived from two-verse fragments recorded by Hamish Henderson from two different singers [Andrew Stewart and William Sharp Lonie, respectively] in the 1950s. I loved the fragments, the melodies and the singing styles and I also loved

the fact that they were fragmentary, as it allowed me to add to them in my own way. In this case I added to them mostly from printed versions. Other ballads in my repertoire are sort of stitched together from multiple sources. For example, my version of "The Cruel Mother" [20], which is probably the ballad I sing most often. That has a bit in it of Shirley Collins (again), Lizzie Higgins, and the seventies folk-rock band Silly Wizard. I go back and forth with the ballads. At certain times, I'm very concerned to explore and interpret them, but at other times I'm more concerned with my own writing and different forms of creation—although of course my own writing is often so stitched in with the older sources and forms in various ways.

Perhaps the Child Ballads' most astonishing transition, however, has been into the deepest realms of experimental music, when the west London musical workshops being held by drummer Eddie Prevost were suddenly infused with the flavor of songs that were as traditional as the students' ideas were futuristic.

The project grew out of American singer-songwriter Ed Pettersen's helming of the 2007 Grammy-nominated *Songs of America* collection, a compilation of fifty songs telling the history of the United States in popular and public domain songs. "Researching it, I kept coming across these English songs with 'Child' written alongside them, and that made me curious. So I found out what it meant and, over the next six or seven years I cultivated this, I read every book on it, got the book of the ballads, and collected I guess the best twenty-five or thirty Child Ballads that made sense to me personally."[6]

He had no immediate plan for the songs beyond the enjoyment he got from playing them. However, relocating with his wife to London in 2016 brought him to the realization that "I was dissatisfied with the way my own musical career was going. I was really bored being a singer-songwriter, I didn't see a purpose in it anymore." To remedy his mood, his wife suggested he start attending a nearby free improvisation workshop.

Within a year, Pettersen's entire musical career had been upended. The London Experimental Ensemble, as the workshop members called themselves, had completed their first project, a musical realization of Cornelius Cardew's *Treatise*. Now they were discussing what to do next.

"I suggested we do something where we perhaps 'explore Englishness a bit more.' The others asked what I meant, so I said 'Are any of you familiar with the Child Ballads?' Some of them sort of knew, so I told them about their [role in] conveying current events and political situations from two hundred years ago and before. They went, 'Tell us more,' and then everybody got as obsessed as I was."

Pettersen proceeded to introduce the musicians to the ballads that he was most confident performing ("nobody else in the group at that time could sing"), and some six months were then spent cutting his original

The London Experimental Ensemble, during the recording of their first Child Ballads collection. (L–R) John Eyles, Shane Shanahan (engineer), Tony Hardie-Bick, Joe Wright, Edward Lucas, Carole Chant, NO Moore, Keisuke Matsui, Ken Ikeda. Courtesy Ed Pettersen

list down and augmenting it with other peoples' suggestions, until finally they had whittled the selection down to eight songs.

The next step was to decide which of the multitude of variations for each ballad they should perform, a conundrum resolved by opting for the very oldest version they could find. First websites, then manuscripts, and finally experts in the field were consulted, with the only significant deviation coming when Pettersen presented the team with one particular ballad, sung entirely in medieval Scots Gaelic, and band member Joe Wright, a native Scot, admitted that even he had no idea what it meant.

"We had a group meeting and they said, 'Let's look up the meaning of every word.' We weren't messing around. Child's glossary helped a little, but you're also trying to convey the true essence of the text and how do you do that in a modern context without diluting it? So it was challenging, months and months of doing homework and then experimenting with substitute phrases and words from different versions."

They also needed to confront the sheer length of some of the ballads they chose. "There are certain Child Ballads that have like four hundred stanzas," Pettersen joked, "so we discussed how do we deal with that, and I said, 'Well, we want it to make sense,' and so we went through line by line and found where duplicates or repetition came in, trying to create a linear narrative for each text, but doing it very carefully. Because when you're talking about the 'ferny brae,' we wanted to be very careful to represent what the ancestors meant when they used that term, and not cut the corners. And when we were done, we were all very proud." So proud that they approached folk scholar Steve Roud to ask if he would be willing to contribute liner notes to the eventual album. He declined.

"He was appalled at what we did," Pettersen continues. "Absolutely flabbergastedly appalled. He wanted nothing to do with it. But we were not upset when Stephen had such a physical reaction, because that's what we were going for. What would be the purpose of doing it exactly like everyone else did?"

The spontaneous nature of the recording naturally negated any urge the musicians may have had to repeat their accomplishment in concert, for it would be performed in a different manner on every occasion. Besides, the Ensemble had achieved what it set out to do. Any further performance would be redundant.

However, with *Child Ballads* completed, the idea of a record release party arose and, with it, a revolutionary approach to this most conventional of promotional activities. The Ensemble *would* play live. But they would perform a completely different repertoire of Child Ballads, drawn from those that had been discussed and worked upon, but had not made the finished disc. "So that's what we did. We didn't play the record at the party, we played the songs that weren't on the record."

That was not, however, the end of the Ensemble's interest in the *ESPB*. Pettersen alone immediately plunged into a new project, *Installations*, described as "a series of recordings I did for a museum in London late last year to be combined with audio-generated random visuals." Amid some five hours of experiment and sound, Pettersen voiced nine further Child Ballads, only for the pandemic to stymy the project. *Installations* was subsequently released on his Bandcamp page.

All the while, too, he was casting around for another Child-related project that the full Ensemble might be interested in tackling. He found it at the very back of the *ESPB*, and the final six ballads in the collection. Offered as a free download with this book, they would also comprise the Ensemble's next album.

Each of these ballads could claim to be among the most obscure in the entire *ESPB*. Indeed, five of them—"Blancheflower and Jellyflorice" (300), "The Queen of Scotland" (301), "Young Bearwell" (302), "The Holy Nunnery" (303), and "Young Ronald" (304)—are known from just one solitary manuscript, Buchan's *Ballads of the North of Scotland*. The sixth, the positively epic (up to seventy-four stanzas) "The Outlaw Murray" (305) exists in three variations, including that which Scott saw fit to include in his *Minstrelsy*.

That obscurity does not, however, dent their flavor. The stories these ballads relate are as engrossing (and, sometimes, fantastical) as any in the *ESPB*. Child 300 tells of the maid, Blancheflower, who falls in love with the wonderfully-named Prince Jellyflorice and is punished, by his mother, by being placed on a wild steed and let loose. Fortunately, the prince is able to rescue her.

In Child 301, the Scottish Queen is spurned by a young man, whom she sends out to lift a large stone, knowing a deadly serpent lives beneath it. As it is about to strike, his lover, a maid, distracts the serpent by cutting off her own breast and is rewarded with both marriage and the miraculous regrowth of the severed flesh.

> *As heaven was pleasd, in a short time*
> *To ease her first sad pain*
> *Sae was it pleasd, when she'd a son*
> *To hae a pap again.*

Child 302 tells of a young man exiled for falling in love with the mayor's daughter but who then rises to a position of power at a foreign court; in Child 303 a young man is driven to desperation when his lover enters a nunnery, so he disguises himself as a woman and takes Holy Orders alongside her; and in 304, Young Ronald must slay a multi-headed giant in order to win the love of the king's daughter. And finally, 305 tells the story of a Scottish landowner's battle with the king.

No melodies have ever been discovered for these ballads; no collectors or field recorders have ever stumbled across a singer who knows them. Child himself was wary about including them in the *ESPB*, discarding "The Outlaw Murray" on at least one occasion before restoring it, and admitting "some of the [ballads] . . . I have admitted have very weak claims." "The Queen of Scotland" he describes as "[an] insipid ballad [that] may have been rhymed from an insipid tale."

Yet still he included it, although it is likely that illness and exhaustion ultimately played as much of a role in these ballads' ultimate elevation as any opinion Child may have entertained regarding either their quality or their worth. They were similarly overlooked for the century following their publication in the *ESPB*. All six, however, have seen some action in the twenty-first century.

For obvious reasons, they formed the conclusion of Australian singer/ guitarist Raymond Crooke's marathon YouTube trek through the entirety of the Child Ballads.

"I actually started recording the Child Ballads in order on a small cassette recorder when I was still in my teens," Crooke reflects. "Not sure how far I got, probably only the first dozen or so. It was not until I started putting up videos on YouTube in 2007 that I decided to seriously attempt at least one version of each of the Child Ballads." It took close to a decade for him to complete the task, "but I have continued to put up alternative versions of the ballads as I come across them." Neither was he shy about borrowing tunes for other ballads when he came across one that had no set melody, or composing his own from scratch. "I think 300 to 305 would be mainly my own tunes, but I don't keep a record of such things."[7]

Quite coincidentally, it was another Australian, Daniel Kelly, who next chose to shed light upon the last pages of the balladry. His decision to record "Blancheflower and Jellyflorice" in his *Love, Murder, Magic and Song* collection of Child Ballads, however, was for a very specific and personal reason. Across his career, Kelly had uploaded 299 performances to YouTube (31 of which were Child Ballads). He chose Child 300 because it would be his 300th posting.

Still the London Experimental Ensemble approach to the six is both unique and audacious. Recorded at London's Pool Studio in September 2022, and again wholly improvised around the lyric, *Child Ballads: The Final Six* represented the first ever commercial studio recording of these ballads. Equally excitingly, the project drew in contributions from Richard Thompson (voicing an icy "The Queen of Scotland"), John Wesley Harding, Gina Fergione, Marissa Nadley (bewitching across "Young Ronald"), Freedy Johnston and Pettersen's own cousin, the Norwegian star Sivert Høyem (the epic "Outlaw Murray").

Yet, even among these artists, no matter how familiar one may be with any other Child Ballads in their repertoire, this time around, every one is a stranger.

Chapter Forty-Eight

BE GLAD, FOR THE BALLADS HAVE NO ENDING

We've come a long way, and a long time, from Percy Grainger trudging the backroads of Lincolnshire in search of unknown singers to record. Technology, so often viewed as the enemy by the staunchest supporters of the traditional song, can also be viewed as its closest ally—one that, far from wiping out every last vestige of the old ways, has in fact ensured their survival. On the internet store Bandcamp, the streaming services Soundcloud and Spotify, the video jukebox that is YouTube, no listener is more than a few clicks and search terms away from a wealth of new—this year, this month, this very week— interpretations of ancient songs. Some are simply rehashes of versions that we have heard a thousand times before. Others are taken, and say so, from rediscovered songbooks and collections of the past. Some are wholly new versions, some are newly gathered—or, at least, newly unearthed.

Field research as it had been conducted for so many decades in the past, is at an end, or close enough. The year 2020 marked the centenary of the birth of America's first commercial radio station, KDKA Pittsburgh, and it was not alone for long. Two years later, the BBC marked the same milestone. All of which means that, for maybe forty years before these anniversaries, the chances of finding a source singer who did not grow up with, and draw inspiration from, the radio age were growing slimmer with every passing funeral.

But if there are no new finds, there are fresh revelations in the digitization and subsequent public availability of so many historical collections, some wholly online, others on CD too. Released in 2007–2008, the Dust to Digital label's two-volume *Art of Field Recording* box sets uncovered a host of tapes made by folklorist Art Rosenbaum (1938–2022) in far more recent years. For example, we have Bobby McMillon's "The Devil Song" (278), recorded in Lenoir, North Carolina, in 1980; Stan Gilliam's "Gypsy Davy" (200), taped in Athens, Georgia, in 1984; and Mary Lomax's rendition of the same song from 2008. Indeed, Rosenbaum's liner notes could be speaking of many of the artists he recorded when he writes of Mary Lomax, "[She] would have been considered an important 'find' as a ballad singer decades ago, and it is next to amazing that she retains the melodies . . . and the ability and motivation to sing them well in a totally traditional style in the first decade of the 21st century."[1]

Priceless, too, is the same label's 2015 exhumation of collector Henry Glassie's 1960s sessions with Ola Belle Reed in Oxford, Pennsylvania, with its raw, banjo-fired "Black Jack Davy" (200). It was, Glassie writes in the accompanying booklet, a shorter version of the ballad than some he had encountered, just four stanzas compared to the ten he heard from another player, James Perry of Ashe County, North Carolina. But it tells the story nevertheless, and that, when every other argument is stripped away, is what matters.

A new edition of the *ESPB* was published across five volumes by Loomis House in 2006, alongside fresh versions of both Bronson's *Traditional Tunes* and Sharp's Appalachian collection. And another fascinating horde of material was revealed—or, rather, rediscovered—in 2022, when Martin Carthy pooled resources with Sir Stephen Sedley, the creator, more than half a century ago, of the ballad collection *The Seeds of Love*, to create a new ballad collection, *Who Killed Cock Robin? British Folk Songs of Crime and Punishment*.

Sedley had always intended following up his original book, only for his legal career to get in the way. Retiring from the bench in 2011, he resolved to complete the project, and reflected upon his working methods as he discussed compiling this latest garland: "Doing my initial research, I noted each song about love, and all its traceable sources, on a card index. (In recent times this procedure has been made obsolete by Steve Roud's online index.) That was the working basis of *The Seeds of Love*. I also kept two side-indexes: one was of songs I encountered about soldiers and sailors; the other, songs about crime and punishment. When I retired. . . I began thinking about returning to the latter."[2]

His first thought was to contact Carthy, whom he had known since 1962. They met, the guitarist recalls, "at The Troubadour in Earl's Court," the basement folk club that hosted some of the key performers of the age. Sedley "arrived with a small but very excited train of people," fresh from the recording of an album of "bawdy songs,"[3] *Songs of Love, Lust and Loose Living* album. Label head Nat Joseph, Sedley continues, "wanted to trail it to the folk world while he still had the performers together. Hence the

Troubadour invasion." Carthy was the headlining act that night, and "we probably still owe [Martin] an apology for barging in."

The two became friends and occasional associates; it was Sedley who penned liner notes to Carthy's 1965 album with the Three City Four, for example. Around 2016, then, Sedley wrote to Carthy outlining his latest project, "and he readily agreed to collaborate on what became *Who Killed Cock Robin*. (The original working title was *Farewell to all Judges and Juries*.)" Work on the book was undertaken whenever touring deposited Carthy in Sedley's neighborhood, "And we would spend a day or two selecting and editing material from my index and/or his repertoire. It took us three or four years in all . . . and hopefully it was worthwhile."

It was. Some sixty ballads appear with words and music, including a clutch that will be familiar, if not from Carthy's catalog, then a wealth of others—"Little Musgrave and Lady Barnard" (81), "Sheath and Knife" (16), "The Two Magicians" (44), "The Gypsy Laddie" (200), and "Geordie" (209) among them. Indeed, reflecting upon the book's contents, Sedley rates Carthy's "The Famous Flower of Serving Men" (106) as "the most gripping" ballad of them all.

With these examples and resources in mind, what is the difference between any new treatment of a traditional song, Child Ballad or otherwise, unearthed "in the field"—by Sharp, Bronson, Creighton, Lomax, Lumpkin, whoever—and gleefully added to the songbooks and the modern "listener" doing the same thing via LP, CD, mp3, video, or ballad book? In 2019, the Irish duo Ye Vagabonds released a version of Child 100 that was learned partly from an uncle who used to sing it at family gatherings. We do not know where *he* learned it, but how can that not be considered a part of the tradition?

As for the many sins of the modern music industry that also get cited in these arguments, most of the artists who handle the Child Ballads today exist so far outside of the mainstream that they might easily *be* sitting in cottages in the islands off Newfoundland, waiting for someone to come along and record them.

The difference is they no longer need to wait. They can record their music themselves and send it out to the whole world. Names like the Witches of Elswick, Geordie McIntyre, Spiers and Boden, and Alison McMorland, to name but a few, have been as active in the dustier corners of English balladry as any folk-rock era enthusiast—more so, in fact, as the imperative to uncover ever more obscure (and thus original) material has only grown stronger over the decades. These acts' world might be one of internet radio and online videos, podcast documentaries, download albums, and self-released CDs, but while there are many sage souls who will tell them that the "old ways" were better, the new ways are easier.

They also save artists from the rapacious industry devils that haunted so many generations of their forebears.

These freedoms have also permitted artists—not just in the traditional arena but across every genre—to follow their own hearts, with no care whatsoever for whatever the industry is currently demanding, secure in the knowledge that their social media following, and the word of mouth that accompanies it, is often as powerful an advertisement as any mention in the music press (or what remains of it) or a play on the radio (ditto).

Would the Unthanks, to name but one, have established themselves among the most cherished of modern British folk (and beyond) acts had they been reliant upon a major record label to oversee their career? In under two decades, they have released close to an album a year, at a time when the industry standard demands a gap of three or four. The late Prince once wrote the word "slave" on his face to protest such strictures. Would a similar gesture by Becky Unthank have received even a fraction of the attention?

Yet there has not been a wasted moment across any of their releases, and the versions of "The Cruel Sister" (10) and "The Fair Flower of Northumberland" (9), with which Rachel Unthank's *Cruel Sister* album launched the band's career in 2005; "Annachie Gordon" (239) on 2009's *Here's the Tender Coming*, and "The Great Silke of Sule Skerry" (113), from 2022's *Sorrows Away* can be rated among the most-beloved and remarked upon Child Ballads of the twenty-first century.[4]

Indeed, with so many artists now thoroughly unbound from convention, the last years of the twentieth century and the first decades of the twenty-first have seen as many Child Ballads recorded and released commercially as at any time in the past, including the booms of the 1950s, and the folk-rock era of a decade later.

In 2013, Fairport Convention's Bruce Rowland reflected, "It is heartening that these ballads are still being performed. If the *ESPB* is not on the comprehensive school English Literature syllabus, it bloody well should be."[5]

That so much of what is now being released absolutely subverts the purist vision of how the ballads should be performed is beside the point. Again, as Rowland put it, "If people want to sit backwards on a chair and sing the ballads through their noses, they can do it. But if I was just starting out now, I'd be sitting at my computer making all manner of noises to accompany them." There is room for all. While "wyrd folk," as the modern skein is now generally known, continues to push boundaries (and, sometimes, the patience of listeners), more traditional renderings of the Child Ballads have continued unabashed; and scholarship, too, continues to develop.

Randall Krieger's Unquiet Grave is one of three 2010s-era acts knowingly named for Child Ballads, alongside the English vocal harmony

The Unquiet Grave, 2022. (L–R) Elise Krieger, Jim Hurley, Randall Krieger, Bronwyn Hagerty, Phoenix Thanatos, Tom Dreiham. Courtesy Randall Krieger

trio Lady Maisery, and Burd Ellen, the vision of Scottish singer Deborah Armour, an occasional collaborator with Alasdair Roberts and Grey Malkin. Krieger explains his choice of name: "'The Unquiet Grave' is a little more poetic than some of the matter-of-fact sounding titles. Also, the story of the ballad is a little more 'poetic,' for lack of a better word."[6] The Unquiet Grave recorded their namesake ballad on 2013's *Mayday* album.

Krieger's own musical background lies in his mother's love for singing fragments of folk songs while accompanying herself on the piano, "songs like 'Loch Lomond' and 'Lagan Love' that now, when I hear them, have an odd nostalgic feeling, being very familiar, activating some old memories that I forgot I had." But he also studied classical guitar and composition at university, before moving onto a graduate degree in early music, while his bandmate (and wife) Elise Krieger was trained in classical singing from around the age of fourteen, although she acknowledges, "A lot of my early repertoire was made up of traditional and folk music. I always have had an interest in fantasy and folklore, but I didn't know any of the Child Ballads until I found a ballad book in my parents' garage when I was in my late teens. I remember thinking the stories were really interesting and different than most things you see and hear in popular culture."[7]

Originally a duo of the Kriegers alone, Unquiet Grave debuted in 2019 with the internet single "Bessie Bell and Mary Gray" (201). It was a precursor for the *Ballades of Old* album, a twelve-track exploration comprised mostly of Child Ballads, arranged to take advantage of the couple's classical training. Randall Krieger continues, "I wanted to set the ballads to new music, so the music and the stories would be intertwined, and the music would match the mood of the story, somewhat like a mini opera or a theatrical performance." It's a magical operation, in some ways reminiscent of Alfred Deller's 1950s approach to the music, but ever conscious, too, of the ballads' early role not only as vehicles for storytelling, but also for action and exposition.

There is an almost Brechtian feel to many of the duo's performances, an approach that has only been broadened by the subsequent expansion of the lineup. Early into their career as a quintet in 2022, the Unquiet Grave added a seething "King Henry" (32) to their repertoire, based around a notated melody Krieger found in the *Oxford Book of Ballads*. "But, instead of using it as the main melody, it is played in the violin during the chorus sections, where the demon is demanding meat and drink. I then composed additional parts for the guitar, cello, and vocals, with the original melody as a harmonic foundation. This partly informed how I composed the rest of the song because I wrote the chorus first. This song is fun to perform live, especially in the right tavern setting where the audience can participate in demanding more meat and drink!" Krieger also has plans "to adapt a larger tale, or a collection of tales that tells a larger epic like . . . the Robin Hood ballads, that could be performed as one large piece like an opera or musical of some sorts."

Krieger is not alone in sensing the value of the Child Ballads as a spectacle in their own right, although the Man, Woman and Child Festival, that was staged three years running (2013–2105) at Dublin's National Library, also had a secondary goal—to disprove the age-old canard that the Child Ballads had no roots on Irish soil, adhered to still by scholars despite decades of evidence to the contrary. Accordingly, almost every performer across the three events, each of which was spread over four days, was of Irish stock (Scotland's Alasdair Roberts was the sole exception), and many of the one-hundred-plus ballads performed throughout that span were rooted in Irish variants.

Ireland's heritage was not the only area ripe for excavation. In 1992, and again in 2008, Martyn Wyndham-Read recorded versions of "Jamie Douglas" (204) that he recalled having learned "years ago in Australia from either Glen Tomasetti, or Brian Mooney, or, perhaps, both of them." He agrees that the song "most definitely" is not Australian. But could it have been transported there among the British prisoners who first colonized the place?[8] Between 1788 and 1868, Britain dispatched over one hundred sixty thousand criminals to the Australian continent, often for infractions as insignificant as shoplifting. (More serious crimes—murder, and the like—were punished with death.) Largely overlooked for so long, the musical legacy of the transported unfortunates is more than overdue for exploration. "Jamie Douglas" might be a good place to start.

The ballads continued to appear, too, in some surprising settings, including in the grasp of Ritchie Blackmore, doyen of hard rock guitarists of the 1970s, but now performing medieval-style music with wife Candice Knight in the very sensibly named Blackmore's Night.

> I first knew about "Barbara Allen" (84) from singing it in school when I was eleven or twelve. I always thought it had a haunting melody, and I got Candy to hum the top line before she learned the song, to see if it would suit her voice, which it did, and it's one of the best songs we do on stage. She puts incredible feeling into the song. Very, very sad. The funny part of the song is it's written about a guy called William. And I have some very colorful friends where we live, some people would say "crazy people." And one is called William. His actual name is "Bill from the Hill." Whenever she sings this very melancholy song, when it gets to the William part, we often look at each other and smile because we think of our crazy friend, William, whom I met in a tavern out at the end of Long Island. I was explaining a tune that Candy and I were about to play, that was written in the 1300s in Spain, and Bill from the Hill shouted from the end of the bar—"King Alfonse the Tenth!" He was correct, and I couldn't believe that someone had ever heard of King Alfonse. So he's been my friend ever since, but I digress.[9]

The stories live on, even when no story is being told. Dylan Carlson and Coleman Grey's 2015 album *Falling with a 1,000 Stars and Other Wonders from the House of Albion* features lengthy, droning guitar performances of "Alison Gross" (35), "Tamlane" 39), "King Orfeo" (19), and "The Elfin Knight" (2), and it is wholly instrumental. Yet the snatches of familiar melody that percolate through the pieces are sufficient.

Critically and maybe musically too, the most successful of all twenty-first-century adaptations of the Child Ballads thus far has been Jefferson Hamer and Anaïs Mitchell's 2013 album titled simply *Child Ballads*. Widely acclaimed on release, the record grew out of the two musicians frequently sharing a car as they made their way from gig to gig, and singing favorite folk songs as they drove along. The Child Ballads just happened to be those they most frequently agreed upon.

"I didn't grow up in a folk music family," Hamer acknowledged. "I was playing electric guitar in high school and college and listening to whatever my white, suburban, middle-class American friends were into." In fact, he was "in the midst of a Frank Zappa obsession" when his professor at the University of Colorado handed him a stack of folk records.

> That was the first time I heard Fairport, Richard Thompson, Martin Carthy, and Planxty. I liked the haunting, modal melodies and exotic, not-American-sounding lyrics. I was also floored by Thompson's guitar playing. I didn't

start thinking categorically about song "collections" until much later, when I moved to New York City and got more entangled in the East Coast folk scene. Writing and recording with people like Anaïs and Eamon O'Leary—my bandmate in the Murphy Beds—sharpened my perception of what any song, traditional or not, can and ought to be.[10]

Another influence was Nic Jones.

He's one of my all-time favorites. But the catch is, you can't sound like any of these people. You don't have their voice. So the real, hard work comes in figuring out what *you* sound like. I might be influenced by Bob Dylan or Nic Jones or Anne Briggs or whoever, but I still have to be able to stand up in front of an audience and deliver my own rendition of a song, standing in my own shoes. Traditional songs give you the great lyrics up front. But you've got to differentiate yourself from your heroes who've already set a high-water mark. There's no shortcut to figuring out how to do that. You can try and have it both ways, and work with the lyrics and melody, until the words and dialect feel good coming out in your own voice. You can sift through the books and all the existing versions. Shop around, just try not to break anything. That was the goal of the *Child Ballads* album.

One of the goals, at least. Another, as Mitchell told the *Daily Telegraph* in 2013, is that "being Americans, Jefferson and I wanted to be able to sing these ballads in the States and have people understand them, rather than see them as museum pieces. But we also wanted to preserve this very weird, archaic culture, which is part of why we love those songs in the first place."[11]

As well as being a collection of the ballads that the duo felt worked best for their intended presentation, *The Child Ballads* also permitted them to pay tribute to other performers whose works they admired. "Riddles Wisely Expounded" (1), for example, was the last ballad they worked on before recording the album, held up by the search for a suitable melody. Hamer continues,

There was this alternate melody to "Geordie" (209) floating around: the upbeat version that the Silly Sisters recorded with Martin Carthy on guitar. We borrowed the first line of that melody for our "Riddles," and put the song in a major key. The rest of the melody just fell into place. We also stole a line out of one of the verses, "you'll beguile a lady soon," and stuck it with Ewan's "lay the bend to the bonny broom" to make a two-line refrain. The real fun, and challenge, with that song was its centerpiece, the riddles section. All the questions portray tactile, worldly objects: "what is greener than the grass, smoother than a glass, louder than a horn, thorns, the sea, etc." But the answers represent psychological or emotional states that are consequences of a love affair: envy, shame, rumor, regret, love. We found most of that in the Child Ballads, but we might have bushwhacked a bit to get it feeling consistent.

"Riddles Wisely Expounded" is, surprisingly, not among the ballads most commonly recorded, despite being the very first one in the *ESPB*. "Tam Lin" (39) on the other hand, ranks among the most popular, with at least some of the challenge for Mitchell and Hamer being to divorce it from its recorded past. As Hamer explains,

> I was always excited to work up a version of "Tam Lin." I knew the Fairport version from way back, and I knew our version would be completely differ-ent, otherwise we wouldn't have done it. We made up a lot of lines for this one, and the melody sounds pretty original to me, although there's traces of Sandy Denny in there for sure. I don't think we set out at the beginning to take the fairies out of the story. But at some point we realized we were *way* more excited about the strange love affair between Janet and Tam Lin than the specific supernatural details of his curse. I understand that the subplot of the Fairie Queen enriches Tam Lin's character with a specific motivation to impregnate the heroine Janet, thereby ensnaring her as a reluctant partner in his only shot at freedom. All those details didn't fit into the arc of the song we wanted to sing. People meet, fall in love, get pregnant, and fight it out under strange circumstances, fairies or no fairies. I love singing this one.

And again, it is traditional song's willingness to be remolded again and again that plays such a major part in its survival, as Fairport Con-vention's Bruce Rowland pointed out. "I would love to know what Child would think of the unique and brilliant version of 'Tam Lin' by The Imagined Village,[12] complete with computerized back projection of Ben-jamin Zephaniah rapping the text. I think he would be mighty pleased with what has been done with his labors. It is a shame Ewan MacColl didn't live to see it."[13]

It is the discovery of Child Ballads in such unexpected places—or even the promise thereof—that lends so much to their continued enjoyment. Yes, anyone can tap "Child Ballads" into a search engine and be rewarded with sufficient renderings to while away several evenings of listening. How much more rewarding, however, to stumble upon them completely unawares?

June Tabor understands that concept, although she would like to reverse it. Back in 1978, she was hired to sing the jingle for a Golden Vale margarine commercial and, over three decades later, she confessed to writer Peter Paphides, "The words [to the jingle] remain tattooed in my memory: 'Morning has come to the bright golden vale.' Even now, I'm frequently tempted to drop it in at a show, possibly between two harrow-ing Child Ballads."[14]

In 1994, Barry Dransfield recorded a "Lily Bulero" (278) that he first heard over a meal in a Mayfair restaurant, being performed by early music player Joe Skeaping. In 2004, a Middle English manuscript of "Sir Orfeo" (19), edited by J. R. R. Tolkien, was published in *The Tolkien Studies Volume 1*, marking its first appearance in print since it appeared as an uncredited booklet dating from 1943–1944, when it was intended for a naval cadets' course. (Tolkien's modern English version, first published in 1975, was recorded by the Hurricane Party in 2012.)

In 2015, a blood-chilling invocation of "The Unquiet Grave" (78), performed by Helen McCrory, surfaced in an episode of TV's *Penny Dreadful*; the following year, Elizabeth Fraser, once the voice of eighties alternative darlings the Cocteau Twins, contributed a brief but startling "The Lover's Ghost" (248) to an episode of the BBC's *The Living and the Dead*. In 2017, P. J. Harvey and Harry Escott combined for an eldritch "An Acre of Land" (2) for the mystery *Dark River*.

The most unlikely appearance of all, however, was surely the inclusion of "Gallows Pole" (95) on the debut album by Swedish death metal band The Storm Dream Troopers. Mercifully, in this case, both recording and band are figments wholly of author Andrew Cartmel's imagination, merely key notes within *Attack and Decay*, the sixth (2022) installment of his *Vinyl Detective* series of novels. But it proves, once again, that the Child Ballads get everywhere.

Not even the darkest recesses of the canon have remained immune to the inquisitiveness of the modern era, and it is among the internet's great virtues that, for the first time in history, it is now possible to listen to at least one recorded English-language performance of every ballad in the *ESPB*—including close to seventy that had never been heard by even the most persistent of collectors. Yet, if the internet has established itself as the twenty-first century's principal medium for the Child Ballads—as it is for most other forms of music—and if constantly shuffled playlists and streams are the primary means of digesting that music, still the age-old concept of the "album" remains powerful. And so, in the concept of such releases, do the Child Ballads.

In May 2022, *The Guardian* newspaper elected as its Folk Album of the Month a new release by Angeline Morrison, a Birmingham-bred, Cornwall-based singer and academic who had already impacted upon the folk horror scene through both solo work and her collaborations with the Rowan Amber Mill. Now she was turning her attention, at least in part, to F. J. Child, with his selections not only populating but also titling *The Brown Girl and Other Folk Songs*.

It was Frankie Armstrong's "brilliantly emotive version" that inspired Morrison's rendering of "The Brown Girl" (295). "I wanted the song to shiver with feeling, and I wanted to really inhabit the inner emotional world of the Brown Girl as much as I could. Nick Duffy's tender guitar work adds real depth and feeling to the storytelling."[15] But she acknowledges, too,

> I also had my own, secret relationship with it. When I listened to it or sang it, I imagined the Brown Girl as my sort of brown—in other words, someone of color. I kept these dreamings to myself as a lonely teenage folkie. It seemed absurd. After all, I knew all about the archaic beauty myth of pale skin signifying wealth and status (and therefore beauty and desirability), and sun-darkened skin signifying hours and hours spent laboring out of doors—therefore, poverty or low social standing (and as a result, beauty and desirability's opposites). When I later began to learn about the hidden histories of the UK's Black populations, it really changed my relationship to this song. I stopped keeping my secret interpretation to myself. And that's exactly what it is—one of many possible interpretations. Whether she was a White girl with a suntan, a White girl with a Black ancestor, a Romany girl, a girl with Asian ancestry, or whatever else, we can't ever know for certain. And as a fictional character in a song, she is open to as many interpretations or readings as there are people who like to think about these things. . . . And so for me, I like to imagine her in my singing as a young woman of color.

It is through such "modern" manipulations and interpretations that the ballads have retained their relevance, because the manner in which twenty-first-century listeners respond to the stories therein is very different from how the original listeners experienced them. The archetypes remain pure, it is true, but it is only by transporting—if not translating—them into the modern idiom that they can truly grow.

That, after all, is what has always happened, from the moment Percy Grainger placed the unaccompanied voice of Joseph Taylor onto a wax cylinder; or Henry Burr took a song he knew from his father's singing, and put a band behind it. From the first time an electric guitar sounded where once a lute had been heard, or an age-old Scottish folk ballad was reimagined as a blues song, a classical air, or a heavy metal rampage. In 1976, the Ratcliffe Stout Band even introduced the Sidmouth Folk Festival audience to what they termed "medieval reggae" and "boogie tunes from 1610."

Different ears hear different things, and, although some might recoil, others will be absorbed. It's the nature of progress, but it is also the nature of evolution—and without that, the alternative is decay. And who are we, any of us, for whatever reasons we might have, to wish that upon a body of work that so many people have, over the decades, eulogized, but that seem to find its most potent analogy in the words of Martyn Bates, as he and I concluded our interview in May 2022:

To me, these songs are *earth and sky music*. It doesn't really belong to us, and yet it does, you know? It's really ours, truly. It's made from tears, death, joy, beauty, ugliness. The thing about the Child Ballads is, they show us how beautiful music and words can be, like hymns, like the rich poetry of the Bible. They're full of texts that fire the imagination—they all contain veiled undercurrents of magic, full of mythological powers, speaking to the collective unconscious. . . . Songs like these tap into the collective unconscious, because this is music that is out there waiting like an escaped genie, and we're all picking up on it—we all *get it*.

It's a romantic notion, but it still stands. It still has that currency.

APPENDIX

PLAYLISTS

These playlists are designed to offer a wide and representative sampling of (generally) commercially recorded/available Child Ballads, divided into eight categories: 78s, classical music, unaccompanied, acoustic and electric (folk-rock) versions, the twenty-first century, BBC performances, and field recordings. Included are a number of artists who, for a variety of reasons, passed unmentioned in the main text but who are equally worthy of investigation.

The categories are not exclusive. Many of the recordings listed could appear in two or more lists beyond that into which they have been entered—for example, number 18 in The Acoustic Child might more accurately have appeared in Child on 78. However, a strict policy of just one recording of a Child number per playlist precludes this.

Neither is inclusion here necessarily intended to suggest these are the "best" versions of the ballads available—in some cases they are the *sole* versions; in others, they're the only ones that were available to hear. And in a few, a choice needed to be made between several competing favorites, so if you find yourself disagreeing with various entries, know that I probably share your opinion.

Ballads are listed according to their Child number, followed by the title as it appears on the record. In general, the artist, the source (label and catalog number for singles and 78s, title for albums), and the year of release then follow. For the field recordings, only the performer and collector's names are given. Missing numbers in the sequence indicate no applicable recording has been noted.

Note: for ease of reference, the ballad "George Collins," generally accepted to be a combination of Child 42 and 85. is listed under the latter number.

Playlist 1–Child on 78

#1: "The Devil's Nine Questions"—Burl Ives (*Ballads and Folk Songs Volume I*) 1948.

#2: "An Acre of Land"—The English Singers (Roycroft 158) 1929.

#4: "The Willow Tree"—Richard Dyer Bennett (*Twentieth Century Minstrel Folk Songs and Ballads*) 1949.

#12: "Billy Boy"—The Almanac Singers (*Songs for John Doe*) 1941.

#13: "Edward"—G. Marston Haddock (Musicraft 262) c. 1944.

#18: "Bangum and the Boar"—Bentley Ball (Columbia A3084) 1919.

#27: "The Keyhole in the Door"—Holland "Si" Puckett (Challenge G12818) 1928.

#46: "The Riddle Song"—Burl Ives (Okeh 6315) 1941.

#53: "Lord Bateman"—Joseph Taylor (*Percy Grainger's Collection of English Folk-Songs Sung by Genuine Peasant Performers*) 1908.

#58: "Sir Patrick Spens"—Ewan MacColl (HMV B 10260) 1951.

#68: "Henry Lee"—Dick Justice (Columbia 3521) 1929.

#76: "The Storms Are on the Ocean"—The Carter Family (Victor 20937) 1927.

#79: "Lady Gay"—Buell Kazee (Brunswick 212) 1928.

#81: "Little Mattie Groves"—John Jacob Niles (*American Folk Lore Vol. 3*) 1941.

#84: "Barbara Allen"—Maxine Sullivan (Columbia 35710) 1940.

#85: "George Collins"—Henry Whitter (Herwin 75536) 1926.

#95: "Gallows Tree"—Bentley Ball (Columbia 3084) 1920.

#155: "The Fatal Flower Garden"—Nelstone's Hawaiians (Victor 40193) 1929.

#162: "Chevy Chase"—Jack Armstrong (Manor M506) n.d.

#167: "Henry Martyn"—Burl Ives (*The Wayfaring Stranger*) 1944.

#170: "The Death of Queen Jane"—John Jacob Niles (*American Folk Lore Vol. 3*) 1941.

#188: "Escape of Old John Webb"—John and Lucy Allison (*Early American Ballads*) 1943.

#200: "Black Jack David"—Cliff Carlisle (Decca 66015) 1939.

#204: "Cockleshells"—Burl Ives (*A Collection of Ballads and Folk Songs*) 1945.

#223: "Eppie Moray"—Ewan MacColl (HMV B10260) 1951.

#226: "Leezie Lindsay"—Margaret Woodrow Wilson (Columbia 39267) 1914.

#243: "The House Carpenter"—Clarence Ashley (Columbia 15654) 1931.

#250: "Young Henry Martin"—Phil Tanner (Columbia 372 M) 1937.

#274: "Cabbage Head Blues"—Lena Kimbrough (Meritt 2201) 1926.

#277: "Nickety Nackety Now Now Now"—Chubby Parker (Silvertone 5011) 1927.

#278: "The Old Lady and The Devil"—Bill and Belle Reed (Columbia 15336) 1928.

#286: "Sinking in the Lonesome Sea"—The Carter Family (Vocalion 03160) 1936.

#289: "The Raging Sea, How It Roars"—Ernest V. Stoneman and the Blue Ridge Corn Shuckers (Victor 21648) 1928.

#293: "Jock of Hazeldean"—Henry Burr (Victor 16961) 1911.

Playlist 2–The Classical Child

Also included here are spoken-word performances and a miscellany of recordings that do not comfortably fit elsewhere.

#1: "The Devil's Questions"—Prunella Scales (*Rhyme and Rhythm: Poems and Songs for Children: Record 2—Blue Book*) 1965.

#2: "Scarborough Fair"—Pennsylvania All-State Concert Band/ Andrew Boysen Jr. (Alfred Music) 2014.

#3: "The False Knight on the Road"—Benjamin Britten (*Folk Songs*) 1942–1947.

#4: "Lady Isabel and the Elf Knight"—Kathleen Danson Read (*Spoken Literature of Early English Ballads*) 1959.

#7: "Medley: Douglas Tragedy . . ."—Gordon Mooney (*O'er the Border—Music of the Scottish Borders Played on the Cauld Wind Pipes*) 1989.

#9: "The Fair Flower of Northumberland"—Jack Armstrong (*Bagpipes of Britain and Ireland*) 1996.

#12: "Lord Randall"—Kathleen Danson Read (*Spoken Literature of Early English Ballads*) 1959.

#13: "Edward"—C. R. M. Brookes (*Poetry of Robert Burns and Scottish Border Ballads [Border Ballads—a Selection of Ancient Scottish Verse]*) 1959.

#20: "The Cruel Mother"—Alfred Deller (*The Cruel Mother and Other English Ballads and Folk Songs*) 1961.

#22: "St. Stephen and Herod"—V. C. Clinton-Baddeley (*The Jupiter Book of Ballads*) 1959.

#24: "Banks of Green Willow"—George Butterworth (Academy of St Martin-in-the-Fields: *A Shropshire Lad / Two English Idylls / The Banks of Green Willow / Variations on a Theme of Frank Bridge*) 1975.

#26: "The Three Ravens"—Kathleen Danson Read (*Spoken Literature of Early English Ballads*) 1959.

#28: "Burd Ellen and Young Tamlane"—Christopher Maitman/Duke Quartet/William Butler Yeats (*The English Song Series 4*) 2003.

#34: "The Laidley Worm o' Spindleston Heugh"—Owen Brannigan (*Drives Home*) 1972.

#35: "Alison Gross"—John Laurie (*The Jupiter Book of Ballads*) 1959.

#37: "Thomas the Rhymer"—C. R. M. Brookes (*Poetry of Robert Burns and Scottish Border Ballads [Border Ballads: A Selection of Ancient Scottish Verse]*) 1959.

#38: "The Wee Wee Man"—Carmina Chamber Choir (*Contemporary Danish Choral Music*) 2016.

#46: "I Will Give My Love an Apple"—Alfred Deller (*The Three Ravens: Elizabethan Folk and Minstrels Songs*) 1955.

#55: "King Herod and the Cock"—Benjamin Britten (*Folk Songs*) 1947–49.

#56: "Variants of Dives and Lazarus"—The Philharmonia Orchestra of London (*Sinfonica Antarctica, 5 Variants of "Dives and Lazarus"*) 1993.

#58: "Sir Patrick Spens"—C. R. M. Brookes (*Poetry of Robert Burns and Scottish Border Ballads [Border Ballads: A Selection of Ancient Scottish Verse]*) 1959.

#60: "King Estmere"—Gustav Holst/Guildford Chorale Society (*Choral Ballets*) 1995.

#69: "Clerk Sanders"—C. R. M. Brookes (*Poetry of Robert Burns and Scottish Border Ballads [Border Ballads: A Selection of Ancient Scottish Verse]*) 1959.

#74: "Fair Margaret and Sweet William"—Josef Haydn (Anderson/ MacDougall/Haydn Trio Eisenradt (*Haydn Edition*) 2008.

#76: "Who's Going to Shoe Your Pretty Little Foot?"—Alfred Deller (*The Three Ravens: Elizabethan Folk and Minstrels Songs*) 1955.

#77: "Sweet William's Ghost"—Kathleen Danson Read (*Spoken Literature of Early English Ballads*) 1959.

#78: "The Unquiet Grave"—V. C. Clinton-Baddeley and Pauline Letts (*The Jupiter Book of Ballads*) 1959.

#79: "The Wife of Usher's Well"—John Laurie (*The Jupiter Book of Ballads*) 1959.

#81: "The Ballad of Little Musgrave and Lady Barnard"—Benjamin Britten (*Folk Songs*) 1942–47.

#83: "Gil Morris"—Josef Haydn (Anderson/MacDougall/Haydn Trio Eisenradt (*Haydn Edition*) 2008.

#84: "Barbara Allen"—The Roger Wagner Chorale (*Folk Songs of the Old World*) 1956.

#105: "The Bailiff's Daughter of Islington"—Jim and Mindy (*Music for Relaxation Featuring the Recorder*) 2012.

#106: "The Lament of the Border Widow"—C. R. M. Brookes (*Poetry of Robert Burns and Scottish Border Ballads [Border Ballads: A Selection of Ancient Scottish Verse]*) 1959.

#112: "Blow Away the Morning Dew"—Alfred Deller (*The Three Ravens: Elizabethan Folk and Minstrels Songs*) 1955.

#125: "Robin Hood and Little John"—Ed McCurdy and Michael Kane (*The Legend of Robin Hood*) 1973.

#129: "Robin Hood and the Prince of Aragon"—Ed McCurdy and Michael Kane (*The Legend of Robin Hood*) 1973.

#139: "Robin Hood and the Fifteen Foresters"—Ed McCurdy and Michael Kane (*The Legend of Robin Hood*) 1973.

#141: "Robin Hood Rescuing Will Stutly"—Ed McCurdy and Michael Kane (*The Legend of Robin Hood*) 1973.

#147: "Robin Hood's Golden Prize"—Kathleen Danson Read (*Spoken Literature of Early English Ballads*) 1959.

#152: "Robin Hood and the Golden Arrow"—Ed McCurdy and Michael Kane (*The Legend of Robin Hood*) 1973.

#155: "Little Sir William"—Benjamin Britten and Peter Pears (*English and French Folk Ballads*) 1948.

#162: "Chevy Chase"—Kathleen Danson Read (*Spoken Literature of Early English Ballads*) 1959.

#170: "King Henry"—Alfred Deller (*The Three Ravens: Elizabethan Folk and Minstrels Songs*) 1955.

#173: "Mary Hamilton"—John Laurie and Isla Cameron (*The Jupiter Book of Ballads*) 1959.

#181: "The Bonnie Earl o' Moray"—Benjamin Britten and Peter Pears (*English and French Folk Ballads*) 1948.

#184: "The Lads of Wamphray"—Sidney Chamber Choir, Melbourne SO Chorus and Melbourne SO (*Percy Grainger—Works for Large Chorus and Orchestra*) 2013.

#187: Jock o the Side—Gordon Mooney (*O'er the Border: Music of the Scottish Borders Played on the Cauld Wind Pipes*) 1994.

#191: "Hughie Graham"—Josef Haydn (Anderson/MacDougall/Haydn Trio Eisenradt (*Haydn Edition*) 2008.

#195: "Lord Maxwell's Last Goodnight"—BBC Philharmonic Orchestra and Richard Hickox (*The Grainger Edition Vol. 15: Orchestral Works 3*) 2000.

#200: "The Wraggle Taggle Gypsies"—Alfred Deller (*The Three Ravens: Elizabethan Folk and Minstrels Songs*) 1955.

#201: "Bessy Bell and Mary Gray"—Josef Haydn (Anderson/MacDougall/Haydn Trio Eisenradt (Haydn Edition) 2008.

#204: "Oh Waly Waly"—Benjamin Britten (*Folk Songs*) 1942–47.

#209: "Geordie"—Alfred Deller (*The Cruel Mother and Other English Ballads and Folk Songs*) 1961.

#214: "The Braes o Yarrow"—Josef Haydn (Anderson/MacDougall/Haydn Trio Eisenradt (Haydn Edition) 2008.

#217: "The Broom of Cowdenknows"—Josef Haydn (Anderson/MacDougall/Haydn Trio Eisenradt (*Haydn Edition*) 2008.

#226: "Leezie Lindsay"—Benjamin Britten (*Folk Songs*) 1942–47.

#248: "The Lover's Ghost"—Alfred Deller (*Vaughan Williams Folk Song Album*) 1959.

#250: "Henry Martyn"—Alfred Deller (*Western Wind and Other English Folk Songs and Ballads*) 1958.

#273: "A Pleasant Ballad of King Henry II and the Miller of Mansfield"—Peasants All (*A Handful of Pleasant Delites*—A Collection of Popular English Music from the 13th. to the 17th. Century) 1977.

#274: "Our Goodman"—Kathleen Danson Read (*Spoken Literature of Early English Ballads*) 1959.

#275: "Get Up and Bar the Door"—Kathleen Danson Read (*Spoken Literature of Early English Ballads*) 1959.

#277: "Risslety Rosslety"—Ruth Crawford (*Works by: Henry Cowell / Wallingford Riegger / John J. Becker / Ruth Crawford Seeger*) 1978.

#278: "The Farmer's Curst Wife"—Kathleen Danson Read (*Spoken Literature of Early English Ballads*) 1959.

#284: "John Dory"—The London Madrigal Singers and Christopher Bishop (*Vaughan Williams—The Collector's Edition*) 2008.

#285: "High Barbaree"—Isla Cameron (*The Jupiter Book of Ballads*) 1959.

#286: "The Golden Vanity—A Vaudeville for Boys and Piano after the Old English Ballad"—Benjamin Britten/Wandsworth School Boys Choir (*Noye's Fludde/The Golden Vanity*) 1993.

#293: "Jock O'Hazeldean"—John Laurie (*A Junior Anthology of English Verse Part Two*) 1960.

Playlist 3–The Unaccompanied Child

#1: "Lay the Bent to the Bonny Broom"—Isla Cameron (*The Waters of Tyne—Northumbrian Songs and Ballads*) 1961.

#2: "Scarborough Fair"—Shirley Collins (*False True Lovers*) 1959.

#3: "The False Knight"—Sheila Clark (*The Legend of Tum Dula and Other Tragic Love Ballads*) 1986.

#4: "The Outlandish Knight"—A. L. Lloyd (*English and Scottish Popular Ballads: Vol. 2*) 1956.

#7: "The Bold Dragoon"—The Young Tradition (*So Cheerfully Round*) 1967.

#9: "The Fair Flower of Northumberland"—Ewan MacColl and Peggy Seeger (*Blood and Roses: Vol. 2*) 1981.

#10: "Minorie"—Ewan MacColl (*English and Scottish Popular Ballads: Vol. 1*) 1956.

#11: "The Cruel Brother"—Katherine Campbell (*The Songs of Amelia and Jane Harris: Scots Songs and Ballads from Perthshire Tradition*) 2004.

#12: "Lord Randal"—Ewan MacColl (HMV B110259—78 rpm) 1951.

#13: "My Son David"—Jeannie Robertson (*Folk Song Today*) 1955.

#14: "The Bonnie Banks o Airdrie"—Ewan MacColl and Betsy Miller (*A Garland of Scots Folk Song*) 1960.

#16: "Sheath and Knife"—Jean Redpath (*There Were Minstrels*) 1977.

#17: "The Old Beggar Man"—Sandy Ives (*Folk Songs of Maine*) 1959.

#18: "Bold Sir Rylas"—A. L. Lloyd (*English and Scottish Popular Ballads: Vol. 8*) 1956.

#19: "King Orfeo"—Alva (*Love Burns in Me—Medieval and Traditional Songs and Fiddle Music from Britain and France*) 2012.

#20: "The Greenwood Side—Ian and Sylvia (*Four Strong Winds*) 1963.

#21: "The Well Below the Valley"—Frankie Armstrong (*Till the Grass O'ergrew the Corn*) 1997.

#24: "The Banks of Yarrow"—Alison McMorland and Peta Webb (*Alison McMorland and Peta Webb*) 1980.

#25: "Among the Blue Flowers and the Yellow"—Ewan MacColl (*English and Scottish Popular Ballads: Vol. 5*) 1956.

#26: "Twa Corbies"—Spindlewood (*Spindlewood*) 1988.

#27: "The Whummil Bore"—Moira Cameron (with light percussive accompaniment) (*Sands of the Shore*) 1983.

#34: "Kemp Owen"—Bryony Griffith (*Nightshade*) 2014.

#35: "Alison Gross"—Dave and Toni Arthur (*Hearken to the Witches Rune*) 1971.

#37: "Thomas the Rhymer"—Ewan MacColl (*English and Scottish Popular Ballads: Vol. 1*) 1956.

#39: "Young Tambling"—Anne Briggs (*Anne Briggs*) 1971.

#41: "Hind Horn"—Ewan MacColl (*English and Scottish Popular Ballads: Vol. 1*) 1956.

#42: "Clerk Colvin"—Jean Redpath (*There Were Minstrels*) 1977.

#43: "The Maid on the Shore"—Eliza Carthy (*Rough Music*) 2007.

#44: "Hares on the Mountain"—Frankie Armstrong (*My Song Is My Own—Songs from Women*) 1979.

#45: "King John and the Bishop"—Elmer George (*Burly Banks of Barbry O: Eight Traditional British-American Ballads*) 1953.

#47: "Proud Lady Margaret"—Ewan MacColl (*The English and Scottish Popular Ballads (Child Ballads): Vol. 2*) 1964.

#49: "The Twa Brothers"—Jeannie Robertson (*Sings Twa Brothers, Davy Faa,* etc.) 1959.

#50: "The Bonny Hind"—June Tabor (*Abyssinians*) 1983.

#51: "Lucy Wan"—Ewan MacColl (*The Long Harvest: Vol. 8*) 1968.

#52: "Lady Jean"—Jo Miller (*Old Songs and Bothy Ballads—There's Bound to Be a Row*) 2010.

#53: "Lord Bateman" (American)—Peggy Seeger (*The Long Harvest: Vol. 8*) 1967.

#54: The Cherry-Tree Carol—Isla Cameron (*Through Bushes and Briars and Other Songs of the British Isles*) 1956.

#55: "Herod and the Cock"—The Watersons (*Frost and Fire*) 1965.

#56: "Dives and Lazarus"—The Young Tradition (*The Young Tradition*) 1966.

#57: "The Guilty Sea Captain"—Dave and Toni Arthur (*Morning Stands on Tiptoe*) 1967.

#58: "Sir Patrick Spens"—Jean Redpath (*Father Adam*) 1979.

#62: "Fair Annie"—Sylvia Barnes (*The Colour of Amber*) 2007.

#63: "Child Waters"—Frankie Armstrong (*Till the Grass O'ergrew the Corn*) 1997.

#65: "Lady Maisry"—Ewan MacColl (*Blood and Roses: Vol. 4*) 1986.

#67: "Glenkindle"—Ewan MacColl (*Blood and Roses: Vol. 3*) 1982.

#68: "The Proud Girl"—Frankie Armstrong (*Till the Grass O'ergrew the Corn*) 1997.

#69: "Clerk Sanders"—Crackerhash (*Napoleon Crossing the Rhine*) 1978.

#72: "The Clerk's Twa Sons o Owensford"—Ewan MacColl and Peggy Seeger (*Blood and Roses: Vol. 4*) 1986.

#74: "Lady Margaret"—Sheila K. Adams (*Loving Forward, Loving Back*) 1987.

#75: "The New Ballad of Lord Lovel"—Peggy Seeger (*The Long Harvest: Vol. 5*) 1967.

#76: "Lord Gregory"—Ewan MacColl (*English and Scottish Popular Ballads: Vol. 7*) 1956.

#77: "Sweet William's Ghost"—Len Graham (*Ye Lovers All*) 1985.

#78: "The Unquiet Grave"—A. L. Lloyd (*English and Scottish Popular Ballads: Vol. 1*) 1956.

#79: "The Wife of Usher's Well"—Ewan MacColl (*The Long Harvest: Vol. 5*) 1967.

#81: "Matty Groves"—Dillard Chandler (*Old Love Songs and Ballads from the Big Laurel, NC*) 1964.

#83: "Gil Morice"—Ewan MacColl (*Blood and Roses: Vol. 2*) 1982.

#84: "Bawbee Allen" (Scots)—Ewan MacColl and Peggy Seeger (*The Long Harvest: Vol. 4*) 1966.

#85: "George Collins"—A. L. Lloyd (*English and Scottish Popular Ballads: Vol. 3*) 1956.

#86: "Young Benjie"—Rosaleen Gregory (*Sheath and Knife*) 2012.

#88: "Young Johnstone"—Ewan MacColl and Peggy Seeger (*Blood and Roses: Vol. 3*) 1982.

#91: "Fair Mary of Wallington"—June Tabor (*The First Folk Review Record*) 1974.

#92: "The Lowlands of Holland" (American)—Peggy Seeger (*The Long Harvest: Vol. 10*) 1968.

#93: "Long Lankin"—Martin Carthy (*But Two Came By*) 1968.

#94: "Young Waters"—Heather Heywood (*By Yon Castle Wa'*) 1993.

#95: "The Hangman Song"—Jean Ritchie (*Kentucky Mountain Songs*) 1954.

#98: "Brown Adam"—Ewan MacColl and Peggy Seeger (*Blood and Roses: Vol. 5*) 1986.

#99: "Johnie Scott"—Seán Corcoran (*Sailing into Walpole's Marsh*) 1981.

#100: "John Barbour" (Canadian)—Peggy Seeger (*The Long Harvest: Vol. 7*) 1967.

#104: "Prince Heathen"—Frankie Armstrong (*. . . Out of Love, Hope and Suffering*) 1974.

#106: "The Famous Flower of Serving Men"—Ewan MacColl (*English and Scottish Popular Ballads: Vol. 3*) 1964.

#110: "Knight William"—The Young Tradition (*So Cheerfully Round*) 1967.

#112: "The Shepherd Lad"—Ewan MacColl (*English and Scottish Popular Ballads: Vol. 2*) 1956.

#113: "The Great Silkie of Sule Skerry"—The Hare and the Moon (*Wood Witch*) 2015.

#114: "Johnnie O'Breadisley"—Ewan MacColl (*English and Scottish Popular Ballads: Vol. 3*) 1956.

#126: "Robin Hood and the Tanner"—A. L. Lloyd (*English and Scottish Popular Ballads: Vol. 2*) 1956.

#132: "The Bold Pedlar and Robin Hood"—A. L. Lloyd (*English and Scottish Popular Ballads: Vol. 4*) 1956.

#144: "Robin Hood and the Bishop of Hereford"—John Roberts and Tony Barrand (*A Present from the Gentlemen — A Pandora's Box of English Folk Songs*) 1992.

#155: "It Rained a Mist" (American)—Peggy Seeger (*The Long Harvest: Vol. 5*) 1967.

#163: "The Battle of Harlaw"—Ewan MacColl (*English and Scottish Popular Ballads: Vol. 1*) 1956.

#170: "The Death of Queen Jane"—Ewan MacColl (*The Long Harvest: Vol. 9*) 1968.

#173: "Mary Hamilton"—Jean Redpath with Abby Newton (*Lowlands*) 1980.

#178: "Edom o Gordon"—Ewan MacColl (*Poetry and Song: Vol. 12*) 1968.

#181: "The Bonnie Earl o' Moray"—Ewan MacColl (*English and Scottish Popular Ballads: Vol. 7*) 1956.

#182: "The Laird o Logie"—Ewan MacColl and Peggy Seeger (*Blood and Roses: Vol. 3*) 1982.

#183: "Willie Macintosh"—Ewan MacColl and Peggy Seeger (*Blood and Roses: Vol. 4*) 1986.

#187: "Jock o the Side"—Andrew Calhoun (*Rhymer's Tower: Ballads of the Anglo-Scottish Border*) 2016.

#189: "Hobie Noble"—Andrew Calhoun (*Rhymer's Tower: Ballads of the Anglo-Scottish Border*) 2016.

#190: Jamie Telfer of the Fair Dodhead—Andrew Calhoun (*Rhymer's Tower: Ballads of the Anglo-Scottish Border*) 2016.

#191: "Hughie Graham"—Ewan MacColl (*English and Scottish Popular Ballads: Vol. 6*) 1956.

#194: "The Laird of Wariston"—Gordeanna McCulloch (*In Freenship's Name*) 1997.

#199: "Bonnie House o' Airlie"—Ewan MacColl (*English and Scottish Popular Ballads: Vol. 2*) 1961.

#200: "Gypsies-O"—A. L. Lloyd (*English and Scottish Popular Ballads: Vol. 6*) 1956.

#201: "Bessy Bell and Mary Gray"—Martin Carthy (*Shearwater*) 1972.

#203: "The Baron of Brackley"—Glenn Muir (*Muckle Sangs and Ither Thangs*) 2020.

#204: "Oh Waly Waly"—Ewan MacColl and Peggy Seeger (*Two Way Trip*) 1961.

#208: "Derwentwater's Farewell"—Dave Webber and Anni Fentima (*Away from It All*) 2003.

#209: "Geordie"—Peter Bellamy (*Mainly Norfolk*) 1968.

#212: "The Duke of Athole's Nurse"—Ewan MacColl (*The Long Harvest: Vol. 11*) 1969.

#214: "The Dowie Dens o' Yarrow"—Jean Redpath (*Song of the Seals*) 1978.

#215: "Willie's Rare"—Jean Redpath (*Father Adam*) 1979.

#216: "Clyde's Water"—Ewan MacColl (*English and Scottish Popular Ballads: Vol. 3*) 1961.

#217: "The Broom of Cowdenknows"—Ewan MacColl (*English and Scottish Popular Ballads: Vol. 7*) 1956.

#218: "Honey for the Bee"—The Witches of Elswick (*Out of Bed*) 2001.

#221: "The Green Wedding"—John Langstaff (*Sings American and English Folk Songs and Ballads*) 1956.

#223: "Eppie Morrie"— Ewan MacColl (*English and Scottish Popular Ballads: Vol. 2*) 1956.

#225: "Rob Roy"—Jean Redpath (*There Were Minstrels*) 1977.

#231: "The Earl of Errol"—Sheena Wellington (*Hamely Fare*) 2003.

#232: "Richie Story"—Ewan MacColl (*English and Scottish Popular Ballads: Vol. 2*) 1956.

#233: "Andrew Lammie"—Ewan MacColl (*The Long Harvest: Vol. 11*) 1969.

#235: "The Earl of Aboyne"—Ewan MacColl (*English and Scottish Popular Ballads: Vol. 7*) 1956.

#236: "The Laird o Drum"—Jeannie Robertson (*The Cuckoo's Nest and Other Scottish Folk Songs*) 1963.

#238: "Glenlogie"—Ewan MacColl (*English and Scottish Popular Ballads: Vol. 3*) 1964.

#240: "The Rantin Laddie"—Jean Redpath (*Jean Redpath's Scottish Ballad Book*) 1962.

#243: "The Daemon Lover"—A. L. Lloyd (*English and Scottish Popular Ballads: Vol. 7*) 1956.

#248: "The Lover's Ghost"—A. L. Lloyd (*English and Scottish Popular Ballads: Vol. 7*) 1956.

#249: "Auld Matrons"—Ewan MacColl and Peggy Seeger (*Blood and Roses: Vol. 3*) 1982.

#250: "Henry Martyn"—A. L. Lloyd (*English and Scottish Popular Ballads: Vol. 7*) 1956.

#251: "Lang Johnny More"—Ewan MacColl (*Blood and Roses: Vol. 1*) 1979.

#267: "The Heir o' Linn"—Ewan MacColl (*English and Scottish Popular Ballads: Vol. 5*) 1956.

#269: "Lady Diamond"—Frankie Armstrong (*Songs and Ballads*) 1975.

#272: "The Suffolk Miracle"—Peggy Seeger (*Blood and Roses: Vol. 1*) 1979.

#273: "King Jamie and the Tinker"—John Kirkpatrick (*Voices: English Traditional Songs*) 1992.

#274: "Our Gudeman"—Ewan MacColl (*English and Scottish Popular Ballads: Vol. 1*) 1956.

#275: "Get Up and Bar the Door"—Ewan MacColl (*English and Scottish Popular Ballads: Vol. 2*) 1956.

#277: "Rissilty Rossity"—Peggy Seeger (*The Long Harvest: Vol. 9*) 1968.

#278: "The Devil and the Ploughman"—A. L. Lloyd (*English and Scottish Popular Ballads: Vol. 1*) 1956.

#279: "The Gaberlunzie Man"—Isla St. Clair (*Great Songs and Ballads of Scotland*) 2008.

#280: "The Beggar-Laddie"—Rachel McDonogh (*Queen of Elfan*) 2020.

#281: "The Keach and the Creel"—A. L. Lloyd (*English and Scottish Popular Ballads: Vol. 4*) 1956.

#282: "Jock the Leg"—Ewan MacColl (*English and Scottish Popular Ballads: Vol. 7*) 1956.

#283: "The Crafty Farmer"—Ewan MacColl (*English and Scottish Popular Ballads: Vol. 6*) 1956.

#286: "Golden Vanitee"—John Faulkner and Sandra Kerr (*Poetry and Song: Vol. 3*) 1967.

#287: "Captain Ward and the Rainbow"—Tundra (*A Kentish Garland*) 1978.

#291: "Chylde Owlet"—Maddy Prior (*Ballads*) 1997.

#293: "Jock O'Hazeldean"—Jean Redpath (*Father Adam*) 1979.

#295: "The Brown Girl"—Frankie Armstrong (*Lovely on the Water*) 1972.

#298: "Young Peggy"—Ewan MacColl (*Saturday Night at the Bull and Mouth*) 1977.

#299: "The Brewer's Daughter"—Ewan MacColl (*The Long Harvest: Vol. 10*) 1968.

Playlist 4–The Acoustic Child

#1: "A Riddle Wisely Expounded"—Hanita Blair (*Minstrel*) 1992.

#2: "Sing Ivy"—Tony Wales (*Sussex Folk Songs*) 1957.

#3: "False Knight on the Road"—Maddy Prior and Tim Hart (*Summer Solstice*) 1971.

#4: "May Colvin"— Ewan MacColl and Peggy Seeger (*The Long Harvest: Vol. 6*) 1967.

#6: "Willie's Lady"—Jefferson Hamer and Anais Mitchel (*Child Ballads*) 2013.

#7: "The Dragoon and the Lady"—Bandoggs (*Bandoggs*) 1978.

#9: "The Fair Flower of Northumberland"—Sara Grey (*Sara Grey*) 1970.

#10: "The Twa Sisters"—Frankie Armstrong (*Lovely on the Water*) 1972.

#11: "The Cruel Brother"—Archie Fisher (*The Man with a Rhyme*) 1976.

#12: "Lord Randall"—Fiddler Beers and Evelyne (*Walkie in the Parlor*) 1960.

#13: "The Murdered Brother"—John Jacob Niles (*The Ballads of . . .*) 1960.

#14: "The Bonnie Banks o' Fordie"—Dick Gaughan (*No More Forever*) 1972.

#16: "Sheath and Knife"—Gordeanna McCulloch (*Sheath and Knife*) 1978.

#17: "The Bleacher Lassie of Kelvinhaugh"—Ewan MacColl (*Still Love Him—Traditional Love Songs*) 1958.

#18: "Wild Hog in the Woods"—Lonesome Luke and His Farm Boys (Champion 6229—78 rpm) 1931.

#19: "Young Orphy"—Frankie Armstrong (*Till the Grass O'ergrew the Corn*) 1997.

#20: "The Cruel Mother"—Blue Lobelia (*Folk Songs and Broadside Ballads from the Helen Creighton*) 2021.

#21: "Jesus Met the Woman at the Well"—Mahalia Jackson (*Sings America's Favorite Hymns*) 1971.

#24: "The Banks of Green Willow"—Dick Gaughan (*Kist O'Gold*) 1976.

#25: "Amang the Blue Flowers and the Yellow"—Eyeless in Gaza (*Song of the Beautiful Wanton*) 2010.

#26: "The Twa Corbies"—Ray and Archie Fisher (*Bonnie Lass Come O'er the Burn*) 1965.

#27: "The Keyhole in the Door"—Mike Harding (*A Lancashire Lad*) 1975.

#29: "The Boy and the Mantle"—Allan Taylor (*The Lady*) 1971.

#31: "The Half Hitch"—Pete Seeger (*Story Songs*) 1961.

#32: "King Henry"—Martin Carthy (*Sweet Wivelsfield*) 1974.

#33: "Kempy Kaye"—Jock Tamson's Bairns (*The Lassie's Fashion*) 1982

#34: "King Knapperty"—Martin Carthy/Dave Swarbrick (*Crown of Horn*) 1976.

#35: "Alison Cross"—Jon Rennard (*The Parting Glass*) 1971.

#36: "The Laily Worm and the Machrel of the Sea"—Celtic Nots (*Not Music*) 1998.

#37: "True Thomas"—Danny Carnahan and Robin Petrie (*Journeys of the Heart*) 1984.

#38: "The Wee Wee Man"—Jim and Holly Lawrence (*Caledonian Shadows*) 2011.

#39: "Tam Lin"—Moira Craig (*The Fairy Dance—Myth and Magic in Celtic Songs and Tunes*) 1996.

#40: "The Queen of Elfan's Nourice"—Daniel Kelly (*Love, Magic, Murder and Song*) 2021.

#42: "Clerk Colville"—Michael Raven and Joan Mills (*Can Y Melinydd [The Miller Song]*) 1976.

#43: "The Broomfield Hill"—Dave and Toni Arthur (*Hearken to the Witches Rune*) 1973.

#44: "The Two Magicians"—Bob Fox and Stu Luckley (*Wish We Had Never Parted*) 1982.

#45: "King John and the Bishop"—Margaret MacArthur (*Ballads Thrice Twisted*) 1999.

#46: "I Will Give My Love An Apple"—Iona (*Heaven's Bright Sun*) 1997.

#47: "Proud Lady Margaret"—Peter and Chris Coe (*Out of Season, Out of Rhyme*) 1976.

#48: "The Death of Young Andrew"—Martin Carthy and Dave Swarbrick (*Because It's There*) 1979.

#49: "The Twa Brothers"—Nic Jones (*Nic Jones*) 1971.

#50: "The Bonny Hind"—Martin Carthy with Dave Swarbrick (*Signs of Life*) 1998.

#51: "Lucy Wan"—Hedy West (*Ballads*) 1967.

#53: "Lord Bateman"—Unthank Smith (*Nowhere and Everywhere*) 2023.

#54: "The Cherry-Tree Carol"—Shirley Collins and Davy Graham (*Folk Roots, New Routes*) 1964.

#55: "Herod and the Cock"—Mary Faith Rhoads (*Le Dulcimer*) 1973.

#56: "Dives and Lazarus"—Rick Lee (*There's Talk about a Fence*) 1999.

#57: "William Glenn"—Nic Jones (*From the Devil to a Stranger*) 1978.

#58: "Sir Patrick Spens"—Martin Carthy and Eliza Carthy (*Sings of Life*) 1998.

#62: "Fair Annie"—Steve Tilston and Maggie Boyle (*All under the Sun*) 1996.

#63: "Child Waters"—Peggy Seeger (*Blood and Roses: Vol. 1*) 1979.

#64: "Fair Janet"—Jack Rutter (*Gold of Scar and Shale*) 2019.

#65: "Mother, Go Make My Bed"—Eliza Carthy (*Eliza Carthy and the Kings of Calicutt*) 1997.

#67: "Jack O'Rion"—Martin Carthy and Dave Swarbrick (*But Two Came By*) 1968.

#68: "Love Henry"—Bob Dylan (*World Go Wrong*) 1993.

#69: "Clerk Sanders"—Martin Simpson (*Kind Letters*) 2005.

#73: "Lord Thomas and Fair Annie"—Ewan MacColl and Peggy Seeger (*Classic Scots Ballads*) 1959.

#74: "Fair Margaret and Sweet William"—Dee Strickland Johnson (*The Unquiet Grave and Other British Ballads*) 1976.

#75: "Lord Lovell"—June Bugg (*Hootenanny Folk Festival*) 1964.

#76: "Lord Gregory"—Judy Collins (*Fifth Album*) 1965.

#77: "Sweet William's Ghost"—Bill Shute and Lisa Null (*The Feathered Maiden and Other Ballads*) 1977.

#78: "Lost Jimmy Whalen"—Tia Blake and Her Folk Group (*Folk Songs and Ballads*) 1971.

#79: "The Wife of Usher's Well"—Peggy Seeger (*11 American Ballads and Songs*) 1957.

#81: "Mattie Groves"—Paul Clayton (*Dulcimer Songs and Solos*) 1957.

#82: "The Bonny Birdy"—Ray Fisher (*The Bonny Bird*) 1972.

#83: "Bill Norrie"—Martin Carthy (*Right of Passage*) 1988.

#84: "Barbara Allen"—Art Garfunkel (*Angel Clare*) 1973.

#85: "George Collins"—Obray Ramsey (*Folk Songs from the Three Laurels*) 1961.

#86: "Young Benjie"—Pete and Chris Coe (*Out of Season Out of Rhyme*) 1976.

#87: "Lord Abore and Mary Flynn"—Al O'Donnell (*Al O'Donnell* 2) 1978.

#88: "Young Johnstone"—June Tabor (*An Echo of Hooves*) 2003.

#89: "King O'Lurve"—Hermes Nye (*Ballads Reliques—Early English Ballads . . .*) 1957.

#90: "Jellon Grame"—Peggy Seeger (Songs of Love and Politics) 1992.

#91: "Bonnie Earl of Livingston"—Phil Cooper (*Written in Our Eyes—Ballads and Sketches: Vol. 1*) 2005.

#92: "The Lowlands of Holland"—Martin Carthy and Dave Swarbrick (*Second Album*) 1966.

#93: "Bo Lankin"—Frank Profitt (*Sings Folk Songs*) 1962.

#94: "Young Waters"—June Tabor (*Airs and Graces*) 1976.

#95: "Hangman"—Tia Blake and Her Folk Group (*Folk Songs and Ballads*) 1971.

#98: "Brown Adam"—Martin Carthy (*Landfall*) 1971.

#100: "Willie o' Winsbury"—Anne Briggs (*Anne Briggs*) 1971.

#102: "Robin Hood"—Allan Taylor (*Sometimes*) 1971.

#103: "The Marriage of Robin Hood"—Estampie (*Under the Greenwood Tree*) 1997.

#104: "Prince Heathen"—Martin Carthy and Dave Swarbrick (*Prince Heathen*) 1969.

#105: "The Bailiff's Daughter of Islington"—Jon Rennard (*Brimbledon Fair*) 1970.

#106: "The Famous Flower of Serving Men"—Martin Carthy (*Shearwater*) 1972.

#110: "The Shepherd's Daughter and the King"—John Jacob Niles (*The Ballads of . . .*) 1960.

#112: "Blow Away the Winds"—Eliza Carthy (*Rice*) 1998.

#113: "The Great Silkie of Sule Skerry"—Judy Collins (*Golden Apples of the Sun*) 1962.

#114: "Fair John and the Seven Foresters"—John Jacob Niles (*The Ballads of . . .*) 1960.

#117: "A Little Gest of Robyn Hood"—Bob Frank (*A Little Gest of Robyn Hood*) 2001.

#120: "Robin Hood's Death and Burial"—Wallace House (*Robin Hood Ballads*) 1953.

#122: "Robin Hood and the Butcher"—Ed McCurdy and Michael Kane (*The Legend of Robin Hood*) 1973.

#123: "Robin Hood and the Curtal Friar"—Estampie (*Under the Greenwood Tree*) 1997.

#124: "The Jolly Pinder of Wakefield"—Wallace House (*Robin Hood Ballads*) 1953.

#125: "Robin Hood and Little John"—Roy Harris (*By Sandbank Fields*) 1977.

#126: "Robin Hood and the Tanner"—St George's Canzona (*A Tapestry of Music for Robin Hood and His King*) 1976.

#131: "Robin Hood and the Ranger"—Wallace House (*Robin Hood Ballads*) 1953.

#132: "The Bold Pedlar and Robin Hood"—Ed McCurdy (*Badmen, Heroes and Pirates*) 1957.

#138: "Robin Hood and Allen a Dale"—Sherwood Rise (*From the Wood*) 1981.

#139: "Robin Hood and the Fifteen Foresters"—Robin Goodluck (*The Suffolk Miracle*) 1974.

#140: "Robin Hood Rescuing Three Squires"—John Kirkpatrick (*Ballads*) 1997.

#144: "Robin Hood and the Bishop of Hereford"—Tony Rose (*Young Hunting*) 1970.

#147: "Robin Hood's Golden Prize"—Hermes Nye (*Ballads Reliques: Early English Ballads*) 1957.

#150: "Robin Hood and Maid Marian"—Wallace House (*Robin Hood Ballads*) 1953.

#154: "A True Tale of Robin Hood"—Wallace House (*Robin Hood Ballads*) 1953.

#155: "Little Sir William"—John Kirkpatrick and Sue Harris (*Shreds and Patches*) 1977.

#156: "Queen Elinor's Confession"—Chad Mitchell Trio (*Singin' Our Mind*) 1963.

#157: "Gude Wallace"—Max Dunbar (*Songs and Ballads of the Scottish Wars*) 1956.

#161: "The Battle of Otterburn"—John Timpany and Audrey Smith (*Come All You Tender-Hearted Christians*) 1973.

#162: "Chevy Chace"—Bob Davenport, Isla Cameron, Jack Armstrong and The Rakes (*Northumbrian Minstrelsy*) 1964.

#163: "The Battle of Harlaw"—Ian Campbell (*The Cock Doth Craw—Ballads from Scotland*) 1968.

#164: "The Fency King and the English King"—John Jacob Niles (*The Ballads of . . .*) 1960.

#167: "Henry Martyn"—Dick Wilder (*Badmen, Heroes and Pirates*) 1957.

#168: "Flodden Field"—Andrew Calhoun (*Rhymer's Tower: Ballads of the Anglo-Scottish Border*) 2017.

#169: "Johnie Armstrong"—Katherine Campbell (*The Songs of Amelia and Jane Harris—Scots Songs and Ballads from Perthshire Tradition*) 2004.

#170: "The Death of Queen Jane"—Joan Baez (*Joan 5*) 1964.

#173: "Mary Hamilton"—Paul Clayton (*Dulcimer Songs and Solos*) 1957.

#178: "Edom o' Gordon"—Folkal Point (*Folkal Point*) 1972.

#181: "The Bonnie Earl o' Moray"—The Ian Campbell Folk Group (*Four Highland Songs* EP) 1966.

#182: "Geordie Laird Logie"—Bandoggs (*Bandoggs*) 1978.

#183: "The Burning of Auchindoon"—Silly Sisters (*Silly Sisters*) 1976.

#186: "Kinmont Willie"—Max Dunbar (*Songs and Ballads of the Scottish Wars*) 1956.

#188: "The Escape of Old John Webb"—The Kingston Trio (*String Along*) 1960.

#190: "Jamie Telfer of the Fair Dodhead"—Andrew Calhoun (*Rhymer's Tower: Ballads of the Anglo-Scottish Border*) 2016.

#191: "The Lamentation of Hughie Graham"—Steve Tilston and Maggie Boyle (*Of Moor and Mesa*) 1992.

#192: "The Blind Harper"—Nic Jones (*From the Devil to a Stranger*) 1978.

#193: "The Death of Parcy Reed"—Graham Pitt (*Fyre and Sworde—Songs of the Border Reivers*) 2000.

#195: "Lord Maxwell's Last Goodnight"—Jean Tabor (*Ashes and Diamonds*) 1977.

#199: "The Bonnie House o' Airlie"—Kate Rusby (*The Girl Who Couldn't Fly*) 2005.

#200: "Gypsy Davy"—Margaret MacArthur and Family (*Folk Songs of Vermont*) 1963.

#201: "Betsy Bell"—Maddy Prior (*Ballads and Candles*) 2000.

#203: "The Baron of Brackley"—Ian Campbell Folk Group (*New Impressions Of*) 1967.

#204: "Waly Waly"—Buffy Sainte-Marie (*Little Wheel Spin and Spin*) 1966.

#206: "The Battle of Bothwell Bridge"—Max Dunbar (*Songs and Ballads of the Scottish Wars*) 1956.

#208: "Derwentwater's Farewell"—Louis Killen (*Old Songs, Old Friends*) 1977.

#209: "Geordie"—Sandy Denny (demo/ *The Notes and the Words: A Collection of Demos and Rarities*) 1966.

#210: "Bonnie James Campbell"—The Livingstones (*The Livingstones, I Presume*) 1969.

#212: "Little Duke Arthur's Nurse"—Frankie Armstrong (*Songs and Ballads*) 1975.

#214: "Dowie dens o' Yarrow"—Davie Stewart (*Davie Stewart*) 1978.

#215: "Annan Water"—Kate Rusby (*Evolving Tradition 2*) 1996.

#216: "Clyde Waters"—Nic Jones (*Penguin Eggs*) 1980.

#217: "Bonny May"—June Tabor (*Airs and Graces*) 1976.

#218: "The False Lover Won Back"—Ewan MacColl and Peggy Seeger (*Classic Scots Ballads*) 1959.

#219: "The Gardener's Child"—Martin and Jessica Simpson (*Red Roses*) 1994.

#220: "The Bonny Lass of Anglesey"—Cindy Mangsen (*Long Time Travelling*) 1983.

#221: "Katherine Jaffrey"—Ewan MacColl (*Poetry and Song: Vol. 5*) 1967.

#223: "Eppie Morrie"—Lori Holland (*Scottish Folksongs for Women*) 1958.

#225: "Rob Roy"—Hermes Nye (*Ballads Reliques: Early English Ballads . . .*) 1957.

#226: "Leezie Lindsay"—Finbar and Eddie Furey (*Finbar and Eddie Furey*) 1968.

#228: "Kilbogie"—Ray and Archie Fisher (*Far over the Forth*) 1961.

#231: "The Earl of Errol"—Dick Gaughan (*Kist O'Gold*) 1976.

#232: "Richie Story"—Shirley Collins (*False True Lovers*) 1959.

#233: "Mill O'Tifty's Annie"—Ray Fisher (*The Bonny Bird*) 1972.

#235: "The Earl of Aboyne"—June Tabor (*Ashes and Diamonds*) 1977.

#236: "The Laird o' Drum"—Tom Kines (*Canadian Folk Songs: A Centennial Collection*) 1967.

#237: "The Duke of Gordon's Daughter"—Dave Burland (*The First Folk Review Record*) 1974.

#238: "Glenlogie"—Shirley and Dolly Collins (*Love, Death and the Lady*) 1970.

#239: "Annachie Gordon"—John Wesley Harding (*Trad Arr Jones*) 1999.

#240: "The Rantin Laddie"—Gordon Bok and Cindy Kallet (*Neighbors*) 1996.

#241: "The Baron o' Leys"—Ewan MacColl and Peggy Seeger (*Traditional Songs and Ballads*) 1964.

#243: "House Carpenter"—Bob Dylan (*The Bootleg Series: Vols. 1–3*) 1961.

#245: "Young Allan"—Jim and Sylvia Barnes (*Mungo Jumbo*) 1991.

#248: "The Night Visiting Song"—Spindlewood (*Spindlewood*) 1988.

#250: "Henry Martin"—Donovan (*HMS Donovan*) 1971.

#251: "Long John, Old John and Jackie North"—Martin Carthy (*Because It's There*) 1979.

#252: "Lord Gordon's Kitchen Boy"—Rod Paterson (*Smiling Waving Goodbye*) 1988.

#255: "Willie's Fatal Visit"—Ray Fisher (*Willie's Fatal Visit*) 1991.

#269: "Lady Diamond"—Tim Crahart (*Faith, Hope and Common Folk*) 2000.

#270: "The Earl of Mar's Daughter"—Aoife Clancy (*Silvery Moon*) 2014.

#272: "The Suffolk Miracle"—Dean Gitter (*Ghost Ballads*) 1957.

#274: "Seven Drunken Nights"—The Dubliners (*A Drop of the Hard Stuff*) 1967.

#275: "John Blunt"—Martin Carthy (*Shearwater*) 1972.

#276: "The Friar in the Well"—Paul Marks (*Live at Christchurch Folk Club*) 1968.

#277: "Risselty-Rossalty"—Pete Seeger (*With Voices Together We Sing*) 1958.

#278: "The Farmer's Curst Wife"—Gryphon (*Gryphon*) 1973.

#281: "The Keach and the Creel"—Subway to Sally (*Album 1994*) 1994.

#283: "The Fair Damsel from London Town"—Peggy Seeger (*The Long Harvest: Vol. 5*) 1968.

#284: "John Dory"—The John Renbourne Group (*Live in America*) 1982.

#285: "Barbaree"—Peter Bellamy (*Both Sides Then*) 1979.

#286: "The Golden Vanity"—Ronnie Gilbert (*Come and Go with Me*) 1961.

#287: "Ward the Pirate"—Peter Bellamy (*Tell It Like It Was*) 1975.

#289: "The Mermaid"—The Clancy Brothers/Tommy Makem (*The First Hurrah*) 1963.

#291: "Chylde Owlet"—Mick West (*Sark O'Snaw*) 2015.

#293: "Jock O'Hazeldean"—Dick Gaughan (*No More Forever*) 1972.

#295: "The Rich Irish Lady"—Hedy West (*Old Times and Hard Times*) 1967.

#298: "Peggy and Jaime"—Clandestine (*To Anybody at All*) 1999.

#299: "The Trooper and the Maid"—The Blue Water Folk (*The Blue Water Folk*) 1970.

#300: "Blancheflour and Jellyflorice"—Daniel Kelly (*Love, Magic, Murder and Song*) 2021.

Playlist 5—The Electric Child

Outlining the folk-rock boom, with help from a few of its antecedents and descendants.

#2: "Y'Acre of Land"—The Albion Dance Band (*The Guvnor: Vol. 3*) 1977.

#3: "The False Knight on the Road"—Fiddler's Dram (*To See the Play*) 1978.

#4: "The Outlandish Knight"—Spriguns (*Revel Weird and Wild*) 1976.

#6: "Willie's Lady"—The Owl Service (*His Pride. No Spear. No Friend.*) 2016.

#7: "Awake Awake"—The Gigspanner Band (*Natural Invention*) 2020.

#10: "The Cruel Sister"—Pentangle (*Cruel Sister*) 1970.

#11: "The Cruel Brother"—The Battlefield Band (*The Battlefield Band*) 1977.

#12: "Lord Randall"—Steeleye Span (*Horkstow Grange*) 1999.

#13: "Edward"—Steeleye Span (*Back in Line*) 1986.

#14: "The Bonnie Banks o' Fordie"—Blind Dogs (*New Tricks*) 1992.

#16: "Sheath and Knife"—Sol Invictus (*The Death of the West*) 1994.

#17: "Hind Horn"—Maddy Prior (*Flesh and Blood*) 1998.

#19: "Orfeo Nathan's Reel"—Steeleye Span (*Rocket Cottage*) 1976.

#20: "The Cruel Mother"—Emily Smith (*A Day Like Today*) 2002.

#21: "The Well Below the Valley"—Planxty (*The Well Below the Valley*) 1973.

#22: "Stephen"—Steeleye Span (*Bedlam Born*) 2000.

#26: "The Twa Corbies"—Steeleye Span (*Hark! The Village Wait*) 1970.

#27: "The Keyhole in the Door"—Fiddler's Dram (*To See the Play*) 1978.

#29: "The Boy and the Mantle"—Steeleye Span and Sophia Yates (*Est 1969*) 2019.

#32: "King Henry"—Steeleye Span (*Below the Salt*) 1972.

#35: "Alison Gross"—Steeleye Span (*Parcel of Rogues*) 1973.

#36: "The Mackrel of the Sea"—Spriguns (*Revel Weird and Wild*) 1976.

#37: "Thomas the Rhymer"—Steeleye Span (*Now We Are 6*) 1974.

#38: "The Wee Wee Man"—Steeleye Span (*Parcel of Rogues*) 1973.

#39: "Tam Lin"—Fairport Convention (*Liege and Lief*) 1969.

#40: "Elf Call"—Steeleye Span (*Commoner's Crown*) 1975.

#42: "Dance with Me"—Steeleye Span (*All Around My Hat*) 1975.

#43: "The Broomfield Hill"—Gallery (*The Wind That Shakes the Barley*) 1972.

#44: "The Two Magicians"—Spriguns of Tolgus (*Jack with a Feather*) 1975.

#46: "Captain Wedderburn"—Bellowhead (*Hedonism*) 2010.

#49: "The Twa Brithers"—Silly Wizard (*Caledonia's Hardy Sons*) 1978.

#53: "Lord Bateman"—Steve Ashley / Albion Band (*Stroll On*) 1974.

#54: "The Cherry-Tree Carol"—Pentangle (*Solomon's Seal*) 1972.

#56: "Dives and Lazarus"—June Tabor and The Oyster Band (*Freedom and Rain*) 1990.

#57: "Sir William Gower"—Fairport Convention (*Angel Delight*) 1971.

#58: "Sir Patrick Spens"—Fairport Convention (*Full House*) 1970.

#61: "Sir Colvin"—Spriguns (*Revel Weird and Wild*) 1976.

#65: "Bonny Susie Clelland"—June Tabor and the Oyster Band (*Freedom and Rain*) 1990.

#67: "Jack Orion"—Fairport Convention (*Tippler's Tales*) 1978.

#68: "Henry Lee"—Nick Cave and PJ Harvey (*Murder Ballads*) 1996.

#74: "Lady Margaret"—Trees (*The Garden of Jane Delawney*) 1970.

#75: "Lord Lovell"—Spriguns (*Revel Weird and Wild*) 1976.

#76: "Lord Gregory"—Steeleye Span (*Bloody Men*) 2006.

#78: "The Unquiet Grave"—Gryphon (*Gryphon*) 1973.

#79: "The Wife of Usher's Well"—Steeleye Span (*All around My Hat*) 1975.

#81: "Matty Groves"—Fairport Convention (*Liege and Lief*) 1969.

#82: "The Bonny Birdy"—Steeleye Span (*Horkstow Grange*) 1999.

#90: "Jellon Grame"—Broadside Electric (*With Teeth*) 1999.

#92: "The Lowlands of Holland"—Maartin Allcock (*Maart*) 1990.

#93: "Long Lankin"—Steeleye Span (*Commoner's Crown*) 1975.

#95: "Gallows Pole"—Led Zeppelin (*Led Zeppelin II*) 1970.

#96: "The Gay Goshawk"—Stone Angel (*Stone Angel*) 1975.

#98: "Brown Adam"—Brian Dewhurst and Tom Tiddler's Ground (*The Hunter and the Hunted*) 1975.

#100: "Willie o' Winsbury"—Pentangle (*Solomon's Seal*) 1972.

#102: "Willie and Earl Richard's Daughter"—Venereum Arvum (*John Barleycorn Reborn—Dark Britannica*) 2007.

#106: "The Famous Flower of Serving Men"—The High Level Ranters (*A Mile to Ride*) 1973.

#110: "The Knight and the Shepherd's Daughter"—Five Hand Reel (*5 Hand Reel*) 1976.

#112: "The Baffled Knight"—Lehto and Wright (*The Further Adventures of Darling Cory*) 2002.

#113: "The Great Silkie"—Trees (*The Garden of Jane Delawney*) 1970.

#114: "Johnnie O'Brady's Lea"—Planxty (*The Woman I Loved So Well*) 1980.

#132: "Robin Hood and the Pedlar"—Barry Dransfield (*Barry Dransfield*) 1972.

#155: "Little Sir Hugh"—Steeleye Span (*Commoner's Crown*) 1975.

#163: "The Battle of Harlaw"—The Battlefield Band (*At the Front*) 1978.

#164: "King Henry Fifth's Conquest of France"—Richard Thompson (*1000 Years of Popular Music*) 2003.

#168: "Flodden Field"—Spriguns of Tolgus (*Jack with a Feather*) 1975.

#170: "The Death of Queen Jane"—The Bothy Band (*After Hours*) 1984.

#181: "The Bonnie Earl o' Moray"—Five Hand Reel (*Earl O'Moray*) 1978.

#183: "The Burning of Auchandoon"—Hedgehog Pie (*The Green Lady*) 1975.

#199: "Bonnie House o' Airlie"—Five Hand Reel (*A Bunch of Fives*) 1979.

#200: "Black Jack Davy"—The Incredible String Band (*I Looked Up*) 1970.

#201: "Betsy Bell and Mary Gray"—Steeleye Span (*Tempted and Tried*) 1989.

#203: "The Baron of Brackley"—Pentangle (*So Early in the Spring*) 1990.

#204: "The Water Is Wide"—Bob Dylan and Joan Baez (*Bootleg Series: Vol. 5—Live 1975*) 1975.

#210: "Sir Gavin Grimbold"—Gryphon (*Glastonbury Carol*) 2003.

#212: "Little Duke Arthur's Nurse"—Mara! (*Images*) 1984.

#213: "Sir James the Rose"—Steeleye Span (*Rocket Cottage*) 1976.

#214: "The Dowie Dens of Yarrow"—Shelagh McDonald (*Stargazer*) 1971.

#215: "Annan Water"—The Decemberists (*Live in Texas, 2008*) 2008.

#217: "The Broom of Cowdenknows"—Silly Wizard (*Caledonia's Hardy Sons*) 1978.

#219: "The Gardener"—Hedgehog Pie (*The Green Lady*) 1975.

#220: "The Bonny Lass of Anglesey"—Tempest (*The Gravel Walk*) 1997.

#225: "Rob Roy"—Orealis (*Orealis*) 1988.

#226: "Leezie Lindsay"—Music Box (*Songs of Sunshine*) 1972.

#228: "Glasgow Peggie"—Silly Wizard (*Caledonia's Hardy Sons*) 1978.

#231: "The Earl of Errol"—The Battlefield Band (*Out for the Night*) 2004.

#243: "House Carpenter"—Pentangle (*Basket of Light*) 1969.

#250: "Henry Martyn"—New Celeste (*High Sands and the Liquid Lake*) 1977.

#251: "Lang Johnny More"—The Battlefield Band (*At the Front*) 1978.

#269: "Lady Diamond"—The Tannahill Weavers (*Passage*) 1984.

#274: "Cabbage Head"—Dr. John (*Going Back to New Orleans*) 1992.

#279: "Little Beggarman"—Fiddler's Green (*King Shepherd*) 1995.

#285: "High Barbaree"—Skibbereen (*Skibbereen*) 1976.

#287: "Captain Ward"—The Tannahill Weavers (*Capernaum*) 1994.

#289: "The Mermaid"—Fiddler's Green (*King Shepherd*) 1995.

#295: "The Brown Girl"—Steeleye Span (*Rocket Cottage*) 1976.

#299: "The Trooper and the Maid"—Five Hand Reel (*Earl O'Moray*) 1978.

Playlist 6–The Twenty-First-Century (or Thereabouts) Child

A sampling of "modern" and/or "current" artists, alongside still-extant older acts—a demonstration of the sheer complexity and variety of approaches to traditional music.

#1: "Riddles Wisely Expounded"—Jefferson Hamer and Anaïs Mitchell (*Child Ballads*) 2013.

#2: "An Acre of Land"—PJ Harvey and Harry Escott (*Dark River* original soundtrack) 2018.

#3: "The False Knight on the Road"—Fleet Foxes (*Fleet Foxes*) 2008.

#4: "Lady Isabel and the Elf Knight"—Paula Paulusma (*Invisible Music*) 2021.

#6: "The Witch Mother"—Timothy Renner (*Strange Familiars* podcast) 2021.

#9: "The Fair Flower of Northumberland"—Rachel Unthank and the Winterset (*Cruel Sister*) 2005.

#10: "Wind and Rain"—Martha Spencer (*Wonderland*) 2022.

#11: "The Cruel Brother "—Martin Simpson (*Kind Letters*) 2005.

#12: "Lord Donald"—Emily Smith (*Traveller's Joy*) 2011.

#13: "Edward"—The Hare and the Moon (*The Grey Malkin*) 2010.

#14: "The Banks of Fordie"—Martyn Bates (*Murder Ballads* [*Passages*]) 1997.

#16: "Sheath and Knife"—Ellie Bryan (*Am I Born to Die*) 2012.

#17: "Hind Horn"—Brian Peters (*Lines*) 2001.

#18: "Old Bangum"—Sharron Kraus (*Songs for the Twins*) 2005.

#20: "The Cruel Mother"—The Hare and the Moon (*Wood Witch*) 2015.

#21: "The Maid and the Palmer"—Paula Paulusma (*Invisible Music*) 2021.

#23: "Judas"—Daniel J. Townsend (*Iscariot*) 2014.

#25: "Amang the Blue Flowers and Yellow"—London Experimental Ensemble (*Child Ballads*) 2019.

#26: "The Three Ravens"—The Hare and the Moon (*The Hare and the Moon*) 2009.

#27: "Keyhole in the Door"—The Seadogs (*Spank the Monkey, Blow the Man and Other (Not) Child-Friendly Sailor Songs*) 2018.

#31: "The Marriage of Sir Gawain"—Lisa Theriot (*The Keys of Canterbury*) 2009.

#32: "King Henry"—The Unquiet Grave (*forthcoming*) 2023.

#34: "Kemp Owen"—Fay Hield (*Looking Glass*) 2010.

#35: "Alison Cross"—Malinky (*Last Leaves*) 2000.

#36: "The Laily Worm and the Machrel of the Sea"—Celtic Knots (*Untied*) 2000.

#37: "Thomas Rhymer"—Ed Pettersen (*Installation*) 2022.

#38: "The Wee Wee Man"—Carl Peterson (*A Faerie Place*) 2012.

#39: "Tam Lin"—The Imagined Village (*The Imagined Village*) 2007.

#40: "The Queen of Elfland's Nourice"—Rachel Newton (*Changeling*) 2014.

#41: "Hind Etin"—Jim Moray (*Skulk*) 2012.

#44: "Oh Thou Coal Black Smith"—Current 93 (*Swastikas for Noddy*) 1989.

#46: "Captain Wedderburn's Courtship"—Alasdair Roberts and Karen Poiwart (*Captain Wedderburn's Courtship*) 2011.

#48: "Young Andrew"—Andrew King (*The Bitter Harvest*) 1998.

#49: "The Rolling of the Stones"—Owl Service (*The Garland Sessions*) 2007.

#50: "The Bonny Hind"—Martyn Bates (*Murder Ballads* [*Incest Songs*]) 1998.

#51: "Lizzie Wan"—Frankie Armstrong (*Cats of Coven Lawn*) 2021.

#52: "Fair Rosie Ann"—Maureen Jelks (*Eence upon a Time*) 2000.

#53: "Lord Bateman"—Stephanie Hadowski and C. Joynes (*The Wild Wild Berry*) 2012.

#54: "The Cherry-Tree Carol"—Antler and Ivy (internet single) 2013.

#55: "King Herod and the Cock"—Belshazzar's Feast (*Frost Bits*) 2009.

#56: "Dives and Lazarus"—Andrew King (*Untitled*) 2005.

#57: "Brown Robyn's Confession"—The Unquiet Grave (*Ballads of Old*) 2019.

#58: "Sir Patrick Spens"—Jefferson Hamer and Anaïs Mitchell (*Child Ballads*) 2013.

#59: "Sir Aldingar"—Brian Peters (*Songs of Trial and Triumph*) 2008.

#62: "Fair Annie"—Martin Simpson (*The Bramble Briar*) 2001.

#63: "Fair Ellen"—Ed Pettersen (*Installations*) 2022.

#65: "Lady Maisry"—Lady Maisery (*Mayday*) 2013.

#67: "Jack Orion"—Harvestman (*Lashing the Rye*) 2005.

#68: "Love Henry"—Jolie Holland (*The Living and the Dead*) 2008.

#69: "Clerk Sanders"—Eliza Carthy (*Heat, Light and Sound*) 1996.

#73: "Lord Thomas and Fair Ellendor"—Naomi Bedford (*Tales from the Weeping Willow*) 2011.

#74: "Little Margaret"—Carolina Chocolate Drops (*Dona Got a Ramblin' Mind*) 2006.

#75: "Lord Lovell"—Country Parish Music (*Introducing . . .*) 2013.

#76: "Roving on a Winter's Night"—Steve Tilston and Maggie Boyle (*Midwinter—the Folk Music and Traditions of Christmas and the Turning of the Year*) 2007.

#77: "Sweet William's Ghost"—Cara Long (*Long Distance Love*) 2010.

#78: "The Unquiet Grave"—Widow's Weeds (*The Revenant*) 2021.

#79: "The Wife of Usher's Well"—The Hare and the Moon (*Wood Witch*) 2015.

#81: "Matty Groves"—Jay Tausig (*Ancient Roots, Modern Branches*) 2020.

#83: "Bill Norrie"—Lucy Ward (*Pretty Warnings*) 2018.

#84: "Barbara Allen"—Lucy Wainwright Roche (*Old Wine, New Skins*) 2007.

#85: "George Collins"—Gavin Davenport (*Brief Lives*) 2010.

#86: "Young Benjie"—Moira Cameron (*Sands of the Shore*) 2008.

#87: "Lord Abore and Mary Flynn"—Jackie Oates (*Jackie Oates*) 2006.

#88: "Young Johnstone"—Alasdair Roberts and Amble Skuse and David McGuinness (*What News*) 2018.

#89: "East Muir King"—Katherine Campbell (*The Songs of Amelia and Jane Harris—Scots Songs and Ballads from Perthshire Tradition*) 2004.

#90: "Jellon Grame"—The Maledictions (*Shallow Graves*) 2019.

#91: "Fair Mary of Wallington"—James Findlay (*Sport and Play*) 2011.

#92: "The Lowlands of Holland"—United Bibles Studies (*The Jonah*) 2009.

#93: "Long Lankin"—Jimmy Crowley and Eve Telford (*Hello! Child Ballads Learned From Irish Travellers*) 2023.

#94: "Young Waters"—Suzanne Langille and Neel Murgai (*Wild and Foolish Heart*) 2010.

#95: "The Pricklie Bush"—United Bible Studies (*Soregh, Murne and Fast*) 2015.

#96: "Goshawk"—Ffynon (*Celtic Music from Wales*) 2002.

#98: "Brown Adam"—Spiers and Boden (*Below*) 2004.

#99: "Johnie Scott"—Susan McKeown (*Sweet Liberty*) 2004.

#100: "Willie o' Winsbury"—Meg Baird (*Leaves from Off the Tree*) 2005.

#102: "Willie and Earl Richard's Daughter"—The Owl Service and Alison O'Donnell (*The Fabric of Folk*) 2008.

#104: "Prince Heathen"—Kitchen Cynics and Grey Malkin (*The Wonder Room*) 2019.

#105: "The Bailiff's Daughter of Islington"—Laura Cortese (*Hush*) 2004.

#106: "Sweet William (The Famous Flower of Serving Men)"—London Experimental Ensemble (*Child Ballads Exclusive Bonus Tracks*) 2020.

#110: "The Royal Forester"—The Bedlam Boys (*Made in Bedlam*) 2004.

#112: "The Baffled Knight"—You Are Wolf (*Keld*) 2018.

#113: "The Great Silkie of Sule Skerry"—Maz O'Connor (*This Willowed Light*) 2014.

#114: "Fair John and the Seven Foresters"—Crwydryn (*Taleisen*) 2006.

#118: "Robin Hood and Guy of Gisborne"—Hester NicEilidh (*The Robin Hood Ballad Project*) 2006.

#119: "Robin Hood and the Monk"—Hester NicEilidh (*Robin Hood Ballad Project*) 2006.

#120: "Robin Hood's Death"—The Unquiet Grave (*Ballads of Old*) 2019.

#122: "Robin Hood and the Butcher"—Hester NicEilidh (*The Robin Hood Ballad Project*) 2006.

#130: "Robin Hood and the Scotsman"—Hester NicEilidh (*Robin Hood Ballad Project*) 2006.

#132: "The Bold Pedlar and Robin Hood"—Freyja Cox Jensen (*The Ballad Singer in Georgian and Victorian London*) 2021.

#136: "Robin Hood's Delight"—Hester NicEilidh (*Robin Hood Ballad Project*) 2006.

#137: "Robin Hood and the Pedlars"—Hester NicEilidh (*Robin Hood Ballad Project*) 2006.

#149: "Robin Hood's Birth, Breeding, Valor and Marriage"—Hester NicEilidh (*Robin Hood Ballad Project*) 2006.

#155: "Sir Hugh"—Andrew King (*The Bitter Harvest*) 1998.

#156: "Queen Eleanor's Confession"—Furrow Collective (*Wild Hog*) 2016.

#161: "The Battle of Otterburn"—June Tabor (*An Echo of Hooves*) 2003.

#162: "Chevy Chase"—Jerry Bryant and Starboard Mess (*Roast Beef of Old England*) 2000.

#168: "Flodden Field"—Owl Service with Alison O'Donnell (*The Fabric of Folk*) 2008.

#169: "The Betrayal of Johnnie Armstrong"—David Wilkie and the Cowboy Celtic (*The Drover Band*) 2001.

#170: "The Death of Queen Jane"—10,000 Maniacs (*Twice Told Tales*) 2015.

#173: "The Queen's Maries"—Scocha (*Bordering On . . .*) 2001.

#178: "Edom o' Gordon"—Malinky (*The Unseen Hours*) 2005.

#181: "The Earl o' Murray"—Ed Petersson (*Installations*) 2022.

#182: "Young Logie"—Katherine Campbell (*The Songs of Amelia and Jane Harris—Scots Songs and Ballads from Perthshire Tradition*) 2004.

#183: "The Burning of Auchindoun"—Pumajaw (*John Barleycorn Reborn*) 2007.

#184: "The Lads of Wamphray"—Scocha (*Bordering On . . .*) 2001.

#186: "Kinmont Willie"—Ross Kennedy (*Fyre and Swords—Songs of the Border Reivers*) 2000.

#188: "Bold Archer"—Brass Monkey (*Steam*) 2009.

#189: "Hobie Noble"—Scocha (*The Land We Love*) 2004.

#191: "Hughie Graham"—Bob Hay and the Jolly Beggars (*Toils Obscure: Songs by Robert Burns*) 2004.

#192: "The Blind Harper"—Kate Rusby (*Underneath the Stars*) 2003.

#195: "Lord Maxwell's Last Goodnight"—June Tabor (*An Echo of Hooves*) 2003.

#199: "Bonnie House o' Airlie"—Ed Pettersen (*Installations*) 2022.

#200: "Black Jack Davey"—White Stripes (B side) 2003.

#201: "Bessy Bell and Mary Gray"—The Unquiet Grave (*Ballads of Olde*) 2019.

#203: "The Baron of Brackley"—Malinky (*Handsel*) 2019.

#204: "The Water Is Wide"—Noel Paul Stookey (*Fazz Now and Then*) 2022.

#206: "Bothwell Bridge"—Celticburn (*Shake Loose the Border*) 2006.

#208: "Lord Allenwater"—Blue Blokes 3 (*Stubble*) (2008).

#209: "Geordie"—Jefferson Hamer and Anaïs Mitchell (*Child Ballads*) 2013.

#210: "Bonnie James Campbell"—Eamon O'Leary and Jefferson Hamer (*The Murphy Beds*) 2012.

#212: "The Duke of Athole's Nurse"—Concerto Caledonia (*Late Night Sessions—Live at the Edinburgh International Festival, 2009*) 2010.

#214: "The Dowie Dens o' Yarrow" Alasdair Roberts and Karine Poiwart (*Captain Wedderburn's Courtship*) 2011.

#215: "Rare Willie"—June Tabor (*An Echo of Hooves*) 2003.

#216: "Clyde Waters"—Martyn Wilde (*The Child Ballads: Vol. 1*) 2016.

#217: "Bonnie May"—10,000 Maniacs (*Twice Told Tales*) 2015.

#218: "False Lover Won Back"—The Furrow Collective (*Fathoms*) 2018.

#219: "The Gardener Child"—The Owl Service (*Garland Sessions*) 2007.

#220: "The Bonny Lass of Anglesey"—Scarecrow (*Bonnie Lass of Anglesey*) 2021.

#221: "The Green Wedding"—The Woodbine and Ivy Band (*Woodbine and Ivy Band*) 2011.

#223: "Epie Morrie"—Jessica Haines and Mark Kaiser (*So Here's to You*) 2006.

#225: "Rob Roy Frae the Highlands Cam'"—Jacobites by Name [*Somewhat Less*] *Scottier Than Thou*) 2019.

#226: "Leezie Lindsay"—Eddi Reader (*Peacetime*) 2007.

#228: "Glasgow Peggie"—Highland Reign (*Scotland Girl*) 2021.

#231: "The Earl of Errol"—Alistair Hulett and Dave Swarbrick (*Saturday Johnny and Jimmy the Rat*) 2005.

#232: "Richie Story"—Trembling Bells (*Shirley Inspired*) 2015.

#233: "Andrew Lammie"—Kate Rusby (*Awkward Annie*) 2007.

#235: "The Earl of Aboyne"—Katherine Campbell (*The Songs of Amelia and Jane Harris—Scots Songs and Ballads from Perthshire Tradition*) 2004.

#238: "Glenlogie"—London Experimental Ensemble (*Child Ballads*) 2020.

#239: "Annachie Gordon"—The Unthanks (*Here's the Tender Coming*) 2009.

#240: "The Rantin Laddie"—Ed Pettersen (*Installations*) 2022.

#243: "The House Carpenter"—Stone Breath (*Lanterna Lucis Viriditatis*) 2008.

#244: "James Hatley"—Martin Carthy (*Waiting for Angels*) 2006.

#246: "Redesdale and Wise William"—Chris Coe (*A Wiser Fool*) 2001.

#248: "The Lover's Ghost"—The Owl Service (*View from a Hill*) 2010.

#250: "Henry Martin"—Rhiannon Giddens/Elftones (*All the Pretty Horses*) 2009.

#251: "Long John More"—Bill Jones (*Turn to Me*) 2000.

#255: "Willie's Fatal Visit"—The Furrow Collective (*Wild Hog*) 2016.

#256: "My Luve She Lives"—Katherine Campbell (*The Songs of Amelia and Jane Harris—Scots Songs and Ballads from Perthshire Tradition*) 2004.

#258: "Burd Helen"—Katherine Campbell (*The Songs of Amelia and Jane Harris—Scots Songs and Ballads from Perthshire Tradition*) 2004.

#260: "Lord Thomas and Lady Margaret"—Phil Cooper and Margaret Nelson (*Lady's Triumph*) 2007.

#265: "The Knight's Ghost"—Kathryn Roberts and Sean Lakeman (*Personae*) 2018.

#267: "The Heir of Linne"—Steeleye Span (*They Called Her Babylon*) 2004.

#269: "Lady Diamond"—Bryony Griffith and Will Hampton (*Lady Diamond*) 2011.

#270: "The Earl of Mar's Daughter"—Lisa Theriot (*The Keys of Canterbury*) 2009.

#272: "The Suffolk Miracle"—Jim Moray (*Sweet England*) 2003.

#274: "Nights Drunk"—Brian Peters (*Songs of Trial and Triumph*) 2008.

#275: "John Blunt"—Frankie Armstrong (*Till the Grass O'ergrew the Corn*) 1997.

#276: "The Friar in the Well"—Brass Monkey (*Park at 25*) 2013.

#277: "Wether's Skin"—Cath and Phil Tyler (*Dumb Supper*) 2008.

#278: "The Devil and the Farmer"—Tempest (*Going Home*) 2022.

#281: "The Wee Toun Clerk"—Gordeanna McCulloch (*Old Songs and Bothy Ballads—Nick-knack on the Waa*) 2008.

#283: "Well Sold the Cow"—Maura Volante (*Safe and Sound: Traditional Canadian Folk Songs*) 2022.

#285: "Coast of High Barbary"—Joseph Arthur (*Rogue's Gallery: Pirate Ballads, Sea Songs and Chanteys*) 2006.

#286: "The Golden Vanity"—Alasdair Roberts (*Too Long in this Condition*) 2010.

#287: "Captain Ward"—Steve Tilston (*Of Many Hands*) 2005.

#289: "The Mermaid"—Martin Carthy and the UK Group (*Rogue's Gallery: Pirate Ballads, Sea Songs and Chanteys*) 2006.

#291: "Child Owlet"—Steeleye Span (*They Called Her Babylon*) 2004.

#293: "Jock o' Hazeldean"—Martin Wylde (*The Child Ballads: Vol. 1*) 2014.

#295: "The Brown Girl"—Angeline Morrison (*The Brown Girl and Other Folk Songs*) 2022.

#299: "As I Roved Out"—the Real Motherfolkers (*Sounds Like Whiskey*) 2017.

And so, to "the final six": #300: "Blancheflour and Jellyflorice"; #301: "The Queen of Scotland"; #302: "Young Bearwell"; #303: "The Holy Nunnery"; #304: "Young Ronald"; and #305: "The Outlaw Murray." Bemoaning, in conversation with Ed Pettersen, the utter absence of commercial recordings of what are, in print, among my personal favorite Child Ballads, he and the London Experimental Ensemble graciously offered to record them and give them new life.

Even more excitingly, an amazing array of artists then volunteered to give voice to the unknown melodies, with Pettersen (the High Line Riders and the Black Country) joined by Richard Thompson, John Wesley Harding, Sivert Høyem (Madrugada), indie artist Marissa Nadler, and mezzo-soprano Gina Fergione.

A private stream of the resultant album *Child Ballads: The Final Six* (or download with free Soundcloud account) is available to readers of this book via this QR code.

For more information www.londexperimentalensemble.com

Playlist 7–Child at the BBC

Note: the following is as much a wish list as a playlist. While many of the listed performances are available on CD and more via the internet, a number have also been included simply to document their existence, with no hope that recordings actually exist. This is particularly true of broadcasts from the 1920s and 1930s, but might also be the case until as late as the 1970s and 1980s.

Many thanks to Colin Harper, Chris J. Brady, Jim Carroll, and members of the John Peel radio show discussion group for their assistance here.

#1: "Lay the Bent to the Bonny Broom"—Rosemary and Hugh Gentleman (*London Folk Song Cellar*) 1966/67.
#2: "Scarborough Fair"—Martin Carthy (*London Folk Song Cellar*) 1966.
#3: "False Knight on the Road"—Steeleye Span (*Folk on 1*) 10.17.1970.

#4: "The Outlandish Knight"—Kate Rusby (*Hyde Park Festival*) 09.13.2015.

#6: "Willie's Lady"—Martin Carthy (*John Peel*) 12.07.1977.

#7: "Awake Awake"—Sheila K. Adams (*Folk Connections: Cecil Sharp's Appalachian Trail*) 2016.

#10: "Two Sisters of Binnorie"—The Strawberry Hill Boys (*London Folk Song Cellar*) 1967.

#12: "Lord Randall"—The Gareth Francis Group (*London Folk Song Cellar*) 1966/67.

#13: "Edward"—Jeana Leslie and Siobhan Miller (*BBC Radio 2 Folk Awards*) 2009.

#14: "The Bonnie Banks o Fordie"—Nic Jones (*John Peel*) 11.07.1974.

#18: "Bold Sir Rylas"—John Spiers and Jon Boden (*BBC Radio 2 Folk Awards*) 2006.

#20: "The Cruel Mother"—Gillian Welch and David Rawlings (*Folk Connections: Cecil Sharp's Appalachian Trail*) 2016.

#21: "Jesus Met the Woman by the Well"—Peter, Paul and Mary (*Tonight in Person*) 1965.

#24: "The Banks of Green Willow"—John Spiers and Jon Biden (*A Place Called England*) 2003.

#26: "Twa Corbies"—Nigel Denver (*London Folk Song Cellar*) 1966/67.

#32: "King Henry"—Steeleye Span (*Pete Drummond Show*) 06.01.1972.

#35: "Alison Gross"—Steeleye Span (*Electric Folk—live at Thoresby Great Hall, Notts*) 03.27.1974.

#37: "Thomas the Rhymer"—Steeleye Span (*John Peel*) 02.26.1974.

#39: "Tamlin"—Dave and Toni Arthur with Paddy Kingsland (*Arthur's Folk*) 07.01.1977.

#40: "Elf Call"—Steeleye Span (*Electric Folk: Live at Warwick Castle*) 03.27.1975.

#42: "Dance with Me"—Steeleye Span (*Electric Folk: Live at Warwick Castle*) 03.27.1975.

#43: "The Maid on the Shore"—Anne Briggs (*Folk on 2*) 02.20.1991.

#44: "The Two Magicians"—Steeleye Span (*Bob Harris Show*) 03.11.1974.

#46: "I Will Give My Love an Apple"—Ernest Eady (*A Night with Folk Songs*) 01.03.1924.

#49: "Two Pretty Boys"—Dave and Toni Arthur (*Folk on Friday*) 1971.

#51: "Lucy Wan"—Martin Carthy (*John Peel*) 09.07.1976.

#53: "Lord Bateman"—June Tabor (*John Peel*) 02.22.1977.

#54: "The Cherry-Tree Carol"—Shirley Collins (*Sing Christmas and the Turn of the Year*) 12.25.1957.

#55: "The Carnal and the Crane"—John Kirkpatrick (*Traditional Celebration of English Midwinter*) 12.09.1995.

#56: "Dives and Lazarus"—Nic Jones (*John Peel*) 11.07.1974.

#57: "Sir William Gower"—Fairport Convention (Folk on 1) 03.27.1971.

#58: "Sir Patrick Spens"—Fairport Convention (*Top Gear*) 09.27.1969.

#65: "Lady Maisry"—Chris Foster (*BBC session*) 06.22.1977.

#67: "Glasgerion"—Tree (*Stuart Henry Show*) 05.21.1970.

#68: "False True Love"—James Yorkston and the Athletes (BBC Scotland) 03.11.2003.

#73: "Lord Thomas and Fair Eleanor"—Martin Carthy and Dave Swarbrick (*BBC Radio 2 Folk Awards*) 2007

#75: "Lord Lovell"—Jeannie Robertson (unknown) 1963.

#76: "Lord Gregory"—Elizabeth Cronin (*As I Roved Out*) 12.31.1954.

#78: "The Unquiet Grave"—The Furrow Collective (*BBC Radio 2 Folk Awards 2016*) 2016.

#79: "The Wife of Usher's Well"—Martin Carthy (*Folk on 2*) 03.11.1997.

#81: "Matty Groves"—Fairport Convention (*Night Ride*) 04.1988.

#84: "Barbara Allen"—Cecil Sharp Project (*In Tune*) 03.25.2011.

#85: "Lady Alice"—Nic Jones (*John Peel*) 12.07.1972.

#92: "Lowlands of Holland"—Fotheringay (*Folk on 1*) 11.21.1970.

#93: "Long Lankin"—Steeleye Span (*Pete Drummond Show*) 09.30.1971.

#94: "Young Waters"—June Tabor (*John Peel*) 09.13.1976.

#95: "The Prickle Holly Bush"—The Watersons (*The Uproot Festival, Hull*) 07.04.2017.

#96: "The Gay Goshawk"—Mr. Fox (*Top of the Pops* transcription disc) 11.24.1970.

#98: "Brown Adam"—Martin Carthy (*John Peel*) 12.07.1977.

#100: "Willie o' Winsbury"—Anaïs Mitchell and Jefferson Hamer (*BBC Folk Awards*) 2014.

#104: "Prince Heathen"—Trees (*Pete Drummond Show*) 02.03.1972.

#106: "The Famous Flower of Serving Men"—Martin Carthy (*Andy Kershaw Show*) 09.15.1988.

#110: "The Royal Forester"—Steeleye Span (*John Peel*) 03.10.1972.

#113: "The Silkie of Sule Skerry"—Val and Roy Bailey (*London Folk Song Cellar*) 1966/67.

#114: "Johnie O'Braidslea"—The JSD Band (*Radio 1 in Concert*) 10.21.1972.

#132: "Robin Hood and the Pedlar"—June Tabor (*Folkweave*) 1976

#155: "Little Sir Hugh"—Steeleye Span (*Electric Folk—Penshurst Place, Kent*) 1974.

#156: "Queen Eleanor's Confession"—The North West Three (*London Folk Song Cellar*) 1966/67.

#162: "Chevy Chase"—Jack Armstrong and Patricia Jennings (*London Folk Song Cellar*) 1966/67.

#163: "The Battle of Harlaw"—Jeannie Robertson (studio recording) 08.14.1963.

#167: "Sir Andrew Barton"—Peter Bellamy and Louis Killen (*Folk on 2/ We Have Fed Our Sea*) 12.28.1982.

#173: "The Four Maries"—Elizabeth Cooper (*Recital of Scots Folk Songs*) 01.25.1929.

#181: "The Bonnie Earl o' Moray"—Rory McEwan and Martin Carthy (*London Folk Song Cellar*) 1966.

#188: "The Bold Archer"—Tony Rose (*Folkweave*) 1976

#191: "Hughie Graeme"—June Tabor (*Later . . . with Jools Holland*) 2003.

#200: "The Raggle-Taggle Gypsies"—The Waterboys (*Cambridge Folk Festival*) 2007.

#203: "The Baron of Brackley"—Tom Spiers (*Stories Are for Singing*) 1966.

#204: "The Water Is Wide"—Ian Campbell Folk Group (*London Folk Song Cellar*) 1966/67.

#209: "Geordie"—Julie Felix and the Incredible String Band (*Once More with Felix*) 02.03.1968.

#214: "Yarrow"—Pentangle (*Folk on 2*) 12.1986.

#216: "The Drowned Lover"—Albion Dance Band (*Folk on 2*) 02.24.1988.

#217: "The Broom of Cowdenknows"—Silly Wizard (*Cambridge Folk Festival*) 10.28.1980.

#218: "The False Lover Won Back"—Martin Carthy (*Folkweave*) 1978.

#223: "Eppy Moray"—Fotheringay (*Folk on One*) 11.21.1970.

#226: "Leezie Lindsay"—Belle Stewart (*London Folk Song Cellar*) 1966/67.

#239: "Annachie Gordon"—Nic Jones (*John Peel*) 07.23.1976.

#243: "The House Carpenter"—Isla St Clair (*Stories Are for Singing*) 04.12.1966.

#245: "Young Allan"—June Tabor (*John Peel*) 09.13.1976.

#248: "The Lover's Ghost"—Elizabeth Fraser (*The Living and the Dead*) 2016.

#251: "Long John"—Martin Carthy (*John Peel*) 04.18.1983.

#255: "Willie's Fatal Visit"—Lizzie Higgins (*Ballad Folk*) 1977–1978.

#269: "Lady Dysie"—Martin Carthy (*John Peel*) 04.18.1983.

#274: "Three Nights Drunk"—Unknown artist (circulating tape cuts out) (*Folkweave*—recorded at Horsham Folk Club) 07.10.1975.

#277: "The Wee Cooper O'Fife"—Ian Campbell Folk Group (*London Folk Song Cellar*) 1966/67.

#278: "The Devil and the Feathery Wife"—Martin Carthy (*John Peel*) 04.18.1983.

#279: "The Jolly Beggar"—Planxty (*Bob Harris Show*) 10.29.1973.

#281: "Keach in the Creel"—Jean Redpath (*Ballad Folk*) 1977.

#287: "Captain Ward"—The Demon Barbers (*BBC Radio 2 Folk Awards*) 2011.

#289: "The Mermaid"—Jack and Margaret King (*London Folk Song Cellar*) 1966/67.

#293: "Jock o' Hazeldean"—Dick Gaughan (*John Peel*) 02.13.1973.

#295: "The Brown Girl"—Martin Carthy (*Folk on* 2) 09.17.1997.

#299: "The Trooper and the Maid"—Archie Fisher and friends (*My Kind of Folk*) 11.27.1968.

Playlist 8–Child in the Field

In June 2022, I canvassed members of the Child Ballads Facebook page for their favorite field recordings. The following list was partly compiled from their responses. Thanks to everybody who participated.

Many of these recordings are available online, although it should be noted that many of the earliest are taken from wax cylinders, with all the audio deficiencies that process was heir to. Others are frustratingly brief, as several collectors chose to record only enough of the performance to capture the melody (it also saved expensive recording media).

Key to Collections

AKD—Arthur Kyle Davis Jr.
AL—Alan Lomax
AL/PK—Alan Lomax and Peter Kennedy
BC—Bob Copper
BGL—Ben Gray Lumpkin
BL—Bill Leader
CLT/RS—Charles L. Todd and Robert Sonkin
DH—Diane Hamilton
EF—Edith Fowke
GC—George Derrington
GD—Gwilym Davies
HC—Helen Creighton
HG—Henry Glassie
HH—Hamish Henderson
HHa—Herbert Halpert
HHF—Helen Hartness Flanders
JC/PG—John Cohen/Peter Gott
JC/PM—Jim Carroll/Pat MacKenzie
JL—John Lomax
JR—Jean Ritchie
JMC—James Madison Carpenter
MEB/TC—Mary Elizabeth Barnicle/Tilman Cradle

MH—Max Hunter
MK—Maud Karpeles
ML—MacEdward Leach
MS/PS-S—Marie Slocum and Patrick Shuldham-Shaw
MV—Margaret Valiant
MY—Mike Yates
PC/BL—Paul Carter/Bill Leader
PD—Philip Donnellan
PG—Percy Grainger
PK—Peter Kennedy
PK/HH—Peter Kennedy and Hamish Henderson
PS-S—Patrick Shuldham-Shaw
RH—Reg Hall
RWG—Robert Winslow Gordon
S'OB—Sean O'Boyle
SE—Séamus Ennis
SP—Sandy Paton
SRC—Sidney Robertson Cowell
TE/TR—Tony Engle/Tony Russell
TM—Tom Munnelly

#1: "The Devil's Nine Questions"—Texas Gladden (AL).
#2: "True Lover of Mine" ("This is a song that hasn't got any title, but it's something about an impossibility. I think.")—George Vinton Graham (SRC).
#3: "False Knight on the Road"—Ben Henneberry (HC).
#4: "Pretty Polly"—Donia Cooper (MH).
#7: "The Seven Sleepers"—Victoria Morris (AKD).
#9 "The Fair Flower of Northumberland"—Bell Duncan (JMC).
#10 "The Two Sisters"—Beulah Greer (BGL).
#11: "The Cruel Brother"—Bell Duncan (JMC).
#12: "Billy Boy"—William T. Day (SRC).
#13: "How Come That Blood on Your Coat Sleeve"—Clyde Johnson (MH).
#14: "Three Sisters on the Bonnie, Bonnie Banks of the Rye-O"—Mrs. Norman Engler (MH).
#17: "Hind Horn"—Leander MacCumber (HC).
#18: "Sir Lionel"—Buna Hicks (SP).
#19: "King Orfeo"—John Stickle (PS-S).
#20: "The Cruel Mother"—Pat MacNamara (JC/PM).
#21: "The Well Below The Valley"—John Reilly (THE).
#22: "St. Stephen and King Herod"—George Edwards (HHF).
#24: "Green Banks of Yarrow"—Mrs. Maguire (S'OB).

#26: "Two Old Crows"—Mrs. Oscar Allen (MK).
#27: "The Keyhole in the Door"—Paralee Weddington (MH).
#34: "The Laidley Worm"—Ewan MacColl (AL).
#37: "Thomas the Rhymer"—Duncan Williamson (JC/PM).
#39: "Tam Lin"—Willie Whyte (HH).
#41: "Young Akin"—Bell Duncan (JMC).
#43: "The Maid on the Shore"—John Lyons (JC/PM).
#44: "Blackbirds and Thrushes"—Charles O'Boyle (BC).
#45: "The Bishop of Canterbury"—Warde Ford (SRC).
#46: "Captain Wedderburn's Courtship"—John Sutherland (JMC).
#47: "Lady Margaret"—John James (ML).
#49: "Two Little Boys"—Ollie Gilbert (MH).
#51: "Fair Lucy"—Mrs. Alice Sicily (HHF).
#52: "Fair Rosy Ann"—Elizabeth Robb (JMC).
#53: "Lord Bateman"—Tom Willet (PC/BL).
#54: "Cherry Tree Carol"—Kris Ann Parker (MH).
#55: "The Carnal and the Crane"—George Derrington (BBC).
#56: "Lazarus"—Molly Jackson (AL).
#57: "William Glen"—unknown singer (JMC).
#58: "Sir Patrick Spens"—Black Jimmie Mason (JMC).
#62: "The King's Daughter"—LaRena Clark (EF).
#63: "Fair Ellen"—Elizabeth Robb (JMC).
#64: "Fair Janet"—Bell Duncan (JMC).
#65: "Lady Maisry"—Bell Duncan (JMC).
#67: "Glenkindle"'"—Mary Thain (JMC).
#68" "Lou Bonnie"—Ollie Gilbert (MH).
#70: "William and Lady Marjorie"—Joe Rae (MY).
#73: "Lord Thomas"—George Vinton Graham (SRC).
#74: "Lady Margaret"—John James (ML).
#75: "Lord Lovel"—Ethel Findlater (PK).
#76: "Who Will Shoe Your Pretty Little Feet"—John T. Alexander (BGL).
#77: "Lady Margaret"—Paddy Tunney (TE/TR).
#78: "Jimmy Whalen"—Mary Dunphy (ML).
#79: "Lady Gay"—Almeda Riddle (MH).
#81: "Matty Groves"—Din Dobbin (ML).
#83: "Child Norris"—Martha Stewart (HH).
#84: "Barbara Allen"—Sarah Makem (JR).
#85: "George Collins"—Mary Sullivan (CLT/RS).
#87: "Lord O'Bore"—Frank Feeney (THE).
#88: "Young Johnstone"—Betsy Whyte (HH).
#90: "Jellon Grame"—Alex Robb (JMC).
#91: "Fair Maid of Wallington"—Bell Duncan (JMC).

#92: "The Lowlands of Holland"—Harry Curtiss (ML).

#93: "Bol' Lamkin"—Nathan and Rena Hicks (Hha).

#95: "Ropes I Man, Ropes I Man"—Vernon Allen (CLT/RS).

#99: "Johnnie Scott"—Mrs. H. H. Power (HC).

#100: "There Was a Lady Lived in the West"—Robert Cinnamond (DH).

#102: "Robin Hood's Birth"—Aunt Molly Jackson (MEB/TC).

#105: "The Bailiff's Daughter of Islington"—Bob Lewis (MY).

#106: "The Famous Flower of Serving Men"—Mrs. R.W. Duncan (HC).

#110: "Knight and Shepherd's Daughter"—Nathan Hall (HC).

#112: "Blow Away the Morning Dew"—Sam Larner (PD).

#113: "The Great Selchie o' Sule Skerry"—Lizzie Higgins (HH).

#114: "Johnnie O'Braidslea"—John Strachan (AL).

#125: "Robin Hood and Little John"—Edith Cummings Taylor (BGL).

#132: "Bold Pedlar and Robin Hood"—Catherine Gallagher (HC).

#139: "Robin Hood's Progress to Nottingham"—Ben Henneberry (HC).

#140: "Robin Hood and the Three Squires"—Dean Robinson (PG).

#155: "The Jew's Garden"—Celia Costello (MS/PS-S).

#156: "Queen Eleanor's Confession"—Boyce Davis (MH).

#163: "The Battle o' Harlaw"—Lucy Stewart (PK/HH).

#164: "King Henry the Fifth's Conquest"—E. C. Green (HHF).

#167: "The Lofty Tall Ship"—Sam Larner (PD).

#169: "Johnny Armstrong"—Willie Beattie (MY).

#170: "Jane Was a Neighbor"—Nellie Gait (RWG).

#173: "The Four Maries"—Charlotte MacInnes (SRC).

#178: "Edom o' Gordon"—Alex Robb (JMC).

#181: "The Bonny Earl of Murray"—Vance Randolph (MH).

#182: "Young Logie"—Bell Duncan (JMC).

#186: "Kinmont Willie"—Willie Beattie (MY).

#187: "Jock O' The Side"—Ewan MacColl (AL).

#188: "The Brothers"—Duncan Williamson (JC/PM).

#190: "Jamie Telfer O' the Fair Dodhead"—Willie Scott (HH).

#191: "Hughie Graham"—Ewan MacColl (AL).

#199: "Bonnie House o'Airlie"—Mrs. Edward Gallagher (HC).

#200: "Black Jack Davey"—Ola Belle Read (HG).

#201: "Two Bonnie Lasses"— Mrs. A Goldenberg (EF).

#203: "The Baron O'Brackley"—Mary Stewart Robeson (JMC).

#204: "Waly Waly"—James Mason (JMC).

#208: "The King's Love Letter"—Mrs. G. A. Griffin (JL).

#209: "Georgie"—Nancy Weaver Stikeleather (RWG).

#210: "Bonny George Campbell"—Duncan Williamson (JC/PM).

#212: "The Duke of Athol's Nurse"—Elizabeth Robb (JMC).

#213: "James the Ross"—John Molly (MacEdward Leach).

#214: "The Dowie Dens o' Yarrow"—Jean Matthew (SE).
#215: "Wille Drowned in Ero"—Eva Bigrow (EF).
#216: "The Clattering of the Child Waters"—Stanley Robertson (BL).
#217: "The Maid of the Cowdie and Knowes"—Ethel Findlater (PK).
#218 "False Lover Won Back"—Mrs. Alex Campbell (JMC).
#219: "The Gardener Lad"—Bell Duncan (JMC).
#221: "The Green Wedding"—Cecilia Costello (MS-PS-S).
#222: "Bonny Baby Livingston"—John Strachan (HH).
#226: "Lizzie Lindsay"—Mrs. John Baird (JMC).
#228: "Glasgow Peggy"—Mrs. Buchan Bull (JMC).
#231: "The Earl of Errol"—Bell Duncan (JMC).
#232: "Richie Story"—Bell Duncan (JMC).
#233: "Andrew Lammie"—Jeannie Higgins (PK).
#235: "The Earl of Aboyne"—Bell Duncan (JMC).
#236: "The Gates of Drum"—Togo Crawford (SE).
#237: "The Duke of Gordon's Daughter"—Mrs. William Duncan (JMC).
#238: "Glenlogie"—John Adams (HH).
#239: "Johnny Doyle"—Berzilla Wallin (JC/PG).
#240: "The Bonny Rantin Laddie"—William Mathieson (AL).
#243: "The House Carpenter"—Beulah Greer (BGL).
#245: "Young Allan"—Jessie Davidson (JMC).
#248: "The Pretty Crowing Chicken"—Jane Gentry (SP).
#250: "Andrew Batan"—Warde Ford (SRC).
#251: "Lang Johnny Moore"—John Strachan (HH).
#252: "The Kitchie Boy"—Elizabeth Robb (JMC).
#255: "Willie's Fatal Visit"—Jeannie Robertson (AL/PK).
#264: "The White Fisher"—Bell Duncan (JMC).
#267: "The Heir O Lynn"—Alex Robb (JMC).
#269: "Lady Eliza"—Winnie Campbell (BL).
#272: "The Holland Handkerchief"—Tom Lenihan (JC/PM).
#273: "The King and The Tinker"—Fred Shorthill (EF).
#274: "I Come in the Other Night"—Ernie Alston (CLT/RS).
#275: "Get Up and Bar the Door"—Mrs. E.H. McKeen (HC).
#276 "Friar in the Well"—Charlie Hill (GD).
#277: "Little Old Man Come in from the Plow"—Joy and Russ Pike (CLT/RS).
#278: "The Devil Out of Hell"—George Vinton Graham (SRC).
#279: "The Gaberlunzie Man"—Maggie and Sarah Chambers (S'OB).
#280: "The Beggar's Dawtie"—Mrs. John Catto (JMC).
#281: "The Keach in the Creel"—Belle Luther Richards (HHF).
#282: "Yorkshire Bite"—Euclid I. Williams (HHF).
#283: "Oxford Merchant"—Warde Ford (SRC).
#285: "High Barbary (Coast of High Barbary)"—Bob Roberts (RH).

#286: "The Merry Golden Tree"—Almeda Riddle (AL).

#287: "Captain Ward and the Rainbow"—Peter Christie (JMC).

#288: "The Young Earl of Essex's Victory Over the Emperor of Germany"—Bell Duncan (JMC).

#289: "The Mermaid"—Edith Cummings (BGL).

#293: "Jock O'Hazeldean"—Margaret Letson (HC).

#295: "Rich Lady"—Ollie Gilbert (MH).

#299: "The Trooper and the Maid"—Harry List (AL/PK).

The Unrecorded Child

#5: "Gil Brenton"

#8: "Erlinton"

#15: 'Leesom Brand"

#30: "King Arthur and King Cornwall"

#66: "Lord Ingram and Chiel Wyet"

#71: "The Bent Sae Brown"

#80: "Old Robin of Portingale"

#97: "Brown Robin"

#101: "Willie o Douglas Dale"

#107: "Will Steward and John"

#108: "Christopher White"

#109: "Tom Potts"

#111: "Crow and Pie"

#116: "Adam Bell, Clim of the Clough and William of Cloudesly"

#121: "Robin Hood and the Potter"

#127: "Robin Hood and the Tinker"

#128: "Robin Hood Newly Revived"

#133: "Robin Hood and the Beggar, I"

#134: "Robin Hood and the Beggar, II"

#135: "Robin Hood and the Shepherd"

#142: "Little John a Begging"

#143: "Robin Hood and the Bishop"

#145: "Robin Hood and Queen Katherine"

#146: "Robin Hood's Chase"

#148: "The Noble Fisherman, or, Robin Hood's Preferment"

#151: "The King's Disguise, and Friendship with Robin Hood"

#153: "Robin Hood and the Valiant Knight"

#158: "Hugh Spencer's Feats in France"

#159: "Durham Field"

#160: "The Knight of Liddesdale"

#165: "Sir John Butler"

#166: "The Rose of England"

#171: "Thomas Cromwell"
#172: "Musselburgh Field"
#174: "Earl Bothwell"
#175: "The Rising in the North"
#176: "Northumberland Betrayed by Douglas"
#177: "The Earl of Westmoreland"
#179: "Rookhope Ryde"
#180: "King James and Brown"
#185: "Dick o' the Cow"
#196: "The Fire of Frendraught"
#197: "James Grant"
#198: "Bonny John Seton"
#202 "The Battle of Philliphaugh"
#205: "Loudon Hill, or, Dromclog"
#207: "Lord Delamere"
#211: "Bewick and Graham"
#222: "Bonny Baby Livingston"
#224: "The Lady of Arngosk"
#227: "Bonny Lizie Baillie"
#229: "Earl Crawford"
#230: "The Slaughter of the Laird of Mellerstain"
#234: "Charlie Mac Pherson"
#242: "The Coble o' Cargill"
#247: "Lady Elspat"
#254: "Lord William, or, Lord Lundy"
#257: "Burd Isabel and Lord Patrick"
#259: "Lord Thomas Stuart"
#261: "Lady Isabel"
#262: "Lord Livingston"
#263: "The New-Slain Knight"
#266: "John Thomson and the Turk"
#268: "The Twa Knights"
#271: "The Lord of Lorn and the False Steward"
#290: "The Wylie Wife of the Hie Toun Hie"
#292: "The West-Country Damosel's Complaint"
#294: "Dugall Quin"
#296: "Walter Lesly"
#297: "Earl Rothes"

NOTES

INTRODUCTION

1. Julie Hennigan, author interview, 2022.
2. Dom Flemons, author interview, 2022.
3. Tennessee born banjo player and singer Louis Marshall "Grandpa" Jones (1913–1998) recorded "The Brown Girl and Fair Eleanor" on his 1974 album *What's for Supper?*
4. Polly Paulusma, author interview, 2022.
5. Citation from *Oxford English Dictionary*, 1971
6. Judy Collins, author interview, 2014.
7. Collins interview.
8. Brian Peters, author interview, 2022.
9. Published in 1959, Bronson's "The Traditional Tunes of the Child Ballads" collected the available melodies for as many Child Ballads for which one could be found.
10. Hester NicEilidh, author interview, 2017.
11. Jefferson Hamer, author interview, 2013.
12. Jim Carroll, talk given at Limerick University, June 2022.
13. Jean Ritchie, *Singing Family of the Cumberlands*. Oxford: Oxford University Press, 1955.
14. Timothy Renner, author interview, 2017.
15. https://www.childballadrecordings.com.
16. *Radio Times* 41, no. 526 (29 October 1933).

CHAPTER ONE: THE VERY FIRST RECORD

1. Steven Roud, "Percy Grainger and English Folk Song," British Library, *Sound and Vision* (blog), https://blogs.bl.uk/sound-and-vision/2018/02/percy-grainger-ethnographic-wax-cylinders.html.

CHAPTER TWO: UNTO BRIGG FAIR

1. Grainger was quoted in E. Marion Hudson's memoir *Brigg Fair: A Memoir of Joseph Taylor by His Grand-Daughter E. Marion Hudson,* edited by Peter Collinson, 2003, and published on the website www.family-trees.org.uk.
2. Hudson.
3. Brigg Fair was established in 1236 under the Charter of King John, granting that "'Ersinius Neville, he and his heirs may have for ever one market every week on Thursday at the bridge of Glanford [Brigg] and one fair there in every year during four days, viz: St James's Day, and the three days following, so that it be not to the nuisance of neighbouring fairs, and neighbouring markets."
4. Quoted in the memoir *Brigg Fair: A Memoir of Joseph Taylor by His Grand-Daughter E. Marion Hudson,* edited by Peter Collinson, 2003, and published on the website www.family-trees.org.uk.
5. Kennedy recorded Mary Taylor herself singing elements of "Lord Bateman" during that 1953 interview, solo and in duet with Kennedy. Kennedy would also record Mary's brother John in 1944. The transcript of this interview can be found in the British Library collection, https://sounds.bl.uk/World-and -traditional-music/Peter-Kennedy-Collection/025M-C0604X0080XX -0001V0https://sounds.bl.uk/World-and-traditional-music/Peter-Kennedy -Collection/025M-C0604X0080XX-0001V0.
6. *The Delius Society Journal,* no. 129 (Spring 2001).
7. Mary Taylor, author interview.
8. Hudson, *Brigg Fair.*
9. John Roberts and Tony Barrand, liner notes to the album *Heartoutbursts* (1998).
10. Percy Grainger, liner notes to 78 rpm album *Percy Grainger's Collection of English Folk-Songs Sung by Genuine Peasant Performers* (1908).
11. https://www.vwml.org.

CHAPTER THREE: 2,000 YEARS BC (BEFORE CHILD)

1. See "The Story of Ahikar," in the *Arabian Nights.*
2. See W. Norman Brown, "The Silence Wager Stories: Their Origin and Their Diffusion," *American Journal of Philology* 43, no. 4 (1922): 289–317.
3. A. L. Lloyd, liner notes to the album *A Selection from the Penguin Book of English Folk Songs,* 1960.

4. A. L. Lloyd, liner notes to the album *The Bird in the Bush: Traditional Songs of Love and Lust*, 1966.

5. Lloyd, liner notes to *The Bird in the Bush*.

6. Jean Redpath, liner notes to the album *Scottish Ballad Book*, 1962.

7. In its original form, "Little Sir Hugh," a.k.a. "The Jew's Garden," relates to the belief that Jewish settlers in medieval England regularly murdered Christian children. Most circulating versions today omit these particular details.

8. A. L. Lloyd, liner notes to the album *Lovely on the Water* by Frankie Armstrong, 1972.

9. Child cites Manuscript B. 14, 39, of the thirteenth century, Library of Trinity College, Cambridge, as printed in Thomas Wright and James Orchard Halliwell's *Reliquae Antiquae: Scraps from Ancient Manuscripts Illustrating Chiefly Early English Literature and the English Language* in 1845.

10. "Riddles Wisely Expounded" can be found in Bodleian Rawlinson D.328, and "Robin Hood and the Monk" in Cambridge University manuscript Ff.5.48.

11. https://www.bl.uk/collection-guides/sloane-manuscripts.

12. Throughout the *ESPB*, Professor Child sought to place ballads of specific type—supernatural, historical, tragedy, etc.—in close proximity to one another. All but one of the above are concerned with Scots history.

13. In fact, Pepys was something of a ballad aficionado himself; among the items he gifted to Magdalen College in Cambridge (the basis of the Pepysian library) was what amounted to five scrapbooks filled with 1,800 old English ballads. These were published in their own right in 1922.

14. Also published as *The Defence of Poesie*.

15. Quoted by Jim Carroll, author interview.

16. Sandy Paton, liner notes to the album *The Traditional Music of Beech Mountain, North Carolina, Volume 1*, 1964.

17. Flemons, author interview, 2022.

18. This title was one of the earliest of the newly founded Folklore Society's republications, in 1881.

CHAPTER FOUR: BANNING THE BALLADS

1. Julie Henigan, *Literacy and Orality in Eighteenth-Century Irish Song* (London: Routledge, 2012).

2. Flemons, author interview.

3. Discussing the ballad "The Lochmaben Harper" (192) in the liners to 1990's *Life and Limb* album, Martin Carthy refers to the harper as "a busker."

4. "The Fryar Well Fitted" (276) was known to Samuel Pepys; "A Merry Jeste of a Shrewde and Curste Wyfe Lapped in Morelles Skin for her Good Behaviour" (277) can be dated to 1575 at the latest.

5. Patrick Colquhoun, *A Treatise on the Functions and Duties of a Constable: Containing Details and Observations Interesting to the Public, as They Relate to the Corruption of Morals, and the Protection of the Peaceful Subject against Penal and Criminal Offences* (1803).

6. Jim O'Connor, liner notes to the album *A Merry Progress to London* by the Critics Group, 1967.

7. Oskar Cox Jensen, *The Ballad Singer in Georgian and Victorian London* (Cambridge: Cambridge University Press, 2021).

8. Sean Shesgreen, *Images of the Outcast: The Urban Poor in the Cries of London* (New Brunswick, NJ: Rutgers University Press, 2002).

9. "The Hunting of the Cheviot" (162), "Lord Bateman" (53), "Fair Rosemund" (156) and any one of the Robin Hood epics (117–54).

10. Henigan, *Literacy and Orality.*

CHAPTER FIVE: A GARLAND OF BALLADRIES

1. Cambridge University Press, 1922; reprinted by Harvard University Press, 1971.

2. The first recorded reference to a "garland" as a collection of literary pieces, usually prose and ballads, was made in 1526. The word remained in common, if increasingly dated, usage until the late nineteenth century.

3. Part of the Bodleian collection, the Ashmole Library was created by the antiquarian Elias Ashmole (1617–1692).

4. Peters, author interview.

5. Brian Peters, liner notes on the album *Gritstone Serenade*, One Row Records, 2010.

6. Subscribers named in the first volume included His Royal Highness the Prince of Wales (the future George IV), His Royal Highness Prince Edward, the Duchess of Argyle, the Earl Bute, and a virtual Who's Who of aristocracy and royalty.

7. Although it is seldom cited among the most beloved of the Child Ballads, "Little Margaret" nevertheless captivates all who hear it. Dave Arthur, Pete Cooper, and Chris Moreton recorded a version in 2003, and recalled the following anecdote in the liner notes for the album *Return Journey*. "During the final session of a recent storytelling residency in a primary school, I gave the children the option of requesting anything that we'd done over the ten weeks, the top choice was the supernatural ballad of 'Little Margaret.'"

CHAPTER SIX: THE BALLAD OF SILAS WEGG AND THE TRIPE-SKEWER

1. John Gibson Lockhart, *Memoirs of the Early Life of Sir Walter Scott, Written by Himself*, vol. 1 (Boston: Houghton Mifflin, 1901).

2. Flemons, author interview.

3. Grey Malkin, author interviews, 2015–2022.

4. Robert Bell. *Early Ballads Illustrative of History, Traditions and Customs* (London: Griffin, Bohn and Company, 1861).

CHAPTER SEVEN: THE VOICE OF SOME PEOPLE

1. Alasdair Roberts, author interview, 2015.
2. Ranald Thurgood, author interviews, 2022.
3. Johann Gottfried von Herder, *Auszug aus einem Briefwechsel über Ossian und die Lieder alter Völker* [Extract from a correspondence about Ossian and the songs of ancient peoples] (1773; Berlin: F. Schöningh, 1926).
4. A. L. Lloyd, liner notes to the album *First Person*, 1966.
5. Shirley Collins, liner notes for the album *The Power of the True Love Knot* (1967).
6. Flemons, author interview.
7. Quoted in Charles Seeger, *Selected Reports of the Institute of Ethnomusicology, University of California*, 1, no. 1 (1966). See https://www.loc.gov/folklife/LP/BarbaraAllenAFS_L54_sm.pdf.
8. Martin Carthy, liner notes to the album *Signs of Life*, 1998.

CHAPTER EIGHT: SONGS AROUND EVERY CORNER

1. Shirley Collins, liner notes to the album *Lodestar*, 2016.
2. Steve Byrne, author interview, 2022.
3. Martin Carthy, liner notes to the album *Shearwater*, 1972.
4. Blue Blokes 3, liner notes to the album *Stubble*, 2008.
5. John Roberts and Tony Barrand, liner notes to the LP *Dark Ships in the Forrest* (1977).
6. Sproatly Smith, author interview, 2015.
7. Smith.
8. Formed from the 1932 merger between the Folk Dance Society and the Folk Song Society, the organization is headquartered today at the appropriately named Cecil Sharp House in Camden, north London.
9. Mary Humphreys and Anahita, liner notes for the album *Sharp Practice*, 2003.
10. William Wells Newell, *Games and Songs of American Children* (New York: Harper Brothers, 1883).
11. Alan Lomax, liner notes to the Peggy Seeger album *Peggy Seeger* (1957).
12. According to Bert Lloyd, writing in 1967's *Folk Song in England*, "The last version of it found in the British Isles was noted down in 1883 from an elderly fisherman at Bridgnorth, Shropshire."
13. Erika Brady. *A Spiral Way: How the Phonograph Changed Ethnography* (Jackson: University of Mississippi Press, 2012).

CHAPTER NINE: THE MERMAID AND THE ASTRONOMER

1. Finest Kind, liner notes to the album *Hearts Delight*, 1999.
2. G. Eberhard, A. Kohlschütter, and H. Ludendorff. *Handbuch der Astrophysik* (Berlin: Springer Verlag, 1932).
3. Henigan, author interview.

CHAPTER TEN: THE ORIGINAL SOUTHERN JOURNEY

1. Cotton himself would subsequently embark upon his own career in ballad collecting, coproducing *A Syllabus of Kentucky Folk Songs* with Professor H. G. Shearin in 1911.

2. Ritchie, *Singing Family*.

3. "Barbara Allen" was popular among English children, too. Shirley Collins first heard it from her grandmother, as a child growing up in early 1940s Hastings; and Linda Peters (later Thompson) recalls learning "Barbara Allen" at school in Glasgow in the 1950s. As English singer Louis Killen remarked in 1975, schoolchildren of that era had "many good songs . . . dinned into [them] in those days, though I'm not sure I always appreciated their goodness at the time." By the time Linda Peters hit the folk club circuit, her schooldays behind her, she was happier "singing 'Katy Cruel,' 'The Blackleg Miner,' that kind of song."

4. Cecil Sharp and Olive Dame Campbell, *English Folk Songs from the Southern Appalachians* (New York: Putnam's, 1917).

5. Maud Karpeles, *Cecil Sharp: His Life and Work* (Chicago: University of Chicago Press, 1967).

6. Karpeles.

7. Four of these letters were published circa 1917 as the booklet *Ballad Hunting in the Appalachians*.

8. Flemons, author interview.

9. *Folk Connections: Cecil Sharp's Appalachian Trail*, presented by Andy Kershaw, BBC Sunday Feature, first broadcast July 31, 2017, https://www.bbc.co.uk/programmes/b06yp4cv.

10. *Folk Connections*.

11. Flemons, author interview.

12. *Folk Connections*.

13. Peters, author interview.

14. Flemons, author interview.

15. Ritchie, *Singing Family*.

16. Ritchie. A peculiarly Southern custom, play parties developed in the 1830s as a way of dancing to music while not breaking religious prohibitions on such merriment. Folk songs were particularly popular, with participants each acting out choreographed lines from the song, while the rest of the room sang and clapped.

17. Canadian collector Helen Creighton wryly speculated that many older singers omitted the whistled element of this and other ballads because they no longer possessed enough teeth to do it.

18. Ritchie, *Singing Family*.

CHAPTER ELEVEN: APPALACHIAN AFTERSHOCKS

1. Profitt's work has been widely covered over the years, but of especial appeal is his "Pretty Cowing Chicken," a variant on "The Lover's Ghost," as revisited

by Martin Simpson on 2007's *Prodigal Son*. Pay particular attention to the closing revelation that "This chicken proved false-hearted."

2. Bert Lloyd, liner notes for Hedy West, *Ballads*.

3. Henigan, author interview.

4. Gentry's great grand-niece Sheila K. Adams performs the Gentry "Awake Awake" during the BBC Radio documentary *Folk Connections: Cecil Sharp's Appalachian Trail*.

5. Flemons, author interview. Giddens subsequently returned to "Little Margaret" in tandem with Roger Gold and Mara Shea, and also on her 2019 solo album *There Is No Other*—described by *The Guardian*'s Jude Rodgers as "a 21st-century version of Shirley Collins and Davy Graham's *Folk Roots, New Routes*."

6. Peters, author interview.

7. With wife Toni, Arthur also recorded the ballad for the BBC's *Folk on Friday*, under the title "Two Pretty Boys."

8. Dave Arthur, liner notes to the album *No Use in Cryin'*, 2010.

9. Maud Karpeles, "A Return Visit to the Appalachian Mountains," *Journal of the English Folk Dance and Song Society* 6, no. 3 (1951).

10. Cecil Sharp's diary; online at https://www.vwml.org/topics/sharp-diaries/SharpDiary1918.

11. Neil Leyshon, "Folk's Unsung Heroines—the Sisters Who Saved English Music," *The Guardian*, January 5, 2022.

12. Leyshon.

13. The vocal trio Coope, Boyes and Simpson's 2005 CD *Triple Echo* comprises their versions of a handful of Butterworth's discoveries, alongside material collected by Grainger and Vaughan Williams.

CHAPTER TWELVE: CABBAGE HEAD BLUES

1. Flemons, author interview.

2. Joel Whitburn, *Pop Memories 1890–1954: The History of American Popular Music* (Menomonee Falls, WI: Record Research Inc., 1991).

3. Harry Smith interview with John Cohen, 1968, quoted in booklet accompanying the 1997 reissue of *Anthology of American Folk Music*.

4. Flemons, author interview.

5. Among the other artists to be recorded during Columbia's Johnson City sessions, albeit the following year, was the above-mentioned Clarence Ashley. However, he was neither an unknown nor unrecorded by this time.

6. Ted Olson and Tony Russell, booklet included with *The Johnson City Sessions 1928–1929* (Bear Family Records, 2013).

7. Flemons, author interview.

CHAPTER THIRTEEN: SONG OF THE TANNER

1. Margaret Bulger points out that "it is difficult to say" whether the ballad is a "true variant form . . . or merely a version of the love lyric 'Who Will Shoe Your

Pretty Little Foot.'" *The Carter Family: Traditional Sources for Song, Presented to the Faculty of the Center for Intercultural Studies*, thesis, Western Kentucky University, 1976.

2. He was not alone in this practice. Vernon Dalhart's musical arranger Carson Robison claimed the writing credit for "Barbara Allen" in 1927; Sylvester Kimbrough was noted as composer of "Cabbage Head Blues" in 1926; and there were many more besides.

3. Bulger, *The Carter Family*.

4. The Carter Family's full repertoire is best represented by Bear Family's 12-CD box set *In The Shadow of Clinch Mountain*.

5. A belated tribute to Tanner, compiled and narrated by J. Mansel Thomas, was broadcast by the BBC on April 30, 1952, under the title *The Singer of Gower*.

CHAPTER FOURTEEN: HUNTERS AND GATHERERS

1. Carroll, author interview.

2. Margaret W. Beckwith, *The English Ballad in Jamaica: A Note upon the Origin of the Ballad Form. PMLA* 39, no. 2 (June 1924).

3. Ronald D. Cohen, *Depression Folk: Grassroots Music and Left Wing Politics in 1930s America* (Chapel Hill: University of North Carolina Press, 2016).

4. Stikeleather was "rediscovered" around 1930, when Dorothy Scarborough visited the area for her book *A Song Catcher in the Southern Mountains*. She and her husband, Jim, were "prominent in musical circles in Asheville . . . [and] knew folk songs, mountain ballads, traditional folk songs and Negro songs, and knew well how to sing them."

5. Henigan, author interview.

6. Henigan.

CHAPTER FIFTEEN: SEEKING FRESH DIRECTIONS

1. Combs was studying at Berea College in Kentucky; his thesis was published by the Sorbonne University in Paris in 1925.

2. Sidney Cowell Robertson's writings are held in the WPA California Folk Music Project Collection, 1938–1940, at the Library of Congress.

3. Kerst, addressing the Library of Congress on May 9, 2017.

4. Kerst.

5. Margaret MacArthur, liner notes to the album *Make the Wildwood Ring*, 1981.

6. MacArthur.

7. Sturgis's work, also championed by Margaret MacArthur, is best sampled through Tony Barrand and Keith Murphy's 2010 CD *On the Banks of Coldbrook: Atwood Family Songs from the Hills of Vermont*. "Barbara Allen" (84) is included among its fourteen tracks.

8. MacArthur, liner notes, *Make the Wildwood Ring*.

9. MacArthur.

10. Phillips Barry, Fannie Hardy Eckstorm, and Mary Winslow Smith, *British Ballads from Maine — The Development of Popular Songs with Texts and Airs* (New Haven, CT: Yale University Press, 1929).

11. Sandy Ives, liner notes to the album *Folk Songs of Maine*, 1959.

CHAPTER SIXTEEN: BRITTEN, IVES, AND NILES

1. Gabe Meline, "Folk Balladeer: John Jacob Niles' Songs of Hill Folk," *North Bay Bohemian*, January 18–24, 2006.

2. John Jacob Niles, *The Ballad Book of John Jacob Niles* (Boston: Houghton Mifflin, 1961).

3. Niles.

4. Evelyn Kendrick Wells, *The Ballad Tree* (New York: The Ronald Press Company, 1950).

5. Richard Thompson, author interview, 2015.

6. Arlo Guthrie, author interview, 2017.

7. Mark Milhofer, quoted in the liner notes to Brilliant Classics' 2021 edition of Britten's *Complete Folk Songs for Voice and Piano*, performed by pianist Marco Scolastra and Milhofer himself.

8. Burl Ives, *Wayfaring Stranger* (Indianapolis: Bobbs-Merrill, 1962).

9. Ives.

10. Ives.

11. Maura Volante, author interview, 2022.

CHAPTER SEVENTEEN: A NOVA SCOTIAN SONGBOOK

1. Thurgood, author interview.

2. Quoted in Edith Fowke, *Traditional Singers and Songs from Ontario* (Hatboro, PA: Folklore Associates, 1965).

3. Anita Best, liner notes to the album *Cross-Handed*, 1997.

4. Helen Creighton, *A Life in Folklore* (New York: McGraw-Hill Ryerson, 1975).

5. Several years later, on a visit to England, Creighton met Sharp's sister, Mrs. Nevanson, and mentioned to her this tribute. "I felt she wasn't too complimented."

6. Clary Croft, author interview, 2022.

7. Creighton, *A Life*.

8. Creighton.

9. Pete Seeger credited Creighton with the version of "False Knight on the Road" (3) he featured on his *The Bitter and the Sweet* live album.

10. Helen Creighton, liner notes to the album *Maritime Folk Songs*, 1962.

11. Since reissued by the Creighton Foundation as *Sankofa Songs: African Nova Scotia Songs from the Collection of Helen Creighton*.

12. Thurgood, author interview.

13. Clary Croft, *Helen Creighton — Canada's First Lady of Folklore* (Halifax, NS: Nimbus Publishing, 1999).

CHAPTER EIGHTEEN: A CANADIAN CACHÉ

1. Volante, author interview.
2. Volante.
3. Edith Fulton Fowke and Richard Johnston, *Folk Songs of Canada* (Waterloo, ON: Waterloo Music Company, 1954).
4. Volante.
5. Thurgood, author interview.
6. Edith Fowke, liner notes to the album *Irish and British Songs from the Ottawa Valley*, 1957.
7. Thurgood, author interview.
8. Volante, author interview.
9. Thurgood, author interview.
10. Thurgood.
11. Thurgood.
12. The revised song title is possibly a corruption of "Burgeo," a town in Newfoundland.
13. Null passed away in July 2022, as this book was being completed. Her recorded legacy, while small, nevertheless includes some of the finest Child Ballad recordings of the 1970s–1980s.
14. Moira Cameron, author interview, 2022.
15. Cameron.
16. Found on Null and Bill Shute's 1977 album *The Feathered Maiden and Other Ballads*.
17. Cameron, author interview.

CHAPTER NINETEEN: THE LOMAX CONNECTION

1. https://jeanne-trembeth.medium.com/ruth-crawford-seegers-composition-rissolty-rossolty-ultramodernism-mingles-with-american-folk-a495771f1c6a.
2. In fact, the series ceased after eighteen volumes.
3. The performance was also selected for inclusion on Topic's first ever twelve-inch LP, an untitled compilation (released in a plain white sleeve) featuring MacColl, Isla Cameron, and the Topic Singers.
4. Ewan MacColl, liner notes for the album *Bothy Ballads of Scotland*, 1961.
5. Ewan MacColl, *Journeyman: An Autobiography* (London: Sidgwick & Jackson, 1990).
6. Ewan MacColl interviewed by Alan Lomax, February 12, 1951.
7. MacColl.
8. Carroll, author interview.

9. A seventeen-song collection of these recordings was released in 2011 under the wonderful title *Whaur the Pig Gaed on the Spree.*

10. https://betterknowachildballad.wordpress.com.

11. Sarah Brody, author interview, 2022.

12. Henderson would continue working with Mathieson for several years to come, under the aegis of the School for Scottish Studies in Edinburgh. He ultimately gathered a haul amounting to 450 songs, including around 30 that were not included in Mathieson's treasured notebooks! Henderson was also permitted to copy those notebooks, but only if their owner accompanied them to Edinburgh. Mathieson admitted that it was the first time he had ever set foot outside of the northeast of Scotland.

13. Flemons, author interview.

CHAPTER TWENTY: BROADCASTING THE BALLADS

1. MacColl, *Journeyman.*

2. Creighton, liner notes to *Maritime Folk Songs.*

3. Writing in *Sing!* magazine later, Lloyd also recalled a version of "Lord Franklin" that he claimed to have collected from a Welsh blacksmith named Edward Harper at a whale factory in Port Stanley, Falkland Islands, around 1936.

4. Peter Kennedy and Alan Lomax, liner notes for the album *Folk Songs of Britain: The Child Ballads No.1* (1961).

5. Roger Glover, author interview, 1998.

6. Kenneth S. Goldstein, liner notes for the album *Lucy Stewart: Traditional Singer from Aberdeenshire, Scotland — volume 1: Child Ballads* (1961).

7. Quoted from East Anglian Traditional Music Trust, https://www.eatmt .org.uk/sam-larner/.

8. Judy Dyble, author interview, 2016.

9. MacColl, Seeger, and producer Charles Parker produced eight hour-long Radio Ballads for the BBC, each one focusing on a different aspect of society, from boxing to the construction of the country's first motorway. The final installment, *The Travelling People,* dealt with the singing traditions of the Romany.

10. Carthy, liner notes to *Signs of Life.*

11. Martin Carthy, liner notes to Waterson-Carthy CD *A Dark Light* (2002).

12. Colin Harper, "The Wheels of the World," *fRoots* magazine, December 2015.

13. Roberts, author interview.

CHAPTER TWENTY-ONE: THE GIRL FROM VIPER COUNTY

1. Jean Ritchie, liner notes for the album *Clear Waters Remembered* (1973).

2. Ritchie, *Singing Family.*

3. Mike Yates, liner notes for Jean Ritchie CD *Ballads from Her Appalachian Family Tradition* (2003).

4. Ritchie, *Singing Family*.

5. Broadcast in the April 2008 Radio 2 special *Jac Holzman's Elektra Story*.

6. Quoted in Jac Holzman and Gavan Daws, *Follow the Music: The Life and High Times of Elektra Records in the Great Years of American Pop Culture* (Santa Monica, CA: FirstMedia Books, 1998).

7. Mick Houghton, *Becoming Elektra: The True Story of Jac Holzman's Visionary Record Label* (London: Jawbone Press, 2010).

8. Mick Houghton, *Becoming Elektra*.

9. Ritchie, *Singing Family*.

10. Creighton, liner notes to *Maritime Folklore*.

CHAPTER TWENTY-TWO: THE BIRTH OF THE BOOM

1. Ritchie Blackmore, author interview, 2017.

2. Judy Collins, author interview.

3. Judy Collins, *Sweet Judy Blue Eyes: My Life in Music* (New York: Crown, 2011).

4. Judy Collins, author interview.

5. According to Joel Whitburn's *Pop Memories 1890–1954* (Menomonee, WI: Record Research, 1986), Stafford racked up thirty-six hit songs between January 1944 and the end of 1948. By 1954, she had more than doubled that tally.

6. Judy Collins, author interview.

7. Judy Collins, *Sweet Judy Blue Eyes*.

8. Shirley Collins, *All in the Downs: Reflections on Life, Landscape and Song* (Cambridge, MA: Strange Attractor Press, 2018).

9. Judy Collins, author interview.

10. Pete Seeger, liner notes to the album *American Ballads* (1957).

11. Quoted by Dave Arthur in his liner notes to Dave Arthur, Pete Cooper, and Chris Moreton's CD *Return Journey* (2003).

12. "Songs to Keep: Documenting the Adirondack Songbook of Marjory Lansing Porter," Performance Marine, http://perfmar.com/songs-to-keep-documenting-the-adirondack-songbook-of-marjorie-lansing-porter/.

13. Reed recorded versions of "Lord Randall" (12), "The Riddle Song" (46), "Barbara Allen" (84), "The Wraggle Taggle Gypsies" (200), "Wallie Wallie" (204), "The Devil and the Farmer's Wife" (278), "The Golden Vanity" (286), and "The Soldier and the Lady" (299).

14. Reed also recorded "If I Had a Ribbon Bow," the song that became Fairport Convention's first single, at almost precisely the same time as the Maxine Sullivan 78 that inspired the band to cover it.

15. *Montana Kaimin*, February 9, 1962.

CHAPTER TWENTY-THREE:
THE CURIOUS TALE OF ROBIN HOOD

1. Roberts, author interview.

2. Bertrand Harris Bronson, *Traditional Tunes of the Child Ballads: With Their Texts, According to the Extant Records of Great Britain and America* (Princeton, NJ: Princeton University Press, 1959).

3. The melody that Larcombe sang has since been associated with no fewer than ten other Robin Hood ballads, as well as "Arthur a Bland," a selection from the anonymous ballad opera, *The Jovial Crew* (1731).

4. Malkin, author interviews.

5. Wallace House, liner notes for the album *Robin Hood Ballads* (1953).

6. Hermes Nye, liner notes to the album *Ballads Reliques: Early English Ballads from the Percy and Child Collections* (1952).

7. Nye.

8. Nye.

9. Nye.

10. Nye.

11. NicEilidh, author interview.

12. NicEilidh.

13. NicEilidh.

14. Randall Krieger, author interview, 2022.

CHAPTER TWENTY-FOUR: DOWN BY THE RIVERSIDE

1. Kenneth S. Goldstein, liner notes for the album series *Popular Ballads of England and Scotland* (1956).

2. Ewan MacColl, *Journeyman*.

3. Shirley Collins recorded White's version on her 1967 LP *The Sweet Primroses*, and acknowledged in her liner notes, "Of all the ballads I have heard, none has really chilled me like this one. Originally it concerned a mortal man who became a lover of a water-sprite. He leaves her, and in revenge she kills him with a poisoned kiss. Several girls die of sorrow. The effectiveness of the ballad comes partly from the matter-of-fact manner in which the characters accept their fate, and the way the death of six girls hints at George Collins' great attractiveness."

4. Emily Portman, liner notes to Furrow Collective CD *At Our Next Meeting* (2014).

5. House, liner notes for *Robin Hood Ballads*.

6. Ewan MacColl, liner notes to the album *No Tyme Lyke the Present* (1976).

7. Maddy Prior, liner notes to Fellside anthology *Ballads* (1997).

8. Peter Bellamy, liner notes to the album *Sond Wind* (1985).

9. Cameron, author interview.

10. A key release in the early sixties folk revival, *The Folk Box* was released in 1964, a four-LP set featuring themed sequences of primarily traditional material.

11. Henigan, author interview.

12. The Ballad and Blues Club became the Singers Club in June 1961.

13. Ewan MacColl, *Journeyman*.

14. Writing to her brother Charles, Seeger invoked Child 200 when she told him, "I'm not coming home for quite a while. . . . [I] am following a sort of Black Jack Davey."

15. Ewan MacColl, *Journeyman*.

CHAPTER TWENTY-FIVE: MACCOLL'S LONG HARVEST

1. Royston Wood, liner notes for the Young Tradition album *The Young Tradition* (1966).

2. Bert Lloyd remarks, "The terrible story has had a particular fascination for children and the ballad became a game-song. A folklorist saw the game being played in a Lancashire orphanage in 1915. The children called it *The Lady Drest in Green*." It was, in fact, a ring game, with two children representing the mother and her child in the center of the circle, acting out the lyric as it develops. Their companions surround them, singing the refrains, until finally three policemen arrive to take the murderous mother away.

3. Ewan MacColl and Peggy Seeger, liner notes to the LP series *The Long Harvest* (1966–1968).

4. Ewan MacColl and Peggy Seeger, liner notes to the LP series *Blood and Roses* (1979–1985).

5. MacColl Seeger.

6. In 1977, two manuscripts of poetry and balladry, dating to the seventeenth century, were discovered among the papers of the Dalhousie family at the Scottish Record Office in Edinburgh. Although the bulk of the contents were poems by John Donne, the ballads included a number of previously unknown variants.

7. Gordeanna McCulloch, liner notes to the album *In Freenship's Name* (1997).

8. Jessica Simpson, author interview, 2022.

CHAPTER TWENTY-SIX: JUDY AND JOAN

1. Judy Collins, *Sweet Judy Blue Eyes*.

2. Tom Rush, author interview, 2014.

3. Rush.

4. Rush's version appears on his 1965 album *Blues Songs Ballads*, recorded for the Prestige label immediately before he signed with Elektra Records.

5. Tom Rush, ibid.

6. Steve Tilston, author interview, 2022.

7. Jean Redpath, liner notes to the album *Scottish Ballad Book*, 1962.

CHAPTER TWENTY-SEVEN: CHILD GOES TO NEWPORT

1. The album upon which Odetta's performance of this ballad appears, 1957's *At the Gate of Horn*, was in fact recorded live at that same venue.

2. Collins, *Sweet Judy Blue Eyes*.

3. The other "standard" melody is that sung to Swedish folklorist Dr. Otto Andersson by John Sinclair on the island of Flotta, Orkney, in 1934. Sinclair later recorded it for the BBC; versions have also been recorded by Jean Redpath (1975), and Alison McMorland in 1977.

4. *Folk Connections*.

5. Judy Collins, author interview.

6. Collins.

7. Melanie Safka, author interview.

CHAPTER TWENTY-EIGHT: THE CLANCYS LEAD THE WAY

1. David Burke. "Liam Clancy—Last Man Standing," *R2/Rock'n'Reel*, January 2008.

2. Henigan, author interview.

3. Jim Carroll, author interview, 2022.

4. Henigan, author interview.

5. Henigan, *Literacy and Orality*.

6. Another distinctly Irish retelling, "Buried in Kilkenny" (12), was included on Jimmy Crowley and Eve Telford's 2023 album *Hello! Child Ballads Learned From Irish Travellers*.

7. Roberts, author interview.

8. This is not the only version of Child 20 to seem wholly to lose its original horror. In 1980, Lisa Null and Bill Shute recorded an almost shockingly jaunty version they found in Bronson's *Traditional Tunes*. As they remark in their liner notes, "'The Cruel Mother' is a gut-level nightmare for any unmarried woman. Pregnant by her father's clerk, the lady in question murders her twin babies and goes home as if nothing has happened. The ghosts of her babies return to taunt her and to expose the dark underside of her maternal sentiments. Yet while such subject matter should be related in terms as desolate and grisly as the lyric, in the version that Null and Shute discovered, "the monotony of its tune and childish little refrain ['tra-la-lee-and a-laddi-o'] give it the macabre feel of a nursery rhyme gone berserk."

9. *Folk Connections: Cecil Sharp's Appalachian Trail*, presented by Andy Kershaw, BBC Sunday Feature, first broadcast July 31, 2017, https://www.bbc.co.uk/programmes/b06yp4cv.

10. Dave Van Ronk, liner notes for the Patrick Sky album *Patrick Sky* (1965).

CHAPTER TWENTY-NINE: ENTER . . . AND EXIT . . . BOB DYLAN

1. All Stookey quotes from author interview, February 2022.
2. Killen recorded the ballad on his and Sally Killen's 1975 album *Bright Shining Morning*.
3. The performance is included on the 1961 various artists LP *Blues in a Bottle*.
4. Ellie Bryan, author interview, 2012.
5. It was published in late 1961 by Cooper Square.
6. A substitute event, featuring Judy Garland, Dave Brubeck, Bob Hope, and others was arranged for Freebody Park. It passed off peacefully but lost $70,000.

CHAPTER THIRTY: SHIRLEY SHINING

1. Gershon Legman, *The Horn Book: Studies in Erotic Folklore and Bibliography* (University Books Inc., 1964).
2. Mike Butler, *Sounding the Century: Bill Leader and Co.*, volume 2 (Matador Books, 2022).
3. Butler.
4. Frankie Armstrong, author interview, 2022.
5. *A Jug of Punch, A Pinch of Salt—British Sea Songs* and *Rocket Along* (all HMV, 1960).
6. Among Marshall's other achievements can be numbered two films, one featuring Jimi Hendrix and the other The Incredible String Band. The latter, *Be Glad, for the Song Has No Ending,* is a must-see for anybody intrigued by that band's so subtle rending of the rock-folk fabric of the pre-*Liege and Lief* late sixties. In addition to his work with Shirley Collins and Steve Ashley, Marshall also produced albums by The Wooden O and Arcadium, and singles by Bert Jansch and Tiger Lily, forebears of 1980s superstar Ultravox. Perhaps his greatest (if sadly most obscure) achievement was the folk opera *The Great Smudge,* written and recorded in 1977 and featuring contributions from Collins, Ashley, Barry Dransfield, Dave Pegg, and Robert Kirby, among others. Still unreleased almost fifty years later, it ranks among the most vivacious manifestations of "folk music" ever conceived.
7. Shirley Collins, author interview, 2013.
8. Gus Dudgeon, author interview, 1986.

CHAPTER THIRTY-ONE: TALKING THE TUNES

1. Other singers that Carter recorded included George Townsend, Pop Maynard, and Paddy Tunney and his family. Material from these excursions is spread across the Topic catalog of the period, with several highlights later released within the multivolume *The Voice of the People* series.

2. Paulusma also considered "Sheath and Knife" (16) during the sessions, and she did record "The Twa Sisters" (10). "But it didn't sit right. I'd love to have a go at 'Tam Lin' [39] one of these days."

3. O'Connor's aching "The Grey Selkie" appeared on her 2014 album *The Willowed Light*.

4. Paulusma, author interview.

5. https://www.mustrad.org.uk/obits/p_carter.htm.

6. Bill Leader, author interview, 2022.

7. "Broomfield Hill" (43), "Geordie" (209), and "The Outlandish Knight" (4).

CHAPTER THIRTY-TWO: THE CRITICS GROUP

1. Alex Petridis, "Gone but Not Forgotten." *The Guardian*, August 2, 2007.

2. Petridis.

3. Armstrong, author interview.

4. Topic Records' *Folk Music of Bulgaria*, recorded by Lloyd and released in 1964.

5. Actress Prunella Scales delivers a fine "The Devil's Nine Questions" (1) on the fourth and final volume in the 1965 series.

6. Angeline Morrison, author interview, 2022.

CHAPTER THIRTY-THREE: NIGHTCLUBBING

1. This performance was released in 1989 on the CD *The Attic Tracks Volume 3*. It is also included in the career spanning box set *A Boxful of Treasures*.

2. *Sussex Folk Songs and Ballads*, Folkways (1957).

3. Al Stewart, author interview, 2021.

4. Richard Byers, author interview, 2013.

5. Marianne Faithful, author interview, 2018.

6. Judy Dyble and Dave Thompson, *An Accidental Musician: The Autobiography of Judy Dyble* (London: Soundcheck Publishing, 2017).

7. Dyble and Thompson.

8. David Burke, *Singing Out: A Folk Narrative of Maddy Prior, June Tabor and Linda Thompson* (London: Soundcheck Publishing, 2015).

9. Steve Tilston, author interview, 2022.

10. Hedy West, liner notes for album *Old Times and Hard Times*, 1965.

11. Hedy West, liner notes for album *Pretty Saro*, 1966.

12. Simpson was also the recipient of several unreleased West recordings, the property of her daughter, including "The Death of Queen Jane" (170). In the liners to 2019's *Rooted* album, he recalled, "I assumed before hearing it that it was a version of 'The Death of Queen Jane,' and was wholly unprepared to find instead one of Hedy's greatest banjo arrangements and vocal performances of a US version of "The King's Daughter Lady Jean" (Child 52).

13. Cameron, author interview.

14. Tilston, author interview. Child 214 appears on Tilston's 1995 album *And So It Goes . . .*

15. Steve Ashley and Dave Thompson, *Fire and Wine: An Armchair Guide to Steve Ashley* (Createspace, 2013).

16. Sylvia Barnes, liner notes for the album *The Colour of Amber*, 2017.

17. Martin Simpson, liner notes for the album *The Bramble Briar*, 2001.

18. Ashley and Thompson, *Fire and Wine*.

19. Malkin, author interviews.

20. Cameron, author interview.

21. "Down Among the Hop Poles" by Steve Ashley, lyric reproduced courtesy Steve Ashley. Published by Topic Records Ltd.

CHAPTER THIRTY-FOUR: THE BALLAD OF PAUL AND MARTIN

1. Art Garfunkel interview by James McNair, *Mojo*, September 2015.

2. It was included on Gentry's 2018 *The Girl from Chickasaw County* anthology.

3. Ewan MacColl, liner notes for the album *Classic Scots Ballads*, 1959.

4. Shirley Collins, liner notes for the album *False True Lovers*, 1960.

5. Folklorist Hugh Shields may have been referring to this in his 1972 article "Old British Ballads in Ireland," where he notes, "Peigín Is Peadar" ("Our Goodman") is one of just four Child Ballads known to have been reborn in Gaelic. The others are the aforementioned "And Amhrán Na hEascainne" ("Lord Randall"—(12) although it is more accurately translated as "The Song of the Eels"; "Hymn Na Cásca" or "Muire agus Naomh Ioseph" ("The Cherry Tree Carol"—54) and "Baile Leo" (10).

6. Quoted in "When Dubliners' 'Seven Drunken Nights' was banned by RTÉ for being too rude," Irish Central.com.

7. "Scarborough Fair" was not released as a single in its own right in Britain; it did, however, appear on the 1968 *Mrs. Robinson* EP, which reached number 9.

CHAPTER THIRTY-FIVE: ANOTHER CHILD OF SKIFFLE

1. From the internationally syndicated BBC Radio show *Folkweave*, presented by Toni Arthur.

2. An online resource dedicated to the presentation and promotion of audio recordings capturing the cultural history of Scotland via songs, music, poetry, stories, and more. See https://www.tobarandualchais.co.uk.

3. Byrne, author interview, 2022.

4. Karl Dallas, *Melody Maker*, November 11, 1967.

5. Karl Dallas, *Melody Maker*, November 25, 1967.

6. Dave Swarbrick, author interview, 1983.

7. Scott Alarik, "Frances James Child: The Man Who Saved the Ballads." *Sing Out: The Folk Music Magazine*, 2006, https://scottalarik.com/blog/stories/Articles/11.

8. Martin Carthy, liner notes from the album *Two Came By*.

9. *Folk Music Journal*, no. 1, 1965.

10. Martin Carthy, liner notes to LP *Selections*, 1971.

11. Carthy, liner notes, *Two Came By*.

12. A. L. Lloyd, liner notes for the album *First Person*, 1966.

13. Lloyd was delighted to share his versions around the folk scene, frequently carrying several copies of his lyrics around with him, to hand out to anybody who seemed interested.

14. There were two BBC shows bearing this title, the original UK edition and, during the mid- to late 1970s, an international edition, presented by Toni Arthur and spotlighting two artists per show.

15. Felix recorded, and may have broadcast, "Geordie" (209); in 1966 Carthy and Swarbrick accompanied her on record. Two years later, the Incredible String Band joined her on her show for a highly idiosyncratic performance of the same ballad.

16. A massive, multi-disc anthology of Carthy's BBC recordings was in preparation as this book was being written. Compiler Colin Harper estimates some fifty performances of Child Ballads will be included across its more than fifty-year span.

17. Dave Cousins, author interviews, 2021–2022.

18. Cousins, author interviews. Cousins reflected, "We were extremely well known because of the BBC, but I still couldn't get anyone interested in giving us a record deal. We recorded with Steve Benbow, the first album that had our name on it. . . . I went to Phillips, which was the label he was on; 'sorry not interested.' I went to lots of companies, same response."

CHAPTER THIRTY-SIX: PLUCKING THE PENTANGLE

1. Stephen Sedley, author interview, 2022.

2. Karl Dallas, *Melody Maker*, February 4, 1967.

3. Jerry Gilbert, "Pentangle: The End," *Sounds,* January 13, 1973.

4. Nick Coleman, "Britain's Grateful Dead," *The Guardian*, March 16, 2007.

5. *The Song Carriers: Folk-Songs Introduced by Ewan MacColl*, BBC Radio, January 28, 1965.

CHAPTER THIRTY-SEVEN: ANY FAIRPORT IN A STORM

1. MacColl and Seeger, liner notes for the *Blood and Roses* LP series.

2. Swarbrick, author interview.

3. Here and the following quotes from Richard Thompson, author interview, 2001.

4. Tim Hart, author interview, 1986

5. Cousins, author interview.

6. Thompson, author interview.

7. Or did it? While "Willie O'Winsbury" certainly employs a traditional melody, it's not the one it originally had. According to Johnny Moynihan, of the band Swee-

ney's Men, when singer Andy Irvine came to record the ballad and went seeking the tune, "he got his numbers confused and emerged with the wrong air. By chance it suited the song very well." This is the melody that Thompson borrowed.

8. Brian Hinton and Geoff Wall, *Ashley Hutchings: The Governor and the Rise of Folk Rock* (London: Helter Skelter Publishing, 2001).

9. Bruce Rowland, author interview, 2015.

10. Hinton and Wall, *Ashley Hutchings*.

11. Rowland, author interview.

12. Rowland.

13. Rowland.

14. Rowland.

CHAPTER THIRTY-EIGHT: LEADER OF THE PACK

1. Sproatly Smith, author interview, 2015.

2. Bill Leader, author interview, 2022.

3. Bob Fischer, "Casting the Runes: Dave and Toni Arthur's *Hearken to the Witches Rune*," *Fortean Times*, no. 403, March 2021.

4. Leader, author interview.

5. The book has since enjoyed several revivals, first in 1971, when it finally saw a reprint; then in the twenty-first century when John Spiers and Jon Boden recorded Williams's published text for "Bold Sir Rylas"; Rosie Hood cut his "Lord Lovel" and "The Cruel Mother"; and June Tabor his "The Broomfield Wager."

CHAPTER THIRTY-NINE: KEEPING UP WITH THE JONESES

1. Nic Jones, liner notes for the album *Unearthed*, 2001.

2. Jon Boden liner notes for the download album, *A Folksong for a Day*, February 2011.

3. Carthy, liner notes to *Signs of Life*, 1998.

4. Nic Jones, liner notes to the album *Nic Jones*, 1971.

5. Colin Irwin, "What the Folk! Nic Jones Is back," *The Guardian*, June 28, 2012.

6. Tim Cooper, "Nic Jones," *Record Collector*, no. 494, July 2019.

7. Martin Simpson, author interview.

8. John Roberts, liner notes for the album *Sea Fever*, 2007.

9. Leader, author interview.

10. John Wesley Harding, author interview, 1999.

CHAPTER FORTY: PITY POOR STEELEYE SPAN

1. Hart, author interview, 1986.

2. As was the venue for the second volume's cover shoot. The St. Albans pub Ye Olde Fighting Cocks had been in operation since 793 AD. It remained in business until COVID restrictions led to its closure in February 2022.

3. Sandy Roberton, author interview, 2016.

4. Jerry Gilbert, "Steeleye Span: The Folk Who Plugged In," *Sounds*, December 6, 1975.

5. Gilbert.

6. Jerry Gilbert, "Steeleye Span," *Sounds*, January 6, 1973.

7. Roberton, author interview.

8. Ashley and Thompson, *Fire and Wine*.

9. Shirley Collins, author interview.

10. Austin John Marshall, author interview.

11. Ashley and Thompson, *Fire and Wine*.

12. Ed Haber interview, 1978.

CHAPTER FORTY-ONE: DON'T PITY POOR STEELEYE SPAN

1. Martin Carthy, liner notes for the album *Sweet Wivelsfield*, 1974.

2. Martin Carthy, liner notes for *The Carthy Chronicles* box set, 2001.

3. Gilbert, "Steeleye Span."

4. Hart, author interview.

5. Hart.

6. Gilbert, "Steeleye Span."

7. Malkin, author interviews.

8. Hart, author interview.

CHAPTER FORTY-TWO: SILLY WIZARDS AND THE SPRIGUNS OF TOLGUS

1. Fred Gerlach, liner notes for *Gallows Pole and Other Folk Songs*.

2. Chris Welch, "Led Zeppelin: Page on Zeppelin III," *Melody Maker*, October 24, 1970.

3. Michael Hann, "Jimmy Page and Robert Plant: How We Made *Led Zeppelin III*," *The Guardian*, May 26, 2014.

4. Hart, author interview.

5. Steve Turner, "Steeleye Span: Ye Olde Rocke & Rolle," *Rolling Stone*, September 12, 1974.

6. Child Ballads played an immediate role in each of these artists' repertoires, featuring across debut albums by Hedgehog Pie ("Jack O'Rion"—67), Gryphon ("The Unquiet Grave"—78; and "The Farmer's Curst Wife"—278), and the JSD Band ("Johnny O'Braidsley"—114).

7. *DADGAD Tuning* (Mel Bay Publications, 2015).

8. Henigan, author interview.

9. Leo O'Kelly, author interview.

10. A posthumous live album and a collection of unused demos for a projected third album have since appeared.

11. The full *Reliques* "Sir Cawline" has yet to see a complete rendering, with even the indefatigable Raymond Crooke (2007) calling a halt around the fourteen-minute mark.

12. Alasdair Roberts, liner notes to the album *No Earthly Man*, 2005.

13. Martin Carthy, liner notes to the album *Sweet Wivelsfield*, 1974.

14. Timothy Renner, author interview, 2016.

15. Rowland, author interview. Carthy explained that the melody "is from a song from the State of Utah called "Kate and the Cowhide" which Dave Swarbrick and I heard Hedy West playing in 9/8 (2-2-2-3). The original was in a much more mundane time signature and Hedy was trying different and more dramatic time sigs for the fun of it, but I've no idea how she counted it." Ed Vulliamy, "Martin Carthy: 'I'm Not Interested in Heritage: This Stuff Is Alive,'" *The Observer*, April 16, 2011.

16. Martin Carthy, liner notes to the album *Because It's There*, 1979.

17. Martin Carthy, liner notes to the Waterson-Carthy album *Common Tongue*, 1996.

CHAPTER FORTY-THREE: THE ELECTRIC MUSE

1. Bob Fischer, "Casting the Runes."

2. Burke, *Singing Out*.

3. Idris Walters, "Playing Silly Sisters," *Street Life*, May 1, 1976.

4. Walters.

5. June Tabor, liner notes to the LP *Airs and Graces*, 1976.

6. Fred Dellar, "Sensuous Librarian Reveals All," *New Musical Express*, October 2, 1976.

7. June Tabor, liner notes to the anthology *Always*, 2005.

8. Tabor.

9. Martin Simpson, liner notes to the album *Kind Letters*, 2005.

CHAPTER FORTY-FOUR: OLD ROOTS, NEWER ROUTES

1. Irwin, "What the Folk!"

2. Robert Shelton, Dave Laing, Karl Dallas, and Robin Denselow, *The Electric Muse Revisited: The Story of Folk into Rock and Beyond* (New York: Omnibus Press, 2021), xvii.

3. Jeanette Leech, *Seasons They Change: The Story of Acid and Psychedelic Rock* (London: Jawbone Press, 2010).

4. Len Brown, "The Oyster Band and the Dinner Ladies: A Total Oyster Time?" *New Musical Express*, July 30, 1988.

5. Itself subject to a radical cover version in 2007 by New Jersey's Schizo Fun Addict.

6. Tilston, author interview.

7. NicEilidh, author interview.

8. Gillian Welch, *Folk Connections: Cecil Sharp's Appalachian Trail.*

9. Daniel Kelly, author interview, 2022.

10. Maddy Prior, liner notes to the album *Bloody Men*, 2006.

11. Len Brown, *Wide Blue Yonder* album review, *New Musical Express*, September 28, 1987.

CHAPTER FORTY-FIVE: MURDEROUS BALLADS

1. The original Canterbury-based act that recorded for September Productions, as opposed to the later American jazz fusion combo. Just in case anyone is confused.

2. David Keenan, *England's Hidden Reverse*, second edition (Cambridge, MA: Strange Attractor Press, 2014).

3. Leech, *Seasons They Change.*

4. David Tibet, e-mail to author, 2022.

5. Len Brown, "The Dinner Ladies."

6. Malkin, author interview.

7. Timothy Renner, author interview, 2015.

8. Klemen Breznikar and Amadeus Wⱥchtler, "In Gowan Ring Interview," *It's Psychedelic Baby*, March 16, 2013.

9. This and the several following quotes are from Martyn Bates, author interview, 2022.

10. Malkin, author interview.

CHAPTER FORTY-SIX: OF OWLS AND HARES

1. Renner, author interview, 2015.

2. This same Carthy performance was also the inspiration behind Delia Sherman's novel *Through a Brazen Mirror* (2015).

3. Renner, author interview, 2015.

4. Malkin, author interview.

5. Child 78 appears as "Cold Blows the Wind" on Wynn Shannon's 2007 album *Courting Autumn*. Another version, recorded live at the 2011 Leigh Folk Festival, was included on the festival compilation album *Fire Feathers Felony and Fate.*

6. Malkin, author interview.

7. Steven Collins, author interview, 2016.

8. Diana Collier, author interview, 2016.

9. Collins, author interview.

10. Alison O'Donnell, author interview, 2016.

11. Steven Collins, author interview, 2022.

CHAPTER FORTY-SEVEN: AND OTHER STORIES

1. Angeline Morrison, author interview, 2022.
2. Harvey returned to the *ESPB* in 2018, when she joined with Harry Escott to contribute "An Acre of Land" (2) to the soundtrack of the movie *Dark River*.
3. Nick Cave, author interview, 1996.
4. See Chapter 11.
5. Frankie Armstrong, liner notes to the album *The Garden of Love*, 2000.
6. Ed Pettersen, author interview, 2022.
7. Raymond Crooke, author interview, 2022.

CHAPTER FORTY-EIGHT: BE GLAD, FOR THE BALLADS HAVE NO ENDING

1. Art Rosenbaum, liner notes for the box set *The Art of Field Recording Volume 2*, 2008.
2. Stephen Sedley, author interview, 2022.
3. Martin Carthy, e-mail correspondence, 2022.
4. As this book was going to press, a new related album, Becky Unthank and Paul Smith's *Nowhere and Everywhere*, arrived, bearing a beautifully wrought "Lord Bateman" (53).
5. Rowland, author interview.
6. Randall Krieger, author interview, 2022.
7. Elise Krieger, author interview, 2022.
8. Martyn Wyndham-Read, liner notes to the album *Jackeroo*, 2008.
9. Blackmore, author interview.
10. Jefferson Hamer, author interview, 2013.
11. Rob Hughes, "Anais Mitchell, Interview," *Daily Telegraph*, March 5, 2013.
12. Recorded with Eliza Carthy and Trans-Global Underground, "Tam Lin Retold" was released in 2007 on the eponymous album by The Imagined Village, a collective that also included Billy Bragg, Chris Wood, Sheila Chandra, Paul Weller, and others.
13. Rowland, author interview.
14. Peter Paphides, "June Tabor: Watery Not Grave," *The Guardian*, February 10, 2011.
15. Morrison, author interview.

BIBLIOGRAPHY

BIOGRAPHIES AND TEXTS

Arthur, Dave. *Bert: The Life and Times of A. L. Lloyd*. Pluto Press. 2012.

Ashley, Steve, and Dave Thompson. *Fire and Wine: An Armchair Guide to Steve Ashley*. Createspace, 2013.

Baez, Joan. *And a Voice to Sing With*. Summit Books, 1987.

Bean, J. P. *Singing from the Floor: A History of British Folk Clubs*. Faber & Faber, 2014.

Bell, Robert. *Early Ballads Illustrative of History, Traditions and Customs*. Griffin, Bohn and Company, 1861.

Brady, Erika. *A Spiral Way: How the Phonograph Changed Ethnography*. University Press of Mississippi, 1999.

Brown, Mary Ellen. *Child's Unfinished Masterpiece*. University of Illinois Press, 2011.

Burke, David. *Singing Out: A Folk Narrative of Maddy Prior, June Tabor and Linda Thompson*. Soundcheck Publishing, 2015.

Butler, Mike. *Sounding the Century: Bill Leader and Co. Volume 1. Glimpses of Far-Off Things: 1855–1956*. Matador, 2021.

———. *Sounding the Century: Bill Leader and Co. Volume 2. Horizons for Some: 1956–1962*. Matador, 2022.

Caldwell, Conor. *"The Wee Wee Man": The Evolution of a Song through Musical and Geographic Boundaries*. www.academia,edu.

Cohen, Ronald D. *Depression Folk: Grassroots Music and Left-Wing Politics in 1930s America*. University of North Carolina Press, 2016.

Collins, Judy. *Sweet Judy Blue Eyes: My Life in Music*. Thorndike Press, 2012.

Collins, Shirley. *All in the Downs*. Strange Attractor Press, 2018.

———. *America over the Water*. White Rabbit, 2022.

Creighton, Helen. *A Life in Folklore*. McGraw-Hill Ryerson Ltd., 1975.

Croft, Clary. *Helen Creighton: Canada's First Lady of Folklore*. Nimbus Publishing, 1999.

Dyble, Judy, and Dave Thompson. *An Accidental Musician: The Autobiography of Judy Dyble*. Soundcheck Publishing, 2017.

Elder, Madge. *Ballad Country; The Scottish Border*. Oliver and Boyd, 1963.

Fowke, Edith. *Traditional Singers and Songs from Ontario*. Folklore Associates, 1965.

Freedman, Jean R. *Peggy Seeger: A Life of Music, Love and Politics*. University of Illinois Press, 2017.

Friedman, Susan O. *Body Count. Death in the Child Ballads*. Loomis House Press, 2016.

Garner, Ken. *In Session Tonight: The Complete Radio 1 Sessions*. BBC Books, 1993.

Henigan, Julie. *Literacy and Orality in Eighteenth-Century Irish Song*. Pickering & Chatto, 2012.

Hinton, Brian, and Geoff Wall. *Ashley Hutchings: The Guv'nor and the Rise of Folk Rock*. Helter Skelter, 2002.

Holzman, Jac, and Gavan Daws. *Follow the Music: The Life and High Times of Elektra Records in the Great Years of American Pop Culture*. FirstMedia Books, 1998.

Houghton, Mick. *Becoming Elektra: The True Story of Jac Holzman's Visionary Record Label*. Jawbone Press, 2010.

Huber, Patrick. *Linthead Stomp: The Creation of Country Music in the Piedmont South*. University of North Carolina Press, 2008.

Hudson, E. Marion. Edited by Collinson, Peter. *Brigg Fair: A Memoir of Joseph Taylor by His Grand-Daughter E. Marion Hudson*. www.family-trees.org.uk, 2003.

Ives, Burl. *Wayfaring Stranger*. Bobbs-Merrill, 1962.

Jensen, Oskar Cox. *The Ballad-Singer in Georgian and Victorian London*. Cambridge University Press, 2021.

Karpeles, Maud. *Cecil Sharp: His Life and Work*. University of Chicago Press, 1967.

Keenan, David. *England's Hidden Reverse*, second edition. Strange Attractor Press, 2014.

Leech, Jeanette. *Seasons They Change. The Story of Acid and Psychedelic Folk*. Jawbone Press, 2010.

Legman, G. *The Horn Book: Studies in Erotic Folklore and Bibliography*. University Books Inc., 1964.

Lloyd, A.L. *The Singing Englishman: An Introduction to Folksong*. Workers' Music Association, 1944.

Lockhart, John Gibson. *Memoirs of the Early Life of Sir Walter Scott, Written by Himself*, vol. 1. Houghton Mifflin, 1901.

Lowry, Charles Wimberley. *Folklore in the English and Scottish Ballads: Ghosts, Magic, Witches, Fairies, the Otherworld*. University of Chicago Press, 1928.

MacColl, Ewan. *Journeyman: An Autobiography*. Sidgwick & Jackson, 1990.

Massimo, Rick. *I Got a Song. A History of the Newport Folk Festival*. Wesleyan University Press, 2017.

Muir, Willa. *Living with Ballads*. Oxford University Press, 1965.

Newell, William Wells. *Games and Songs of American Children*. Harper Brothers,1883.

Potter, Lois. *Playing Robin Hood: The Legend as Performance in Five Centuries*. University of Delaware Press, 1998.

Ritchie, Fiona, and Doug Orr. *Wayfaring Strangers: The Musical Voyage from Scotland and Ulster to Appalachia*. University of North Carolina Press, 2014.

Ritchie, Jean. *Singing Family of the Cumberlands*. Oxford University Press, 1955.

Roud, Steve. *Folksong in England*. Faber & Faber, 2017.

Shelton, Robert, Dave Laing, Karl Dallas, and Robin Denselow. *The Electric Muse Revisited: The Story of Folk into Rock and Beyond*. Omnibus Press, 2021.

Szwed, John. *Alan Lomax: The Man Who Recorded the World*. Viking Penguin. 2010.

Three Score and Ten: A Voice to the People — 70 Years of the Oldest Independent Record Label in Great Britain. Topic Records, 2009.

Von Schmidt, Eric, and Jim Rooney. *Baby Let Me Follow You Down: The Illustrated History of the Cambridge Folk Years*. Anchor Press, 1979.

Wells, Evelyn Kendrick. *The Ballad Tree*. The Ronald Press Company, 1950.

Whitburn, Joel. *Pop Memories: 1890–1954*. Record Research Inc., 1986.

Wiggington, Eliot, ed. *Foxfire*. Vols. 1–12. Anchor Books, 1972–2004.

Williamson, Duncan. *The Horsieman: Memories of a Traveller 1928–58*. Birlinn Books, 2008.

Young, Rob. *Electric Eden: Unearthing Britain's Visionary Music*. Faber & Faber Inc., 2010.

BALLAD COLLECTIONS AND SONG BOOKS

Barry, Philips, Fannie Hardy Eckstorm, and Mary Winslow Smyth. *British Ballads from Maine: The Development of Popular Songs with Texts and Airs*. Oxford University Press, 1929.

Beattie, William. *The Penguin Poets: Border Ballads*. Penguin Books, 1952.

Bronson, Bertrand Harris. *The Ballad as Song*. University of California Press, 1969.

———. *Traditional Tunes of the Child Ballads: With Their Texts, According to the Extant Records of Great Britain and America*. Princeton University Press, 1959.

Creighton, Helen. *Songs and Ballads from Nova Scotia*. J. M. Dent & Sons, 1933.

Darke, Tamsin. *Live on the Light and Other Broadcasts, Volume Two: Rock, Pop, Folk and Jazz at the BBC 1962–1967*. Lulu.com, 2021.

Dickens, Charles, W. M. Thackeray, and George Cruikshank. *The Loving Ballad of Lord Bateman*. Charles Tilt, Fleet Street, London, 1839.

Friedmann, Albert B. *The Viking Book of Folk Ballads of the English-Speaking World*. The Viking Press, 1956.

Hales John, and Frederick J. Furnivall (editors). *Bishop Percy's Folio Manuscript* (three volumes). N. Trübner & Co., 1867.

Johnson, R. Brimley. *Popular British Ballads*. J. M. Dent/Everyman's Library, 1912.

Kinsley, James. *The Oxford Book of Ballads*. Oxford University Press, 1969.

Leach, MacEdward. *The Ballad Book*. Harper & Brothers, 1955.

Lloyd, A. L. *Singing Englishmen: A Collection of Folk-Songs Specially Prepared for a Festival of Britain Concert Given in Association with the Arts Council of Great Britain*. 1951.

Lloyd, A. L. *Folk Song in England*. Lawrence & Wishart. 1967.

Lomax, Alan. *The Folk Songs of North America in the English Language*. Doubleday & Co., 1960.

Lyle, Emily, Kaye McAlpine, and Anne Dhu McLucas. *The Song Repertoire of Amelia and Jane Harris*. The Scottish Text Society. 2002.

Niles, John Jacob. *The Ballad Book of John Jacob Niles*. Houghton Mifflin Company, 1961.

Percy, Thomas. *Reliques of Ancient English Poetry consisting of Old Heroic Ballads, Songs and Other Pieces*. Henry G. Bohn, 1857.

Rieuwerts, Sigrid (editor). *The Ballad Repertoire of Anna Gordon, Mrs. Brown of Falkland*. Scottish Text Society, 2011.

Ritson, Joseph. *Robin Hood: A Collection of All the Ancient Poems, Songs, and Ballads Now Extant, Relative to That Celebrated English Outlaw*. Cambridge University Press facsimile, 1975.

Rollins, Hyder E. *A Pepysian Garland—Black Letter Broadside Ballads of the Years 1595–1639*. Harvard University Press, 1971.

Round, Steve, and Julia Bishop. *The New Penguin Book of English Folk Songs*. Allen Lane, 2012.

Sedley, Stephen, and Martin Carthy. *Who Killed Cock Robin? British Folk Songs of Crime and Punishment*. Reaktion Books/English Folk Dance and Song Society, 2022.

Sharp, Cecil, and Olive Dame Campbell. *English Folk Songs from the Southern Appalachians*. Putnam's, 1917.

Stubbs, Ken. *The Life of a Man—English Folk Songs from the Home Counties*. E.F.D.S. Publications, 1970

Williams, Ralph Vaughan, and A. L. Lloyd. *The Penguin Book of English Folk Song*. Penguin Books, 1959.

INTERNET RESOURCES

http://ballads.bodleian.ox.ac.uk (Brodside ballads)

http://bluegrassmessengers.com/the-305-child-ballads.aspx (vast American folk authority)

http://www.csufresno.edu/folklore/BalladIndexDisc.html (Traditional Ballad index)

http://www.folkworld.eu (news)

http://getangelacarter.co.uk/angela-carters-folksong-and-music-concert (Angela Carter site)

https://archive.culturalequity.org (Alan Lomax digital archive)

https://birthplaceofcountrymusic.org (exploration of the Bristol scene)

https://carthyarchive.wordpress.com (Martin Carthy archive)

https://collections.mun.ca (Memorial university of Newfoundland digital archives)

https://cudl.colorado.edu/luna/servlet/UCBOULDERCB1~25~25 (Ben Gray Lumpkin archive)

https://www.efdss.org/ (English Folk, Dance & Song Society)

https://folkcatalogue.wordpress.com (discographies)

https://mainlynorfolk.info/folk/ (authoritative English folk site)

https://maxhunter.missouristate.edu (Max Hunter collection)

https://monologues.co.uk (English Music Hall)
https://mudcat.org/ (discussion and information)
https://www.mustrad.org.uk/votp.htm (*The Voice of the People* reference site)
https://sounds.bl.uk/ (British Library sound archive)
https://tradfolk.co (news, reviews and podcasts)
https://web.sheffieldlive.org/shows/thank-goodness-its-folk/ (Radio Sheffield, *Thank Goodness It's Folk*)
https://www.childballadrecordings.com (Child Ballads Database)
https://www.clarelibrary.ie/eolas/coclare/songs/cmc/carroll_mackenzie.htm (Carroll MacKenzie collection)
https://www.loc.gov/collections/sidney-robertson-cowell-northern-california-folk-music/articles-and-essays/sidney-robertson-cowell-ethnographer-and-folk-music-collector/ (Sidney Robertson Cowell collection)
https://www.loc.gov/collections/todd-and-sonkin-migrant-workers-from-1940-to-1941/ (Charles Sonkin archive)
https://www.middlebury.edu/library/special-collections/collections/flanders (Helen Hartness Flanders collection)
https://www.mun.ca/folklore/leach/ (MacEdward Leach collection)
https://www.mustrad.org.uk/votp.htm (Topic Records' *Voice of the People* series)
https://www.peterkennedyarchive.org (Peter Kennedy archive)
https://www.vwml.org/archives-catalogue (Vaughan Williams Memorial Library)

ACKNOWLEDGMENTS

It's fifty years since I heard my first Child Ballads, courtesy of my school woodwork teacher Steve Miles and his eight-track of Steeleye Span's *Parcel of Rogues*. The first "thank-you," then, belongs to him.

I gathered more across the years that followed, first as a child of British folk-rock, but also through sheer curiosity. I picked up my first Joan Baez LP because she performed "Matty Grove"—a song I knew from Fairport Convention—and my first Dylan bootleg for "The House Carpenter" (ditto, Steeleye Span). But it was not until 1976 or so, when I chanced upon a very battered copy of the abridged *ESPB*, that I realized the true vastness of the canon—and, by comparison, the puniness of my collection. But it was already too late to stop.

I discovered a full set of Caedmon's *Folk Songs of Britain* LPs at my local Tottenham library and recorded them all—long afterward, I learned that June Tabor did the same thing, probably with the exact same copies, during her time working at that same library a few years previous; and with my ears now open to both field and popular recordings, I at last appreciated, and embraced, the sheer magnitude of my quest.

Pursuing a career in music journalism across the decades since then, I've complemented this musical hoard with a broad archive of Child-related interviews and notes, an invaluable resource that went a long way toward enabling me to write this book. In chronological terms, the earliest of these interviews dates back to what was, coincidentally, my very first piece of "paid writing" in a magazine, an overview of Fairport Convention for *Record Collector* in 1983. The Dave Swarbrick interview was set up for that purpose. Unfortunately, his schedule was such that we didn't finally speak until sometime *after* the piece went to press. I've been sitting on it ever since.

Here, I should also mention the journalist Colin Irwin, alongside whom I worked at Melody Maker during the 1980s. Sharing my love of folk, he pointed me toward some remarkable (and remarkably obscure) records and artists. My only regret is that Colin passed away while this book was in production, and never got to see what I did with all that he taught me.

The Tim Hart and Gus Dudgeon interviews are (largely) unpublished and date from my research for a David Bowie book I was writing in the mid-1980s, *Moonage Daydream* (1987) Of glancing interest, I intended asking Tim about Bowie's appearance on Steeleye's *Now We Are 6* LP; in fact, we talked about anything but.

The Nick Cave quotes are taken from our interview for *Alternative Press* in 1996, as he celebrated the release of his *Murder Ballads* album. The interview with John Wesley Harding, re his Nic Jones tribute album, was conducted for *No Depression* magazine in 1999. The majority of Richard Thompson's quotes are from a *Goldmine* feature a couple of years later.

Conversations and communications with Austin John Marshall, Bruce Rowland, Karl Dallas, Richard Byers, Dave Pegg, and Shirley Collins trace back to my work with Steve Ashley for his 2013 autobiography *Fire and Wine: An Armchair Guide to Steve Ashley*; from this same period, Edward Haber kindly provided me with some monumental rarities from the Austin John Marshall archive.

Judy Dyble's recollections (alongside some additional Richard Thompson material) are taken from our collaboration on her book *An Accidental Musician* (2016) A nod, too, to her son Daniel De La Bedoyere, for permission to include here my favorite photograph of his mother.

Elements of my conversations with Noel Paul Stookey, Melanie Safka, Jefferson Hamer, Ellie Bryan, Steven Collins, Al Stewart, and Dave Cousins appeared in *Goldmine* over the years; that with Judy Collins in the liner notes to her 2014 collection *Both Sides Now: The Very Best of*.

Interviews with Leo O'Kelly, Alison O'Donnell, David Colohan, Sproatly Smith, and Diane Collier date from 2015, during the writing of *A Séance at Syd's: An Anthology of Modern Acid-Folk-Haunt-Psych-Prog-Space-Kraut-Radiophonic-Rock Etcetera Quotes*. I spoke with Hester NicEilidh during research for my book *Robin Hood FAQ: All That's Left to Know about England's Greatest Outlaw and His Band of Merry Men* (2017) Stephen Sedley and Martin Carthy's contributions date from a *Goldmine* feature on their book *Who Killed Cock Robin?* in May 2022.

Other interviews were undertaken specifically for this book, between 2013 and 2022:

Frankie Armstrong, Jon Bartlett, Martyn Bates, Sarah Brody, Steve Byrne, Moira Cameron, Jim Carroll, Clary Croft, Raymond Crooke, Don

Flemons, Colin Harper, Julie Henigan, Fiona Hunter, Daniel Kelly, Randall Krieger, Bill Leader, Grey Malkin, Angeline Morrison, Paula Paulusma, Brian Peters, Timothy Renner, Sandy Roberton, Alasdair Roberts, Rika Ruebsaat, Tom Rush, Jessica Simpson, Jay Tausig, Ranald Thurgood, Steve Tilston, and Maura Volante. Less formal chats with Linda Thompson and David Tibet also date from this period. Thank you everyone.

Special thanks to Julie Hennigan and Jim Carroll for conversation, music, and invaluable guidance, and to Ed Pettersen and the members of the London Experimental Ensemble, first for bringing life to "the final six" ballads in the *ESPB*, and then for offering the resultant album as a free download with this book.

And . . . to Amy, who has lived with the ballads for as long as we've known one another but has really heard a lot of them in recent times. To Jo-Ann Greene and Grey Malkin for making their way through early drafts of this book and making comments and suggestions; Chris Haug for seeking out ever more arcane performances of the ballads, the Fruits de Mer fishermen, Karen and Todd, Miranda and Todd, and Pat Prince.

To everyone at Backbeat Books, for allowing me to finally cross this book off the to-do list.

And finally, to George, Trevor, Dennis, Frankie, a couple of fish and a lot of snails, Geoff Monmouth, Barb East, the gremlins that live in the heat pump, a host of Thompsons and more for forbearance.

INDEX

INDEX OF BALLADS